The debate on European spatial planning spans over two decades, but has gained currency and legitimacy with the inclusion of 'territorial cohesion' as an objective of the European Union in the Lisbon Treaty. Although no consensus exists on the specific problems territorial cohesion policy should address, it recognizes the diversity of European regions and their particular development potentials. Moreover, it has the clear ambition, like spatial planning and regional policy, of being evidence-based. This raises the crucial question: what kind of knowledge is needed for this emerging policy area, how is it being (re)produced and by whom?

This book answers the call by chronicling how various 'epistemic communities' are developing in the field of European spatial planning in central and east European (CEE) countries and what this means for the future spatial development agenda of the Union. In so doing, the book treats some very interesting and often neglected subject matter, since the literature in this area has focused almost exclusively on north-west Europe. Despite their modest role in setting the spatial planning/territorial cohesion agenda, CEE countries are in some ways more receptive to European spatial planning/ territorial cohesion policy, and have in recent years become more active in the discussions on its development, than some of the member states pioneering this policy area. Finally, as much of the literature on EU spatial planning is more descriptive than explanatory, the critical reflection and theoretical rigour of this book is a very welcome addition to this growing body of literature.

> Dr. David Evers, Senior researcher at the Netherlands Environmental
> Assessment Agency (Planbureau voor de Leefomgeving)

Territorial Development, Cohesion and Spatial Planning

This book examines some of the evolving challenges faced by spatial planning in Europe post enlargement, assessing these challenges through a knowledge perspective on the study of processess contributing to policy stability and change. Focusing on the experiences in Central and Eastern Europe (CEE), the different chapters reflect on the diversity of approaches to spatial planning and the politics of policy formation and multi-level governance operations – from local to transnational agendas.

It promotes increased awareness and understanding of the links between the 'hard' regulatory spaces of planning systems and the 'soft' spaces of territorial governance beyond the geographical and professional boundaries of these systems. And it highlights the potential for both conflict and learning among expert and non-expert actor communities in policy development processess, and their contribution as both institutionally enabling and constraining factors. In this regard, the main purpose of the book sets out to explore how, and to what extent knowledge resources (data, ideas and arguments) are channeled by these communities through various knowledge arenas where they are tested, debated and validated in efforts to shape or frame spatial policy. The recently acquired CEE dimension to EU territorial governance provides a unique opportunity to examine the evolution of this agent interactivity, whilst offering a conceptualization of the role of knowledge in the policy process as a useful departure point into understanding the complex adaptive processes inherent in territorial development, cohesion and spatial planning.

The book will be of interest to academics, researchers, practitioners, project managers and policy advisors active in the fields of European territorial development and spatial planning, particularly concerning issues of territorial cohesion, development, EU regional and sectoral policies, EU enlargement and the transition of former Soviet and Socialist countries, especially in light of the widespread participation throughout Europe of these groups in EU funded projects and research. It will be most relevant to under and post-graduate students studying regional development and European spatial planning.

Neil Adams is Senior Lecturer at London Southbank University, Department of Urban, Environmental and Leisure Studies. **Giancarlo Cotella** is Research Fellow at Politecnico di Torino, Eupolis, Dipartimento Interateneo Territorio (DITER). **Richard Nunes** is Senior Lecturer in Spatial Planning and Governance, Department of Planning at Oxford Brookes University.

Regions and cities

Series editors:
Ron Martin
University of Cambridge, UK
Gernot Grabher
University of Bonn, Germany
Maryann Feldman
University of Georgia, USA
Gillian Bristow
University of Cardiff, UK

Regions and Cities is an international, interdisciplinary series that provides authoritative analyses of the new significance of regions and cities for economic, social and cultural development, and public-policy experimentation. The series seeks to combine theoretical and empirical insights with constructive policy debate and critically engages with formative processes and policies in regional and urban studies.

Territorial Development, Cohesion and Spatial Planning

Knowledge and policy development
in an enlarged EU

**Edited by Neil Adams,
Giancarlo Cotella and Richard Nunes**

Routledge
Taylor & Francis Group

LONDON AND NEW YORK

First published 2011
by Routledge
2 Park Square, Milton Park, Abingdon, Oxon OX14 4RN

Simultaneously published in the USA and Canada
by Routledge
270 Madison Avenue, New York, NY 10016

Routledge is an imprint of the Taylor & Francis Group, an informa business

Typeset in Times by Wearset Ltd, Boldon, Tyne and Wear
Printed and bound in Great Britain by CPI Antony Rowe, Chippenham, Wilshire

British Library Cataloguing in Publication Data
A catalogue record for this book is available from the British Library

Library of Congress Cataloging in Publication Data
Territorial development, cohesion and spatial planning : building on EU
enargement / edited by Neil Adams, Giancarlo Cotella and Richard Nunes.
p. cm.
1. Regional planning–European Union countries. 2. Regionalism–
European Union countries. I. Adams, Neil, 1966– II. Cotella, Giancarlo,
1979– III. Nunes, Richard, 1973–
HT395.E85T48 2010
307′1094–dc22

2010011588

ISBN13: 978-0-415-55194-6 (hbk)
ISBN13: 978-0-2038-4297-3 (ebk)

A policy process based on regulation and expertise, on the one hand, and a more politicized context, on the other, can be either an explosive combination or a corroborating alchemy

(C. M. Radaelli 'The public policy of the European Union', *Journal of European Public Policy*, 1999, 6(5): 771)

Contents

Figures

Tables

About the editors

Neil Adams is a Senior Lecturer in Spatial Planning at London South Bank University. His main research interests are the internal and external dimensions of EU territorial governance, European spatial planning and spatial planning in Europe at the national and regional levels within the context of EU enlargement and with a particular focus on Central and Eastern Europe. He has participated in various EU-funded research projects (including INTERREG and ESPON) and was previously employed as a consultant leading and participating in international regional development and spatial planning projects in Europe generally and in the Baltic States in particular. Neil has published various journal articles and co-edited a book 'Regional Development and Spatial Planning in an Enlarged EU' (Adams, Alden and Harris, 2006) focusing on planning in the Celtic and Baltic peripheries.

Giancarlo Cotella is a Research Fellow and teaching assistant at the Inter-university Department of Territorial Studies and Planning (DITer) of Politecnico di Torino. His research focuses on European territorial governance, in particular on the mutual influence between European spatial planning and domestic spatial planning contexts. His recent contributions deal with the eastward enlargement of the EU and with the impact of the latter on spatial development and planning in Central and Eastern Europe and on the new models of territorial and urban governance consolidating in this area in the pre-accession period. He has taken part in several international research projects and published widely on CEE countries in scientific journals. Since 2005 he has been actively involved in the Association of European Schools of Planning (AESOP), at first as coordinator of the AESOP Young Academic Network and currently as member of the AESOP Executive Committee.

Richard Nunes is a Senior Lecturer in Spatial Planning and Governance at Oxford Brookes University, Department of Planning. His main research interests include European territorial governance and spatial planning, and industry restructuring, regional innovation and economic development. The focus of his current research explores the cognitive and institutional dimensions of strategic planning and governance of industry and regional development, and the role of evidence and expertise in urban development policies. Richard has contributed to research on topics including regional foresight and technological innovation, and has held lectureship posts at the University of Westminster (London) and University College London.

Contributors

Mark Tewdwr-Jones is Professor in Spatial Planning and Governance. He teaches and researches at the Bartlett School of Planning and the UCL Urban Laboratory, University College London. As the author of several books, he has published widely in the fields of the politics and governance of planning, including spatial planning, urban and regional development, governance and devolution.

Bas Waterhout is a Researcher at OTB Research Institute for Housing, Urban and Mobility Studies of Delft University of Technology in the Netherlands. He has participated in various research projects in the field of European spatial planning including EU-funded ESPON and INTERREG projects. His publications and research focus on territorial governance and spatial planning from the regional to the European level.

Maroš Finka is Professor in Spatial Planning, Director of the SPECTRA Centre of Excellence and Vice-Rector at the Slovak University of Technology in Bratislava, researcher and planner, widely published in books and planning journals and considered to be one of the leading academics on spatial planning in Central and Eastern Europe.

Karina Pallagst is Professor in International Planning Systems at Kaiserslautern Technical University, Germany. Karina previously worked as the Director of the Shrinking Cities Programme at the University of California, Berkeley. Her research focuses on comparative urban and regional studies, planning cultures and the emergence of epistemic communities.

Dominic Stead is a Senior Researcher at OTB Research Institute for Housing, Urban and Mobility Studies within Delft University of Technology. He has been involved in a wide range of research projects related to European spatial planning, including EU-funded ESPON, INTERREG and Framework Programme projects. He has published widely in international planning journals.

Vincent Nadin is Professor in Spatial Planning and Strategy at the Department of Urbanism, Faculty of Architecture, Delft University of Technology. He is Visiting Researcher at the Institute of Environmental Planning, Leibniz University, Hannover, and was previously Professor of Town Planning at the University of the West of England, Bristol.

Naja Marot is a PhD researcher with the Urban Planning Institute of the Republic of Slovenia. She has been a visiting researcher at the German Federal Office for Building and Regional Planning and a Fulbright scholar at the Taubman College of Architecture and Urban Planning, University of Michigan, Ann Arbor.

Marcin Dąbrowski is finalizing his PhD in the Business School at the University of West Scotland. Marcin has studied in France and now Scotland. His research addresses questions related to Europeanization, institutional capacity building and partnership within regions and he has published in *Europe-Asia Studies* and various French language journals.

Beatrix Haselsberger is a Researcher at the University of Natural Resources and Applied Life Sciences, Vienna and the Vienna University of Technology. Beatrix is active in various European research projects and conferences, and has written various book chapters, viewpoints and journal articles. In 2008–2009, Beatrix chaired AESOP's (Association of European Schools of Planning) Young Academics Network.

Paul Benneworth is a Senior Researcher at the Centre for Higher Education Policy Studies at the University of Twente, the Netherlands. A geographer and planner by background, Paul is currently leading the (UK) Economic and Social Research Council project 'Universities' engagement with excluded communities'.

Karel Maier is Professor in Planning at the Czech Technical University in Prague. Karel is published in numerous books and international planning journals and has participated in several national as well as international (INTERREG, ESPON) research projects dealing with spatial development and sustainable urban and regional development. He has emerged as one of the most prominent spatial planning academics and researchers in CEE countries in recent years.

Laila Kule is finalizing her PhD on rural-urban aspects in post soviet city-regions at the University of Latvia where she is lecturer in human geography and regional planning. She previously worked as head of the spatial planning division at the responsible Latvian ministry and has been adviser to the Baltic Sea Region intergovernmental initiatives.

Zaiga Krisjane is Professor and Head of the Department of Human Geography of the University of Latvia. Her scientific interests lie in population geography, urbanization, migration, settlement systems and regional planning. Zaiga is chair of the Latvian Geographical Society; she has a number of local and international publications.

Maris Berzins is working on his PhD at the Department of Human Geography of the University of Latvia. The subject of his dissertation is population mobility and urbanization dynamics over the past few decades in Latvia. He has participated in research projects on Latvian labour mobility.

Paweł Capik is a Lecturer in International Business at the Sheffield Business School. His research explores interdependencies between international business strategies and operations and regional development theory and practice, particularly in the context of transition economies.

Konrad Ł. Czapiewski completed his PhD at the Polish Academy of Sciences. Konrad is an active member of the Polish Geographical Society (treasurer of Main Board), Committee for Spatial Economy and Regional Planning PAS, and European Rural Development Network. He has participated in various international and national research projects concerning rural and local development, intraregional differences and human capital.

Krzysztof Janc is a Researcher at the Institute of Geography and Regional Development, University of Wrocław. Krzysztof has participated in many applied research projects for national and regional ministries and agencies, concerning human and social capital, spatial differentiation of educational potential. His research interests are connected also with geography of the internet and applications of quantitative methods in social science.

Matti Fritsch is a Researcher at the Karelian Institute and Doctoral Student at the Department of Geographical and Historical Studies of the University of Eastern Finland in Joensuu, Finland. He is currently entering the concluding stages of his PhD, which deals with EU-Russian cooperation in spatial planning and territorial development. He has authored and co-authored several articles on European and cross-border spatial planning issues in international journals and edited volumes.

Natalia Razumeyko is Deputy Dean at the Faculty of Public Administration and Associate Professor in Regional Economics at the prestigious North-West Academy of Public Administration in St Petersburg in the Russian Federation. Natalia has published in a number of Russian journals and has a reputation as one of the emerging academics in the field of regional planning and development in Russia.

Editors' preface

The topic of this book builds on a cooperation between the editors and many of the contributors to this edited volume, which started at a meeting organized by the Young Academics Network of the Association of European Schools of Planning (AESOP) in Bratislava, Slovakia in February 2007. The theme for the meeting sought to explore ways of engaging with Central and Eastern European countries within the context of the recent enlargements of the European Union (EU). On the basis of that meeting and the quality of the papers presented and discussed on spatial planning in Europe and, more specifically on Central and Eastern European engagement, we explored the possibility of publishing selected works in conjunction with the contributions of more established academics in the field. The result has been a rewarding experience and we hope this will prove to be a worthwhile contribution to the topic area of spatial planning in the enlarged EU.

Our professional and academic backgrounds and interests vary, although we share a common interest in the heterogeneous and ever-evolving landscape for spatial planning in Europe in the context of the most recent EU enlargements. Still, as editors and authors on this book project, we have found an additional area of common interest, which we have encouraged in the contributions to this edited volume; that is, the complex interplay of knowledge and policy development. Albeit well documented, in our view, this relationship remains highly contested in the academic literature and therefore highly relevant to spatial policy at all territorial scales. This understanding begins with the cross-sector and multi-disciplinary nature of spatial planning, which in recent decades has been embraced by many countries throughout Europe as a means of promoting more balanced patterns of development, integrating the territorial impacts of sectoral policies, and more recently as a means of promoting 'territorial cohesion'. The cross-sector and multi-disciplinary nature of spatial planning also provides an appropriate and dynamic context for experimenting with different approaches to territorial governance arrangements and processes of policy development. All in all, the diversity of territorial governance practices or arrangements, evident within the enlarged EU, consist of everyday processes of formal and informal institutional change and organizational learning, which reflect the extremely heterogeneous and ever-evolving challenges of spatial development in Europe.

In this context, we make a distinction between spatial planning in Europe and European spatial planning (see Chapter 1 for elaboration). At the most basic level of this distinction we consider spatial planning in Europe to be an umbrella term that refers primarily to spatial planning activities in the domestic contexts of the Member States but that can also include European spatial planning, which we use to refer to spatial planning activities focusing on the EU level or on EU-inspired transnational 'soft' spaces. Soft spaces are unlike the hard spaces bordered by administrative boundaries that generally provide the focus for 'hard' regulatory planning instruments. They seek to reflect the reality of functional areas where diverse interactions do not necessarily respect administrative jurisdictions, and therefore require innovative and creative 'soft' (informal/ad hoc) spatial planning instruments and practices. There has been an increased focus in recent academic literature on the potential of such soft spaces to address spatial challenges at diverse scales and this will be discussed further in Chapter 1.

The inherent diversity of the territorial governance practices and spatial challenges ensures that the results of the above-mentioned everyday processes of institutional change and organizational learning are context specific, and their implications often contested as demonstrated by the growing institutional and organizational diversity between European regions and cities. These potentially path-shaping processes also can facilitate the emergence of new forms of territorial governance and radical policy change, notwithstanding the persistence of path-dependent processes of policy development. Together these emerging arrangements consist of a complex layering of agent interaction within existing institutional and political geographies. These interactions often transcend and/or challenge established jurisdictions at varying territorial scales (cross-scalar) and across different institutional remits or responsibilities (multi-jurisdictional). These cross-scalar and multi-jurisdictional environments involve an ever increasing number and diversity of public and private networks whereby formal authority has been transferred beyond core representative institutions. These systems of multi-level governance are the result of both the rescaling of formal authority up to supranational institutions and down to sub-national governments. Within this context, we stress that the increased diversity of agents interacting across this multi-jurisdictional and polyarchic space of European governance, consisting of multiple and/or overlapping territories and changing boundaries, requires a consideration of both the 'soft' (informal/ad hoc) and 'hard' (formal/regulatory) aspects of spatial planning practices mentioned earlier.

Our aim as editors of this book is to explore this understanding of the dynamics of a multi-jurisdictional policy environment and the interplay of knowledge and policy development in relation to spatial planning and territorial development. We address this understanding in light of the evolving context of spatial planning in Europe and the recently acquired east-west dimension since the enlargements of 2004 and 2007. This departure point offers a unique opportunity to examine the transformation of existing 'territorial knowledge communities' as well as to explore the potential emergence of new ones. Our conceptualization of 'territorial knowledge communities' builds on the knowledge focus of 'epistemic communities', whilst referring to several other notions of communities or networks of actors relevant to the theoretical basis of, or the knowledge perspective for this book. More specifically, the book places an emphasis on the knowledge base of 'causal beliefs' as well as the values base of 'belief systems' underpinning advocacy groups, which factor into the production and use of 'knowledge'. Thus, the knowledge perspective that we bring to this book positions itself on recent debates about the role of knowledge in the policy development process, offering an interpretative lens through which to explore the stability and change of spatial planning policy approaches to territorial development challenges in an enlarged EU.

Furthermore, we consider this knowledge perspective to be particularly relevant to the continuing study of spatial planning in Europe, including European spatial planning, because of the increasingly complex interplay of knowledge and policy development in the institutionally dynamic and multi-jurisdictional space of European territorial governance. Further to our understanding of this multi-jurisdictional policy environment, we find that a number of existing arenas have evolved and new ones have emerged, within which spatially relevant knowledge is generated, debated and validated. The European Observation Network on Territorial Development and Cohesion (ESPON, formerly European Spatial Planning Observation Network) and the ongoing debate around the territorial dimension of the cohesion principle are testimony to this evolution. The resulting knowledge claims may be used, to a greater or lesser extent, to influence policy development and to increase the legitimacy of spatial planning practices in Europe. In other words, our consideration of how knowledge translates into the organizational and institutional forces that shape or 'frame' the course of spatial policy development is more akin to understanding the 'sticky places' of knowledge and power, which ground the 'slippery spaces' of knowledge flows. That is, to explore how and to what extent data, ideas and argument (knowledge resources) are channelled through 'arenas of action' (knowledge arenas) in an effort to shape or 'frame' policy. And to analyze what role 'territorial knowledge communities' have in this policy development process and how they utilize the organizational structures at the interface of knowledge resources and knowledge arenas – 'territorial knowledge channels' in our terminology.

In this regard, the key issues we want to consider are set within the evolving context of spatial planning in Europe as both a signifier of a growing body of diverse territorial governance practices, as well as an institutionalized arena for the interplay of knowledge and policy development:

- How do 'territorial knowledge communities' contribute to the transformation of institutional geographies of agent interaction as both institutionally enabling and constraining factors on policy development?
- How do different knowledge arenas link with the 'hard' regulatory spaces of planning systems, and the 'soft spaces' of territorial governance beyond the geographical and professional boundaries of these systems?

In the context of this book, a combination of emerging and more established academics have been encouraged to reflect on the above-mentioned issues in relation to the recent eastward enlargement of the EU. To facilitate this process, as editors we provided the contributors with flexible guidelines intended to encourage them to reflect on their own unique experiences and insights in light of the issues raised above. As time progressed, the editing process provided us with a series of extremely rich inputs in the form of drafts written by the various contributors and this review process stimulated the evolution of our theoretical exploration and allowed us to refine it and develop it further. The theoretical framework for the book, presented in detail in Chapter 2, is therefore the product of both the preliminary considerations behind this project as well as the continuous interaction between the editors and the individual contributors throughout the editing process. The various elements of the framework were discussed with the contributors at various stages, strengthening reciprocal understanding and stimulating the fine tuning of the different elements.

The book thus provides a collection of different experiences and perspectives built around a common goal for which its shape and scope has evolved since the inception of the idea over three years ago. Far from being discouraging, the process of incremental readjustment and the sharpening of our main focus has been extremely rewarding because it has allowed us to dig deeper and deeper into the different issues and to better grasp those aspects that once seemed blurred. This process has been possible thanks to the proactive attitude of the different contributors, whose enriching comments allowed us to put things into perspective more effectively. In some ways the process has generated as many questions as answers but if the book provides an input into the debates surrounding European territorial development, cohesion and spatial planning in an enlarged EU, and generates additional engagement and critical reflections, then this will be the greatest reward for our work and we will consider our goal achieved.

Acknowledgements

The publication of this book represents the end of a journey that began during the 1st Aesop Young Academics Meeting, 'Central and Eastern European Engagement', in Bratislava, Slovakia in February 2007. Before starting to unfold the main issues of the discussion, we would like to thank all the people who, through their professional and/or personal support, participated in the translation of our passion for the themes of enquiry into written form. The network that was established at that initial meeting has since been consolidated and extended. The considerations presented in the book have been continuously stimulated and fuelled by a proactive interaction between all contributors that has demonstrated a level of commitment above and beyond what we expected and without which we would not have been able to bring the process to such a satisfying conclusion. All contributors have participated fully in the process and engaged positively with the rigorous editorial process, which involved several rounds of comments and revisions to individual contributions. We therefore owe a debt of gratitude to all of the contributors and look forward to working with them again in the future.

The meeting in Bratislava was the first occasion when the three of us met, two being there as organizers of the event and the third as invited guest. The interesting considerations emerging from the seminar, as well as the quality and scientific relevance of the contributions presented there, provided us with the necessary enthusiasm to start the extremely demanding process that lies behind this project. During these three years various people have contributed directly or indirectly to the operations that allowed this book to come into being. In the first place, we would like to thank the supporters of the meeting where all this started, i.e. on one side the Association of European Schools of Planning (AESOP) and particularly former president Peter Ache and all the executive committee members, and on the other side the Faculty of Architecture of the Slovakian University of Technology, and especially Maroš Finka and Dagmar Petrikova who were directly involved in the organization of the meeting and provided us with financial and logistical support. We would also like to thank our publishing Editor and the team at Routledge for their patience and support, and the various colleagues who, at various stages, have provided us with valued feedback on the drafts of various parts of the book. Special thanks go to Stephen Ward and Tim

Marshall of Oxford Brookes University, Gordon Dabinett of University of Sheffield, and Dominic Stead and Bas Waterhout of Delft University of Technology. Their valuable comments and insights have undoubtedly enabled us to strengthen the quality of the book. Jo van Hees also deserves a big thank you for providing the necessary support for the graphics in Chapter 2.

In addition, Neil Adams would like to thank his colleagues at London South Bank University for their support. A special thank you also goes to Professor Jeremy Alden for inspiration and to Lowie Steenwegen with whom my passion for Central and Eastern Europe was ignited during numerous projects in the Baltic States and elsewhere. Finally the biggest thank you of all goes to my family, especially to Tracy, Kelly and Molly for their patience and support. Giancarlo Cotella would like to thank his colleagues at the Inter-University Department of Territorial Studies and Planning of the Polytechnic University of Torino for the continuous confrontation on territorial themes. Special thanks go to Umberto Janin Rivolin and Loris Servillo, with whom I share an interest in the evolution of spatial planning domestic systems within the framework of EU territorial governance. Finally, warm thanks go to my family, to Valentina and to all those who, despite living outside the academic environment, have supported with their love the completion of this project. And lastly Richard Nunes would like to close with added heartfelt thanks to Teresa for her patience and understanding, and to Sophia whose reassuring smiles are beyond words.

1 Spatial planning in Europe

The interplay between knowledge and policy in an enlarged EU

Neil Adams, Giancarlo Cotella and Richard Nunes

Introduction

The overall aim of this book is to explore the interplay between knowledge and policy development[1] in the evolving landscape of spatial planning in Europe, within the context of the two most recent enlargements of the European Union (EU). The geographical focus of this book is appropriately centred on Central and Eastern Europe (CEE), a spatial planning environment that has undergone significant changes as a consequence of EU accession and a relatively unknown planning terrain when compared to North-western European casework in mainstream Anglo-American academic journals. In this regard, this region is taken to be a particularly useful context for the exploration of new territorial development issues, new planning ideas and approaches, new actors, and new forms of engagement and arenas of action. The context provided by European spatial planning, including the drafting process of the Territorial Agenda, the consolidation of the European Observation Network for Territorial Development and Cohesion (ESPON, formerly European Spatial Planning Observation Network) and the publication of the *Green Paper on Territorial Cohesion*, has led to the intersection of new ideas, data and argument, and to the emergence of new arenas at both EU and Member State levels. At the same time, the complex processes of institutional change and organizational learning characterizing the CEE domestic contexts have stimulated new and evolving territorial governance arrangements and processes of policy development, which in turn influence European spatial planning. The outcomes of these EU and domestic level responses to the eastwards enlargement merit an exploration of the interplay of knowledge and policy development. In order to do this, the rationale for the volume draws on a number of theories and case studies, which form the basis for the elaboration of a theoretical framework to explore how emergent ideas and approaches translate into the organizational and institutional forces that shape or frame spatial policy. In so doing, we will examine some of the evolving challenges with respect to territorial development, cohesion and spatial planning in the EU in light of enlargement and, more generally, within the framework of the ongoing processes of Europeanization, internationalization and globalization.

The book assesses some of the approaches and trends in terms of spatial planning policy and practice that are emerging out of these processes, both at the European level as well as within different domestic contexts. In the context of the book, CEE is interpreted as including ten of the twelve new Member States that have joined the EU since 2004 – eight of the 2004 entrants, Czech Republic, Estonia, Hungary, Latvia, Lithuania, Poland, Slovakia and Slovenia, and the two most recent entrants, Bulgaria and Romania. Despite being a heterogeneous grouping, CEE countries share some common characteristics in terms of relatively low prosperity levels compared to the EU average at the time of their accession, and their ongoing transition and transformation from a former Soviet or socialist state to democracy and a market economy. As the different contributions to the present volume highlight, these characteristics have significant implications for current territorial development trends, challenges and identities. At the same time, a pivotal role is played by the endogenous features of the different national and local contexts. This complexity is reflected in the growing heterogeneity of approaches to spatial planning in the enlarged EU and merits close scrutiny of the politics of policy development and multi-level governance operations (Hooghe and Marks 2001), from transnational to local agendas. In this context, we hope that the book will not only promote increased awareness and understanding of these issues, but also harness some of the extensive 'knowledge' within CEE countries and promote discussion that will enrich the discourse within an enlarged European spatial planning community of academics, practitioners and policy-makers.

It is not the intention of this book to provide a comprehensive account of the spatial planning systems and policies of the CEE countries individually. A variety of sources exist in this regard such as the EU-funded Baltic Sea Conceptshare (COMMIN), which provides details of the planning systems in the Baltic Sea Region, and the project ESPON 2.3.2 *Governance of Territorial and Urban Policies from EU to Local Level* (ESPON 2007), for which the aim (amongst others) was to update and extend the *EU Compendium of Spatial Planning Systems and Policies* (CEC 1997) to include the new EU Member States. In addition, there is a growing academic literature focusing on spatial planning challenges and approaches in different countries post enlargement (Adams *et al.* 2006a; Altrock *et al.* 2006; Cotella 2007; Knieling and Othengrafen 2009). However, the post-enlargement scenario examined in the book offers a unique opportunity to explore the evolution of the heterogeneous landscape for spatial planning in Europe. The complex cross-scalar and multi-disciplinary nature of spatial planning practice in an enlarged EU stimulates many planning practitioners to take part in multiple professional communities and networks. Participation in these communities and networks often leads them to seek modes of reference from their domestic planning system and approaches in the course of developing strategic actions on transnational or cross-border spatial challenges. In support of our belief in the importance of the spatial dimension of policies with a territorial impact, we argue that the future success of EU territorial development policy may, to a large degree, depend on the extent and nature of the engagement of academics, practitioners and policy-makers with a politics of expertise. Furthermore we argue that, by way of this interaction, a better understanding is necessary of the changes and challenges that have been 'mapped out' or 'framed' in terms of spatial planning both between and within the regions of the enlarged EU. In light of this particular concern, an understanding of the contribution that CEE academics, practitioners and policy-makers will provide to the process of shaping and framing spatial policy, as well as their influence in shaping the channels through which knowledge and expertise are translated into policy and practice, is of utmost importance.

By way of introduction, this chapter outlines the aims of the book and sets the context for this exploration in more detail. After a brief introduction to the multi-jurisdictional policy environment of the EU, the discussion explores the heterogeneous landscape for spatial planning in Europe in more detail. The historical context, the impact of the enlargements and the emergence of a new east-west dimension that requires the consideration of a broader geographical context are all examined. Subsequently, the focus of the chapter shifts to European spatial planning and examines the increased focus on knowledge that has characterized the informal process of its institutionalization. The emergence of multiple arenas of action within the complex field of European spatial planning is discussed in the light of the road toward, and the aftermath of the eastwards enlargement. Then, the territorial turn of EU policies is taken into account, and potential future directions and perspectives are discussed. Finally the structure of the book is explained and the individual contributions introduced.

Building on EU enlargement in a multi-jurisdictional policy environment

The most significant contextual elements for this book are the heterogeneous landscape for spatial planning in Europe in the context of enlargement – as it manifests within the various domestic contexts (cf. Nadin and Stead 2008) – and the still somewhat ambiguous set of European guidance documents, policies and interventions characterized by a specific 'spatial' or 'territorial' focus, often referred to as European spatial planning (Williams 1996; Faludi 2001; Husson 2002; Janin Rivolin 2004; Waterhout 2008).[2] Within this framework, the concepts of 'hard' and 'soft' spaces, and 'hard' and 'soft' forms of planning have recently gained prominence as part of the rescaling processes that have taken place in territorial governance responses to the perceived inadequacies of planning within the regulatory scope and remit of statutory planning systems, as well as to wider processes such as EU enlargement and the devolution of power in domestic contexts. Faludi (2010 forthcoming) points out that in reality all spaces or jurisdictions are historical and social constructs rather than objective facts. Over time such spaces become naturalized as national or sub-national spaces, although these 'hard' administrative boundaries are subject to change through either catastrophic events such as war or through more peaceful but nevertheless dramatic processes such as the collapse of the Soviet Union or EU enlargement.

The idea of 'hard' spaces with fixed borders fits well with the rationale for 'hard' or regulatory forms of planning. The fact that in reality movements of people and goods, functions and activities and a whole range of challenges and opportunities do not respect these 'hard' borders implies that regulatory forms of planning are unlikely to provide ideal solutions. Haughton *et al.* argue for a combination of 'hard' and 'soft' spaces and forms of planning, suggesting that 'soft' spaces 'are valued as a mechanism for encouraging more creative thinking, unconstrained by regulation and national guidance, and providing greater opportunities for a range of non-planning actors to engage more productively with the planning process' (2010: 240). The potential effectiveness of spatial planning may depend on the ability that planners demonstrate to work creatively with a combination of 'hard' and 'soft' spaces and instruments. The utilization of 'soft' spaces in particular is likely to require engagement with a broader group of actors and involve the creation of new channels and arenas and could potentially have a significant impact on the policy development process.

The key components of these contextual elements require a consideration of the entwined dynamics of knowledge (in relation to mechanisms and processes of its production, diffusion and validation) and power (in relation to competency issues, and the relative power of the different actors within decision making processes to shape policy development by influence, force or control). While the importance of knowledge in planning in different contexts is widely recognized (Sandercock 2003; Rydin 2007), it is by no means the only important factor. The capacity to develop and cultivate knowledge and to be able to apply it in an appropriate manner to achieve identified goals is also crucial (Levin 2007). This process of development, cultivation and application of knowledge is strongly subjected to power logics. In turn, it also influences those logics, and the balance of existing power relations. Within this process, a crucial role is played by networks or communities of actors – 'territorial knowledge communities' in our terminology. Along with the resources they produce ('knowledge resources') and the arenas within which they operate ('knowledge arenas'), these communities are central to the main focus of the rationale for this book and to the theoretical framework in relation to 'territorial knowledge channels' (Nunes *et al.* 2009; Cotella *et al.* 2010), which we use to explore the interplay between knowledge and policy development. A more detailed elaboration of the concepts of knowledge resources (in terms of ideas, data and argument) and knowledge arenas, and a further exploration of the meaning and role of territorial knowledge communities and territorial knowledge channels is provided in Chapter 2.

In the context of the above discussion, detailed consideration is required of the new east-west dimension of European territorial governance due to the major spatial consequences of the enlargements of 2004 and 2007. The continuous interaction of domestic and supranational arenas both within the EU and beyond (for example in the context of the Council of Europe, cf. CEMAT 1984) has promoted the transfer of planning ideas, techniques and approaches both horizontally between countries and vertically between different levels within this multi-jurisdictional policy environment. Due to the complex two-way interactions between supranational and domestic contexts, it can be argued that European spatial planning operates as a form of governance but also as a form of metagovernance, as its discursive and operative elements trickle down to influence domestic spatial planning debates and agendas. Metagovernance refers to the governance of governance systems or, in other words, to the guidance of governance systems in a way that seeks to ensure that they are complementary and mutually reinforcing (Haughton *et al.* 2010); though in practice this would appear to reflect an idealized view rather than reality. As Kule *et al.* discuss in the case of Latvia in this volume (Chapter 12; cf. also Fritsch, Chapter 15, and Razumeyko, Chapter 16), such interactions are not necessarily restricted to within the EU or intra-European interactions often referred to as 'Europeanization' (cf. among others Olsen 2002; Radaelli 2004; Radaelli and Saurugger 2008). More importantly, in recent years these processes of Europeanization – and more generally processes of internationalization – have taken place within a context that has seen an increased focus on knowledge and evidence to underpin the course of policy development (Faludi and Waterhout 2006a, 2006b; Davoudi 2006a). The institutionalization of the European Observation Network on Territorial Development and Cohesion (ESPON) and the elaboration of the *Territorial State and Perspectives of the European Union* (DE Presidency 2007a), which provided the evidence base for the *Territorial Agenda of the European Union* (DE Presidency 2007b), clearly illustrate this increased emphasis on knowledge in policy development. More recently, the publication of the *Green Paper on Territorial Cohesion* (CEC 2008) has broadened the debate, representing the latest manifestation of the evolution of European spatial planning. In the remainder of this section, we seek to draw out the heterogeneous landscape of spatial planning *in* Europe as well as the ever evolving activity of spatial planning *for* Europe (Böhme 2002), commonly referred to as European spatial planning, both of which have clearly taken on new facets as a result of the recent eastwards enlargements.

The heterogeneous landscape for spatial planning in Europe

In this section the heterogeneous landscape for spatial planning in Europe will be explored, particularly in relation to the various domestic contexts. The historical reasons behind the evolution of planning in Europe are briefly discussed before some of the implications and consequences of enlargement for planning practices in the Member States are outlined. Finally, the new east-west dimension that has emerged as a result of enlargement is examined, along with the broader geographical context that has created new challenges for the Member States at the micro, meso and macro scale.

Emergence of planning in Europe

A wide diversity of events and processes has transformed Europe in a number of ways in the post-war period and in spatial development terms Europe has experienced rapid urbanization during this time. Increases in personal wealth and car ownership rates, higher expectations regarding housing quality and a movement of population away from employment in agriculture towards the industrial and services sectors have been associated with the effects of this rapid urbanization. These processes have increased development pressures dramatically in many locations in order to house the growing urban population, to accommodate industries or offices, to develop transport networks to link to new uses and to provide for national and international movements of people and goods (Williams 1984). The impact of these phenomena has been such that all European countries have deemed it necessary to establish some effective procedure to channel these pressures and resolve conflicts between competing land uses or, in former socialist and Soviet countries of CEE, to plan and control their organization through centrally defined rational plans. Legislation has been introduced in each country to establish the principle that public authorities should be empowered to monitor and control territorial development and prepare plans, identifying what types of development will be permitted and where they would be most appropriate. Such legislation was introduced at different times in different countries from the late nineteenth century onward, depending on political attitudes to the acceptability of these regulatory powers, which may be regarded as infringing individual rights to exploit private property, and on diverse perceptions of the value of planning in different contexts.

Healey and Williams argued that the diversity of planning systems and practices in Europe is therefore the result of a range of related issues such as 'specific histories and geographies of particular places, and the way these interlock with national institutional structures, cultures and economic opportunities' (1993: 716). The fascination of taking an international view of planning lies exactly in the great diversity to be found within spatial planning systems and approaches (both formal and informal) that have been established; that is, a diversity apparent both in the associated legal and administrative structures and procedures as well as in the policies and priorities that are pursued in different contexts and at different territorial levels. On the one hand, there has been an increasing recognition that much can be learnt from studying these differences and this is reflected in the growing academic literature examining different spatial planning systems (among others cf. Newman and Thornley 1996; CEC 1997; ESPON 2007; Adams *et al.* 2006a, Nadin and Stead 2008).[3] On the other hand, only limited efforts have been made at the EU level to capitalize on this diversity of spatial planning practices (Finka, Chapter 5), which can more readily present itself as an obstacle in terms of coordination capacity and mutual understanding than as an asset.

Consequences of enlargement

Several authors (Adams 2008; Nadin and Stead 2008; Stead 2008) have identified a range of external pressures, including globalization, sustainable development, economic competitiveness, European integration, economic reforms, increasing environmental challenges and demographic change – all of which are influencing the evolution of domestic planning systems. However, one of the key drivers of change in the context of this book has been the enlargement of the EU, which has clearly had a dramatic impact in terms of increasing the diversity of an already highly heterogeneous EU family. CEE countries were required to undertake institutional, administrative and socio-economic reforms at an unprecedented scale in the pre-accession period, which has impacted all policy fields and institutional and administrative structures. It was for this reason that these countries were the first candidate countries to be offered a substantial package of funds in the pre-accession process in order to facilitate what Williams (1996) referred to as both the transition (referring to the formal institutional changes) and the transformation (a step beyond trans-ition so that structural behavioural changes are achieved) to democracy and a market economy – both pre-requisites to EU membership. Three pre-accession instruments were introduced with the purpose of facilitating administrative reform and building institutional capacity. The PHARE, ISPA and SAPARD [4] programmes promoted economic and social cohesion, improvements to trans-port and environmental infrastructure, and rural development respectively. The intention was to stimulate necessary reforms, to strengthen the capacity of the CEE countries, and to ensure that new institutions would be more able to absorb the more substantial EU funding that would become available to them upon accession. The complexity of managing three separate instruments, with differ-ent time frames and ways of working, provided numerous difficulties for both the European Commission and for the then candidate countries. On the basis of these experiences, they were replaced in 2007 by a single integrated Instrument for Pre-Accession Assistance (IPA). Similarly, a number of geographically and thematically focused neighbourhood instruments (for example CARDS, TACIS and MEDA) have been replaced by a single comprehensive European Neigh-bourhood and Partnership Instrument (ENPI).[5] This evolution clearly demon-strates that, while the EU influences domestic realities through processes of Europeanization (for example, through mechanisms of conditionality linked to the adoption of regulations and to the requirements for accessing funding), the EU policy landscape has also been subject to significant influence and change as a result of enlargement. In other words this implies both top-down and circu-lar interactions between the EU level and Member States, as well as horizontal interactions between Member States (cf. Stead and Nadin, Chapter 7). However, the extent to which Europeanization mechanisms impact on embedded institu-tional practices in reality is open to debate, whether such processes relate to the satisfaction of the accession requirements or later, in the post-enlargement sce-nario, to the embeddedness within EU multi-level governance as a full Member State (cf. Marot, Chapter 8; Dąbrowski, Chapter 9).

The external pressures identified earlier have further stimulated the processes of Europeanization and internationalization. Though, as Healey (2010) identi-fies, such interactions are by no means a new phenomenon. In combination with enlargement, however, these external processes have clearly given an impetus to increased transnational cooperation and networking among spatial planning practices, enabled through European initiatives such as the INTERREG programmes. These interactions have resulted in policy-makers increasingly becoming influenced by and exposed to practices from abroad and to approaches and ideas developed within wider European knowledge arenas. In principle, the processes of Europeanization could contribute to a convergence around particular 'styles' or ideal types of planning. However, the reality is more complex. Despite the integration of EU Directives into domestic legislation and the adoption of a common spatial planning language (Pallagst 2006), as well as the many common challenges facing domestic planning systems, the deeply embedded differences between European countries in terms of political and administrative cultures and structures potentially limit the scope for the Europeanization of spatial planning. In other words, the consequences of Europeanization are different in different places due to the diversity of domestic characteristics (cf. Giannakourou 2005; Dühr *et al.* 2007; Böhme and Waterhout 2008; Waterhout *et al.* 2009; Dühr *et al.* 2010). Be this as it may, one can hardly dispute the fact that the frontier of European integration has experienced a dramatic eastwards shift due to enlargement and this new east-west dimension will now be explored in more detail.

The new east-west dimension and the broader geographical context

Enlargement has created a new east-west dimension for spatial planning in Europe. A Union founded and developed from a strongly western perspective, has been confronted with a dramatically different and challenging reality in terms of economic, social and territorial development (see Davoudi 2006b). Thus the challenging macroeconomic situation affecting many CEE nations present significant social, economic and spatial challenges for diverse strategic policy sectors such as the economy, education, environment and social welfare. Furthermore, the combination of these factors provides a highly challenging context to which domestic planning systems and approaches (formal and informal) have had to adapt. As a result, the new east-west dimension of EU territorial governance has had considerable impact on the spatial planning discourse in an already heterogeneous spatial planning landscape and took the existing heterogeneity to a new and unprecedented level. The spatial planning discourse has been opened up to new questions, new challenges and issues, new actors, and new forms of engagement and 'arenas of action' (Steinmo *et al.* 1992; Hall and Taylor 1996; Lowndes 1996), which have generated new planning ideas and approaches. In our opinion, the participation of these new actors in existing and emerging knowledge arenas is likely to lead to new knowledge resources being generated which may potentially have a significant impact on spatial planning policy and practice in both the EU and domestic contexts.

In addition to the pressures for change and the enlargement process, which are shaping domestic planning systems and approaches, enlargement has also created new pressures in the form of new geopolitical tensions and power relations at various territorial scales. Coupled with increasing environmental challenges (e.g. climate change) and energy resource concerns, this means that the EU and its Member States are constantly facing a different set of relations that are embedded in their role within a broader region. This broader region overlaps with the territorial scale of Europe as a continent, further emphasizing the importance of the newly acquired east-west dimension mentioned above, although the implications of this new dimension play themselves out in different ways at various territorial scales. Discussions and cooperation in relation to spatial development in the broader European context take place in the framework of the Council of Europe (CoE), within the long established European Conference of Ministers for Spatial/Regional Planning (CEMAT). At the same time, there has been increased attention post enlargement from both academics (Kunzmann 2008) and the European Commission on this external dimension. The desire to shed some light on the global role played by the EU is demonstrated by the recent launch of several research projects funded under the ESPON programme (*Territorial cooperation in transnational areas and across internal/external borders* and *Continental territorial structures and flows (globalization)*) and 7th Framework Programme (FP7. Socio-Economic Science and Humanities for 2010: *EU regions and their interaction with the neighbourhood regions* and *Analysis of the impacts of global changes*) – all of which focus on the further exploration of the position of the EU within a broader geographical context.

It is clear that such initiatives will contribute to the evolution of a knowledge base that can inform future policy, implying a growing recognition of the importance of looking beyond the borders of the EU. In the context of the geographical focus of this book on CEE, it is the Eastern external border and more specifically the external border with North-west Russia that is the most relevant. For reasons related to history, geopolitics, culture, scale and geography, the relationship between the EU and Russia is one of the principal challenges for the EU on the global political stage; although these challenges will manifest themselves not only at the macro-level but also at the meso- and micro-levels as will be discussed later in the book (cf. Fritsch, Chapter 15, and Razumeyko, Chapter 16).

European spatial planning: building on the eastwards enlargement

The second key contextual element in relation to this book is the somewhat ambiguous field of European spatial planning. In this section we focus on European spatial planning, first examining the extent of the progressive institutionalization of this rather esoteric field of policy and research (Evers 2007) and the increasing emphasis on knowledge and evidence. The road to enlargement is then described, before the focus shifts to some of the key knowledge arenas within which European spatial planning has been discussed and debated in the period since the publication of the *European Spatial Development Perspective* (ESDP. CEC 1999). Finally, potential new directions for European spatial planning in the future are debated in the light of the rationale for this book.

Institutionalization and increased focus on knowledge

European spatial planning is not new and, as Faludi (2009) has pointed out, the EU has had an implicit territorial agenda since its inception. Spatial and regional planning has a history at the EU level going back to the 1960s, when the Council of Europe focused increasingly on the need for regional planning. Since then, there has been an increasing realization of the need to consider the spatial impacts of sectoral spending programmes. Despite this regional policy concern, only 20 years ago, when the Member States' ministers responsible for spatial planning informally met for the first time in Nantes under the French Presidency, even the more enthusiastic experts would have been reluctant to affirm the importance of a spatial dimension for EU policy, mainly because of the lack of legitimate EU competence in this field (Williams 1996). During this 20 year period, elements of European spatial planning became more institutionalized (cf. Waterhout 2008 and in Chapter 4) through a process that led to the publication of the ESDP (CEC 1999) and, more recently, to the *Territorial Agenda for the European Union* (DE Presidency 2007b). With the inclusion of territorial cohesion in the recently ratified Lisbon Treaty, Faludi (2009) has argued that a turning point has been reached in relation to the competence issue, whereby the Member States now seem to appreciate the importance of the territorial dimension of EU policy.

As with many policy fields relevant to the multi-jurisdictional policy environment of the EU, the evolution of European spatial planning has experienced an increased focus on knowledge to support policy. The provision of an evidence base for the more recent reference documents with a spatial or territorial focus illustrates this growing emphasis. The increased focus on knowledge in spatial policy development, matured within the ongoing process of European integration, has provided opportunities for mutual learning processes (Faludi and Waterhout 2006a). This increased focus on knowledge has also resulted in the creation of a diversity of arenas where such knowledge is shared, tested, validated and recreated. Waterhout (Chapter 4) refers to the ESPON Programme, the European Territorial Co-operation objective (INTERREG), the Territorial Agenda and the debate on territorial cohesion as the pillars of European spatial planning. In addition, arenas such as INTERREG and ESPON also contribute to the institutionalization of European spatial planning. More importantly in the context of this book, they function (along with the other pillars identified by Waterhout) as both knowledge arenas in their own right whilst at the same time generating other arenas within which knowledge resources in relation to spatial planning *in* and *for* Europe are shared, tested, validated and recreated. Previously the ESDP process also performed such a role. Given that INTERREG and ESPON can be viewed in these different ways suggests that European spatial planning today remains a heterogeneous – and not always coherent – set of actions, procedures and guidelines on spatial matters that are continuously evolving in light of the reciprocal influences occurring between the supranational and domestic spheres.

The 'power' component of European spatial planning has also evolved. That is, the limited institutionalization of a spatial dimension of European policies can be related to the absence of legitimate power or competences of the EU in the field of spatial planning. Several authors (including Williams 1996; Janin Rivolin 2008; Waterhout 2008 and in Chapter 4) have identified the lack of references to spatial planning or territorial governance in any of the EU Treaties. To some extent it is therefore surprising that an informal policy domain (i.e. a policy domain in which the EU does not possess any competence, either exclusively or in coordination with the Member States), such as spatial planning, has such a long history in the context of the EU. Notwithstanding this competence issue, the spatial dimension has incrementally and progressively consolidated its position within the EU political agenda, most recently with the ratification of the Lisbon Treaty. At the same time, the EU exerted a degree of influence over spatial development issues, mainly through its regional policy and funding mechanisms, which additionally contribute to the power component of European spatial planning. While discussing the various stages in the increased spatialization of EU policies, Waterhout explores a set of tensions that clearly illustrate the overlap between the components of power and capital in the complex and multiple interactions between the EU and the Member States, whereby the EU utilizes capital as a means of exerting influence and power via conditionality processes (2008; cf. also Schimmelfenning and Sedelmeier 2005). This helps to explain how, in this complex cross-scalar policy environment, the focus on the extent and nature of the way that knowledge and power are intertwined in European spatial planning has received a significant impetus in the reality of the post-enlargement EU.

Road to enlargement and emergence of post-ESDP knowledge arenas for European spatial planning

The impact of enlargement on spatial planning discourse in the domestic contexts of Member States was identified earlier in this chapter. However, the reciprocal nature of the transnational and national interactions in the multi-jurisdictional policy environment of the EU, mean that similar new questions, challenges, issues, actors, forms of engagement and arenas have also significantly impacted the European spatial planning field.

To a certain extent, European spatial planning has emerged and started to mature in institutional and policy terms simultaneously with the recent enlargement processes. Discussions regarding possible EU membership for the so called Visegrad countries (Czech Republic, Hungary, Poland and Slovakia), the Baltic States (Estonia, Latvia and Lithuania), the former Yugoslav Republic of Slovenia, and for the countries of Romania and Bulgaria all commenced in the early 1990s. The official opening of EU doors to post-socialist countries occurred during the European Council of Copenhagen in 1993 and formal candidatures were submitted for all countries by 1996. During the same period, the inter-governmental Committee for Spatial Development, established under the Dutch

Presidency in 1991, was promoting a discourse about a spatial vision for Europe that ultimately resulted in the publication of the ESDP in 1999 (CEC 1999). The preparation process and the role of the various actors within the ESDP arena has been well documented (see Faludi and Waterhout 2002) and the importance of the document is recognized as the 'proudest achievement of European spatial planning' (Faludi 2001: 245). Despite claims that the ESDP was nothing more than a paper tiger (Kunzmann 2003), it ultimately evolved into an influential source of knowledge and learning that consequently has represented a watershed moment for European spatial planning – not only because it was the product of almost a decade of discussion and negotiation, but also because in many ways it defined what European spatial planning had become.

Partly as a result of the ESDP, a number of knowledge arenas have since emerged and/or consolidated, within which the European planning community (cf. Waterhout, Chapter 4) have continued the discourse over territorial development and spatial planning. Two of the most important knowledge arenas in the post-ESDP period have been the former Community Initiative INTERREG and ESPON. The former was introduced in 1989 but consolidated itself as an influential arena for European spatial planning partly as a result of the attention of the ESDP for transnational cooperation (Stead and Waterhout 2008). The latter was established as a response to the lack of an evidence base underpinning the ESDP, which reduced its legitimacy among some sectoral actors.

INTERREG now forms part of the European Territorial Cooperation objective, which has been mainstreamed to become one of the three regional policy priorities of the EU in the current 2007–2013 programming period. It has provided a distinct arena within which spatially relevant ideas, data and approaches have been discussed and debated by planners and others. While a systematic analysis of the results and outputs of INTERREG is well beyond the scope of this book, it can be assumed that the knowledge arenas and resources generated amongst the INTERREG community have been amongst the most significant. Much of this knowledge has been in the form of so called 'good and best practices', but the extent to which this can be classed as policy relevant or usable knowledge is open to debate (cf. Stead and Nadin, Chapter 7). The various INTERREG secretariats have been united in applying more stringent approval criteria to projects in recent years, insisting that all applications demonstrate policy relevance and the transferable likelihood of project outputs. For European spatial planning, some of the most significant resources generated from INTERREG have been the various transnational spatial strategies (cf. Zonneveld 2005). Building upon the ethos established by the ESDP, these documents were highly strategic and non-binding spatial visions that were the product of an exclusive group of spatial planners with some of the characteristics of an 'epistemic community' of expert professionals with an authoritative claim on a shared policy-relevant knowledge base. The concept of an 'epistemic community' was introduced by Haas (1992) and, along with related concepts of 'communities of practice' (Lave and Wenger 1991; Wenger 1998) and 'advocacy coalitions' (Sabatier 1988), forms an important part of the basis of the theoretical framework for this book. It is communities and networks such as these that provide many of the key ingredients of the territorial knowledge communities mentioned earlier. The concepts and their interrelationships are explained in more detail in Chapter 2. Nevertheless, it can be argued that the learning and knowledge generated during the processes that have contributed to the institutionalization of European spatial planning have been more important than the European documents themselves. This further reinforces the sense of European spatial planning as an arena for learning and the generation of knowledge, and potentially stimulates further consolidation of professional networks and communities throughout the EU.

Ultimately, the establishment of ESPON, under the umbrella of INTERREG, has been perhaps the most significant consequence of the ESDP. During the preparation process for the ESDP, it became apparent that 'usable' spatially relevant knowledge (Haas 2004) was at best fragmented and in some cases virtually non-existent – especially in the relation to CEE countries where integration into the EU was very much a relevant issue by the time the ESDP was published. Initially ESPON was established as an arena within which research institutions and networks throughout the EU could undertake research to generate knowledge arenas and resources to aid the Committee on Spatial Development in its discussions and deliberations. The current mission of ESPON, as identified on its website, is 'to support policy development and to build a European scientific community in the field of territorial development. The main aim is to increase the general body of knowledge about territorial structures, trends and policy impacts in an enlarged European Union' (www.espon2013.panteion.gr, accessed March 2010). The emphasis on the interplay between knowledge and policy development here is clear. One of the main criticisms of the ESPON 2006 Programme was that the benefits were primarily for the scientific community, identifying the need to generate knowledge arenas and resources that are policy relevant and in a form that can be transferred via relevant channels into the policy development process, which is one of the main challenges for the ESPON 2013 Programme. This will inevitably mean closing the gap between the research community that has traditionally been active in ESPON projects and policy-makers and practitioners, although the inherent differences between research and policy in terms of power relations and dynamics mean that this will be a difficult tension to resolve.

The territorial turn

The availability of substantial knowledge resources generated through the ESPON programme was one of the key differences between the preparation of the ESDP and the drafting of its long-awaited successor – the *Territorial Agenda of the European Union*, which was adopted during an informal meeting of ministers in Leipzig in May 2007 (DE Presidency 2007b). Although the Territorial Agenda had evolved into a short rhetoric document that lacked any substantial detail by the time it had been adopted, its preparation process had been driven by a desire to produce an evidence-based document that would strengthen the legitimacy of European spatial planning with diverse sectoral actors. The fact that the evidence base was ultimately consigned to a separate document, the *Territorial State and Perspectives of the European Union* (DE Presidency, 2007a), which was not placed before ministers for consideration, does not detract from the progress made in the provision of robust knowledge resources to underpin discussions about European spatial planning. Davoudi (2006a) argues that the current enthusiasm for evidence-based policy has its roots in an instrumental view of the policy-evidence interface, whereby there is a clear linear and direct relationship between evidence and policy. If this is the case, then that assumes, she argues, that either research/evidence drives policy or, vice versa, research follows policy. Davoudi appeals for a more enlightened approach, which she refers to as 'evidence-informed' policy-making, whereby the relationship between knowledge and policy development is more indirect. In this context, the aim of relevant knowledge arenas is to generate knowledge resources that can enlighten the debate and the context within which decisions are made.

The most recent arena within which European spatial planning and, more generally, spatial planning in Europe has been debated is represented by the ongoing discourse on theoretical boundaries and operational applications of the territorial dimension of the cohesion objective. Initially included in the Amsterdam Treaty as a secondary goal in 1997, the principle of 'territorial cohesion' has been enriched by the reflections published in the second, third and fourth Commission reports on economic and social cohesion (respectively: CEC 2001, 2004 and 2007). Eventually it became listed among the competences shared between the EU and the Member States in the Treaty establishing a constitution for Europe (Rome, 29 October 2004) and in the natural follow-up, the Lisbon Treaty (Lisbon, 13 December 2007). The territorial cohesion agenda has recently received an added dimension through the publication of the Commission's *Green Paper on Territorial Cohesion* (CEC 2008). As a matter of fact, the Green Paper provides little or no clarification as to the meaning of the idea (cf. Evers 2007 and Evers *et al.* 2009). Rather it has sought to stimulate the reactions of a wide diversity of actors with regard to the value and possible interpretations of the principle. In this sense, it represents a clear attempt by the European Commission to widen the discourse beyond the narrow expert community that has traditionally been engaged in European spatial planning. The 388 responses to the Green paper, from a variety of bodies, organizations and individuals, are available on the Commission website,[6] which provides an extremely valuable resource in relation to current interpretations of the principle. Over 150 responses were received from a wide diversity of interest groups from throughout the EU. Ten EU institutions such as the European Parliament and the Committee on Regional Development and seven different EU programmes including various INTERREG secretariats submitted responses, giving a clear indication that the territorial cohesion discourse has attracted the interest of a broad spectrum of EU institutional actors. National Governments and responsible ministries from all 27 Member States, except for Ireland, submitted responses – with the vast majority stating that they highly valued the potential of the principle. Regional and local authorities and organizations also submitted over 100 responses. More than 20 submissions were received from universities and research institutions from throughout the EU though, interestingly in the context of this book, only three of these university and research institutions were from CEE countries – two from Poland and one from Slovakia. This may imply an imbalance in the geographical distribution of the academic actors engaged in the territorial cohesion discourse, but it could equally reflect different cultures of engagement. Either way this may imply that the heterogeneity of the post-enlargement EU does not appear to be fully reflected yet in the territorial cohesion discourse (cf. Finka, Chapter 5).

New directions for European spatial planning?

Despite a continuous evolution, progressive institutionalization and the reaching of a potential turning point in relation to the competence issue, European spatial planning remains a somewhat ambiguous arena whose evolution is ongoing. Various authors in this volume, including Tewdwr-Jones (Chapter 3) and Waterhout (Chapter 4), emphasize the importance of European spatial planning demonstrating its added value to a broader audience. However, it can be argued that influential actors such as the European Commission, politicians and sectoral actors are seeking to move away from the high-level strategic aspirational style of the ESDP and the transnational spatial visions towards more pragmatic and action oriented forms of planning.[7] The move towards the evidence-based Territorial Agenda and the more pragmatic approach adopted in the most recent initiatives focusing on transnational spaces such as the EU Strategy for the Baltic Sea Region (CEC 2009, cf. Fritsch, Chapter 15) may reflect this and implies that spatial planning may need to reinvent itself in order to remain relevant. Interestingly, this pragmatic turn has already been adopted in the Danube area and is currently being considered for the North Sea Region and the Mediterranean area. Such a transition may imply a move away from what de Vries (2002) refers to as planning as communication (whereby planning is required to provide a context within which spatial development can be discussed and interpreted) towards planning as programming (whereby the active implementation of specific actions is the main aim). De Vries argues that planning processes in a cross-border or transnational context are unlikely to achieve consensus when planning is considered as programming and that therefore planning needs to be considered as communication, at least initially as an essential first step. Although in reality a combination of the two is likely to be necessary, any move towards the programming end of the spectrum would have significant implications not only for discussions about 'hard' and 'soft' spaces for planning action but also for the type of knowledge resources that existing and emerging knowledge arenas will be required to generate.

Road map for the reader

The final section of this introductory chapter provides an overview of the structure of the book, the various sections and the individual contributions. The book contains 14 contributions from a combination of widely published authors as well as emerging academics with expertise in European territorial development and spatial planning issues. All of the contributors provide critical and reflective commentary on the evolution of, and future challenges and opportunities for the territorial development agenda within the context of recent EU enlargement. This chapter sets the context for the discussion before we establish our theoretical framework for the book (Chapter 2). The remainder of the book is divided into four interrelated sections followed by a concluding discussion (Chapter 17). An editorial introduction precedes each part of the book, which focuses respectively on: (Part I) the challenges for, and cognitive bounds of, spatial planning in the enlarged EU, (Part II) the motivating factors underpinning the institutionalization and deinstitutionalization of territorial governance and spatial planning approaches, (Part III) the process of policy formation around increasing disparities and inequalities in the new regions of Europe, and (Part IV) a forward-looking reflection on the EU Eastern border with the Russian Federation – without which any book examining European territorial development would be incomplete.

Chapter 2 introduces the main theoretical basis upon which the rationale for the book is built and establishes the key theoretical elements that are used to explore the interplay between knowledge and policy development in the field of spatial planning. Building on those elements, the theoretical framework is presented as an interpretative lens through which the reader can view the various individual contributions. The introduction of the concept of territorial knowledge channels within this framework allows for the opening of a knowledge perspective on stability and change in the development of spatial policies in the multi-jurisdictional policy environment of an enlarged EU. The theoretical framework is enriched by an exploration of the concept of Europeanization within the broader context of EU multi-level governance, and by a discussion of the variables upon which Europeanization mechanisms are based.

Part I of the book examines some of the key territorial challenges and debates in the context of an enlarged EU. Mark Tewdwr-Jones (Chapter 3) explores some of the complexities and tensions in relation to the dual pursuance of competitiveness and cohesion and assesses the implications that this has for territorial development and spatial planning in Europe. The author examines the paradoxes in the notions of 'balanced economic competitiveness' and the more recent competitiveness and economic growth agendas. Trends in regional economic development and the role and implications of foreign direct investment (FDI) on spatial development in the EU are examined in detail. The role of spatial planning and accumulated spatial knowledge as a means of embedding investments within their new regions is discussed, setting the context for the discussions in the chapters that follow.

Bas Waterhout (Chapter 4) sets the context for the evolution of European spatial planning by examining its current state and future challenges. While acknowledging the importance of a 'European planning community' in the preparation of the ESDP, the author explores the extent to which this community has been able to consolidate and play a role in influencing EU policy fields. The discussion focuses on four 'pillars' of European spatial planning that have provided arenas within which knowledge resources have been debated since the publication of the ESDP: ESPON, EU Territorial Co-operation (INTERREG), the Territorial Agenda of the EU and the Commission Green Paper on Territorial Cohesion. The author explores the evolving context of European spatial planning in light of these pillars, with particular regard for its organizational ability and transformative capacity. The ability and capacity to engage with wider discourses by what Waterhout refers to in previous work as the 'European planning community' will clearly have a significant impact on the future of territorial development policy.

Drawing on the previous two chapters, Maroš Finka (Chapter 5) examines some of the evolving frameworks for regional development and spatial planning in the new regions of the EU, providing an initial CEE perspective on the evolution of spatial planning in Europe. The author examines some of the commonalities and differences impacting on territorial development in 'old' and 'new' Member States before considering the complexities of differentiation and integration among the diverse planning communities in the enlarged EU. Finka questions the logic of thinking about these issues in geographical terms and laments the fact that the processes in relation to both the ESDP and the Territorial Agenda have not capitalized on the potential offered by the diversity of planning communities in the enlarged EU, identifying this as a key challenge for the future.

Karina Pallagst (Chapter 6) examines the emergence of epistemic communities in the post-enlargement landscape and explores some of the theoretical implications for territorial development and for the spatial agenda of the EU. The chapter builds on earlier work by the same author (Pallagst 2006), which identified two possible scenarios for the evolution of European spatial planning and, more specifically, for the evolution of the community involved with spatial planning in Europe in the context of enlargement. The two scenarios, 'retention' and 'merger', are re-examined as the author seeks to conceptualize European spatial planning under enlargement conditions. This exercise provides a valuable contribution to the theoretical framework for the book as it attempts to tease out the complexities of the knowledge/policy interface and assesses some of the theoretical implications in relation to the discourse around European spatial development policy. This final chapter of the first part provides a thought provoking context for the discussions that follow in Parts II–IV, and it has been a motivating element of the editors' overall rationale for this book.

Part II directs the geographical focus more specifically on the CEE Member States that have joined the EU since 2004. This section explores some of the complexities of multi-level governance and the evolution of the institutional landscape within the rapidly evolving environment of a 'new Europe', giving consideration to engaging systems of multi-level governance by analysing different national realities from various territorial levels. Dominic Stead and Vincent Nadin (Chapter 7) explore the shifts in territorial governance and the issue of Europeanization of spatial planning. The authors begin by looking at some common spatial development challenges across the EU before focusing on the concept of Europeanization, which is explained with reference to the flows of policy, information and experience among EU Member States and among relevant actors. The chapter makes a valuable contribution to the book by exploring the interplay between knowledge and policy development within these processes and assessing the role of epistemic communities in this context. Following on from a further discussion of spatial development trends in both Western Europe and CEE, the authors conclude with a discussion of the extent to which a convergence in planning systems and policies can be detected.

Naja Marot (Chapter 8) explores new planning jurisdictions and local public responsibility in a context characterized by scarce resources. The study focuses on the delivery of spatial planning in Slovenia, reflecting on the limited use of knowledge generated within planning arenas in the policy development process, and discussing the challenges that this creates for the delivery of spatial planning at the sub-national level. The discussion is appropriate to other parts of CEE where similar challenges are emerging in a fluid, rapidly evolving and highly politicized context. Marcin Dąbrowski (Chapter 9) focuses on the institutional change, partnerships and networks in relation to the implementation of the Structural Funds in Poland and the impact that this has had on institutional practices and processes of collective learning. The case study focuses on the management of Structural Funds in Lower Silesia and provides some valuable insights into the realities of collective learning in practice and the practical consequences of the conditions imposed by the EU in order to satisfy the accession requirements. The final chapter in this section is written by Beatrix Haselsberger and Paul Benneworth (Chapter 10) who examine the evolution of cross-border communities on the basis of a case study of the dynamics of territorial cooperation in the Austrian–Slovakian border region, providing useful insights into one of the key pillars discussed by Waterhout (Chapter 4). The chapter begins by examining the importance of borders in the European planning context before focusing more specifically on cross-border planning in a multi-jurisdictional policy environment. The chapter adds significant depth to the theoretical basis for the book by examining the concepts of 'epistemic communities' and 'communities of practice' within this context.

Part III examines one of the enduring challenges for regional policy; that is, the prospects of addressing increasing disparities and inequalities in the new regions of the EU. It deals with the complexities of pursuing territorial cohesion at the EU level in the face of new socio-economic realities of increasing interregional disparities within many Member States. The opening chapter in this section assesses the realities and the complexities of the cohesion agenda in parts of CEE. The author, Karel Maier (Chapter 11), focuses on elements of the European spatial planning discourse that are well established among the planning community in the 'old' EU Member States such as disparities, territorial cohesion, polycentric development and territorial capital, and examines them from a CEE perspective. In so doing, the chapter makes a particularly useful contribution to a discourse that has until now received relatively little attention in many

CEE countries, partially due to the fragmented nature of different planning communities. The discussion also focuses on the extent to which the integration of the planning community in Europe appears to be more of an obsession within the community of the 'old' Member States, and this not only provides food for thought but also has important implications with regard to the scenarios discussed by Pallagst (Chapter 6).

Laila Kule, Zaiga Krisjane and Maris Berzins (Chapter 12) focus on the rhetoric and reality of pursuing territorial cohesion in Latvia. Latvia provides an interesting context for this discussion because it encapsulates many of the tensions and contradictions of the simultaneous pursuance of competitiveness and cohesion already discussed by Tewdwr-Jones and others in the book (cf. Adams *et al.* 2006b; Paalzow 2006). The discussion explores the evolution of the Latvian networks and communities involved in planning arenas, and the extent to which they have become internationalized. The role of these networks and communities in the various arenas opened by the enlargement – what Waterhout refers to as the 'pillars of European spatial planning' – is examined along with the influence that this has had on policy development in Latvia. The contribution by Pawel Capik (Chapter 13) is more thematic, focusing strongly on regional promotion and the various approaches to attracting FDI. The discussion builds on some of the issues already covered by Tewdwr-Jones and provides detailed case studies of approaches to FDI attraction in the Czech Republic, Poland and Slovakia, although readers are likely to find the discussion relevant to many other CEE countries. The author examines the extent of current knowledge and evidence upon which the place promotion agenda is built, and in so doing makes a valuable contribution to the knowledge perspective that we have put forth as editors. Konrad Czapiewski and Krzysztof Janc (Chapter 14) author the final chapter in Part III, examining accessibility to higher education and its impact on regional development in Poland. The authors explore the extent to which there appears to be a relationship between diverse levels of accessibility in different parts of the country and different levels of regional development. The implications of these challenges and the policy response are then examined. This chapter offers an interesting case study due to the relatively polycentric structure of urban settlements in the country and the ongoing transformation processes that seem to favour the main urban centres over the more geographically peripheral areas.

Part IV broadens the geographical focus of Parts II and III, and revisits the broader discussion of EU enlargement in Part I, shifting toward the external dimension of EU territorial governance and, more specifically, to its engagement with the Russian Federation. It seeks to highlight the cross-border nature of emerging territorial challenges by examining certain aspects of planning and development practice in the Russian Federation, without which any discussion of EU territorial development would be incomplete. Existing geopolitical tensions between the EU and the Russian Federation provide a challenging context within which any assessment of the Russian dimension needs to be placed. Matti Fritsch (Chapter 15) examines the interfaces of the internal and external territorial governance of the EU in the context of the Baltic Sea Region (BSR). The BSR provides an interesting case study due to the long history of cooperation and its special status as a region where the internal and external dimensions of EU territorial governance come together. Fritsch focuses primarily on two specific initiatives: the long standing VASAB initiative and the recent EU Strategy for the BSR – both providing contexts for mutual learning and knowledge exchange. The chapter makes a valuable contribution to the rationale of the book by assessing the impact of these initiatives on policy development at various levels, and emphasizes the importance of looking beyond knowledge by taking account of geopolitics and the realities of power relations when considering interactions between actors in the EU and Russia. It also provides some excellent insights into the complexities of EU-Russian relations and questions the extent to which the EU is able or willing to integrate the Russian Federation into its territorial governance.

Natalia Razumeyko (Chapter 16) examines the emergence of strategic planning in North-west Russia. Razumeyko builds on the discussion of the complexities of geopolitical relations between the EU and the Russian Federation by Fritsch, emphasizing the importance of relations at all levels between actors on both sides of the external EU border. The author examines some of the challenges and obstacles to the application of strategic planning, and how emergent networks and communities are trying to address these in practice. The North-west Federal region generally, and the City of St Petersburg in particular have played an important role in the emergence of strategic planning in Russia as a result of containing a significant concentration of relevant actors, networks and communities. While Razumeyko identifies the significant potential for, and importance of integrating these communities into wider international communities and arenas, she also acknowledges that much remains to be done so as to make this a reality.

Finally, as editors, we provide our reflections on the individual contributions when viewed through the interpretive lens of a knowledge perspective in a concluding chapter (Chapter 17). Building on the considerations of the different authors, we try to shed some light on the complexity of the interplay of knowledge and policy development in the field of spatial planning, highlighting new and emerging challenges that characterize the enlarged and heterogeneous European landscape, and identifying complementary strands among the diverse contributions.

Notes

1 For the purposes of this book, policy development implies both policy process and product. This understanding includes process attributes such as issue identification and analysis, consultation, and performance monitoring, and product attributes such as policy purpose, logics and evidence (argument), and presentation (informing or communication).

2 As already highlighted in the preface, we distinguish between spatial planning in Europe and European spatial planning. We consider 'European spatial planning' to

refer to spatial planning activities focusing on the EU level or on EU-inspired transnational 'soft' spaces. On the other hand, we employ 'spatial planning in Europe' as an umbrella term that refers primarily to spatial planning activities in the domestic contexts of the Member States, but which can also include European spatial planning as defined above.

3 The academic literature does not seek to identify the 'best' planning system nor is it the intention of this volume to do so. Although the terminology, aims and objectives of spatial planning may be similar in different domestic contexts, they are interpreted and applied in different ways. As a result, individual approaches need to be context-sensitive and thus appropriate to the specific endogenous characteristics of different areas (cf. Stead and Nadin, Chapter 7). However, the nature of spatial challenges themselves means that similar issues are being faced in different places and, in that sense, the study of different techniques, procedures or policies to address such challenges is a natural subject of interest to planning academics and professionals.

4 The PHARE programme (the acronym of the French *Pologne Hongarie Assistance à la Reconstruction des Economies*), which was introduced in 1989, aimed to promote economic and social cohesion in a similar manner to the European Regional Development Fund and the European Social Fund. ISPA (Instrument for Structural Policies for Pre-Accession) and SAPARD (Special Accession Programme for Agriculture and Rural Development) were introduced in the year 2000. The former, with its focus on transport and environmental infrastructure, possessed many similarities to the Cohesion Fund, whereas SAPARD was aimed at preparing the countries for the Common Agricultural Policy.

5 Until 31 December 2006, EU assistance to neighbouring countries via the European Neighbourhood Policy was provided under various geographical programmes including CARDS (Community Assistance to the Countries of South-Eastern Europe for the Balkan Countries), TACIS (Technical Assistance for CIS countries for eastern neighbours and Russia) and MEDA (an abbreviation of the French *mesures d'accompagnement*, referring to the EU instrument for cooperation with its southern Mediterranean neighbours), as well as thematic programmes.

6 For additional information see: http://ec.europa.eu/regional_policy/consultation/terco/contrib_en.htm accessed March 2010.

7 This may be explained also by the fact that, although the ESDP was generally well received, it had little direct impact on policy development in other sectors and the transnational spatial visions generated within INTERREG even less so (cf. ESPON 2007).

References

Adams, N. (2008) 'Convergence and policy transfer: an examination of the extent to which approaches to spatial planning have converged within the context of an enlarged EU', *International Planning Studies* 13(1): 31–50.

Adams, N., Alden, J. and Harris, N. (2006a) *Regional Development and Spatial Planning in an Enlarged EU*, Aldershot: Ashgate.

Adams, N., Ezmale, S. and Paalzow, A. (2006b) 'Towards regional development in Latvia: the experience of the Latgale Region', in Adams, N., Alden, J. and Harris, N. (eds) *Regional Development and Spatial Planning in an Enlarged EU*, Aldershot: Ashgate.

Altrock, U., Gunther, S., Huning, S. and Peters, D. (2006) *Spatial Planning and Urban Development in the New Member States: From adjustment to reinvention*, Aldershot: Ashgate.

Böhme, K. (2002) *Nordic Echoes of European Spatial Planning*, Stockholm: Nordregio.

Böhme, K. and Waterhout, B. (2008) 'The Europeanization of spatial planning', in Faludi, A. (ed.) *European Spatial Research and Planning*, Cambridge (MA): Lincoln Institute of Land Policy: 225–248.

CEC – Commission of the European Communities (1997), *EU Compendium of Spatial Planning Systems and Policies*, Luxembourg: Office for the Official Publication of the European Communities.

—— (1999) *European Spatial Development Perspective: Towards balanced and sustainable development of the territory of the EU*, Luxembourg: Office of the Official Publications of the European Communities.

—— (2001) *Second Report on Economic and Social Cohesion: Unity, solidarity, diversity for Europe, its people and its territory*, Luxembourg: Office for Official Publications of the European Communities.

—— (2004) *Third Report on Economic and Social Cohesion: A new partnership for cohesion: convergence competitiveness cooperation*, Luxembourg: Office for Official Publications of the European Communities.

—— (2007) *Fourth Report on Economic and Social Cohesion: Growing regions, Growing Europe*, Luxembourg: Office for Official Publications of the European Communities.

—— (2008) *Green paper on territorial cohesion: Turning territorial diversity into strength*, Luxembourg: Office for Official Publications of the European Communities.

—— (2009) Communication from the Commission to the European Parliament, the Council, the European Economic and Social Committee and the Committee of the Regions concerning the European Union Strategy for the Baltic Sea Region, available online HTTP: http://ec.europa.eu/regional_policy/sources/docoffic/official/communic/baltic/com_baltic_en.pdf (accessed March 2010).

CEMAT (1984) *European Regional/Spatial Planning Charter*, available online HTTP: www.dgotdu.pt/cemat/site%20CEMAT/Rec(84)2.pdf (accessed March 2010).

COMMIN Baltic Sea Conceptshare National Spatial Planning Systems, available online HTTP: http://commin.org/en/planning-systems/national-planning-systems/nations.html (accessed March 2010).

Cotella, G. (2007) '(R)Evolution of Central and Eastern European spatial planning systems: Trends towards divergence or uniformity?' in Nunes, R., Cidre, E. and Cotella, G. (eds) *Central and Eastern European Engagement: Planning, development and sustainability. ALFA SPECTRA, Central European Journal of Architecture and Planning*, special issue, 11(2): 11–19.

Cotella, G., Adams, N. and Nunes, R. (2010) 'Territorial knowledge channels: mapping territorial governance arrangements in the European Union', paper presented at the conference *Socio-economic Spatial Systems and Territorial Governance*, 3–5 March 2010, Tartu, Estonia.

Davoudi, S. (2006a) 'Evidence-based planning: Rhetoric and reality', *disP* 165 2/2006: 14–24.

—— (2006b) 'EU enlargement and the challenges for spatial planning systems in the new member states', in Altrock, U., Guntner, S., Huning, S. and Peters, D. (eds) *Spatial Planning and Urban Development in New EU Member States*, Aldershot: Ashgate: 31–38.

DE Presidency (2007a) *The Territorial State and Perspectives of the European Union: Towards a stronger European territorial cohesion in the light of the Lisbon and Gothenburg ambitions – A background document to the territorial agenda of the European Union*, available online HTTP: www.bmvbs.de/Anlage/original_1005296/The-Territorial-State-and-Perspectives-of-the-European-Union.pdf (accessed March 2010).

—— (2007b) *Territorial Agenda of the European Union: Towards a more competitive and sustainable Europe of diverse regions – Agreed at the occasion of the informal ministerial meeting on urban development and territorial cohesion on 24/25 May 2007*, available online HTTP: www.bmvbs.de/Anlage/original_1005295/Territorial-Agenda-of-the-European-Union-Agreed-on-25-May-2007-accessible.pdf (accessed March 2010).

Dühr, S., Colomb, C. and Nadin, V. (2010) *European Spatial Planning and Territorial Co-operation*, London: Routledge.

Dühr, S., Stead, D. and Zonneveld, W. (2007) 'The Europeanization of spatial planning through territorial cooperation', *Planning Practice and Research*, 22(3): 291–307.

ESPON (no date) www.espon.eu (accessed March 2010).

—— (2007) ESPON 2.3.2 Governance of Territorial and Urban Policies from EU to Local Level, available online HTTP: www.espon.eu/main/Menu_Projects/Menu_ESPON2006Projects/Menu_PolicyImpactProjects/governance.html (accessed March 2010).

Evers, D. (2007) 'Reflections on territorial cohesion and European spatial planning', *Tijdschrift voor Economische en Sociale Geografie*, 99(3): 303–315.

Evers, D., Tennekes, J., Borsboom, J., Heiligenberg, H. van den and Thissen, M. (2009) A Territorial Impact Assessment of Territorial Cohesion for the Netherlands, Netherlands Environmental Assessment Agency (PBL), available online HTTP: www.eukn.org/binaries/eukn/netherlands/research/2009/07/tia_tc_webversie.pdf (accessed March 2010).

Faludi, A. (2001) 'The application of the European spatial development perspective: Evidence from the North-West Metropolitan Area', *European Planning Studies*, 9(5): 663–675.

—— (2002) 'Positioning European spatial planning', *European Planning Studies*, 10(7): 897–909.

—— (2009) A Turning Point in the Development of European Spatial Planning? The Territorial Agenda of the European Union and the First Action Programme, Progress in Planning 2009, doi:10.1016/j.progress.2008.09.001.

—— (2010 forthcoming) *Cohesion, Coherence, Cooperation: European spatial planning coming of age?* London: Routledge.

Faludi, A. and Waterhout, B. (2002) *The Making of the European Spatial Development Perspective: No masterplan*, London: Routledge.

—— (2006a) 'Introducing evidence-based planning', *disP* 165 2/2006: 4–13.

—— (2006b) 'Debating evidence-based planning', *disP* 165 2/2006: 71–73.

Giannakourou, G. (2005) 'Transforming spatial planning policy in Mediterranean countries: Europeanization and domestic change', *European Planning Studies* 13: 319–331.

Haas, P. (1992) 'Introduction: Epistemic communities and international policy coordination', *International Organization*, 46(1), Knowledge, Power, and International Policy Coordination (Winter, 1992): 1–35, The MIT Press.

—— (2004), 'When does power listen to truth? A constructivist approach to the policy process', *Journal of European Public Policy*, 11(4), August 2004: 569–592.

Hall, P. and Taylor, R. (1996) 'Political science and the three new institutionalisms', *Political Studies*, 44: 936–957.

Haughton, G, Allmendinger, P., Counsell, D. And Vigar, G. (2010) *The New Spatial Planning: Territorial management with soft spaces and fuzzy boundaries*, London: Routledge (RTPI Library Series).

Healey, P. (2010) 'Introduction: The transnational flow of knowledge and expertise in the planning field', in Healey, P. and Upton, R. (eds) *Crossing Borders: international exchange and planning practices*, London: Routledge (RTPI Library Series).

Healey, P. and Williams, R. (1993) 'European urban planning systems: diversity and convergence', *Urban Studies*, 30: 701–720.

Hooghe, L. and Marks, G. (2001) *Multilevel Governance and European Integration*, Lanham MD: Rowman and Littlefield.

Husson, C. (2002) *L'Europe sans territoire: essai sur le concept de cohésion territoriale*, Paris: Datar/L'aube.

Janin Rivolin, U. (2004) *European Spatial Planning*, Milano: Franco Angeli.

—— (2008) 'EU Territorial governance and the innovation cycle of planning: time for sharing benefits?', paper presented at the 4th joint conference ACSP-AESOP Bridging the divide: Celebrating the city, Chicago IL, 6–11 July.

Knieling, J. and Othengrafen, F. (eds) (2009) *Planning Cultures in Europe: Decoding cultural phenomena in urban and regional planning*, Farnham, Surrey: Ashgate.

Kunzmann, K. (2003) 'Does Europe really need another ESDP – an ESDP+ – and, if so, what should it look like?' in Tewdwr-Jones, M. *What Does Europe Want from the Next ESDP?*, Report for European Council of Town Planners Seminar Report, 24 October 2003, available online HTTP: www.ceu-ectp.eu/images/files/Conferences/cp20041231.pdf (accessed March 2010).

—— (2008) 'Futures for European Space', *Journal of Nordregio: European Space 2020 Planning, Energy and Transport*, 2(8), June 2008: 12–21.

Lave, J. and Wenger, E. (1991) *Situated learning: Legitimate peripheral participation*, Cambridge: Cambridge University Press.

Levin, M. (2007) 'Knowledge and technology transfer: Can universities promote regional development?' in Harding, A. Scott, A., Laske, S. and Burtscher, C. (eds) *Bright Satanic Mills: Universities, regional development and the knowledge economy*, Aldershot: Ashgate.

Lowndes, V. (1996) 'Varieties of new institutionalism: A critical appraisal', *Public Administration*, 74(2): 181–197.

Nadin, V. and Stead, D. (2008) 'European spatial planning systems, social models and learning', *disP* 172, January: 35–47.

Newman, P. and Thornley, A. (1996) *Urban Planning in Europe: International competition, national systems, and planning projects*, London: Routledge.

Nunes, R., Adams, N. and Cotella, G. (2009) 'Policy framing and evidence-based planning: Epistemic communities in the multi-jurisdictional environment of an enlarged Europe', RSA Annual International Conference, Leuven, Belgium, 6–8 April.

Olsen, J. P. (2002) 'The many faces of Europeanization', *Journal of Common Market Studies*, 40(5): 921–952.

Paalzow, A. (2006) 'Barriers to regional development in the new Member States: the Latvian experience', in Adams, N., Alden, J. and Harris, N. (eds) *Regional Development and Spatial Planning in an Enlarged European Union*, Aldershot: Ashgate.

Pallagst, K. (2006) 'European spatial planning reloaded: Considering EU enlargement in theory and practice', *European Planning Studies*, 14(2), February 2006: 253–272.

Radaelli, C. M. (2004) 'Europeanization: Solution or problem?', European integration online papers (EIoP), 8(16), available online HTTP: http://eiop.or.at/eiop/texte/2004-016a.htm (accessed March 2010).

Radaelli, C. M. and Saurugger, S. (eds) (2008) 'The Europeanization of public policies: New research directions', *Journal of Comparative Policy Analysis: Research and Practice*, 10(3).

Rydin, Y. (2007) 'Re-examining the role of knowledge within planning theory', *Planning Theory 2007*, 6(1): 52–68.

Sabatier, P. (1988) 'An advocacy coalition framework of policy change and the role of policy-oriented learning therein', *Policy Sciences*, 21: 129–168.

Salgado, S. R. and Woll, C. (2004) 'L'européanisation et les acteurs non-étatiques', paper presented to the conference *Europeanization of public policies and European integration*, IEP-Paris, 13 February 2004.

Sandercock, L. (2003) *Cosmopolis II: Mongrel cities in the 21st century*, London: Continuum.

Schimmelfenning, F. and Sedelmeier, U. (eds) (2005) *The Europeanization of Central and Eastern Europe*, Ithaca, NY: Cornell University Press.

Stead, D. (2008) 'Assessing the convergence of national spatial planning systems in Europe', paper presented at the 4th joint conference ACSP-AESOP Bridging the divide: Celebrating the city, Chicago IL, 6–11 July.

Stead, D. and Waterhout, B. (2008) 'Learning from the application of the ESDP: Influences on European territorial governance', *DisP*, 172(1): 21–34.

Steinmo, S., Thelen, K. and Longstreth, F. (1992) *Structuring Politics: Historical institutionalism in comparative analysis*, Cambridge [England]; New York: Cambridge University Press.

Vries, J. de (2002) 'Grenzen verkend, Internationalisering van de ruimtelijke planning in de Benelux' (Exploring Borders: the internationalisation of spatial planning in the Benelux), *Stedelijke en Regionale Verkenningen* 27, Delft: Delft University Press.

Waterhout, B. (2008) *The Institutionalisation of European Spatial Planning*, Amsterdam: IOS Press.

Waterhout, B., Mourato, J. and Böhme, K. (2009) 'The impact of Europeanisation on planning cultures', in Knieling, J. and Othengrafen, F. (eds) *Planning Cultures in Europe: Decoding cultural phenomena in urban and regional planning*, Farnham, Surrey: Ashgate: 239–253.

Wenger, E. (1998) *Communities of Practice: Learning, meaning, and identity*, Cambridge: Cambridge University Press.

Williams, R. H. (eds) (1984) *Planning in Europe*, London: George Allen & Unwin.

—— (1996) *European Union, Spatial Policy and Planning*, London: Paul Chapman.

Zonneveld, W. (2005) 'Expansive spatial planning: The new European transnational spatial visions', *European Planning Studies*, 13(1), January 2005: 137–155.

2 Territorial knowledge channels in a multi-jurisdictional policy environment

A theoretical framework

Neil Adams, Giancarlo Cotella and Richard Nunes

Introduction

> Planning [...] is both a form of governance and metagovernance, as it provides a vehicle for greater spatial coherence among different strategic, sectoral governance systems. In turn, through its intersection with other strategic work, planning itself becomes subject to their shaping influence.
>
> (Haughton *et al.* 2010: 50)

The new east-west dimension, created since the most recent enlargement of the European Union (EU), has been discussed in light of the turning points of EU eastwards enlargement for the context of diverse spatial planning practices in Europe and the evolving context of European spatial planning (Adams *et al.* Chapter 1). This discussion has contemplated two main considerations. The first and more immediately obvious one lies with the emergence of a new socio-economic and political landscape, within which both established and new Member States pursue the dual goals of 'cohesion' and 'competitiveness' (Tewdwr-Jones, Chapter 3). As further elaborated in the Introduction to Part I of this book, despite the prominence of territorial cohesion in the EU policy rhetoric, the increased emphasis on regional competitiveness and employment since the adoption of the Lisbon Agenda (EC 2000) and the increasing disparities within many Member States, continue to demonstrate the complexities and tensions inherent in the simultaneous pursuance of these two goals. The second consideration with respect to this east-west dimension lies within the diversity of planning cultures, styles and approaches that characterize the EU. Whilst this diversity was already significant between the EU-15, its extent has been taken to a new level by the recent eastwards enlargements, posing questions about the unique historical and cultural significance of the socialist and Soviet pasts of the 'new' Member States and how it can influence stability and change in the course of policy development.

Both of these considerations have been factored into the knowledge perspective proposed by this book for the study of processes contributing to policy stability and change, which will be discussed later in this chapter in relation to the concept of 'territorial knowledge channels'. This exploration of the 'role of knowledge in the policy process' (Radaelli 1995) concerns the interplay of knowledge and policy development[1] within the polyarchic, multi-agent and cross-scalar policy landscape of spatial planning in Europe. In this respect, we understand territorial knowledge channels to be the multi-agent, cross-scalar governance arrangements manifesting across and within different territorial knowledge communities, that can impart an influence on policy development as a result of having acquired the powers to shape or frame new 'policy images' (Kingdon 1995) for future policy change or safeguard existing policy approaches (Nunes *et al.* 2009). As introduced in Chapter 1, this understanding of territorial knowledge channels is built on the notion that 'knowledge resources' (ideas, data and argument) are channelled into 'knowledge arenas' where they are tested/validated or subject to debate/institutionalized rules of policy evaluation, or employed selectively in the representation of policy problems/opportunities or in the advancement of vested interests (cf. Figure 2.1). In so doing, the rationale for this book focuses attention on the potential for conflict and agreement between communities of actors with respect to the 'power [struggles] and preferences' over the development and selection or utilization of 'knowledge and information' (cf. Conzelmann 1998; Haas 2004; Davoudi 2006; Krizek *et al.* 2009); that is, the complex adaptation paths and interactive institutional and discursive logics of path-dependent and path-shaping processes of policy development to which different communities of actors contribute.

The above-mentioned conceptual framework is elaborated in more detail later in this chapter and is accordingly suggested as a means for the exploration of these logics at the interplay of knowledge and policy. Figure 2.1 illustrates the location of the territorial knowledge channels at the intersection of knowledge resources and knowledge arenas in a multi-jurisdictional policy environment.

Territorial knowledge channels embody the spatio-temporal, socio-cultural factors that condition agent interactivity within and between territorial knowledge communities. In this regard, they directly contribute to knowledge development and utilization, and the transformation of existing institutional and political geographies of agent interaction, whereby it is possible for individual actors to be members of more than one community. Thus these geographies of agent interaction transcend and/or challenge established jurisdictions at varying territorial scales ('cross-scalar') and across different institutional remits or responsibilities ('multi-jurisdictional'). Furthermore, the resulting reciprocation of knowledge within and between territorial knowledge communities reflects both the endogenous and exogenous elements of the study of policy stability and change, whereby conflict and learning among actors is triggered by 'exogenous shocks' (Radaelli 1999) or changes to the policy environment. Both of these elements, upon which this chapter further elaborates below, seek to offer the necessary explanatory power to elucidate the processes associated with the utilization of knowledge and development. That is, the intra-/extra-community links of territorial governance arrangements evident in the knowledge resources-based interpretation of policy relevant events, and the framing of policy problems and opportunities. In this context, certain knowledge arenas are then pursued to ensure these resources can be best employed in the representation of individual/collective interests through the promotion of policy images, which are intended to stimulate policy change or safeguard existing policy approaches.

Taking the path emerging within planning and more broadly in public policy research circles, which focuses on evidence-based planning (Davoudi 2006; Faludi and Waterhout 2006) and evidence-based policy (Clarence 2002), the proposed territorial knowledge channels framework looks to explore the complex adaptation processes of knowledge and its role in policy stability and change. More specifically, this framework explores the contribution of multi-agent, cross-scalar governance arrangements within and across 'territorial knowledge communities' to path-shaping and path-dependent processes of policy development. These processes reflect a symbiotic relationship between knowledge and political interests whereby knowledge resources are channelled into knowledge arenas where they are tested, debated and validated. Moreover, this view acknowledges the role of organizations as key sites for knowledge production and utilization. At the same time, it also recognizes that organizations and the agents that occupy them are social units within the spaces of institutionalized

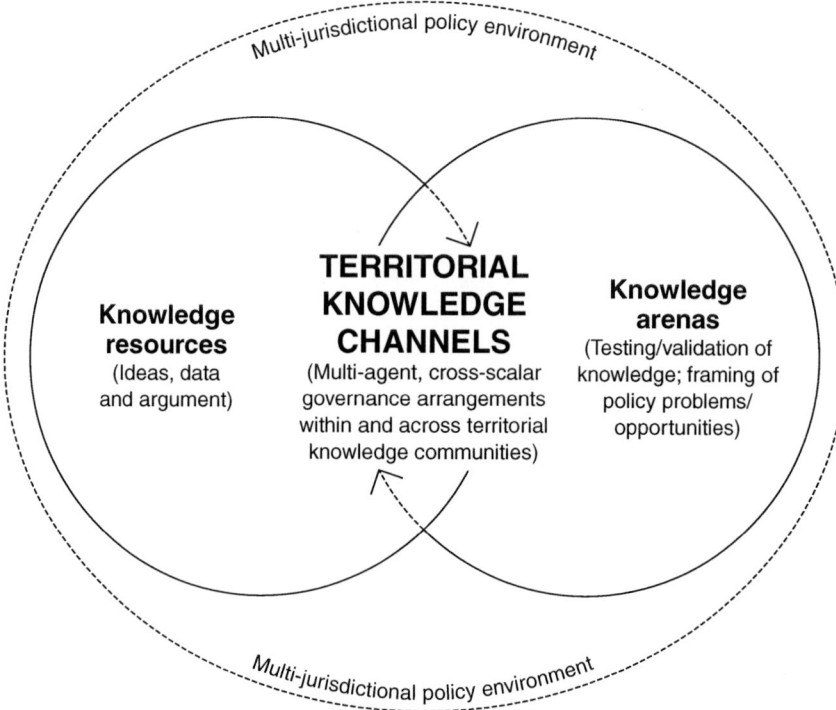

Figure 2.1 Territorial knowledge channels (source: Nunes *et al.* 2009, Graphics Jo Van Hees).

practices that can have a constraining and/or enabling influence on the competing logics and legitimacies of human agency whilst simultaneously being the product of that agency.

Healey (2010: 2) uses the notion of 'cultures of practice' among 'communities of experts, advocates, officials and lobbyists who promote or work in distinct fields' to denote the existence of various communities of actors presenting peculiar characteristics of aggregation, action and focus. These communities of actors can include 'policy communities' with a range of actors clustered around a particular area of public policy (Rhodes 1997), 'epistemic communities' of expert professionals with a shared knowledge base (Haas 1992), and 'communities of practice' among diverse actors engaging in a task, job or profession (Wenger 1998). In this view, Healey notes that these cultures of practice 'vary in relation to national priorities and governance cultures, and in relation to disciplinary backgrounds'. The assumption claims that all of these communities have cultures in terms of 'their way of doing things' whereby a 'planning culture may perhaps best be understood as evolving through the infusions from all three forms of community' mentioned above (Healey 2010: 21).

The focus on 'cultures of practice' offers a useful starting point into the exploration of 'what planners do'. However, the exploration of 'who learns what, when, to whose benefit, and why' (Adler and Haas 1992: 370) lies at the core of this book. In order to address these further questions it is necessary to extend our consideration of epistemic communities to include the concept of communities of practice in addition to that of 'advocacy coalitions' of shared interests and 'deep core' policy principles (Sabatier and Jenkins-Smith 1993; Sabatier 1998) under the expression of 'territorial knowledge communities'. The combination of these three concepts offers an opportunity to elucidate the above-mentioned multi-agent cross-scalar governance arrangements of territorial policy development as well as the contribution of interactive institutional and discursive logics to the 'institutional construction of interests' (Parsons 2003).

In light of this, the first of the remaining sections of this chapter identifies and explores the significance of a policy environment of competing logics and legitimacies, which is characterized by the ideas, concepts and planning approaches that potentially can impart an influence on the complex adaptation processes of both the path-dependent as well as the path-shaping course of policy development. Subsequently, the chapter focus shifts to the implications of the Europeanization mechanisms for these competing 'knowledge claims' in the European space of multi-level territorial governance (Rydin 2007; cf. Haas 1990 for 'reality tests'); that is, the exogenous shocks to the policy environments of new and old Member States, triggering the cross-scalar multi-agent links of governance arrangements looking to frame new policy problems and opportunities and/or re-frame old ones. Lastly, bulding on this discussion, the theoretical framework is elaborated, further detailing the concept of territorial knowledge communities and highlighting the territorial knowledge channels that are situated at the intersection of knowledge resources and knowledge arenas in a multi-jurisdictional policy environment (see Figure 2.1).

Territorial governance and the 'metaphors we live by'

Policy development phenomena such as the influence of Europeanization mechanisms and the resulting 'institutional construction of interests' (Parsons 2003), which have been expressed through the emergence of diverse policy images in the spatial planning discourse in Europe, are all relevant to a consideration of the interplay of knowledge and policy development. On a European level, spatial planning approaches and metaphors, developed by academics during the 1980s and 1990s to conceptualize spatial development in the EU-15 (e.g. the 'Blue Banana', Brunet 1989), have become outdated and require revision to take account of post-enlargement realities. New sets of heterogeneous claims and ideas have been put forward to underpin a range of Member States' interests, not least their inclusion in EU funding priorities (Nadin 2002; Dühr 2007). A review of these metaphors also reveals a transition from a core-periphery model to an approach promoting more balanced patterns of development throughout Europe (Dühr *et al.* 2010). Some attempts have already been made by experts from both the 'old' and 'new' Member States to elaborate more contemporary conceptualizations that take account of these new realities, notably the Central and Eastern European (CEE) 'Boomerang' (Gorzelak 1996; cf. Pallagst, Chapter 6) and a series of attempts to apply the concept of polycentric development through the individuation of potential 'global zones of economic integration' (French Presidency 2000; Mehlbye 2000). However, in spite of achieving varying degrees of visibility, none of these policy images gained a hegemonic role in driving policy development. This highlights particular challenges in the interplay of knowledge and policy development in relation to both the norms and values underpinning spatial policies as well as to the set of powers that permeate the arenas where discussion and negotiation take place. That is to say, how the qualities of knowledge resources, filtered through power struggles and conflicts, translate into the organizational and institutional forces that shape the course of policy development for different European places and communities (cf. Giannakourou 1996; Böhme *et al.* 2004).

Some spatial metaphors, such as the 'Blue Banana' (Brunet 1989), the 'Bunch of Grapes' (Kunzmann and Wegener 1991) and the 'Pentagon' (Schön 2000), appear to have been more influential than others – such as the above-mentioned 'Boomerang'. Thus one might assume that the general inability of European spatial planning to effectively visualize such spatial metaphors and concepts emphasizes the fact that once something is 'on the map', even in abstract form, it becomes more politically contentious (cf. Dühr 2007). Despite the vague and contradictory nature of these spatial concepts and precepts, these signifiers of territorial governance and policy remain 'metaphors we live by' (Lakoff and Johnson 1980; cf. Schön 1963, 1978). Reference to these signifiers of territorial governance and policy however, is not to suggest professional or academic compliance or submission to these concepts and precepts. Rather it suggests the presence of ongoing debates in relation to the simultaneous embrace of, and apprehension and confusion over European rhetoric as the more recent discussions and consultations on territorial cohesion illustrate (Evers *et al.* 2009; CEC 2009; cf. also Adams *et al.*, Chapter 1; Tewdwr-Jones, Chapter 3). The following sections explore the extent to which these debates parallel professional apprehension and confusion over the meaning of 'spatial' for planning practice, the convergence of these debates on a preference for the territorial over the spatial, and the implications of these developments for spatial policy development.

From 'hard' to 'soft' and from spatial to territorial planning

The debates mentioned above are paralleled, and in some respects even mirrored, in ongoing and long-standing discussions over the meaning of the spatial approach to planning and, more generally, over the meaning of space and territory. Just as with the ambiguity associated with territorial cohesion, spatial planning also has its share of professional and academic embrace and apprehension (Haughton *et al.* 2010). After all, a spatial concept like 'polycentricity', which was given political kudos in the spatial approach put forward by the European Spatial Development Perspective (ESDP, CEC 1999), has been translated into recent interpretations of the precept of territorial cohesion (Meijers *et al.* 2007; Waterhout 2008; Evers *et al.* 2009). In other words, the above signifiers of territorial governance and cohesion policy are intertwined with the equally ambiguous notion of spatial planning.

The UNECE (2008: 11) report on this issue, highlights the fact that 'there is no single ideal model of spatial planning'. In a similar vein, Glasson and Marshall (2007: 4) argue that 'there is no such thing as an abstract "correct" definition of planning valid for any place or time'. In fact, the precise nature of spatial planning has remained ambiguous despite extensive discussion in academic literature (Tewdwr-Jones 2001; Alden 2006; Healey 2006a, 2006b; Nadin 2007; Tsenkova 2007), and in numerous reports (CEC 1997, ESPON 2007) and policy documents since the adoption of the European Regional and Spatial Planning Charter (CEMAT 1984).[2] Nevertheless, spatial planning has provided a new sense of direction or purpose for those who have embraced its ethos. Interestingly, although living the oxymoron of both an embrace of its ethos in policy documents and an apprehension or skepticism with respect to its ability to deliver where traditional planning practices have failed (cf. Haughton *et al.* 2010; Faludi 2010), not to mention the ambiguity of its highly interpretative quality and potentially confusing nature, the advocates of spatial planning have gained momentum within different knowledge arenas in light of the ESDP (CEC 1999). This has been evident in arenas such as the INTERREG Community Initiative and the ESPON Programme, and in the making of national and regional strategic planning documents within the different domestic contexts.

On a European level, ironically, the European rhetoric on territorial cohesion has more recently fuelled the continued search for legitimacy and influence of spatial planning practice (cf. Tewdwr-Jones, Chapter 3; Waterhout, Chapter 4).

In other words, the precept of territorial cohesion potentially offers a unifying normative direction for the diversity of European planning styles and systems in the same way that the spatial approach was applied to the ESDP. In fact, the different contributions to this book reveal how CEE countries tend to be characterized by spatial planning approaches of a more formal and regulatory nature (cf. Adams *et al.* 2006; Altrock *et al.* 2006; ESPON 2007; Cotella 2007, 2009), partially in contrast with the prominence of 'softer' non-regulatory approaches that characterize spatial planning activities in many old Member States (particularly in North-West Europe, cf. Haughton *et al.* 2010 on 'soft spaces'). Then again, there is evidence to suggest that European level initiatives promoting greater coordination and consistency, such as the elaboration of various transnational spatial visions under the framework of INTERREG and, more recently, the EU Strategy for the Baltic Sea Region (cf. Fritsch, Chapter 15), have influenced the ways in which spatial ideas and planning approaches are evolving in domestic contexts. This can be related to processes of Europeanization involving socialization and collective learning, which will be discussed later in this chapter (cf. also Dühr *et al.* 2010).

Consequently, the professional apprehension, confusion and skepticism that justifiably can be attributed to debates over the meaning or implications of an embrace of the spatial planning and territorial cohesion ethos seems to have converged on a preference for the *territorial* over the *spatial*. Waterhout (Chapter 4) argues that this implies European spatial planning discourse and rhetoric is taking on a more 'neutral territory matters focus'. Waterhout traces this change in terminology back to the power struggles between the European Commission and Member States over competency (in planning) issues in the making of the ESDP (Faludi and Waterhout 2002), pointing to the adoption of a 'spatial development' perspective as opposed to a 'spatial planning' one and, more recently, to the adoption of a 'territorial agenda' as opposed to a spatial one. Other reasons echo similar territorial sovereignty tensions embedded in the conception of planning as land use regulation (Janin Rivolin 2008), and the subsequent incorporation of territorial cohesion in the language of the Treaty establishing a Constitution for Europe. The result is a 'shift in institutional balance' with the ratification of the Lisbon Treaty and a newly bestowed role for the European Commission in the as yet ambiguous practice of delivering on territorial cohesion (Waterhout, Chapter 4).

Spatial policy development between knowledge and interests

The context discussed above raises two questions of concern for this book, which reflect the tension over competing logics and legitimacies in the institutionalization of interests:

- How do territorial knowledge communities contribute to the transformation of institutional geographies of agent interaction as both institutionally enabling and constraining factors on policy development?

• How do different knowledge arenas link with the 'hard' regulatory spaces of planning systems, and the 'soft spaces' of territorial governance beyond the geographical and professional boundaries of these systems?

There are no clear cut answers to these questions, but an attention to the role of knowledge in policy stability and change clearly again implies an attention to competing knowledge claims within spatial planning policy processes and its inherent power struggles across diverse knowledge arenas (cf. Rydin 2007; Tewdwr-Jones 2002). Healey associates these competing logics and legitimacies with a 'disembedding process' that can involve the making of 'new, more horizontal intergrations' across different communities of actors by breaking with 'current discourses, arenas and practices' rather than a shift of policy focus (2006c: 73–74). An attention to, or concern for policy integration is implicit in this long-held acknowledgement of the 'wicked problems' of planning practice for which 'solutions in the sense of definitive and objective answers' is futile (Rittel and Webber 1973). More recently, this recognition has brought some academics to refer to the search for joint solutions through the integration of (sectoral) policies as the 'administrative Holy Grail' (Jennings and Crane 1994). Stead and Meijers (2009) provide a useful review of the existing research on 'policy integration', distinguishing this occurrence from its lower tiers of 'policy coordination' and 'policy cooperation'.

Whereas the resulting efficiency of sectoral policies benefits from the recognition of compatibility in policy cooperation and of a degree of comprehensiveness and accessibility between policy sectors in policy coordination, policy integration is evident in the interaction and interdependence of a new joint policy; though a number of 'facilitators' and 'inhibitors' condition the processes to greater policy integration, which include political factors; institutional/organizational factors; economic/financial factors; process, management and instrumental factors; and behavioural, cultural and personal factors. These facilitators and inhibitors of the processes of policy integration can be identified among the links within and between territorial knowledge communities in response to policy environment changes that present new territorial development issues and opportunities. This reasoning echoes the different dimensions of policy integration, such as intra-/inter-organizational considerations and sectors with/without shared or adjacent boundaries. These dimensions are often conflated in policy discourses that 'fail to recognize the tensions that can exist between them [...] or neglect the fact that each dimension involves quite different actors, processes and/or institutions' (ibid. 320). A similar logic applies to the different actors and tensions that are implied in the interactions within and between territorial knowledge communities, which constitute cross-scalar multi-agent territorial governance arrangements (further elaborated later in this chapter).

Above all, this reflects a close and mutualistic relationship between knowledge and interests. That is, knowledge resources are channelled into knowledge arenas where they are tested/validated or subject to debate/institutionalized rules of policy evaluation, or employed selectively in the representation of policy problems/opportunities or in the advancement of vested interests.

In these struggles over discourse, arenas and practices, the arenas of the planning system and its practices are caught up in many complex tensions. On the one dimension, there is tension between which territory is in focus in place-focused development strategies: is it that of a formal politico-administrative jurisdiction, a territory of material functionality such as a land or labour market, a place of identity such as a historic city or ancient shire county? On the other dimension, there are the struggles over the logics of legitimacy for a strategy: is it that of a political mobilization movement which has recognized critical connectivities within a sub-region? Is it the logic of functional relations, such as a travel-to-work area? Is it the logic of elected politicians? Is it the logic of the construction of arguments that have standing in judicial arenas?

(Healey 2006c: 74)

Healey (2006c) refers to the arenas of planning systems as 'key sites for the performance of multi-level and multi-actor governance', yet emphasizes that 'this is to be done in a situation of competing arenas and multiple policy networks and coalitions, all encouraged to develop horizontal or multi-scalar relations in contexts where national power and traditions of nested hierarchy remain strong' (ibid. 69). This passage echoes the above-mentioned symbiotic relationship between knowledge and interests whereby political interests can be best explored in terms of process rather than outcome; that is, the continuing critique and embrace of knowledge resources that are advanced through the power struggles and preferences of new policy images in policy shaping processes. It also echoes the importance of 'historical explanations' of path dependency in the form of an historical 'situation' of actors and structures together at a given point in time or time period, and the historical 'legacy' of pre-existing structures within which actors individually or collectively interact and the influence that these processes have upon the shaping or framing of policy (Roness 2001; Pierson 1996; Mahoney 2000). In the context of the collective Soviet and socialist past, this is particularly relevant for many CEE countries.

Together these combined considerations of path-shaping and path-dependent processes of policy change and stability determine that the organizational structures of territorial governance arrangements are not the products of the uniform force that a 'generative metaphor' (Schön 1978) exerts on the policy development process. On the contrary, the powers of influence that knowledge resources acquire in their interplay with policy development are the product of policy processes being constantly subjected to the different sets of power-relations within and between territorial knowledge communities that permeate the knowledge arenas themselves.

The rather esoteric and seemingly all encompassing nature of European spatial planning (Evers 2007), as well as the lack of a spatial planning competence at the level of the EU, exacerbates the above-mentioned complexities of the intra-/extra-community links among territorial governance arrangements in response to policy environment change. Despite an apparently increased legitimacy, granted by the inclusion of the principle of territorial cohesion alongside economic and social cohesion as an EU competence, European spatial planning and territorial cohesion remain vague and ambiguous in terms of content, meaning and application. That is, in spite of a relatively long history, the battle for legitimacy amongst a broader group of sectoral actors, who tend only to make use of spatial planning documents when they help to justify funding requirements, continues – with spatial planning remaining the focus of an intense discourse amongst a relatively small group of academics and practitioners spread throughout the EU (cf. Waterhout, Chapter 4).

The extent to which diverse knowledge resources can contribute to the search for legitimacy amongst a broader group of stakeholders remains to be seen. Be this as it may, the following sections explore how, in a multi-jurisdictional policy environment, the resultant learning within European territorial governance practices, as a function of numerous formal and informal territorial knowledge communities, can contribute to the 'vertical', 'horizontal' and 'circular' reciprocation of knowledge common in Europeanization processes (Stead and Nadin, Chapter 7). The context sensitivity of the governance arrangements where these processes mature can be highest when new policy windows emerge, evoking the responses from a diverse range of actors on particular policy areas or issues. In light of the significant institutional and administrative transformation among new Member States, both pre- and post-accession to the EU, the new multi-jurisdictional landscape of the enlarged EU-27 requires planning discourse to be extended to focus on its new east-west dimension referred to in Chapter 1. In order to achieve this it will be necessary for CEE actors to become engaged in this discourse and for new institutional arrangements and spatial planning approaches to be operationalized.

EU multi-level governance and Europeanization of spatial planning

The EU, which has been described as the first postmodern political organization (Johnson 2009), does not have a traditional institutional structure. A number of academics have studied the consequences of the open-ended character of the process of European integration in terms of the coexistence of domestic and supranational authorities. Within this framework, Hooghe and Marks (2001) described the EU model as 'EU multi-level governance' (cf. also Scharpf 1994, 2001; Sbragia 1992; Marks 1992; Hooghe 1995, 1996; Benz 2002), highlighting the dispersion of decision-making power among different territorial levels as a result of the two specific processes that characterized the second half of the twentieth century. On the one hand, the competence transfer in various policy domains from the Member States to the European institutions and, on the other hand, the process of regionalization that has led to a devolution of the political authority from the national to the sub-national levels within Member States (Brenner 1999, 2004).

Whereas the process of European integration led to the consolidation of a specific multi-level polity characterized by the dispersion of competences between a number of entwined but independent institutions, such a governance system is by no means immutable. On the contrary, the EU, as a multi-jurisdictional policy environment, is characterized by a high degree of uncertainty, thus making EU multi-level governance an unstable configuration, mainly due to the absence of a defined constitutional framework and of shared consensus on the scope and goals of integration (Waterhout 2008). As a result, the distribution of competences between domestic and supranational levels remains ambiguous and its process defined through the interaction of multiple actors, consequently having significant implications for both domestic and supranational realities.

The outcomes of such reciprocal interaction are often referred to as Europeanization, to indicate a process of institutionalization specifically connected to European integration (Waterhout 2008; Böhme and Waterhout 2008). The concept of Europeanization does not have a univocal meaning and has been used to describe a variety of processes and phenomena (cf. among others: Olsen 2002; Featherstone and Radaelli 2003; Lenschow 2006). Radaelli (2004) argued that the concept goes beyond the theories of European integration and, rather than focusing on the reasons for the latter, focuses more on the impact of such a process on the domestic and supranational sphere. Whereas European integration theories mainly focus on the dynamics that regulate the precarious equilibrium of power and competences between the EU and the Member States (Borzel 2004), Europeanization studies concentrate more on the adaptation to, and of, the European dimension within this equilibrium. This implies an interactive understanding of Europeanization that is no longer seen as unidirectional process of 'reaction to Europe' (Salgado and Wool 2004: 4), but goes beyond a static and mechanistic top-down impact on domestic contexts, towards an analysis of complex adaptation paths and interactive logics of co-evolution (cf. Olsen 2002; Gualini 2003; Megie and Ravinet 2004; Radaelli 2004).

In this context, the concept of Europeanization is not intended as a phenomenon in itself, but as a particular approach to a problem, a cause in search of an effect (Goetz 2001) or, as Gualini (2003) puts it, not the *explanans* but the *explanandum*. Hence an investigation into Europeanization is not an attempt to understand whether a nation is Europeanizing or not, but rather seeks to explore the complex dynamics – either vertical, horizontal or circular in nature – that entwine and contribute to the modification of the supranational and domestic spheres (cf. Stead and Nadin, Chapter 6).

Exploring mechanisms of Europeanization

The described processes, characterized by continuous interactions between 'domestic contexts → EU → domestic contexts' (Lenschow 2006), suggest the crucial role of 'Europeanization' as 'the main transmission belt of the process of European integration' (Borzel and Risse 2000, 1–3; cf. also Böhme and Waterhout 2008). Several attempts have sought to shed light on the mechanisms that regulate the mutual adaptation and co-evolution of supranational and domestic spheres, analyzing both in terms of reactions to adaptation pressures (Borzel and Risse 2003) as well as taking place within complex socialization processes around specific political spheres (Jacquot and Woll 2003; Tatcher 2004). Starting from a similar approach, Conzelmann (1998) argues how, within the multi-jurisdictional policy environment of an enlarged EU, the evolution of political spheres, and supranational and domestic levels is attributable to two distinct – but coexisting – models based on 'conflict' and 'knowledge' respectively characterized by variables of 'power and preferences' and 'knowledge and information'. Conzelmann explores how the 'power and preferences' and 'knowledge and information' of the actors taking part in the policy development process are strongly embedded within EU multi-level governance and how, in pursuing this logic further, it is possible to redirect these variables to specific 'mechanisms of Europeanization'.

On the one hand, the EU influences domestic realities through mechanisms of 'conditionality' that have an impact on the 'power and preferences' of domestic actors through the setting of rules and the provision of external incentives (c.f Schimmelfenning and Sedelmeier 2005). In the first case, conditionality processes follow a logic based on the predisposition of sanctions to be put into practice in case of non-compliance with specific rules by Member States or candidate countries. Such a mechanism mainly concerns the policy areas in which the EU retains legitimate competences, and applies also to the process of transposition of the 'acquis communautaire' by candidate countries, as the EU has the power to interrupt negotiations (the so-called 'acquis conditionality'). In the second case, the process of conditionality is driven by the predisposition of financial rewards to be awarded in relation to specific actions to be taken at the domestic level. In this process, the EU defines the adoption of specific logics as a necessary condition to obtain certain benefits, therefore influencing the cost-benefit logics of domestic actors and stimulating the adoption of particular practices. Policy development at the EU level is clearly influenced by mechanisms in relation to the variable of 'power and preferences'. This can be seen in the processes of negotiation typical of the Conzelmann (1998) conflict model. A pivotal role is played within such processes by the influence of costs and benefits on the preferences of the different actors involved (Schimmelfenning and Sedelmeier 2002) and by the set of power relations embedding those actors within the negotiation arena.

On the other hand, Europeanization mechanisms can also be understood in a broader sense, starting from the assumption that changes in terms of rules, norms and behaviour at both the supranational and domestic levels are generated and/or influenced by complex processes based on variables of knowledge and information. The emergence and exchange of new knowledge resources is reinterpreted in such processes within deeper 'socialization' mechanisms by territorial knowledge communities that have an influence on the policy development process. Socialization mechanisms view the EU as an institution defined by a specific set of values and norms and by a variable number of territorial knowledge communities, producing, discussing and exchanging knowledge within specific knowledge arenas, potentially contributing to changing the logics of the different actors themselves. They follow the logics of appropriateness and describe the adaptation of specific domestic logics to supranational perspectives. The processes driven by socialization mechanisms are based on the progressive persuasion of domestic actors by the legitimacy and appropriateness of logics promoted by the EU, as well as their appropriateness to fit domestic needs and challenges. EU logics may in turn be influenced by the emergence of new knowledge resources matured within diverse knowledge arenas. Although an analytical distinction can be made between the variables behind them, it is important to stress how the described mechanisms, as well as their effects, overlap, making it hard to attribute changes in an unambiguous cause-effect manner. Indeed, as introduced in the previous section, the process of policy development is influenced simultaneously by the knowledge and interests, that is to say by an overlapping of 'conflict' and 'knowledge' acting through variables of 'power and preferences' and 'knowledge and information'. This complexity is recognizable in the processes that gave birth to the ESDP, where the desire to adopt maps as visual knowledge resources was opposed by the majority of Member States worried that any graphical representation would undermine the benefits of their use and the possibility of reaching consensus (Faludi and Waterhout 2002). At the same time, as the discussion in various contributions in this book illustrate (e.g. Dąbrowski, Chapter 8; Czapiewski and Janc, Chapter 14), it can be argued that some of the reforms undertaken in the candidate countries have followed the logic of maximizing EU financial support rather than a real belief in the adopted solution. In the next section, this consideration of the knowledge and interests embedded in the reciprocal processes of policy development is considered in light of EU enlargement as a window of opportunity. That is, the logics of EU mechanisms through to the socialization processes that in turn have the potential to shape new ideas, metaphors and scenarios at an EU level.

Europeanization in the field of spatial planning

Whereas the impact of Europeanization is undeniable in those fields where the EU retains legitimate competences, either autonomously or shared with the Member States, it is more difficult to demonstrate influence on those policy fields where no supranational competence exists. This is the case for spatial planning where, as discussed earlier in this chapter, competences remain the sovereignty of the Member States, notwithstanding the adoption of the territorial cohesion objective with the ratification of the Lisbon Treaty. In order to address this issue, it is important to recall how changes that punctuate the generally stable characteristics of much public policy, which are caused by the mechanisms of Europeanization presented above, are not necessarily path-dependent. Rather these changes are a response to power struggles and a multiplicity of exogenous and endogenous factors as well as to the specific opportunities linked to particular polity events (Buitelaar *et al.* 2007). Building on Buitelaar *et al.*

(2007) and Kingdon (1995), Waterhout (2008) describes how such processes presuppose the coincidence of a series of critical elements, respectively: to 'perception of problems', 'suggested solutions' and 'political development', favouring the opening of a so-called 'window of opportunity'. Such windows 'set up specific developments in the political sphere, thus modifying existing agendas, or structuring completely new agendas' (Winn 1998: 124). In this context, Kingdon (1995) argues how, thanks to specific 'spillover' effects that often occur between different policy fields, the opening of a window of opportunity may induce changes within fields where the EU does not possess any legitimate competence, and may even lead to the creation of new fields (Pallagst 2006). This coincides with the view of Radaelli (2004) that Europeanization processes present different characteristics in relation to different policy fields. More particularly, the absence of legitimate EU competence does not prejudice the triggering of Europeanization processes in a specific domain. Rather it influences the mechanisms through which these processes are manifest.

In this context it is possible to understand why some authors optimistically suggest an advance, albeit limited, of the institutionalization of 'spatial planning' at the European level (Waterhout, 2008), which has had a direct influence on national planning systems' consideration of cross-sectoral planning approaches. Evidence to support such a hypothesis is provided by the number of authors who have explored the impact of the European dimension on spatial planning activity as it manifests itself within different Member States (Tewdwr-Jones and Williams 2001; Böhme 2002; Janin Rivolin 2003, Adams *et al.* 2006; Altrock *et al.* 2006; Cotella 2007a, 2009; Waterhout 2008) and conversely the influence of the different national perspectives on European spatial planning (Böhme 2002; Janin Rivolin 2004; Janin Rivolin; Faludi 2005). This implies a form of reciprocation in the field of spatial planning, which may include new ideas, metaphors and scenarios as well as new actors and approaches to spatial planning from the 'new' EU entrants of CEE as a result of the enlargement process.

EU enlargement as a window of opportunity

The discussion in the previous section helps us to understand how the enlargement process, a change clearly originating from the EU polity level, can trigger Europeanization processes and therefore produce changes within the generally stable policy process. Pallagst argues that enlargement and Europeanization are two strongly linked phenomena from a theoretical perspective (2006: 262–8). Heritier (1999) claims that specific polity changes may end up opening special policy windows that provide the opportunity to develop radical processes of change at the policy level. The opening of such windows does not define *a priori* the details of the actions and changes that will take place at the policy level, but establishes general themes and issues that later need to be 'filled with contents' by specific proposals whose definition is delegated to a complex intersection of negotiation, deliberation and socialization processes (Kingdon 1995). Once a window is open, the different actors interact within different arenas in a complex game simultaneously characterized by the two sets of variables described by Conzelmann (1998). On the one hand, actors seek to maximize their own benefits, following action paths determined within different political and cognitive spheres, and proposing different issues with the aim to upload them onto the policy agenda. On the other hand, they are subject to the influence of other actors playing the game within the same arenas under similar rules – although following different assumptions – therefore being constantly subject to the potential questioning of the elements underpinning their own logics of actions.

Pallagst (2006: 265–266) argued that, throughout the incremental process of European integration, the EU created 'official windows of opportunities' extending its territory and involving an increasing number of Member States within its political system. The recent enlargement rounds clearly constituted an unprecedented event in relation to both the number of nations involved – 15 Member States and 12 candidate countries – as well as to the political, socio-economic, cultural and territorial challenges implicit in the process. According to this logic, it is possible to assume that spatial planning, both at the European and domestic levels, would be highly influenced by such a pivotal event. The different facets of European spatial planning were influenced by the specific, institutional, administrative and legal characteristics of the nations that were progressively moving towards full membership, by the specific character of their spatial planning systems and cultures, and by the priorities that the different domestic actors tried to upload onto the community agenda. The enlargement process also strongly impacted on the domestic sphere of spatial planning, with Member States being exposed to new spatial challenges and approaches and needing to modify existing systems in relation to both endogenous and exogenous conditions. The old Member States meanwhile tried to strengthen their position within the new EU reality by focusing on instruments to support the competitiveness of their own regions while the then candidate countries pursued rapid reforms in order to conform to accession requirements and take full advantage of structural support.

This heterogeneous and ever-evolving landscape for spatial planning in Europe provides the context within which the theoretical framework has been elaborated and this framework will be explained in more detail in the next section, highlighting how the concept of territorial knowledge channels provides an interesting knowledge perspective for the understanding of stability and change in the development of spatial policies.

Territorial knowledge channels: a knowledge perspective on stability and change in development of spatial policies

Agent interactivity in policy-shaping processes often involves new policy ideas, preferences and images, and new governance arrangements in a multi-jurisdictional policy environment (Jensen and Richardson 2004). At the same time, these changing cross-scalar multi-agent arrangements of agent interactivity can also continue along the path-dependent trajectories of vested interests among political alliances, and/or conform to the traditional silo-mentality of sectorally organized institutions or government departments (Almendinger and Tewdwr-Jones 2000; Benz 2000). For example, whilst many new Member States have undergone significant administrative and institutional transformation as a result of their accession to the EU (cf. Schimmelfennig and Sedelmeier 2005; Pridham 2005, Cotella 2007b, 2009), they continue to be faced concurrently with the legacy of their socialist and Soviet pasts – upon which new identities have been forged (Paalzow 2006).

An appreciation of the dynamics of newly framed policy issues and opportunities, and the historical legacy of socialist and Soviet pasts, demands an attention to the interplay of knowledge resources and knowledge arenas. As already mentioned, this consideration of path-shaping and path-dependent processes of policy development reflects the conflicts (power and preferences) and learning (knowledge and information) associated with competing institutional and discursive logics (Conzelmann 1998). It also reflects the uncertainties concerning territorial development futures (Abbott 2005), not to mention the 'historical explanations' of current policy developments (cf. Roness 2001).

These processes are evident in the above-mentioned territorial governance arrangements – territorial knowledge channels in our terminology – between knowledge resources and knowledge arenas, which are structured on the extra-/intra-community links between/within territorial knowledge communities (see Figure 2.1). Moreover, territorial knowledge channels can impart an influence on policy development as a result of having acquired the powers to shape or 'frame' new policy images or safeguard existing policy approaches. In effect, these knowledge channels are the structures within which agents interact in a multi-jurisdictional policy environment. As actors within these structures can be members of more than one community, it is possible for individual actors to be part of more communities of practice, whilst at the same time a member of such communities can also be part of an advocacy coalition or epistemic community (Figure 2.2).

In order to clarify, this consideration of the interplay of knowledge and policy development, agent interactivity requires an attention to both 'powers and preferences' (conflict) and 'knowledge and information' (learning) between actors in the study of the processes of policy stability and change (cf. Conzelmann 1998; Lave and Wenger 1991 on 'situated learning'). This approach is particularly significant in a consideration of policy environment tensions where there are territorial knowledge communities who push for technocratic solutions and those who push for more political debate. That is, knowledge has become the 'terrain of politics' at the same time that the public sphere has become 'depoliticized' due to the increasingly complex governance arrangements involving an ever increasing number of agencies, which can insulate public policy from public scrutiny (Radaelli 1999). Within this framework, the knowledge base of epistemic communities and communities of practice in a shared activity or professional discipline may be consensual. However, whereas epistemic communities share common beliefs and interests, the same does not apply to communities of practice whose interests are usually varied and unshared. Similarly, whereas a disputed or absent knowledge base is common within interest groups or advocacy coalitions, and other policy communities of legislators and bureaucratic coalitions, interests can be shared among different interest groups but unshared among legislators (Haas 1992: 18).

This symbiotic relationship between knowledge and interests requires a consideration of both exogenous and endogenous factors, both of which are inter related. Whereas the former constitute 'exogenous shocks' to a policy environment (e.g. political change, economic crisis or new research findings), which can trigger agent responses such as the framing of new policy images, the latter constitute the intra-/extra-community links of communities of actors. In this light, the first of the following three sections will identify and briefly discuss the underlying notions of 'punctuated equilibrium' and 'multiple streams', which are useful in comprehending the nature of policy stability and change in a multi-jurisdictional policy environment. The second will focus more specifically on the endogenous factors of cross-scalar multi-agent intra-/extra-community links among governance arrangements, which are central to a full appreciation of the complex adaptive processes within/between territorial knowledge communities. A third section on the indeterminate nature of power and preferences concludes the presentation of the theoretical framework.

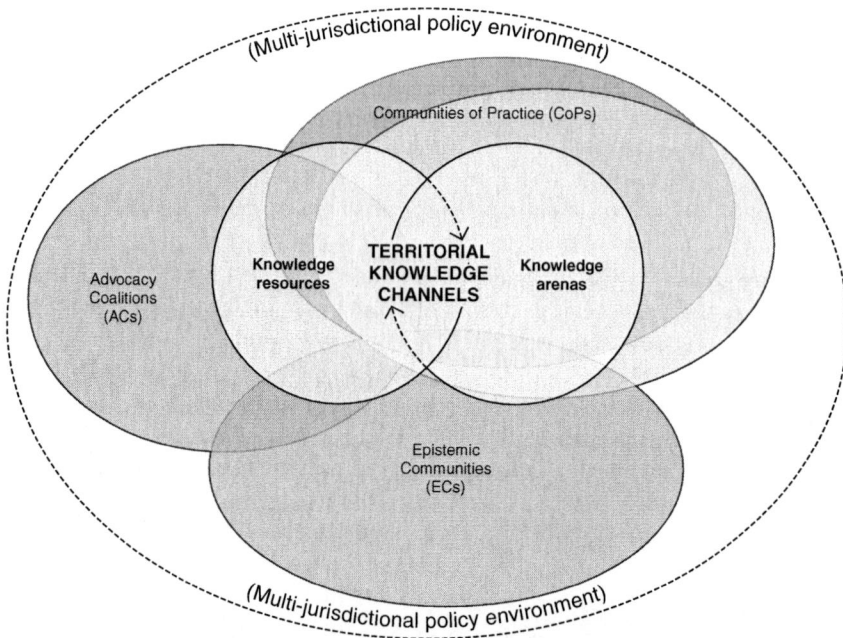

Figure 2.2 Territorial knowledge channels. Intra-community and extra-community links constituting governance arrangements within and across territorial knowledge communities (source: Authors' elaboration; graphics Jo Van Hees).

Endogenous/exogenous factors

Following Radaelli (1999: 769), the view outlined above would maintain that 'knowledge has less to do with specific actors than with the structure in which actors act'. In this regard, Radaelli stresses that the interaction between knowledge and interests are closely related, and that a comprehensive look at the utilization of knowledge in the policy process must integrate both endogenous and exogenous elements of policy change and stability. This is a consideration of how both external shocks (e.g. the perceived political demands of global financial crisis and European enlargement) and agent interactivity can produce path-shaping policy change through the framing of new policy images or the addition of new dimensions to existing policy that 'punctuate' (Baumgartner and Jones 1993, 2002) path-dependent processes of policy stability. The potential reframing of policy problems and/or opportunities as a result of external shocks to a policy environment can trigger complex adaptive processes that involve the politics of learning and conflict with potential knock-on effects on knowledge transfer within/across policy domains.

Furthermore, an appreciation of the potential knock-on effects of these exogenous shocks is evident in the 'multiple streams' of problems, politics and policies (Kingdon 1995; cf. Zahariadis 1999) that generate new knowledge resources. It is also evident in the pursuit of knowledge arenas where these resources can be best employed in the representation of policy problems by advancing new policy options and/or new policy images. The problem stream refers to the pragmatic, albeit contested, application of knowledge and its inherent value judgments and causal beliefs. The policy stream, on the other hand, refers to the causal beliefs embodied in a varied and contradictory 'policy primeval soup' of ideas (Zahariadis 1999: 76) and planning approaches with regard to policy problems and opportunities. Finally, the political stream refers to the value base of influential forces that can influence how problems are recognized and framed such as 'national mood', legislative and political turnover, and pressure from various interest groups.

In other words, the forces acting upon the course of policy development are borne out of evidence, argument and persuasion, and the dynamics of uncertainty, interpretation of problems and path-dependency. The interplay of these resources and arenas with policy development are thus crucial to an understanding of existing and evolving policy contexts of incremental path-dependent change as well as the path-shaping radical policy change that punctuates or breaks with a state of policy stability or 'institutionalised policy monopoly' (Meijerink 2005). Such radical policy change or 'punctuated equilibrium' of policy development is introduced by the creation of new 'policy images', or the framing of new policy approaches or new dimensions to existing policy (Kingdon 1995). Baumgartner and Jones (1993, 2002; cf. True *et al.* 1999; Meijerink 2005) develop this as the 'punctuated equilibrium' of a prevailing 'policy image' in policy studies. To invoke policy change, the promoters of new policy images must redefine or tack on new policy dimensions to prevailing policy images by seeking out arenas where the chances for support are greatest. Once more, the interplay of knowledge and policy development is evident in the advance of policy images whereby knowledge resources are crucial in challenging prevailing policy support in knowledge arenas and thereby helping to invoke policy change.

The notions of punctuated equilibrium and multiple streams therefore offer useful insights into the consideration of endogenous/exogenous factors in a territorial knowledge channels framework. That is, the contested knowledge (conflict), the co-evolution of knowledge and policy development (learning), and the overlapping and conflicting communities of actors, arenas and resources with which planning systems interact in a multi-jurisdictional policy environment. The following section examines this symbiotic relationship between knowledge and interests in the intra-/extra-community links between cross-scalar multi-agent communities of actors, defining and briefly discussing both complementary and mutually reinforcing characteristics of territorial knowledge communities.

Intra-/extra-community links

Borrowing from Aristotelian dictates on knowledge (Levin 2007), our consideration of knowledge invokes an appreciation for the value base of interest groups or 'advocacy coalitions' (Sabatier and Jenkins-Smith 1993) and the value judgments inherent in new policy preferences or approaches ('phronesis'), the scientific and theoretical 'usable knowledge' base of the causal beliefs of 'epistemic communities' ('episteme'), and finally the application of this knowledge ('techne'). The latter more specifically refers to the interplay between knowledge and policy development through the social or interactive process of 'situated' learning across 'communities of practice' (Lave and Wegner 1991). Again it is important to emphasize at this stage that the interrelationships between these concepts are not mutually exclusive. That is, the emphasis on the symbiotic relationship between knowledge and interests must integrate both above-mentioned intra-/extra-community links in approaches to the study of policy stability and change. Table 2.1 offers insights into the distinct characteristics and conceptual limitations of these territorial knowledge communities, identifying key actors, knowledge emphasis, and treatment of knowledge development and utilization. Together, this comparison exposes issues associated with the potential for learning and conflict within and between territorial knowledge communities.

The use of the epistemic communities concept has been a departure point for this book project because of its explicit emphasis on the utilization of knowledge (cf. Haas 1992, 2004). Unlike a policy community (Rhodes 1997) or 'territorial policy communities' (Healey 2006c), which refer to a range of actors drawn together in an area of policy design and delivery, 'an epistemic community is a network of professionals with recognized expertise and competence in a particular domain and an authoritative claim to policy-relevant knowledge within that domain or issue-area' (Haas 1992: 3).

Table 2.1 Territorial knowledge communities

	Key characteristics	Key actors	Knowledge/policy focus	Knowledge development/utilization focus	Conceptual limitations
Epistemic communities[a]	Driven by technocratic consideration; called upon in times of uncertainty and highly complex policy problems; actors share common world view	Restricted group of experts/professionals – think tanks, regulatory agencies and research bodies	Scientific basis of causal knowledge of policy solutions and/or alternatives	Conditional on demand for neutral (unbiased) opinion on controversial, uncertain and complex policy issues; influence depends on political positioning of the community	'Oblique' with regard to limits with wider public concerns; extra-community links
Advocacy coalitions[b]	Motivated by core policy concerns rooted in normative views and perceived causal relationships, and 'deep core' principles	Interest group lobbyists, agency officials, legislators, politicians, and applied researchers and journalists	Individual/collective values (principles) basis of perceived causal relationships	Policy change largely explained exogenously (original definition) as a response to 'exogenous shocks' to policy environment	Endogenous factors of policy change less explored; that is, interaction among actors (learning) within/between coalitions in a policy process
Communities of practice[c]	Structured on a shared 'way of doing things' – on mutually defining identities, codes of practice and shared discourses; flexible and dynamic therefore difficult to identify precisely	Diverse actors, engaging in a task, job or profession (field of practice); organizations	Knowledge remains largely abstract	Knowledge has a role in processes of participation, identity-construction and practice within the community	Power, trust and predispositions, and size, spatial reach and nature ill-defined; lure of 'community' obscures fluidity/heterogeneity within CoPs, their links with other actors and different contexts

Source: Authors' elaboration.

Notes

a Based on interpretation of 'epistemic communities' by Peter Haas (1992, 2004); cf. Ernst Haas' (1990) usage of concept, which places emphasis on extra-community 'reality tests' consistent with the view argued in this book in terms of learning and conflict within and between different communities of actors or 'territorial knowledge communities'.

b See Radaelli (1999: 768) on 'exogenous shocks' and learning within the policy process and Meijerink (2005: 1062) on unresponsive coalitions resistant to change and conditions for learning between coalitions; cf. Sabatier and Jenkins-Smith 1993 (original definition) and Sabatier (1998) for redress of largely exogenous explanation of policy change.

c Roberts (2006); Handley (2006); see also flexible, shifting and porous nature of the boundaries on communities of practice in 'networks of practice' (Brown and Duguid 2001), 'constellations of practice' (Roberts 2006: 631); and links between local knowledge and expert knowledge (Yanow 2004) and change and innovation of shared 'ways of doing' things (Fox 2000).

The theoretical basis of this knowledge perspective begins with Pallagst (2006), who conceptualized the post-enlargement community of actors engaged in European spatial planning as an 'epistemic community'. Work by Haas (2001, 2004), and by others including Hajer (1995) and Radaelli (1995, 1999), can be drawn upon to reinforce the arguments by Pallagst (2006 and Chapter 6). In addition, Zito (2001a, 2001b) re-examined the concept of epistemic communities and argued that a wider conceptual framework was necessary in order to engage a broader group of actors and coalitions in the policy development debate. Similarly, the concept of 'communities of practice' (Lave and Wenger 1991) provides another lens through which knowledge is created, debated, transformed and transferred. Lave and Wenger define a 'community of practice' as 'a system of relationships between people, activities and the world; developing with time and in relation to other tangential and overlapping communities of practice' (1991: 98). The works by Handley *et al.* (2006) and Roberts (2006) undertake a similar re-examination of the concept of communities of practice as was undertaken by Zito (2001a, 2001b) in relation to epistemic communities. More than epistemic communities, the concept of 'communities of practice' focuses on the social and interactive aspects of the socio-cultural dynamic of socialization processes of intra-community links through participation, identity-construction and practice (see Lave and Wenger 1991 on 'situated learning'). However Roberts (2006) re-examines this concept and argues that an understanding of how existing community practices are internalized, challenged or rejected remains unclear. Handley *et al.* (2006) echo this view on the basis of the wider socio-cultural context in which communities of practice are embedded.

An appreciation of the mutually reinforcing and interacting nature of these concepts (see Figure 2.2 and Table 2.1) is extremely useful as they can all focus strongly on the knowledge dimension. As the policy environment changes, knowledge resources are modified or new ones generated in response to the interpretation of policy dilemmas. This in turn triggers harmonious and conflictual relationships between new and existing 'advocacy coalitions' of actors who are driven by normative and perceived causal beliefs in their representation of policy problems (Sabatier and Jenkins-Smith 1993; Sabatier 1998). Certain dimensions of policy dilemmas or issues can be illuminated by the scientific basis of policy solutions from epistemic communities from which interests can be deduced by advocacy coalitions. It is also important to note that the boundaries between these communities are porous whereby epistemic communities can exercise an element of advocacy using their expertise to advance particular policy objectives. Conversely, advocacy coalitions can incorporate scientifically based knowledge through the inclusion of expert actors in advancing their interests. Nevertheless, the theoretical rationale for observing the interplay between these two territorial knowledge communities is that knowledge and interests are often in symbiotic relationship. Lastly, this interplay can in turn have an effect on the intra-community processes of communities of practice in terms of changes to shared 'ways of doing things' but more importantly the utilization of knowledge in light of differing interests (cf. Handley *et al.* 2006; Roberts 2006).

Moreover, the co-consideration of these complementary conceptual frameworks within the overall consideration of territorial knowledge communities may begin to shed light on questions concerning the complex forces shaping spatial development policies (Dabinett and Richardson 1999, 2005) and the competing legitimacies and logics that can inhibit 'integrated' policy development outcomes (cf. Healey 2006c; Stead and Meijers 2009). Once more, the underlying relationship between knowledge and interests in this regard suggests political interests can be best explored in terms of process rather than outcome as addressed in the final section.

Knowledge and the indeterminate nature of power and preferences

The above theoretical framework is a process-oriented conceptualization of knowledge development and utilization, which assumes that the power struggles and indeed preferences are often underspecified or indeterminate. This coincides with the above discussion of the symbiotic relationship between knowledge and interests whereby political interests can be best explored in terms of process rather than outcome. This process-oriented approach involves the continued critique and embrace of concepts and ideas that are advanced through power struggles and preferences with support of data and persuasive argument, and that have the potential to be progressively embedded in the institutional construction of interests. Again, this view further acknowledges the contingency and open-endedness of social contexts for human agency and institutionalized practices (i.e. rules, norms or routines), whilst recognizing that organizations remain the key sites for knowledge and meaning production.

As potentially temporally fixed outcomes of social relations, organizations can be the sites for new and emerging modes of territorial governance that constitute multi-agent, cross-scalar interactions of differing interests and influences in a multi-jurisdictional policy environment. This echoes the view by Allmendinger and Haughton (2009; cf. Haughton *et al.* 2010) who argue that planning, despite the persistence of silo mentalities and clear geographical and professional boundaries, is increasingly open and porous to new expertise, priorities and insights. Thereby, whilst planning continues to exercise its regulatory functions within the legal boundaries or hard spaces of formal plans, it also needs to step out of established working patterns or communities of practice and to operate across 'fuzzy boundaries' into other administrative/political spaces and scales, or 'soft spaces'. This is a befitting view in light of the process-oriented framework on knowledge development and utilization that has been developed in this book.

Furthermore, the agent choices implicit in this process-oriented conceptualization of knowledge development and utilization are bounded by what they make of their policy environment. In other words, this refers to the influential forces or political events such as national mood or legislative and political turnover that can shape agents' interpretation of policy problems (framed by knowledge) encapsulated in the value judgments or meaning attributed to their understanding of policy-related issues. The theoretical framework therefore contemplates both constitutive and structural causes evident in agents' shared and unshared causal beliefs (both scientifically based in the case of epistemic communities and perceived in the case of advocacy coalitions). It reflects the constitutive implications of path-dependent and path-shaping policy processes with respect to the utilization of knowledge. According to Haas, this 'presumes that outcomes, and indeed preferences, are often underspecified or indeterminate, and thus that regimes and political interactions can best be appraised in terms of process [of the intervention of institutionalized norms or rules] rather than outcome' (Haas 2004: 575). It also recognizes the structural implications evident in agent responses to direct environmental pressures or constraints in light of constant preferences or collective material concerns like security or economic welfare. These pressures or constraints could, for example, implicate the long-standing issues of competitiveness and territorial development.

Lastly, these constitutive and structural considerations can be evident in both the formal and informal 'institutional construction of interests' (Parsons 2003). That is, the formal institutional processes of regulatory planning practices acting within hard geographical (jurisdictional) and professional bounds of planning systems, and its potential linkages and conflicts with the soft social structures of informal institutional processes evident in social norms, customs and traditions. Following Lopez and Scott (2000), this particular consideration of the institutional dimension of social structures (rules, norms and traditions) also embraces the interrelated dimensions of language and communication ('relational') and principled beliefs ('embodied') as expressed through ideas, data and argument or knowledge resources.

The discussions in Chapter 1 and in the earlier sections of this chapter established that this book is firmly set within the contexts of an increasingly heterogeneous and ever evolving landscape of spatial planning in Europe at all territorial scales from the supranational to the local. These contexts have taken on uniquely distinct turning points with the latest rounds of EU enlargement, adding an indisputable east-west dimension to the already heterogeneous landscape of spatial planning. In addition there has been a shift from the 'spatial' focus of the legacy of the ESDP to the 'territorial cohesion' emphasis of the latest developments in the maturing and increasingly institutionalized environment of European spatial planning. The specific process-oriented knowledge focus of the above-mentioned territorial knowledge channels framework has implications for any consideration of the diverse form and nature of engagement among territorial knowledge communities. Thus consequently a recognition of the consensual/disputed or absent knowledge bases, and the shared/unshared interests within and across these communities of actors can begin to elucidate 'cultures of practice' or the way of doing things as well as begin to identify who learns what, when, to whose benefit, and why.

In fact it is through this symbiotic relationship between knowledge and interests that the potential for both learning and conflict among territorial knowledge communities becomes evident. In line with this process-oriented approach to policy stability and change this potential for learning and conflict is ultimately evident in the intra-/extra-community links between communities of actors, which constitute the multi-agent cross-scalar governance arrangements of territorial knowledge channels. In a context where knowledge resources have become the terrain of politics at a time when public engagement has become marginalized as a result of a growing number of agencies and knowledge arenas that are able to insulate policy-relevant knowledge from public scrutiny, the nature of these links as well as their inhibiting and facilitating factors is essential to the process-oriented study of policy stability and change. This territorial knowledge channels framework can offer a lens into the chapters that follow, and a useful departure point for future reflections on the complex adaptive processes inherent in territorial development, cohesion and spatial planning in an enlarged EU.

Notes

1 For the purposes of this book, policy development implies both policy process and product. This understanding includes process attributes such as issue identification and analysis, consultation, and performance monitoring, and product attributes such as policy purpose, logics and evidence (argument), and presentation (informing or communication).
2 The European Regional and Spatial Planning Charter, often referred to as the 'Torremolinos Charter', was adopted by the European Conference of Ministers responsible for Regional Planning (CEMAT) in 1984.

References

Abbott, J. (2005) 'Understanding and managing the unknown. the nature of uncertainty in planning', *Journal of Planning Education and Research*, 24: 237–251.

Adams, N., Alden, J. and Harris, N. (2006) *Regional Development and Spatial Planning in an Enlarged EU*, Aldershot: Ashgate.

Adler, E. and Haas, P. M. (1992) 'Conclusion: epistemic communities, world order, and the creation of a reflective research program', in P. M. Haas (ed.) 'Knowledge, Power and International Policy Coordination', *International Organization*, Monographic Issue 46(1): 367–390.

Alden, J. (2006) 'Regional development and spatial planning', in N. Adams, J. Alden and N. Harris (eds) *Regional Development and Spatial Planning in an Enlarged EU*, Aldershot, Ashgate: 17–42.

Allmendinger, P. and Haughton, G. (2009) 'Soft spaces, fuzzy boundaries, and metagovernance: the new spatial planning in the Thames Gateway', *Environment and Planning*, A 41: 617–633.

Allmendinger, P. and Tewdwr-Jones, M. (2000) 'Spatial dimensions and institutional uncertainties of planning and the "new regionalism"', *Environment and Planning C*, 18: 711–726.

Altrock, U., Gunther, S., Huning, S. and Peters, D. (eds) (2006) *Spatial Planning and Urban Development in the New Member States: from adjustment to reinvention*, Aldershot: Ashgate.

Baumgartner, F. R. and Jones, B. D. (eds) (2002). *Policy Dynamics*, Chicago: University of Chicago Press.

—— (1993) *Agendas and Instability in American Politics*, Chicago: University of Chicago Press.

Benz, A. (2002) 'How to reduce the burden of coordination in European spatial planning', in A. Faludi (ed.) *European Spatial Planning*, Lincoln Institute of Land Policy, Cambridge (MA): 149–155.

—— (2000) 'Two types of multi-level governance: inter-governmental relations in Germany and European regional policy', *Regional and Federal Studies*, 10(3): 21–44.

Böhme, K. (2002) *Nordic Echoes of European Spatial Planning*, Stockholm: Nordregio.

Böhme, K. and Waterhout, B. (2008) 'The Europeanization of spatial planning', in A. Faludi (ed.) *European Spatial Research and Planning*, Cambridge (MA): Lincoln Institute of Land Policy: 225–248.

Böhme, K., Richardson, T., Dabinett, G. and Jensen, O. B. (2004) 'Values in a vacuum? Towards an integrated multi-level analysis of the governance of European space', *Journal of European Planning Studies*, 12(8): 1175–1188.

Borzel, T. (2004) 'How the European Union interacts with its member states', in C. Lequesne and S. Bulmer (eds) *Member States and the European Union*, Oxford, Oxford University Press.

Borzel, T. and Risse, T. (2000) 'When Europe hits home: Europeanization and domestic change', *European Integration Online Papers (EioP)* 4(15).

—— (2003) 'Conceptualizing the domestic impact of Europe', in K. Featherstone and C. Radaelli (eds) *The Politics of Europeanization*, Oxford: Oxford University Press: 57–80.

Brenner, N. (1999) 'Globalization as reterritorialization: the re-scaling of urban governance in the European Union', *Urban Studies*, 36(3): 431–451.

—— (2004) *New State Spaces: urban governance and the rescaling of statehood*, Oxford and New York:Oxford University Press.

Brown, J. S. and Duguid, P. (2001) 'Knowledge and organization: a social-practice perspective', *Organization Science*, 12(2): 198–213.

Brunet, R. (1989) *Les Villes Européennes, Rapport pour la DATAR*, Délégation à l'Aménagement du Territoire et à l'Action Régionale, under the supervision of Roger Brunet, with the collaboration of Jean-Claude Boyer *et al.*, Groupement d'Intérêt Public RECLUS. Paris: La Documentation Française.

Buitelaar, E. A., Legendijk, A. and Jacobs, W. (2007) 'A theory of institutional change: illustrated by Dutch city-provinces and Dutch land policy', *Environment and Planning A*, 39: 891–908.

CEC – Commission of the European Communities (1997) EU Compendium of Spatial Planning Systems and Policies Luxembourg: Office for the Official Publication of the European Communities.

—— (1999) *European Spatial Development Perspective: Towards Balanced and Sustainable Development of the Territory of the EU*. Luxembourg: Office of the Official Publications of the European Communities.

—— (2009) *Green Paper on Territorial Cohesion - Turning Territorial Diversity into Strength*. Contributions to the Consultation. Online. Available HTTP: http://ec.europa. eu/regional_policy/consultation/terco/contrib_en.htm (accessed March 2010).

CEMAT (1984) European Regional/Spatial Planning Charter, Online. Available HTTP: www.dgotdu.pt/cemat/site%20CEMAT/Rec(84)2.pdf (accessed March 2010).

Clarence, E. (2002) 'Technocracy reinvented: the new evidence based policy movement', *Public Policy and Administration*, 17(1): 1–11.

Conzelmann, T. (1998) 'Europeanization of regional development policies? Linking multi-level governance approach with theories of policy learning and policy change', *European Integration Online Papers (EIoP)*, 2(4), Online. Available HTTP: http://eiop.or.at/eiop/texte/1998–004a.htm (accessed March 2010).

Cotella, G. (2007a) '(R)Evolution of Central and Eastern European spatial planning systems: trends towards divergence or uniformity?' in R. Nunes, E. Cidre and G. Cotella (eds) *Central and Eastern European Engagement: planning, development and sustainability. ALFA SPECTRA, Central European Journal of Architecture and Planning*, special issue, 11(2): 11–19.

—— (2007b) 'Central and eastern Europe in the global market scenario: evolution of the system of governance in Poland from socialism to capitalism', in B. Leubolt (ed.) 'Approaches to governance', special issue of *Journal für Entwicklungspolitik*, XXIII (1): 98–124.

Dabinett, G. and Richardson, T. (1999) 'The European spatial approach: the role of power and knowledge in strategic planning and policy evaluation', *Evaluation*, 5(2): 220–236.

—— (2005) 'The Europeanization of spatial strategy: shaping regions and spatial justice through governmental ideas', *International Planning Studies*, 10(3): 201–218.

Davoudi, S. (2006) Evidence-based planning: rhetoric and reality, *disP*, 165(2): 14–24.

Dühr, S. (2007) *The Visual Language of Spatial Planning: exploring cartographic representations for spatial planning in Europe*, London: Routledge.

Dühr, S., Colomb, C. and Nadin, V. (2010) *European Spatial Planning and Territorial Co-operation*, London: Routledge.

EC – European Council (2000) *Presidency Conclusions of the Lisbon European Council*, 23–24 March 2000, Council documents Nr. 100/1/100.

ESPON (2007) ESPON 2.3.2 Governance of Territorial and Urban Policies from EU to Local Level. Final report. Online. Available HTTP: www.espon.eu/main/Menu_Projects/Menu_ESPON2006Projects/Menu_PolicyImpactProjects/governance.html> (accessed March 2010).

Evers, D. (2007) 'Reflections on territorial cohesion and European spatial planning', *Tijdschrift voor Economische en Sociale Geografie*, 99(3): 303–315.

Evers, D., Tennekes, J., Borsboom, J., Heiligenberg, H. van den and Thissen, M. (2009) *A Territorial Impact Assessment of Territorial Cohesion for the Netherlands*, Netherlands Environmental Assessment Agency (PBL), Online. Available HTTP: www.eukn.org/binaries/eukn/netherlands/research/2009/07/tia_tc_webversie.pdf (accessed March 2010).

Faludi, A. (2010 forthcoming) *Cohesion, Coherence, Cooperation: European spatial planning coming of age?* London: Routledge.

Faludi, A. and Waterhout, B. (2002) *The Making of the European Spatial Development Perspective: no masterplan*, London: Routledge.

—— (2006a) 'Introducing evidence-based planning', *disP* 165 2/2006: 4–13.

Featherstone, K. and Radaelli, C. M. (eds) (2003) *The Politics of Europeanization*, Oxford: Oxford University Press.

French Presidency (2000) *Contribution to the Debate on the Long-term ESDP Polycentric Vision of Europe. Elaboration of a long-term polycentric vision of the European space*. Final report – Volume 2, Paris: DATAR.

Fox, S. (2000) 'Communities of practice, Foucault and actor-network theory', *Journal of Management Studies*, 37(6): 853–867.

Giannakourou, G. (1996) 'Towards a European spatial planning policy: theoretical dilemmas and institutional implications', *European planning studies*, 5(4): 595–613.

Glasson, J. and Marshall, T. (2007) *Regional Planning*, Abingdon: Routledge.

Goetz, K. H. (2001) 'European integration and national executives: a cause in search for an effect?', in S. Hix and K. H. Goetz (eds) *Europeanized Politics? European integration and national political systems*, Frank Cass: 211–231.

Gorzelak, G. (1996) *The Regional Dimension of Transformation in Central Europe*, London: Jessica Kingsley.

Gualiini, E. (2003) *Multi-level Governance and Institutional Change: the europeanization of regional policy in Italy*, Aldershot: Ashgate.

Haas, E. B. (1990) *When Knowledge is Power*, Berkley: University of California Press.

Haas, P. (1992) 'Introduction: Epistemic Communities and International Policy Coordination', *International Organization*, 46(1), 'Knowledge, Power, and International Policy Coordination' (Winter, 1992): 1–35, The MIT Press.

—— (2001) 'Epistemic communities and policy knowledge', *International Encyclopedia of Social and Behavorial Sciences*, New York: Elsevier: 11578–11586.

—— (2004) 'When does power listen to truth? A constructivist approach to the policy process', *Journal of European Public Policy*, 11(4), August 2004: 569–592.

Hajer, M. (1995) *The Politics of Environmental Discourse: ecological modernization and the policy process*, Oxford: Oxford University Press.

Handley, K., Sturdy, A., Fincham, R. and Clark, T. (2006) 'Within and beyond communities of practice: making sense of learning through participation, identity and practice', *Journal of Management Studies*, 43(3): 641–653.

Haughton, G, Allmendinger, P., Counsell, D. and Vigar, G. (2010) *The New Spatial Planning: territorial management with soft spaces and fuzzy boundaries*, London: Routledge (RTPI Library Series).

Healey, P. (2006a) *Collaborative Planning: shaping places in fragmented societies*, (London: Palgrave Macmillan).

—— (2006b) 'Relational complexity and the imaginative power of strategic spatial planning', *European Planning Studies*, 14(4): 525–546, May.

—— (2006c) 'Territory, integration and spatial planning', in M. Tewdwr-Jones and P. Allmendinger (eds) *Territory, Identity and Spatial Planning: spatial governance in a fragmented nation*, London: Routledge: 64–79.

Heritier, A. (1999) *Policy-making and diversity in Europe: escape from deadlock*, Cambridge: Cambridge University Press.

Hooghe, L. (1995) 'International mobilization in the European Union', *West European Politics*, 18: 175–198.

—— (1996) *Cohesion Policy and European Integration: building multi-level governance*, New York: Oxford University Press.

Hooghe, L. and Marks, G. (2001) *Multilevel Governance and European Integration*, Lanham MD: Rowman and Littlefield.

Jacquot, S. and Woll, C. (2003) 'Usage of European integration: Europeanization from a sociological perspective', *European integration online papers (EIoP)*, 7(12), Online. Available HTTP: http://eiop.or.at/eiop/texte/2003–012a.htm (accessed March 2010).

Janin Rivolin, U. (2003) 'Shaping European spatial planning. How Italy's experience can contribute', *Town Planning Review*, 74(1): 51–76.

—— (2004) *European Spatial Planning*, Milan: Franco Angeli.

—— (2008) 'EU Territorial governance and the innovation cycle of planning: time for sharing benefits?', paper presented at the 4th joint conference ACSP-AESOP Bridging the divide: Celebrating the city, Chicago IL, 6–11 July.

Janin Rivolin, U. and Faludi, A. (2005) 'The hidden face of European spatial planning: innovations in governance', *European Planning Studies*, 13(2).

Jennings, E. T. and Crane, D. (1994) 'Coordination and welfare reform: the quest for the philosophers stone', *Public Administration Review*, 54(4): 341–348.

Jensen, O. B. and Richardson, T. (2004) *Making European Space*, London: Routledge.

Johnson, C. (2009) 'Cross-border regions and territorial restructuring in Central Europe: room for more trans-boundary space', *European Urban and Regional Studies*, 16(2): 177–191.

Kingdon, J. W. (1995) *Agendas, Alternatives and Public Policies*, 2nd edition, New York: Harper Collins.

Krizek, K., Forsyth, A. and Slotterback, C. S. (2009) 'Is there a role for evidence-based practice in urban planning and policy?' *Journal of Planning Theory and Practice*, 10(4): 459–478.

Kunzmann, K. and Wegener, M. (1991) *The Pattern of Urbanisation in Western Europe 1960–1990*. Report for the Directorate General XVI of the Commission of the European Communities as Part of the Study 'Urbanisation and the Function of Cities in the European Community'. Dortmund: IRPUD.

Lakoff, G. and Johnson, M. (1980) *Metaphors We Live By*, Chicago and London: University of Chicago Press.

Lave, J. and Wegner, E. (1991) *Situated Learning: legitimate peripheral participation*, Cambridge: Cambridge University Press.

Lenschow (2006) 'Europeanization of public policy', in J. Richardson (ed.) *European Union: power and policy making*, Abingdon: Routledge, 55–71.

Levin, M. (2007) 'Knowledge and technology transfer: can universities promote regional development?' in A. Harding, A. Scott, S. Laske and C. Burtscher (eds) *Bright Satanic Mills: universities, regional development and the knowledge economy*, Aldershot: Ashgate.

Lopez, J. and Scott, J. (2000) *Social Structure*, Buckingham: Open University Press.

Mahoney, J. (2000) 'Path dependence in historical sociology', *Theory and Society*, 29: 507–548.

Marks, G. (1992) 'Structural policy in the European Community', in A. Sbragia (ed.) *Euro-politics: institutions and policy-making in the 'new' European Community*, Washington, D.C.: Brookings Institution Press: 191–224.

Megie, A. and Ravinet, P. (2004) 'Contrainte de cooperation intergouvernementale et processus d'europeanisation, la construction des espaces européens de l'enseignement supérieur et de la justice', paper presented at the conference *Europeanization of public policies and European integration*, IEP-Paris, 13 February 2004.

Mehlbye, P. (2000) 'Global integration zones: neighbouring metropolitan regions in metropolitan clusters', *Informationen zur Raumentwicklung*, 11/12: 755–762.

Meijerink, S. (2005) 'Understanding policy stability and change. The interplay of advocacy coalitions and epistemic communities, windows of opportunity, and Dutch coastal flooding policy 1945–2003', *Journal of European Public Policy*, 12(6): 1060–1077.

Meijers, E. J., Waterhout, B. and Zonneveld, W. A. M. (2007) 'Closing the GAP: territorial cohesion through polycentric development', Refereed Articles, Oct 2007, no 24, *European Journal of Spatial Development*, Online. Available HTTP: www.nordregio. se/EJSD/refereed24.pdf (accessed March 2010).

Nadin, V. (2002) 'Visions and visioning in European spatial planning', in A. Faludi (ed.) *European Spatial Planning*, Cambridge (MA): Lincoln Institute of Land Policy.

—— (2007) 'The emergence of the spatial planning approach in England', *Planning Practice and Research*, 22 (1): 43–62.

Nunes, R., Adams, N. and Cotella, G. (2009) 'Policy framing and evidence-based planning: epistemic communities in the multi-jurisdictional environment of an enlarged Europe', RSA Annual International Conference, Leuven, Belgium, April 6–8.

Olsen, J. P. (2002) 'The many faces of Europeanization', *Journal of Common Market Studies*, 40(5): 921–952.

Paalzow, A. (2006) 'Barriers to regional development in the new Member States: the Latvian experience', in N. Adams, J. Alden and N. Harris (eds) *Regional Development and Spatial Planning in an Enlarged European Union*, Aldershot: Ashgate.

Pallagst, K. (2006) 'European spatial planning reloaded: considering EU enlargement in theory and practice', *European Planning Studies*, 14(2), February 2006: 253–272.

Parsons, C. (2003) *A Certain Idea of Europe*, Ithaca: Cornell University Press.

Pierson, P. (1996) 'The path to European integration: a historical institutionalist analysis', *Comparative Political Studies*, 29: 123–163.

Pridham, G. (2005) *Designing Democracy: EU enlargement and regime change in post-Communist Europe*, Basingstoke: Palgrave Macmillan.

Radaelli, C. M. (1995) 'The role of knowledge in the policy process', *Journal of European Public Policy*, 2(2): 159–183.

—— (1999) 'The public policy of the European Union: whither politics of expertise?', *Journal of European Public Policy*, 6(5): 757–774.

—— (2004) 'Europeanization: solution or problem?', European integration online papers (EIoP), 8(16), Online. Available http://eiop.or.at/eiop/texte/2004–016a.htm (accessed March 2010).

Rhodes, R. A. W. (1997) *Understanding Governance: policy networks, governance, reflexivity and accountability*, Milton Keynes: Open University Press.

Rittel, H. W. J. and Webber, M. M. (1973) 'Dilemmas in a general theory of planning', *Policy Sciences*, 4: 155–169.

Roberts, J. (2006) 'Limits to communities of practice', *Journal of Management Studies*, 43(3): 623–639.

Roness, P. G. (2001) 'Historical explanations, structural features and institutional characteristics', paper presented at 17th ESGOS Colloquium, Sub Themes 2 'Re-discovering History in Studying Organizations', Lyon, France, July 2001.

Rydin, Y. (2007) 'Re-examining the role of knowledge within planning theory', *Planning Theory*, 6(1): 52–68.

Sabatier, P. A. and Jenkins-Smith, H. C. (eds) (1993) *Policy Change and Learning: an advocacy coalition approach*, Boulder, CO: Westview Press.

Sabatier, P. A. (1998) 'The advocacy coalition framework: revisions and relevance for Europe', *Journal of European Public Policy*, 5(1): 98–130.

Salgado, S. R. and Wool, C. (2004) 'L'européanisation et les acteurs non-étatiques', paper presented to the conference *Europeanization of public policies and European integration*, IEP-Paris, 13 February 2004.

Sbragia, A. (ed.) (1992) *Euro-politics: institutions and policy-making in the 'new' European Community*, Washington, D.C.: Brookings.

Scharpf, F. W. (1994) 'Community and autonomy: multi-level policy making in the European Union', *Journal of European Public Policy*, 1: 219–242.

Schimmelfennig, F. and Sedelmeier, U. (2002) 'Theorizing EU enlargement: research focus, hypotheses, and the state of research', *Journal of European Public Policy*, 9(4): 500–528.

—— (eds) (2005) *The Europeanization of Central and Eastern Europe*, Ithaca NY: Cornell University Press.

Schön, D. (1963) *Displacement of Concepts*, New York: Humanities Press.

—— (1978) 'Generative Metaphor: a perspective in policy setting in social policy', in A. Ortony (ed.) *Metaphor and Thought*, Cambridge: Cambridge University Press.

Schön, P. (2000) 'Einführung – Das Europäische Raumentwicklungskonzept und die Raumordnung in Deutschland', *Informationen zur Raumentwicklung*, 3/4: I–VII.

Stead, D. and Meijers, E. (2009) 'Spatial planning and policy integration: concepts, facilitators and inhibitors', *Planning Theory and Practice*, 10(3): 317–332.

Tatcher, M. (2004) 'Winners and losers of Europeanization: reforming the national regulation of telecommunications', *West European Politics*, 27(2): 284–309.

Tewdwr-Jones, M. (2001) 'Complexity and interdependency in a kaleidoscopic spatial planning landscape for Europe', in L. Albrechts, J. Alden and A. da Rosa Pires (eds) *The Changing Institutional Landscape of Planning*, Aldershot: Ashgate.

Tewdwr-Jones, M. (2002) *The Planning Polity Planning, Government and the Policy Process*, London: Routledge.

Tewdwr-Jones, M. and Williams, R. H. (2001) *European Dimension of British Planning*, London: Spon.

True, J. L., Jones, D. and Baumgartner, F. R. (1999) 'Punctuated-equilibrium theory, explaining stability and change in American policymaking', in P. A. Sabatier (ed.) *Theories of the Policy Process*, Boulder CO: Westview Press: 97–115.

Tsenkova, S. (2007) 'Reinventing strategic planning in post-socialist cities: experiences from Sofia', *European Planning Studies*, 15(3): 295–317.

UNECE – United National Economic Commission for Europe (2008) *Spatial Planning: Key Instrument for Development and Effective Governance with Special Reference to Countries in Transition*, New York; Geneva: United Nations.

Waterhout, B. (2008) *The Institutionalisation of European Spatial Planning*, Amsterdam: IOS Press.

Wenger, E. (1998) *Communities of Practice: learning, meaning, and identity*, Cambridge: Cambridge University Press.

Winn, N. (1998) 'Who gets what, when and how? The contested conceptual and disciplinary nature of governance and policy making in the European Union', *Politics*, 18(2): 119–132.

Yanow, D. (2004) 'Translating local knowledge at organizational peripheries', *British Journal of Management*, 15: 9–25.

Zahariadis, N. (1999) 'Ambiguity, time, and multiple streams', in P. A. Sabatier (ed.) *Theories of the Policy Process*, Boulder CO: Westview Press: 73–93.

Zito, A. (2001a) 'Epistemic communities, European Union governance and the public voice', *Science and Public Policy*, 28(6): 465–476.

—— (2001b) 'Epistemic communities, collective entrepreneurship and European integration', *Journal of European Public Policy*, 8(4): 585–603.

Part I

Territorial challenges and the cognitive bounds of spatial planning in the enlarged European Union

Editors' introduction to Part I

Neil Adams, Giancarlo Cotella and Richard Nunes

As already introduced in the first chapter of this volume, evidence clearly suggests that recent enlargements of the European Union (EU) have drastically shifted the frontier of European integration eastward. This is true both in terms of the challenges faced by the EU and those facing the old and new Member States, and has important implications also in relation to the production of relevant 'knowledge resources' within the 'knowledge arenas' of spatial planning in Europe (cf. Adams *et al.*, Chapters 1 and 2). From the first half of the 1990s, and particularly since the Copenhagen European Council in 1993, the EU started to broaden its horizons beyond its eastern border, for the first time bringing into question the western-oriented perspective under which it was born (cf. CEC 1994, 1996).

Whereas the most recent enlargement rounds have initiated a set of political, democratic, cultural and socio-economic challenges, the territorial dimension of these new challenges constitutes a challenge in itself. The importance of the territorial dimension of the eastwards enlargement of the EU is clear if one considers that it led, in less than three years, to the expansion of the EU territory by nearly 40 per cent, while increasing the population by approximately 120 million up to a total of almost 500 million. At the same time, evidence on the spatial distribution of economic development illustrates how the challenges initiated by the enlargement process were far from being solved at the time of its formal completion: more than 92 per cent of the population of CEE Member States live in regions with a GDP per capita below 75 per cent of the EU average whilst the combined GDP of the recent entrants is only 10 per cent of the overall EU output (CEC 2007).

The negative macroeconomic trends affecting CEE nations present considerable social, economic and spatial challenges for a variety of strategic policy sectors such as the economy, education, environment and social welfare and, in turn, the combination of these factors provides a highly challenging context for spatial planning in the enlarged EU. Furthermore, the progressive institutionalization of spatial planning at the European level (Waterhout 2008) has had a direct influence on cross-sectoral planning approaches within the domestic contexts of national planning systems. This influence on national planning systems includes both the old Member States as well as the EU entrants from CEE, partly as a result of their preparations for accession to the Union, including but not limited to their eligibility for Structural funding. In this concern, there is some evidence to suggest a degree of convergence in ideas and approaches to spatial planning throughout the EU (Adams 2008; Stead 2008) due to specific processes of Europeanization (Adams *et al.*, Chapter 2). Such a shift manifests through the everyday processes of institutional change and organizational learning referred to in Chapter 1, which seek to address the diverse territorial development challenges in the different regions of Europe. Notwithstanding the above-mentioned convergence of ideas and practices, the variety of these challenges and of the contexts within which these challenges are being faced determines that the results of these processes are context specific, as reflected by the growing institutional and organizational diversity between European regions and cities.

Drawing on the above discussion, the Part I of this book explores the territorial challenges and the cognitive bounds that are contributing to shape the evolution of spatial agendas at the different territorial levels in diverse territorial contexts, all within the framework of the enlarged EU. In so doing, the various contributions discuss some of the approaches and trends in terms of spatial planning policy and practice that are emerging out of the recent enlargement processes. This exploration is undertaken from different points of view corresponding to the diverse backgrounds and expertise of the authors as well as their geographical location and experience, spread throughout western, central and eastern Europe. The heterogeneity of the contributors and the diversity of the chosen themes and approaches provides an opportunity to explore the evolution of spatial planning in Europe from multiple perspectives: first, from a general consideration of the economic forces and interests implicit in the dichotomy between cohesion and competitiveness; second, an extensive analysis of the process of institutionalization of European spatial planning and the reasons and means behind it; third, a more geographically focused reflection on the evolving framework for regional development in CEE; and, finally a consideration of the future perspectives for epistemic communities and the potential for their integration in the western and eastern part of the continent. Despite the heterogeneity described above, each author considers its specific theme in relation to the role of diverse communities of actors and the interplay between knowledge and policy development and this provides a unifying theme and links this section to the overall rationale for the book. The strong focus on knowledge creation inherent in the 'epistemic communities' concept (Haas 1992), which in the context of our theoretical framework has been extended to 'territorial knowledge communities' (Chapter 2), means that it is particularly relevant to elucidating this interplay between knowledge and policy development and the ways in which knowledge resources are created, contested, mobilized and controlled across governance architectures (cf. Radaelli 1995). As discussed in Chapter 2 the generation of such knowledge resources is not sufficient and this cognitive capacity to generate knowledge requires concrete actions to put it to use. How territorial knowledge communities articulate this knowledge is therefore crucial in determining its influence and this is particularly relevant in the context of contemporary communicative planning theory. Benz (2002) refers to this as the combination of the cognitive task of analysis and goal formulation with the political task of overcoming conflicts of interest and the integration of divergent policies.

Considerable resources are committed within the EU to sharing experience between these communities, in an attempt to overcome cultural and cognitive boundaries that may inhibit the sharing of ideas on policy and approach and the effective utilization of knowledge resources. There seems to be a shared consensus around the fact that emerging territorial challenges require both old and new Member States to build on the enlargement through the activation of new investment and a more effective utilization of 'territorial knowledge channels', in order to address increasing spatial polarization, economic disparities and environmental damage. However, as widely debated in the literature (Stead 2008; Stead and Nadin, Chapter 7) the appropriateness of sharing and transferring elements of successful approaches from context to context is somehow undermined by the diversity of planning cultures, styles and approaches that, already significant between the EU-15, has now reached an unprecedented level due to recent eastwards enlargements (Knieling and Othengrafen 2009).

In order to seek answers to old and emerging territorial challenges, policy approaches need to reflect the new east-west dimension that is characterized by the emergence of a new socio-economic and political landscape, within which both established and new member states pursue the dual goals of 'cohesion' and 'competitiveness'. However, whilst the pursuit of territorial cohesion and balanced and/or sustainable development continue to be central to the rhetoric of the EU policy agenda, the unrelenting emphasis on 'regional competitiveness and employment' since the adoption of the Lisbon Agenda (EC 2000) has increased the complexity of the context within which those goals are being pursued. The continuing emphasis on 'balanced competitiveness' is currently echoed in the latest territorial reference documents developed at the EU level, and more specifically in the Territorial Agenda of the European Union (DE Presidency 2007a) that is centred on the 'global competitiveness and sustainability' of European regions (cf. Böhme and Schön 2006). These tensions are further mirrored by current EU regional policy measures that, in spite of their apparent success in terms of economic convergence between Member States, continue to fuel increasing internal disparities within many Member States whereby national growth has been driven by a small number of dynamic regions (Ezcurra *et al.* 2007) in a process that Kunzmann (2008) refers to as metropolization. These challenges are evident in the presented contributions and are reflected in the different interpretations the various authors seem to have of similar issues. These issues illustrate both the cognitive bounds and at the same time the main challenges for spatial planning in Europe at present time, and it is within this context that the contributions in this section should be read. Despite the shared ambition to increase attention for the spatial dimension of EU policy, which facilitated the adoption of ESDP (CEC 1999) and more recently the Territorial Agenda (DE Presidency 2007a), the different authors show how contradictions remain evident in the EU spatial planning discourse. As Waterhout (2008) argues, this may be partly due to the lack of identity amongst the 'European planning community', and the lack of a common understanding of what form European spatial planning could or should take at least in terms of broad guiding principles, possible future institutionalization and its fields of intervention. Pallagst reflects on the future of such a European planning community in terms of its potentials to integrate experts and communities from both 'old' and 'new' Member States. However, as pointed out by Finka, until now efforts in this direction seem to have been in vain and new ways need to be found in order to overcome existing cognitive bounds, to integrate knowledge effectively and to valorize the inherent diversity of the enlarged EU.

The first contribution in this part is written by Mark Tewdwr-Jones (Chapter 3) and examines the existing tensions between the dual pursuance of economic competitiveness and territorial cohesion in the cross-scalar framework of the EU. In so doing, it illuminates the main features of the present and future context for territorial development in an evolving European landscape. In the beginning of the twenty-first century, the affirmation of the territorial cohesion objective in the official documents of the EU appears to have legitimized territorial actions at the European level. Explicit references to the principle of territorial cohesion have been included in the Treaty establishing a Constitution of Europe and eventually in the most recent version of the latter, the Lisbon Treaty. Nevertheless, despite its official legitimization, the interpretation of the concept of territorial cohesion remains open to debate, especially when national economic interests conflict with ideals of territorial re-equilibrium. Notwithstanding the wide appeal of the concept at the supranational level, the lack of uniform interpretation seems to imply that whilst the multidimensional nature of the concept could constitute an asset, it also introduces a set of unresolved tensions. An exploration of this dichotomy between cohesion and economic growth and competitiveness, which lies at the heart of these tensions, forms the basis for Chapter 3.

More specifically the contribution focuses on a reflection about a persisting tension embodied in the concept of territorial cohesion and explores the potential mismatch between the implementation of the political objective of territorial cohesion and its contextual economic reality. In so doing, the author discusses the paradox associated with the notion of 'balanced economic competitiveness', central to several EU territorial guidance documents as well as to Commission policies associated with planned economic growth.

The chapter illustrates this debate and makes a useful contribution to the conceptual development of territorial cohesion. It does so by focusing its attention on the ongoing regional economic trends concerning foreign direct investment (FDI) and the spatial impacts of this mobile capital, and situates them in the context of regional competitiveness. The author focuses more on the economic rather than the political concept of territorial cohesion and draws out some of the implications for spatial development in Europe. The quest to attract FDI is not new and lagging regions have traditionally sought to devise means of attracting this mobile capital. Given the socio-economic characteristics of many CEE countries it is not surprising that many of them have made extensive efforts to

planning and policy systems of CEE countries. The author argues how the different dynamics that regulate the development of socio-spatial systems and the problems they generate concern both the established and the new EU Member States, though with a different intensity. In this context, the problems that the regions in the new EU Member States have been facing are not issues specific to contemporary European spatial planning theory and practice, nor are they specific for CEE countries. The majority of such problems have been experienced in many Western European regions and other parts of the world in recent decades. These concerns therefore demonstrate the need to re-evaluate traditional spatial classifications at the European and global scales and to base theoretical and political approaches on these classifications.

Building on the above considerations, Finka examines current trends in spatial planning policy in the context of EU integration. In so doing, he assesses the extent of the potential for developing approaches in terms of theory, policy-making and practice, which reflect the new realities of spatial development in Europe. The liberal flavour that characterized the first years of the transition resulted in scarce political priority to development policy and planning issues (Sykora 1999) and, while the removal of outdated Communist institutions took place almost immediately after 1989, their substitution with a new and effective operational framework came to be a much less certain process. To some degree this links to the discussion by Dąbrowski (Chapter 9) who identifies the ease with which the old structures are replaced but the much more difficult and long-term task of adapting old ways of working in practice to new realities. The developments of new institutional frameworks have been influenced heavily by the diversity of national contexts, pre-accession initiatives and European spatial policy documents, leading to an unprecedented reorganization of the spatial planning systems that are now operational in the new Member States. In this context, despite CEE countries clearly forming a highly heterogeneous group, the majority of them are currently bound by similar socio-economic characteristics compared to the EU-15 and many are facing similar challenges in terms of dealing with the legacy of their socialist past whilst at the same time trying to look towards a more prosperous future within the EU. To a certain extent CEE countries have been forced to adopt some elements of North-west European approaches to territorial development and spatial planning. Finka explores some of these issues and discusses how approaches to territorial development have evolved in some of the new regions of the EU within this context. The contribution examines the extent to which CEE countries have so far been engaged in the discourse in relation to EU territorial development policy and how this is likely to evolve in the future. The author goes on to consider the practical application of the territorial cohesion agenda and its implications for CEE countries before finally exploring ways in which the regions in CEE can make a significant contribution to this process by highlighting their key issues and concerns and how these could be addressed at both the EU and national levels. While acknowledging that CEE experts are not yet fully engaged in the knowledge arenas of European spatial planning, Finka questions the logic of conceptualizing such issues in geographical terms or in terms of 'old' and 'new' Member States. He identifies the harnessing of the diversity of spatial planning in Europe as a means of generating innovative approaches to addressing context sensitive issues as one of the key challenges for planners throughout the EU. Finka's argument also seems to imply the need for the creative use of the 'soft' planning and 'soft' spaces mentioned on numerous occasions elsewhere in this book.

Part I concludes with a contribution by Pallagst (Chapter 6), which examines the impact of recent EU enlargements on the emergence of 'new' and 'hybrid' epistemic communities and assesses some of the theoretical implications of this approach in relation to the discourse around European spatial planning. The adopted focus on the role of territorial knowledge communities in the 'framing' of policy intervention, which constitutes one of the main transversal themes of the book, is particularly relevant here. This 'framing' of policy intervention becomes apparent if one considers the manner in which new epistemic communities develop as an influential factor in determining how discourse, in relation to the EU spatial development policy, evolves at all levels across policy sectors within the complex multi-scalar reality of spatial policy intervention in the EU-27.

Whereas the last 20 years were characterized by a boost in spatial planning at the European level, the process of enlargement and the ongoing transition process in CEE countries constitutes a major challenge for European integration and the spatial dimension of EU policy. Pallagst argues that enlargement and European spatial planning are closely related from a theoretical perspective, as enlargement challenges European spatial planning in several ways. On the one hand, the territorial dimension of the integration of a group of countries in a clearly unfavourable socio-economic situation has dramatic implications on spatial planning at the EU level. On the other hand, as numerous new CEE actors joined the planning arena, they introduced a legacy of planning approaches, styles and cultures substantially different from those of western European countries, offering opportunities for a systematic and reciprocal exchange of planning knowledge. Hence, enlargement should constitute a major input for change within the policy field of European spatial planning, requiring a further conceptualization of the knowledge-aspects of the notion of change. In this concern, it is becoming increasingly apparent how previous spatial planning approaches and spatial metaphors, developed by academics during the 1980s and 1990s to conceptualize spatial development in the EU-15 territory, have become outdated and require revision to take account of the new reality. This will involve the development of new knowledge resources and planning approaches, the formulation of new institutional arrangements and the de-institutionalization of others.

Here, Pallagst points out that an influential role in the evolution of the discursive dimension of European spatial planning is played by the new level of complexity and diversity of policy approaches in the enlarged EU. This situation has provided a fertile breeding ground for the emergence of new territorial knowledge communities and a new relationship between these communities and policymakers in the framing of policy. As a result, the author argues, one of the most significant challenges for planners in the new EU will be how best to engage in new relationships and networks in order to broaden the discourse on territorial issues. Within this context, Pallagst explores the interplay between knowledge and policy at the heart of this book in relation to the role of the concept of epistemic communities as defined by Haas (1992) in contemporary planning theory and practice. On the basis of this, she presents a detailed discussion of present and future perspectives for European spatial planning in the enlarged EU, taking further her previous work debating the emergence of either a new European epistemic community or the evolution of two separate communities divided roughly along the line of the Iron Curtain. By revisiting these two scenarios Pallagst makes a useful contribution both to the theoretical framework for this book and to the theoretical discussions of European spatial planning generally.

References

Adams, N. (2008) 'Convergence and policy transfer: an examination of the extent to which approaches to spatial planning have converged within the context of an enlarged EU', *International Planning Studies*, 13(1): 31–50.

Benz, A. (2002) 'How to reduce the burden of coordination in European spatial planning', in A. Faludi (ed.) *European Spatial Planning*, Lincoln Institute of Land Policy, Cambridge (MA): 149–155.

Böhme, K. and Schön, P. (2006) 'From Leipzig to Leipzig: territorial research delivers evidence for the new territorial agenda of the European Union', *disP* 165, 42(2): 61–70.

CEC – Commission of the European Communities (1994) *Europe 2000+. Cooperation for the development of the European territory*, Luxembourg: Office for the Official Publications of the European Communities.

—— (1996) *Scenarios of Spatial Development of Central and Eastern European Countries*, Luxembourg: Office for the Official Publications of the European Communities.

—— (1999) *European Spatial Development Perspective (ESDP) Towards Balanced and Sustainable Development of the Territory of the EU*, Luxembourg: Office for Official Publications of the European Communities.

—— (2007) *Growing Regions, Growing Europe. Fourth relation on economic, and social cohesion*, Luxembourg: Office for the Official Publications of the European Communities.

—— (2008) *Green paper on Territorial Cohesion – Turning territorial diversity into strength*. Luxembourg: Office for Official Publications of the European Communities.

DE Presidency (2007a) *Territorial Agenda of the European Union: Towards a more competitive and sustainable Europe of diverse regions* – Agreed at the occasion of the informal ministerial meeting on urban development and territorial cohesion on 24/25 May 2007. Online. Available HTTP: www.bmvbs.de/Anlage/original_1005295/Territorial-Agenda-of-the-European-Union-Agreed-on-25-May-2007-accessible.pdf (accessed March 2010).

—— (2007b) *The Territorial State and Perspectives of the European Union: Towards a stronger European territorial cohesion in the light of the Lisbon and Gothenburg ambitions* – A background document to the territorial agenda of the European Union. Online. Available HTTP: www.bmvbs.de/Anlage/original_1005296/The-Territorial-State-and-Perspectives-of-the-European-Union.pdf (accessed March 2010).

EC – European Council (2000) *Presidency Conclusions of the Lisbon European Council*, 23–24 March 2000, Council documents Nr. 100/1/100.

Ezcurra, R., Pascual, P. and Rapun, M. (2007) 'The dynamics of regional disparities in Central and Eastern Europe during transition', *European Planning Studies*, 15 (10), 1397–1421.

Faludi, A. (2010 forthcoming) *Cohesion, Coherence, Cooperation: European spatial planning coming of age?* London: Routledge.

Faludi, A. and Waterhout, B. (2006a) 'Introducing Evidence-based Planning', *disP*, 165, 42(2): 4–13.

—— (2006b) 'Debating Evidence-based Planning: Conclusions from the International Workshop', *disP*, 165, 42(2): 71–72.

Haas, P. (1992) 'Introduction: Epistemic Communities and International Policy Coordination', *International Organisation*, 46(1): 1–35.

Haughton, G., Allmendinger, P., Counsell, D. and Vigar, G. (2010) *The New Spatial Planning: territorial management with soft spaces and fuzzy boundaries*, London: Routledge (RTPI Library Series).

Kingdon, J. W. (1995) *Agendas, Alternatives and Public Policies*, 2nd edition, New York: Harper Collins.

Knieling, J. and F. Othengrafen (eds) (2009) *Planning Cultures in Europe: decoding cultural phenomena in urban and regional planning*, Farnham, Surrey: Ashgate.

Kunzmann, K. (2008) 'Futures for European space', *Journal of Nordregio: European Space 2020 Planning, Energy and Transport*, 2(8), June 2008: 12–21.

Radaelli, C. M. (1995) 'The role of knowledge in the policy process', *Journal of European Public Policy*, 2(2): 159–183.

Stead, D. (2008) 'Assessing the convergence of national spatial planning systems in Europe', paper presented at the 4th joint conference, ACSP-AESOP Bridging the divide: Celebrating the city, Chicago IL, 6–11 July.

Sykora, L. (1999) 'Local and regional planning and policy in East Central European transitional countries', in M. Hampl (eds) *Geography of societal transformation in the Czech Republic*, Prague: Charles University, Department of Social Geography and Regional Development: 153–179.

Waterhout, B. (2008) *The Institutionalization of European Spatial Planning*, Delft: IOS Press.

3 Cohesion and competitiveness

The evolving context for European territorial development

Mark Tewdwr-Jones

Introduction

Adding to the previous notions of economic and social cohesion identified in Articles 3 and 158 of the EC treaty, the text of the Constitution for Europe, and of its natural follow-up, the Lisbon Treaty, has embodied the territorial dimension of European development policies with greater political significance than ever before. This book provides the reader with a wide-ranging discussion on the development, ethos and possible delivery mechanisms of 'territorial cohesion' across the enlarged European Union (EU). This chapter, more specifically, is centred on a reflection about a persisting tension embodied in the concept of 'territorial cohesion' and explores the potential mismatch between the implementation of the political objective of 'territorial cohesion' and its contextual economic reality. The discussion will provide the reader with an introduction to some of the current issues in relation to territorial development in the EU and in doing so provide part of the context within which the chapters that follow can be read.

'Territorial cohesion' has the aim of combating territorial disparities to achieve a more spatially balanced pattern of economic development by securing the coordination and coherence of development policies (CEC 2004: 28). The main concern with this objective relates to the unevenness and, by implication, the concentration of economic activity within particular territories of the European Union. The message outlined by the Commission of the European Communities (CEC) is clear: market forces alone will not result in balanced economic development across the Union as a whole and Eastern enlargement only has served to double existing regional disparities (CEC 2003: 38).

This chapter's key objective is to discuss the paradox associated with the notion of 'balanced economic competitiveness' in the European Spatial Development Perspective (ESDP) and the subsequent Commission policies associated with planned economic growth (Davoudi 2003). It is possible to suggest that the ongoing emphasis on polycentric development in spatial strategies across the EU, in the aftermath of the ESDP's publication in 1999, might have informed a shift toward spatial planning as a vehicle for the generation of economic growth in regions away from concerns to redistribute or compensate such regions (Ezcurra *et al.* 2007). But, in practice, 'polycentricity' and 'balanced competitiveness' remain somewhat abstract phrases at the present time (Dühr 2007). This is largely a consequence of the lack of an evidence base behind the terminology of the ESDP as it was developed in the 1990s (Meijers *et al.* 2007). These abstract phrases allowed for different interpretations across Member States and the resultant planning policy nomenclature within nations and regions have had uncertain but variable impacts on urban form, development patterns and mobility. Furthermore, the economic performance of Member States was in a different state in 1999 compared to the present day, and the disparities between them were far less dramatic than they have been in the current post-enlargement scenario. In light of the recent global economic recession in 2008, the importance of stimulating economic growth within European cities and regions is likely to find stronger political footing as a pan-European agenda within the EU and thereby challenge aspects of both the ESDP's agenda and to the spatial planning concepts within 'territorial cohesion'.

The following chapter has been structured to illustrate this debate and to try and inform the conceptual development of 'territorial cohesion'. Following a critical review of how economic competition is addressed in the ESDP, this chapter turns its attention to the ongoing regional economic trends concerning foreign direct investment (FDI) and their spatial impact. The debate situates the latter trends in the context of regional competitiveness, drawing conclusions on the economic rather than the political concept of 'territorial cohesion' and its implications for European spatial development. In this context, the extent to which current policy is knowledge-based, the role that knowledge plays and who the agents involved in the generation of that knowledge are, will be discussed and this also provides a central theme that is discussed elsewhere in this book (cf. Adams, N. *et al.* in Chapters 1 and 2). Salient points are drawn out before returning to consider the spatial implications of 'territorial cohesion' and 'balanced competitiveness' in an enlarged EU.

The ESDP, economic growth and 'balanced competitiveness'

One of the key objectives of this chapter is to try and inform the development of a spatial implementation strategy contained within the 'territorial cohesion' concept (Faludi 2005). This is in the spirit of the recently published Commission Green Book on Territorial Cohesion (CEC 2008), which aims to constitute the basis of a discussion platform for different stakeholders in order to define the operational outlines of 'territorial cohesion'. Notwithstanding uncertainty concerning its existing political validation, as one of the main principles in the Lisbon Treaty, it remains to be seen how this reshuffle of competences concerning cohesion policies will actually translate into a territorial dimension (Doucet 2006, Evers 2008). As other commentators have suggested (e.g. Faludi 2006, 2007), the concept of 'territorial cohesion' has been seen as a suitable conceptual follow-up to the ESDP process. According to the Commission of the European Communities, the rationale behind the formulation of the ESDP in 1999 involved strengthening economic and social cohesion and achieving the sustainable development of the EU territory as a whole (CEC 2003). But the EU goals of competitiveness on the one hand and economic and social cohesion on the other are ultimately different and possibly contradictory (Lawton-Smith *et al.* 2003: 865). Whilst the management of EU economic competition-related tensions is clearly embedded in the ESDP, it nonetheless failed to address the competitiveness concept. The ESDP flagship objective of a shared vision of the European territory (CEC 1999: 3) was structured on a development model of competition between regions and cities in order to secure a better balance between competition and cooperation (Jensen and Richardson 2004: 21). This objective, which was eventually included in the final document, envisaged the preservation of an 'optimum level of competitiveness' (CEC 1999: 2).

The ESDP outlined a new vision for European space, introducing a new scale of spatial planning in order to pursue polycentric urban systems – that of transnational infrastructure networks and growth zone development. Growth zone development, in particular, has underlined the importance of promoting complementary relations between cities and regions through simultaneously building on the advantages and overcoming the disadvantages of economic competition between them. Nonetheless, the ESDP also advocated that this complementarity should not be focused solely on economic competition. Rather it also should be expanded to all urban functions such as culture, education and knowledge, and social infrastructure (CEC 1999: 21). In reality, the ESDP developed and shared a co-existence with the interventionist policies intended to overcome the problems of the lagging regions (i.e. cohesion policies), and those of anti-interventionist character (i.e. competition policy) that are designed to remove existing barriers to full market integration (Lawton-Smith *et al.* 2003: 859). It is interesting to note the inclusion of both competitiveness and cohesion objectives within the document, reflecting perhaps differing attitudes within those Member States participating in the drafting process of the document (see Faludi and Waterhout 2002, Waterhout 2008).

Critical insights may be introduced as the ESDP championed – among other objectives – a vital goal of EU spatial policy: the need to proactively counterbalance the negative effects of increased inter-European competitiveness brought about by the single market and globalization. Breaking down this objective raises interesting debates that underline, for instance, the lack of absolute reasoning on the impacts of globalization. As has been debated at length (see, for example, Cooke and Morgan 1998, Swyngedouw and Baeten 2001), the uniform and constraints-free single-market Europe, upheld by some EU policy-makers, has failed to materialize. From another angle, the noticeable market and competition-orientated spatial development content of the ESDP (Jensen and Richardson 2004: 21) raises the issue of how coherent and effective this strategic spatial document has been in advancing the EU ideals of equity, justice and political legitimacy (Getimis 2003: 85) – if it does not directly address the management of its conflicting interests. Faludi's (2009) recent reflection on the making of the Territorial Agenda highlights the dual elements of 'territorial cohesion' and 'territorial capital'; both of these notions continue to be emphasized in the Territorial Agenda in much the same way that 'cohesion' and 'competition' featured within the development of the ESDP. In this regard, it is useful to recall Evers' (2008) assertion that European spatial planning can, at times, prove to be somewhat 'elusive'.

Another significant issue in this discussion concerns EU regional policy and its important contribution towards convergent economic development (e.g. Rodriguez-Pose and Fratesi 2004). As intense agglomeration of corporate and research and development (R&D) activity has developed in key areas of Europe that privilege distinct geographies within the EU, a great increase in regional disparities has not been witnessed. However, Rodriguez-Pose and Fratesi (2004) have concluded that economic cohesion and convergence targets show low levels of compatibility and that there remain doubts about the capacity of development funds to actually foster a further higher degree of 'territorial cohesion', a point previously pre-empted by Morgan and Nauwelaers (1999: 16). They have produced a set of recommendations for future use that emphasize the risks of disproportionately focusing on certain development axes as a disrupting strategy for establishing long-term sustainable growth patterns. They suggest a regionally tailored development strategy, taking into consideration factors as diverse as premature exposure to the market, 'brain-drain', or subsidization of non-competitive local firms, and it would not seem too far-fetched to extend this suggestion into notions of 'territorial capital'. The subsidization argument reverts to the discussion on competition policy and its direct impact on achieving economic and social cohesion, as well as the reduction in inter- and intra-regional disparities as targeted in Article 158 of the Treaty of Rome. Indeed, Article 92(1) of the Treaty provided a general ban on so-called State aids for economic development (Lawton-Smith *et al.* 2003: 867); State aid would be possible, but under the ruling regulatory role of the European Commission. This mechanism, known as Regional Selective Assistance (RSA), is then regulated by determining the type of assistance allowed and by examining how assisted area maps are determined (Armstrong 2001: 252).

Therefore, the current EU economic development approach is argued to have had, to some extent, a positive impact in lagging regions via a set of policies that places competitiveness in a central position in determining objectives, and in designing measures (Hall and Soskice 2001). In this context, some authors state that the systemic choices underlying EU development policy are adequate considering the uncertain challenges that lie ahead (e.g. Molle 2002); a reconsideration of the fundamentals of this approach is not, consequently, a priority. Molle (2002) identifies two crucial tasks for sustainable evolution: first, to reintroduce knowledge accumulated into the policy-making system in order to optimize the effectiveness and efficiency of these policies; and, second, to distinguish between problems resulting from adaptation processes and systemic faults. However, regardless of the placement of structural and cohesion funds under different objectives, the real coordination mechanisms behind these development policies remain unclear. Faludi (2004) has discussed these issues extensively in the context of the 'territorial cohesion' concept. The rationale behind this concept, originally outlined in the third cohesion report (CEC 2004), encompassed, among other objectives, the promotion of greater coherence and coordination between regional and sectoral policies with a spatial impact. Before going on to look at these implications further, it is necessary to outline trends of regional economic development in the EU and the spatial implications of the impacts of globalization.

EU trends in regional economic development

As global economic integration continues to create interdependencies among nations and localities, competition for inward investment continues to intensify (see Phelps and Raines 2003). The economic geography literature reminds us that internationally mobile investors nevertheless remain, to a greater or lesser extent, embedded in particular places (Yeung 1998), while the political geography literature points to the contribution of local politics to processes of economic globalization (Jessop 1999). Under conditions of rapid international economic integration, the quality and efficiency of markets for the factors of production – such as labour, land and property – become, if anything, more important to economic competitiveness. Most academic and policy concern has, to date, focused on debates surrounding the significance of labour skills and flexibility in economic performance. However, MacLennan (1995: 397) pointed out that where international competition is speeding up,

> competitive responses need not be limited to making labour markets more flexible. The role of housing, land and planning policies may play a critical role in shaping which places, even nations, adjust successfully to the new international economic order.

Land use and spatial planning practices are an important and neglected element of such national and local modes of social regulation (Berry and McGreal 1995: 8). An exploration of how planning systems contribute to the competition for FDI has been lacking, but it could provide an invaluable window onto the articulation of global and local economic and political processes (cf. Capik, Chapter 13).

On the one hand, the recent history of inward investment attraction in the EU suggests that planning systems have been largely by-passed as a result of promotional bodies wishing to minimize disruption to prospective investors (Tewdwr-Jones and Phelps 2000, Phelps and Tewdwr-Jones 2001). A planned approach evident in the 1960s and 1970s gave way to an approach customized to the needs of inward investors. Arguably, planning systems have played their role in ensuring that inward investors have rarely been integrated into existing clusters of economic activity. This might be viewed as almost globalization from below in that agents of local governance are helping to reinforce the mobility of these companies. This is also reconfiguring the planning system from a purely regulatory mechanism into a supporting, enabling and collaborating spatial process, with a renewed emphasis on policy and agency integration, regional and spatial differentiation, and development management.

On the other hand, more recent EU and regional interest in issues of sustainability, territorial-based interventions and clusters, implies a return to potentially more plan-led approaches to economic development and to the steering of inward investment in particular. Here, robust local responses and the development of spatial plans might offer more progressive attempts to embed otherwise mobile companies. Devolution and the incorporation of these new concerns with clusters and sustainability (along with the increasing potential influence of new spatial development perspectives) is likely to be geographically uneven, not least because of the variable development pressures faced across different territories within the EU, but also as a consequence of the high political support within devolution.

Underlying the developments of the past 25 years or so has been a political agenda to open up the EU regions (space economy) as a viable and efficient location within the international market for mobile investment. As part of a much broader agenda of regulatory reform, the planning systems of some EU countries have undergone immense structural and policy changes over the past two decades and successive governments have reoriented the system to ease the externality costs facing businesses and investors. This has affected planning within Central and Eastern European states in particular, but it has also started to occur within older Member States, eager to modernize their planning systems to address twenty-first century problems while also taking into account new planning regimes in the East that may, potentially, create better conditions and provide a competitive advantage for investment and growth. This process may not solely relate to further deregulation of planning regimes, but rather may concern the redesigning of internal administrative borders to reflect spaces of flows, and reconfigure responsibilities between tiers of governance to embed EU funding and inward investment more smoothly within spatial governance arrangements (cf. Dąbrowski, Chapter 9, on Poland, and Marot, Chapter 8, on Slovenia).

These political agendas and regulatory reforms have been evident in the UK, but have also been apparent in planning within other EU Member States – where competing models of social welfare and national economic management have persisted (Rhodes and van Appledoorn 1998). These reforms affect planning systems but, more pertinently, they may also affect planning cultures (Nadin and Stead 2008). To an extent, these have touched upon planning systems that are very different in organization and practice to the UK system (Newman and Thornley 1996). On the surface, it may seem that the centralized and essentially regulatory nature of mainland European planning systems may well be ill-suited to the attraction of FDI (cf. Healey and Williams 1993). It seems clear that even the comparatively flexible British planning system has, in some instances, hindered development (Evans 2003, Healey and Williams 1993). This gives rise to the notion that the varying form of planning systems across Europe and their ability to become more flexible to meet inward investment objectives either supports or inhibits different European regions to attract greater or lesser FDI. And yet the relationship of planning to broader regional economic development issues remains under-assessed.

A UK Government report (ODPM 2003), for instance, highlighted just how contentious and yet unresolved this issue has been. For instance, problems associated with passive land ownership and land valuation overshadowed planning as a constraint on land supply and, by implication, economic development – including that through FDI (Adams, D. *et al.* 1994, Adams, D. *et al.* 2002). Moreover, although planning systems may, in principle, embody important 'non-tariff barriers' (Healey and Williams 1993) to FDI, there is evidence to suggest that, in practice, planning has been an important part of rules-based competition for, or the incentive of, FDI (Tewdwr-Jones and Phelps 2000).

It should not be a surprise that different views of planning and spatial strategy-making as a constraint coexist within particular national contexts. In fact, a key feature in respect of the above is the geographically unbalanced nature of economic growth, land and property markets and hence the policy latitude open to planning system responses within national territories and across Europe (MacLennan 1995). With the heightened competition for FDI across Europe recently and probably in the future, there are signs of renewed inter-authority cooperation and strategic planning at the city-region scale (Tewdwr-Jones and McNeill 2000, Harrison 2007) and, as Brenner (2003) notes, "metropolitan governance is today being mobilized as a mechanism of economic development policy [...] to enhance place-specific socio-economic assets" and unblocking growth constraints, as in the case of the Cambridge high technology cluster (While *et al.* 2004). Critically, centrally conceived 'one size fits all' national planning policies are unlikely to match the needs of a Europe of the regions in which divergence in economic performance remains the order of the day. With the accession of Central and Eastern European countries, the tensions between the planning and FDI needs of overheated 'core' capital city regions and lagging 'peripheral' regions is likely to be greater still. Ironically, the push by national governments to encourage FDI within these regions has occurred simultaneously to the rolling out of regional devolution, thereby reinforcing aspects of the central state (Phelps and Tewdwr-Jones 2001).

Spatial planning implications for foreign direct investment

Clearly as part of the continued trend across Europe towards a Europe of the regions (Keating 1999), with greater decentralization and regional autonomy (Batchler and Turok 1997), development agencies and government bodies adopt proactive development strategies to ensure economic growth of particular regions. This economic growth strategy, founded on competition between cities and regions, is not necessarily led by or constrained within spatial planning frameworks, but is rather led by economic development personnel and political actors; their active bidding for FDI places regions on the global map as possible locations for multinational companies' mobile investment. Given the scale and employment size of these developments, politicians and economic developers are more than aware of the possible positive impacts on existing firms in their locality, and of the economic benefit to their regions more prominently.

During the 1980s and 1990s, certain countries within Western Europe were particularly successful at winning these developments (Cooke and Morgan 1998), but over the last decade strategic development projects have been more spatially concentrated in Central and Eastern Europe (Carstensen and Toubal 2004). This spatial unevenness is resulting in the promotion of competitive strategies by western regions of Europe as they attempt to out-compete the new accession countries of the EU where economic and labour conditions are more favourable (Bevan and Estrin 2004).

Examination of examples of FDI (such as BMW's development in Leipzig, Germany, LG in Newport, UK, and Volkswagen/Ford in Setubal, Portugal) indicates that each of the multinationals have been reliant on large-scale financial incentives offered by national and regional governments to support the investments in particular locations (Lung 2004, Phelps and Tewdwr-Jones 1998, Moniz 1994). The European Commission's competition laws have been checked, but the EU has given approval for the incentives packages offered in each case. The finance utilized has not been EU money, but rather that of individual Member States. In all cases, the planning process has played a less than significant role in the investment process. The attraction of companies to particular regions is not related to traditional economic matters alone. As Moniz (1994: 11) highlights:

> The question where to locate production sites does not lie on labour costs or technical competencies. The so-called comparative advantages can show up from the type of available infrastructures, on the location, social environment or even on the political and fiscal.

All regional authorities have utilized strategies to promote the region, galvanize institutional support among a range of relevant actors, and to develop a team approach. But these strategies have not been spatial by nature. If planning has played a part, it has been to remove the impediments to development, given that the investment deal had been won in each case prior to securing planning approval.

This is the reality of the market: the continued move towards regionalization across Europe is creating enhanced regional competitiveness between and sometimes within regions. Economics, politics and the power of multinational firms are setting the framework for major inward investment developments that have strategic significance. National and regional finance is assisting the development decisions. The key question therefore is what role can planning really play in achieving more 'balanced competitiveness' and in providing spatial certainty and cohesion across and between territories.

Implications for and future of European spatial policy

Drawing down the benefits to territories

A degree of convergence in European planning systems has already been detected some time ago (Healey and Williams 1993). However, even if there are reasonably commonly felt pressures of inter-locality competition and regulatory arbitrage by foreign direct investors, there nevertheless remain important differences in the structure, consistency, administration and nature of national and sub-national planning systems alongside differences in the dynamics of land and property markets within Europe. These differences have periodically been documented and their implications for the likes of housing markets explored. There appears to be a dearth of systematic studies of variations in European planning systems and their impacts on economic performance, a large part of which rests on the contribution of FDI to national and local economies. Environmental appraisals and sustainable development obligations across the EU have increasingly provided a benchmark against which to evaluate individual projects, but do not capture subtle differences comparatively across the territory in land, infrastructure and regulatory permeability.

What is required is a study to uncover the mechanisms through which there is or is not a degree of convergence in planning for FDI in the EU and in the role of Member States in creating conditions to enhance regional economic growth. This 'internationalization of the state' occurs in less overt, more concrete, terms through ad hoc and Commission-sponsored transnational cooperation through which there is the prospect of knowledge transfer and the transformation of institutions and their norms. The picture is complicated further still by the proliferation of quasi-governmental bodies such as investment promotion agencies (IPAs), EU initiatives, entrepreneurial cities, and competitive regions across Europe that frequently benchmark the rapid transmission of what may be termed 'best practice'. Multinational enterprises (MNEs) themselves exert pressures on local and central governments, not least in the expediting of planning processes, by virtue of their experiences of operating in many nations globally. Intermediaries such as location consultants also play a role in transmitting particular norms and practices regarding the successful attraction of MNEs – including presumably those relating to planning – among potential host countries. The reinvention and reinvigoration of spatial planning rests significantly on the acquisition of new attitudes, and of skills of persuasion on the part of professional staff (Harris 2001, Healey 2001) and indeed elected local politicians as has been seen in an improved UK planning system. Finally, the planning profession itself is unevenly developed across Europe with different disciplinary orientations and credentials (cf. Healey and Williams 1993 and also Maier, Chapter 11), which is likely to exert an effect upon practices in 'territorial cohesion' and planning for FDI. In the UK, for example, economists' lack of influence on planning has been evident (Evans 2003, Barker 2007). The influence of economists may be greater given the sectoral planning legacy of Central and East European countries while architects (rather than land use planners) exert a more widespread influence on mainland Europe (Healey and Williams 1993, Nadin and Stead 2008).

These considerations indicate that:

> Competition for investment is not just any kind of competition. Unlike competition in goods markets, there can be no presumption that competition for

investment is efficiency enhancing [...] it clearly has the potential to result in races to the bottom in terms of wages, social protections, environmental standards, and tax base degradation [...] Conscious intervention is necessary to prevent these negative outcomes.

(Thomas 2000: 271)

Therefore, liberalization in advanced nations has not been associated simply or directly with deregulation per se, but also with creative processes of re-regulation (Vogel 1996). The challenge remains, as Healey has noted, to remake planning and effective national and local institutional capacities – including those pertaining to planning – capable of the 'drawing down of benefits from companies into the social and economic life of a place in environmentally sensitive way' (Healey 1997: 202). This might involve a broader vision of 'balanced competitiveness' as contained in the ESDP (CEC 1999). Here, an emphasis upon polycentric development might inform a shift toward viewing FDI and planning as ingredients in the *production* of economic growth in regions away from concerns to redistribute to, or compensate such regions (Amin *et al.* 2003). This, in turn, is likely to rest on the regionally differentiated practice of planning as a regulatory and facilitative activity.

The paradox of 'balanced competitiveness'

In terms of the form of European spatial planning as well as the principles of the ESDP and 'territorial cohesion' in the future, regions and national states may already recognize the benefit of and commitment towards European spatial development. As the European Community increases in size, with enhanced markets, greater territorial competition and economic unevenness, it is right that issues such as 'sustainable development', 'balanced competitiveness' and 'territorial cohesion' are assessed in a meaningful way across the continent. The interests in these issues are checked by an economic and political expediency for the regional advantage that is becoming more apparent in different parts of Europe, in order to address growing regional economic disparities and to market territories as major players in the global arena. But this behaviour may run counter to the accepted principles of European spatial planning as governments, government agencies and non-governmental agencies become more entrepreneurial and competitive.

Wooing major multinational companies, identifying land, the availability of cheap labour, the offer of incentives, and the hard sell between particular companies and individual city-regions are the factors that carve out customized spaces for businesses. Finance plays a significant part in this wooing process: older industrial regions, recipients of EU structural funds, form a dependency culture on the Commission for their economic development; 'successful' EU regions (in terms of their economic profile and growth) rely on national and regional governments' finance to create their advantage, bound up with strong institutional capacity and presence. The link between spatial planning policy and financial incentives must be addressed more prominently in the future if spatial development strategies are going to make a difference and contribute towards the goal of 'territorial cohesion' and 'balanced competitiveness'. But this also means the planning culture has to change, and the knowledge of the economic processes accumulated in the planning policy-making system has to be garnered and optimized to ensure the effectiveness and efficiency of future spatial policies.

Conclusions

Attempting to develop European spatial planning further is a goal worth pursuing. And attempts by the European Commission in the wake of the ESDP to make enhanced links between spatial development policy, land use decisions and finance should be welcomed by making qualifications about the allocation and spending of EU structural and cohesion funds. These attempts have assisted in promoting greater spatial awareness within and across a range of territorial scales, and in reinforcing the role of planning in development decisions. But the spatial planning practice relationship between a reliance on the knowledge of existing spatial situations and regional economic development, and an economic logic of profit maximization remains out-of-sync and unrelated at present. National and regional development actors have preferred to negotiate with multinational companies directly and impose minimum externalities on firms as part of an incentives package to attract industries to particular territories. Such incentives, resting on finance and the creation of customized spaces, rely on bargaining, negotiation and flexible institutional structures and strategies, and do not build upon accumulated spatial knowledge.

Previous instances of FDI suggest that firms are highly mobile and require fast decisions on potential locations, and regional authorities are either successful or unsuccessful in attempting to embed companies into particular territories. Faced with market concentration, lucrative financial incentives, the availability of land and cheap labour, and political and economic actors who are enthusiastic to attract companies partly on the latter's terms, planning becomes an externality in itself rather than a promotional tool. But there are differences between regions in the form of inward investment attraction and the degree to which companies are encouraged to embed to support the region's economy more broadly. In some cases, there has been a noticeable absence of planning in the attraction process, making attempts by governments to extract gain from companies problematic. This could be one step in the right direction in the future, where planning – having arranged incentives to attract a firm to locate to a region initially – then utilizes the gain extracted from the development as a basis for further development on the site and as a way of embedding the company within the territory. There are challenges in achieving a more embedded form of economically-aware spatial governance, particularly in linking up the skills of planning practitioners with other 'communities of practice'. But overall such an approach could be thought of as a robust form of strategic spatial development and 'territorial cohesion'.

It is possible to identify European spatial planning, and national and regional spatial planning strategies as playing a proactive role in territories to identify spatial locations and create the broad conditions for territorial development. Specific attention could be devoted to the relationship between finance, financial incentives and land. It may also perform a role in developing institutional capacity, team-building and collaboration between a range of relevant actors to ensure the delivery of development and the removal of potential barriers at the appropriate stage once a multinational company has expressed interest. Spatial planning may also assume a reactive role after a company has been approached by regional actors or when regional actors have already secured a firm's interest. Thus the role of spatial planning would not be in the regulation of development but rather in the attempt to territorially embed companies by integrating disparate development opportunities into a more cohesive whole, directly related and linked to the inward investment industry and site. The ability of the market and the dominance of multinational companies to select strategic sites for investment, however, will continue in the years ahead as the EU pulls out of recession; as the EU territory expands, so too will the competition between city-regions in the attraction and wooing of companies to customized sites. Nevertheless, if European 'territorial cohesion' is going to play any sort of role in planning for territorial development, it must be recognized for its limits and opportunities in the regional economic development process – a process that will always remain highly political.

Acknowledgement

The author is grateful to Nick Phelps, Joao Morais Mourato, Claire Colomb and the editors of this book for comments and suggestions on previous versions of this chapter.

References

Adams, D., Disbury, A., Hutchison, N. and Munjoma, T. (2002) 'Vacant urban land: exploring ownership strategies and actions', *Town Planning Review*, 73: 395–418.

Adams, D., Russell, L. and Taylor-Russell, C. (1994) *Land for Industrial Development*, London: Spon Press.

Adams, N., Cotella, G. and Nunes, R. (2010) 'Spatial planning in Europe: the interplay between knowledge and policy in an enlarged EU', in N. Adams, G. Cotella and R. Nunes (eds) *Territorial Development, Cohesion and Spatial Planning: Knowledge and policy development in an enlarged EU*, London: Routledge.

Adams, N., Cotella, G. and Nunes, R. (2010) 'Territorial knowledge channels in a multi-jurisdictional policy environment. A theoretical framework', in N. Adams, G. Cotella and R. Nunes (eds) *Territorial Development, Cohesion and Spatial Planning: Knowledge and policy development in an enlarged EU*, London: Routledge.

Amin, A., Massey, D. and Thrift, N. (2003) 'Decentring the nation: A radical approach to regional inequality', *Catalyst Paper 8*, London: Catalyst.

Armstrong, H. W. (2001) 'Regional selective assistance: Is the spend enough and is it targeting the right places?', *Regional Studies*, 35(3): 247–257.

Batchler, J. and Turok, I. (eds) (1997) *The Coherence of EU Policy*, London: Jessica Kingsley Publishing.

Barker, K. (2007) *Barker Review of Land Use Planning*, London: HM Treasury.

Berry, J. and McGreal, S. (1995) 'European cities: The interaction of planning systems, property markets and real estate investment', in J. Berry and S. McGreal (eds) *European Cities, Planning Systems and Property Markets*, London: Spon Press: 1–16.

Bevan, A. and Estrin, S. (2004) 'The determinants of foreign direct investment into European transition economies', *Journal of Comparative Economics*, 32(4): 775–787.

Brenner, N. (2003) 'Metropolitan institutional reform and the rescaling of state space in contemporary western Europe', *European Urban and Regional Studies*, 10: 297–324.

Capik, P. (2010) 'Regional promotion and competition: An examination of approaches to FDI attraction in the Czech Republic, Poland and Slovakia', in N. Adams, G. Cotella and R. Nunes (eds) *Territorial Development, Cohesion and Spatial Planning: Knowledge and policy development in an enlarged EU*, London: Routledge.

Carstensen, K. and Toubal, F. (2004) 'Foreign direct investment in Central and Eastern European countries: A dynamic panel analysis', *Journal of Comparative Economics*, 32(1): 3–22.

CEC – Commission of the European Communities (1999) *European Spatial Development Perspective: Towards Balanced and Sustainable Development of the Territory of the EU*, Luxembourg: Office of the Official Publications of the European Communities.

—— (2003) *Structural Policies and European Territories: Competitiveness, Sustainable Development and Cohesion in Europe – From Lisbon to Gothenburg*, Luxembourg: Office for Official Publications of the European Communities.

—— (2004) *A New Partnership for Cohesion: Convergence, Competitiveness, Cooperation – Third Report on Economic and Social Cohesion*, Luxembourg: Office for Official Publications of the European Communities.

—— (2008) *Green Paper on Territorial Cohesion: Turning territorial diversity into strength*, Brussels: Commission of the European Communities.

Cooke, P. N. and Morgan, K. (1998) *The Associational Economy*, Oxford: Oxford University Press.

Dąbrowski, M. (2010) 'Institutional change, partnership and regional networks: Civic engagement and the implementation of the structural funds in Poland', in N. Adams, G. Cotella and R. Nunes (eds) *Territorial Development, Cohesion and Spatial Planning: Knowledge and policy development in an enlarged EU*, London: Routledge.

Davoudi, S. (2003) 'Polycentricity in European spatial planning: From an analytical tool to a normative agenda', *European Planning Studies*, 11(8): 979–999.

Doucet, P. (2006) 'Territorial cohesion of tomorrow: A path to co-operation or competition?', *European Planning Studies*, 14(10): 1473–1485.

Dühr, S. (2007) *The Visual Language of Spatial Planning: Exploring cartographic representations for spatial planning in Europe*, London: Routledge.

Ezcurra, R., Pascual, P. and Rapún, M. (2007) 'Regional disparities in the EU: An analysis of regional polarization', *The Annals of Regional Science*, 41(2): 401–429.

Evans, A. E. (2003) 'Shouting very loudly: Economists, planning and politics', *Town Planning Review*, 74: 195–212.

Evers, D. (2008) 'Reflections on Territorial Cohesion and European Spatial Planning', *Tijdschrift voor Economische en sociale geografie*, 99(3): 303–315.

Faludi, A. (2004) 'The open method of co-ordination and "post-regulatory" territorial cohesion policy', *European Planning Studies*, 12(7): 1019–1034.

—— (2005) 'Territorial cohesion: An unidentified political objective', *Town Planning Review*, 76(1): 1–13.

—— (2006) 'From European spatial development to territorial cohesion policy', *Regional Studies*, 40(6): 667–678.

—— (ed.) (2007) *Territorial Cohesion and the European Model of Society*, Cambridge MA: Lincoln Institute of Land Policy.

—— (2009) 'A turning point in the development of European Spatial Planning? The Territorial Agenda of the EU and the first action programme', *Progress in Planning*, 71(1): 1–42.

Faludi, A. and Waterhout, B. (2002) *The Making of the European Spatial Development Perspective: No masterplan*, London: Routledge.

Getimis, P. (2003) 'Improving European union regional policy by learning from the past in view of enlargement', *European Planning Studies*, 11(1): 77–87.

Hall, P. A. and Soskice, D. (2001) *Varieties of Capitalism: The institutional advantages of comparative advantage*, Oxford: Oxford University Press.

Harris, N. (2001) 'Spatial development policies and territorial governance in an era of globalisation and localisation', in OECD (ed.) *Towards a New Role for Spatial Planning*, Paris: OECD: 33–58.

Harrison, J. (2007) 'From competitive regions to competitive city-regions: A new orthodoxy, but some old mistakes', *Journal of Economic Geography*, 7(3): 311–332.

Healey, P. (1997) *Collaborative Planning: Shaping Places in Fragmented Societies*, Basingstoke: Palgrave MacMillan.

—— (2001) 'New approaches to the content and process of spatial development frameworks', in OECD (ed.) *Towards a New Role for Spatial Planning*, Paris: OECD: 143–163.

Healey, P. and Williams, R. (1993) 'European urban planning systems: Diversity and convergence', *Urban Studies*, 30: 701–720.

Jensen, O. B. and Richardson, T. (2004) *Making European Space: Mobility, power and territorial identity*, London: Routledge.

Jessop, B. (1999) 'Reflections on globalization and its (il)logics', in P. Dicken, K. Olds, P. Kelly and H. Yeung (eds) *Globalisation and the Asia-Pacific*, London: Routledge.

Keating, M. (1999) *The New Regionalism in Western Europe*, Cheltenham: Edward Elgar.

Lawton-Smith, H., Tracey, P. and Clark, G. L. (2003) 'European policy and the regions: A review and analysis of tensions', *European Planning Studies*, 11(7): 859–873.

Lung, Y. (2004) 'The changing geography of the European automobile system', *International Journal of Automotive Technology and Management*, 4(2/3): 137–165.

MacLennan, D. (1995) 'Property, planning and European progress', in J. Berry and S. McGreal (eds) *European Cities, Planning Systems and Property Markets*, London: Spon Press: 395–408.

Maier, K. (2010) 'The pursuit of balanced territorial development: The realities and complexities of the cohesion agenda', in N. Adams, G. Cotella and R. Nunes (eds) *Territorial Development, Cohesion and Spatial Planning: Knowledge and policy development in an enlarged EU*, London: Routledge.

Marot, N. (2010) 'New Planning Jurisdictions, Scant Resources and Local Public Responsibility: Delivering Spatial Planning in Slovenia', in N. Adams, G. Cotella and R. Nunes (eds) *Territorial Development, Cohesion and Spatial Planning: Knowledge and policy development in an enlarged EU*, London: Routledge.

Meijers, E. J., Waterhout, B. and Zonneveld, W. A. M. (2007) 'Closing the GAP: Territorial cohesion through polycentric development', *European Journal of Spatial Development*, 24: 1–25.

Molle, W. (2002) 'Globalization, regionalism and labour markets: Should we recast the foundations of the EU regime in matters of regional (rural and urban) development?', *Regional Studies*, 36: 161–172.

Moniz, A. (1994) 'The automobile sector and the organisation of the industrial space: the case of Setubal Region (Portugal)', Munich Personal RePEc Archive, Paper No. 7503, posted on 6 March 2008. Online. Available HTTP: http://mpra.ub.uni-muenchen. de/7503 (accessed July 2009).

Morgan, K. and Nauwelaers, C. (eds) (1999) *Regional Innovation Strategies: The challenge for less-favoured regions*, London: Routledge.

Nadin, V. and Stead, D. (2008) 'European planning systems, social models and learning', *disP*, 172, 1/2008: 35–47.

Newman, P. and Thornley, A. (1996) *Urban Planning in Europe*, London: Routledge.

ODPM (2003) *Planning, Competitiveness and Productivity. Select Committee on Office of the Deputy Prime Minister: Housing, Planning, Local Government and the Regions. Fourth Report*. London: Stationery Office. HC 114-I.

Phelps, N. A. and Raines, P. (eds) (2003) *The New Competition for Inward Investment: Firms, institutions and territorial development*, Cheltenham: Edward Elgar.

Phelps, N. A. and Tewdwr-Jones, M. (1998) 'Institutional capacity building in a strategic policy vacuum: The case of the Korean firm LG in South Wales', *Environment & Planning C, Government & Policy*, 16 (6): 735–755.

—— (2001) 'Globalisation, regions and the state: Exploring the limits of economic modernisation through inward investment', *Urban Studies*, 38(8): 1253–1272.

Rhodes, M. and van Appledoorn, B. (1998) 'Capital unbound? The transformation of European corporate governance', *Journal of European Public Policy*, 5: 406–427.

Rodriguez-Pose, A. and Fratesi, U. (2004) 'Between Development and Social Policies: The impact of European Structural Funds in Objective 1 Regions', *Regional Studies*, 38(1): 97–113.

Swyngedouw, E. and Baeten, G. (2001) 'Scaling the City: The political economy of 'glocal' development – Brussels' conundrum', *European Planning Studies*, 9(7): 827–849.

Tewdwr-Jones, M. and McNeill, D. (2000) 'The politics of city-region planning and governance: Reconciling the national, regional and urban in the competing voices of institutional restructuring', *European Urban and Regional Studies*, 7(2): 119–134.

Tewdwr-Jones, M. and Phelps, N. A. (2000) 'Levelling the uneven playing field: Inward investment, inter-regional rivalry and the planning system', *Regional Studies*, 34(5): 429–440.

Thomas, K. P. (2000) *Competing for Capital: Europe and North America in a global era*, Washington DC: University of Georgetown Press.

Vogel, S. (1996) *Freer Markets, More Rules: Regulatory reform in advanced industrial countries*, Ithaca: Cornell University Press.

Waterhout, B. (2008) *The Institutionalization of European Spatial Planning*, Delft: IOS.

While, A., Jonas, A. and Gibbs, D. (2004) 'Unblocking the city? Growth pressures, collective provision and the search for new spaces of governance in Greater Cambridge, England', *Environment & Planning A*, 36: 279–304.

Yeung, H. W. C. (1998) 'Capital, state and space: contesting the borderless world', *Transactions of the Institute of British Geographers*, 23: 291–309.

4 European spatial planning

Current state and future challenges

Bas Waterhout

Introduction

About a decade ago the institutional capacity that the European Spatial Development Perspective (ESDP. CEC 1999) had created was 'in danger of evaporating' (Faludi and Waterhout 2002: 177). This was also the conviction of the author of the ESDP, the Committee of Spatial Development (CSD), which consisted of representatives of the then 15 Member States plus the European Commission. During a CSD seminar in 1998 serious questions were raised, such as: Who really needs European spatial planning? What can European spatial planning achieve and with what instruments? What are the necessary arrangements for European spatial planning? And also, 'we have been very focused on the ESDP text; we missed the wider picture!' and 'we must become more professional!' (Faludi and Waterhout 2002: 169). Clearly, serious doubts existed.

This chapter picks up on these doubts and sheds light on how the situation has been changed and what this means in terms of planning becoming part of EU mainstream policy or, in other words, becoming institutionalized. The institutionalization of European spatial planning is a complex, multi-facetted, multi-actor and multi-layered process. It requires existing (mainstream) institutions to change in the way that they take on board planning perspectives and solutions. Although, by nature, institutions are in a process of continuous change, there are no proven recipes to change or design institutions into a desired direction. European spatial planning therefore faces a tough challenge, as was aptly recognized by the CSD members. Leaning on the general theoretical framework of this book, this chapter analyses the institutionalization of European spatial planning a decade after the ESDP. A major question is whether the 'epistemic community', which the CSD formed, has been able to spread its wings and influence important EU policy spheres and, in terms of this book, 'knowledge arenas'.

The focus in this chapter is on the post-ESDP period, from 1999 until summer 2009, in which the European spatial planning organizational framework has been extended with some important new pillars. ESPON was set up in 2002. In 2007 the ministers adopted the Territorial Agenda of the European Union (DE Presidency 2007a) and in 2008 the European Commission tabled the Green paper on Territorial Cohesion (CEC 2008). Combined with the already existing

INTERREG IIIB/IVB programme (now coming under the name European Territorial Cooperation – ETC), European spatial planning is currently organized around four pillars: ESPON, ETC, the Territorial Agenda and the Green Paper on Territorial Cohesion. All of these pillars bear elements of the ESDP, illustrating that the institutional capacity apparently had not evaporated. Yet, despite all these impressive initiatives, the impression remains that planning is still a game in the margin of EU policy-making. So, what then, is the meaning of European spatial planning in a wider policy context, how has it evolved and what are the main challenges ahead?

This chapter explores these questions in two parts. The first part elaborates on the evolution and the four pillars of European spatial planning. After having displayed the organizational set-up and the evolution of central ideas and concepts, the second part discusses the meaning of the framework for the wider EU policy context. In fact, it appears that planning finds itself back in the midst of a discourse coalition urging, against the backdrop of the 2013 regional policy reform, that territory matters! The chapter rounds off with some concluding remarks.

The pillars of European spatial planning

As indicated, European spatial planning is organized around a number of interrelated programmes and initiatives. In May 1999, when the ESDP was published, these were: the INTERREG IIC programme, the Tampere ESDP Action Programme (TEAP) (as from September 1999) and the Study Programme on European Spatial Planning (SPESP). Currently, a decade later, these pillars have evolved in various ways, but in general they do still exist. Now they come under the labels of European Territorial Co-operation, ESPON, the Territorial Agenda of the EU and last but not least Territorial Cohesion. Together they can be regarded as the four interrelated pillars of what still could be termed (in legacy of the ESDP) the European spatial planning organizational framework.

ETC – implementing European spatial planning messages

The first pillar, European Territorial Cooperation (ETC) includes the earlier INTERREG IIC and IIIB programmes and is often referred to as INTERREG IVB. The former INTERREG IIC programme ran from 1997 until 1999 and promoted transnational cooperation in the field of spatial planning. European planners considered it a true test ground for applying ESDP messages. The programme was a so-called Community Initiative, which means that it was completely financed and controlled by the European Commission – in this case represented by the Directorate General Regio, in short DG Regio. In the EU programming period 2000–2006, it was followed up by INTERREG IIIB, which had more or less the same objectives and way of working. In the current programming period 2007–2013 it has become a mainstream initiative, as a part of the European Territorial Cooperation objective. Apart from the transnational cooperation strand, which often is referred to as INTERREG IVB, the ETC objective also promotes cross-border cooperation and interregional cooperation, the former INTERREG IIIA and IIIC programmes respectively. Of the total budget of €8,6 billion, €1,8 billion is reserved for transnational cooperation, which is being subdivided in 13 transnational cooperation areas.

The ETC programmes have a firm bottom-up character: regions, or stakeholders within regions, submit proposals that are accepted on the basis of a set of criteria. Each of the 13 cooperation areas hosts a couple of hundred projects, with each project consisting of at least three but often more partners from different countries (i.e. regions and communities). The total network involved in the transnational cooperation strand of ETC consists of several thousand partners distributed throughout Europe (following Ahlke *et al.* 2007; some 6500 partners were involved in INTERREG IIIB). This is a significant increase compared to INTERREG IIC.

In terms of creating 'knowledge arenas', it should be emphasized that each transnational cooperation project functions on its own and forms a learning environment for the stakeholders involved (Colomb 2007). However, there is little mutual contact between the projects, and between the ETC objective and other pillars of European spatial planning. Knowledge gathered at the local level, by applying concepts developed at the EU level, barely finds its way back to the offices of Territorial Agenda or Green paper policy-makers (Waterhout and Stead 2007). A considerable amount of knowledge is collected at the 13 programme secretariats, but their main task is to allocate budgets and monitor projects. Small projects are carried out that relate projects dealing with similar topics to each other as well as to ESPON through a programme called INTERACT. Mostly this results in a report, not in further cooperation. Continuation is a moot point because of the financing structure. Once a project is finished, usually after three years, little remains of what once was a learning environment.

Over time the focus of the programme has changed. Whereas the INTERREG IIC programme heavily focused on spatial planning issues, and was strongly influenced by the ESDP, the attention in current programmes has shifted toward growth and jobs in line with the broad discourse underlying EU Cohesion Policy (CEC 2005). With this concentration on growth and jobs the programme's focus has shifted toward an emphasis on tangible outcomes that, preferably, are more visible to the people on the street. In terms of institutionalization, the ETC objective has become an end-of-line application framework, in which project learning experiences remain limited to the project participants and barely feed into the overall EU spatial planning debate.

ESPON – delivering the evidence

ESPON was originally named the European Spatial Planning Observation Network, but since the current programming period is termed (whilst retaining its acronym) European Observation Network for Territorial Development and Cohesion. It was preceded by the Study Programme on European Spatial Planning, which functioned as a pilot programme from 1997 to 2000. ESPON came into operation in 2002 and has continued during the current 2007–2013 budget period of the EU. ESPON aims at a systemized analysis of spatial development trends, territorial structures and territorial impact of policies across the territory of the EU. It can be considered one of the major achievements of the ESDP planners, who, already back in the early 1990s, asked for detailed and comparable data and knowledge regarding the EU territory (Faludi and Waterhout 2002). The new name, however, reflects the shifting policy discourse from planning towards territorial cohesion and development (see below). The programme is financed by both the Commission (50 per cent) by means of the structural funds, under the interregional cooperation strand of ETC objective in particular, and the Member States (50 per cent), including four non-Member States: Norway, Switzerland, Liechtenstein and Iceland.

Just as ETC, ESPON is organized as a network with a small coordination unit located in Luxembourg, a Monitoring Committee composed of Member State and DG Regio officials and several transnational project groups. The monitoring committee decides on the type of projects to be carried out, agrees on the terms of reference for these projects and evaluates the tendering documents by transnational project groups. Transnational project groups are composed of researchers from institutes all over Europe. Under ESPON 2006 some 30 research projects have been carried out. A similar amount will be carried out under the ESPON 2013 programme. The total budget has increased to around €60 million, which is approximately twice as much as the 2006 programme, but still modest when compared to the over €1 billion budget of the Commission's central statistical office: Eurostat.

ESPONs primary objective is to generate knowledge. As a 'knowledge arena', however, it suffers from a similar continuation problem as ETC. Two ESPON seminars per year, where each project presents its intermediate findings, provide for the exchange of knowledge between projects. Generally, these seminars are characterized by a good atmosphere in which participants (project partners, policy-makers, monitoring committee members) get to know each other quite well, addressing one of the objectives of ESPON: to build a scientific community in the field of territorial development. Peter Mehlbye, director of the ESPON coordination unit, in this sense sometimes refers to the 'ESPON family' (for an overview of participants in ESPON, see ESPON 2006). However, this family, apart from some core members, is held together thanks to project budgets that generally extend for two years. Thus, because of the tendering system, the family changes continuously and well-known members may leave, and be missed.

Nevertheless, the ESPON programme as such has acquired a central position in the European spatial planning framework. It feeds both the Member States working on the territorial agenda and the Commission working on territorial cohesion and on a new regional policy in general. In so doing, it operationalizes the planning principle that European spatial planning policy should be evidence-based (cf. Adams *et al.* in Chapter 1). This should provide the ministers responsible for spatial development with a stronger position vis-à-vis their colleagues and the European Commission. The evidence-based principle is interpreted differently by researchers and policy-makers and sometimes leads to tensions between them (Gløersen *et al.* 2007; Bengs 2006; Prezioso 2007). In order to deliver 'hard' evidence the ESPON programme is dominated by quantitative research models, even in cases where this approach is not very relevant (Hague and Hachmann 2008).

The Territorial Agenda of the EU: the intergovernmental track

The Territorial Agenda can be regarded as the continuation, albeit in a somewhat bumpy way, of the intergovernmental ESDP track. Also, as we will see, the track gradually loses its exclusive intergovernmental character as most follow-up events and decisions are made jointly with the Commission. Nevertheless, the Territorial Agenda process itself has been run primarily by the Member States. The upcoming EU enlargement and the European Commission, getting the single 'right of initiative' to propose territorial cohesion policy once the EU Constitution (now Lisbon Treaty) is ratified, urged the Member States in 2003 to come together and made them agree on a forward defence strategy: the Territorial Agenda of the EU.

The making of the Territorial Agenda was reminiscent of the ESDP process, with informal ministerial gatherings prepared by DG-meetings (replacing the CSD), working meetings and an editorial group formed of representatives of the Coming Presidencies Group and complemented with some consultant-prepared drafts. The role of the Commission, DG Regio, was different; it was less centrally involved, albeit always present. Subsequent EU Presidencies (Netherlands, Luxembourg, UK, Finland and Germany) contributed in one way or the other to the Territorial Agenda (see Faludi 2009a for a detailed overview). A difference with the ESDP was that, in the spirit of the evidence-based policy principle, two documents were prepared at the same time: the Territorial Agenda and the Territorial State and Perspectives, with the latter providing the analytical background (mainly on the basis of ESPON results) for the former. The Territorial Agenda for the EU (DE Presidency 2007a) was accepted by the EU ministers responsible for spatial development and planning on the 25 May 2007 in Leipzig. The Territorial State and Perspectives (DE Presidency 2007b), not being tabled in Leipzig, has remained an unofficial background document. As a political document, the Territorial Agenda does not replace the ESDP, but complements it according to the document itself.

Its complementary status is reflected by its contents, which can be characterized merely as an evolution of the ESDP. The two enlargements did not influence spatial planning's main message. There is still a European 'core area' (referred to as 'pentagon' by the ESDP) in the EU-27 where 46.5 per cent of the GDP is produced by one third of the population on just 14 per cent of the territory, which needs to be balanced by polycentric development elsewhere (DE Presidency 2007b). Due to new insights delivered by ESPON, the 'core area' concept, however, is losing some of its political and explanatory power. For example, the third ESPON synthesis report speaks of an 'enlarged pentagon' with Manchester, Paris, Genoa, Venice and Berlin as its cornerstones (ESPON 2006). Furthermore, 'in terms of economic performance and in particular with relation to the Lisbon aims [...] the Northern parts of Europe are on an equal footing with the core and even outperform the core on some indicators' (DE Presidency 2007b: 13). Also the relative wealth is highlighted of regions such as Rome, Lisbon, Madrid, Athens as well as Budapest, Bratislava and Prague in the new Member States, whilst the importance of medium-sized cities like Valencia, Gothenburg, Tallinn, Riga, Vilnius, Cork and Seville is also recognized (ESPON 2005). As regards conceptualizing the EU territory, a picture emerges of capital regions forming islands of economic growth. The Territorial Agenda itself, however, refrains from invoking EU-wide spatial conceptualizations. This is not surprising as EU-wide conceptualizations have always been politically highly sensitive. Another reason for why no EU-wide conceptualizations emerge is simply that, as is indicated above, the data on the EU territory illustrate that there are no clear visible structures.

Compared to the ESDP the EU territory is now being approached in a more diversified way, taking more and different indicators on board. There is no standard recipe for success, 'the reasons for a prosperous region can be manifold' (DE Presidency 2007b: 19) and depend on a region's territorial capital. 'Territorial capital', originally introduced by the OECD's Territorial Outlook 2001 has been adopted as a new concept by the makers of the Territorial Agenda, although it is not mentioned explicitly in the document. Basically the concept refers to the endogenous potential of regions. Judging from two ESPON synthesis reports with such telling names as 'In search of territorial potential' and 'Territory matters for competitiveness and cohesion' (ESPON 2005; ESPON 2006), the theme has become central in ESPON research too. Disguised as 'regional potential' and 'territorial assets', the concept also prominently figures in the Green Paper.

The Territorial Agenda, with the Green Paper in its wake, also introduces new topics such as climate change, energy resources, uneven territorial opportunities, demographic change and the possible occurrence of natural hazards. Obviously, these topics are inspired by recent events and political debates. The underlying assumption is that once such a topic really takes off and planning can make a contribution, the political profile of planning will rise.

In terms of planning principles, the Territorial Agenda (and the Green Paper) no longer refer to the 'spatial approach', but uses a new umbrella term: 'territorial governance'. Rather than proposing an approach, 'territorial governance' is presented as a challenge. This challenge not only involves coping with the territorial impact of EU policies, for example through the potential future establishment of a territorial impact assessment instrument (something which ESPON is focusing on), but also aims to 'integrate the territorial dimension in EU and national policies' instead of 'creating a top-down and separate EU territorial cohesion policy' (DE Presidency 2007b: 9). 'Territorial governance' is based on four principles: '(a) integration, (b) no new procedures or rules but better use of existing possibilities, (c) subsidiarity, and (d) facilitating development and thus supporting efficiency in achieving cohesion' (DE Presidency 2007b: 9). Similar to the ESDP, the most important instruments of this governance method are dialogue and communication.

In institutional terms the concept of 'territorial governance', but also that of 'territorial capital', indicates a shift in thinking in which leadership is relocated to the local or regional level. Planners have become more aware of their institutional position and subsequently more realistic in terms of the strings they can pull. Whereas the ESDP boldly spoke of developing global economic integration zones to counterbalance the dominant pentagon area, the Territorial Agenda and Territorial State and Perspectives, with the Green Paper in their footsteps, focus on the development of existing regions and modestly speak of investigating possibilities for transnational clustering based on synergies and complementarities. Perhaps, now that the Strategy for the Baltic Sea Region (CEC 2009a) has been tabled, and plans are being prepared to develop a similar strategy for the Danube area, this may change again.

After the Territorial Agenda had been accepted, the First Action Programme (PT Presidency 2007), jointly written by the Commission and the Portuguese presidency, was approved at a ministerial gathering on territorial cohesion and regional policy in the Azores. The following Slovenian Presidency lifted it off the ground by means of installing a number of working groups where not only Member State and Commission representatives met, but also representatives from institutions and organizations such as Eurocities and the European Council of Spatial Planners (ECTP – the acronym referring to its former name: European Council of Town and Country Planners). Also the Slovenian Presidency was to include the Territorial Agenda in the Spring European Council, something it did not succeed in. Territorial cohesion was also discussed in the Conference on the Future of Cohesion Policy, in May 2008 in Maribor, but not with planners in the lead.

The French Presidency, in the second half 2008, carried on with the working groups that delivered their reports just before the Commission published its Green Paper. The working groups were visited by a host of institutions like the Organization for Economic Co-operation and Development (OECD), the Committee of the Regions, the European Parliament, the Association of European Border Regions, Council of Maritime and Peripheral Regions, ESPON, but also two directors-general from DG REGIO and DG EMP (Employment). In terms of this book, the working groups can be considered temporary 'knowledge arenas', but also ad hoc platforms that provided the key players with another opportunity to meet. Also the French organized a ministerial meeting in Marseille in November (Faludi 2009b).

As regards follow-up presidencies, it is worth mentioning that the Czech Presidency (first half 2009) organized a DG-meeting immediately after a conference on the 'Future of the Cohesion Policy and Territorial Cohesion'. It also called for an informal meeting of ministers responsible for Regional Policy and an ESPON seminar (over the years it has become standard practice that each presidency hosts an ESPON seminar). The Swedes (second half 2009) never intended to organize a ministerial meeting on territorial cohesion. Instead they organized back-to-back a High-Level Conference on Sustainable Cities and a Conference on Macro Regional Strategies with the EU Baltic Sea Strategy as a case study (cf. also Fritsch Chapter 15). The Baltic Sea Strategy deserves further comment later on in this chapter as this comes closest to what ESDP planners hoped to achieve, but never did, with INTERREG IIC. Sweden also organized an ESPON seminar as well as a conference under the theme 'Make Use of the Territorial Potential', which not without reason was organized in December in Kiruna, well above the Polar Circle. Currently, it is unclear what Spain (first half 2010) will do next year, whereas Belgium (second half 2010) will likely assist Hungary (first half 2011) in its evaluation of the Territorial Agenda. Whether true or not, rumours are that Poland (second half 2011) will try to organize a formal council on cohesion policy. This would be the first time ever because cohesion policy never had its own council; the topic (and related budget) is considered too important for a sectoral council. Until now the topic is dealt with by the Ministers of Foreign Affairs, forming 'the Council', and the European Council of heads of State and Government leaders.

The Green Paper on Territorial Cohesion: the Commission track

A fourth pillar concerns Territorial Cohesion as guiding principle. The concept of 'territorial cohesion' has been in the air since the Treaty of Amsterdam (1997), where it appeared in Article 16. At that time the ESDP planners hardly took notice, mainly because the concept was specifically related to the provision of general (economic) services of interest. This changed with the EU Constitution, now called the Lisbon Treaty, which mentions 'territorial cohesion' in Article 2 alongside with economic and social cohesion as one of the objectives of the EU. Former European Commissioner Michel Barnier, having a policy such as the French *l'aménagement du territoire* in mind, played an important role in the process of introducing the concept in the Treaty (Faludi 2009c).

It was expected that the European Commission would soon bring out a White Paper on Territorial Cohesion, of which draft versions of the Territorial Agenda had been requested (Faludi forthcoming). The no-votes to the Constitution in 2004, however, changed everything and it took the Commission time to come up with a new strategy to address the situation. In the meantime, the Lisbon Strategy had been revitalized into a Growth and Jobs agenda and, in the context of the Sapir report (Sapir *et al.* 2004) and the Financial Perspectives 2007–2013, Regional Policy (as well as Common Agricultural Policy) had come under severe threat. Net-contributors, the UK in the lead, required a thorough evaluation of the policy's rationale and effectiveness, the ultimate aim being the 'renationalization' of this policy. In defence, the Community Strategic Guidelines (CEC 2005) formed a first answer and pointed out how regional policy and, with reference to territorial cohesion, geography matter to the Growth and Jobs Agenda. Member States were asked to submit National Strategic Reference

Frameworks, outlining how regional funds in their countries would be allocated to achieve economic, social as well as territorial cohesion, and also how this would contribute to the Growth and Jobs agenda. It was a first signal that the Commission had considered its position and, despite a non-ratified treaty, deemed it appropriate to make work of the new territorial cohesion objective. Other signals that the Commission was serious about territorial cohesion already had become apparent in the ESPON arena, in which the Commission has a considerable stake, not to mention its interests in the Territorial Agenda process. European Commissioner, Danuta Hübner, was present at all ministerial meetings, which all refer to territorial cohesion in their titles. Subsequently, the Commission tabled its Green Paper on Territorial Cohesion in early October 2008.

The making of the Green Paper has been less transparent than that of the ESDP or the Territorial Agenda, and mainly took place within the offices of the European Commission. The main preparations took place in the unit 'Territorial Cohesion, Urban Matters' but, after some internal struggles, the final editing was carried out by the Economic Analysis Unit. The Green Paper went through inter-service consultations where representatives of all Commission services were allowed to comment on drafts. In particular, DG AGRI asked about the treatment of rural areas, whereas DG BUDG and the Secretariat General were concerned about the interference with the budget review (Faludi forthcoming).

In terms of its contents, the Green Paper on Territorial Cohesion, accounting for a mere 12 pages, is downright disappointing. An answer to one of the key questions 'what does territorial cohesion mean?' is not even attempted by the document. This may suggest that the Commission sides with the reasoning that there is no single recipe for what 'territorial cohesion' may involve in one part of Europe or another. Also, from a political standpoint, it may have considered how the inclusion of a definition in a policy document, which is not fully crystallized, may provide opponents with too clear a target for criticism.

Nevertheless, in a speech at the Marseille ministerial, Hübner (2008) pointed out what the Commission had in mind. She emphasized that 'territorial cohesion' was about harnessing territorial diversity for more competitiveness, that no territory can be treated as an island and that there was a need for territorial coordination at all levels (Faludi 2009b). She also indicated that 'territorial cohesion' was not an attempt to establish an EU competence for 'land use and spatial planning'. Also, it was not a rationale for the automatic compensation for territorially handicapped regions, nor was it a brand new objective. Ultimately, however, the Green Paper is foremost an invitation to stakeholders to react and, in that sense, an instrument for the Commission to generate ideas and assess political sensitivities.

Indeed, the mobilizing power of the Green Paper turned out to be enormous. The conference in Paris attracted over 1,000 participants and the consultation round, open until February 2009, saw no less than 388 reactions being submitted by Member States, regions, EU organizations (European Parliament, Committee of the Regions and European Economic and Social Committee), NGOs (Assembly of European Regions, Council of Maritime and Peripheral Regions,

Association of European Border Regions) and other parties, such as the ECTP and the German Academy for Spatial Research and Planning, institutes and individuals from all over Europe (all reactions can be found on the website of the Commission). Responses differed, with Member States like Germany and the UK only attributing a marginal role to 'territorial cohesion', but with Hungary, Poland and EU institutions embracing it. The Commission's reaction to the consultation round can be found in the Sixth Progress Report (CEC 2009b), but there is nothing said about future steps apart from a summary of the reactions.

Hübner herself has been elected a member of European Parliament where she will chair the EP Regional Development Committee. Also, just before resigning her post as Commissioner, the Barca Report (Barca 2009), an independent report written under the responsibility of Italian Fabrizio Barca, was presented. It answers the questions raised by the Sapir Report by, amongst other things, referring to a place-based approach for future Regional Policy. The future of territorial cohesion clearly depends on the next Commissioner and whether he or she, first, is a supporter of regional policy and, second, regards territorial cohesion as a useful addition to regional policy, also with the view to safeguard it from renationalization.

Organizational framework of European spatial planning

When looking at the interaction between the pillars from a somewhat distant perspective, they can be characterized in the following ways. For example, speaking in metaphors, the intergovernmental track forms the machine chamber. Here consensus is reached between the Member States about what European spatial planning should or could be. Other pillars are influenced by this machine; however, the extent to which they are influenced depends on the power the engine produces. Over time this power output fluctuates. INTERREG IIC, for example, was influenced much more by the end of the 1990s than it is now, although this may differ between transnational cooperation areas.

Clearly, the Commission track has been heavily influenced, amongst others, by the Territorial Agenda and ESDP discourse. What is more, the Commission track differs from the intergovernmental track in a sense that it has become much more exposed to the 'outside world'. It forms, much more than any other pillar, the showroom of the European spatial planning organizational framework. Simply because it has been stated that 'territorial cohesion' will become official EU policy, all stakeholders concerned eagerly watch the Commission's moves. Even if there is little to care about, such as with the contents of the Green Paper, a lot of fuss is created, at least, much more than when Member States agreed over the Territorial Agenda. In fact, although efforts have been made to integrate stakeholders beforehand (Eser and Schmeitz 2008), the consultations after the Territorial Agenda have been limited. This was evidently different when, in absence of the territorial cohesion concept, the ESDP was in the full spotlight and attracted similar levels of attention as does the Green Paper now.

Turning back to the metaphor, the engine needs fuel, and this is the purpose of ESPON. However, like with most types of fuel its use is not restricted to just one engine, and so, as intended, the Commission also makes use of it. Moreover, ESPON results are used by a range of actors, varying from Commission services and the European Parliament to national departments and regions and also private stakeholders as well as non-governmental organizations like the OECD.

The transformative capacity of European spatial planning

We can return to the central question of the chapter now that we have an idea of the European spatial planning organizational framework: is European spatial planning institutionalizing and does it lead to the *spatializing* of EU policy? As indicated above, institutionalization of European spatial planning is a complex, multi-actor, multi-scalar and multi-facetted affair. Looking at the performance of individual pillars does not bring us much further in answering this question. A first part of the answer lies in a more detailed look at how the pillars interact between them and with the 'outside world'. A second part of the answer concerns the direction in which this outside world, as a contextual environment, develops and whether this endangers or benefits the cause of European spatial planning.

Important for influencing institutions, or institutional design, is an actor's 'transformative capacity'. This capacity should be used once an opportunity for change occurs. In line with the introduction by the editors of this book, intentional change may occur once a so-called 'policy window' opens (Kingdon 1995). The occurrence of these critical moments is explained in terms of several semi-independent 'streams' coming together (Kingdon distinguishes between: (1) problem perception, (2) available solutions, (3) political development). The direction in which these streams move depends on many different factors, innovation being one of them. New ideas, new conceptualizations or new solutions by planners may, in theory, induce change and lead to the opening of policy windows. For example, it could be argued that the ESDP has helped create the policy window that encouraged the set-up of ESPON. However, contextual events more often lead to the opening of policy windows. Examples of such events are the droughts and near-river floods in 1995 that propelled the need for transnational cooperation and led to INTERREG IIC, with planners seizing the opportunity. In a similar way the Constitutional Treaty opened up the territorial cohesion policy window, which is still open. Likewise the Sapir report and the Financial Perspectives 2013 negotiations require an overhaul of Regional Policy, providing possibilities for planning to propose innovative solutions.

However, because of the very nature of institutions, with irrational aspects and asymmetric power balances, policy solutions proposed by the European spatial planners will not be immediately adopted. This refers to what March and Olsen (1989: 23–24) call the 'logic of social appropriateness'. Transformative capacity, therefore, is determined by at least two factors: first, the ability 'to gain societal recognition, trust and legitimacy ... [and] second, the capacity ... to learn and to act upon this learning, that is, the capacity for institutional reflection' (Buitelaar *et al.* 2007: 895). In other words, European spatial planners must be able to critically reflect on contextual changes, and must become visible as a trustworthy and legitimate agent.

Planning messages in EU and Member State politics

Has European spatial planning become a factor in policy debates in domains or at other administrative levels? The answer to this question is mixed. Undeniably the territorial dimension receives more attention now than a decade ago, also because more actors have become involved. The extent, however, to which planning messages are taken on board by targeted stakeholders and leads to impact varies.

One indication of the 'social appropriateness' of planning solutions concerns the extent and manner in which the ESDP, being a main carrier of the discourse, has been applied. This has been analyzed, amongst others, in the ESPON 2.3.1 project. As regards the EU level it was found that, except for DG Regio which is part of the community, other DG's welcomed the ESDP, but they did not find it useful because of its abstractness (ESPON 2007). At the Member State level the ESDP has aroused considerable interest in most Member States, particularly in Member States or at administrative levels where spatial planning policy is relatively new. Nevertheless, the ESDP's influence has remained limited in the sense that, generally speaking, only spatial planners, not sector policies, were inspired by it. Though, as regards ETC and INTERREG, it has been found that the abstract ESDP messages are taken on board at various steps of the process, but that they are interpreted in increasingly flexible ways toward the implementation level (Waterhout and Stead 2007).

Of the more recent initiatives like ESPON and the Territorial Agenda, it is, as indicated, generally the former that receives much of the attention and from which outcomes are used increasingly by other stakeholders. In fact, ESPON maps and outcomes are frequently showing up in national and regional policies. Also, inspired by ESPON, Member States and regions engage in studies of their own 'spatial position' in a wider context (Williams 1996; Böhme and Waterhout 2008). As for the Territorial Agenda, reference has been made above to the low profile consultation round that was mainly web-based, but not made public. Its main objective was to influence the Commission and its Green Paper, which in fact it did. So altogether, the 'social appropriateness' of planning seems limited, although this changes with ESPON, which however is not strictly about planning, but about territorial trends and characterization.

Terminology: territory matters

'Social appropriateness', institutional reflection and becoming a trustworthy partner also have to do with language and terminology, and this has undergone a significant change. Following March and Olson (1989), institutions, such as the EU, in a sociological sense, also represent certain symbolic values, which provide them with cultural significance. In this sense, the change in terminology from spatial planning to territorial development and cohesion, as transpired from the above-mentioned course of events, is not without significance.

Spatial planning, a Euro-English term (Williams 1996), focuses on land use. This is different from territorial development and territorial cohesion, whose focus is targeted on the development, in the widest sense, of regions. To further elaborate: *spatial* and *territorial* are not exact synonyms. In general *territory* is considered a warm-hearted term that refers to socially constructed places or regions. *Spatial* on the other hand has an analytical connotation that refers to areas of land in general, regardless of scale, structure or, for example, history and local identities. These do matter, however, when speaking about territory (Schön 2005; Guigou 2000; Sykes 2006); 'space', for example, may thus encompass several territories.

Apart from the shift in terminology from 'spatial' to 'territorial', there is also the shift from *planning* to *cohesion* and *development* – ESPON's change of name being a prime example. There are several reasons for this. One is that 'territorial cohesion' has become part of the Lisbon Treaty, which is why planners, in the context of 'social appropriateness', started to rephrase their own ideas in similar terms. A second reason has to do with the two recent enlargements seeing a number of former socialist countries joining the EU, where the term 'planning' is related to central steering approaches of the past and has a negative connotation (cf. also Finka Chapter 5 and Maier Chapter 11). The term 'planning' also has been contested during the ESDP period, which, not without reason, refers to spatial development in its title (Faludi and Waterhout 2002).

The shift from spatial planning to territorial cohesion and development also indicates something else: a shift of institutional balance. It is well known that during the ESDP process there was the so-called competency issue: Member States did not grant the Commission the initiative and, vice versa, the Commission wanted to take control (Faludi and Waterhout, 2002). With 'territorial cohesion' being mentioned in the Lisbon Treaty it was clear that the Commission would get the right of initiative. The Member States responded with the Territorial Agenda. With ratification of the Treaty still pending, the Member States and the Commission move into each other's political turf. The reason is both that territorial cohesion policy run by the Commission cannot do without the Member States and provides excellent opportunities to the Member States to formalize European spatial planning concepts. In other words, the Commission (DG Regio) and the Member States need one another, and realize this fact.

Not only do Member States and the DG Regio (i.e. the unit on Territorial Cohesion and Urban Matters and some higher ranked officials) move closer, also a whole range of other stakeholders becomes more deeply involved. The talk is about territorial cohesion, which, although still an open concept, is the official language. The broad consensus behind it refers to territorial diversity and the idea that regions have their own territorial assets (or capital) the exploitation of which forms the basis for cohesion in Europe. The uniform message of all these stakeholders is: 'Territory matters!'

'Territory matters' is what is exclaimed by the Green Paper, basically as its one and only message. This message is also captured in the European Parliament by means of the 2005 and 2009 resolutions (EP 2005; EP 2009) based on the Guellec and Van Nistelrooij reports respectively, and by the Committee of the Regions and the already mentioned ESPON synthesis reports. More importantly, respected organizations such as the OECD and the World Bank talk a similar language, as does the above mentioned Barca report. As such the policy window to fundamentally overhaul regional policy sees the rise of a territorial cohesion/territory matters discourse coalition. Planners form one of the stakeholders of this coalition, and, whilst retaining their own ideas and concepts, adhere to the coalition's language.

Coalition forming and the European spatial planning framework

The 'territory matters' coalition is growing and extends well beyond the four pillars forming, for lack of a better name, the European spatial planning organizational framework. When looking more closely at both the growing coalition behind the 'territory matters' discourse and the planning framework, it becomes clear that the level of mutual dependence and the intricateness of relations has increased over the years. Here the framework is discussed as well as its relationship with the coalition.

The European spatial planning organizational framework involves: planners from the beginning of the ESDP, new generation territorial cohesion policymakers, new Member States, officials monitoring programmes such as INTERREG and ESPON, and regional and local policy-makers carrying out transnational projects. They meet in one or more of the committees, most of which have overlapping representation, that keep the pillars going. A second circle involves stakeholders such as the European Parliament and Committee of the Regions, interest and lobby groups, researchers, commentators and so forth. Many of the actors already have showed interest in the ESDP and so really have formed a circle around the planning framework. Now the situation changes, the group of stakeholders is still interested in planning, but its main focus is on the changing regional policy and the contents of territorial cohesion. So the 'territory matters' coalition is organized around regional policy and sees the ideas developed in the planning framework as an interesting contribution to their case. The challenge for planners now is to remain a trusted partner of this coalition and to further influence it.

The planners' framework now includes thousands of individuals and organizations, which results in more heterogeneity regarding interests and objectives. In the times of the ESDP, the network, with just 12 and later 15 Member States, was still overseeable, with everybody more or less knowing each other and making it appropriate to speak of an 'epistemic community' (Faludi *et al.* 2000; cf. also Adams *et al.* Chapter 2 and Pallagst Chapter 6). The vast scale of the current network requires closer analysis.

The committees, organizations and working groups mentioned are the platforms where people meet; they form 'communities of practice' (Wenger 1998).

They cannot, however, be regarded 'epistemic communities' in the sense of Haas' (1992) definition whereby they are a network of professionals with an authoritative claim to policy-relevant knowledge within the domain of planning or territorial cohesion. The committees are far too heterogeneous for that. Because these committees have a highly political character, many of the actors participating in them are not planners or adhere to the planning messages (i.e. many officials are from national departments for economic development or the interior). Some sit there for a different purpose, like gate-keeping, staying informed or, in some cases, just because none of their colleagues wanted to go (Börzel 2002). Also the turn-around time of delegations can be high; delegations themselves or the messages they convey may be completely changed after national elections.

Rather, if there is such a thing as an 'epistemic community' in European spatial planning, then this should be conceived of as a group of officials and individuals at key positions in their Member State or organization (ESPON, ETC, DG Regio, consultants, researchers) who know each other well, have cell phone numbers and e-mail addresses and meet regularly at one of the various platforms as well as bilaterally. Now, with the 'territory matters' coalition this 'epistemic community' is getting closer to tiers with representatives of the European Parliament, Committee of the Regions, Economic and Social Committee, lobby groups and so on. By means of an example of how this works, the public hearing on 7 November 2007, organized by the European Peoples Party and the European Democrats (EPP-ED), chaired by van Nistelrooij, on 'A new regional policy: Innovative ideas for the post 2013 reform', saw several speakers invited – ranging from the Committee of the Regions and a large electronics firm, to the German Metropolitan Regions, President of the European wide cities network METREX and an old-hand planning consultant with a central role in ESPON amongst others. There are numerous other examples in the past that worked in a similar fashion.

Because the members of this 'epistemic community' are located at various positions, scattered all over Europe, they can pull different strings and influence various relevant domains. However, their stretch should not be overestimated as this often concerns individuals or small organizations within a larger institutional framework. Also, to the uninitiated and, in fact, even for close watchers, this heterogeneous group of European spatial planners is hard to pinpoint and hardly visible and therefore the label 'epistemic community' may be less appropriate to use, although it is not clear what label then could be attached to theorize this group.

Concluding remarks

The objective of this chapter has been to analyze the current state of affairs as regards European spatial planning. The picture is all but clear. Though, within the last decade since the ESDP, what can be concluded is that: (1) the organizational European spatial planning framework has been further built up, with

ESPON and territorial cohesion being the most notable additions, that (2) to a varying extent EU and Member State policies have taken on board planners' messages, that (3) the planning discourse itself has evolved towards a more neutral 'territory matters' sound, and that, arguably, (4) a growing network or coalition that extends well beyond the organizational framework is forming around regional policy and invokes this discourse.

Whereas the last decade has not witnessed major shifts or achievements, behind the scenes things have been set in motion. The enlargements, the Lisbon Treaty, the announced evaluation of regional policy have all fundamentally impacted on European spatial planning as such. Planning and spatial development that, judging by the Territorial State and Perspectives (DE Presidency 2007b: 9), still has a wider focus than regional policy or territorial cohesion policy alone, already focused on regional policy, but always as one of the EU's policies to be influenced. With the policy window having been opened on regional policy and territorial cohesion, and with 12 new Member States, most of which are net-receivers, and with the emergence of a 'territory matters' discourse conveying similar messages as the European planners, the focus on regional policy has become dominant. This is reflected amongst others in the adoption of a new terminology, of which the terms territory, diversity and development are the main components.

Currently, the territorial cohesion policy window is still wide open and will remain open at least until the next Commission is installed and regional policy has been evaluated. An overhaul of regional policy is considered the main opportunity for planning messages to become implemented and formalized in EU policies. Whether this will be achieved depends on (1) the new Commissioner and whether he or she considers territory an important policy dimension, (2) the outcome of the regional policy evaluation, and (3) the transformative capacity of the 'territory matters' coalition. At this moment, little can be said about the first two. The transformative capacity of the coalition will be crucial for the continuation of regional policy as the alternative will be the renationalization of this policy.

If the 'territory matters' coalition is to be successful, then planners are in a good position, thanks to ESPON amongst others, to influence how the new regional policy will be operationalized in the future. One of the outcomes also may be that a formal regional policy council will be installed (something that the Polish Presidency may try to establish during its term in 2011), offering a more permanent platform that planners can scrutinize, influence and/or intervene. The extent to which planning messages have influenced policies is rather limited until now, mostly due to the vagueness of these messages. Planners therefore should make their ideas more concrete. One way of doing this is to get involved in concrete projects and show the added value of the planning approach. What is also uncertain is the impact of the Strategy for the Baltic Sea Region and whether upcoming strategies such as the Danube strategy will be appreciated and effective. If so, this may open up another policy window that planners can use.

References

Adams, N., Cotella, G. and Nunes, R. (2010) 'Spatial planning in Europe: the interplay between knowledge and policy in an enlarged EU', in N. Adams, G. Cotella and R. Nunes (eds) *Territorial Development, Cohesion and Spatial Planning: Knowledge and policy development in an enlarged EU*, London: Routledge.

Adams, N., Cotella, G. and Nunes, R. (2010) 'Territorial knowledge channels in a multi-jurisdictional policy environment: a theoretical framework', in N. Adams, G. Cotella and R. Nunes (eds) *Territorial Development, Cohesion and Spatial Planning: Knowledge and policy development in an enlarged EU*, London: Routledge.

Ahlke, B., Görmar, W. and Hartz, A. (2007) 'Territoriale Agenda der Europäischen Union und transnationale Zusammenarbeit', *Informationen zur Raumordnung*, Heft 7/8.2007: 449–463.

Barca, F. (2009) *An Agenda For a Reformed Cohesion Policy. A place-based approach to meeting European Union challenges and expectations*. Independent report prepared at the request of Danuta Hübner, Commissioner for regional policy. Online. Available HTTP: www.interact-eu.net/news/barca_report/7/2647 (accessed 28 September 2009).

Bengs, C. (2006) 'ESPON in context', *European Journal of Spatial Development*, October. Online. Available HTTP: www.nordregio.se/EJSD/.

Böhme, K. and Waterhout, B. (2008) 'The Europeanisation of planning', in A. Faludi (ed.) *European Spatial Research and Planning*, Cambridge MA: Lincoln Institute of Land Policy: 227–250.

Börzel, T. A. (2002) 'Pace-setting, foot-dragging, and fence-sitting: Member State responses to Europeanization', *Journal of Common Market Studies*, 40(2): 193–214.

Buitelaar, E., Lagendijk, A. and Jacobs, W. (2007) 'A theory of institutional change: illustrated by Dutch city-provinces and Dutch land policy', *Environment and Planning A*, 39: 891–908.

CEC – Commission of the European Communities (1999) *European Spatial Development Perspective: towards balanced and sustainable development of the territory of the EU*. Luxembourg: Office of the Official Publications of the European Communities.

—— (2005) *Cohesion Policy in Support of Growth and Jobs: community strategic guidelines 2007–2013*, COM (2005) 0299, Luxembourg: Office for official publications of the European Communities.

—— (2008) *Green Paper on Territorial Cohesion – turning territorial diversity into strength*, Brussels: Commission of the European Communities. Online. Available HTTP: http://ec.europa.eu/Regional_policy/consultation/terco/index_en.htm (accessed 28 September 2008).

—— (2009a) *European Union Strategy for the Baltic Sea Region*, Brussels, 10.6.2009 COM(2009) 248 final.

—— (2009b) *Sixth Progress Report on Economic and Social Cohesion*, Luxembourg: Office for official publications of the European Communities.

Colomb, C. (2007) 'The added value of transnational cooperation: towards a new framework for evaluating learning and policy change', *Planning Practice and Research*, 22(3): 347–372.

DE Presidency (2007a) *Territorial Agenda of the European Union: Towards a more competitive and sustainable Europe of diverse regions – Agreed at the occasion of the informal ministerial meeting on urban development and territorial cohesion on 24/25 May 2007*. Online. Available HTTP: www.bmvbs.de/Anlage/original_1005295/Territorial-Agenda-of-the-European-Union-Agreed-on-25-May-2007-accessible.pdf (accessed 28 September 2009).

—— (2007b) *The Territorial State and Perspectives of the European Union: towards a stronger European territorial cohesion in the light of the Lisbon and Gothenburg ambitions – A background document to the territorial agenda of the European Union.* Online. Available HTTP: www.bmvbs.de/Anlage/original_1005296/The-Territorial-State-and-Perspectives-of-the-European-Union.pdf (accessed 28 September 2009).

EP – European Parliament (2005) *European Parliament Resolution on the Role of Territorial Cohesion in Regional Development*, (2004/2256(INI)), rapporteur Ambroise Guellec, 28 September 2005.

—— (2009) *European Parliament Resolution of 24 March 2009 on the Green Paper on Territorial Cohesion and the State of the Debate on the Future Reform of Cohesion Policy*, (2008/2174(INI)).

Eser, T. W. and Schmeitz, P. (2008) 'The making of the Territorial Agenda of the European Union: policy, polity and politics', in A. Faludi (ed.) *European Spatial Research and Planning*, Cambridge MA: Lincoln Institute of Land Policy: 249–270.

ESPON – European Spatial Planning Observation Network (2005) *In Search of Territorial Potential – Midterm results by Spring 2005*, ESPON Synthesis Report II, Esch-sur-Alzette: ESPON Secretariat.

—— (2006) *Territory Matters for Competitiveness and Cohesion – facets of regional diversity and potential in Europe – Results by Autumn 2006*, ESPON Synthesis Report III, Esch-sur-Alzette: ESPON Secretariat.

—— (2007) *ESPON Project 2.3.1 – Application and Effects of the ESDP in the Member States*, Final Report, Stockholm/Luxembourg: Nordregio/ESPON Secretariat. Online. Available HTTP: www.espon.eu.

Faludi, A. (2009a) 'A turning point in the development of European spatial planning? The Territorial Agenda of the European Union and the First Action Programme', *Progress in Planning*, 71: 1–42.

—— (2009b) 'The Portuguese, Slovenian and French Presidencies 2007–2008: a sea change in European spatial planning?', Refereed May 2009, *European Journal of Spatial Development*. Online. Available HTTP: www.nordregio.se/EJSD/refereed36.

—— (2009c) 'Territorial cohesion under the looking glass: Synthesis paper about the history of the concept and policy background to territorial cohesion', Online. Available HTTP: http://ec.europa.eu/regional_policy/consultation/terco/pdf/lookingglass.pdf (accessed 28 September 2009).

—— (forthcoming) *Cohesion, Coherence, Cooperation: European spatial planning coming of age?*, London: Routledge.

Faludi, A. and Waterhout, B. (2002) *The Making of the European Spatial Development Perspective: no masterplan*, London: Routledge.

Faludi, A., Zonneveld, W. and Waterhout, B. (2000) 'The Committee on Spatial Development: Formulating a spatial perspective in an institutional vacuum', in T. Christiansen and E. Kirchner (eds) *Committee Governance in the European Union*, Manchester/New York: Manchester University Press: 115–131.

Finka, M. (2010) 'Evolving frameworks for regional development and spatial planning in the new regions of the EU', in N. Adams, G. Cotella and R. Nunes (eds) *Territorial Development, Cohesion and Spatial Planning: Knowledge and policy development in an enlarged EU*, London: Routledge.

Frisch, M. (2010) 'Interfaces of European Union internal and external territorial governance: the Baltic Sea Region', in N. Adams, G. Cotella and R. Nunes (eds) *Territorial Development, Cohesion and Spatial Planning: Knowledge and policy development in an enlarged EU*, London: Routledge.

Guigou, J. L. (ed.) (2000) *Aménager la France de 2020: Mettre les territoires à mouvements*, Paris: La Documentation française.

Gløersen, E., Lähteenmäki-Smith, K. and Dubois, A. (2007) 'Polycentricity in transnational planning initiatives: ESDP applied or ESDP reinvented?', *Planning Practice and Research*, 22(3): 417–437.

Haas, P. (1992) 'Introduction: epistemic communities and international policy coordination', *International Organisation*, 46(1): 1–35.

Hague, C. and Hachmann, V. (2008) 'The European Spatial Planning Observation Network: organization, achievements and future', in A. Faludi (ed.) *European Spatial Research and Planning*, Cambridge MA: Lincoln Institute of Land Policy: 21–42.

Hübner, D. (2008) *Presentation of the Green Paper on Territorial Cohesion*, speech, Informal meeting of Ministers, Marseille, 26 November 2008. Online. Available HTTP: http://europa.eu/rapid/pressReleasesAction.do?reference=SPEECH/08/651&format=HTML&aged=0&language=EN&guiLanguage=en (accessed 28 September 2009).

Kingdon, J. W. (1995) *Agendas, Alternatives and Public Policies*, 2nd edition, New York: Harper Collins.

Maier, K. (2010) 'The pursuit of balanced territorial development: the realities and complexities of the cohesion agenda', in N. Adams, G. Cotella and R. Nunes (eds) *Territorial Development, Cohesion and Spatial Planning: Knowledge and policy development in an enlarged EU*, London: Routledge.

March, J. G. and Olsen, J. P. (1989) *Rediscovering Institutions: the organizational basis of politics*, New York: The Free Press.

Pallagst, K. (2010) 'The emergence of "Epistemic Communities" in the new European landscape: some theoretical implications for territorial development and the spatial agenda of the EU', in N. Adams, G. Cotella and R. Nunes (eds) *Territorial Development, Cohesion and Spatial Planning: Knowledge and policy development in an enlarged EU*, London: Routledge.

Prezioso, M. (2007) 'Why the ESPON Programme is concerned more with "policy implications" than with "good science"', *European Journal of Spatial Development*, March. Online. Available HTTP: www.nordregio.se/EJSD.

PT Presidency (2007) *First Action Programme for the Implementation of the Territorial Agenda of the European Union (agreed 23 November 2007, at Ponta Delgada, Azores)*. Online. Available HTTP: www.dgotdu.pt/rimotr/UE-doc/AP1_23NovembroVfinal.pdf (accessed 28 September 2009).

Sapir, A., Aghion, P., Bertola, G., Hellwig, M., Pisany-Ferry, J., Rosita, D., Viñals, J., Wallace, H., with Butti, M., Nava, M. and Smith, P. M. (2004) *An Agenda for a Growing Europe: The Sapir Report*, Oxford: Oxford University Press.

Schön, P. (2005) 'Territorial cohesion in Europe?', *Planning Theory and Practice* 6(3): 387–398.

Sykes, O. (2006) 'Space the final frontier?', *Town and Country Planning*, 75(5): 158–160.

Waterhout, B. (2008) *The Institutionalisation of European Spatial Planning*, Amsterdam: IOS Press.

Waterhout, B. and Stead, D. (2007) 'Mixed messages: how the ESDP's concepts have been applied in INTERREG IIIB programmes, priorities and projects', *Planning Practice and Research*, 22(3): 395–415.

Wenger, E. (1998) *Communities of Practice*, Cambridge (UK): Cambridge University Press.

Williams, R. H. (1996) *European Union Spatial Policy and Planning*, London: Chapman Publishing.

5 Evolving frameworks for regional development and spatial planning in the new regions of the EU

Maroš Finka

Introduction

The development of European society at the start of the twenty-first century has been characterized by the increased dynamics of transformation processes toward a knowledge-based society, wider and deeper integration, demographic changes and globalization. As a result, there have been increased imbalances and tensions due to the contradictions between the different dynamics that regulate social development and the development of spatial systems.

These development dynamics and the problems they generate concern both the established and the newer EU Member States, though with a different intensity. A variety of factors determined the level of this intensity, including the dynamics of societal transformation, the affectivity to relevant changes, the structural sensitivity, the ability to absorb the disturbances and the internal adaptability of individual regions. In this context, the problems that the regions in the new EU Member States have been facing are not issues specific for contemporary European spatial planning theory and practice. Some of these problems, such as suburbanization and inner-city blight, have been experienced in many Western European regions in recent decades, whilst others, such as the re-use of brownfields, the sustainable and efficient use of land and metropolitanization, constitute subjects of ongoing discussions in many parts of the world. In addition, some of the problems, such as demographic change or non-EU migration, represent an even more pressing problem in certain Western European regions than in the regions of new EU Member States.

The specific situation in the new EU Member States results from the intensity and mutual synergy of different, often contradictory, development processes as well as from the specific new contexts within which these processes are operating. The development dynamics in the Central and Eastern European (CEE) regions have been, in some cases, several times higher than the average in the EU. Gross Domestic Product (GDP) grew 2.3 per cent in the EU in 2007/2008, compared to an average of 8.7 per cent in Slovakia, 8.2 per cent in Romania and 6.8 per cent in Lithuania (Eurostat 2009). Such high rates of growth in combination with specific local circumstances have created multiple problems that require rapid and pragmatic responses. Global financial crisis seems to exacerbate natural selective processes of economic and spatial development displaying hidden imbalances. This is caused by deformed development policies that focus only on rapid GDP growth in certain regions rather than development sustainability in the transition countries (cf. Tewdwr-Jones Chapter 3). The decline of the global economy has increased the pressure on spatial planning to react quickly and to offer efficient solutions to reduce the dramatic effects of the crisis in some EU Member States and to support the way out of the recession.

Thus effective spatial planning needs to offer integrated and cross-sector spatial policies to these context-specific problems. At the same time, these territorial development concerns demonstrate the need to re-evaluate traditional spatial classifications at the European and global scales and to base theoretical and political approaches on these classifications. Building on the above considerations, this chapter will examine current trends in spatial planning policy in the context of EU integration. It will aim to assess the extent of the potential for developing approaches in terms of theory, policy-making and practice, which reflect the new realities of spatial development in Europe.

Differentiation in the contexts of territorial cohesion policy

The dramatic increase in diversity of the EU territory has led EU enlargement to become almost synonymous with a distinction between 'old' and 'new' Member States and this has reinforced the feeling of an EU that is divided into two separate blocks (Horký 2008). For the purposes of clarity, references to 'old' EU Member States in this chapter refer to the former EU-15. The references to 'new' EU Member States refer to the countries that have joined the EU in the two most recent enlargements in 2004 and 2007, the majority of which are CEE countries. This distinction appears to be logical and necessary in many aspects. However, the use of 'new' and 'old' or 'Western' and 'Eastern' as criteria in the context of spatial development is an oversimplification that does not always correspond with the existing situation or the spatial characteristics of the regions in question. In this section a number of common features shared by regions in the 'old' and 'new' Member States will be identified, along with a number of differences within the group of 'old' EU Member States and within the group of 'new' EU Member States. This ratio of differentiation may offer new views in spatial planning theory (Finka and Petríková 2000) or open the way for appropriate new solutions in spatial development policy. If this is the case, then we should start with analyses and classifications that are independent from the often used schematic differentiations (Newman and Thornley 1996). The main challenge for spatial planners in an enlarged EU seems to be connected with the sharing of information and ideas about territorial development issues, with a view to producing innovative approaches to address the specific territorial challenges of the diverse European regions (cf. Pallagst 2006 and Chapter 6). The sharing of information and ideas occurs within diverse knowledge arenas and the effectiveness of this interaction will determine the quality of the knowledge resources generated in these arenas (cf. Adams *et al.* Chapter 2).

An analysis of the main features of the process framing spatial development in the 'old' and 'new' EU Member States during the last two decades reveals some common and specific characteristics. However, it is essential to understand the spatial context of these characteristics in order to develop measures to promote 'territorial cohesion' in its multiple interpretations and at different territorial scales (Evers *et al.* 2009).

Common features impacting on territorial development processes in 'old' and 'new' EU Member States

There seem to be a number of structural changes and processes with an impact on spatial development that appear to be common to both 'old' and 'new' Member States. The transformation from an industrial to a post-industrial knowledge-based society is occurring throughout the EU, facilitated by the evolution in information and communications technology (ICT). The resulting structural changes include changes in the dominance of the production sectors, ICT development, the flexibility of production structures and the automation of production. Globalization is an ongoing process and the European economic space has changed dramatically as a result of the most recent enlargements. The prominence of the sustainability and environmental agendas is also a common feature among all Member States of the EU. For example, structural changes have resulted as a consequence of the greening of the economy and attempts to ensure more sustainable forms of development through a reduction in the use of energy and raw materials, and the use of greener production and building practices. The evolution of ICT and the rise to prominence of knowledge is also facilitating changing employment practices and altering the relationship between employees and their place of work. Many people throughout the EU now work some or all of the time from home or in a number of different locations. The pull factors attracting dominant economic activities also appear to have changed in recent years with soft factors relating to image, the cultural environment and quality of social infrastructure appearing to increase in importance. The final feature common to both 'old' and 'new' Member States is the increased devolution of powers and decision-making autonomy to the regional and local levels. However, the extent of the devolution and the resulting autonomy is diverse as can be seen from the examples of Wales and Scotland in the UK, northern Spain and southern Slovakia. The processes discussed in this section do not respect territorial boundaries and impact all Member States. The extent and nature of their impact will depend on the local context, but the important point here is that this local context does not necessarily depend on the criteria of 'new' and 'old' or 'Western' and 'Eastern'.

Spatial development features specific to 'new' EU Member States

There are also a number of features that one can argue are specific to the 'new' EU Member States and generally this is due to the similar nature of their recent histories. All of the former socialist CEE countries have undergone massive structural changes as a result of the transformation to a market-based economy. CEE countries also share the experiences of economic and social transformation resulting from the EU accession processes. This transformation has had a number of consequences that have had an impact in all of these countries to a greater or lesser extent. The restructuring of the economies of CEE countries has been intense in terms of the rapid transition from industrial towards service and knowledge-based economies. The transition resulted in the decline of vast state-owned industrial monopolies, the disintegration of State service providers, the privatization of social infrastructure and the consequences of land privatization and restitution. There has been a drastic reduction in State ownership, rapid privatization and a significant influx of foreign capital, all of which have had significant spatial consequences. In fact, qualitative structural changes were required in the cities in reaction to the dynamic urbanization process connected to the rapid and centrally controlled post-war industrialization in some CEE countries. These were political decisions that resulted in the inefficient use of local and regional potentials and reflected limits to the quantitative growth of cities without the necessary qualitative changes. Many cities and their suburban areas were characterized by mono-functional and monocentric employment areas, which resulted in large-scale short-distance migration patterns and a high proportion of commuters.

In addition, increased global competition and the limited availability of mobile capital have led to the transformation of many national centres toward metropoles. One characteristic of many CEE countries in socialist times was the spatial concentration of specific branches of industry with highly qualified labour, such as the armament or glass industries. Many of these concentrations have been unable to adapt to the new economic market-based realities and have declined, resulting in the loss of major employers in many regions. In other regions, some of these concentrations have survived. In the automotive and textile industries, for example, industry transformation has contributed to territories with a limited economic base and low levels of economic diversification. Since 1989 all of the former socialist CEE countries have had to realign their economies toward new markets away from total reliance on states of the Eastern bloc and the former Soviet Union. The breakdown of the Council for Mutual Economic Aid (COMECON) in 1991 removed not only the security of former markets but also the security of sources of raw material, which required a dramatic adaptation to these new realities on behalf of CEE countries. To a degree, the 'Iron Curtain' had sheltered CEE countries from the effects of globalization. And this meant that they were collectively late entering the global competition arena. Exposure to these new forces and processes had a dramatic social impact in terms of increased social polarization and decreased social cohesion. The transformation process, in some cases, led to the division of some multinational states into independent national states with dramatic consequences for institutional and administrative structures, the economy and society. The immediate effects of these transformation processes have provided opportunities for these late-comer countries, particularly due to the reduction in the level of isolation and peripherality in this post-socialist context. However, new limits to territorial development have been introduced due to certain demographic trends and migration, 'brain drain' and stringent EU environmental regulation.

Although these latter aspects also apply to 'old' EU Member States, the resulting synergies were not applied to the same extent during the comparable development phases, which occurred over a period of decades in the West. In the next section the characteristics of spatial planning systems in some of the CEE countries will be discussed.

Spatial planning systems between differentiation and integration

The process of looking for optimal spatial patterns and organizational models of spatial systems in the regions of the 'new' EU Member States has been logically linked with the reactions to the specific development contexts described above. At the same time, it was more or less framed by the overall processes of the adaptation of spatial structures to new societal developments and challenges. An important role has been played by relations demonstrating a new comprehension of societal objectives and value systems in the European knowledge-based society. This can be seen in the national strategies of 'new' EU Member States, which seek to combine the competitive and knowledge-based focus of the Lisbon Strategy (EC 2000) with the cohesion-based aims of more and better jobs, greater social cohesion and improved access to public health, education and information (cf. Tewdwr-Jones Chapter 3).

The deciding factor in determining the specific nature of territorial development in a particular context is related to the dynamics of the integration processes and the intensity of mutual interactions between the regions in the 'old' and 'new' Member States. For example, the dynamics and intensity of these interactions are determined by the characteristics of a border region, a metropolitan region or a gateway region. The planning cultures of the different CEE countries played only a marginal role in the approximation processes whereby the accession States had to approximate their legal system to the EU system, which was an obligatory part of the accession process. This is illustrated by the disparities between regions in the Czech Republic and Slovakia, which had almost identical planning systems and yet experienced different dynamics, reaction times and responses to development trends (Muller *et al.* 2005). Taken together with the arguments of Stead and Nadin in Chapter 7, in relation to the marginal role of best practices, this implies that new ways of conceptualizing stability and change are required.

The thesis that the planning traditions in CEE differ from those in Western European countries is rational to a degree, but its interpretation as an overall feature is misleading and shows a lack of knowledge and understanding of planning cultures, and this is reflected in some classifications (Sanyal 2005) quoted in official EU documents. Contrary to what some in Western Europe may believe, the Central European planning culture is not defined by, or related to the socialist culture of plan-making. Rather it is a phenomenon embedded in the Hapsburg monarchy reforms of the eighteenth and nineteenth centuries and the functionalistic traditions from the inter-War period. The evolution of planning culture in some Central European countries was deformed, but not interrupted under the communist regime. The highly progressive practice which character-ized the inter-War period, transformed itself into personal experiences that enabled it to survive among the planning community. Planning practice was undoubtedly influenced by highly centralized political decision making. This was especially the case for the socio-economic dimension of spatial planning, which created an ulterior planning system parallel to the so-called territorial planning. Nevertheless numerous similarities can be detected between the plan-ning systems of the 'old' and 'new' Member States, and some of these can also be traced back to the planning systems of the socialist period. For example, the planning system, methodology and instruments introduced by the Act on Terri-torial Planning and Building Code in former Czechoslovakia in 1976 are similar to those in Austrian or German spatial planning. With some minor revisions, reflecting the democratization of public life, the 1976 legislation has also pro-vided the basis for the current territorial planning legislation in both the Czech Republic and Slovakia (Finka *et al.* 1997).

It can be argued that the transformation processes in the 'new' EU-Member States created false expectations and an overestimation of the self-regulative func-tion of the market mechanism and this thesis is similar to those often presented today in the context of the current global financial crisis. The synergies between a variety of factors have combined to contribute to the development problems in the 'new' EU Member States, including an underdeveloped market environment, a culture of protectionism, the absence of natural control mechanisms such as ethical business principles, a lack of political culture and a public sensitivity to political failures. This has undermined the role of public sector interventions generally, and in the field of planning in particular. In addition, the lack of faith in the ability of the public sector to provide objective and efficient interventions, rooted in the defi-ciencies of the previous centralized planning and political decision making system, created a diffuse mistrust of any form of public sector led planning.

The spatial planning system in some Central European countries, such as Slo-vakia, the Czech Republic and Hungary, integrates territorial planning with social, economic and environmental planning into one system focusing on land-use and structure planning. This type of system, including its instruments, methods and procedures is comparable to the spatial planning systems in many 'old' EU Member States, which was in many cases the only long- and medium-term public sector planning activity in the decade after 1989 – often having to substitute for other planning activities such as strategic development planning. At the regional level, the EU accession process provided a considerable impetus for the development of spatial planning activities in the context of the implemen-tation of EU-regional policy. In many cases spatial planning strategies were a pre-condition for accessing EU funding for regional development.

Integrated spatial planning has traditionally consisted of three main pillars: land-use planning, strategic socio-economic development planning and landscape planning. The influence of integrated spatial planning over sectoral activities with a spatial impact has been widely discussed in the academic literature (Petríková 2002; Kováč and Komrska 2000; Maier 2000). The spatial planning systems in 'new' Central European EU-Member States belong first and foremost to those systems where the ex-ante planning activities were absolutely dominant. Spatial planning activity in these countries relied heavily on the development of concepts in the form of images illustrating future functional and spatial structures. This approach, strengthened by the strong functionalistic tradition developed in the first half of the twentieth century in Central European countries, interfered with the political paradigms of socialism. Planning in the Central European 'new' Member States has also had to overcome other problems apart from the problems of poor public perception mentioned above. A culture of broad stakeholder engagement and consensus building needed to develop and this clearly would take time. In addition, spatial planning did not possess the necessary instruments to be able to mediate conflicts effectively and react quickly to changing demands, which reduced its credibility amongst sectoral policy actors.

Thus spatial planning systems in both the 'new' and the 'old' Member States include a hierarchy of documents elaborated on the basis of 'subsidiarity' from national down to regional and local levels. The independence of local municipalities is formally preserved, subject to a degree of State control to protect national interests in fields such as nature protection, health and national defence. Regulatory instruments tend to dominate in these types of planning systems for historical reasons and this limits opportunities to develop proactive interventionist instruments and mechanisms. As a result, there tends to be a reliance on compulsion and statutory powers in such systems, with little room for flexibility and informal non-statutory instruments. The extent and nature of knowledge exchange and the potential for valorizing the increased diversity in the enlarged EU will be discussed in more detail in the next section.

Knowledge exchange and valorization of diversity as a way forward

The highly dynamic nature of the transformation processes in the 'new' EU-Member States, in combination with stronger limitations and higher vulnerability of social and physical environments, has been one the challenges for spatial planning systems in CEE countries. In many cases the ability of CEE countries to develop new instruments, methods and solutions that reflect emerging problems and react to development dynamics also can serve as an inspiration for the planning practice among 'old' Member States. The greater capacity of Western European spatial systems to absorb disturbances created by the societal transformation towards the knowledge-based society caused the delay of some necessary structural transformation processes in settlement systems in comparison to CEE countries. At the same time, spatial planning in the 'new' EU Member States has had to face some problems that are new for them, albeit already well known to planning practice in Western European countries. The interplay of knowledge and policy, and its future implications for planning practice and the transfer of 'best practices' can provide useful insights into the further development of planning theories in this context (cf. Pallagst 2006; Pallagst Chapter 6; Stead and Nadin Chapter 7).

There are a variety of diverse factors, including current societal trends, which provide an extremely challenging context for further discussions on planning theory as well as on the future orientation of EU spatial development policy. The parallel existence of different 'epistemic communities' that have been created on the basis of diverse philosophical backgrounds, independent of geographical location and across different planning cultures, exacerbates these complexities in a context where knowledge development and sharing and the provision of evidence is becoming increasingly important to policy-making (Davoudi 2006, Faludi and Waterhout 2006a, 2006b). The dominance of the representatives from the 'old' EU Member States in the planning process for the preparation of the European Spatial Development Perspective (ESDP: CEC 1999) has been replicated to a large extent in the process leading to the most recent reference documents of EU spatial policy: the Territorial States and Perspectives of the European Union (DE Presidency 2007b) and the Territorial Agenda (DE Presidency 2007a). Unfortunately, therefore, these processes have not reflected the reality of EU diversity and its potential for finding innovative solutions to current challenges in European spatial development.

In other words, the complexity and depth of the transformation processes in the 'new' EU Member States has meant that the spatial impacts have been large-scale and therefore the need for spatially coordinated integrative policies has been intense. This concerns not only the national level but also the European dimension of territorial development. The development processes and their effects in the new EU Member States have a trans-European dimension that is visible in the former EU-border regions as well as in the inner regions, albeit with different intensity. Thus the effects of more or less coherent EU policies are much more visible among the 'new' EU Member States because of their higher sensitivity to these spatial policies, the larger scale of transformation processes among their regions and the dominance of EU interventions over the national level of interventions.

Furthermore, many processes contribute to a natural process of convergence in terms of the contents, instruments and methods related to territorial development policies, including globalization, increased EU integration and the intensification of mutual interactions, inter-dependencies and synergies in the European socio-spatial system. However, this does not mean that territorial development policies and instruments are universal because clearly it is necessary that they reflect specific problems in specific contexts (cf. Stead and Nadin Chapter 7). In fact, it has become increasingly evident that efficient public interventions cannot be achieved unless they are adapted to and are appropriate in a specific regional reality. Therefore, the division between 'West' and 'East' or 'old' and 'new' seems to be irrelevant in this context. This calls into question the logic of a classification of 'epistemic communities' based on this division. The crucial question is, whether the growing complexity and stochasticity of the socio-spatial systems, which are the objects of spatial planning in combination with the accepted plurality of (not only) professional approaches, will support the 'retention' or 'merger' scenarios for 'epistemic communities' discussed by Pallagst (cf. Pallagst 2006, as well as Pallagst Chapter 6 and Adams *et al.* Chapter 2).

In addition, the evolution of contemporary planning theory seems to be characterized by a general delay in relation to the actual development of space and society. This can be seen in the political and theoretical debates on many current topics, including 'territorial cohesion', the spatial effects of EU enlargement and the scenarios of EU spatial development policy needs. Thus there is the danger that some theoretical frameworks are already surpassed by practice by the time they are introduced. On the one hand, there is always an inevitable delay acquired in post hoc academic reactions to current practice because of the time-consuming process of knowledge presentation, consolidation and debate in the form of books, journal articles and other papers. Furthermore, the transfer of knowledge is hampered by a lack of access to appropriate media channels, the time consuming nature of the topics, not to mention the often irrelevant formal requirements for the submission of papers. On the other hand, the attention of planning professionals is generally and necessarily devoted to everyday problems, leaving them unable to devote significant time to the development or application of planning theory. As a result, in those works where a future direction for practice is argued, the 'solution' often can appear to be lagging behind the reality of territorial development dynamics.

In this context, theoretical discussions on spatial planning systems in Europe, which are based on the scenarios of division or approximation of Eastern and Western spatial planning, belong to the last century. Territorial development processes in all European countries are either directly or indirectly affected by the overall processes of globalization, of European integration, of a knowledge-based society and of the development and transformation of civic society. The similarity and coherence of the territorial development challenges and policy frameworks, which national spatial planning systems are facing, suggests that they are increasingly interrelated and mutually influenced despite national jurisdictions and certain historically developed planning cultures. In other words, this development has been reflected in the approximation processes in respective planning systems regardless of their Western or Eastern location, as demonstrated by recent evolutions in planning legislation in the Netherlands, United Kingdom, Germany, Czech Republic, Slovakia and other countries (Finka *et al.* 2008; COMMIN 2007).

In this regard, the diversity of planning cultures in Western as well as in Eastern European countries and the existence of a plurality of planning theories can be perceived as a potential for mutual enrichment in a collaborative yet competitive planning environment and also as a precondition for sustainable development. If this is to be achieved, then the inherent diversity should be reflected in European spatial planning policies to the same degree as the diversity of development trajectories and problems in different European regions and their respective national States, as highlighted in the Green Paper on Territorial Cohesion (CEC 2008). The basic precondition for achieving the desired synergic effects in a joint European spatial policy seems to be mutual acceptance and understanding based on mutual acquaintance and shared knowledge. The differences characterizing European regions, regardless of whether they belong to 'new' or 'old' Europe, can be mirrored in the differentiation of goals and adaptation of joint strategies. In this way the heterogeneity of the regions as well as the heterogeneity of planning cultures can be valorized as an asset of the European space.

Several reasons can be identified for the dominance of the representatives of certain planning cultures, as well as of certain theoretical schools (Young 2008) in the current European spatial planning environment. Not only is the professional profile of planners generally higher in Western Europe compared to some CEE countries (cf. Maier Chapter 11), but there has been an evolution in the perceived view of planning as a scientific activity, a pragmatic plan-making activity, or an artistic and creative discipline. Furthermore, international discourse has been hindered due to diversity of languages throughout Europe, and this has limited the engagement of CEE planners with spatial planning in Western Europe as well as the engagement of Western European planners in CEE debates. This not only concerns the division between the 'old' and the 'new' EU Member States, but it also does not correspond with the efficiency and progressiveness of respective planning systems. The separation of Europe in two blocks for 40 years and the ongoing tendencies of isolation, in combination with the language barriers mentioned above, severely limited the transfer of theoretical works produced in CEE on spatial planning to Western European spatial planners and theorists.

The plurality of professional approaches and experience in relation to contemporary topics in spatial development, and the ability to provide well grounded and diverse solutions are a precondition for strong links in the triangle between spatial systems, spatial planning practice and spatial planning theory. Theory that is relevant, understandable and applicable to practice is essential. This, together with the positioning within the international theoretical discussion, is one of the most important challenges for spatial planning theory in CEE countries and will not be easy to solve under the pressure of current territorial development dynamics in the new EU Member States. If 'territorial cohesion' is understood as the new quality in spatial development in Europe regardless of its different interpretations (Evers *et al.* 2009), then the unbalanced knowledge streams and decisions, which are more or less connected to the dominance of certain planning approaches and theoretical backgrounds within many 'knowledge arenas', can potentially pose a danger for European spatial development policy. Thus this misleading one-sided interpretation of the position of disparities in spatial development has been a typical example of the failure of such imbalanced approach, limiting and lowering the efficiency of European spatial development policy in the last two decades (see also Maier Chapter 11). In the next section some of the lessons that the European spatial planning community can learn from recent experience in CEE will be discussed, along with the question of integration and/or differentiation of spatial planning in Europe.

Integration and/versus differentiation: lessons learned?

The need for the new approaches in European spatial development policy in the context of European integration is illustrated in relation to the ESDP (CEC 1999). Though the document emphasized the need for enlarging spatial development cooperation beyond the EU-15 territory (CEC 1999; Adams *et al.* 2006), and though it outlined a European spatial policy framework that included the period within which the enlargement would proceed, the treatment of enlargement was highly superficial and vague. The influence and implications of enlargement on spatial development were not considered either in relation to the 'old' or the 'new' Member States. Moreover, the excessive complexity and time consuming nature of involving the then accession States in the ESDP preparation process is dubious as a justification for this omission. The significant impacts of the integration process on spatial structures and development were already evident in the early 1990s. Nevertheless, despite the fact that several documents in the early 1990s recognized the impacts of regional integration (Bachtler 1992; CEC 1994, 1996), the candidate countries were never invited to participate fully in this process. Reflection on existing trends and prognosis for future spatial development patterns, as a result of enlargement, was left to professional networks in diverse 'knowledge arenas'. Internal divisions on spatial development issues on the basis of Western and Eastern European realities deformed the overall concept of European 'integration', and delayed the application of an integrated spatial policy in relation to both European sectoral policies (e.g. in the field of transport infrastructure) and in relation to actual regional needs. This was particularly the case in the regions on both sides of the former Eastern EU-borders.

As stated by Peyrony:

> The effects of the underestimated integrative policies have been the unused opportunities or the problems of transnational character requiring the intervention from the upper level. In the language of economists, the problems, where the discrepancy between the administrative frontiers of the states and the economic and social reality generates 'externalities' which can justify an intervention by the higher level: European networks (TEN); cross-border cooperation, when the persistence of linguistic, legal or cultural barriers hampers the growth of cross-border conurbations, transnational cooperation implementing networks of cities or development corridors, the sustainable development of transnational sea and river basins or mountain ranges.
>
> (Peyrony 2005: 2)

The character of the ESDP represented the kind of conceptual document whereby political options were defined and connected to the system of intervention instruments. An ESDP of this nature could be seen as an important impulse for planning practice in the new Member States. It represented a high-level framework for the development of national spatial development concepts and with its implementation instruments, it could have provided inspiration for the evolution of new planning systems. In fact, the style and approach offered an alternative to the predominantly regulatory instruments in many CEE Member States. The accelerated dynamics of territorial development in CEE countries required a balanced intervention and response at the supranational level. And CEE countries were prepared for, and felt the need for internationally coordinated regulative measures to support territorial development dynamics and to ensure their sustainability during the long accession process. At this time, a clear spatial development concept at the European level was required to frame the development of transnational settlement structures, cross-border and transnational transport infrastructure and cooperative networks, and industry clusters. The lack of such conceptual frameworks has led to different tensions at, and between different levels. Such tensions are illustrated in the cross-border development in the Czech-German or Slovak-Austrian border regions. The dynamics of territorial development, the development of infrastructure and the mobility of workers in such areas lag behind the needs of the economy and this reduces the competitiveness of the European economic space. Thus there was a clear opportunity for the ESDP to play an important role in this context. Although this task was partially fulfilled at the level of identifying basic global spatial development trends and objectives, it did not overcome the shadow of the 'Iron Curtain' – defining the continent within the boundaries of the EU-15.

The need for a coordinated approach has also been clearly illustrated in a number of INTERREG initiatives such as the Vision Planet Project (Vision Planet 1999), developed within the framework of the INTERREG IIC initiative. The project had partners in Austria, Bulgaria, Croatia, the Czech Republic, Germany, Hungary, Italy, Poland, Romania, the Slovak Republic, Slovenia and Serbia, and focused on the Central European, Danubian, Adriatic and South-East European Space (CADSES). The objective of this transnational project was to develop a common understanding of problems, challenges and strategic perspectives for spatial development in CADSES. Whereas the ESDP was understood to promote cooperation and identify spatial policy options for EU Member States, the emphasis of Vision Planet outputs focused more on the non-EU member countries of CADSES, their interregional relations and links with EU-15 Member States. The principal function of Vision Planet for partners from the EU Member States was to look outwards, beyond EU boundaries, and to strengthen spatial development cooperation with and between these countries. This approach clearly contrasts with the inward looking approach adopted in the ESDP.

The result of Vision Planet was not only a vision of future spatial development for CADSES space; it also reflected the attitudes of different actors involved in the project panel. The panel consisted of representatives of state and regional administrations, and local self-governments from partner countries as well as experts and academics. One of the follow up strategies for Vision Planet was to integrate its main content into the Guiding Principles of Sustainable Spatial Development of the European Continent (CEMAT 2002). The fact that the ESDP was not addressed in this context demonstrates the focus on a pan-European document in preference to the anticipated revised version of the ESDP.

The tensions between new development impulses and problems arising with EU enlargement and EU spatial development policy, as reflected in the ESDP, catalyzed an intensive discussion on the future of the ESDP as well as on new principles for territorial development and a competitive and integrated Europe based on notions of a knowledge-based economy (Barroso and Verheugen 2005; CEC 2001). Gustedt (2005) claims that this discussion has been influenced significantly by the historical model of integration in the EU ('integration sui generis') and a lack of consensus about the final quality targeted by the integration process. This question is closely related to the vision of the quality of an enlarged EU spatial structure. Since the solution to the problem of a new spatial quality is balanced between territorial sovereignty and optimization at the supranational level, it is perhaps surprising that the term 'territorial cohesion' was included in the proposed EU Constitution. However, this can be understood as a definition of one aspect of spatial quality in respect of the needs of a European society that is undergoing transformation processes toward a knowledge-based society. Yet again, then, the purpose of this reflection is to emphasize the importance of the appearance of the term 'territorial cohesion' in the Lisbon Treaty, albeit with the much more developed background of the Territorial Agenda, which was agreed at the (DE Presidency 2007a) Informal Ministerial Meeting on Urban Development and Territorial Cohesion in Leipzig in May 2007. The Territorial Agenda and the extent to which it offers new opportunities for more balanced patterns of development will be examined in the next section.

The Territorial Agenda – new opportunities for 'balanced' development?

The concept of 'territorial cohesion' in the EU (DE Presidency 2007a) has been seen by the 'new' EU Member States as an opportunity for a new approach in European spatial development policy, despite the lack of clarity about a specific definition for the term. This highlights the need to take problems into account that result from the current situation and challenges in spatial development, but more specifically the challenges resulting from the transformation toward a knowledge-based society, EU integration and the reality of increased diversity in the EU. This has been connected with the aim of understanding the complexities of cohesion, which recognizes that each territory has assets and faces constraints that development policies have to take into account in order to be efficient. These expectations in the regions of the 'new' EU Member States reflected the need for a broader view of cohesion in this context. Such a view would need to encompass all dimensions of spatial development and horizontal interactions in harmony with the main strategic development goals of the EU in relation to equity, competitiveness, sustainability and good governance (Finka 2007).

Enlargement clearly increased the diversity of the EU in terms of cultures, natural eco-systems, religions, value systems and other aspects. This European diversity should be seen as a challenge for EU spatial policy, focusing on reducing regional disparities whilst simultaneously promoting sustainability and competitiveness. In this context, the concept of 'territorial cohesion' opens up the EU territory and seeks to identify and strengthen the economic development potential of all territories in order to harness their endogenous potentials and territorial capital to achieve sustainable economic growth (cf. Maier Chapter 11). The endogenous development potential is made up of place-specific territorial capital that can potentially offer a comparative advantage. In order to compete effectively in the global market the utilization of this territorial capital can be regarded as one of the central aims connected to 'territorial cohesion'.

Regional authorities in both the 'new' and 'old' EU need to utilize their own specific territorial capital, and to activate the potential place-based organizational capacity of their territories in order to optimize what their territorial structures have to offer. This can be done through the development of new cross-border and transnational networks and structures. Unfortunately, spatial planning has often been unable to cope with such challenges (cf. Hasselberger and Benneworth Chapter 10) and has tended to react to development pressure from production sectors. The Vienna-Bratislava-Gyor region at the border of Austria, Slovakia and Hungary highlights how such integration processes have been starved in the absence of appropriate structures and frameworks. In this context, for example, Laissy has stated that it is important to underline that:

> the concept of 'territorial cohesion' extends beyond the notion of economic and social cohesion by both adding to it and reinforcing it. In policy terms, the objective is to help achieve a more balanced development by reducing existing disparities, preventing territorial imbalances and making both sectoral policies, which have a spatial impact and regional policy more coherent. The concern is also to improve territorial integration and encourage cooperation between regions.
>
> (Laissy 2004: 27)

Thus the degree of optimization of territorial organizational capacity should be judged by the quality of the conditions that territorial structures create for social processes over the long term. A critical part of the transformation process in the 'new' Member States is the evolution toward a knowledge-based society as defined in the Lisbon Strategy (EC 2000) and summarized in the 'Partnership for Growth and Jobs' document prepared for the Gothenburg EU Council meeting (CEC 2005). Both documents played the role of beacons in the storm of diverse and contested views expressed during the complex economic and social reforms in 'new' EU Member States. These documents also highlighted the interconnections between economic development and human capital, which represent the core values for development in the transition countries. The priorities identified in these documents often have been used by spatial planners as justification against short-term development concepts, which are promoted by politicians who seek immediate results to satisfy vested interests. In this sense, it is a pity that the political will to be more consistent in the implementation of the Lisbon Strategy was lacking even in the policy areas in which the EU has appropriate competences.

The processes connected with the realization of the Lisbon Strategy introduced new requirements concerning the quality and organization of territorial structures that are, to a large degree, independent from a location in either Western or Eastern Europe. It concerns innovations like new space-time structures, virtual spatial structures, self-learning structures and intelligent cities and regions. However, the most important requirement concerns the optimization of the environment for the development and dispersal of organizational innovation across existing administrative borders. The outputs from the ESPON programme, which are based upon national statistical data, neither reflect the formation of such structures (ESPON 2006) nor do they reflect the agglomeration effects in new cross-border regions with their valuable internal diversity. In other words, even when the potential was identified over a decade ago as in the metropolitan region Vienna–Bratislava, there remains a lack of effective integrated regional structures (cf. Hasselsberger and Benneworth Chapter 10).

Therefore, despite ESPON being the 'knowledge arena' (cf. Adams *et al.* introduction to this volume) within which the background information was generated for the preparation of the Territorial State and Perspective of the European Union (DE Presidency 2007b) to provide the evidence base for the political document the Territorial Agenda of the European Union (DE Presidency 2007a), the lack of 'inside' knowledge included in the ESPON outputs represents a potential danger in terms of the objectivity of the political priorities at the European level. This can be critical in the context of the above-mentioned spatial-structural innovations connected with the development of a knowledge-based society in Europe. In other words, these innovations have common requirements concerning their spatial quality, density, intensity of interconnections, and capacity and efficiency as a result of the necessary precondition for the spread of innovation in production sectors. Furthermore, the development and existence of territorial systems with high quality internal and external relationships between various elements is one of the aspects of the quality of 'territorial cohesion'. In this context, a variety of crucial questions remain open for consideration, not to mention those reflections on the impacts of the recent global economic crisis. The optimal type of territorial organization in support of the efficient functioning of societal processes, especially the efficient use of territorial capital, and the development and spread of 'technological' and 'social' innovation, forms one of the basic preconditions for competitiveness of the European economic space. However, the form of this optimal territorial organization remains elusive. Territorial development policy in the 'new' EU Member States, similar to the policies in Western European states, continues to seek an appropriate mode of territorial development that can balance between various contradictions. One such contradiction is the quest to reduce regional disparities on the one hand and the promotion of development poles and internationally competitive centres according to the strategic goals of the Lisbon Agenda on the other. Further contradictions can be seen in the ignorance of the increasing complexity and mutual dependence of human activities in combination with the continuing dominance of sectoral approaches, the weak position of spatial planning in many EU Member States and the lack of a competence in spatial planning at the European level. A number of such contradictions among uncoordinated sectoral policies are visible, such as the plethora of EU-funded industrial and technology parks being developed on greenfields and agricultural land whilst old industrial brownfields are being starved of investors.

The weakness of integrative planning approaches compared to sectoral planning activities at the European level also impairs the position of spatial planning at the national level. This is especially true in the 'new' EU Member States where the institutional structure and policy domains of the European Commission are often followed uncritically. The strong position of sectoral policies such as transport, economics, social infrastructure, environment and agriculture, and the weak position of integrated spatial planning is also reflected in the official distance of the European Commission in terms of its responsibility for spatial development, not to mention the ongoing discussions over the meaning of 'territorial cohesion'.

An important tension can be detected between new development impulses, arising out of EU enlargement and the negative effects of ongoing globalization that has been catalyzed by European integration. The negative effects especially can be seen where the vulnerability of spatial structures (social, environmental, settlement structures) and the weakness of integrated approaches and control instruments have been confronted with the power of global capital. The importance of integrated spatial development policies, as a means of balancing the range of contradictions mentioned above and supporting more balanced and sustainable patterns of development in the EU, has been increased due to the need to tackle the complex transformation processes and, more recently, in order to tackle the effects of the global financial crisis. Thus one of the crucial points seems to be finding the necessary balance between integrative approaches and territorial differentiation, which is not based on outdated schemes but on serious spatial analyses of the problem situation. Again, 'territorial cohesion', as a theoretical concept, incorporates a concern for the coordination of a comprehensive integrated approach to territorial development and for actively pursuing balanced development throughout the territory concerned (Faludi 2004). The concept has the potential to evolve into a political concept via the Territorial Agenda (DE Presidency 2007a). One of the key aims of the Territorial Agenda document was to contribute to greater coherence both vertically and horizontally between EU policies with a territorial impact, and to capitalize on the potential of the territorial and cultural diversity of the EU.

The pragmatic nature of the priorities defined in the Territorial Agenda enhances the potential for achieving them successfully. However, the added value of the implementation of 'territorial cohesion' in spatial planning, through its implicit dimensions of 'cooperation', 'cohesion', 'coherence' and 'coordination', does not create the potential for securing the above-mentioned spatial quality of territorial development (Finka 2000) in policy practice. In other words, the interpretations of 'territorial cohesion' in the Territorial Agenda do not appear to represent a new approach, not even for the 'new' EU Member States. It can be understood more as an expression of the need to follow system linkages between different dimensions of cohesion across territorial socio-cultural systems in the EU. As such, the import of this term for ongoing policy-making processes is limited.

However, numerous questions still remain. How can the introduction of this concept catalyze the latest knowledge on the future territorial development of the EU? To answer this question, it is important first to highlight how the preparation of the EU Territorial Agenda did not involve adequate professional discussion with the equitable participation of specialists from the EU Member States. Such equitable participation and discussion could have contributed to the discovery of the value-added potential of a 'territorial cohesion' concept to future European spatial development. This could have moved the term beyond being a political buzzword toward being a political and theoretical concept, which would embrace a comprehensive integrated approach to territorial development that respects and harnesses the spatial diversity of the EU. The ESPON descriptions of the existing spatial structure of the EU, which are often prepared with scarce representation of spatial planners from 'new' EU Member States, seek to translate statistical data without aspiring to identify and to describe territorial potentials and development trends. It can be argued that this does not provide an appropriate basis for a deeper understanding of the current and future dynamics of development processes, and its associated risks. A broader professional discussion of the interpretation of 'territorial cohesion' could have avoided the current ambiguity in relation to the concept, which currently weakens its integrative potential. At the same time, the equitable participation of specialists also could have strengthened the stabilizing role of the concept in the context of different short-term local as well as global disturbances, such as the national responses to the recent global financial crisis during the spring of 2009.

In closing, the events of the last two years, since the Informal Ministerial Meeting on Urban Development and Territorial Cohesion in Leipzig 2007, have left us with the impression that only mutual understanding and closer collaboration in the field of spatial planning can contribute to the effective pursuance of a coherent framework for sustainable development, which simultaneously strives for the increased competitiveness of the whole EU. In this context, the harmonization process of spatial planning systems and approaches needs to reflect globalization and economic integration whilst simultaneously respecting diverse planning cultures in Europe, thus a more nuanced consideration of territorial differentiation and its spatial components in future EU Cohesion Policy, encouraging greater coherence between national policy priorities and those of transnational and interregional cooperation.

References

Admas, N., Alden, J. and Harris, N. (eds) (2006) *Regional Development and Spatial Planning in an Enlarged European Union*, Aldershot: Ashgate.

Adams, N., Cotella, G. and Nunes, R. (2010) 'Territorial knowledge channels in a multi-jurisdictional policy environment: a theoretical framework', in N. Adams, G. Cotella and R. Nunes (eds) *Territorial Development, Cohesion and Spatial Planning: knowledge and policy development in an enlarged EU*, London: Routledge.

Bachtler, J. (ed.) (1992) *Socioeconomic Situation and Development of the Regions in the Neighbouring Countries of the Community in Central and Eastern Europe*, Report to the European Commission, Luxembourg: Office for Official Publications of the European Commission.

Barroso, J. M. and Verheugen, G. (2005) *Working Together for Growth and Jobs: a new start for the Lisbon Strategy*, Communication to the Spring European Council, SEC (2005) 192, SEC(2005) 193, Brussels: European Commission.

CEC – Commission of the European Communities (1994) *Europe 2000+. Cooperation for territorial development*, Luxembourg: Office for Official Publication of the European Communities.

—— (1996), *Scenarios of Spatial Development of Central and Eastern European Countries*, Luxembourg: DG-Regio.

—— (1999) *European Spatial Development Perspective: towards balanced and sustainable development of the territory of the EU*. Luxembourg: Office of the Official Publications of the European Communities.

—— (2001) *A Sustainable Europe for a Better World: a European Union strategy for sustainable development*, Commission's proposal to the Gothenburg European Council, Brussels: Commission of the European Communities.

—— (2005) *Working Together for Growth and Jobs: a new start for the Lisbon Strategy*, COM 24 (05), Luxembourg: Office for Official Publications of the European Commission.

—— (2008) *Green paper on Territorial Cohesion – turning territorial diversity into strength*, Brussels: Commission of the European Communities.

CEMAT (2002) *Guiding Principles of Sustainable Spatial Development of the European Continent*, Recommendation Rec(2002)1 of the Committee of Ministers to Member States on the Guiding Principles for Sustainable Spatial Development of the European Continent, adopted by the Committee of Ministers on 30 January 2002 at the 781st meeting of the Ministers' Deputies, Council of Europe.

COMMIN (2007) *COMMIN Project*, INTERREG III C. Online. Available HTTP: www.commin.org (website officially launched 2007, accessed August 2009).

Davoudi, S. (2006) 'Evidence-based planning: rhetoric or reality?', *DisP*, 165, 42(2): 14–24.

DE Presidency (2007a) *Territorial Agenda of the European Union: towards a more competitive and sustainable Europe of diverse regions – Agreed at the occasion of the informal ministerial meeting on urban development and territorial cohesion on 24/25 May* 2007. Online. Available HTTP: www.bmvbs.de/Anlage/original_1005295/Territorial-Agenda-of-the-European-Union-Agreed-on-25-May-2007-accessible.pdf.

—— (2007b) *The Territorial State and Perspectives of the European Union: towards a stronger European territorial cohesion in the light of the Lisbon and Gothenburg ambitions – A background document to the territorial agenda of the European Union*. Online. Available HTTP: www.bmvbs.de/Anlage/original_1005296/The-Territorial-State-and-Perspectives-of-the-European-Union.pdf.

EC (2000) *Employment, Economic Reforms and Social Cohesion – towards a Europe based on innovation and knowledge*, Document from the presidency 5256/00, Lisbon/Brussels.

ESPON (2006) *ESPON Atlas – mapping the structure of the European territory*, Luxembourg: ESPON. Online. Available HTTP: www.espon.eu/mmp/online/website/content/publications/98/1235/index_EN.html.

—— (2007) *ESPON 2.3.2 – Governance of Territorial and Urban Policies from EU to Local Level. Final Report*, Luxembourg: ESPON.

EUROSTAT (2009) *Real GDP Growth Rate*. Online. Available HTTP: http://epp.eurostat.ec.europa.eu.

Evers, D., Tennekes, J., Borsboom, J., van den Heiligenberg, H. and Thissen, M. (2009) *A Territorial Impact Assessment of Territorial Cohesion for the Netherlands*, The Hague/Bilthoven: Netherlands Environmental Assessment Agency (PBL).

Faludi, A. (2004) 'The open method of co-ordination and 'post-regulatory' territorial cohesion policy', *European Planning Studies*, 12(7): 1019–1033.

—— (2005) 'Territorial cohesion: an unidentified political objective. Introduction to the Special Issue', *Town Planning Review*, 76 (1): 1–13.

Faludi, A. and Waterhout, B. (2006a) 'Introducing evidence-based planning', *DisP*, 165, 42(2): 4–13.

—— (2006b) 'Debating evidence-based planning: conclusions from the International Workshop', *DisP*, 165, 42(2): 71–72.

Finka, M. (2000) *Interdisciplinary Aspects of Spatial Quality Development in Settlement Systems*, Bratislava: Central European Training Centre in Spatial Planning.

—— (2002) 'The role of planning in increasing ethical behaviour', in D. Petrikova (ed.) *Planning, Ethics and Religion II*, Bratislava: FA STU Spectra Centre – ROAD: 146–151.

—— (2007) 'Territorial cohesion – between expectations, disparities and concept', in D. Scholich (ed.) *German Annual of Spatial Research and Policy*, Berlin/Heidelberg/New York: Springer: 23–40.

Finka, M., Jamečný, Ľ. and Petríková, D. (2008) *Legislative Environment for Spatial Planning in the EU-counties: analyses for a proposal of new act on spatial planning in Slovak Republic (Analýzy právnych predpisov územného plánovania štátov EÚ ako podklad pre tvorbu územnoplánovacej legislatívy v SR)*, Bratislava: CPTŠ/URBION.

Finka, M. and Petríková, D. (eds) (2000) *Spatial Development and Planning in the Context of EU Enlargement*, Bratislava/Hannover/Newcastle/Grenoble: Central European Training Centre in Spatial Planning.

—— (2002) 'Achieving social equity through effective spatial planning policies and tools', in D. Petríková (ed.) *Planning, Ethics and Religion II*, Bratislava: FA STU Spectra Centre – ROAD: 192–205.

Finka, M., Prikryl, Z., Scholich, D. and Turowski, G. (1997) *Deutsch-Slowakisch-Tschechisches Handbuch der Planungsbegriffe*, Hannover: ARL.

Gustedt, E. (2005) 'Territorial cohesion of Europe – From a vague notion, to clear idea', paper presented at the AESOP Congress *The Dream of a Greater Europe*, AESOP, 13–17 July.

Haselsberger, B. and Benneworth, P. (2010) 'Cross-border communities or cross-border proximity? Perspectives from the Austrian–Slovakian border region', in N. Adams, G. Cotella and R. Nunes (eds) *Territorial Development, Cohesion and Spatial Planning: knowledge and policy development in an enlarged EU*, London: Routledge.

Horký, O. (2008) *Development policy in new EU Member States – re-emerging donors on the way from compulsory altruism to global responsibility*, Online. Available HTTP: www.ceeisaconf.ut.ee/orb.aw/class=file/action=preview/id=166463/horky.pdf.

Kováč, B. and Komrska, J. (eds) (2000) *Recent Developments in Urban and Rural theories and New Trends in Spatial Planning*, Bratislava/Newcastle-upon-Tyne/Grenoble/Hannover: ROAD.

Laissy, A. P. (2004) Ministerial Meeting on Territorial Cohesion on 29 November 2004, Rotterdam: CEC: 27.

Maier, K. (2000) 'Proměny urbanizmu – teorie, pojetí a činnosti urbanismu od II. světové války', in B. Kováč and J. Komrska (eds) *Recent Developments in Urban and Rural theories and New Trends in Spatial Planning*, Bratislava/Newcastle-upon-Tyne/Grenoble/Hannover: ROAD.

—— (2010) 'The pursuit of balanced territorial development: the realities and complexities of the cohesion agenda', in N. Adams, G. Cotella and R. Nunes (eds) *Territorial Development, Cohesion and Spatial Planning: knowledge and policy development in an enlarged EU*, London: Routledge.

Muller, B., Finka, M. and Linz, G. (eds) (2005) *Rise and Decline of Industry in Central and Eastern Europe*, Berlin/Heidelberg/New York: Springer.

Newman, P. and Thornley, A. (1996) *Urban Planning in Europe*, London: Routledge.

Pallagst, K. M. (2006) 'European spatial planning reloaded: considering EU enlargement in theory and practice', *European Planning Studies*, 2/2006: 253–272.

—— (2010) 'The emergence of "epistemic communities" in the new European landscape: some theoretical implications for territorial development and the spatial agenda of the EU', in N. Adams, G. Cotella and R. Nunes (eds) *Territorial Development, Cohesion and Spatial Planning: knowledge and policy development in an enlarged EU*, London: Routledge.

Petríková, D. (ed.) (2002) *Planning, Ethics and Religion II*, Bratislava: FA STU Spectra Centre.

Peyrony, J. (2005) 'Territorial cohesion: evolutionary background, implementation in the frame of 2007/2013 EU policies', AG TC ARL – working material, Hannover: ARL.

Rechnitzer, J. (2000) *The Features of the Transition of Hungary's Regional System*, Pecs: Centre for Regional Studies.

Sanyal, B. (ed.) (2005) *Comparative Planning Cultures*, New York/London: Routledge.

Stead, D. and Nadin, V. (2010) 'Shifts in territorial governance and the Europeanization of spatial planning in Central and Eastern Europe', in N. Adams, G. Cotella and R. Nunes (eds) *Territorial Development, Cohesion and Spatial Planning: knowledge and policy development in an enlarged EU*, London: Routledge.

Tewdwr-Jones, M. (2010) 'Cohesion and competitiveness: the evolving context for European territorial development', in N. Adams, G. Cotella and R. Nunes (eds) *Territorial Development, Cohesion and Spatial Planning: knowledge and policy development in an enlarged EU*, London: Routledge.

van Gestel, T. and Faludi, A. (2005) 'Towards a European Territorial Cohesion Assessment Network. A bright future for ESPON?', in *Town Planning Review*, 76(1): 81–92.

Vision Planet (1999) *Strategies for an Integrated Spatial Development of the Central European, Danubian, and Adriatic Area*. Online. Available HTTP: www2.units.it/~vplanet/general.html.

Young, G. (2008) *Reshaping Planning with Culture*, Aldershot: Ashgate.

6 The emergence of 'epistemic communities' in the new European landscape

Some theoretical implications for territorial development and the spatial agenda of the EU

Karina Pallagst

Introduction

Transformative processes during the 1990s among countries of Central and Eastern Europe gradually contributed to a break with their socialist past, and a move toward democratic societies and market-oriented economies. Eastern enlargement finally took place during the 2000s with Czech Republic, Estonia, Hungary, Latvia, Lithuania, Poland, Slovakia and Slovenia becoming EU members in 2004, and Bulgaria and Romania in 2007. It turns out that integrating a large number of countries is a challenge in itself, as the last rounds of enlargement create large-scale disparities due to the accession of countries with a significantly lower socio-economic level, as compared to the EU-15 (Avery and Cameron 1998).

The territorial dimension of the enlargement, as well as the disparity issue that came along with it, has significant implications for spatial planning at the European level. At the same time, European spatial planning can contribute to democratic and more effective governance structures in Central and Eastern European countries, and can foster the benefits of knowledge exchange on a European scale (Pallagst 2000). In this regard Faludi and Waterhout argue that 'attitudes towards European spatial planning are shaped by people's attitudes towards European integration' (Faludi and Waterhout 2002: 17).

The 1990s saw a boost in spatial planning on the European level, driven by the EU member states and supported by the European Commission. The European Spatial Development Perspective (ESDP) (CEC 1999) and the broad discursive process leading to its creation has played a crucial role in this regard. However, the main territorial focus of the document concerned itself with the former EU-15 Member States and their spatial development policy priorities, while the Central and Eastern European countries were only addressed in a marginal way. The 2000s finally delivered a view of European spatial planning, integrating Western and Eastern European countries with an enlarged ESPON[1] approach and the European Territorial Agenda (DE Presidency 2007) at hand. Thus, in the light of this recent evolution, European spatial planning has begun to engage Central and Eastern European countries, pertinently considering whether a new 'epistemic community' with Central and Eastern European development as its focal point will emerge.

This chapter presents a detailed discussion of the future prospects for EU spatial planning in an enlarged Europe, suggesting that a new quality of conceptualizing European spatial planning has to be found. The argument is based on discussions of a theoretical basis for the informal policy area of European spatial planning, taking into account enlargement issues and thus spatial planning for Central and Eastern European countries. Moreover, the main institutional steps that have been taken to prepare and accomplish the accession of Central and Eastern European countries will be characterized. In this regard, structural policy instruments that have been applied in recent years to support these countries, as well as recent changes in EU structural policy, will be examined. Furthermore, the involvement of Central and Eastern European countries from a European spatial planning perspective will be outlined. Here the question is how far their integration might induce changes in the administration of European spatial planning. This chapter considers the potential shifts in European spatial planning, as an 'epistemic community', due to the appearance of new actors from these countries with an interest and possible influence on spatial planning. Two scenarios, 'retention' and 'merger', suggested by the author in 2006 (Pallagst 2006), will be revisited in this concern, assuming knowledge transfer to either create an 'epistemic community' around spatial planning for Central and Eastern Europe, or to shape an enlarged 'epistemic community' on European spatial planning.

Theoretical thoughts on enlargement and European spatial planning

From a theoretical perspective, the process of enlargement and the evolution of European spatial planning have a close affinity. Both are based on political sciences and, among these, international relations. This link becomes obvious when looking at theoretical discussions that focus on enlargement (e.g. Schimmelfennig and Sedelmeier 2002) and theoretical considerations of European spatial planning (Faludi 2002a; Faludi and Waterhout 2002). For this reason, exploring the theoretical basis of these contributions might assist with highlighting the future of European spatial planning in an enlarged European Union. In this regard, the following discussion will focus on policy process models that examine the relationship of enlargement and spatial planning (cf. Pallagst 2006). Here, a closer observation of the concepts of 'policy windows' (Kingdon 1995) and 'epistemic communities' (Haas 1992) is carried out.

Regarding the enlargement of the EU, two potentially interrelated levels must be considered. At one level we are dealing with EU as a polity that has to conduct the selection of candidates. The second level involves the policy dimension with particular regard to the outcome of accession processes in specific policy areas. Closely related to this aspect is the concern over the impact of enlargement on the EU territory, which implies the need for, and concern over the effectiveness of spatial planning policies. The modes by which powers are divided and/or shared across different institutions of the EU is of special importance for the successful interplay of both levels. Similarly, this raises issues of the particular norms and goals attributed to these institutions.

The following paragraphs seek to employ a closer look at spatial planning for Central and Eastern European countries from a policy process perspective. The chapter begins with an adaptation of the ideas of Faludi (2002a), who has emphasized that mid-range theories such as policy networks, 'epistemic communities' and multi-level governance offer valuable theoretical explanations for European spatial planning. Moreover, the contributions by Böhme (2002) on the relationship of multi-level governance and policy networks to European spatial planning will be debated as well as the contributions by Kingdon (1995) with the notion of 'policy windows' and those by Héritier (Héritier 1999) on the European polity. The application of these models of policy-making to European spatial planning and the ESDP policy process has been characterized, to a large extent, in the literature mentioned above, and they will be used here to shed some light on the influence of the enlargement on European spatial planning.

The challenges that enlargement might trigger in European spatial planning are evident. One of the principal challenges is on-going incorporation of new Central and Eastern European actors in the European spatial planning arena. That is, their planning traditions – formerly embedded in socialist plan-making – differ from those in Western European countries (Pallagst 2001; see also Finka Chapter 5). This indicates the need for a systematic and reciprocal exchange of planning knowledge. At the same time, enlargement might be fuelled by new actors and differing traditions, hence placing demands on planning as a forceful initiator of change within the policy field of European spatial planning. In the author's opinion, the new European focus on the territorial dimension, with 'territorial cohesion' as a new policy field (cf. Evers 2007) embodied in the Territorial Agenda, is a manifestation of the acknowledgement of the territorial impact of enlargement that has been reflected in the new East-West disparities among EU Member States. To understand this evolution requires a further examination of the concept of open 'policy windows' (Kingdon 1995), articulating the notion of institutional change and policy outcomes through a consideration of 'epistemic communities'.

Changes at the polity or institutional level usually take place incrementally. From time to time, however, there is a chance that political changes break ground for more radical policy changes. Kingdon (1995) refers to these opportunities as 'policy windows' (see also 'policy windows' as outlined in Héritier 1999). Policy windows help to facilitate an opportunity for action. Once a 'policy window' has opened, the actors try to take advantage of it. In these exercises, various participants bring their issues to the deliberation process. This follows from the logic of participants' hope that their solutions will be considered in an upcoming political agenda. As indicated by Kingdon, the negotiations are driven by 'policy entrepreneurs' who sense the opportunity that a window has to offer. Interestingly, they tend to 'develop their ideas, expertise, and proposals well in advance of the time the window opens' (Kingdon 1995: 169).

The changes taking place on a European level, following the decision to include new Member States, can be characterized, to a great extent, as the result of the major political shift for the European Union during the last decade. Consequently, there are many arguments that explain why the accession as such has to be seen as a forceful window of opportunity. Indeed, the current state of the enlargement process, with particular respect for its political and institutional significance, in the new Member States as well as on the EU level, has facilitated varying degrees of all-embracing change. This is manifested in adaptations of existing policy areas. Moreover, Kingdon (1995) and Héritier (1999) also highlight the potential of 'policy windows' in the initiation of new policy fields. The implication of this observation is that policy change in the sphere of regional policy inevitably would take place. In the case of the reform process of the structural funds, for example, these changes can be characterized as the expression of a typical EU-policy stream where a variety of participants from Member States and other European institutions seize the opportunity and try to influence the negotiations by means of their proposals.

Kingdon (1995) argues further that spillover effects from one policy field to another are frequently taking place when open 'policy windows' offer the opportunity for more radical policy change. This leads us to consider the political changes associated with enlargement not only as a window of opportunity for structural policy, but also for the policy arena of European spatial planning. There is much evidence to support this argument, based on the rudimentary observation that EU structural policy and European spatial planning both have the territorial dimension in common. Indeed, a close relation between EU structural policy and European spatial planning has been established during the last funding periods with the option to apply structural funding for spatial development issues by means of the Community Initiative INTERREG. For this reason, an informal field such as European spatial planning, which operates without formal competences, is likely to be influenced by a window of opportunity initiated by enlargement and its impacts on structural policy. Then again it is the nature of informal institutional processes that lack binding regulations and timelines, which might force the actors in these processes to respond directly to changes. By providing well thought-out and funded programmes such as ESPON and INTERREG, however, the European Commission takes control of an informal sphere by linking European spatial planning to its regulative framework. Perceiving enlargement as a 'policy window' thus could provide a reference point for explaining changes in the administration of European spatial planning.

For this argument, two strands can be identified. First, new Member State actors are at the table. One can assume that they are not acting as advocates in favour of all Central and Eastern European countries, but rather in regard to the spatial planning issues in their respective Member State. Furthermore, it can be assumed that these actors will try to shape the implementation of EU programmes such as INTERREG, and to participate in informal spatial planning exercises such as ESPON. This is where the second component comes in. It also can be assumed that the actors most likely intend to widen the policy area on the European level by articulating specific spatial development tasks of their countries. New issues – just to mention a few – are rural development in border regions of eastern Poland, suburban sprawl in Slovenia, ecological regional development in Latvia, and transit concerns in the Czech Republic. Involving the spatial planning issues of these countries will lead most likely to shifts in long-term perceptions of European spatial planning. For example, within this process, there now is evidence that the long-term struggle over North-South disparities has been replaced by an East-West divide (Ezcurra *et al.* 2007). Here the following adoption of the concept of 'epistemic communities' can contribute to a better understanding. 'Epistemic communities' – like policy networks – are encapsulated in an environment of multi-level governance. But unlike policy networks, 'epistemic communities' can offer a more nuanced insight into the factors that have influenced policy outcomes.

It is the character of multi-level governance to perceive EU policy-making as a complex structure where national governments are supplemented by supranational and sub-national players (Marks *et al.* 1998). Embedded in a multi-level environment, the policy network approach seeks to identify actors or stakeholders within EU's policy areas. A policy network reflects the multiplicity of actors organized around a certain policy problem. The question of stable actor relationships is a critical activity in forming the network (Richardson 2001). Moreover, policy networks are stated to be a typical medium for transporting policy agendas between policy-makers and turning them into policy proposals (Richardson 2001). This is the case in terms of the Western European-centred look at European spatial planning, which 'produced' the ESDP. But this policy actor interactivity is also to some extent characteristic of spatial planning among Central and Eastern European countries.

'Epistemic communities' and policy networks are closely related to each other. However, the idea of 'epistemic communities' (as first promoted in Haas 1992) adds the aspect of 'knowledge' to the network concept, which more accurately reflects policy-makers' demand for specialist advice in the formulation of their decisions. According to Haas 'an 'epistemic community' is a 'network of professionals with recognized expertise and competence in a particular domain and an authoritative claim to policy-relevant knowledge within that domain or issue-area' (1992: 3). These principles involve the aspect of producing and applying knowledge within the 'epistemic community'. It has been argued that the 'politics of expertise' are especially relevant in situations where loose networks and a high level of uncertainty exist (Richardson 2001). Here, again, the assumptions are echoed in European policy areas.

Thus uncertainty and 'knowledge' demand – as generators of 'epistemic communities' – are necessary if a new quality of conceptualizing European spatial planning is to be achieved. The first discussion of European spatial planning as an 'epistemic community' was articulated by Faludi (2000). In this respect,

Faludi refers to the ESDP policy process, and describes it as an 'anarchic field' where 'there was uncertainty regarding content as well as on the positions of the various actors' (Faludi 2000: 249). He comes to the conclusion that 'what has emerged is an "epistemic community", *admittedly with its roots in Northwest Europe*' (Faludi 2000: 249, emphasis added). The implication here is that experts within the 'epistemic community' of European spatial planning assume that the policy area might have geographical limitations.

Moreover, a policy-network approach can be recognized in the fact that the process of shaping structural policy takes place in an open discussion, offering not only experts, but all internet-connected citizens (no matter whether inside or outside EU) the possibility to share their thoughts, ideas and comments. Increasing use of web-based communication is facilitating the participation of all kinds of individuals in the EU's agenda in a non-hierarchical way. As Winn has argued: 'politics is therefore becoming less hierarchical, more diverse, and organized into porous, ever changing networks' (Winn 1998: 124). Moreover Winn observes that 'the power of epistemic communities [...] is also constrained by the need for policy-makers – at both the EU and national levels – to involve other actors' (Winn 1998).

Building upon the work of Zito (2001a, 2001b), the editors of this book propose to expand the notion of 'epistemic communities' toward advocacy groups and a public voice (cf. Adams *et al.* Chapter 2). This would – in theory – facilitate the day-to-day work of policy-makers across the EU's multi-jurisdictional environment. The necessity to engage the wider public in a knowledge exchange about European planning is apparent. However, this may be something new to European planning traditions, particularly on a supranational level where expert groups dominate the practice of planning.

Héritier (1999) explicitly argues that, in the light of evolving 'policy window' opportunities, changes are likely to emerge within one policy field as well as bring about new areas for policy intervention. In the sphere of European spatial planning, the integration of Central and Eastern European countries could generate a new policy area that concentrates on these countries and their specific spatial development requirements. Stepping back to theoretical thoughts on 'epistemic communities', the question arises whether spatial planning for Central and Eastern Europe is prepared to be subsumed into the policy arena of European spatial planning, or whether it encompasses qualities that shape a policy environment of its own. Some of the developments with respect to European spatial planning and enlargement will be discussed later in this chapter in an effort to address the possibility of these two scenarios for spatial planning in Central and Eastern Europe.

Central and Eastern European integration and its role in European spatial planning

Central and Eastern European countries and EU structural funding

Since the beginning of the 1990s, the consensus has maintained that a close connection has to be established between the former EU-15 and Central and Eastern

European countries. In seeking to strengthen this relationship, the preamble of the Treaty of the European Union has specifically emphasized the achievement of a closer cooperation of all European nations. All European countries are encouraged to participate in this effort. Meanwhile ten Central and Eastern European countries have reached the status of full EU members albeit clearly continuing to represent a challenge for joint European spatial development due to their significantly lower levels of economic prosperity. Then again it should be noted that enlargement also offers these countries an almost unique opportunity for European integration.

Already during the 'association' period between the EU and Central and Eastern European countries, it became clear that it would require great transformation efforts for Central and Eastern European countries to establish within a relatively short time structures that have been developed over a period of decades by EU member states. During the pre-accession phase, the main funding processes designed to support Central and Eastern European countries in coping with economic transformation processes included the EU programmes PHARE, ISPA and SAPARD (CEC 2000a). With the enlargement, the EU outer borders have shifted, and the definition of 'accession country' has changed. Taking this into consideration, EU policy is once more supporting neighbouring countries among which are the new members-to-be. The new policy instruments created in this respect are the Instrument for Pre-Accession Assistance (IPA)[2] and the European Neighbourhood and Partnership Instrument (ENPI).[3]

Moreover, the Community Initiative INTERREG for transnational spatial planning was launched to foster the exchange of knowledge and information. In fact, this was the first time an operational programme was articulated in support of spatial planning at the European level with INTERREG II C and its follow-up programme III B. The aim of the INTERREG initiative is to encourage sustainable, harmonious and balanced development across the Community's territory, and to develop better cooperation between candidate countries and neighbouring countries (CEC 2000b). Transnational INTERREG II C/III B spaces were created throughout Europe. Of special importance for the integration of Central and Eastern European countries were the two INTERREG spaces – Baltic space and CADSES-space. The process of cooperation is still a critical activity in the approach to enlargement and integration because it can especially contribute to the creation of a joint spatial planning language, to develop common spatial planning strategies and perspectives, and to encourage joint actions. While in retrospect the Community Initiative INTERREG could be seen as an experimental playground of European spatial planning, for this and other reasons it is now a mainstream tool in spatial development on a European scale (Faludi 2006a).

Having initially struggled with the modes of providing financial support both to the regions of the current Member States as well as to its new Central and Eastern European member regions, the European Commission has redesigned its structural policy in light of this challenge under the new ongoing programming period for 2007–2013. The former candidate countries always rigorously rejected a two speed EU-integration, fearing a second class status within the EU. But they now have their fair share in policy support under the current structural funding programme. Nevertheless, changing structural policy to fit the requirements of an enlarged Union was a difficult task; the significance of the new policy design cannot be underestimated because any redistribution process through structural funding is a question of 'who wins and who loses' (Héritier 1999).

Despite the fact that the European Commission has no competency for spatial planning, a close link between EU structural funding and European spatial planning can be traced. This connection can be observed in several publications tackling the historical development of both fields. Williams' thorough description of a broad range of spatial policies at EU level reveals that there is no turning back from 'thinking European in spatial planning' (Williams 1996: 91). Moreover, Tewdwr-Jones and Williams (2001: 18) witness a rising interest of the European Union in spatial planning issues during the 1980s and 1990s, bringing about a 'European "spatial" planning system' consisting of a variety of Community activities, such as INTERREG. Then again Faludi and Waterhout (2002), arguing from a formal point of view, consider the link between spatial planning and structural policy as rooted in the influence of French *aménagement du territoire* on regional policy design, which requires the accompaniment of a larger-scale plan or concept. This requirement is manifested by article 10 of the European Regional Development Fund (ERDF), which allowed for the development of spatial strategies in support of regional policy programmes. The regional policy–spatial planning connection is thus nicely captured by the notion of EU regional policy as 'the cradle of European spatial planning' (Faludi and Waterhout 2002: 6). In practical terms, with the Community Initiative INTERREG, EU structural policy introduced an application tool of European spatial development. INTERREG has offered a platform for transnational cooperation in spatial planning since 1996, supplying European spatial planning with the structural policy means that Williams metaphorically describes as 'the pot of gold at the end of the rainbow' (Williams 1996: 114). The following section will further address this described link between spatial planning and structural policy, and will depict the overall mounting impact of the enlargement on European spatial planning.

Conceptualizing European spatial planning under enlargement conditions

While European integration offers support and sets out demands for Central and Eastern European countries, it appears that informal policy areas such as European spatial planning initially struggled to pay sufficient attention to enlargement. The conceptualization of spatial planning on the EU-level had reached its peak with studies such as Europe 2000 (CEC 1991), Europe 2000+ (CEC 1994) and the ESDP in the 1990s. Though, as mentioned earlier in this chapter, the recent integration of Central and Eastern European countries has dramatically changed the established balance of disparities in the EU long since the advent of these studies. Nevertheless, as documented in selected studies, Central and Eastern Europe has raised some interest in European spatial planning prior to their accession in 2004 and 2007. In fact, the opening of the Iron Curtain in 1989 and the subsequent reform processes initiated in Central and Eastern European countries can be interpreted as a major development impulse for European spatial planning (Pallagst 2000). And, as the following paragraphs demonstrate, exercises in European spatial planning have increasingly sought to integrate Central and Eastern European countries.

The need for a coordination of spatial development at the European level remains centred on the fact that spatial planning in Central and Eastern European countries has to ensure a solid connection to European spatial planning through a consideration of the territorial impact of policy, and an attention to policy formation and governance processes – especially when it comes to joint transnational projects. Though, despite the fact that the development tendencies in Central and Eastern European countries offered much room for speculation, at the beginning of the 1990s it had already been argued that geopolitical shifts would cause a closer orientation of Central and Eastern European countries with the EU (Grimm 1995; Bachtler 1992). Aware of economic struggles and political instabilities among the EU's neighbouring countries to the East, which could affect the Union's overall economic prosperity, the European Commission decided to more closely observe the development in Central and Eastern Europe in an effort to estimate the implications for EU territory.

Since the reforms in Central and Eastern Europe could be perceived as one of the decisive factors for development in European spatial planning, at least for the document Europe 2000+, the European Commission initiated several studies that were specifically related to Central and Eastern Europe. Among them was the 1990 report on the *Socio Economic Situation and Development in the Regions of Central and Eastern Europe*, which was the first to investigate regional development conditions in Central and Eastern European countries (Bachtler 1992). However, the geopolitical constellations have been changing dramatically since then. Subsequently, the European Commission initiated another study on the *Scenarios of Spatial Development of Central and Eastern European Countries* in 1993. Its purpose was to analyze the territorial impacts of the development of Central and Eastern European countries on spatial development in the EU (CEC – Directorate General Regional Policy and Cohesion 1996). This report highlighted general trends such as higher transit volumes, increasing migration and a dynamic development of border regions.

However, only a limited number of studies focused solely on Central and Eastern European spatial planning issues. One of them is the *Central and Eastern European 'Boomerang'* (Gorzelak 1996), presenting a more conceptualized idea of the Central and Eastern European territory. The document involves a visualization of centres in the transformation process of Central and Eastern European countries. The use of the 'Boomerang' as a spatial metaphor for the Central and Eastern European territory is unique from a conceptual perspective. The study could have set the basis for a more proactive discussion of the conceptualization of Central and Eastern European space, yet the 'Boomerang' never made its way into the set of European visions. In fact, Faludi displays a collection of widely discussed conceptualizations and maps for the European space, suggesting how the different 'images of Europe tell their own story' (Faludi 2002b). But the 'Boomerang', or comparably something that specifically concerns Central and Eastern European countries, is not part of it. With the shift from a centralized or concentrated notion of (Western) Europe toward a more diversified and polycentric view of the European space, however, the conceptual integration of Central and Eastern European countries needs to be addressed.

Lastly, the Conference of European Ministers Responsible for Regional Planning (CEMAT) conducted the study on *Guiding Principles for a Sustainable Spatial Development of the European Continent* (CEMAT 1999), which set out to provide a joint European view on spatial development. Although representatives of all EU member states, and Central and Eastern European countries were at the table, the study never obtained the same popularity as the ESDP. Jensen and Richardson conclude in this respect that 'the document is very brief, and unlike the ESDP contains no detailed analysis or discussion' (2001: 707). From a policy process perspective this implies that – as a reaction to the first draft of the ESDP – the Council of Europe developed the document under time constraints whilst the ESDP process swept through Western Europe. Looking back, the document failed to receive the same political backup of the Member States *and* the accession countries.

Altogether, spatial development on the European level was very much characterized by the elaboration of the *European Spatial Development Perspective* (ESDP) during the 1990s. It is often argued that the ESDP is the expression of an informal consensus, but the involvement of 15 Member States in the making of the document indicates that its content can only represent the least common denominator (Pallagst 2000). In this regard the ESDP is defined as a conceptual framework that is not supposed to state how to link together relevant spatial development policies. Rather, the document cultivates familiar EU goals: economic and social cohesion, sustainable development and competitiveness of the European space. The long-term deliberation process that shaped the document and the roles of different actors is vividly portrayed in the 2002 publication by Faludi and Waterhout in *The Making of the European Spatial Development Perspective – No Masterplan*. According to the authors, it turns out that the EU was confronted with new spatial challenges under accession conditions during the ESDP process. Thus, integration aspects and enlargement were added in a separate (the last) chapter of the ESDP. Here, the role of integrating Central and Eastern European countries into European spatial planning is stressed. Thus, in principle, the ESDP suggests the application of its political options in the candidate countries, and it calls for cooperative and conceptual development on the European level together with Central and Eastern European countries.

However, at this stage, Central and Eastern European actors were more or less observing the ESDP process. In fact, Central and Eastern European experts only had a marginal role in shaping the ESDP document. Paradoxically, nevertheless, Central and Eastern European countries showed an overwhelming interest in the issues addressed in the document. This is understandable as these countries were under pressure to update their planning systems, and to re-establish spatial planning, once a tool of the socialist regimes, under democratic conditions. In so doing, the ESDP's policy options were encapsulated in numerous national spatial planning conceptions in countries such as Hungary and the Slovak Republic. However, this does not mean that Central and Eastern European country experts were involved thoroughly in the ESDP process; rather they used and referred to the document as a knowledge source.

Nevertheless, one of the most significant outcomes of the ESDP process was the launch of ESPON. A key aim of ESPON is to undertake spatial research through a network of spatial planners and researchers throughout Europe. ESPON was initiated by the European Commission and deals primarily with current trends in spatial development at the European level. With the ESDP process finalized, ESPON can be seen as the major ongoing spatial planning exercise at the EU level. One problem in this development is that the focus of ESPON's decentralized studies principally has been to gather quantitative data on the European territory with little effort in the way of quantitative analysis (Böhme and Schön 2006). In this respect, ESPON has helped to revive the notion of 'evidence-based planning' (cf. Faludi and Waterhout 2006a, 2006b). As for Central and Eastern European involvement, meanwhile, ESPON has taken into consideration the territorial impact dimension of EU enlargement, and it has extended its organizational network as well as its content through the involvement new member countries; this has been a significant opportunity for the evolution of European spatial planning in an enlarged territory whereby a large number of Central and Eastern European experts can be found within ESPON's organizational structure (i.e. ESPON monitoring Committee or expert database). Moreover, the visions and strategies around the Baltic Sea Region (VASAB) (cf. also Fritsch Chapter 15 and Kule *et al.* Chapter 12) and those for the so called V4+2 countries (Poland, Czech Republic, Slovak Republic, Hungary, Romania and Bulgaria) are actively discussed under ESPON (Tunka 2009; Lindblad 2009).

Furthermore, while strategies for the Baltic Sea Region have a far-reaching history with the VASAB documents, the conceptualization for the V4+2 countries is something comparably new, yet it reminds one of the Central and Eastern European 'Boomerang'. This document, which is a genuine product by Central and Eastern European experts, will be finalized in the year 2010. It aims at visualizing new development spaces and transportation axes in these countries. Interestingly, the making of this document refers to a so called 'New Banana', a potential second core area of Europe (Tunka 2009), that lies somewhat parallel to the 'Blue Banana' (RECLUS 1989). Though, despite the fact that not all ESPON projects have included Central and Eastern European countries, and that Central and Eastern European experts have not been as actively involved in the overall ESPON process as their Western European counterparts, the institutional development of ESPON – from its creation as a predominantly Western

European exercise through to its formal incorporation of Central and Eastern European countries under the current ESPON 2013 programme – might suggest that this process is creating a platform for the evolution of an 'epistemic community' for European spatial planning.

Moving still further from the ESDP, studies had been conducted by the European Commission during the 2000s to capture the notion of 'territorial cohesion' for a soon-to-be enlarged Europe. For example, DG Regio's *Interim Territorial Cohesion Report* from 2004 summarizes ESPON and DG Regio findings for an enlarged Europe (CEC – Directorate General Regional Policy, 2004). The report states that 'territorial imbalances' will increase in an enlarged Europe, requiring better coordination of European Community and national policies. Subsequently, a major step was taken in 2007. With the ESDP process finalized for some time and the ESPON projects database at hand, the time was ripe to launch a new policy document for an enlarged EU: The *Territorial Agenda of the European Union* (DE Presidency 2007; cf. also Waterhout Chapter 4). The Territorial Agenda is an offspring of the informal European ministerial meetings on spatial planning. The Agenda process had already started in 2003 with an expert document on *Managing the Territorial Dimension of EU policies after Enlargement* followed by several more ministerial meetings (Faludi 2009). The Agenda highlights 'territorial cohesion' as the major goal for European spatial development (cf. Faludi 2009). It points out new challenges and new priorities for addressing the European territory in the future, and a set of actions to implement these priorities. However, Evers (2007) claims that the strength of 'territorial cohesion' lies in its vagueness. According to Evers it is not clear if 'territorial cohesion' means a reduction of socio-economic disparities between EU's regions, or – following the Lisbon path – whether it provides a strategy for economic growth and competitiveness.

The disparity issue is of high importance for the Central and Eastern European Member States, although they are explicitly mentioned only once in the Territorial Agenda when it comes to overcoming disparities. Nevertheless, this represents a progress in European spatial planning for an enlarged Europe! Though unlike the broad discursive process that had delivered the ESDP, the timeline for launching the Territorial Agenda was short. Therefore, the validation of the document was seen to be the evidence-base produced by ESPON (Böhme and Schön 2006). Here it becomes obvious that different planning styles are operating at the level of European spatial planning: a discursive style demonstrated by the ESDP process, and a more traditional expert-based style with the ESPON exercise. Yet the document's imminent claim for networking suggests that there is still a tremendous need for knowledge exchange with a broad stakeholder involvement that is evidence-based and links evidence to policy-making, which would stress the editors' claim to redefine or expand the 'epistemic community' of European spatial planning (cf. Adams *et al.* in Chapter 2). Again, as regards the involvement of Central and Eastern European actors in the agenda process, Faludi describes the European Commission's Directorate General for Regional Policy (DG Regio) as the key player behind the Agenda. That is, the recent appointment of commissioner in charge of regional policy for DG Regio was given to Pawel Samecki of Poland. This can be taken to reasonably signify a display of Central and Eastern European expertise at a crucial position for decision-making unfamiliar in EU policy processes in the past. Thus, in other words, this could be understood, at least at a formal EU level, as the potential merger of Central and Eastern European experts and an existing 'epistemic community' around European spatial planning.

Another important step towards 'territorial cohesion' is outlined with the Lisbon Treaty, signed on December 23, 2007, formally making 'territorial cohesion' one of the EU's spatial development aims (Evers 2007). However, the Treaty may have implications for further enlargement: As the proceedings of further enlargement of the EU depend on the ratification of the Lisbon Treaty by all Member States,[4] it is still unclear when the enlargement process will continue. To further communicate the notion of 'territorial cohesion', the European Commission (CEC 2008) published the *Green Paper on Territorial Cohesion.* This document highlights the diversity of the European territory, including its disparities. Its purpose is to launch a debate on 'territorial cohesion', following a questionnaire that addresses aspects such as the understanding of 'territorial cohesion' and its practice. The Green Paper mentions the disparity issue with the border regions to the east, and their need of coordinated development in terms of infrastructure and economic collaboration.

In closing, the above-mentioned documents and programmes illustrate that the spatial development of Central and Eastern European countries had not been integrated sufficiently in studies concerning European spatial planning during the 1990s. However, during the 2000s ESPON and the Territorial Agenda provided a significant 'policy window' (Kingdon 1995) for spatial planning in an enlarged EU territory. Nevertheless, the Central and Eastern European territory, from a European spatial development point of view, leaves many unanswered questions. This includes the major task of addressing the immanent disparities of an enlarged EU for spatial planning policy in years to come. Indeed, this might be one of the reasons why the Territorial Agenda has not offered a further conceptualization of the newly enlarged European space.

The 'merger' and 'retention' scenarios revisited

Taking the theoretical insights from 'epistemic communities' and 'policy windows' into consideration, in an earlier publication (Pallagst 2006) the author suggested, with particular regard for Central and Eastern Europe, two possible scenarios when imagining future spatial planning on the European level. This part of the chapter will briefly sketch these two scenarios, and will attempt to further discuss the scenarios' validity in light of above discussion of European spatial planning under enlargement conditions.

The first scenario, 'retention', proposes a persistence of current trends. In particular, spatial development perspectives for the European territory would be developed based on Western European countries, while Eastern Europe would remain separately conceptualized as a European spatial unit of its own. Here, once more, competencies are divided mainly between multi-level expert groups that shape planning processes on a European level, while specializing either on one or another part of Europe. On the one hand, this scenario assumes that EU funding is channelled differently between the eastern and western parts of Europe. The advantage of the 'retention' scenario lies in the fact that expert knowledge, regarding the Central and Eastern European territory, would be comparably high, and that Central and Eastern European countries would be able to receive strong advocacy in support of their specific spatial planning objectives. On the other hand, the gap between Eastern and Western Europe would continue. This would imply that a mental barrier between Eastern and Western European countries would remain,[5] which might even be fuelled by distinctive approaches to transferring EU funds between the east and west of Europe. Nevertheless, this scenario would help to sharpen the view of spatial planning for Central and Eastern Europe as an 'epistemic community'.

In contrast, the second scenario, 'merger', proposes a close integration between European spatial planning for Central and Eastern, and Western Europe. It relies on the idea that 'barriers' to spatial planning practice between the eastern and western parts of Europe, which used to be backed by creating maps and spatial development studies, would vanish. The European Commission would take on this aspect of European spatial development and similarly handle all of its structural funding programmes for the whole of the EU territory. In this regard, networking and transnational cooperation could be perceived as the keys to a more regionalized Europe. This approach also would be characterized by a vital transfer of spatial planning knowledge. Then again, however, this could weaken efforts to establish an 'epistemic community' around Central and Eastern European spatial planning. Nevertheless, the 'merger' scenario would require that spatial planning for Central and Eastern Europe find its role within the 'epistemic community' of European spatial planning, thus strengthening the latter.

The question is how do these scenarios hold up today in the era of the EU-27? There is evidence that, since the adoption of the Lisbon Treaty, competitiveness is of growing importance on an EU scale and thus for the Member States (Faludi 2006b; Colomb 2007; Dühr and Nadin 2007; Adams 2008). This is a fact that all Member States must face, regardless of their location in the eastern or western parts of Europe. Competitiveness, alongside the need to gain access to EU funding, might diminish the interest of Central and Eastern European experts to cultivate an 'epistemic community' of their own. Adams (2008), for instance, traces notions of growing convergence within the planning styles of old and new EU member states, which suggests this might lead to the conclusion that a 'merger' scenario is the more realistic option in the long run. This suggestion also would be underpinned by the fact that ESPON provides a platform for experts from western and Central and Eastern European countries alike. Likewise, many activities in the European spatial planning realm (e.g. the Territorial

Agenda and its First Action Programme) are driven by the various EU presidencies in charge, whose experts provide knowledge for the shaping of EU policies (cf. Faludi 2009), including Central and Eastern European experts. Even so it has to be noted that 'the level of diversity between the EU-27 in terms of socio-economic and cultural characteristics and collective memory should not be underestimated' (Adams 2008: 36). Indeed, persistent disparities divide the EU map significantly, as noted by academics and the EU likewise (see for example Ezcurra *et al.* 2007; CEC – Directorate General Regional Policy 2004). As Chapter 9 by Dąbrowski demonstrates, the implementation of EU structural funding conditions also has been a challenge among new Member States. For example, the new governance structure created in order to facilitate structural funding in Poland was too complex to function effectively. But the initial policy process of 'learning-by-doing' proved to be a great exercise in knowledge expansion, and subsequently may generate a platform for networking toward the creation of future 'epistemic communities'.

However, spatial development disparities and planning approaches have to be acknowledged in the light of their historical roots and the legacy of planning cultures (cf. Finka Chapter 5 and Maier Chapter 11). This might give way to the retention scenario – and possibly in the interest of Member States. Furthermore, it should not be forgotten that there is a territory beyond the EU-27. The new external eastern border and the countries beyond that border provide an immense challenge for cross border and transnational cooperation, and thus 'territorial cohesion' (cf. Razmeyko Chapter 16 and Fritsch Chapter 15). Indeed, this point is reflected in the fact that ESPON have initiated a call for proposals to study 'Territorial Co-operation in Transnational Areas and Across Internal/External Borders' (ESPON, 2009). While the new Central and Eastern European Member States have access to, and are integrated in European expert networks, their counterparts further east have yet to gain access. Razumeyko (in Chapter 16) observes that Russian regions and municipalities in the North-West Federal District are gradually becoming part of a European 'epistemic community' by means of projects funded under various European programmes. It will, however, be difficult to integrate countries like Russia when it comes to maintaining a strategy of competitiveness for EU regions.

Building on the above elements, it can be stated that neither 'retention' nor 'merger' scenarios are completely off the table. Engaging the wider public in these 'epistemic communities', as the editors suggest on the basis of works by Zito (2001a, 2001b) seems more than a legitimate goal for European spatial planning. However, in these complex planning structures, which at a supranational level are presently dominated by expert groups and ministerial meetings, it seems a difficult task for 'mainstream' European spatial planning to truly expand their networks to a wider range of stakeholders. This may be the case even more so for the Central and Eastern European spatial planning arenas where facilitating democratic planning processes has been something new for the professionals involved (Pallagst 2000; cf. also Dąbrowski Chapter 9).

Conclusions

As this paper has demonstrated, the inclusion of 12 new Member States induces changes in the EU's structural funding modalities as well as for European spatial planning. Moreover, the new regional disparities require more than just an eastward extension of the EU's existing policies. Introducing 'territorial cohesion' as one of EU's main goals demonstrates this recognition.

As for the policy side of these changes, significant progress has been made. Previous studies in the field of European spatial development predominantly have not included Central and Eastern European countries. Though, today the effort for coordination is greater, encouraging the EU as well as Central and Eastern European countries to address the future spatial development of the European territory through a consideration of the potential territorial impacts of EU enlargement. If the idea of European spatial planning as an 'epistemic community' is to evolve, then spatial planners in Eastern as well as in Western Europe should embrace these new tasks as an opportunity to deepen and widen their shared knowledge base in this regard. Also, the idea of European spatial planning as an 'epistemic community' offers valuable insights like other midrange theories well known in the study of European spatial planning. But we have seen that a consideration of EU enlargement can bring about other theoretical approaches such as the policy process model of EU enlargement as a 'policy window', initiating wide-ranging changes to the EU's structural policy and affecting the interrelated practices of European spatial planning.

Finally, the 'merger' and 'retention' scenarios have been revisited in this chapter to investigate whether spatial planning for Central and Eastern European countries has meanwhile formed an 'epistemic community' of its own or triggered adaptations within the 'epistemic community' European spatial planning. In the light of this retrospective, the ESPON programme, as it stands now and hopefully in future generations of programming, does offer the possibility for a joint 'epistemic community' around spatial planning. This would follow the suggestions of the 'merger' scenario. Though, one aspect is still crucial in this respect: knowledge transfer and mutual learning between Eastern and Western European experts – evidence-based albeit less decentralized and better institutionalized – will be a major spatial planning task in the future.

Notes

1 The European Spatial Planning Observation Network (ESPON) is currently referred to as the European Observation Network on Spatial Development and Cohesion.
2 IPA is supporting the Western Balkan countries and Turkey.
3 ENPI is a successor of the MEDA and TACIS programmes; eligible countries are the southern and eastern EU neighbors: Algeria, Armenia, Azerbaijan, Belarus, Egypt, Georgia, Israel Jordan, Lebanon, Libya, Moldova, Morocco, Palestinian Authority of the West Bank and Gaza Strip, Russian Federation, Syria, Tunisia, Ukraine.
4 Up to now (June 2009) 23 out of 27 EU member states have ratified the treaty.
5 On the concept of 'mental geographies' see Hedetoft 1999.

References

Adams, N. (2008) 'Convergence and policy transfer: an examination of the extent to which approaches to spatial planning have converged within the context of an enlarged EU', *International Planning Studies*, 13(1): 31–50.

Adams, N., Cotella, G. and Nunes, R. (2010) 'Territorial knowledge channels in a multi-jurisdictional policy environment: a theoretical framework', in N. Adams, G. Cotella and R. Nunes (eds) *Territorial Development, Cohesion and Spatial Planning: knowledge and policy development in an enlarged EU*, London: Routledge.

Avery, G. and Cameron, F. (1998) *The Enlargement of the European Union*, Sheffield: Sheffield Academic Press.

Bachtler, J. (ed.) (1992) *Socio-economic Situation and Development of the Regions in the Neighbouring Countries of the Community in Central and Eastern Europe. Report to the European Commission*, Luxemburg: Office for Official Publications of the European Communities.

Böhme, K. (2002) *Nordic Echoes of European Spatial Planning: discursive integration in practice*, Stockholm: Nordregio.

Böhme, K. and Schön, P. (2006) 'From Leipzig to Leipzig: territorial research delivers evidence for the new territorial agenda of the European Union, *DisP*, 165, 42(2): 61–70.

CEC – Commission of the European Communities (1991) *Europe 2000: outlook for the development of the Community's territory*, Luxemburg, Office for Official Publications of the European Communities.

—— (1994) *Europe 2000+: cooperation for European territorial development*, Luxemburg: Office for Official Publications of the European Communities.

—— (1997) *European Spatial Development Perspective*: First Official Draft. Presented at the informal meeting of Ministers responsible for spatial planning of the member states of the European Union. Nordwijk, 9 and 10 June 1997.

—— (1999) *European Spatial Development Perspective (ESDP): towards balanced and sustainable development of the territory of the EU*, Luxembourg: Office for Official Publications of the European Communities.

—— (2000a) *European Union Enlargement – a historic opportunity*, Luxembourg: Office for Official Publications of the European Communities.

—— (2000b) 'Communication from the Commission to the Member States of 28.4.00 laying down guidelines for a Community Initiative concerning trans-European cooperation intended to encourage harmonious and balanced development of the European territory – Interreg III', *Official Journal of the European Communities*, 23.5.2000: C143-C129. http://europa.eu.int/comm/regional_policy/sources/docoffic/official/reports/contentpdf_en.htm.

—— (2004) *A New Partnership for Cohesion. Third Report on Economic and Social Cohesion*, Brussels: Commission of the European Communities.

—— (2008) *Green Paper on Territorial Cohesion – turning territorial diversity into strength*, Brussels: Commission of the European Communities.

CEC – Directorate General Regional Policy (1996) *The Impact of the Development of the Countries of Central and Eastern Europe on the Community territory*, Luxemburg: Office for Official Publications of the European Communities.

—— (2004) *Interim Territorial Cohesion Report (Preliminary results of ESPON and EU Commission Studies)*, Luxembourg: Office for Official Publications of the European Communities.

CEMAT – European Conference of Ministers Responsible for Regional Planning (1999) *Guiding Principles for a Sustainable Spatial Development of the European Continent*, Strasbourg: Council of Europe.

Colomb, C. (2007) 'The added value of transnational cooperation: towards a new framework for evaluating learning and policy change', *Planning Practice and Research*, 22(3): 347–372.

Dąbrowski, M. (2010) 'Institutional change, partnership and regional networks: civic engagement and the implementation of the Structural Funds in Poland', in N. Adams, G. Cotella and R. Nunes (eds) *Territorial Development, Cohesion and Spatial Planning: knowledge and policy development in an enlarged EU*, London: Routledge.

DE Presidency (2007) *Territorial agenda of the European Union: Towards a more competitive and sustainable Europe of diverse regions* – Agreed at the occasion of the informal ministerial meeting on urban development and territorial cohesion on 24/25 May 2007. Online. Available HTTP: www.bmvbs.de/Anlage/original_1005295/Territorial-Agenda-of-the-European-Union-Agreed-on-25-May-2007-accessible.pdf.

Dühr, S. and Nadin, V. (2007) 'Europeanisation through transnational territorial cooperation? The case of Interreg IIIB North-West Europe', *Planning Practice and Research*, 22(3): 373–394.

ESPON (2009) *Territorial cooperation in transnational areas, between regions and across internal/external borders*, Call for Proposals on Applied Research Projects, Luxembourg: ESPON.

Evers, D. (2007) 'Reflections on territorial cohesion and European spatial planning', *Tijdschrift vor Economische en Sociale Geografie*, 99(3): 303–315.

Ezcurra, R., Pascual, P. and Rapun, M. (2007) 'The dynamics of regional disparities in Central and Eastern Europe during transition', *European Planning Studies*, 15(10): 1397–1421.

Faludi, A. (2000) 'Strategic planning in Europe: institutional aspects', in W. Salet and A. Faludi (eds) *The Revival of Strategic Spatial Planning*, Amsterdam: Royal Netherlands Academy of Arts and Sciences: 243–258.

—— (2002a) 'Positioning European Spatial Planning', *European Planning Studies*, 10(7): 897–909.

—— (2002b) 'Images of Europe tell their own story', in A. Faludi (ed.) *European Spatial Planning*, Cambridge MA: Lincoln Institute of Land Policy: 19–36.

—— (2006a) 'European territorial cooperation and learning – reflections by the Guest Editor on the wider implications', *DisP*, 165, 42(2): 3–10.

—— (2006b) 'From European spatial development to territorial cohesion policy', *Regional Studies*, 40(6): 667–678.

—— (2009) 'A turning point in the development of spatial planning? The "Territorial Agenda of the European Union" and the "First Action Programme"', *Progress in Planning*, 71(1): 1–42.

Faludi, A. and Waterhout, B. (2002) *The Making of the European Development Perspective – no masterplan*. London/New York: Routledge.

—— (2006a) 'Introducing evidence-based planning', *DisP*, 165, 42(2): 4–13.

—— (2006b) 'Debating evidence-based planning: conclusions from the International Workshop', *DisP*, 165, 42(2): 71–72.

Finka, M. (2010) 'Evolving frameworks for regional development and spatial planning in the new regions of the EU', in N. Adams, G. Cotella and R. Nunes (eds) *Territorial Development, Cohesion and Spatial Planning: knowledge and policy development in an enlarged EU*, London: Routledge.

Fritsch, M. (2010) 'Interfaces of European Union internal and external territorial governance: the Baltic Sea Region', in N. Adams, G. Cotella and R. Nunes (eds) *Territorial Development, Cohesion and Spatial Planning: knowledge and policy development in an enlarged EU*, London: Routledge.

Gorzelak, G. (1996) *The Regional Dimension of Transformation in Central Europe*, London/Bristol: Regional Studies Association.

Grimm, F.-D. (1995) 'Der politische und wirtschaftliche Umbruch als Auslöser raumstruktureller Veränderungen im östlichen Europa', in F.-D.Grimm (ed.) *Der Wandel des ländlichen Raumes in Südosteuropa*, Munich: Südosteuropa-Gesellschaft.

Haas, P. M. (1992) 'Introduction: epistemic communities and international policy coordination', *International Organization*, 46(1): 1–35.

Hedetoft, U. (1999) 'The nation-state meets the world: national identities in the context of transnationality and cultural globalization', *European Journal of Social Theory*, 2(1): 71–94.

Héritier, A. (1999) *Policy-making and Diversity in Europe: escape from deadlock*, Cambridge: Cambridge University Press.

Jachtenfuchs, M. (2002) 'Deepening and widening integration theory', *Journal of European Public Policy*, 9(4): 650–657.

Jensen, O. B. and Richardson, T. (2001) 'Nested visions: new rationalities of space in European spatial planning', *Regional studies*, 35(8): 703–717.

Kingdon, J. W. (1995) *Agendas, Alternatives, and Public Policies*, New York: Harper Collins College Publishers.

Kule, L., Krisjane, Z. and Berzins, M. (2010) 'The rhetoric and reality of pursuing territorial cohesion in Latvia', in N. Adams, G. Cotella and R. Nunes (eds) *Territorial Development, Cohesion and Spatial Planning: knowledge and policy development in an enlarged EU*, London: Routledge.

Lindblad, S. (2009) *Baltic Sea Territorial Strategy*, ESPON: Open Seminar 'Territorial Development Opportunities in the Global Economic Recession'. Online. Available at: www.espon.eu/mmp/online/website/content/programme/1455/2112/2327/2372/index_EN.html.

Maier, K. (2010) 'The pursuit of balanced territorial development: the realities and complexities of the cohesion agenda', in N. Adams, G. Cotella and R. Nunes (eds) *Territorial Development, Cohesion and Spatial Planning: knowledge and policy development in an enlarged EU*, London: Routledge.

Marks, G., Hooghe, L. and Blank, K. (1998) 'European integration from the 1980s: state-centric v. multi-level governance', in B. R. F. Nelsen and A. C.-G. Stubb (eds) *The European Union: readings on the theory and practice of European integration*, 2nd edition, Boulder CO: Lynne Rienner Publishers: 273–293.

Pallagst, K. M. (2000) *Raumordnung der Tschechischen Republik: Mittel- und Osteuropa vor dem Hintergrund europäischer Raumordnungsbestrebungen*. Berlin: Berlin Verlag.

—— (2001) 'Planung im Transformationsprozess: Entwicklungstendenzen auf regionaler Ebene in der Tschechischen Republik', *Raumplanung*, 94(1): 21–25.

—— (2006) 'European spatial planning reloaded: considering EU enlargement in theory and practice', *European Planning Studies*, 2/2006: 253–272.

PT Presidency (2007) *First Action Programme for the Implementation of the Territorial Agenda of the European Union (agreed 23 November 2007, at Ponta Delgada, Azores)*. Online. Available HTTP: www.dgotdu.pt/rimotr/UE-doc/AP1_23NovembroVfinal.pdf (accessed 28 September 2009).

Razumeyko, N. (2010) 'Strategic planning practices in North-West Russia: European influences, challenges and future perspectives', in N. Adams, G. Cotella and R. Nunes (eds) *Territorial Development, Cohesion and Spatial Planning: knowledge and policy development in an enlarged EU*, London: Routledge.

RECLUS (1989) *Les Villes Européennes: rapport pour la datar*, Montpellier: RECLUS.

Richardson, J. (2001) 'Policy-making in the EU: interests, ideas and garbage cans of primeval soup', in Richardson, J. (ed.) *European Union Power and Policy-making*, 2nd edition, London/New York: Routledge: 3–26.

Schimmelfennig, F. and Sedelmeier, U. (2002) 'Theorizing EU enlargement: research focus, hypothesis and the state of research', *Journal of European Public Policy*, 9(4): 500–528.

Tewdr-Jones, M. and Williams, R. H. (2001) *European Dimension of British Planning*, London/New York: Spon Press.

Tunka, M. (2009) *Common Spatial Development Document of V4+2 countries*, ESPON: Open Seminar 'Territorial Development Opportunities in the Global Economic Recession'. Online. Available HTTP: www.espon.eu/mmp/online/website/content/programme/1455/2112/2327/2372/index_EN.html.

Waterhout, B. (2010) 'European spatial planning: current state and future challenges', in N. Adams, G. Cotella and R. Nunes (eds) *Territorial Development, Cohesion and Spatial Planning: knowledge and policy development in an enlarged EU*, London: Routledge.

Williams, H. (1996) *European Union spatial policy and planning*, London: Chapman.

Winn, N. (1998) 'Who gets what, when and how? The contested conceptual and disciplinary nature of governance and policy-making in the European Union', *Politics*, 18(2): 119–132.

Zito, A. (2001a) 'Epistemic communities, European governance and the public voice', *Science and Public Policy*, 28(6): 465–476.

—— (2001b) 'Epistemic communities, collective entrepreneurship and European integration', *Journal of European Public Policy*, 8(4): 585–603.

Part II

Engaging systems of multi-level governance

Editors' introduction to Part II

Neil Adams, Giancarlo Cotella and Richard Nunes

Institutional change and organizational learning constitute everyday processes that seek to address the challenges of European territorial development, the results of which are context specific and its implications often contested. This represents the growing diversity within European cities as well as between its regions. It also can set the stage for new and existing territorial governance arrangements. Together these new and existing arrangements constitute a complex layering of institutional and political geographies of agent interaction, which transcend and/or challenge established jurisdictions at varying territorial scales (cross-scalar) and across different institutional remits or responsibilities ('multi-jurisdictional'). These multi-agent, cross-scalar governance arrangements form systems of multi-level governance with interactions within and between 'territorial knowledge communities' (Chapter 2). These processes involve the transfer of formal authority beyond core representative institutions and are the result of both the rescaling of formal authority up to supranational institutions and down to sub-national governments (Hooghe and Marks, 2001). At the same time these processes imply a need to move beyond the 'hard' regulatory spaces formed by administrative borders as well as the spaces defined by professional and disciplinary borders. The flexible and dynamic realities of this post-enlargement cross-scalar and multi-jurisdictional policy environment create challenges but also opportunities for existing and emerging multi-level governance arrangements.

In this consideration there needs to be an appreciation of the dynamic of newly framed policy issues and opportunities in light of particular historical situations and/or legacies (cf. Kingdon 1995; Roness 2001). The processes of accession and enlargement have resulted in many new Member States undergoing significant administrative and institutional transformation. At the same time, the need to address the consequences of the legacy of their socialist and Soviet pasts exacerbates the complexities of their transition. Needless to say, this consideration of the material importance of institutions is by no means a comprehensive appreciation of multi-scalar agent interactivity, as earlier works on the notion of 'governance' and its transformation in a European context can attest (Rhodes 1996, 1997; Kooiman 1993; Kohler-Koch 1999). Altogether, though, organizations and the agents that occupy them are social units within the spaces of institutionalized practices that can have a constraining and/or enabling influence on the competing logics and legitimacies of human agency whilst simultaneously the product of that agency. This is a particularly important element in any thorough consideration of policy stability and change in a policy environment of multi-level governance engagement and transformation.

As some of the contributions in this section illustrate, multi-scalar agent interactivity can contribute to both path-shaping and path-dependent processes of policy development. On the back of rescaling national political processes toward new spaces of territorial governance beyond the professional and geographic boundaries of planning practice (Haughton *et al.* 2010), these changing multi-scalar agent practices often can be subject to the vested interests of loyal political alliances, and the traditional silo-mentality of sectorally oriented organizations or government departments (Almendinger and Tewdwr-Jones 2000; Benz 2000). This understanding largely has been argued in this book on the basis of a close and mutualistic relationship between knowledge and political interests. The symbiotic relationship between knowledge and political interests is one of the key components upon which the theoretical framework is based (see Chapter 2). This point appears to be valid at both the EU level and within various domestic contexts. As Dühr *et al.* argue 'preparing concepts of European space is a political act. Particular models will favour certain interests and be promoted by them' (2010:56). The concepts of European space referred to by Dühr *et al.* correspond with particular types of knowledge resources and this illustrates the relevance of political interests in relation to our theoretical framework. As a result the institutional construction of interests, evident in the mutually constituting processes of knowledge development and utilization, lie at the intersection of knowledge resources and knowledge arenas (Parsons 2003). That is to say, knowledge resources are therefore employed selectively in the representation of policy problems and opportunities or in the advancement of vested interests. Depending on the relative power of these vested interests, they are transmitted via territorial knowledge channels into knowledge arenas where they are tested and validated, or subject to debate and institutionalized rules of policy evaluation.

The discussions in the earlier chapters of this book have started to highlight the complexity of the interplay between knowledge and policy development in the enlarged EU and particularly in relation to spatial planning in Europe. The cross-scalar and multi-agent policy landscape of spatial planning in Europe provides a challenging context within which increasingly diverse spatial development challenges and opportunities are to be addressed. The cross-scalar and multi-level governance arrangements that can influence policy development, encapsulated in the theoretical framework as territorial knowledge channels, will only be able to exert such an influence once they have acquired the powers necessary to frame policy issues and opportunities or to safeguard existing policies or approaches. This takes particular note of the complex adaptation paths, and competing institutional and discursive logics that can potentially influence policy development as the following chapters suggest. Put differently, knowledge and information is the basis upon which all actors perceive or construct their worlds, and derive possible action strategies. Also the preferences over these action strategies can be linked to actors with the capacity or influence to enforce policy change and inspire new actor coalitions, which can alter the distribution of power and influence within a policy domain. Such actors could be in the form of a political champion or a well connected high-level civil servant or academic.

Policy change may result not only from changing preferences and interventions of such actors and the dynamics of actor coalitions, but also from changing perceptions of how the policy problem in question is to be defined and what the appropriate solutions are in a given situation (Conzelman 1998). The relevance and importance of power and preferences and a process-oriented approach have already been discussed extensively in Chapter 2 and these elements form an important part of the theoretical framework. This process-oriented approach implies that the simultaneous critique and embrace of concepts and ideas will be advanced through the preferences of certain actors and the power struggles between them. More than this, however, the approach implies that these power struggles and preferences will be supported by knowledge resources and that this will allow them to potentially become progressively embedded in the institutional construction of interests.

As discussed in Chapter 2, Conzelmann (1998) identifies two approaches to the study of policy change, supplementing the 'conflict-based' (power and preferences) approach discussed above with a 'learning-based' (knowledge and information) approach. He stresses how both sets of variables are useful in 'linking the explanatory strengths of policy-analytical approaches with the descriptive accuracy of the multi-level governance literature' (p. 7). Namely, the potential for redressing these analytical and descriptive qualities of policy stability and change will be evident in any consideration of the different actors and tensions of a multi-jurisdictional policy environment where some push for more technocratic solutions and others push for more political debate. This is evident, for example, in the complexity and growth of independent agencies that can insulate public policy from public scrutiny whereby knowledge has become the 'terrain of politics' whilst the public sphere has become 'depoliticized' (cf. Radaelli 1999, Haughton *et al.* 2010).

Notwithstanding the processes of purposeful misinformation and actors' inaccessibility to information, the theoretical framework particularly highlights the intra-/extra-community links of territorial governance arrangements within and between territorial knowledge communities of diverse actors. That is, the diverse form and nature of engagement among territorial knowledge communities with systems of multi-level governance. Moreover, these links reflect the potential for learning and conflict with regard to consensual/disputed or absent knowledge bases and shared/unshared interests within the complex adaptive processes of incremental and radical policy change.

Styles of territorial governance and spatial planning follow a process of constant incremental adjustment in response to new policy agendas and priorities. During the 1990s however, institutional reform was more rapid and radical in the countries aspiring to join the EU due to the approaching accession. Similar radical change, although not as dramatic, was underway in Western Europe at the end of the decade, with a number of countries undertaking fundamental reforms of governance arrangements (cf. Albrechts *et al.* 2001). In fact, reform and innovation in governance have been defining characteristics in so many countries, both east and west, partly as a result of common challenges such as the 'network society' (Albrechts and Mandelbaum 2005), economic competitiveness, environmental sustainability and, more recently, climate change. In almost all countries the hallmark of reform has been the extension of multi-level governance and particularly the increasing significance of the regional (subnational) level. Innovation also has been encouraged through extensive transnational and cross-border cooperation, which have enhanced opportunities for policy transfer and the exchange of experiences and good practice, and exposed actors increasingly to the influence of European discourse and policy statements on territorial governance. More importantly, however, simple typologies of governance and spatial planning are becoming more difficult to apply as reforms incorporate a greater diversity of arrangements and respond to diverse national and local contexts. This has created a scalar 'layering' of governance arrangements in response to changing imperatives over time, which are superimposed on existing professional/institutional remits and political jurisdictions (cf. Nadin 2002; Brennar 2004; Deas and Lord 2008, Haughton *et al.* 2009). The roles and relations between a greater range of actors horizontally across sectors, vertically between levels of government, and geographically are now much more varied.

In light of these complexities, it is not surprising therefore that the application and effect of the reforms has not always been successful. The transfer and adaptation of 'best practices' from elsewhere in the interests of innovation through policy transfer and integration has not always taken account of local contexts. That is to say, there may be problems with adaptation because of local capacities and other constraints, or more fundamental issues to do with the mismatch of models of territorial governance and the models of society in which they are embedded (see Stead and Meijers 2009 for review). In some places this has contributed to a divergence of formal governance arrangements and the reality of policy and action. In simple terms, plans and policies may be prepared but they have little bearing on the way that places are ultimately governed. Thus there are important lessons, especially for the transposition of approaches to territorial governance and the engagement of systems of multi-level governance. In this regard, Dominic Stead and Vincent Nadin (Chapter 7) explore the shifts in territorial governance and the issue of Europeanization of spatial planning. Their discussion offers an insightful look into the ongoing discussions of the innovation and transformation of European governance as an 'experimental field' of extensive transnational and cross-border cooperation (cf. Janin Rivolin and Faludi 2005, Stead and Meijers 2009). Similar to the contribution by Finka (Chapter 5), the authors start by discussing some common spatial development challenges and explore these in the context of the implications of EU enlargement. The authors focus specifically on the CEE reality and link this to the need for more effective territorial governance structures and practices. The discussion then focuses on the concept of Europeanization, which is explained with reference to the flows of policy, information and experience between diverse actors in the cross-scalar and multi-jurisdictional policy environment of the enlarged EU. The vertical (top-down), horizontal (between Member States) and circular (domestic contexts to EU level and back to domestic contexts) flows are examined in turn and this provides a context within which policy transfer and the value of good and best practices are explored. Both policy transfer and the use of good and best practice have been promoted in a variety of policy fields, and the discussion examines the value and extent of such approaches in the post enlargement reality. In the second half of the chapter the authors examine the diversity of planning traditions and practices in the heterogeneous landscape of spatial planning in Europe and assess the extent to which Europeanization has contributed to any sort of convergence. The chapter makes a valuable contribution to the rationale for the book through its examination of the interplay between knowledge (particularly expert knowledge) and policy development in the context of these wider processes and the role of diverse networks and communities in this context.

In Chapter 8 Marot explores the creation of new jurisdictions and responsibilities for the delivery of spatial planning in Slovenia. She carefully considers these changes to be an outcome of transitional processes or restructuring of political and socio-economic systems within and between new Member States, identifying a host of issues that arise through the creation of these jurisdictions and responsibilities for the delivery of spatial planning. The developmental impact of European enlargement takes on unique characteristics throughout many cities and regions. The consequences not only impact the objects of European enlargement, in other words the new EU Member States, but also the existing Member States or subjects of this process. In fact, the repercussions of European enlargement often involve significant changes caused by transitional processes within and between new Member States by way of socio-economic transformation and modified ways of life. On the one hand, new developments in economic activity and social mobility impact upon land use, while, on the other hand, they reflect the constantly changing needs of individuals. Furthermore, in often concerted efforts to accommodate these changes, new planning jurisdictions are created and planning responsibilities are assigned to deliver on spatial planning requirements. But along with these new planning jurisdictions and assignments comes a host of issues concerning planning delivery. Marot outlines some examples in addition to providing a thought provoking discussion on the delivery of spatial planning in Slovenia. First, the evolution of the Slovenian planning system and legislation is described along with the challenges posed in the context of scant resources and the rapid emergence of new jurisdictions. The small size of Slovenia has clear implications in terms of the extent and nature of the communities and networks engaged in policy development in the field of spatial planning, and the evolution of the territorial cohesion discourse is examined in this context. Finally, Marot uses Krtina to elucidate the challenges to delivering spatial planning in Slovenia, highlighting the implications of scant resources at the local level. The chapter makes a valuable contribution to the rationale for the book through its consideration of the role of knowledge and the role of expert communities in the rapid evolution of a planning system of a small country dealing with the realities and challenges of the post-enlargement EU.

In the first of the remaining two chapters Dąbrowski (Chapter 9) offers an insightful look at the challenges of civic engagement and the implementation of European Structural Funds. The author develops a two-fold approach that examines state efficiency and the potential evolution in institutional arrangements, whilst exploring the extent to which collective learning-by-practice has helped to free Government from organizational features inherited from its socialist past. Dąbrowski explores the possibility for regional planning delivery and the creation of new channels of civic participation in this context, exploring path-dependent notions of institutional change and the embeddedness of socio-cultural features of technocratic networks in Poland, and casting new light on cultural and legal dimensions of Europeanization. The author takes an insightful look at the practice of partnership and the development of civic society in Poland as it seeks to address its enduring socialist legacy, examining the potential for new channels of agent interactivity in the processes of regional policy formulation and the implementation of Structural Funds. First, the challenges of administrative reform when confronted with the realities of dealing with the socialist legacy are discussed. Dąbrowski explores these challenges through the formulation of regional policy and the creation of new channels of participation and focuses upon a case study examining the management of the structural funds in Lower Silesia. The case study allows various barriers to the notion of change to be examined and the implications for collective learning to be assessed. The rhetoric and reality of civic engagement, partnership and the establishment of technocratic networks are unpacked and ultimately the chapter challenges path-dependent notions of institutional change and 'social capital', as it sheds new light on cultural and legal dimensions of Europeanization.

The final contribution by Haselberger and Benneworth (Chapter 10) goes beyond the emphases on 'discursive European integration' of policy communities or networks (Böhme 2002) towards one that examines the influential tactics of agents in multi-jurisdictional environments of intersecting political and economic systems out of which new governance arrangements are created to bridge communication gaps. Using the dynamics of cross-border cooperation in the soft space consisting of the Austrian city-hinterland of the Slovakian capital Bratislava as an example, Haselberger and Benneworth draw out the challenges of multi-jurisdictional regional development, placing emphasis on agent reflexivity and learning. In this context, the authors explore the sustainability of long-standing decentralized cooperation structures that are not necessarily underpinned by policy communities or networks. They build on this attention to sustainable cooperation, held by many EU policy-makers, and explore cross-border planning in the complex governance context in which it is often administered. In light of this objective, the authors suggest cross-border planning can be a matter of perspective. That is, the fruits of cooperation processes often will be discursively framed by those involved, and by their interests in, and readiness for cooperation. Along the course of these planning processes, governance arrangements are made to bridge communication gaps within and between organizations. But the quality and depth of cooperation can be affected or jeopardized by the complexity of conflicting legal frameworks and unstable institutional partnerships, although these are not the only, or sometimes even the most influential threats to effective cross-border cooperation. In their closer look at cross-border cooperation, Haselsberger and Benneworth identify and discuss a multi-dimensional view of 'proximity' between agents in these complex environments, offering new insights into current debates on spatial governance and territorial identity. After an initial examination of the evolution of the concept of borders in the context of European planning and the evolution of cross-border planning in a multi-jurisdictional policy environment, the authors begin to explore the role of expert communities in these processes. The concepts of epistemic communities and communities of practice, two key features of the theoretical framework for this book, are examined in the context of the case study. The discussion provides valuable insights into the context of the roles of territorial knowledge communities in soft planning spaces and is therefore highly relevant and makes a valuable contribution to the theoretical framework for the book.

References

Adams, N., Alden, J. and Harris, N. (eds) (2006) *Regional Development and Spatial Planning in an Enlarged EU*, Aldershot: Ashgate.

Albrechts, L., Alden, J. and da Rosa Pires, A. (2001) *The Changing Institutional Landscape of Planning*, Aldershot: Ashgate.

Albrechts, L. and Mandelbaum, S. J. (2005) 'Introduction. A new context for planning?', in L. Albrechts and S. J. Mandelbaum (eds) *The Network Society. A new context for planning*, Abingdon: Routledge: 1–7.

Almendinger, P. and Tewdwr-Jones, M. (2000) 'Spatial dimensions and institutional uncertainties of planning and the new regionalism', *Environment and Planning C: Government and Policy*, 18: 711–772.

Altrock, U., Guntner, S., Huning, S. and Peters, D. (eds) (2006) *Spatial Planning and Urban Development in the New EU Member States: From Adjustment to Reinvention*, Aldershot: Ashgate.

Arthur, W. B. (1992) *Increasing Returns and Path Dependence in the Economy*, Ann Arbor: University of Michigan Press.

Benz, A. (2000) 'Two types of multi-level governance: Intergovernmental relations in German and EU regional policy', *Regional and Federal Studies*, 10(3): 21–44.

Brenner, N. (2004) *New State Spaces: urban governance and the rescaling of Statehood*, Oxford and New York: Oxford University Press.

Böhme, K. (2002) *Nordic Echoes of European Spatial Planning*, Stockholm: Nordregio.

Büchs, M. (2008) 'How legitimate is the open method of co-ordination?', *Journal of Common Market Studies*, 46(4): 765–786.

Clark, G, Tracey, P. and Lawton-Smith, H. (2003) 'Agents, endowments, and path-dependence: making sense of European regional development', *Revista Território*, September/October, 7(11–13), Rio de Janeiro.

Conzelmann, T. (1998) 'Europeanization of regional development policies? Linking multi-level governance approach with theories of policy learning and policy change', European Integration Online Papers (EIoP), 2(4), available online HTTP: http://eiop.or.at/eiop/texte/1998–004a.htm (accessed March 2010).

Davoudi, S. (2006) 'Evidence-based planning: Rhetoric or reality?', *disP*, 165, 42(2): 14–24.

Deas, I. and Lord, A. (2008) 'From a new regionalism to an unusual regionalism? The emergence of nonstandard regional spaces and lessons for the territorial reorganisation of the state', *Urban Studies*, 43(10): 1847–1877.

Dühr, S., Colomb, C. and Nadin, V. (2010) *European Spatial Planning and Territorial Co-operation*, London: Routledge.

Faludi, A. and Waterhout, B. (2006a) 'Introducing evidence-based planning', *disP*, 165, 42(2): 4–13.

Faludi, A. and Waterhout, B. (2006b) 'Debating evidence-based planning: Conclusions from the International Workshop', *disP*, 165, 42(2): 71–72.

Haas, P. (1992) 'Introduction: epistemic communities and international policy coordination', *International Organization*, 46(1): 1–35.

Haughton, G., Allmendinger, P., Counsell, D. and Vigar, G. (2010) *The New Spatial Planning: territorial management with soft spaces and fuzzy boundaries*, London: Routledge (RTPI Library Series).

Hooghe, L. and Marks, G. (2001) *Multi-level Governance and European Integration*, Oxford: Rowman & Littlefield.

Hillier, J. (2008) 'Plan(e) speaking: A multiplanar theory of spatial planning', *Planning Theory*, 7(1): 24–50.

Janin Rivolin, U. and Faludi, A. (2005) 'The hidden face of European spatial planning: Innovations in governance', *European Planning Studies*, 13(2): 195–215.

Kingdon, J. W. (1995) *Agendas, Alternatives and Public Policies*, 2nd edition, New York: Harper Collins.

Kohler-Koch, B. (1999) 'The evolution and transformation of European governance', in B. Kohler-Koch and R. Eising (eds) *The Transformation of Governance in the European Union*, London: Routledge.

Kooiman, J. (1993) 'Findings, Speculation and Recommendations', in J. Kooiman (ed.) *Modern Governance: New Government-Society Interactions*, London: Sage.

Nadin, V. (2002) 'Visions and visioning in European spatial planning', in A. Faludi (ed.) *European Spatial Planning*, Cambridge (MA): Lincoln Institute of Land Policy.

Pallagst, K. (2006) 'European spatial planning reloaded: Considering EU enlargement in theory and practice', *European Planning Studies*, 14 (2): 253–272.

Parsons, C. (2003) *A Certain Idea of Europe*, Ithaca: Cornell University Press.

Rhodes, R. (1996) 'The new governance: governing without government', *Political Studies*, 44(4): 652–667.

Rhodes, R. A. W. (1997) *Understanding Governance: Policy Networks, Governance, Reflexivity and Accountability*, Milton Keynes: Open University Press.

—— (1995) 'The role of knowledge in the policy process', *Journal of European Public Policy*, 2(2): 159–83.

Radaelli, C. M. (1999) 'The public policy of the European Union: whither politics of expertise?', *Journal of European Public Policy*, 6(5): 757–774.

Roness, P. G. (2001) 'Historical explanations, structural features and institutional characteristics', paper presented at 17th ESGOS Colloquium, Sub Themes 2 'Re-discovering
History in Studying Organizations', Lyon, France, July 2001.

Sabatier, P. (1988) 'An advocacy coalition framework of policy change and the role of
policy-oriented learning therein', *Policy Sciences*, 21: 129–168.

—— (1998) 'The advocacy coalition framework: revisions and relevance for Europe',
Journal of European Public Policy, 5(1): 98–130.

Scharpf, F. (2001) 'Notes toward a theory of multilevel governing', *Scandinavian Political Studies*, 24(1): 1–26.

—— (2002) 'The European social model: Coping with the challenges of diversity',
Journal of Common Market Studies, 40(4): 645–70.

Simon, H. (1956) 'Rational choice and the structure of environments', *Psychology
Review*, 63: 129–138.

—— (1997) *Models of Bounded Rationality: Empirically Grounded Reason*, Cambridge,
MA: MIT Press.

Stead, D. and Meijers, E. (2009) 'Spatial planning and policy integration: concepts, facilitators and inhibitors', *Planning Theory and Practice* 10(3), 317–332.

Tewdwr-Jones, M. (2004a) 'Spatial planning: principles, practices and cultures', *Journal
of Planning and Environment Law*, May: 560–569.

—— (2004b) 'Determinants of the form of territorial governance: assessing relation
between government, governance and spatial strategy-making'; copy available from
the author, Bartlett School of Planning, University College London, London.

Tewdwr-Jones, M. and Williams, R. H. (2001) *The European Dimension of British Planning*, London: Spon.

Waterhout, B. (2008) *The Institutionalization of European Spatial Planning*, Delft: IOS
Press.

Zito, A. R. (2001a) 'Epistemic communities, European Union governance and the public
voice', *Science and Public Policy*, 28(6): 465–476.

—— (2001b) 'Epistemic Communities, collective entrepreneurship and European integration', *Journal of European Public Policy* 8(4): 585–603.

7 Shifts in territorial governance and the Europeanization of spatial planning in Central and Eastern Europe

Dominic Stead and Vincent Nadin

Introduction

From the early 1990s, spatial planning in Europe has experienced rapid and sometimes radical reform. This is especially true for Central and Eastern Europe (CEE). The enlargement of the European Union, economic globalization, increasing competition, the sustainable development agenda, and demographic change have been key factors in shaping the speed and direction of change. At the same time, European-wide policy statements on spatial planning and the recognition of the critical spatial impacts of sectoral policies have been important in stimulating reforms. A wide range of transnational interregional and cross-border networking initiatives have influenced thinking about alternative approaches by exposing planning professionals to planning practices and policies in other countries. The result has been the 'Europeanization' of spatial planning in various ways, although this is not synonymous with the convergence of planning systems or planning approaches.

Cooperation and exchange assumes that dissemination of experiences will help to lead to overall improvements in the performance of spatial planning, and that practices and policies that are successful in one place can also be successful if transposed to another setting (Stone 2004). But notions and practices of spatial planning vary greatly among European countries. These differences are deeply embedded in the social, political and administrative cultures of countries and regions, and there are great divides, particularly between north and south, and west and east Europe. Such differences call into question the applicability of the direct transposition of 'best practices' and potentially put limits on the harmonization or convergence of spatial planning approaches. This is particularly true when considering the transposition of practices in spatial planning to the 'new' from the 'old' Member States (East and West for short), where conditions are fundamentally different.

The purpose of this chapter is to explain and chart general trends in spatial planning systems and policies in Europe with reference to countries of Central and Eastern Europe. It sets the scene for more detailed consideration of recent developments in particular countries. The chapter begins by drawing attention to important European territorial development issues and debates about the apparent Europeanization of spatial planning and convergence of systems and policies. This has taken place within the context of transnational networking, knowledge exchange, learning and policy transfer via European initiatives such as INTERREG and ESPON, both of which help to create and support the work of epistemic communities. We then consider the available evidence on the nature of change in spatial planning systems in Western and Eastern Europe, and offer some tentative conclusions on the impacts of Europeanization and the extent of convergence.

Common spatial development challenges

The UNECE strategy for sustainable quality of life in human settlements (UNECE 2000) outlines four key challenges for human settlements: globalization, European integration and market economy reforms, sustainable development and demographic change. Recent reforms of spatial planning in Europe have been fundamentally influenced by the requirement of governments to try to reconcile the competing demands that arise from these challenges. Arguably, the dominant themes have been the impact of globalization on national and local economies and political systems. There is widespread acceptance of liberal economic systems, with more reliance on market-oriented solutions and private (and often foreign) investment, increasing competition between cities, alongside rapid technological innovation, particularly in information and communications technologies. These trends have profound spatial or territorial effects, including increasing polarization of economic disparities with concentration of services, education and know-how in favoured metropolitan regions and increased social and economic segregation within cities (see also Kunzmann 2008).

For the new EU Member States, entry into the Single Market enhanced the prosperity of regions close to the west, but it also reinforced competition and helped lead to massive restructuring of both urban and rural economies. New Member States enjoyed some economic growth (although from a very low baseline and concentrated in a few main cities), whilst unemployment rates remained generally higher than in the old Member States. While there is some evidence of economic convergence at European level, there is often increasing divergence within Member States, especially in central and eastern Europe (CEC 2007; Ezcurra *et al.* 2007). Types and locations of employment have generally shifted from rural to urban creating new demands for travel and infrastructure. EU enlargement has been an important factor in raising agricultural productivity in Central and Eastern Europe, but this has been accompanied by sharp falls in rural employment (CEC 2008). The share of employment in the service sector, on the other hand, has increased rapidly. By 2005 it was about 60 per cent in many CEE countries, which is approaching the same situation as in Western economies (UNECE 2005).

The CEE region continues to face significant local, transboundary and international environmental problems (UNECE 2003). These include emissions of greenhouse gases, air and water pollution, biodiversity loss, waste generation, technological hazards and risks to human health caused by harmful chemicals. Transition countries in particular face the legacy of air, soil and water pollution due to outdated industrial technologies and lack of environmentally consistent policies. Despite progress in some of these areas, such as the reduction in emissions of some air pollutants and the decoupling of economic growth and energy consumption, more effective measures are needed to protect the environment and human health and close the 'implementation gap' (EEA 2007: 48).

In view of these trends, the situation in Central and Eastern Europe presents unique opportunities for promoting and conserving the environmental and built heritage. Cities and rural areas are generally less affected by the worst excesses of competition and the dispersal of residential, economic and service activities from cities, although there is a considerable legacy of industrial dereliction and underinvestment. This situation is compounded by rapid urbanization and long-term demographic trends. The population of most countries is getting older and more urban (and suburban). In 1970, 63 per cent of the population of UNECE countries lived in urban areas. By 2000, the figure was 72 per cent and by 2030 it is forecast to be 78 per cent (74 per cent in Eastern Europe) (United Nations 2006). At the same time cities are spreading quickly with excessive urban sprawl, declining inner city areas and associated shifts in demand on infrastructure and services (EEA 2006). Some countries, particularly in the south, are experiencing a demographic crisis with ageing and falling economically active population. Rural populations are declining and ageing rapidly with consequent problems in providing local public services.

Current spatial planning activities in Europe's newer Member States give priority to many of these issues and challenges (Buckley and Mini 2000; Stanilov 2007) though economic competitiveness and employment is the paramount concern. Economic restructuring has been particularly severe with the loss of old economic activities creating high unemployment and leaving behind large areas of vacant and sometimes derelict land in and around urban centres. New economic activities have emerged, often in 'unplanned' locations in the suburbs, especially along major roads. Better-off residents too have tended to move out of inner cities to new low-density suburban residential areas. Out-of-town shopping centres have been developed in peripheral locations around most large cities (Pucher and Buehler 2005). In Warsaw for example, nearly 30 out-of-town shopping centres and megastore complexes had been built in the suburbs of the city over the space of ten years up to 2002 (Transit Cooperative Research Program 2003).

This brief rehearsal of some of the more pressing spatial development issues for the EU, and especially the new Member States, explains why in some quarters there are strong demands for more effective territorial governance. Many of the problems described above are similar in all the EU Member States, both old and new. This has led to the assumption by some individuals and organizations that there are common solutions to these common problems. This is not however the case: there are also some profound social, economic and political differences across EU Member States (and also within certain countries), which make the possibility of common solutions (one size fits all) very unlikely.

Europeanization

Since the 1980s, there has been an increasing perception that transnational influences on spatial development are growing and that such trends are accentuated by the processes of European integration (Sykes 2008). Europeanization is the notion that national and sub-national policies and actions are being influenced by European polity (and also vice versa in some cases). The role of the EU is picked out as central to a process whereby rules, procedures, policy themes and norms (among other things) change in common directions. The EU provides a 'massive transfer platform' (Radaelli 2000) for the exchange and diffusion of information and ideas between its Member States (Bulmer and Padgett 2004) and others.

We explain the Europeanization concept here with reference to the flows of policy, information and experience among EU Member States and actors in three ways: (1) top-down (from the EU to the national level), (2) horizontal (between EU Member States) and (3) circular (from the national level to the EU and back to the national (adapted from Lenschow 2006). These relationships are closely linked to processes of learning (Bennett and Howlett 1992), policy transfer (Bomberg and Peterson 2000) and best practice (Vettoretto 2009). It is in these processes, characterized by the complex interplay of knowledge and policy-making, where epistemic communities play a fundamental role in the introduction and validation of knowledge, as outlined by the editors in the introduction to this volume.

Top-down

The EU is said to have a strong top-down impact on spatial planning systems, policies and processes in Member States (Börzel 1999). Whilst the EU does not have formal competence in the field of spatial planning, other EU sectoral policies in environment, transport, rural development and regional policy (among others) have considerable direct or indirect spatial impacts (Dühr *et al.* 2010; van Ravesteyn and Evers 2004). Radaelli (2000) explains how rules, procedures, norms and other informal 'ways of doing things' are first established at the level of the EU institutions and then diffused and institutionalized in the logic of domestic discourse, political structures and public policies. European law may trigger domestic change by prescribing specific institutional requirements with which Member States must comply, often explicitly directed at replacing existing domestic regulatory arrangements (Dühr *et al.* 2010; van Ravesteyn and Evers 2004).

Second, somewhat less directly, European policy or legislation may affect domestic arrangements by altering opportunity structures and hence the distribution of power and resources between domestic actors. For instance, the spatially discriminating effects of the Common Agricultural Policy have (rather counter-intuitively) been concentrated in the core area of Europe (Shucksmith *et al.* 2005).

Third, policy and action at the EU level may also promote change in the attitudes and expectations of domestic actors. This is a change in understanding of the nature or definition of a problem, or 'cognitive logic'. This is the principal top-down effect of the complex processes of transnational spatial policy-making in Europe, and particularly the EU's *European Spatial Development Perspective* (*ESDP*) (CEC 1999), the *Territorial Agenda* (DE Presidency 2007a) and the Council of Europe *Guiding Principles* (CEMAT 2000). All top-down influences will vary in effect in different places, but especially so for changes in attitudes in spatial planning because of the lack of institutional and legal frameworks for this at the EU level (cf. Börzel and Risse 2000). Care should also be taken not to interpret this as 'a question of the implementation of a single core policy document (the ESDP)' (Böhme *et al.* 2004: 1178). Rather this is a complex process of interactions and adaptations within multi-level governance structures, also involving bottom-up and horizontal effects (as explained below).

Horizontal

Horizontal, state-to-state transfer and learning processes can take place independently of EU influences, although EU institutions may be important facilitators. This happens notably through the EU's extensive committee structure that brings national policy-makers and opinion leaders into contact with each other in what might be described as 'knowledge arenas'. The exchange of ideas may diffuse into national practices (Lenschow 2006). The ESDP is one such example, being prepared by the intergovernmental 'Committee on Spatial Development' (CSD) (a community of experts exchanging and generating knowledge) and which during this process and after its publication has had the effect of 'shaping the minds of actors involved in spatial development' (Faludi 2001:664).

One of the most important stimulus for horizontal processes of Europeanization in spatial planning has been the INTERREG initiative (Colomb 2007; Dühr and Nadin 2007; Waterhout 2007). Because of INTERREG professional planners and other actors across Europe are now routinely involved in trans-boundary cooperation networks and exposed to new knowledge arenas where understandings of spatial planning development from the Member States are brought together (Dühr *et al.* 2007). In central and eastern Europe, the PHARE Programme has provided similar opportunities across a broad spectrum of areas, including administrative reforms and infrastructure and environment policies (Pallagst 2006; Stanilov 2007). The European Spatial Planning Observation Network for Territorial Development and Cohesion (ESPON) has provided cooperation opportunities for the planning research sector.

These horizontal activities have supported more informal top-down policy processes, and numerous authors have noted how they have influenced planning systems and policies across Europe by facilitating the sharing and dissemination of experiences and knowledge (Böhme *et al.* 2004; Dabinett 2006; Dabinett and Richardson 2005; Giannakourou 2005; Janin Rivolin 2003; Janin Rivolin and Faludi 2005; Pedrazzini 2005; Shaw and Sykes 2003; Tewdwr-Jones and Williams 2001). INTERREG and ESPON have generated a new discourse on European spatial development characterized by 'new policy ideas and language, new knowledge forms and policies, and new institutional forms for their application' (Böhme *et al.* 2004: 1178). However, the extent to which that exchange has made any significant impacts on practice is questionable. A study of transnational cooperation among eight countries in north-west Europe found that whilst EU funding was a strong incentive to develop joint projects, thinking tends 'to remain firmly locked in their territorial compartments' with 'little evidence of [...] adaptation of institutions or policies' (Dühr and Nadin 2007: 388; see also Dabinett 2006 on cooperation in the North Sea Region).

Circular

Various examples of circular processes of Europeanization and interactive exchanges can be found in relation to spatial planning. In these cases, actors at national and sub-national levels have sought to 'upload' domestic policy models and ideas to the EU and these have then filtered back down to the national, regional and local levels. In the process of preparing the *ESDP*, for example, the main protagonists in North-western Europe were particularly influential in shaping policy in the CSD (Faludi and Waterhout 2002; Faludi 2004) which was to be subsequently influential in reform of domestic planning systems and institutional change (Shaw and Sykes 2003; Davoudi and Wishardt 2005). The adoption of the concept of 'territorial cohesion' is one example where ideas already well established in France were uploaded to EU fora (Faludi 2004). These ideas were then reinterpreted at the European level and mixed with other influences, especially from the Netherlands (Waterhout 2007; Dühr *et al.* 2010). Similarly, the concepts of subsidiarity and proportionality that have become so important in Community policy-making are largely political concepts uploaded from Germany (see, for example, Estella 2002).

The combination of top-down, horizontal and bottom-up learning processes is difficult to distinguish clearly, especially for the countries of Western Europe where there have been very long-term collaborations affecting the world views or cognitive logic of the principal actors. The generation of knowledge among a tight-knit group of planning related experts (an epistemic community) has been a long and iterative process (Martin and Robert 2002). The effects are subtle and often not directly attributable to a certain initiative. The more recent activities and results of intensified INTERREG cooperation and ESPON research networks may yet contribute to a further Europeanization of spatial planning in the longer term both in terms of the consolidation of learning in the European arenas (cf. Waterhout Chapter 4) and their influence on practice at lower levels.

In the new Member States, the general process of Europeanization has been felt since the early 1990s with more rapid and profound impacts on attitudes and norms than in Western Europe (Batt and Wolczuk 1999; Grabbe 2001; O'Dwyer 2006). There has been very little circularity in learning (and this is perhaps also true of Southern Europe). This is because the new Member States have had to make rapid changes to their laws and policies to meet the demands of the *acquis communautaire*, bringing wide-ranging effects on administration, institutions and the distribution of competences (O'Dwyer 2006). In this climate of change, there may be less institutional resistance to policy change than in the old Member States (Grabbe 2001; Pietrzyk-Reeves 2008). Many new Member States have had to create new institutional arrangements for governance in general and for spatial planning in particular. Although these changes to formal institutions are for the most part yet to take practical effect, it may be that old power relations remain firmly in place (see for example Dąbrowski Chapter 9).

Policy transfer

The process of Europeanization entails transfer of policy ideas, institutions, models and programmes. The notion has received significant attention in policy studies though understood in varying ways (Stone 2004). Most studies have examined policy transfer between highly developed countries (e.g. Bennett 1991; Dolowitz and Marsh 1996, 2000; Majone 1991; Robertson 1991; Rose 1993, 2005; Stone 1999; Wolman 1992; Wolman and Page 2002). Enlargement has raised interest in policy transfer and learning between West and East Europe (for example Rose 1993; Randma-Liiv 2005; Stead *et al.* 2008). According to Rose (1993), policy transfer in Central and Eastern Europe was seen as a way of trying to catch up politically and/or economically. Politicians often see policy transfer as the quickest solution to many problems without having to reinvent the wheel (Rose 2005; Tavits 2003). Policy transfer is frequently regarded as a means of avoiding newcomer costs. Using the experience of other countries is cheaper because they have already borne the costs of policy planning and analysis, whereas creating original policies requires more resources (Randma-Liiv 2005). Transfer has been facilitated by EU initiatives for research, territorial cooperation and development assistance.

In the early 1990s supply-based policy transfer on the initiative of the donor was more predominant. Politicians and senior civil servants in Central and Eastern European countries had limited detailed know-how about governmental institutions in liberal democratic economies, and insufficient time to make the institutional and policy changes demanded of them. By the late 1990s, policy transfer became more demand-led, where recipient institutions were more active Randma-Liiv (2005). Either way, fundamental questions have been raised about the validity of transposing solutions from Western Europe to places with very different historical, cultural or political backgrounds (Stone 2004). Although policy transfer to Central and Eastern Europe and questions about its effectiveness are long-standing (Cherry 1986; Masser 1986), empirical evidence of its effectiveness is limited, especially in relation to spatial planning. An important lesson from case studies, especially from new EU Member States (Nedović-Budić 2001; Stead *et al.* 2008), is that policy transfer is not merely a matter of copying or emulation; successful policy transfer involves processes of learning, adaptation of borrowed tools and bespoke solutions (Nedović-Budić 2001). The European knowledge arena 'opens the door for a multilateral learning process' (Colomb 2007: 366) and thus potentially policy exchange, but we should not assume that policy transfer will automatically follow, or indeed, that it is always desirable.

Best and good practices

Whilst there may be limited potential for direct policy transfer, much attention has been paid to learning and the exchange of best (or good) practices. Indeed, the assumption that the dissemination of best practice can lead to policy change 'has become an accepted wisdom within national policies and programmes, as well as in international arenas and networks' (Bulkeley 2006: 1030). The implicit argument is that provision of information about the operation of projects or policies or initiatives in one place will help others to tackle problems in similar ways in other places. They will learn from others' experience and this will lead to policy changes. However, as explained below, best and good practice within the practice of cross-border and transnational cooperation on spatial planning may not get beyond the level of 'illustration' and thus will not constitute 'knowledge' in the sense of a conceptual understanding of problems and solutions.

Nevertheless, numerous European policy documents make reference to best practice, including the *White Paper on European Governance* (CEC 2001) and the revised *EU Sustainable Development Strategy* (CEC 2005). Documents citing the importance of best practice in spatial planning include the *ESDP* (CEC 1999), the *Thematic Strategy on the Urban Environment* (CEC 2006), the *Territorial Agenda* (DE Presidency 2007a) and the *Leipzig Charter on Sustainable Urban Cities* (DE Presidency 2007b).

The *ESDP* suggests that 'the exchange of good practices in sustainable urban policy [...] offers an interesting approach for applying ESDP policy options' (CEC 1999: 22). The Leipzig Charter on Sustainable Urban Cities (DE Presidency 2007b: 7) goes further in calling for 'a European platform to pool and develop best practice, statistics, benchmarking studies, evaluations, peer reviews and other urban research to support actors involved in urban development'. The Territorial Agenda of the European Union contains a whole annex of examples of 'best practices of territorial cooperation' (DE Presidency 2007a). Much of the funding connected to European spatial planning is directed to producing and exchanging case studies of best and good practices including INTERREG, INTERACT, URBACT and IPA (the successor to the PHARE programme). Environment programmes such as LIFE, LEADER do much the same, and even the European Research Framework Programme has directed attention to the production of best and good practice guides and comparisons on spatial planning and governance.

Despite all this activity, the impact of transfer of best practices is poorly understood, as is the extent to which the applicability of best practices in different contexts is considered. Assumptions about the universal value of best practices are especially questionable in transposition from the old to the new Member States where many of the critical conditions vary greatly in 'borrowing' and 'lending' countries. For example, in Central and Eastern Europe there are lower levels of 'trust' in the role of government (van Dijk 2002; Mason 1995), planning often has a much weaker place in government (Maier 1998) and a much shorter history (Adams 2008). This is notwithstanding the general antipathy towards planning in countries where the term is closely associated with central 'command and control' government. It is obvious that great care is needed in promoting Western European best practices to Central and Eastern Europe, but this is also true of transposing solutions north or south, or even between adjacent countries. Two brief examples of east-west transfer of 'best practice' help to illustrate this point.

St. Petersburg's strategic plan was partly funded by USAID under the condition that the strategy be based on experience in western cities (see also Razumeyko's Chapter 16). Officials from St. Petersburg had contact with plan-makers from Barcelona and other cities in Europe and the USA. In the event, both the plan-making process and the eventual strategic plan for St. Petersburg bore little resemblance to the best practice models, although inspiration from Barcelona (coupled with the leverage of the foreign financial and technical assistance) did result in the introduction of a participatory approach. In Wrocław (Poland) and Riga (Latvia), the German Federal Environment Agency funded two similar projects drawing on German best practices, to try to establish public transport executives (*Verkehrsverbünden*) as a way of promoting more integrated public transport. The intentions were worthy: more coordinated public transport services, common information and integrated ticketing. However, because the underlying conditions for organizing public transport is quite different in Poland, Latvia and Germany, the transfer of German best practice did not occur (Stead *et al.* 2008).

Much of the design and implementation of any project depends on the context and 'tacit' knowledge (personal experiences and commitments) (Bulkeley 2006) or 'knowledge in practice' (Schön 1983). Best practice is a codification of this knowledge but 'in formal language is often clumsy and imprecisely articulated' (Hartley and Allison 2002: 105). The factors that have led to success may be very unclear, especially in the absence of formal evaluation. Moreover, identifying best practice is often 'an exercise in informal polling' and may just represent 'the manifestation of the best advertising and most effective programmatic or municipal spin doctoring' (Wolman *et al.* 1994: 992). Yet best practice examples proliferate as 'success stories', 'winners' and benchmarks that can be useful in gaining competitive advantage for the example donors and in relationships with central government (Benz 2007; Lidström 2007; Carmichael 2005; Heinelt and Niederhafner 2008; Le Galès 2002). Not surprisingly, therefore, in their study of urban regeneration practice, Wolman and Page (2002) found that only a small minority of officials believe best practice plays a significant role in their decision-making. There is little reason to think that the situation may be much different in the field of spatial planning.

Trends in spatial planning in Europe

This section examines the case for a Europeanization of planning by reviewing the actual trends in planning systems and policies in Europe as part of the wider processes of reform of European territorial governance. However, identifying change in something as indeterminate as a 'planning system' or 'planning style' is a problem in itself. Measuring change is even more difficult. Before considering trends in spatial planning in new and old EU Member States we introduce the main sources of evidence.

We should stress at the outset the great variety of approaches to spatial planning. Nevertheless, there is wide agreement on general tendencies in 'traditions' or 'styles' of spatial planning that follow from their embeddedness in alternative social or welfare models (Nadin and Stead 2008). A small number of typologies of styles of spatial planning in Europe have been proposed (Nadin and Stead 2008) but they either ignore the countries of Central and Eastern Europe, treat them as one all-embracing category of 'socialist systems' or apply models from the west.

The *EU Compendium of Spatial Planning Systems and Policies* (CEC 1997) identified four ideal types or 'traditions of spatial planning' in Western Europe. The criteria used to develop the types include the constitutional and legal forms, the scope or breadth of topics addressed, the division of competences to national, regional and local governments, the relative roles of public and private sectors, the extent to which the system was established and enforced in society, and effectiveness of application of the system in shaping outcomes. These criteria are a (limited) range of indicators of the formal and informal institutional arrangements for spatial planning that have influence on the operation and outcomes of planning. The four major traditions of spatial planning proposed are 'ideal types' – and provide benchmarks against which real systems can be compared. The 'traditions' or ideal types are summarized in Figure 7.1 as overlapping, which is intended to illustrate the point that, in practice, any system will exhibit characteristics of more than one ideal type. We explain below how these traditions have had varying impact in the 'knowledge arenas' of European spatial planning. The planning traditions of Central and Eastern Europe are special cases that are being established or re-emerging. Until the 1990s, they were completely outside of any consideration of spatial planning typology, but Figure 7.1 shows them 're-engaging' with western European traditions.

The four 'traditions' of planning were used in a subsequent study of 29 countries, including the new EU Member States in Central and Eastern Europe (ESPON 2007). This ESPON sponsored study on *Governance of Territorial and Urban Policies from EU to Local Level* 'gives a modest update on the movements that took place since' the Compendium was completed in 1997 (ESPON 2007: 112). The report accepts the special position of Central and Eastern Europe by arguing for the term 'planning styles' rather than 'traditions' which are less relevant where there are more profound and complete shifts in approaches to planning. (It might be argued that at least some of these countries have returned to more traditional arrangements, especially as regards the organization of regional and local government.) The limited time available to the project meant that it was necessary to take the four styles created in a study of 15 countries of Western Europe as a given, and apply them to the new Member

States. There was no consideration of alternative or additional traditions or styles. Figure 7.1 indicates the current position of spatial planning styles in Central and Eastern Europe in relation to Western Europe's prevalent planning styles.

The ESPON *Governance* study involved an investigation through 'the government lens' considering reforms in the distribution of competences: state structures, decentralization processes, devolution of powers, the extent of power at the local level and inter-municipal cooperation. Part of the report addresses shifts in 'spatial planning styles'. The four *Compendium* traditions are taken as a starting point from which national experts working independently were asked 'to describe their perception of the style of planning which prevails' in their country (ESPON 2007, Annex B: 251). Unfortunately, this type of analysis rather distorts the Compendium approach as it treats the 'ideal types' as if they are

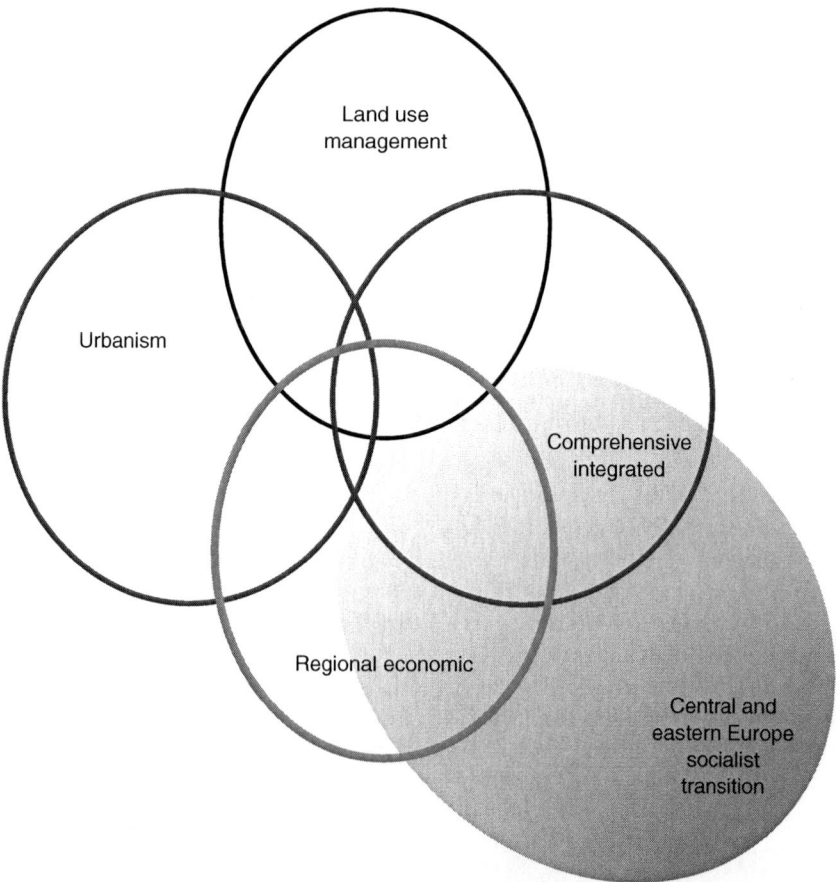

Figure 7.1 Models of spatial planning in Europe (source: Authors' elaboration on Dühr *et al.* 2010, who in turn draw inspiration from the *EU Compendium of Spatial Plans and Policies* (CEC 1997)).

mutually exclusive categories into which countries can be placed. This project's interpretation of the Compendium's ideal types is sometimes questionable although it does help to update our understanding of broad changes in styles of planning in Western Europe and provides a first overall assessment of styles of spatial planning in Central and Eastern Europe.

Western Europe

Before turning to governance and spatial planning reform in the new EU Member States, we first briefly set the context of recent developments in Western Europe. It has been widely recognized for some time that the general direction of spatial planning in Western Europe (given the great variation in starting points) is towards greater flexibility, the loosening of rigid zoning rules, more strategic planning paying more attention to the spatial impacts of sectoral policies, and stricter environmental and conservation controls (Albrechts 1997; Healey and Williams 1993; Healey 1997; Salet and Faludi 2000). More recently, Adams (2008) identifies a general trend towards more collaborative and communicative forms of planning in Western Europe. Allmendinger and Haughton (2007) from a UK perspective draw attention to the shifting scales of spatial planning and the cyclical or repetitive nature of change in response to changing planning doctrine, irresolvable tensions, and wider changes in institutional structures. These tendencies can be clearly seen in the recent path of western European spatial planning.

The dominance of rational procedural and public sector-led approaches in Northern Europe in the post-war era has given way to styles of planning that incorporate citizen and market interests. Most recently, the design of physical layout or the contribution of planning to the 'making of place' has been rediscovered (Hebbert 2006). Conversely, southern European countries, where the urbanism tradition has dominated, are experimenting more with regional strategic planning approaches (Janin Rivolin 2008). These changes reflect not only new problems but also the continuing and irresolvable tensions in planning (Allmendinger and Haughton 2007), especially concerning the need to provide for both certainty and flexibility. Planning also is affected by the more general regionalist trends in Europe, which argue in favour of more competences at regional, provincial and sometimes municipal levels, in efforts to ensure against the loss of competences for national governments (Netherlands Institute for Spatial Research 2006; Nadin and Stead 2008).

Central and Eastern Europe

The ESPON *Governance* report finds that the mixture of national planning is tending to increase (e.g. Portugal is embracing more land use regulation and the UK has moved towards the regional economic approach). The findings also suggest that the countries of Central and Eastern Europe are pressing forward in the creation of more 'comprehensive integrated' forms of spatial planning and to a lesser extent the 'regional economic approach'. It elaborates further on this by assessing the extent of 'comprehensiveness' in terms of the extent of coordination – 'vertical (between levels with competences in spatial planning) and horizontal (between policies with territorial impact)' (ESPON 2007: 41). The Baltic states of Estonia, Latvia and Lithuania, together with Poland and Slovakia, are judged to have 'strong vertical and horizontal coordination' of policymaking. Hungary and Romania are stronger on the vertical dimension of integration and Slovenia stronger on horizontal coordination. There are various qualifications to these observations, not least that intentions or innovation is often held back by lack of capacity and skills at particular points in the system – which arises in part from past traditions and planning cultures.

The overall conclusions of the ESPON *Governance* project support those of the Compendium of Spatial Plans and Policies and also offer some additional detail, especially on the shifting patterns and relations in governance. First, a variety of approaches to spatial planning can be found in the EU and within Central and Eastern Europe. Here, we should beware of any simple classifications. The organization of countries into common groupings will vary depending on the criterion that is given priority. Second, and despite this variation, the report concludes that adaptation is leading to a general convergence of planning systems, and particularly that the comprehensive integrated and regional economic planning styles are becoming more widespread. This supports other claims about the dominance of the 'north-western perspective' on spatial planning (Janin Rivolin and Faludi 2005) which through its elaboration in the ESDP and other documents, is gaining currency elsewhere. Furthermore it argues that these two styles are often combined in one system to create a style of 'neo-comprehensive integrated planning approach'. In a similar vein, Pallagst and Mercier (2007: 478) argue that the most likely outcome from reform in Central and Eastern Europe is a 'merger' of styles of spatial planning with those in Western Europe, rather than a 'retention' or reinforcing of difference.

Whilst the policy discourse in Central and Eastern Europe may have changed substantially over the last two decades or so, practice has not always followed suit. The ESPON *Governance* report recognizes this and warns that 'legislation and policy are valuable as pointers to change but can be misleading' (ESPON 2007: 285). The formal system in theory is one thing; practice may be quite different. This point is also underlined by other contributors to this volume (e.g. Dąbrowski Chapter 9). Undoubtedly, the dramatic economic and political changes in Central and Eastern Europe over the last two decades have had far-reaching consequences for spatial development and the institutional arrangements that are meant to guide them (Altrock *et al.* 2006; Stanilov 2007). However, the form of these changes in practice varies considerably across new Member States, and the reality is difficult to distinguish from the rhetoric (see for example Kule *et al.* Chapter 12).

There is no argument that the former planning systems concerned primarily with state construction projects (Thomas 1998) and with technical aspects of development (Maier 1998) quickly became irrelevant. But reform of planning has seldom been a priority for government, and old laws are still the formal legal basis for decisions in some places. The scale of change required in government is relevant here. For some countries, such as the Baltic states of Estonia, Latvia and Lithuania, entirely new institutional, economic and political systems were required (Downes 1996). More progress has been made since the late 1990s in overhauling planning legislation and institutional structures but many countries and regions are still in the process of developing 'good governance': the transparent, accountable decision-making processes and clear political leadership at the urban and regional levels that could support effective planning (OECD 2001). The implementation of governance reforms, often involving decentralization, was often driven by internal political demands and the requirements of early EU regional policy funding, with little consideration of the longer-term strategic issues (Pallagst and Mercier 2007).

Two decades after the fall of the Iron Curtain, the lack of progress on establishing more effective and democratic planning processes in some parts of Central and Eastern Europe is concerning. Even where the legal requirements are in place, progress in the development of new policy instruments is variable, institutional arrangements are not always complete and the influence of adopted plans and policies are sometimes still limited. Professional capacities are also variable and financial resources to lever the implementation of plans are sometimes lacking, especially where major investments in infrastructure are required (as noted by Maier Chapter 11). Democratization has often been accompanied by devolution and decentralization of competences in more complex multi-level governance arrangements but often without corresponding, but politically difficult, financial and fiscal reforms (Maier 1998; OECD 2001). The legacy of former planning on which new planning could be built is also quite variable (Nedović-Budić 2001). This is not to say however that there is no tradition of planning in Central and Eastern Europe. Various authors (e.g. Fisher 1966; Montias 1962; Shove and Anderson 1997) have highlighted the relative sophistication of the planning system and profession in some of these countries, despite the frequent lack of institutional support. Planning is certainly not a new notion for many parts of Central and Eastern Europe but its nature and rationale has changed significantly.

In sum, since the collapse of the centrally planned system of economic and territorial development, spatial planning has been neglected in many countries in transition (UNECE 2000). The introduction of new planning legislation and institutional structures has often taken a back seat whilst issues such as poverty or macro-economic stability have been dealt with (Tsenkova 2004). Due to its association with the communist regime, the idea of 'planning' has enjoyed little public support in Central and Eastern Europe (Nedović-Budić 2001; UNECE 2000). It has not been a priority for politicians (Shove and Anderson 1997) who have limited experience of the role of regulation in a mixed economy. Indeed the role of planning since the fall of Communism has gradually weakened: a process which Maier (1998 and also Chapter 11) contends began as early as the 1960s.

Whilst some cities retained strict land-use regulations and building codes, much new suburban and exurban development has taken place beyond the jurisdiction of urban authorities, where land-use regulations are often far less demanding, and where virtually any kind of development is permitted in order to attract local jobs, tax revenues and economic development (Pucher and Buehler 2005). During the 1990s planning in Central and Eastern Europe existed 'in an environment where the position of the public is weak in the face of strong private interests which often dominate over elected representatives' (Maier 1998: 362). This view might also be valid in parts of Western Europe but the scale of the problem is quite different. Tasan-Kok (2006) identifies three main problems in the implementation of planning reform: the lack of power of planning organizations and vague implementation processes (due to incomplete regulatory reform); the lack of efficient and effective instruments to regulate development and apply a more strategic and flexible general guidelines for development; and the lack of powers to implement the new plans. An additional problem is the lack of funds and reliance on external sources of finance in some cases (see for example Razumeyko's account of strategic planning in north-west Russia in Chapter 16).

Where progress has been made in establishing more effective spatial planning, it is likely that the requirement for spatial planning as a precondition for accessing EU funding has been important (Adams 2008; Mercier 2005). Despite wide recognition of the limitations of policy transfer and importing best practice as described above (see also Maier 1998), Western models are routinely followed (Mercier 2005), which again supports the notion of 'merger' suggested by Pallagst and Mercier. According to Jaakson, 'Western planning thought has become legitimized and is presented to the East as a culturally and socially superior model, based on the presumption that because the newly independent States are moving towards market economies, Western planning models are appropriate' (Jaakson 2000: 565).

Convergence?

In the context explained above and with strong pressures for Europeanization a measure of convergence of planning systems and policies might be expected. Some writers claim that this is the case although others are much more cautious. In 1994, Davies argued that the growth of mutual learning and cooperation at the regional and local levels of governments will result in 'a gradual convergence of planning policies and practices [... and that] evidence for this is already beginning to be apparent' (Davies 1994: 69). This is not to suggest any simplistic notion of planning styles gravitating to a common denominator. It is rather to argue that the natural diversity of planning styles that arise from the 'specific histories and geographies of particular places, and the way these interlock with national institutional structures, cultures and economic opportunities' (Healey and Williams 1993: 716), will now also manifest characteristics in common arising from the process of Europeanization.

In practice in the 1990s and 2000s it is quite obvious the EU has played a key role in the promotion of a 'European spatial planning agenda' (Colomb 2007), and that changes in practice have been shaped by 'European normative concepts and 'spatial planning ideas' developed within the European planning community (Böhme *et al.* 2004; Jensen and Richardson 2004). The evidence from the major comparative studies of planning systems presented above supports a measure of convergence in the general style of planning although in practice this may be more of an aspiration than a reality. The ESPON *Governance* report highlights the very diverse institutional arrangements within which planning activities play out in different countries, even within the new Member States.

Beyond these very general conclusions, more local studies tend to emphasize difference. Europeanization is certainly underway in the sense of vertical top-down influences from EU and other policies and actions, extensive exchange of experience, and a degree of 'clustered commonality' in experiences (Goetz 2006), but this does not necessarily lead to convergence (de Jong and Edelenbos 2007; Giannakourou 2005). Outside influences are viewed and understood from the local perspective and reinterpreted according to the local context and planning cultures (Börzel 2002; Nadin and Stead 2008). We also should not forget the dominance of national interests in politics: the willingness to share is limited and domestic systems persist and incorporate European themes according to their own institutional logic (de Jong *et al.* 2002; Knill 2001). So the Europeanization process tends to produce varying outcomes in different places or, to put it another way, there are 'differential responses to European policies' (Héritier *et al.* 2001: 257). Moreover, non-convergence may be strength. De Jong and Edelenbos (2007: 704) for example argue that 'continued variety has a greater potential to offer innovative solutions to evolutionary problems'.

In a study of the Europeanization of spatial planning in Southern Europe, Giannakourou (2005) argues that the mechanisms and structures of spatial planning in these countries are neither homogenous nor convergent. On the contrary, she argues that the Europeanization process cannot be identified with hard institutional convergence of domestic policy styles but rather follows soft and alternative paths of socialization and learning, causing at different times different degrees of domestic change. Similarly, Jordan and Liefferink (2004), reporting the results of a comparative study on the Europeanization of national environmental policy in ten countries, conclude that evidence for convergence towards a single model is lacking and that policy styles and structures continue to diverge. Adams (2008) compares spatial planning systems in the United Kingdom and in the Baltic States and reports that, in many respects (e.g. plan focus, plan preparation time, appraisal processes, implementation, monitoring and review), convergence is not evident despite the fact that most plans have a similar structure and topic coverage.

Furthermore, should spatial planning converge, there is no guarantee that outcomes or development patterns will also converge (see also Lenschow *et al.* 2005). Van Dijk (2002) argues that the way in which actors respond to the actions of government and citizens will differ from country to country according to local culture shaped by history, traditions, customs and social models. Considering convergence in an economic sense, Ezcurra *et al.* (2007) argue that, whilst current European regional policy measures appear to be supporting economic convergence between Member States, these processes are simultaneously fuelling increasing internal disparities within many Member States, where national growth continues to be driven by a small number of dynamic regions, usually where the largest urban centres are situated.

For the new EU Member States, the process of Europeanization is arguably faster, and the extent of change is more profound (Batt and Wolczuk 1999; Grabbe 2001; O'Dwyer 2006). Without doubt a shift in approaches has begun, which has taken on board Western European practices. In these new administrations national elites may be more open to external influence (Batt and Wolczuk 1999), and there may be less institutional resistance (or more 'malleable institutions') than in the 'older' Member States (Goetz 2006; Grabbe 2001). However, this in itself does not signify convergence.

Conclusions

This chapter has reviewed the general conditions that are contributing to the Europeanization of spatial planning, the mechanisms of policy transfer, learning and good practice that underlie this process, and the evidence for a coming together of traditions or styles of spatial planning particularly for Central and Eastern Europe. All European countries face common spatial development challenges; there are agreed European-wide policy statements on the form and content of spatial planning; and there is extensive interaction of actors and exchange of experience across European countries through transnational cooperation, sharing of best practice and policy transfer. The *ESDP* itself says that 'the requirement for a "Europeanization of state, regional, and urban planning" is increasingly evident' (CEC 1999: 45).

Various European initiatives, particularly INTERREG and ESPON, have helped to create and support epistemic communities in spatial planning. It is not always the case, however, that epistemic communities are behind Europeanization processes or help lead to policy convergence or policy innovation. It has for example been argued that epistemic communities can also sometimes lead to very technocratic and conservative policy outcomes, particularly in cases where institutional capacity is limited (see, for example, Stevens 2004, who discusses the situation in relation to policy-making processes in the European Commission where in-house technical expertise is scarce).

There is some evidence of common general trends in the style of spatial planning at least in the objective to provide more 'comprehensive integrated systems' that address vertical and horizontal coordination of spatial policy. These formal objectives are not realized in practice, especially in the new Member States that are lagging in establishing meaningful spatial planning. Alongside common general objectives for styles of planning across Europe, at the local level we see a continuing diversity of spatial planning systems and policies from country to country. There is certainly evidence of Europeanization in the sense of sharing knowledge about planning theory and practices and mutual learning about territorial management within specialized 'knowledge communities'. There appears to be an acceptance of general shared principles as set out in European level policy documents and much exchange of experience, but there should be no simplistic projection of this exchange into convergence of spatial planning. In practice, local conditions and traditions tend to demand specific approaches and maintain diversity. Consequently, we seem to be witnessing the contemporaneous Europeanization and diversification of spatial planning.

References

Adams, N. (2008) 'Convergence and policy transfer: an examination of the extent to which approaches to spatial planning have converged within the context of an enlarged EU', *International Planning Studies*, 13(1): 31–49.

Adams, N., Alden, J. and Harris, N. (2006) *Regional Development and Spatial Planning in an Enlarged European Union*, Aldershot: Ashgate.

Albrechts, L. (1997) 'Genesis of a Western European spatial policy', *Journal of Planning Education and Research*, 17: 158–167.

Allmendinger, P. and Haughton, G. (2007) 'The fluid scales and scope of UK spatial planning', *Environment and Planning A*, 39(6): 1478–1496.

Altrock, U., Günter, S., Huning, S. and Peters, D. (2006) *Spatial Planning and Urban Development in the New Member States: From Adjustment to Reinvention*, Aldershot: Ashgate.

Batt, J. R. and Wolczuk, K. (1999) 'The political context: building new states', in P. Hare, J. Batt and S. Estrin (eds) *Reconstituting the Market: The Political Economy of Microeconomic Transformation*, Amsterdam: Harwood Academic Publishers: 33–48.

Bennett, C. J. (1991) 'How states utilize foreign evidence', *Journal of Public Policy*, 11(1): 31–54.

Bennett, C. and Howlett, M. (1992) 'The lessons of learning: reconciling theories of policy learning and policy change', *Policy Sciences*, 25(3): 275–294.

Benz, A. (2007) 'Inter-regional competition in co-operative federalism: new modes of multi-level governance in Germany', *Regional & Federal Studies*, 17(4): 421–436.

Böhme, K., Richardson, T., Dabinett, G. and Jensen, O. B. (2004) 'Values in a vacuum? Towards an integrated multilevel analysis of the governance of European space', *European Planning Studies*, 12(8): 1175–1188.

Bomberg, E. and Peterson, J. (2002) *Policy Transfer and Europeanization: Passing the Heineken Test?* Queen's Papers on Europeanization 2/2000, School of Politics, International Studies and Philosophy, Queen's University of Belfast.

Börzel, T. A. (1999) 'Towards convergence in Europe? Institutional adaptation to Europeanization in Germany and Spain', *Journal of Common Market Studies*, 37(4): 573–596.

—— (2002) *States and Regions in the European Union: Institutional Adaptation in Germany and Spain*, Cambridge: Cambridge University Press.

Börzel, T. A. and Risse, T. (2000) 'When Europe hits home: Europeanization and domestic change', *European Integration Online Papers* (EIoP) 4, Online. Available HTTP: http://eiop.or.at/eiop/texte/2000–015a.htm (31 March 2009).

Buckley, R. M. and Mini, F. (2000) *From Commissars to Mayors: Cities in the Transition Economies*, Washington DC: The World Bank.

Bulkeley, H. (2006) 'Urban sustainability: learning from best practice?' *Environment and Planning A*, 38(6): 1029–1044.

Bulmer, S. and Padgett, S. (2004) 'Policy transfer in the European Union: an institutionalist perspective', *British Journal of Political Science*, 35: 103–126.

Carmichael, L. (2005) 'Cities in the multi-level governance of the European Union', in M. Haus, H. Heinelt and M. Stewart, M. (eds) *Urban Governance and Democracy: Leadership and Community Involvement*, London: Routledge: 129–148.

CEC – Commission of the European Communities (1997) *The EU Compendium of Spatial Planning Systems and Policies*, Luxembourg: Office for the Official Publications of the European Communities.

—— (1999) *The European Spatial Development Perspective*, Luxembourg: Office for the Official Publications of the European Communities.

—— (2001) *White Paper on European Governance*, COM(2001)428 final, Luxembourg: Office for the Official Publications of the European Communities.

—— (2005) *Review of the Sustainable Development Strategy: A Platform for Action*, COM(2005)658 final, Luxembourg: Office for the Official Publications of the European Communities.

—— (2006) *Communication from the Commission to the Council and the European Parliament on Thematic Strategy for the Urban Environment*, COM(2005)718 final, Luxembourg: Office for the Official Publications of the European Communities.

—— (2007) *Growing Regions, Growing Europe: Fourth Report on Economic and Social Cohesion*, Luxembourg: Office for the Official Publications of the European Communities.

—— (2008) *Report on Rural Development in the European Union: Statistical and Economic Information*, Luxembourg: Office for the Official Publications of the European Communities.

CEMAT, Conference of Ministers of Spatial Planning, Council of Europe (2000) *Guiding Principles for Sustainable Spatial Development of the European Continent*, Strasbourg: Council of Europe.

Cherry, G. (1986) 'Problems in cross-national research: an east European perspective', in I. Masser and R. H. Williams (eds) *Learning from other Countries*, Norwich: Geo Books: 59–63.

Colomb, C. (2007) 'The added value of transnational cooperation: towards a new framework for evaluating learning and policy change', *Planning Practice and Research*, 22(3): 347–372.

Dabinett, G. (2006) 'Transnational spatial planning: insights from practices in the European Union', *Urban Policy and Research*, 24(2): 283–290.

Dabinett, G. and Richardson, T. (2005) 'The Europeanization of spatial strategy: shaping regions and spatial justice through governmental ideas', *International Planning Studies*, 10(3–4): 201–218.

Dąbrowski, M. (2010) 'Institutional change, partnership and regional networks: civic engagement and the implementation of the Structural Funds in Poland', in N. Adams, G. Cotella and R. Nunes (eds) *Territorial Development, Cohesion and Spatial Planning: Knowledge and policy development in an enlarged EU*, London: Routledge.

Davies, H. W. E. (1994) 'Towards a European planning system?', *Planning Practice and Research*, 9(1): 63–69.

Davoudi, S. and Wishardt, M. (2005) 'The polycentric turn in the Irish spatial strategy', *Built Environment*, 31(2): 122–132.

DE Presidency (2007a) *Territorial Agenda of the European Union: Towards a More Competitive and Sustainable Europe of Diverse Regions*, agreed at the occasion of the Informal Ministerial Meeting on Urban Development and Territorial Cohesion on 24/25 May 2007. Online. Available HTTP: www.bmvbs.de/territorial-agenda (accessed 31 March 2009).

—— (2007b) *Leipzig Charter on Sustainable European Cities*, agreed at the occasion of the Informal Ministerial Meeting on Urban Development and Territorial Cohesion on 24/25 May 2007. Online. Available HTTP: www.bmvbs.de/en/dokumente/-, 1872.982774/Artikel/dokument.htm (accessed 31 March 2009).

Dijk, T. van (2002) 'Export of planning knowledge needs comparative analysis: the case of applying western land consolidation experience in central Europe', *European Planning Studies*, 10(7): 911–922.

Dolowitz, D. and Marsh, D. (1996) 'Who learns from whom: a review of the policy transfer literature', *Political Studies*, 44(2): 343–357.

—— (2000) 'Learning from abroad: the role of policy transfer in contemporary policy making', *Governance*, 13(1): 5–24.

Downes, R. (1996) 'Regional policy development in central and eastern Europe', in J. Alden and P. Boland (eds) *Regional Development Strategies: A European Perspective*, London: Jessica Kingsley and Regional Studies Association: 256–272.

Dühr, S. and Nadin, V. (2007) 'Europeanization through transnational cooperation: the case of INTERREG IIIB North-west Europe', *Planning Practice and Research*, 22(3): 373–394.

Dühr, S., Colomb, C. and Nadin, V. (2010) *European Spatial Planning and Territorial Cooperation*, London: Routledge.

Dühr, S., Stead, D. and Zonneveld, W. (2007) 'The Europeanization of spatial planning through territorial cooperation', *Planning Practice and Research*, 22(3): 291–307.

Estella, A. (2002) *The EU principle of subsidiarity and its critique*, Oxford: Oxford University Press.

EEA – European Environment Agency (2006) *Urban Sprawl in Europe: the Ignored Challenge*, Copenhagen: EEA.

—— (2007) *Europe's Environment: The Fourth Assessment*, Copenhagen: EEA.

ESPON (2006) *ESPON 3.2 – Spatial Scenarios and Orientations in relation to the ESDP and Cohesion Policy, Final Report*, Luxembourg: ESPON.

—— (2007) ESPON 2.3.2 – *Governance of Territorial and Urban Policies from EU to Local Level. Final Report*, Luxembourg: ESPON.

Ezcurra, R., Pascual, P. and Rapun, M. (2007) 'The dynamics of regional disparities in central and eastern Europe during transition', *European Planning Studies* 15(10): 1397–1421.

Faludi, A. (2001) 'The application of the European Spatial Development Perspective: evidence from the north-west metropolitan area', *European Planning Studies*, 9(5): 663–75.

—— (2004) 'The European Spatial Development Perspective and north-west Europe: application and the future', *European Planning Studies*, 12(3): 391–408.

Faludi, A. and Waterhout, B. (2002) *The Making of the European Spatial Development Perspective*, London: Routledge.

Fisher, J. C. (ed.) (1966) *City and Regional Planning in Poland*, Ithaca NY: Cornell University Press.

Giannakourou, G. (2005) 'Transforming spatial planning policy in Mediterranean countries: Europeanization and domestic change', *European Planning Studies*, 13(2): 319–332.

Goetz, K. H. (2006) *Territory, Temporality and Clustered Europeanization*, IHS Political Science Series No. 109, Vienna: Institute for Advanced Studies (IHS).

Grabbe, H. (2001) 'How does Europeanization affect CEE governance? Conditionality, diffusion and diversity', *Journal of European Public Policy*, 8(4): 1013–1031.

Hartley, J. and Allison, M. (2002) 'Good, better, best? Inter-organizational learning in a network of local authorities', *Public Management Review*, 4(1): 101–118.

Healey, P. (1997) 'The revival of strategic spatial planning in Europe', in P. Healey, A. Khakee, A. Motte and B. Needham (eds) *Making Strategic Spatial Plans: Innovation in Europe*, London: UCL Press.

Healey, P. and Williams, R. H. (1993) 'European planning systems: diversity and convergence', *Urban Studies*, 30(3/4): 701–720.

Hebbert, M. (2006) 'Town planning versus urbanismo', *Planning Perspectives*, 21(3): 233–251.

Heinelt, H. and Niederhafner, S. (2008) 'Cities and organized interest intermediation in the EU multi-level system', *European Urban and Regional Studies*, 15(2): 173–187.

Héritier, A., Kerwer, D., Knill, C. and Lehmkuhl, D. (2001) *Differential Europe: The European Union Impact on National Policy-making*, Lanham: Rowman and Littlefield.

Jaakson, R. (2000) 'Supra-national spatial planning of the Baltic Sea Region and competing narratives for tourism', *European Planning Studies*, 8(5): 565–579.

Janin Rivolin, U. (2003) 'Shaping European spatial planning: how Italy's experience can contribute', *Town Planning Review*, 74(1): 51–76.

—— (2008) 'Conforming and performing planning systems in Europe', *Planning Practice and Research*, 23(2): 167–186.

Janin Rivolin, U. and Faludi, A. (2005) 'The hidden face of European spatial planning: innovations in governance', *European Planning Studies*, 13(2): 195–216.

Jensen, O. B. and Richardson, T. (2004) *Making European Space: Mobility, Power and Territorial Identity*, Routledge: London.

Jong, M. de and Edelenbos, J. (2007) 'An insider's look into policy transfer in transnational expert networks', *European Planning Studies*, 15(5): 687–706.

Jong, M. de, Lalenis, K. and Mamadouh, V. (2002) *The Theory and Practice of Institutional Transplantation. Experiences with the Transfer of Policy Institutions.* Dordrecht: Kluwer Academic Publishers.

Jordan, A. and Liefferink, D. (eds) (2004) *Environment Policy in Europe: The Europeanization of National Environmental Policy*, London: Routledge.

Knill, C. (2001) *The Europeanization of National Administrations: Pattern of Institutional Change and Persistence*, Cambridge: Cambridge University Press.

Kule, L., Krisjane, Z. and Berzins, M. (2010) 'The rhetoric and reality of pursuing territorial cohesion in Latvia', in N. Adams, G. Cotella and R. Nunes (eds) *Territorial Development, Cohesion and Spatial Planning: Knowledge and policy development in an enlarged EU*, London: Routledge.

Kunzmann, K. (2008) 'Futures for European space 2020', *Journal of Nordregio*, 8(2): 12–21.

Le Galès, P. (2002) *European Cities. Social Conflicts and Governance*, Oxford: Oxford University Press.

Lenschow, A., Liefferink, D. and Veenman, S. (2005) 'When the birds sing. A framework for analyzing domestic factors behind policy convergence', *Journal of European Public Policy*, 12(5): 1–20.

Lenschow, A. (2006) 'Europeanization of public policy', in J. Richardson (ed.) *European Union – Power and Policy Making*, Third edition. London: Routledge: 55–71.

Lidström, A. (2007) 'Territorial governance in transition', *Regional and Federal Studies*, 17(4); 499–508.

Maier, K. (1998) 'Czech planning in transition: assets and deficiencies', *International Planning Studies*, 3(3): 351–365.

—— (2010) 'The pursuit of balanced territorial development: the realities and complexities of the cohesion agenda', in N. Adams, G. Cotella and R. Nunes (eds) *Territorial Development, Cohesion and Spatial Planning: Knowledge and policy development in an enlarged EU*, London: Routledge.

Majone, G. (1991) 'Cross-national sources of regulatory policymaking in Europe and the United States', *Journal of Public Policy*, 11(1): 79–106.

Martin, D. and Robert, J. (2002) 'Influencing the development of European spatial planning', in A. Faludi (ed.) (2002) *European Spatial Planning*, Cambridge, Mass, Lincoln Institute: 39–58.

Mason, D. (1995) 'Attitudes towards the market and political participation in the postcommunist states', *Slavic Review*, 54(2): 385–406.

Masser, I. (1986) 'The transferability of planning experience between countries', in I. Masser and R. H. Williams (eds) *Learning from Other Countries*, Norwich: Geo Books: 165–175.

Mercier, G. (2005) 'Which territorial cohesion policy for the new EU members? The example of Slovakia', *Town Planning Review*, 76(1): 57–68.

Montias, J. M. (1962) *Central Planning in Poland*, New Haven CT: Yale University Press.

Nadin, V. and Stead, D. (2008) 'European spatial planning systems, social models and learning', *DisP* 44(1): 35–47.

Nedović-Budić, Z. (2001) 'Adjustment of planning practice to the new eastern and central European context', *Journal of the American Planning Association*, 67(1): 38–52.

Netherlands Institute for Spatial Research (2006) *Spatial Outlook 2006. Spatial Planning Between Government and the Market* – English summary, The Hague: Netherlands Institute for Spatial Research (RPB). Online. Available HTTP: www.pbl.nl/nl/publicaties/rpb/2006 (accessed 31 March 2009).

O'Dwyer, C. (2006) 'Reforming regional governance in east central Europe: Europeanization or domestic politics as usual?', *East European Politics and Societies*, 20(2): 219–253.

OECD (2001) *Cities for Citizens: Improving Metropolitan Governance*, Paris: OECD.

Olsen, J. P. (2002) 'The many faces of Europeanization', *Journal of Common Market Studies*, 40(5): 921–952.

Pallagst, K. M. (2006) 'European spatial planning reloaded: considering EU enlargement in theory and practice', *European Planning Studies*, 14(2): 253–272.

Pallagst, K. M. and Mercier, G. (2007) 'Urban and regional planning in central and eastern European countries: from EU requirements to innovative practices', in K. Stanilov (ed.) *The Post-Socialist City Urban Form and Space Transformations in Central and Eastern Europe after Socialism*, Dordrecht: Springer: 473–490.

Pedrazzini, L. (2005) 'Applying the ESDP through INTERREG IIIB: A southern perspective', *European Planning Studies*, 13(2): 297–317.

Pietrzyk-Reeves, D. (2008) 'Weak civic engagement? Post-communist participation and democratic consolidation', *Polish Sociological Review*, 1(161): 73–87.

Pucher, J. and Buehler, R. (2005) 'Transport policy in post-communist Europe', in K. Button and D. Hensher (eds) *Handbook of Transport Strategy, Policy and Institutions*, Oxford: Elsevier: 725–743.

Radaelli, C. M. (2000) 'Wither Europeanization? Concept stretching and substantive change', *European Integration Online Papers*, 4(8): 1–27.

Randma-Liiv, T. (2005) 'Demand- and supply-based policy transfer in Estonian public administration', *Journal of Baltic Studies*, 36(4): 467–487.

Ravesteyn, N. van, and Evers, D. (2004) *Unseen Europe: A Survey of EU Politics and its Impact on Spatial Development in the Netherlands*, The Hague: Ruimtelijk Planbureau.

Razumeyko, N. (2010) 'Strategic Planning Practices in North-West Russia: European Influences, Challenges and Future Perspectives', in N. Adams, G. Cotella and R. Nunes (eds) *Territorial Development, Cohesion and Spatial Planning: Knowledge and policy development in an enlarged EU*, London: Routledge.

Robertson, D. (1991) 'Political conflict and lesson-drawing', *Journal of Public Policy* 11(1): 55–78.

Rose, R. (1993) *Lesson-drawing in public policy: A Guide to Learning across Time and Space*, New Jersey: Chatham House.

—— (2005) *Learning from Comparative Public Policy: A Practical Guide*, London: Routledge.

Salet, W. and Faludi, A. (2000) *The Revival of Strategic Spatial Planning*, Amsterdam: Edita KNAW.

Schön, D. A. (1983) *The Reflective Practitioner: How Professionals Think in Action*, New York: Basic Books.

Shaw, D. and Sykes, O. (2003) 'Investigating the application of the European Spatial Development Perspective (ESDP) to regional planning in the United Kingdom', *Town Planning Review*, 74(1): 31–50.

Shove, C. and Anderson, R. (1997) 'Russian city planning, democratic reform, and privatization: emerging trends', *Journal of Planning Education and Research*, 16(3): 212–221.

Shucksmith, M., Thomson, K. J. and Roberts, D. (2005) *The CAP and the Regions: The Territorial Impact of the Common Agricultural Policy*, Wallingford, CABI Publishing.

Stanilov, K. (2007) 'Urban development policies in Central and Eastern Europe during the transition period and their impact on urban form', in K. Stanilov (ed.) *The Post-Socialist City Urban Form and Space Transformations in Central and Eastern Europe after Socialism*, Dordrecht: Springer: 347–359.

Stead, D., de Jong, M. and Reinholde, I. (2008) 'Urban transport policy transfer in Central and Eastern Europe'. *DisP* 44(1) 62–73.

Stevens, H. (2004) *Transport Policy in the European Union*, Basingstoke: Palgrave Macmillan.

Stone, D. (1999) 'Learning lessons and transferring policy across time, space and disciplines', *Politics*, 19(1): 51–59.

—— (2004) 'Transfer agents and global networks in the "transnationalization" of policy', *Journal of European Public Policy*, 11(3): 545–566.

Sykes, O. (2008) 'The importance of context and comparison in the study of European spatial planning', *European Planning Studies*, 16(4): 537–555.

Tasan-Kok, T. (2006) 'Institutional and spatial change', in S. Tsenkova and Z. Nedovic-Budic (eds) *Urban Mosaic of Post-Socialist Europe: Space, Institutions and Policy*, Heidelberg: Physica-Verlag: 51–70.

Tavits, M. (2003) 'Policy learning and uncertainty: the case of pension reform in Estonia and Latvia', *Policy Studies Journal*, 31(4): 643–660.

Tewdwr-Jones, M. and Williams, R. H. (2001) *The European Dimension of British Planning*, London: Spon Press.

Thomas, M. J. (1998) 'Thinking about planning in the transitional countries of central and Eastern Europe', *International Planning Studies*, 3(3): 321–333.

Transit Cooperative Research Program (2003) *Transit Operations in Central and Eastern Europe. International Transit Studies Program Report on the Fall 2002 Mission*, Research Results Digest Number 62, Washington DC: Transit Cooperative Research Program.

Tsenkova, S. (2004) *Urban Sustainability. Progress and Challenges in Europe and North America*, Geneva: United Nations Economic Commission for Europe (UNECE).

UNECE (2000) *ECE Strategy for Sustainable Quality of Life in Human Settlements in the 21st Century*, Report HBP/1999/4/Rev.1, Geneva: United Nations Economic Commission for Europe.

—— (2003) *Sustainable Development of Human Settlements in the UNECE Region*, Progress and Challenges (ECE/AC.25/2004/4), Economic and Social Council, Geneva: United Nations Economic Commission for Europe.

—— (2005) *Trends in Europe and North America – The Statistical Pocketbook of the Economic Commission for Europe*, New York: United Nations.

United Nations (2006) *World Urbanization Prospects: The 2005 Revision*, New York: United Nations.

Vettoretto, L. (2009) 'A preliminary critique of the best and good practices approach in European spatial planning and policy-making', *European Planning Studies*, 17(7) 1067–1083.

Waterhout, B. (2007) 'Episodes of Europeanization of Dutch national spatial planning', *Planning Practice and Research*, 22(3): 309–327.

—— (2010) 'European spatial planning: current state and future challenges', in N. Adams, G. Cotella and R. Nunes (eds) *Territorial Development, Cohesion and Spatial Planning: Knowledge and policy development in an enlarged EU*, London: Routledge.

Wolman, H. (1992) 'Understanding cross national policy transfers: the case of Britain and the U.S.', *Governance: An International Journal of Policy and Administration*, January: 27–45.

Wolman, H., Ford, C. C. and Hill, E. W. (1994) 'Evaluating the success of urban success stories', *Urban Studies*, 31(6): 835–850.

Wolman, H., Hill, E. W. and Furdell, K. (2004) 'Evaluating the success of urban success stories: is reputation a guide to best practice?', *Housing Policy Debate*, 15(4): 965–997.

Wolman, H. and Page, E. (2002) 'Policy transfer among local governments: an information theory approach', *Governance*, 15(4): 477–501.

8 New planning jurisdictions, scant resources and local public responsibility

Delivering spatial planning in Slovenia

Naja Marot

Introduction

Slovenia obtained independence in 1991. This year not only represents an important shift in political terms, but it also has brought significant changes in public perceptions of real property. The status of the democratic republic Slovenia implied a change of the economy from nationally regulated to free market oriented (SSDS 2004: 13). Land ceased to be managed only by the State and equally accessible for all, and became open to the private initiatives and investment interests of many actors (Blagajne and Santej 2001). Not only the market but also public policies and regulations, territorial development legislation among them, had to adapt to this new reality. In less than 20 years since Slovenian independence, three spatial planning acts already have been adopted. But, for the moment, none of these acts have been regarded as successful in handling the transformation of the Slovenian planning system.

Redefining the organization and the purpose of a spatial planning system is an enormous challenge, especially under the pressure of the constant inflow of changes in European and wider global policies and economy. After gaining a new geopolitical position in Europe and entering newly established international relations (SSDS 2004: 13), the pre-accession period started in 1993 with the Copenhagen declaration. This period meant that recently formulated national polices and institutions would have to be reshaped to meet the increasingly demanding development challenges. The need for additional policy and institutional adaptation became even more evident when Slovenia formally entered the EU in 2004, becoming officially entitled to the whole range of benefits and constraints of the Union. Although there is no common European planning law, some guidelines and initiatives for a more comprehensive approach to spatial development do exist at the EU level. Additionally, funding is available through the EU Cohesion Policy where, for the 2007–2013 programming period, the whole area of Slovenia constitutes two NUTS2[1] convergence regions which compete and cooperate on the international level (European Regional Policy 2007). In such a mixture of present challenges and future opportunities, we see the establishment of an efficient system of regulations as an even more important driving force to oppose the interests of the different stakeholders constantly putting the planning activity under pressure (ESPON 2007).

Planning activity is also challenged by the diverse Slovenian landscapes and dispersed settlement network in which it is difficult to deliver development and economic prosperity equally. This problem resulted in the occurrence of deprived areas, especially in geographically remote parts of the country. Since the accessibility of these areas and the interconnectivity of the country were among the major problems, construction of the highway network became the primary development priority. Nowadays, the nearly finished highway system is seen rather as a creator of new problems than a solution to the old ones (SDSS 2004). In fact, a substantial increase of suburbanization and everyday commuting has occurred around the capital city and the highway routes; additionally, more freight transit through the country has increased emissions in these areas (Svetic 2006). On one hand, the small settlements exposed to the pressure of suburbanization usually lack sufficient infrastructure and facilities for the newcomers (Music 2000). On the other, bigger towns suffer from emigration; in the past, well established companies failed, and degraded areas such as brownfields occur, which desperately call for urban renewal, not just in environmental and spatial terms but also in economic and social ones (SSDS 2004). So far the government has not developed any national policies specifically targeting urban development and renewal, but it has worked more strongly on environmental protection measures as evidenced by one of the highest terrestrial rates (37 per cent) in the Natura 2000 programme (Natura 2000, 2009). These are all policy areas and issues upon which spatial planning can have an influence, but their success does not depend as much on their scale as it does on the capacity and characteristics of the planning system itself.

In Slovenia traditional land-use planning is still very much alive and evident in the current planning legislation. Three spatial planning acts have been adopted after independence. The first one was only a slight adaptation of an existing one, but the subsequent two acts in 2003 and 2007 brought new concepts into planning. Legislation changes quickly and thus it is seen as a major cause of the current situation in the territory – without questioning the planning system itself and its capacity. By definition, it is the duty of the law to control people's behaviour and decisions, and to guarantee the institutions, instruments and funds to prevent unwanted development (Rakar 2006: 25). This chapter does not naively accept this estimation, but tries to find an explanation by taking a closer look into the implementation of the legislation and the organizational support behind it. The author argues that if the legislation fails in the task of delivering spatial development, as specified in the core planning policy, it is not necessarily the fault of the planning system as it is the result of insufficient implementation and organizational support. In this environment of new jurisdictions and a new conceptual framework, planners are left to operate through knowledge and values insufficiently adapted to these new conditions. During the preparation process of the last planning legislation, a large gap occurred between policy-makers and policy beneficiaries in terms of where to shift the redesign of the planning act.

The guidelines for attaining the qualities of good legislation as defined in the OECD recommendations from 1995 (OECD 1995), in the White Paper on European Governance (CEC 2001), and in national guidelines (Metodologija, 2005) were only partially addressed. Therefore, the last spatial planning act from 2007 was a result of a political will that prevailed over interests of professionals from the field and over the needs of the system, which is not a good precondition for a successful delivery of the desred change in planning delivery.

The chapter shifts attention away from the legislation and tries to reveal the problem in a different manner, i.e. explore the role of knowledge and its transfer throughout the planning system. It is argued that the present situation is not only a result of political and economic development but also a consequence of the lack of knowledge and its exchange among the tiers and actors engaged in the planning activity. The described shortage is evident in different levels of governance and institutional settings, and especially in delivering a 'modern' spatial planning – as defined by Tewdwr-Jones (2004) – which not only integrates different policies into planning, but also emphasizes community participation, agency stakeholding and development management. The chapter is divided into three sections to show how and whether Slovenia is on the way to a successful transformation of its planning system. The first section provides an overview of the development and present state of the Slovenian spatial planning system, unfolding planning legislation and the administrative framework of the country. Major problems are fully revealed in the second section of the chapter, where special focus is placed on the role of knowledge, the inspection of existing 'epistemic communities' and their relations and interflow of information. Also here, public participation is addressed as an important part of the planning process, which needs to be refined in order to follow the principles of openness and legitimacy. Scant resources and negligible planning activity is especially evident in small municipalities. To illustrate the situation some examples of planning performance on the local level are added in the third section. The chapter concludes with recommendations for the improvement of governance in the planning system through an empowerment of the scope of knowledge present in the system; some alterations are subsequently suggested for the future transformation of the Slovenian planning system.

Slovenian spatial planning system

Slovenia has a surface of 20,273 km², inhabited by 2 million people and is located on the intersection of Central, South-east and Southern Europe. Four completely different geographical regions, the Alps, the Mediterranean, Pannonia and Dinaric Karst, influence the diverse cultural landscape, the architectural and settlement heritage, and the varied and extensive natural systems and resources (SSDS 2004: 14). The very first settlements in the territory of Slovenia appeared in 600 AD, but the country remained predominantly rural until the eighteenth century (Vriser 1984). It was in the nineteenth century when towns flourished as an outcome of the industrial revolution; in the 1960s and 1970s they became the essential part of the Slovenian polycentric settlement network (Pogacnik 1983). The Slovenian polycentric structure is based on a system of several hierarchically equivalent centres and nodes (SSDS 2004: 11) established by Vriser (1978) in his geographical theory of settlements. The concept was not restricted only to regional planning and the development of underprivileged towns in the economical and infrastructural sense, but was strongly supported politically as a socialistic type of governance. In this sense it was different from the EU concept of polycentric development which focuses on the creation of different economic integration zones to counteract the dominance of the 'pentagon' area (CEC 1999). Polycentrism was not just a spatial development policy as it had considerable wide political support, but it did not correspond to the needs of the transformation process. This was in part because a great deal of attention to polycentrism was formerly imposed by the socialist government and was supported with mid-term social implementation programmes which ceased to exist after independence, and in part because the diffusion of industrialization was imposed without considering the local potentialities, except for the unemployed and unskilled women's labour force that entered the labour market in the 1970s (Pogacnik 1983). Again, this is in contrast to the European model of polycentrism, which stipulates the use of endogenous potentialities to valorize the diversity in development (CEC 1999). With less concern about the real local potentialities, middle-size towns with formerly artificially imposed production

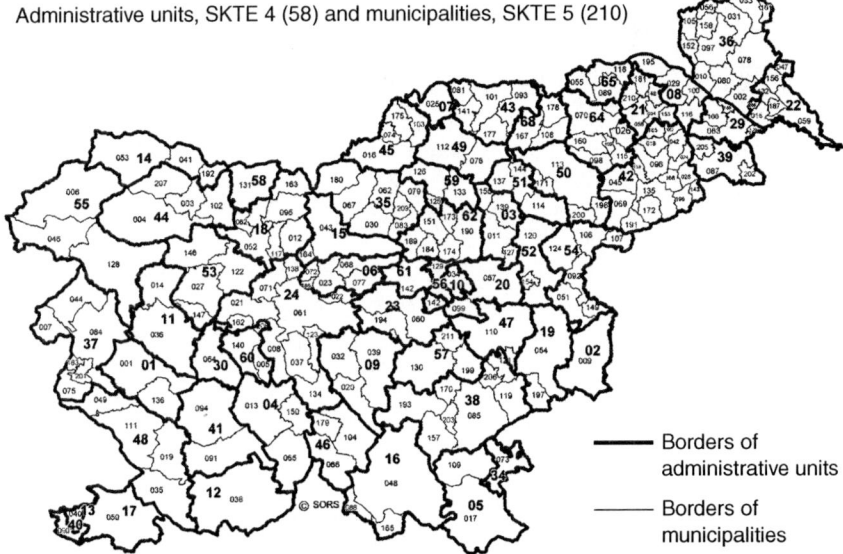

Figure 8.1 Map of administrative units and municipalities in Slovenia (source: Statistical Office of the Republic of Slovenia and Surveying and Mapping Authority of the Republic of Slovenia).

units and remote rural areas with small settlements were immediately put on the spot in 1991. In most cases these settlements were economically not able to overcome the transition period, which resulted in an increase of unemployment, urban decay and environmental problems (Music 2004). Tackling these problems was in addition to the already existing question about the planning system transformation after 1991.

Setting up an efficient and modern planning system has been a challenge since 1991. To overcome the transition period and to acquire additional time to create a new spatial planning system, the old legislation from 1984 was amended to fit the new value and land ownership system because land was no longer socialized and nationally owned (Urejanje prostora, graditev objektov 2003). Adaptations did not consider the new administrative system, which divided the local self-government level and the executive power of the State. In Slovenia there are 6,000 settlements and only 16 of them have more than 10,000 inhabitants (STAT 2009). The number of those with 1,000 to 10,000 inhabitants is 186 and represents the living environment for half of the Slovenian population (STAT 2009). The other half lives in local communities, villages or rural settlements, administratively divided among 210 municipalities, and the main institutions in charge of spatial planning on the local level. The last change in number of municipalities occurred in 2007 and follows the trend of middle-size municipalities dividing into smaller ones in order to ensure their own financial resources.

The change that significantly handicapped the efficiency of spatial planning occurred in 1991. The government established 58 administrative units, derived from former municipalities, and charged them with the tasks not covered by local government or governmental agencies. This artificial division had substantial implications for spatial planning. Since municipalities are in charge of the spatial plan preparation they determine land use and zoning, but the actual development/construction permits are approved by the local administrative offices as spatial bodies of the national government. Additionally, municipalities and administrative offices do not always coincide since 210 municipalities come under the jurisdiction of 58 local administrative districts, which provokes several problems. First, administrative officers are usually neither trained planners nor from a related field of education and consequently lack technical knowledge to interpret land use plans. They also do not have the contextual planning background to rationally support their decisions. For example, they make decisions based on their own individual judgment in the construction permit application process, which is not always in favour of sustainable spatial development (Blagajne and Santej 2001). Second, officials can succumb to the demands of the developers and their willingness to use different means to guarantee them the hope for success. In a survey conducted by the Faculty of Administration at the University of Ljubljana, about the misuse of status and lobbying on the local level, the results have shown that the spatial planning area is one of the most manipulated in the administrative bodies (Kovac 2006).

Spatial Planning Act of 2003

The first spatial planning act in the independence era was brought into force in January 2003 under the name Spatial Planning Act (ZUreP-1 2003). It introduced three levels of planning in Slovenia: the national, the regional and the local municipal levels (see Figure 8.2). The planning documents were divided into strategic spatial conceptions and implementing (detailed) plans. The major national planning policy document is the Spatial Development Strategy of Slovenia, adopted in 2004, which is still in use today. It was prepared by the Ministry of the Environment and Spatial Planning with significant support from planning researchers and experts from fields strongly related to planning, such as environmental protection, transportation and energy. The document presents a comprehensive concept of long-term spatial development in Slovenia, so goals defined in the Strategy should be considered according to the 'subsidiarity'[2] principle on every planning level. The strategy was prepared with reference to the guidelines of the Agenda Habitat (United Nations 1996), the European Spatial Development Perspective (CEC 1999) and other EU policies, which are significantly realized in the vision of Slovenian spatial development. Integration of these guidelines is a result of Slovenian participation in tailoring planning policy at the EU level, which was already in place before the attaining of full membership (cf. Pallagst Chapter 6 and Finka Chapter 5). Thus, the strategy is based on the consideration of social, economic and environmental factors of spatial development, which defines sustainable development as the guiding principle to enforce prudent land use and provides for the safety of life and natural resources (SSDS 2004: 8).

According to the Spatial Planning Act (ZUreP-1 2003), a similar strategic document should have been prepared in every Slovenian municipality regardless of its size and administrative organization. The main purpose of such a document on the local level was to define major guidelines and concepts of spatial development and

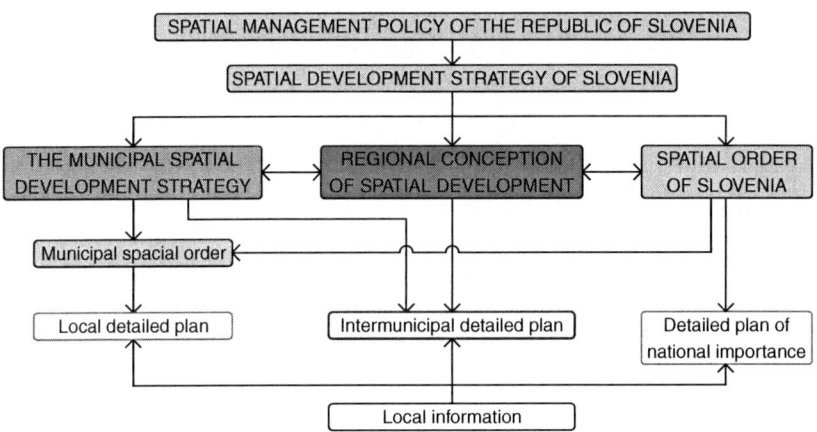

Figure 8.2 Scheme of planning documents from 2003 legislation (source: Author's elaboration on ZUreP-1 2003).

also the land use for the whole area. An additional duty of the Ministry of the Environment and Spatial Planning and the municipalities was to encourage spatial order through exact guidelines and rules for development interventions. The main implementing documents were called national and municipal local detailed plans in which individual spatial development projects were described and presented on the scale of a proposed development area (ZUreP-1 2003). These detailed plans were later applied in the application process for building permits, run under the jurisdiction of an administrative office. Preparation of planning documents on the national level is done by the former national office of spatial planning, now the Spatial Planning Directorate; though, at the municipal level, it is only partially mandated to the municipal planning departments. By law, municipalities are not authorized to prepare the documents themselves but they outsource them to planning consultancy agencies. However, they initiate and lead the process, and finally also deliver the plan to the municipal council that has the authority to adopt it. Participation in the planning process is still rather limited, and the different parties engaged in the process, such as investors, NGOs, citizens, planners and environmentalists, can only have their say in public hearings or by written statements during the public proceedings. This again counteracts the principle of openness defined in modern policy-making. In the older system, the regional level only applied to development, but not in administrative terms since Slovenia had not yet been divided into administrative regions. Nevertheless, the provision of the Regional Conception of Spatial Development in the past would have been guaranteed by the Ministry and the municipalities through the regional council in which representatives from other relevant ministries were presented together with the regional development agency (ZUreP-1 2003). But the actual performance of the regional planning agency did not meet the much needed role of mediator in the hierarchical structure of the planning system, since only three regional conceptions for spatial development were prepared, of which none officially became valid because the system was changed once more. The preparation of these regional conceptions was initiated and also partly financed by the Ministry, and later also terminated by it. This lack of regional spatial planning was recognized later as a weakness of the structure within the ESPON project 2.3.2 (ESPON 2007).

The new Spatial Planning Act

By the time of its promulgation in 2003, some of the solutions of the new Spatial Planning Act were already proclaimed inefficient and unsuitable by several parties (Gerbec 2003). For example, a considerable number of supplementary regulations about the process and exact content of documents should have been adopted together with the law but were delayed up to two years. Because of inadequate guidelines, lack of initiative and 'how-to' knowledge, the majority of municipalities had not started with the preparation of planning documents until 2005. After a major political shift from the left to the right wing in 2005, spatial planning activities on the municipal level were minimal since the Ministry decided to prepare the new law. Both municipal officers and experts belonging to different 'epistemic communities' strongly disagreed with the proposal. First, too little time had passed to objectively assess the implementation of the act from 2003. Also, experiences in other countries have shown that modifications of planning systems present a gradual long-term process that requires time and resources to fully come into practice (ESPON 2007: 22). Thus they advised, first, to provide some adequate knowledge through sound analysis of the present system, and afterwards react in accordance with the findings. Second, they suggested only minor changes to particular articles. Their view was expressed through hearings and written public statements sent to all members of the Parliament (Skupno stališče 2007). Nevertheless, a lot of time had passed without any municipal activities regarding the plans' preparation until the new order came into force three years after former law (ZPNacrt 2007).

The New Spatial Planning Act from 2007 (see Figure 8.3) again emphasizes traditional land-use planning and puts the efforts of the legislation from 2004, for a more strategic, comprehensive approach, on the back-burner. A basic task of municipalities is to prepare a local detailed land-use plan. The scale of the strategic approach and the volume of analyses performed in the preparation process of this plan is under the competence of each municipality, hence it varies based on the size of municipality (ZPNacrt 2007). In comparison to other European countries, where spatial planning is seen more as a coordinating, policy-making activity than a technical one (Tewdwr-Jones 2004), the Act seems to be a step backwards. A greater focus on zoning speaks for itself, in so far as it is allocative planning in its pure form. The New Spatial Planning Act thus covers only a few of the activities that planning should undertake, which is demonstrated by the fact that this act is only a part of the Spatial Planning Code in preparation. Consequently, some of the articles from the 2003 law are still binding today (ZPNacrt 2007).

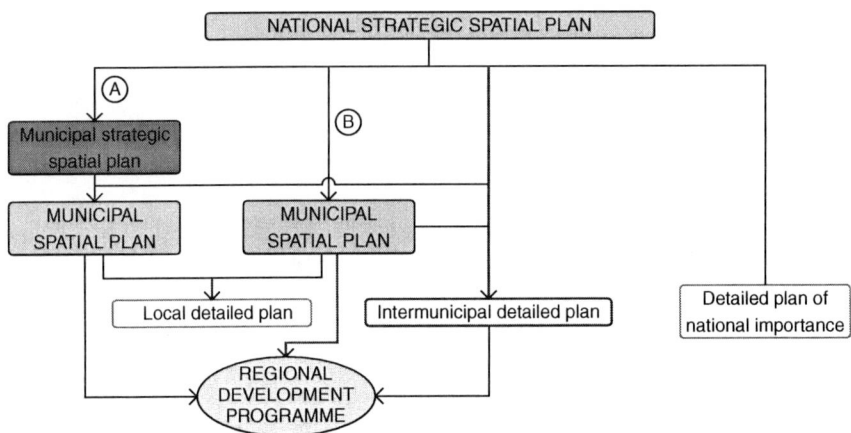

Municipalities decide for one option to follow: A or B.

Figure 8.3 Scheme of planning documents from 2007 legislation (source: Author's elaboration on ZPNacrt 2007).

One of the weakest solutions of the New Spatial Planning Act is the establishment of a non-binding regional level of spatial planning. This decision is contrary to the outcomes of ESPON findings on territorial governance (ESPON 2007), and reveals the weak vertical structure of governance in Slovenia, which should be strengthened with particular concern for regional planning and performance of planning in local communities and municipalities. However, following the Act, municipalities can join consortia, and establish a joint planning office and prepare joint municipal plans, and/or regional detailed spatial plans can be initiated for projects of regional importance (ZPNacrt 2007). The first solution can be applied to small municipalities without requiring a complex hierarchical structure of their administration, or a separate or dedicated planning department. Legally each area, with the status of municipality, should conform to one of the following criteria: having a population of 5,000 (which is not the case for 45 per cent of municipalities), or having at least 3,000 inhabitants and serving as an economic, social and cultural centre of a wider region (SSDS 2004: 9). The list of Slovenian municipalities shows that 57 municipalities out of 210 (i.e. more than 25 per cent) do not meet any of these criteria (Benkovic Krasevec 2006). These numbers strongly correlate with the state of municipal spatial planning, since smaller municipalities established in the last ten years do not possess the administrative capacity to actually carry out the obligations assigned to them by planning law. To prevent inappropriate development, the Act allows such municipalities to hire a joint-planner who compensates for the lack of a planning department (ZPNacrt 2007) or establishes a joint planning office. However, only a few municipalities actually use these possibilities, and even so, they would still prepare the planning documents separately. This joint action demonstrates a need for an intermediate level of planning or, as stated in ESPON, a need for vertical cooperation of different actors, institutions and interest groups on different territorial and administrative levels (ESPON 2007). As Tewdwr-Jones (2004) claims, the regional level is often seen as a good solution, with a desire for coordinating the institutional framework that mediates between conflicting policy priorities and sectoral problems. For now the gap in vertical cooperation between the national and local level is partially covered by regions, but not in an administrative sense.

Role of regional level

Slovenian 'regions' are a constitutional category defined in Article 143 as 'a self-governing local community that manages local affairs of wider importance, and certain affairs of regional importance provided by law' (Constitution of the Republic of Slovenia 1991). The economic and territorial circumstances to have that article fully implemented will outlast the mandate of this and possibly also the next government. Although many researchers (e.g. Albrechts *et al.* 2003) claim that the regional level is crucial in modern, multi-level territorial governance, Slovenian politicians and professionals still have not reached consensus about this matter. Two questions are usually discussed when considering how to configure the region as an administrative unit: first, the number of potential regions and, second, their legal status and jurisdiction. The discussion touches on the competence of many 'epistemic communities', including experts from the government, municipalities and regional development institutions, geographers, lawyers and public policy academia, each of them with their own favourite solution, agenda and interests. Partial agreement was reached about the number of regions: Slovenia should be divided into six to eight administrative regions. But again this would present a large load on the governmental budget; additionally, more human resources would be required (Smidovnik 2007) to deliver this new form of governance.

At present, spatial planning and regional development are guided by two separate policies, one managed through the Spatial Planning Act (ZPNacrt 2007), and the other through the Promotion of Balanced Regional Development Act (1999). Slovenia is divided into 12 development regions, which overlay the statistical division of the country into NUTS3 regions (Figure 8.4). In every region one or more regional development agencies are in charge of preparation and implementation of regional development programmes. However, in practice, no regional spatial conception or strategic plan is required to show the territorial dimension of the proposed projects. Municipalities rarely prepare programmes in search for joint solutions of territorial problems, such as a development of infrastructure, provision of services, etc. The linkage between development and planning was established in the Spatial Planning Act of 2003. To motivate joint

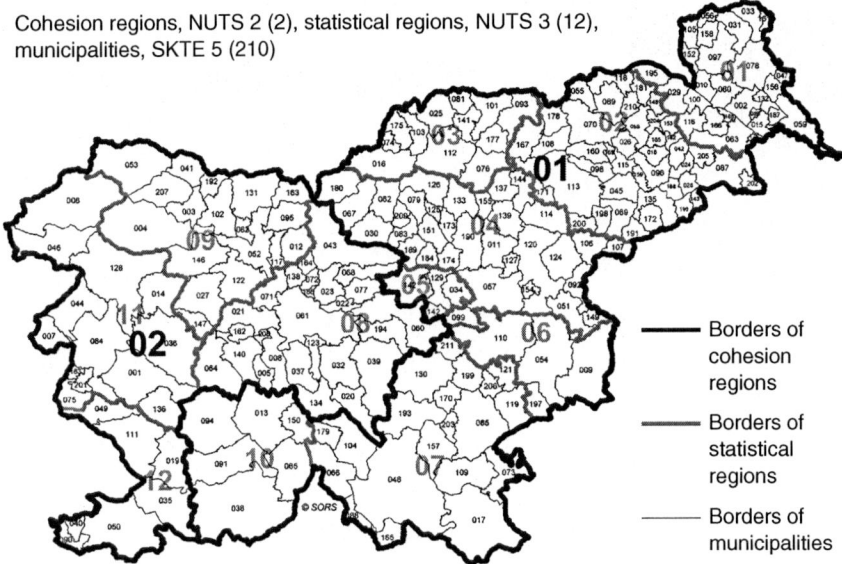

Figure 8.4 Map of development regions in Slovenia (source: Statistical Office of the Republic of Slovenia and Surveying and Mapping Authority of the Republic of Slovenia).

policy-making, the Ministry of Environment and Spatial Planning financed the preparation of regional spatial strategies. However, the Ministry cut off the financial support for the regions after three successful pilot projects. Hence the regional spatial planning strategies only turned out as good research projects, and otherwise did not come fully into force as planning strategies, albeit recognized as a useful mediation and planning tool by several experts (Hudoklin 2007; cf. also Davoudi 2006). The more comprehensive approach to regional spatial planning might be reshaped again with the Act of Regions (Proposal of Act of Regions 2008); however, this is still going through the parliamentary process and for now does not represent the major focus of government policy-making, since it could risk voters' support of political agendas, not to mention have an unpredictable outcome. The proposal states that spatial planning at the regional level should provide public infrastructure, an energy strategy, spatial development plans of regional importance, housing and land policy, and environmental protection measures (Proposal of Act of Regions 2008: Article 13). The government, however, cannot agree to enlarge the administrative apparatus without knowing the potential hazards and benefits during the current economic crisis. At the same time, there is still general disagreement on the way forward among the different 'epistemic communities', and thus experts have not yet managed to provide policy-makers with the 'right and exclusive' solution that would work (Smidovnik 2007).

In such a situation of uncertainty, regional development is still mainly delivered on the basis of the Promotion of Balanced Regional Development Act (1999). This legislation follows the principles of regional planning in Europe, thus fostering economic, social and territorial cohesion within and between regions, and enabling the establishment of a basic institutional framework for the implementation of the EU *acquis* in the field of regional policies and in the coordination of Structural Funds. Development assistance was guaranteed and territorially concentrated to areas whose development was lagging – so called deprived areas. The Promotion of Balanced Regional Development Act (1999) introduced the regional development programme as the main instrument for

> promoting a balanced economic, social and spatial view of development, lessening the differences in economic growth and opportunities between regions, preventing the formation of new problem regions, restoring settlements throughout the entire land of the Republic of Slovenia and promoting environmentally sound economies.
>
> (Promotion of Balanced Regional Development Act 1999: 7674–7675, translation)

Additional funds for regional development were provided from 1992 by the EU Pre-accession programme PHARE, and almost half of the €339 million, obtained until 2004, were spent on setting up an institutional framework for regional development, i.e. for the establishment of regional development agencies throughout the country. Also ISPA and SAPARD programme funding became available to the Slovenian government in 1999 – first, for large scale transport infrastructure, and later for the stimulation of agriculture and development of the rural areas (Pre-accession help 2003).

Slovenia does not only take advantage of Structural Funds, but it also has participated in territorial cooperation initiatives. Cross-border cooperation is strong with all the surrounding countries of Italy, Austria, Hungary and also Croatia. For example, in November 2007 the EU approved Cross-Border Operational programme between Hungary and Slovenia, which aims to develop a competitive and sustainable cooperation area that offers access to work and income opportunity (Cross-Border 2009). In most cases regional development agencies are participating as leading partners while municipalities join projects as pilot areas or supplementary partners. Although they are not directly linked to local planning, these initiatives do have an important impact on territorial development. They provide municipalities with funds, fresh ideas and actual development projects that sometimes cannot be provided solely by planning activity.

An overview of the development of the Slovenian spatial planning field has revealed several issues that still need to be resolved before the system transformation is completed. Constant changes in the planning legislation cause municipalities difficulties in following the jurisdictions. Additionally, the division between the strategic and implementation (administrative) levels hinders the delivery of spatial development, as does the limited administrative capacity planning in small municipalities (Blagajne and Santej 2001). While the limited capacity could have been compensated for with the establishment of a regional spatial planning level, as prescribed by the Spatial Planning Act of 2003, this solution was partially abolished in 2007. Furthermore, this scrutiny seems to hint at a general lack of knowledge and knowledge exchange throughout the different layers of the planning system and its actors, thus implying a problem of scant resources that will be discussed in the following section.

Scant resources and new jurisdictions: challenges of delivering spatial planning in Slovenia

In the first part of this section we argue that constant changes of the system occur due to the lack of consolidated knowledge and information to underpin policy-making activity. In the last 20 years, many analyses and assessments have been conducted (Blagajne and Santej 2001), and many reflections have been written on the Slovenian spatial planning system. Researchers were motivated to express their opinions when the preparation of new legislation was in progress, although they had only minor influence on the final result. These assessments vary in approach and specifications. Some researchers like Gerbec (2003), Pogacnik (2003) and Zavodnik Lamovsek (2003) evaluated the system and implementation of the law in general, while others focused on a specific issue such as governance and planning in small settlements (Ogorelec 1994; Rus 1994; Benkovic Krasevec 2006). However, no system has been established to regularly monitor implementation of the legislation. Planning experts are invited into the ongoing legislation process but, when it comes to the closing arguments, their reasoning will prevail only when it is in line with political preferences. As Miles (1998) and Nelkin (1979) argue in Haas (2004), politicians do not want science, but are often looking for a justification for pre-existing political programmes that are driven principally by political anticipations of gain. Therefore, results of otherwise objective knowledge are only rarely integrated into the policy-making process.

Both the OECD and the EU recommended additional attention be given to evidence-based policy-making in the Recommendations of the Council (OECD 1995), and through the publication of the White Paper on European Governance (CEC 2001) and of several impact assessment guidelines, the latest one from 2009. However, initiatives for better regulation, thus for more knowledge integrated into policy-making processes, has been only partially adopted by Slovenian policy-makers. The Ministry of Public Administration carries out a preliminary Regulatory Impact Assessment that is simply an evaluation, with the aim to diminish bureaucracy as part of the Better Governance Policy of the EU (Metodologija 2005) and the OECD Red Tape initiative. According to the assessment, each piece of legislation should be efficient, transparent, legitimate and comprehensible, and should correspond to existing public needs as well as those of the policy system in question. The latest Planning Act was evaluated in the same way, which means the potential economic, environmental and social impacts were assessed in a one-paragraph description, and the rest of the analysis concentrated on administrative costs. The cost-benefit analysis, one of the most used methods in such cases, was left out, and the potential expenses were stipulated briefly (ZPNacrt 2007). This general approach can hardly be regarded as sufficient for a complex and interdisciplinary field such as spatial planning. In the past, Slovenian planning legislation has undergone a similar implementation analysis, albeit not in a formalized process. For example, in 1972 a study of European foreign and domestic spatial planning systems was published to serve as a foundation for the legislation in 1984. Later on, in the 1990s, the Ministry of Environment and Spatial Planning launched a capacity study among municipal planners. Nevertheless, the collected data were never processed to evaluate the planning state of art. The most recent study of the planning system was conducted in 2001 by the Institute of Environmental Law during the preparation of the Spatial Planning Act from 2003 (Blagajne and Santej 2001). The main survey methods were a questionnaire and an interview, again engaging municipalities and administration offices. The major outcomes focusing on strengths and weaknesses of the system were only partly integrated into the new law. Institutional discrepancies remained unchanged and today still hamper the implementation process (Pogacnik 2003).

If this study shows a fairly good example of cooperation between the scientific society and policy-makers, the policy-making process of the 2007 Spatial Planning Act seems to deny it because its preparation seems to be closer to a political statement than a rational decision. The new legislation was prepared just after the political shift in the government, without any sound analysis or support from the scientific planning field. Public hearings and parliamentary proceedings disclosed mixed opinions of municipalities and a strong opposition from the planning 'epistemic community', which was presented in a statement sent to all political parties and members of the parliament (Skupno stališče 2007). Planning experts were against the abolition of the strategic regional level and were also concerned with the unnecessary change of terminology. They were promoting the new Act as unnecessary and preferred instead the possibility to act through minor changes to the existing legislation. Parliamentary hearings revealed the general idea politicians had about spatial planning. That is, planning should unconditionally serve the interests of developers no matter what the possible implications would be for the environment and society (Transcript of parliamentary hearing 2007). This indirectly demonstrates the pressure under which municipal planners deliver spatial development. The parliamentary discussion also included debate about the (ir)relevance of knowledge in the delivery of planning because the leading party defended a limitation on the amount of preliminary analysis needed for the preparation of a plan and development vision. In fact, at some point they even claimed preliminary analysis as unnecessary and too costly (Transcript of parliamentary hearing 2007), which directly speaks against 'evidence-base planning'.

The transparency of the preparation procedure, which is the level of the so-called social learning included in a policy-making process (Friedman 1987; also cf. Dąbrowski Chapter 9), was also minimal as shown in the research about public participation in policy-making by Umanotera – one of the most active environmental Slovenian NGOs. They investigated 45 acts in the preparation procedure from May 2006 to December 2006, included among which was the new Spatial Planning Act. The evaluation of the communication environment confirmed that the formal procedural requests were met, but the in-depth analysis of the state of the art in planning was missing. In other words, the level of consideration of public proposals required from policy-makers was not evident. Thus, it was difficult to evaluate the degree and possibilities for the inclusion of informal knowledge in the policy-making process (Umanotera 2007).

This introduction to the Slovenian spatial planning system and its resources demonstrate that its current knowledge framework is insufficient. Thus it is likely to impede or constrain the effective delivery of spatial development. 'Epistemic communities' of planners, and other policy-makers and professionals is described in more detail to illustrate the current need for the increased circulation of knowledge in the planning system, especially with regard to the diverse interests of local communities.

Epistemic communities and recognition of territorial cohesion concept

Within the described framework, it is interesting to explore the role played by planning experts and the academic environment in greater depth. Although rather insignificant in number, it is possible to identify the existence of a fairly active 'epistemic community' in planning research. This research is done by the National Urban Planning Institute, which covers broad areas from spatial planning to urban design, and by faculty departments engaged in planning (Geography, Architecture, Landscape Architecture, Civil Engineering) under the patronage of the University of Ljubljana, the University of Maribor and the University of Primorska. Within this framework, a small group of approximately 60 individuals in total competes for the research funds available from the Ministry of Higher Education, Science and Technology, and the Ministry of Environment and Spatial Planning. There is a permanent national research programme called Target Research Programmes, which also sponsors projects to enhance the development of Slovenia in various areas related to spatial development.

Researchers, as scientific partners, also are engaged in several projects funded by the EU, often contributing to integrate European concepts within transnational policy-making. Here it is interesting to underline how, together with the Ministry of Environment and Spatial Planning, the above-mentioned community produced a preliminary attempt to integrate the concept of 'territorial cohesion' into Slovenian planning. Indeed, within the Slovenian context, 'territorial cohesion' represents a rather new concept and so far has been acknowledged mostly by researchers and academia in planning, and by officials working for the Ministry of Environment and Spatial Planning. For example, an extensive debate was held in Slovenia recently during the public consultation period for the Green Paper on Territorial Cohesion (CEC 2008). From the field of policy-making, the following institutions were represented: the Ministry for Environment and Spatial Planning, the Ministry for Agriculture, Forestry and Food, the Government Office for Local Self-government and Regional Policy, and the Government Office for Development and European Affairs. Later on, a public debate also was organized, engaging NGO's, researchers and academia. Participants agreed that 'territorial cohesion' is a fundamental concept for sustainable economic growth and the delivery of social and economic cohesion in light of the territorial potential of different areas.

Throughout the debate, the ambiguous notion of 'territorial cohesion' (cf. Evers *et al.* 2009) stabilized as a means to improve the quality of policy-making processes between sectors of policy, and also as a tool for enhanced multi-level governance and transnational cooperation. Policy-making would improve by equalizing territorial cohesion with economic and social cohesion in consideration of potential policy impacts (Stališče 2009). The Government Office of the Republic of Slovenia for Local Self-Government and Regional Policy (GOSP), and the EU Structural Funds and the Cohesion Fund Managing Authority began a media campaign to promote European Cohesion Policy in March 2009. The campaign was initiated by the EU Communication Plan in order to inform and make the public aware of the role of the European Union in co-financing operations from the Cohesion Fund, the European Regional Development Fund and the European Social Fund, their effects and how they work as well as the opportunities they offer. The media campaign includes mainly television and radio advertisements with recognizable slogans, for example 'EU funds pave the way for further development for the Operational Programme of Environmental and Transport Infrastructure Development' (GOSP 2009). These actions indicate cohesion is gaining recognition as a development concept, and in this case also as a financial opportunity. The campaign does not directly focus on 'territorial cohesion', but it does indirectly promote it through regional development, infrastructure development and images of improved territories throughout the country, such as renewed old city centres. No matter what the dynamics of activities on the national level are, 'territorial cohesion' currently is seen more as 'an important esoteric ideal' (Doucet 2006: 1475) in local planning than a development concept.

However, we can find some evidence of 'territorial cohesion' present in the policy-making in Slovenia. The regional development programmes reflect the demand of 'territorial cohesion' for 'a more balanced development by reducing existing disparities and preventing territorial imbalances' because they are usually structured in economic, social and environmental chapters, just like the pillars of sustainable development (Camagni 2005). As seen in practice, these programmes do well in strengthening access to services, invigorating economic activity and improving the environment, but they fail in enhancing the territorial dimension of regional policy. Above all, they fail in improving the better coordination of sectoral policies. Though the Ministry of Environment and Spatial Planning has financed several projects, including the development of a method for the Territorial Impact Assessment in the country, to fulfil the 'task' of 'territorial cohesion' and 'to make both sectoral policies which have a spatial impact and regional policy more coherent' (Davoudi 2005: 435). The territorial impact assessment is a tool used to measure how singular sector policies have integrated the goals of Slovenian spatial development into their policy documents (Golobic *et al.* 2008). First, the method focused mainly on infrastructure projects (ESPON 2004), but was later also developed for policies and programmes such as the EU Common Agriculture Policy (ESPON 2005). 'Territorial cohesion' is only one of the themes planning researchers investigate in relation to planning, and thus far it has not been recognized widely by practitioners on the local level who approach planning in a less comprehensive and sophisticated way.

Scant resources on the local level

From the policy-making process we now shift to the issue of policy implementation at the local level. According to the spatial planning act every municipality must carry out the same duties regardless of its size, population or institutional support. There is some flexibility in law, suggesting that smaller municipalities without a competent administrative staff can outsource and hire a planning consultant (ZPNacrt 2007), or establish a joint planning office. Smaller municipalities also compensate for insufficient institutional support by consulting the larger neighbouring municipality from which they recently departed. Thus municipalities vary in organizational structure; only a few larger ones have a hierarchical, departmental structure with an independent planning department. A survey conducted in 118 municipalities (56 per cent of all Slovenian municipalities) showed 77 per cent of them have a uniform structure without a specialized body for planning activity. Seventy five per cent of the municipalities surveyed claimed they do not have enough educated and trained employees to successfully cover infrastructure and (urban) planning (Ferfila 2008), which limits the quality and innovation in spatial development. Another query with smaller municipalities in focus shows development and planning funds are spent on infrastructure construction projects without any broader strategic concept or plan behind the projects. This approach evidently wins votes for the next election and, in the short term, solves the most urgent problems. But it does not necessarily deliver sustainable development as defined in the national planning strategy (Benkovic Krasevec 2006). Furthermore, the municipal budget spent on handling planning issues is on average only 2 per cent, and no more than 4 per cent, which provides planners with limited implementation power (Ferfila 2008).

To illustrate the problems of scant resources and insufficient knowledge on the local level mentioned above, the above general descriptions will be upgraded further on with an example of the planning situation in a typical suburban small-scale settlement. Krtina is an example of a recently heavily suburbanized traditional rural settlement situated at a highway junction in one of the most planning rules-free and economically successful municipalities in the Ljubljana urban region, the most developed and one of the above-mentioned 12 development regions. This settlement was chosen because the author has participated in a project of spatial plan preparation and because it adequately illustrates planning issues on the local level. Krtina is a typical example of a smaller community where the major factors influencing its development are as follows: a short distance (only 16 km) to Ljubljana, a major employment centre; location on a highway junction; promising real estate prices of new suburban uniform single family housing that is geographically from areas with traditional rural architecture and a well preserved nature; and where the development initiative has been accepted widely by the governing municipality, but not the community itself. The municipality of Domzale to which Krtina belongs administratively has been very liberal when granting construction permits due to its advantageous location near the capital city, and also has a liberal tax and economic policy (Kusar 2005). The only existing planning document to cope with the rapid changes in Krtina is the long-term spatial development and land use plan of Domzale, which is no longer relevant since it has been valid for almost 20 years and was prepared on the basis of the socialist model (Brusnjak *et al.* 2006). Decisions made in favour of the capital have in practice not always turned out as good for the quality and efficiency of the landscape as for development because smaller settlements were not prepared for such sudden changes (Music 2004). This gap of provisions and data enables developers to realize their projects without significant constraints.

Generally, the problem of data provision is due to lack of financial and human resources so that municipal planners are unable to generate the data they use in their delivery of planning, especially in smaller municipalities where lack of resources is even more evident. They use the data available from the Ministry of Environment and Spatial Planning, public agencies or infrastructure providers. On the national level there are four major institutions: the Statistical Office, the Environmental Agency, the Surveying and Mapping Authority and the Institute of Macroeconomic Analysis and Development. For example, the Statistical Office monitors major demographic, economic and environmental statistics, but it does an insufficient job in providing spatially related data like energy consumption, transport network and land use coverage. Inconsistency in data is especially apparent in the primary phase of the plan preparation when municipalities have to gather the data from different stakeholders, which is not only time consuming and tiring but in some cases even impossible. Both Spatial Planning Acts from 2003 and 2007 have introduced a common spatial information system to overcome this problem, but it is yet to be established. Some similar on-line databases do function, but they provide already processed information. For example, PISO is a web page with municipal spatial plans in which approximately half of the municipalities now participate (PISO 2009). Also, the availability of data for spatial development was tested through the ambitious regulation for monitoring the performance of the national spatial development strategy (Uredba 2004). Theoretically the monitoring system defines indicators that cover all major aspects of planning, but practically the system creates unrealistic expectations for data provision, providing, for example, the frequency of the use of bus routes; additionally no report on the progress toward the goals of a national planning policy has been produced so far.

Another way to retrieve the data is through the public participation process, but that is another failure of the Slovenian planning system. Although a straightforward planning process seems to exist in the legislation, in reality it is never a linear journey from point A to point B. During the process different actors join in to play in the planning game (Dijksman 2006) with the intention of influencing the final consensus about the potential development. The main scenario or vision of spatial development is usually prepared by the planners, though it can be later altered by the mayors in favour of investors who bring the money into the municipality. Thus municipal spatial planning in Slovenia is exceedingly capital and policy led; it is also referred to incidentally as 'mayoral spatial planning' (Gaberscik 2004). On the one hand, mayoral decisions are legitimate since their focus is on invigorating economic development and attracting jobs as a way to ensure votes in future elections and to deliver progress at minimum cost; on the other hand, their accountability for the sustainability of the territory as well as the community's best interests with general regard for a 'quality of life' is low. According to law, the interests of the public can be expressed during the process of a public hearing. Therefore local residents are invited to attend the planning game when it has finished and consequently cannot influence the final outcome (Zakrajsek 1990). This partly originates from the former political system when the state decided the correct course of action; but it is also partly a result of residents' lack of interest in the process because they know the likelihood of acceptance of their proposals is quite low. Indeed, it was not the fact that there was no public participation in the socialist era. On the contrary, residents were more engaged in the development of local communities; they did a lot for free, including helping neighbours, and paying a voluntary financial contribution that went to local infrastructure and development projects. Because of individualism and a lack of time many residents only engage in public consultations when the territorial impacts of development directly affect their private property or way of life. These changes have been reported in several projects in which the author has participated, including one project where locals explain how they perceive, understand and engage in spatial planning (Marot 2005).

All existing analysis about public participation shows public engagement on a small scale (Ogorelec 1994; Vahtar 2002). In the Arnstein scale of measuring the level of participation, which is rather old but still fairly describes the current situation in Slovenia, only the forms of informing (third), consultation (fourth) and placation (fifth) are presented (Arnstein 1969). In placation citizens have a minor influence on policy-making and the final decision more resembles the opinion of policy-makers than that of the public. In practice, the local community usually enters the planning process at the end when a new municipal spatial plan has almost been finalized. Also on the modern scale of public participation in Slovenia, designed by the International Association of Public Participation (IAP2), the public is solely engaged through informing and consulting (the first and the second levels of the Arnstein scale) (Umanotera 2007: 36). This means planning in Slovenia has not turned toward the direction of collaborative planning, which has been strongly advocated by Healey (1997) and Innes (1996) and has encouraged the openness of the planning process and the importance of dialogue and consensus within it. This resistance to any form of dialogue is a result of several factors. First, the Spatial Planning Act (ZPNactr 2007) only defines public hearings and 30 days of public display as obligatory in the process of municipal spatial plan preparation. Second, planners are not familiar with different methods and techniques for public participation, so they are limited in their ability to intervene or influence the process. Third, planning staff numbers are limited, so they have less time to become more involved in public consultations or to advocate for the public interest (Ogorelec 1993). Lately, some positive improvements have been made and some training in communication skills is also available to planners. The Legal Informative Centre of NGOs offers courses in mediation and public participation as part of a masters in planning curricula, and the Institute for Policies of Space is currently working on a project, financed by EEA and Norwegian grants, about open governance (IPOP 2009).

There is also some innovation in public participation present in the field, which can help to overcome the problem of scant resources, especially in the areas with the least knowledge and planning support. For example, in the case of Krtina, a field survey with the help of university students, carried out in the analytical phase of the plan preparation process, illustrates how citizens are capable of judging their current situation and also of expressing their ideas and wishes for the development; so their contribution to the planning process should not be underestimated (Brusnjak *et al.* 2006). Local community representatives, a teacher in lower primary school, representatives of the sport and tourism sectors, two estate investors and some newcomers were chosen as a representative sample for semi-structured interviews since the surveyors – the group of students working on the local land-use plan – did not have time or money to carry out a comprehensive study. These students were part of a larger project group, set up as a cooperation between the Domzale municipality and the Faculty of Geodesy and Civil Engineering at the University of Ljubljana. The project was in part an academic exercise, but it also succeeded in gaining recognition by the local community that published the final results on-line. The most problematic areas of concern, which were revealed in the survey, included insufficient public transportation and parking places, devastation of the rural landscape, atypical housing, no jobs in the area thus requiring daily commuting, an influx of urban ways of life, and above all a serious shortage of service providers such as a bank, a post office, a well-stocked grocery store and early education facilities. The village was simply not prepared for such a rapid increase in the population, which had only increased from 300 to 500 in the past 15 years. Furthermore, no measures against sprawl have been taken by the municipality which granted investors the construction permits to mitigate the changes and the typical suburbanization process that quickly had taken over the area (Brusnjak *et al.* 2006).

In addition to the evaluation of current development, participants in the interviews also expressed their ideas and wishes for future development based on their *a posteriori* knowledge. Like experts, the locals are in favour of more sustainable and nature-friendly development. For example, they would use the potential of their cultural heritage and recreational areas for tourist activity albeit only on a scale of eco-tourism in the interest of preservation (Brusnjak *et al.* 2006). The long-term vision of Krtina, as stated in the proposal that the urban planning students prepared, is to become a qualitatively and functionally regulated, self-sufficient settlement with an emphasis on natural and cultural spatial qualities to fulfil the needs of local residents, newcomers and visitors. Also, besides the detailed description of gradual development phases and design specifications of three major projects, there are policy-making lessons to be learned from this case. First, the local community is the one with the most recent information on the development and needs of a place and its residents should be actively engaged in the planning process – not just during the hearings. In line with 'territorial cohesion' this would ensure that policies are designed and implemented with local knowledge. Second, detailed plans are also needed for smaller communities under development pressures. Lastly, these plans can be prepared with low-budget funds through cooperation between municipalities and planning schools. Although the plan for Krtina has yet to obtain legal status, it was legitimately recognized by local residents and also published on their website. The results of the project were also reported to the Domzale municipality, which can use the report in the preparation process and in the finalization of their municipal spatial plan (Brusnjak *et al.* 2006).

Conclusion

The intention of this chapter was to discuss the challenges that Slovenia as well as many of the new EU Member States face in planning in the era of global changes, focusing on the role of knowledge and 'epistemic communities' in this transition process. Planning is still perceived as traditional land use planning in Slovenia, as one can easily see in the legislation. The first Spatial Planning Act (ZUreP-1 2003) put more emphasis on strategic comprehensive planning. And the introduction of the regional spatial planning level indicated the shift toward planning as an activity that strives for more coordinated and transparent planning policy development (Tewdwr-Jones 2004). Nevertheless, the most recent 2007 Act constitutes a step backwards, allocating land use planning with zoning at its core. Constant changes of the legislation created difficulties for municipalities because some still use 20 year old plans in their development and construction permit applications (Brusnjak *et al.* 2006). Furthermore, municipalities lack human resources and knowledge (Ferfila 2008), and, due to the constant alteration of the regulations, they show a high level of resistance to the new rules. Planners act in line with the law and its minimal requirements instead of playing an active role as mediators between conflicting interests, actors and resources (Innes 1996). To change the current system and open it up to flexibility would first require the empowerment of social capital on the local level, thus potentially encouraging knowledge sharing and teamwork norms of behaviour and interaction within planning arenas (Ekins and Medhurst 2006). Consequently, the staff of planning departments should increase in number, become more competent and interdisciplinary in knowledge, and above all seize the role of initiators instead of passive followers (Ferfila 2008).

Second, an obligatory regional spatial development plan should be reintroduced in the Spatial Planning Act. Regional spatial conceptions, developed under the planning legislation from 2003, confirmed there is a need for such an approach in order to improve cooperation between neighbouring municipalities, policy sectors and stakeholders, and the quality of spatial development (Hudoklin 2007). Similar documents were presented by Doucet (2006) as 'spatial visions', which should identify development operations and key-players for their implementation. At the same time, the ESPON 3.2 project (2007) emphasizes the need for empowering the vertical structure in Slovenia. For now the Government has only partly agreed on the role and legislative status of regions, leaving the question of the number of regions unresolved (Smidovnik 2007).

The weakness of a multi-level governance framework particularly hampers the spatial development of small municipalities, which primarily adopt an incremental approach to planning without any significant strategic component. As shown in the case of Krtina, smaller settlements, which have not gained the status of municipality, only end up with some spatial development guidelines from the municipal plan without any strategic attention (Brusnjak *et al.* 2006). In the current situation of the emerging economic crisis and social problems, to increase the governmental apparatus without knowing the exact results of the measure would be unreasonable. A partial solution would be to decrease the number of municipalities in accordance with the legal requirements for municipality status, which is currently not always implemented (Benkovic and Krasevec 2006). But this again would result in oppression from smaller municipalities. Additionally, the government could experimentally apply the regional administrative reform to one of the Slovenian regions and carefully monitor the outcomes (benefits, costs, difficulties), which could help them redesign, terminate or continue with the reform. Such a method was used for testing the proposal of the new German Federal Spatial Planning Act in which they chose a testing planning office to work in accordance with the proposal and report its weaknesses and strengths (Planspiel 2008). If the administrative regions turned out to be unworkable, the government could stick with the development regions as they are currently configured. The complexity of 'regional discussion' also implies that for any administrative reform of the system we would need stronger evidence in support of policy-making.

At the moment, transparency of the policy-making is ensured by a partial Regulatory Impact Assessment performed in the preparation process (Metodologija 2005). This assessment is very limited in its scope and does include wider public consultation about the policy proposal, but it does not recognize any other 'epistemic communities'. Governmental officials finance research projects and they do acquire some evidence to support their proposals from these knowledgeable communities. But, in most cases, they will still stick to their own judgments when it comes to implementation. If there is no legal force, the argument will be misinterpreted and an opportunist solution will be given priority. As stated in Haas (2004), 'Even when scientists think they have developed truth to power, power appears disinterested at best, and possibly even uninterested.' The rule developed by Fainstein (2000), 'The power of the words depends on the power of the speaker', will somehow prevail.

As seen in practice, comprehensive development concepts can force politicians to open the political process and adopt more sustainable policies (Haas 1992). This is also evident in Slovenia with the introduction of 'territorial cohesion' into planning, which revived the discussion about spatial planning and approaches to it on the national level. 'Territorial cohesion' does primarily focus on delivering sustainable development by acknowledging the territorial potentials of a region (Davoudi 2005). More importantly, 'territorial cohesion' will foster a comprehensive approach to policy-making and better coordination between policy sectors, governmental levels and actors to improve the cohesion on all levels (Stališče 2009). At the moment discussion is established between the Government and researchers, and it has not yet reached the local level. Researchers have been recognized as a network of professionals with recognized expertise who can develop techniques of impact assessments to bring together partial insights on sustainable development from different academic disciplines and also interest groups (Haas 2004). And, following the media campaign for EU cohesion policy, the public will become more familiar with the terminology of cohesion. Thus one can only hope it also will become a buzz-word outside of the scientific community, which could result in a more demanding public regarding policy-making (Schön 2005) and more sustainable spatial development.

In conclusion, the struggle for setting up the Slovenian planning system is a clear example of how planning approaches cannot be unified and universally tailored since they depend on different cultural and historical background. All EU countries cannot apply the same range of solutions or at least they will not necessarily work in the same way (ESPON 2007). Limitations of such transfers were discussed in the theory of policy convergence. As Knill (2005) claims, decision-makers should consider experiences and solutions of those countries with which they share an especially close set of cultural ties such as similarity in socio-economic structures and development (also cf. Stead and Nadin Chapter 7). Also a response to the global or the European challenge is strongly influenced by existing domestic structures and institutions (Caporaso *et al.* 2001). In Slovenia the former political system, perception of property, and government structure and practice require well established regulation and rules to make sure development is steered in the right direction. That is to say, 'epistemic communities' are not strong enough to equally participate in policy-making, and the policy-makers are not confident enough to open up the policy-making process. In such conditions, 'territorial cohesion' can play an important role in harmonizing the national planning systems or in shifting the singular national planning system toward a more feasible and comprehensive integrated approach (Davoudi 2005). If Slovenia continues the practice of participating in transnational, cross-border programmes and other EU initiatives, sharing ideas and good practice will generate additional new knowledge that can help to redefine the role of planning in governance structures (cf. Haselsberger and Benneworth Chapter 10). The continuing discussion about 'territorial cohesion', as initiated by the Ministry of Environment and Spatial Planning, will improve the importance of intersectoral cooperation in shaping the policies and preventing the conflicts among 'epistemic communities'. It will also favourably influence the adaptation of the Spatial Planning Act so that it corresponds to the modern needs of citizens and territorial development.

Notes

1 NUTS (following the French *nomenclature d'unités territoriales statistiques*) is the official nomenclature of territorial units for statistics in the European Union.
2 The principle of 'subsidiarity' implies that government should only undertake those initiatives that exceed the capacity of individuals and organizations. This principle is similarly agreed between the European Union of Member States and the Commission.

References

Albrechts, L., Healey, P. and Kunzmann, K. (2003) 'Strategic spatial planning and Regional governance in Europe', *Journal of the American Planning Association*, 69: 113–129.

Arnstein, S. (1969) *A Ladder of Citizen Participation*, Online. Available HTTP: http://lithgow-schmidt.dk/sherry-arnstein/ladder-of-citizen-participation.html (accessed 15 April 2006).

Benkovic Krasevec, M. (2006) 'Vloga majhnih obcin pri razvoju slovenskega podezelja', *DELA*, 25: 223–243.

Blagajne, D. and Santej, B. (2001) *Studija izvajanja prostorske zakonodaje o urejanju naselij, stavbnih zemljisc in graditve objektov*, Ljubljana: Institut za pravo okolja.

Brusnjak, M., Klemen, M., Marolt, G., Marot, N. and Mikec, U. (2006) *Urban land use plan of Krtina*, unpublished, Ljubljana: Faculty of Geodesy and Civil Engineering.

Camagni, R. (2005) *TEQUILA SIP, Interactive Simulation Package for Territorial Impact Assessment*, presented at General ESPON meeting, Espoo.

Caporaso, J., Cowles, M. and Risse, T. (eds) (2001) *Transforming Europe. Europeanization and Domestic Change*, Ithaca NY: Cornell University Press.

CEC – Commission of the European Communities (1999) *European Spatial Development Perspective: Towards Balanced and Sustainable Development of the Territory of the EU*. Luxembourg: Office of the Official Publications of the European Communities.

—— (2001) *White Paper on European Governance: COM(2001) 428 final*, Brussels: Commission of the European Communities.

—— (2008) *Green paper on territorial cohesion – Turning territorial diversity into strength*, Brussels: Commission of the European Communities.

Constitution of the Republic of Slovenia (1991) Online. Available HTTP: www.svlr.gov. si/en/areas_of_work/local_self_government_department/legislation (accessed 31 January 2009).

Cross-Border Operational Programme 'Slovenia – Hungary' (2009) Online. Available HTTP: http://ec.europa.eu/regional_policy/index_en.htm/ (accessed 25 July 2009).

Dąbrowski, M. (2010) 'institutional change, partnership and regional networks: civic engagement and the implementation of the Structural Funds in Poland', in N. Adams, G. Cotella and R. Nunes (eds) *Territorial Development, Cohesion and Spatial Planning: Knowledge and policy development in an enlarged EU*, London: Routledge.

Davoudi, S. (2005) 'Understanding territorial cohesion', *Planning Practice & Research*, 20(4): 433–441.

—— (2006) 'Evidence-based planning. Rhetoric and reality', *disP*, 165:2: 14–24.

Dijksman, K. (2006) *The Planning Game, How to Play the System and Win Planning Consent: An Insider's Guide to Planning Permission for Newbuilts and Extentions*, Ellington: Ovolo Publishing.

Doucet, P. (2006) 'Territorial cohesion of tomorrow: a path to cooperation or competition?' *European Planning Studies*, 14: 1473–1485.

Ekins, P. and Medhurst, J. (2006) 'The European Structural Funds and Sustainable Development: A Methodology and Indicator Framework for Evaluation', *Evaluation*, 12: 474–495.

ESPON (2004) *ESPON project 2.1.1: Territorial Impact of EU Transport and TEN Policies*. Online. Available HTTP: www.espon.eu/mmp/online/website/content/projects/243/239/index_EN.html (accessed 20 January 2009).

—— (2005) *ESPON project 2.1.3: Territorial impact of CAP and Rural Development Policy*. Online. Available HTTP: www.espon.eu/mmp/online/website/content/projects/243/277/index_EN.html (accessed 20 January 2009).

—— (2006) *ESPON project 3.2 Spatial Scenarios and Orientations in relation to the ESDP and Cohesion Policy. Volume 2. Final thematic bases and scenarios*. Online. Available HTTP: www.espon.eu/mmp/online/website/content/projects/260/716/index_EN.html (accessed 20 January 2009).

—— (2007) *ESPON project 2.3.2 Governance of Territorial and Urban Policies*. Online. Available HTTP: www.espon.eu/mmp/online/website/content/projects/243/374/index_EN.html (accessed 20 January 2009).

European Regional Policy. The Basic Essentials (2007). Online. Available HTTP: http://ec.europa.eu/inforegio (accessed 20 January 2009).

Evers, D., Tennekes, J., Borsboom, J., van den Heiligenberg, H. and Thissen, M. (2009) *A Territorial Impact Assessment of Territorial Cohesion for the Netherlands*, The Hague/Bilthoven: Netherlands Environmental Assessment Agency (PBL).

Finka, M. (2010) 'Evolving Frameworks for Regional Development and Spatial Planning in the New Regions of the EU', in N. Adams, G. Cotella and R. Nunes (eds) *Territorial Development, Cohesion and Spatial Planning: Knowledge and policy development in an enlarged EU*, London: Routledge.

Fainstein, S. (2000) 'New Directions in Planning Theory', *Urban Affairs Review*, 35 (4): 451–478.

Ferfila, B. (2008) *Upravljavska sposobnost in koalicijsko povezovanje v slovenskih občinah. Končno poročilo*, Ljubljana: Fakulteta za družbene vede.

Friedmann, J. (1987) *Planning in the Public Domain: From Knowledge to Action*, Princeton, N.J.: Princeton University Press.

Gaberscik, B. (2004) 'Pogled na prostorski red in strukturno urejanje', in A. Prosen (ed.) *Prostorske znanosti za 21. stoletje*, Ljubljana: Faculty of Geodesy and Civil Engineering.

Gerbec, F. (2003) '(Z)mesani obcutki in ocene', *Pravna praksa*, 22: 3–4.

Golobic, M., Marot, N., Radej, B., Tomsic, M. G., Kontic, B. and Gulic, A. (2008) *Monitoring and Territorial Impact Assessment of Sector Policies. Final Report. Target Research Programme Competitiveness of Slovenia 2006–2013*, Ljubljana: Urban Planning Institute of the Republic of Slovenia.

GOSP (2009) *Media campaign – European Cohesion Policy Promotion*. Online. Available HTTP: www.svlr.gov.si/nc/en/splosno/cns/novica/article/2005/1994/ (accessed 25 July 2009).

Haas, P. M. (2004) 'When does power listen to truth? A constructivist approach to the policy process', *Journal of European Public Policy*, 11: 569–592.

—— (1992) 'Epistemic communities and international-policy coordination – introduction', *International Organization* 46(1): 1–35.

Haselsberger, B. and Benneworth, P. (2010) 'Cross-border communities or cross-border proximity? Perspectives from the Austrian–Slovakian border region', in N. Adams, G. Cotella and R. Nunes (eds) *Territorial Development, Cohesion and Spatial Planning: Knowledge and policy development in an enlarged EU*, London: Routledge.

Healey, P. (1997) *Collaborative Planning: Shaping Places in Fragmented Societies*, Houndmills: Palgrave Macmillan.

Hudoklin, J. (2007) *Regional Spatial Planning*, lecture, Ljubljana: Faculty of Geodesy and Civil Engineering.

Innes, J. E. (1996) 'Planning through consensus building: a new view of the comprehensive planning ideal', *Journal of the American Planning Association*, 62(4): 460–472.

IPOP – Institute for Policies of Space (2009). Online. Available HTTP: www.ipop.si/estart.html (accessed 25 July 2009).

Knill, C. (2005) 'Introduction: Cross-national policy convergence: concepts, approaches and explanatory factors', *Journal of European Public Policy*, 12: 764–774.

Kovac, P. (2006) 'Empiricne ugotovitve o pojavnih oblikah korupcije', in S. Vlaj (ed.) *Eticno upravljanje obcin*, Ljubljana: Institut za lokalno samoupravo pri Fakulteti za upravo.

Kusar, S. (2005) 'Ko se staro umika novemu: nekatere najnovejše prostorske in funkcijske spremembe v Domžalah kot posledica deindustrializacije', *Geografski obzornik*, 52/2: 4–13.

Marot, N. (2005) *Strokovna izhodišča in smernice za prostorsko ureditev na primeru degradiranega jugovzhodnega dela Trbovelj: diplomsko delo*, Ljubljana: Faculty of Arts.

Metodologija za izpolnjevanje in spremljanje Izjave o odpravi administrativnih ovir in sodelovanju zainteresirane javnosti. Začetna ocena učinkov predpisov (2005) Ljubljana: Ministrstvo za javno upravo.

Miles, E., L. (1998) 'Personal reflections on an unfinished journey through global environmental problems of long timescale', *Policy Sciences* 31(1): 1–33.

Music, V. B. (2000) 'Usmeritve in kriteriji za razvoj in urejanje naselij', in P. Wallas (ed.) *Neformalna strokovna srecanja SiP – slovenski prostor*, Ljubljana: Ministry of Environment and Spatial Planning.

—— (2004) 'Mesto in urbanizem med teorijo in prakso', in Z. Mlinar (ed.) *Demokratizacija, profesionalizacija in odpiranje v svet*, Ljubljana: Fakulteta za druzbene vede.

Natura 2000 in Slovenia (2009) Online. Available HTTP: www.natura2000.gov.si/index. php?id=45&L=1 (accessed 30 January 2009).

Nelkin, D. (ed.) (1979) *Controversy*, Beverly Hills, CA: Sage Publications.

OECD (1995) *Recommendation of the Council of the OECD on Improving the Quality of Government Regulation*, Paris: OECD.

Ogorelec, B. (1993) *Tehnike in nacini odnosov z javnostjo v procesu urbanisticnega nacrtovanja: koncno porocilo*, Ljubljana: Urbanisticni institut Republike Slovenije.

—— (1994) 'Administration in land management – the organisation and scope of local bodies', *Urbani izziv*, 26/27: 24–28.

Pallagst, K. (2010) 'The emergence of epistemic communities in the new European Landcape: some theoretical implications for the spatial agenda of the EU, in N. Adams, G. Cotella and R. Nunes (eds) *Territorial Development, Cohesion and Spatial Planning: Knowledge and policy development in an enlarged EU*, London: Routledge.

PISO – Prostorsko-informacijski sistem občin (2009) Online. Available HTTP: www. geoprostor.net/PisoPortal/vstopi.aspx (accessed 25 July 2009).

Planspiel 'Neurodnung des Rechts der Raumordnung'. Ergebnisse und Empfehlungen (2008) Berlin: Deutsches Institut für Urbanistik.

Pogacnik, A. (1983) *Urbanizem Slovenije. Oris razvoja urbanisticnega in regionalnega prostorskega nacrtovanja v Sloveniji*, Ljubljana: Faculty of Geodesy and Civil Engineering.

—— (2003) 'The new spatial "ordnung"', *Urbani izziv*, 14/1: 105–107.

Pre-accession help (2003) Online. Available HTTP: www.svez.gov.si/si/dejavnosti/tehnicna_pomoc/predpristopna_pomoc/?type=98 (accessed 23 April 2009).

Promotion of Balanced Regional Development Act (1999) Online. Available HTTP: www. uradni-list.si/1/objava.jsp?urlid=199960&stevilka=2868 (accessed 30 January 2009).

Proposal of Act of Administrative Regions (2008) Online. Available: www.svlr.gov.si/si/ delovna_podrocja/podrocje_lokalne_samouprave/pokrajine/ (accessed 30July 2009).

Rakar, I. (2006) 'Etika, korupcija in pravo', in S. Vlaj (ed.) *Eticno upravljanje obcin*, Ljubljana: Institut za lokalno samoupravo pri Fakulteti za upravo.

Ravnikar, L. and Tanko, D. (2005) *Land consolidation in Slovenia*, Online. Available HTTP: www.fao.org/REGIONAL/SEUR/events/landcons/docs/Slovenia.pdf (accessed 30 January 2009).

Rus, A. (1994) 'Urban and regional management of small towns – The institution of intermunicipal cooperation', *Urbani izziv*, 26/27: 29–35.

Schön, P. (2005) 'Territorial cohesion in Europe', *Planning Theory and Practice*, 6(3), 389–400.

Skupno stališče o predlogu ZPN-ja za širšo javnost (2007) Ljubljana: Društvo urbanistov in prostorskih planerjev Slovenije, Društvo krajinskih arhitektov Slovenije, UL FGG, UL BF, Zveza geodetov Slovenije, UI RS.

Smidovnik, J. (2007) 'Nevarnosti in pasti pri uveljavljanju ustavnega koncepta pokrajine', *Javna uprava*, 43(2): 281–286.

SSDS – Spatial Development Strategy of Slovenia, SSDS (2004) Ljubljana: Ministry of the Environment, Spatial Planning and Energy.

Stališče do Zelene knjige o teritorialni koheziji – teritorialna raznolikost kot prednost (2009) Ljubljana: MOP. (27. 2. 2009).

STAT: Statistical demographical data of Slovenian settlements (2009) Online. Available HTTP: www.stat.si/pxweb/Database/Ekonomsko/Ekonomsko.asp (accessed 27 January 2009).

Stead, D. and Nadin, V. (2010) 'Shifts in territorial governance and the Europeanization of Spatial Planning in Central and Eastern Europe', in N. Adams, G. Cotella and R. Nunes (eds) *Territorial Development, Cohesion and Spatial Planning: Knowledge and policy development in an enlarged EU*, London: Routledge.

Svetic, D. (2006) *Suburbanizacija v ljubljanski regiji*, thesis, Ljubljana: Faculty of Social Sciences.

Tewdwr-Jones, M. (2004) 'Spatial planning: principles, practices and cultures', *Journal of Planning & Environment Law*, V: 560–569.

Transcript of parliamentary hearing of Spatial Planning Act (2007) Online. Available HTTP: www.dz-rs.si/index.php?id=97&cs=1&st=m (accessed 25 July 2009).

Umanotera (2007) *Umanotera poroca – Ogledalo vladi 2006, praksa in znacilnosti sodelovanja s civilno druzbo*, Ljubljana: Umanotera in Pravno-informacijski center za nevladne organizacije.

United Nations (1996) *Habitat Agenda and Istanbul Declaration*, New York: United Nations, Department of Public Information.

Uredba o vsebini poročila o stanju na področju urejanja prostora in minimalnih enotnih kazalnikih (2004) Online. Available HTTP: http://zakonodaja.gov.si/rpsi/r06/predpis_URED3006.html (accessed 27th July 2009).

Urejanje prostora, graditev objektov: z uvodnimi pojasnili (2003) Ljubljana: Uradni list Republike Slovenije.

Vahtar, M. (2002) *Nacrtovalske igre: tehnike in metode vkljucevanja javnosti v procese odlocanja, ki zadevajo okolje in njegov razvoj*, Domzale: ICRO.

Vriser, I. (1978) *Regionalno planiranje*, Ljubljana: Faculty of Arts, Department of Geography.

—— (1984) *Urbana geografija*, Ljubljana: Faculty of Arts, Department of Geography.

Zakrajsek, F. J. (1990) 'Zapisi ob preobrazbi sistema planiranja in urejanja prostora', in *Prispevki za razvoj sistema urejanja prostora*, 11. Sedlarjevo srecanje, Otocec: Urbanisticni institut Republike Slovenije.

Zavodnik Lamovsek, A. (2003) 'Spatial planning on route to a systems solution', *Urbani izziv*, 14(1): 107–110.

ZPNacrt – Spatial Planning Act (2007) Online. Available HTTP: www.mop.gov.si/fileadmin/mop.gov.si/pageuploads/zakonodaja/prostor/nacrtovanje/prostorsko_nacrtovanje_en.pdf (accessed 30 January 2009).

ZUreP-1 – Spatial Planning Act (2003) Online. Available HTTP: www.dz-rs.si/index.php?id=101&vt=6&new=1 (accessed 14 November 2006).

9 Institutional change, partnership and regional networks

Civic engagement and the implementation of structural funds in Poland

Marcin Dąbrowski

Introduction

European Structural Funds (SF) have generated unprecedented opportunities in Poland, the major recipient of EU funding for the 2007–2013 SF programme. This project funding has helped boost economic development and narrow the country's gap with Western Europe. It also must be considered for its role as a stimulus for new institutional structures, knowledge and skills for the delivery of regional development policy in Poland, which was largely absent throughout the 1990s (e.g. Ferry 2004). SF implementation generally constitutes a potentially powerful driver for institutional change in Central and Eastern European (CEE) member states; it implies the introduction of new norms and/or policy practices that are at odds with the established 'ways of doing things' within administrations in these countries. In fact, some authors, exploring the impact of SFs on policy practices in national administrations, have highlighted the ongoing redefinition of relations between regions and central government (Ferry and McMaster 2005; Aïssaoui 2005; Hughes *et al.* 2004; Keating 2006; Bruszt 2008). Bruszt, for example, has suggested that SFs were instrumental in preparing ground for the introduction of elements of multi-level governance in CEE countries.

> The EU set the rules governing SF policies, attached positive and negative sanctions to these rules, and played an active role in creating conditions that could improve the chances of participating regional and national players to successfully play a role in the framework of the SF programmes.
>
> (Bruszt 2008: 615)

Similarly, other scholars have highlighted the beneficial role of SFs in terms of enhancing administrative capacities and stimulating changes in administrative routines through the adoption of a set of European norms and standards (e.g. Bafoil and Hibou 2003; Beaumelou 2004; Paraskevopoulos and Leonardi 2004). That said, Bafoil and Lhomel (2003) and Lepesant (2005) have emphasized the institutional difficulties of administering SF programmes in light of organizational qualities or features stemming from their limited effectiveness as well as those inherited from their Communist past. They also have suggested, however, that the imposition of new norms governing the implementation of SFs, including multi-annual programming or partnership-working between stakeholders in policy-making, could trigger a 'silent revolution'; that is, widespread collective learning processes within CEE administrations.

The EU 'partnership principle' offers some grounds for the contemplation of new organizational norms of policy practice and widespread collective learning processes, advancing EU regional policy as a driver for multi-level territorial cooperation and the involvement of a diversity of actors (e.g., NGOs, academics or business associations) in regional policy-making. A consideration of this 'partnership principle' by new EU member states could be conducive to a further consideration of the formation of new 'policy networks' and/or 'epistemic communities' (Haas 1992; Pallagst 2006) of academics, practitioners and other actors whose expertise informs policy-making. Indeed, new ideas regarding multi-annual programming, strategic approaches to regional and local development, and partnership were diffused throughout CEE countries using a number of organizational means; these included 'twinning' exercises in training, and in the exchange of knowledge and experience of implementing SF programmes. Organized by the institutions distributing funds, these numerous training courses had the added value of informal knowledge exchange, which enabled the diffusion of technical 'tips' for the successful preparation of bids for EU funding. As a result, new links have been fostered between a variety of regional actors involved in SF programmes – either as distributors or beneficiaries of the grants.

However, the degree of fit between collaborative patterns of policy-making on the back of pre-existing CEE administrative traditions and routines, and the 'ways of doing things' is questionable. Drawing a comparison with the Greek experience, Paraskevopoulos and Leonardi (2004) have concluded that, in the case of CEE countries, the compliance with EU rules might turn out to be purely 'formal' due to the weaknesses of organizational learning capacities for the implementation of EU funds (see also Czernielewska *et al.* 2004). Similarly, Grabbe (2006: 105) has argued that the new member states could be prone to creating dysfunctional institutions due to insufficient resources, lack of adequate leadership or their purely 'symbolic' nature. Such failures might be accidental, but could also 'emerge by design', as 'some CEE policy-makers already were used to creating such institutions as a way of avoiding substantive change and protecting the *status quo*' (2006: 105). In the context of 'Europeanization', Grabbe (2006) has suggested this legacy could generate institutional structures that resemble those functioning in old EU Member States – yet comparably weak and lacking in 'substance', and in policy impact. In this respect, one might ask how pre-existing features of national administrations across CEE – or region-specific socio-cultural features – affect the adoption of elements of this European model of multi-scalar and participative governance. How does the Polish administration, which often is characterized as rooted in centralism and operating from a silo-mentality, not to mention lacking the experience in pro-grammatic approaches and multiple stakeholder cooperation (cf. Bafoil and Lhomel 2003; Hibou and Bafoil 2003; Czernielewska *et al.* 2004), cope with SFs in practice? Are the new practices promoted by the financial 'carrot' of SFs internalized by the regional actors? Or rather are they considered solely as a con-dition for obtaining funding? Finally, does the implementation of EU funds create new opportunities for the involvement of local officials, business repre-sentatives, NGOs and practitioners in policy-making? Or rather does it create new opportunities for promoting one's vested interests and/or those of its polit-ical allies?

Building on the above considerations, this chapter adopts a two-fold approach. First, it will examine the regional system of SF distribution in Poland from 2004 to 2006. It asks whether the centralized and formalized *modus oper-andi* contributes to the inefficiency of SF implementation, exploring the extent to which SF-driven learning among Polish administrations suggests a shift away from the embedded practices and the administrative mindsets of its past. Second, it examines the impact of the implementation of SFs on the participation of sub-national and non-State actors in regional policy delivery and the potential forma-tion of 'epistemic communities'. Lastly, it investigates the extent to which the 'partnership principle' creates new channels for community participation, includ-ing but not limited to the emergence and involvement of 'epistemic communit-ies' in regional policy-making.

The chapter turns to the author's ongoing research of the Lower Silesia region (*Dolnoslaskie*) to the southwest of the country (NUTS II) for answers to the above questions. Lower Silesia recently has enjoyed rapid economic growth, mainly linked with its favourable geographical position close to borders with Germany and the Czech Republic, not to mention a recent wave of foreign investment. That said, its performance in terms of the pace of SF absorption from 2004 to 2006 was one of the poorest among Polish regions. This could be puzzling due to the relatively high level of social capital, and of the administra-tive capacities characterizing the region (cf. Swianiewicz and Lackowska 2007). This makes Lower Silesia an intriguing case study for the following discussion of the state's efficiency, and potential evolution in institutional arrangements, whilst scrutinizing inherited organizational features and examining the extent to which collective learning has helped to free the country from its Communist past. Nevertheless, the findings of the research conducted by the author in this region are relevant to other Polish regions. This is due largely to the implemen-tation of SFs within a similar institutional framework and as part of a single cen-trally designed and managed Integrated Regional Operating Program (IROP). The first of the following sections reviews the existing literature on the institu-tional adjustment prior to Poland's accession to the EU. The subsequent section presents the findings of the research conducted in Lower Silesia, focusing on the regional system of SF distribution in the country and emphasizing the process of collective learning among regional actors. Finally, the third section focuses on civic engagement in the process of SF implementation in Lower Silesia. It stresses the difficulties of complying with the 'partnership principle' as well as the implications of the emergence of regional networks among policy-making and administrative circles.

Institutional adjustment prior to Poland's accession to the EU: impossible decentralization?

As part of the accession 'conditionality' (see e.g. Schimmelfennig and Sedelmeier 2005; Hughes *et al.* 2004), the EU imposed a number of conditions with which the CEE candidate countries needed to comply in order to be granted EU membership. In particular, the CEE countries were obliged to adopt the so called *acquis communautaire* that required administrative reform with respect to regional policy (Chapter 21) in particular, establishing decentralized regional territorial units capable of administering SFs (see, for example, Bafoil and Hibou 2003; Keating 2006). From 1997 onwards the recommendations concerning these adjustments have been formulated in the yearly Commission's Regular Reports, assessing progress in candidate states' adoption of the *acquis* and outlining policy priorities to be tackled. Nevertheless, the Commission's preferences have been expressed in a sufficiently vague manner to allow governments room for manoeuvre. Consequently, the European 'soft expectation' (Brusis 2002) has been reinterpreted within candidate countries' domestic policy and legal systems according to specific institutional heritages, political contexts and cultures. The institutional choices taken by the Polish government, as part of the 1998 administrative reform as well as later on in the wake of preparations for SF management, confirm that adaptation pressures from Brussels have had a rather limited impact. Paradoxically though, despite these pressures from the imposition of numerous reforms and the adoption of the *acquis* by candidate countries as pre-conditions for granting them access to the EU (cf. Grabbe 2003; Schimmelfennig and Sedelmeier 2005; Hughes *et al.* 2004), the old model of centralized territorial administration has been perpetuated if not reinforced. Thus these pressures have been driven partly by efforts of adjustment and preparation for administering SFs in Poland on the one hand, and by the imperative to absorb unprecedented amounts of development aid on the other hand.

Administrative reform: between European adaptation pressure and legacy of the past

During the 1990s administrative reform was a bone of contention between mainstream centre-right parties, viewing decentralization as a continuation of democratic reforms, and left-wing parties that benefited from well established partisan structures within pre-existing territorial units. European pressure for the decentralization of territorial governance systems has opened a 'window of opportunity' for the Polish centre-right government (in power since 1997), which has been keen to bring decentralization back to the political agenda.

After harsh political debates (Regulska 1997; Illner 1998, 2002) the new territorial system in Poland came into effect in 1999 (Law from 5/06/1998, *Dziennik Ustaw* 91/576). The new territorial system is composed of 16 regions, which are structured on elected councils that designate their respective chief executive officers (the Marshals). The new regional authorities acquired wide competences, including the responsibility for delivering regional development policy. The Government, however, has secured measures that allow it to maintain a significant degree of control over the regions. Firstly it has introduced representatives or 'Voivods' into the regions, who are supposed to safeguard national interests and control the legality of decisions taken by the elected regional authorities. Second, the decentralization of competences has not been followed with a decentralization of finance. The regional authorities remain financially dependent on the Government, which considerably limits their discretion in delivering regional policy (Grosse 2004; Lepesant 2005) and thus contradicts their statutory functions. The safeguarding of the Government's trusteeship over the regions was, to some extent, also favoured by the vagueness of the European Commission's recommendations concerning administrative reform (e.g. Brusis 2002). Therefore, the outcome of the reform is paradoxical. In other words, the apparent empowerment of regions hides a de facto recentralization of State power vis-à-vis Government control of funding to the regions (Aïssaoui 2005; Grosse 2004; Lepesant 2005).

2004–2006 programming period: regional planning without regions

This re-centralization tendency has been reinforced with the institutional solutions chosen for the management of SFs for the programming period from 2004 to 2006, which has restrained the role of the regions and reasserted the Government's hegemony over regional development. Instead of preparing separate regional operational programmes for each region, the Polish Government has drafted one integrated programme for all regions (IROP) as a result of the European Commission's insistence, and despite strong opposition from regional actors. The IROP programme was based on the Government's own assessment of developmental needs and priorities for the regions, excluding the participation of the regional authorities that could have provided 'local' knowledge of regional specificities. As legislated, therefore, the regions are responsible for formulating and delivering regional development policy whereby their role in the management of SFs has been limited to the selection of projects under the pretext of their reputed insufficient capacities (Bafoil and Lhomel 2003; Bachtler and McMaster 2008). Nevertheless, regardless of the state or potential of their organizational capacity, these fledgling regional authorities have been deprived of an opportunity to improve their competence for long-term strategic planning. Therefore the European Commission's decision has thwarted the emergence of a regional development policy regime based on the participation of different levels of administrative actors, and it has perpetuated the features of the pre-existing model of centralized administration in Poland (Aïssaoui 2005). In addition, the competences in management of IROP are currently divided between the overlapping responsibilities of the Voivod and the Marshal, resulting in a fragile institutional equilibrium that could hinder the distribution of SFs. In other words, this institutional arrangement has resulted not only in longer procedures but also a risk of rivalry and conflict between the two actors.

Management of the structural funds in Lower Silesia

The persistence of formalism as well as excessive control procedures and continuously changing regulations hampered the effectiveness of the Polish system of SF distribution during the first programming period (2004–2006). However, the author's research findings also point to incremental changes within the involved regional administrations and related processes of learning of new practices. The following section will discuss the main difficulties or obstacles hampering the distribution of European structural funds in Lower Silesia; these obstacles include overregulation, bureaucratic pedantry, legal flaws and a political culture characterized by clientelism and reluctance to cooperate. Second, it will attempt to demonstrate that these obstacles might be gradually overcome through learning and increased practical experience both among employees of the institutions distributing the funds and among their beneficiaries. This view further maintains that opportunities for learning and practical experience can contribute to enhancing the regions' administrative capacities, potentially strengthening their position vis-à-vis government control.

Bureaucratic hurdles and formalism

The Polish system of SF distribution during the 2004–2006 programming period was composed of nearly 100 institutions in charge of the implementation, intermediation and financial management of different sectoral operating programmes and of the IROP. Coordinating such an institutional arrangement of diverse actors proved to be problematic as the competences of institutions often overlapped, such as in the case of the four stage evaluation of bids for IROP funding across three different institutions. First, bids would be submitted to the Marshal Office for a formal verification. If successful, these bids were subsequently evaluated by a panel of experts who listed projects by rank. Next, the list was examined by the Regional Steering Committee, a partnership-based advisory body, which could rearrange the list. Finally, the Voivod Office, in charge of signing contracts with beneficiaries, and of project implementation control and financial transfers, would re-examine the project documentation. This circumspect and complex procedure led to delays and confusion among potential beneficiaries, most of whom lacked the knowledge and experience in preparation of projects eligible for funding.

The main obstacle to the effective absorption of SFs in Poland was the bureaucratic pedantry and risk-averse attitudes of officials involved in project administration, and the multitude of often unclear procedures echoing Communist-era bureaucracy (Dąbrowski 2008). In fact, this finding has been evident, for instance, in the case of SF administration for the European Social Fund component of IROP by the Polish Regional Labour Office, which has returned project applications for correction regardless of its content once 'the first error was found'; the reasons for rejecting a project could be as trivial as the lack of a signature on one page of an attached document, the use of an inadequate colour of ink, or the incorrect format of a date. Furthermore, the potential beneficiaries of funds have been obliged to submit an exorbitant number of supporting documents. For instance, an NGO applying for funding for a training programme had to submit more than ten additional documents, such as an extract from the National Judiciary Registry confirming the status of the organization, documents confirming its financial condition (tax forms, etc.), statements certifying that it regularly pays social security fees and taxes, CVs of people involved in the project, etc. If the project was conceived in a partnership, all partners had to submit a similar amount of additional documents. Therefore, preparing documentation for an application proved to be a real challenge, especially for smaller NGOs. The same problem concerned many poorly staffed local authorities. Unsurprisingly the administration of these applications within distributing institutions, which often were lacking in staff support as well, was extremely time-consuming.

What is more, the regional institutions implementing SFs suffer from a high turnover of staff due to low wages and a lack of effectiveness incentives for overburdened employees In fact, underpaid officials have found more lucrative posts in consultancies due to their sought-after skills in SF-oriented administration. This has led to a massive exodus to the private sector, requiring regional institutions, such as the Regional Labour Office, to constantly recruit new inexperienced staff. Again the bureaucratic pedantry of employees of the Lower Silesian Voivod Office, combined with staff shortages, has caused significant delays in the payment of grants to beneficiaries. As a result of these delays, beneficiaries, who often have resorted to loans in order to secure match funding for proposed projects, have been forced to take further loans to complete the project on time, and in some cases run the risk of bankruptcy. An awareness of these risks has been seriously discouraging for potential beneficiaries of SFs.

Thus the degree of complex formal procedures has pushed many applicants to solicit specialized consultancies, which have flourished as a result of the growing demand for such services not to mention the availability of experienced former officials keen to work for them. Apart from the fact that such services are costly, massive recourse to consultants could create conditions prone to corruption. In fact, some private consultants are simultaneously engaged in the process of project selection as members of expert panels, for instance, which have been commissioned for assessing the quality of projects and their fit with IROP objectives.

Legal framework issues

Furthermore, the creation of an institutional system to implement SFs has not been followed by adequate adjustments in the legal frameworks concerning public-private partnerships (PPP) and invitations to tender. These shortcomings also have added to difficulties in the implementation of SFs. PPPs play a vital role in the implementation of SFs as they can assist local authorities willing to carry out an EU-funded project and overcome the financial shortage of resources for match funding. Even so, the current law regulating PPPs did not come into effect until October 2005. Yet still it remained a de facto dead letter until July 2006, that is, two years after launching the implementation of SFs in Poland as a result of drafting application directives. Meanwhile regional authorities have been obliged to postpone a number of projects, which were often supposed to respond to urgent infrastructure needs. Lastly, concerning the legislation on invitations to tender, there is the often noted problem of the minimum value of investment above which it is necessary to take recourse of this procedure. Both beneficiaries and institutions involved in the distribution of SFs argue that the current minimum value of 6,000 Euros is too low. In fact, this lengthy procedure has to be used even for small-scale projects like those carried out by NGOs. In addition, the process is frequently blocked as unsuccessful bidders can object to its outcome in a trial which might take several months, during which the realization of a project can stall in want of a contractor.

Mistrust, clientelism and politicization

Finally, another factor conflicting with the mode of collaborative and inclusive governance, which was imposed as part of the EU cohesion policy framework and contributed to difficulties in SF implementation, is the predominant political culture in Poland. This predominant political culture is characterized by a mutual distrust between officials and beneficiaries, and a reluctance to cooperate, clientelism and the politicization of administration. A general belief that 'everyone would like to steal European money' (Lower Silesia Voivod Office 2006) resulted in a particular insistence on control procedures that are much more meticulous than those suggested by the European Commission. This was, for instance, the case with respect to the procedures implemented by the Voivod Office in controlling the implementation of projects. But excessive 'control of everyone by everyone' (Lower Silesia Marshal Office 2006) also hindered cooperation between institutions involved in the distribution of the SF. The government has put in place meticulous control procedures of regional authorities' actions: employees of the Lower-Silesian Marshal's Office complained that they had been subjected to 'three controls in two months, all concerning the same issue, which resulted in a paralysis' (ibid.). This reflected Government's lack of trust toward regional authorities and a perception that they were not competent partners. Yet, according to Putnam *et al.* (1993) or Amin and Thrift (1994), it is precisely the mutual trust between regional development actors, which favours the effectiveness of their actions.

Changes to organizational schemes and the mindsets of bureaucratic and political *élites* are a *sine qua non* condition for constructing effective regional policy and for overcoming the administrative culture inherited from the Communist era (Grosse 2004: 59, 279). In fact, clientelism and tendencies to privilege narrowly defined party or even private interests appear to be deeply rooted in Poland and to affect both regional and local authorities. One striking example, illustrating the frequent interference of party politics with administrative decision-making in Poland, was evident in the political struggle over eligibility criteria for EU grants between the heads of the regional executive in Lower Silesia, the Voivod and the Marshal, who represented two fiercely opposed political camps (the former – left-wing SLD, and the latter – conservative PiS). The Voivod claimed that the criteria which were established by his political opponents from the Marshal Office were inadequate and, hence, refused to approve the first bundle of projects to receive funding as part of IROP which were selected by the Board of Voivodship (an executive body elected by the regional council and presided over by the Marshal). As a result of this quarrel the payment of grants allocated to beneficiaries was delayed by nearly a year, consequently placing Lower Silesia behind other regions in terms of SF absorption rates.

On the local level, mayors manifested a reluctance to cooperate with other institutions, resulting in a lack of long-term strategic thinking that could transcend the borders of the commune. Consequently, numerous SF-funded projects were carried out by individual communes when they should have been the product of cooperation between local neighbouring jurisdictions (Lower Silesia Voivod Office 2006). Therefore, it was not uncommon to find part of an SF-funded road renovation terminate exactly at the border between the communes it crossed. In some cases, European grants were spent for building local roads 'in the middle of nowhere', which did not connect to any major district or regional level road networks. Thus a change in the mindsets SF beneficiaries, which would discourage these problems in the future and promote a more efficient and strategic use of SFs, is urgently required. European funds, given that they cover such a large variety of actions from professional training through to the refurbishment of historical monuments, the setup of technological clusters and the construction of roads, should gradually encourage local officials to conceive development initiatives in an integrated and strategic manner. In other words, SFs could contribute to enhancing local organizational capacity through the provision of a financial 'carrot' (funding for projects) and a normative 'stick' (requirements regarding multi-annual local development strategies to which projects must correspond) provided they cooperate between each other (Lepesant 2005).

Collective learning in practice: towards more effective administration of Structural Funds

The bureaucratic barriers, legal shortcomings and a political culture prone to clientelism and mistrust hampered the distribution of SFs in Poland, leading to delays and discouraging beneficiaries. Moreover, both the distributors of SFs and their beneficiaries lacked experience and knowledge useful in acquiring funding. This resulted in considerable difficulties in implementing SFs during the 2004–2006 programming period, which fuelled fears about Poland's capacity to absorb the allocated funds. In fact, the statistics on absorption rates confirmed a significant disproportionate relationship between the high number of submitted projects and the funds actually transferred to beneficiaries. Roughly two years after Poland's accession in 2004, the sum of money claimed in the totality of bids in Lower Silesia was equal to 206.44 per cent of the total allocation to the region via IROP. This is a testament to the great mobilization of beneficiaries. At the same time, the aggregated value of funding contracts signed between the Voivod Office and beneficiaries' co-funding equalled 82.58 per cent of the total allocation. But the value of financial transfers towards beneficiaries accounted for only 13.2 per cent of the available funding, attributing the Lower Silesia to a laggard region in the absorption of SFs among Polish regions.[1]

Nevertheless, it must be highlighted that the imposition of principles governing EU regional policy implementation, such as partnership and programming as well as norms concerning monitoring and evaluation, pushed the actors involved in the distribution of SFs to gradually adapt their practices and to learn how to operate in this new policy environment. This learning process is improvised and lengthy, but it is present at all levels of the system of SF distribution. The institutions involved in this process in Lower Silesia have been confronted with new tasks, requiring specific skills and experience that they had lacked. Therefore, they have been obliged to improvise, to learn from their own mistakes and to enhance their expertise, which ultimately has led to the successful absorption of SFs in the region (Lower Silesia Marshal Office 2006, 2007; Lower Silesia Voivod Office 2006). In fact, in a context of strong pressure for adjustment and absorption of unprecedented amounts of EU funding, the functioning of the system of SF distribution improved gradually and the cumbersome procedures were rationalized. A number of the problems in the implementation of SFs in the region seem to have been linked with the initial rush and pressure to spend European money (Lower Silesia Marshal Office 2006; see also Hibou and Bafoil 2003).

Gradually the system became more flexible and beneficiary-oriented as a result of regional actors' denouncement of procedural flaws (Dąbrowski 2008). And cooperation between regional actors, especially between the Marshal's Office and beneficiaries, improved as they interacted. The situation also has improved progressively at the State level. The creation of the Ministry of Regional Development (MRD), detached from the Ministry of Economy in 2005, reflected the importance of the SF programme on the political agenda and was the first sign of the Government's growing awareness of the need to enhance coordination of actions to ensure that Poland effectively copes with the challenges of SF absorption. The new Ministry boldly defines its priorities in the following way: 'the Ministry's objective is to use all the European Union's funds that are available to Poland both in the current budget for the 2004–2006 programming period and subsequently for 2007–2013 in the most efficient way'.[2] Thus, one of the first endeavours of the 'Ministry of Structural Funds' was carrying out a special programme aimed to eliminate system flaws and accelerate the process of distribution. Initially unresponsive, the MRD's 'repair programme' soon appeared to be successful albeit difficult to assess. Neverthe-less, from the second half of 2006 onwards the aforementioned disproportionate relationship between the high number of submitted projects and the funds actu-ally transferred to beneficiaries has started shrinking rapidly in Lower Silesia and in other Polish regions. On a national scale, whilst the percentage of funds transferred to beneficiaries as part of the IROP grew from 18.91 per cent in June 2006 to 83.46 per cent in April 2008, Lower Silesia grew from 13.2 per cent to 84.24 per cent, respectively.

What is more, it should be highlighted that the Government demonstrates a growing awareness of the opportunities for State modernization, which are gen-erated through efforts to successfully implement SFs, but also demand further and wider reforms at all levels of governance:

> The integration within the EU is an opportunity, which implies a moderniz-ing obligation and offers substantial financial means. However, this oppor-tunity cannot be used without a radical restructuring of the system of governance of developmental processes, above all on the national level, but practically at all levels of governance.
>
> (Ministry of Regional Development 2007)

Concerning the beneficiaries, learning also was apparent in the gradually decreasing number of projects which were rejected in the initial formal assess-ments. Moreover, the constraints imposed by the SF framework force actors to

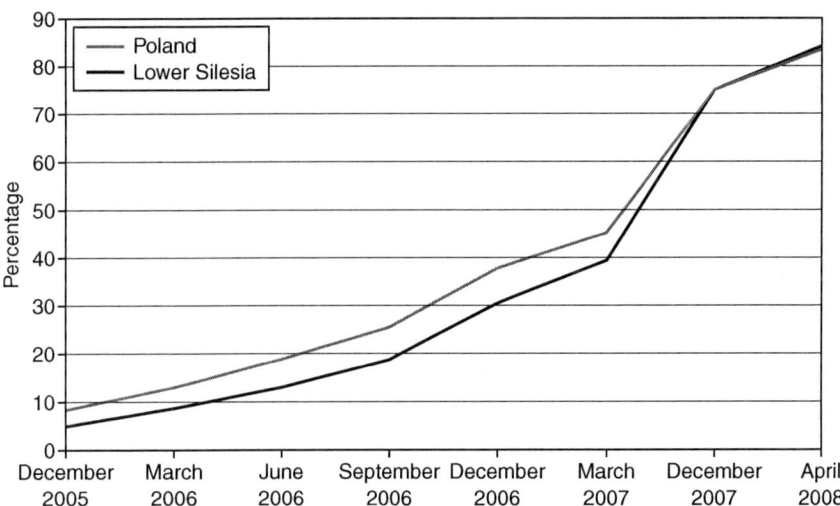

Figure 9.1 Evolution of value of financial transfers towards beneficiaries as percentage of allocation for whole country and for Lower Silesia (IROP) (source: Author's compilation from data available at website of Ministry of Regional Development, www.mrr.gov.pl).

search for new organizational solutions, especially within NGOs and local authorities. What specifically concerns local authorities' drafting of multi-annual local development strategies, to which projects outlined in applications for funding must correspond, is a precondition for benefiting from structural funding. European structural funds therefore have promoted multi-annual strategic development planning. In fact, prior to EU accession, hardly any local authority was taking part in any sort of 'planning' activity, apart from those communes that participated in pre-accession funds programmes. Investment in development projects were based on the commune's yearly budget and, hence, were limited to this short-term perspective. The funding opportunities offered, as part of SF programmes and the conditions imposed for their acquisition, have prompted local authorities to reflect on communes' development, and create broader and more strategic visions of local development, corresponding to relevant planning documents that are meant to be drafted with the participation of local communities (Lower Silesia Marshal Office 2007).

One could ask, however, to what extent these changes correspond to a genuine internalization of EU-imported rules or a rather purely 'formal' compliance with these rules as driven by the willingness to benefit from European funds? For instance, the prospect of influencing decision-making and obtaining valuable first-hand information on project selection criteria that could prove useful in future grant applications by communes had encouraged the participation of local officials in partnership-based committees concerned with SF distribution (e.g. the Regional Steering Committee). The commonplace outsourcing of the preparation of local development strategies to consultancies is another example of such 'formal' adjustment to SF requirements. These strategies are drafted by private consultants, frequently according to the same template, which casts doubt over their fit with local specificities and needs, and hence their purposefulness.[3] Nonetheless, one cannot exclude a gradual internalization of EU-imposed rules by actors involved in SF programmes (see, for example, Goetz 2005; Börzel 2006; Sedelmeier 2006), which could be favoured by factors such as the normative attractiveness of EU rules, the growing experience of implementers and beneficiaries of SFs. These factors also include the diffusion of 'good practice' and the knowledge of regional development through involvement of an increasing number of regional and local actors in SF-oriented training courses, conferences, seminars and informal exchanges. For example, despite the fact that multi-annual strategic planning is imposed as a condition for receiving funding and outsourced to consultancies, local officials seldom question this condition, often emphasizing the merits of strategic approaches and tending to perceive public consultations in the process of drafting local development strategies as 'normal' practice.

Finally, the involvement of regional authorities in the administration of the IROP gave them an opportunity to acquire experience and skills necessary to take full control of the management of SFs within their territories. In fact, for the 2007–2013 programming period, the IROP was replaced by 16 Regional Operating Programs (ROP) prepared and carried through by the Marshals' Offices;[4] this corresponds to a shift towards a more decentralized system of distribution of EU funds and could potentially enhance the prestige and standing of regional authorities in the hierarchy of State governance structures (Bachtler and McMaster 2008). Drawing on the practical experience gained during the implementation of the IROP as well as the expert input from a number of regional stakeholders as part of the formal and informal consultations, all Polish regions have drafted regional development strategies as well as corresponding ROPs. This reflects a relative degree of collective organizational learning that ultimately is a testament to these regional actors' ability to formulate 'evidence-based' regional development policy. ROPs are expected to provide a better response to regions' specific needs because they have been prepared by regional authorities with active participation of regional stakeholders, especially local authorities. As a result, there are variations across ROPs in the number of priorities defined (between six and ten) and in the amount of funding allocated to different areas of policy intervention, such as urban revitalization, environmental protection or research and development. In Lower Silesia, for instance, urban revitalization initially was not included in the ROP; however, it was included later as a result of pressure from potentially concerned local authorities (Wałbrzych Municipal Office 2007).

Though it is early to thoroughly assess ROPs it appears that a number of lessons have been drawn from the IROP experience, which contributes to the establishment of more transparent and efficient institutional solutions. First, the regionalization of SF administration, which involves a concentration of competences within the Marshal Office, eliminates the risk of troublesome conflicts between the Marshal and the Voivod. Second, regional authorities had the upper hand in determining the procedures for SF implementation as part of the ROPs; their hands-on experience (and mistakes) in the 2004–2006 resulted in the elimination of a number of procedural bottlenecks and hurdles. For instance, Lower Silesian authorities introduced a pre-selection procedure for certain types of projects, which enabled beneficiaries to complete the costly preparation of project documentation once the bid had been pre-selected for funding. This procedure eliminated the risk of incurring these costs even when a bid was rejected. Lastly the Marshal Office can take rapid decisions concerning changes in ROP procedures without waiting for Government approval (unlike administrative procedures in the case of the IROP), which can further improve the SF distribution system's flexibility.

Nevertheless, an early observation of ROP management points to a number of persisting problems. SF beneficiaries have noted that the bureaucratic obstacles regarding applications for grants continue to remain significant in the case of ROP. Moreover, the changes in the institutional architecture for SF administration in the current 2007–2013 programming period exacerbated, to some extent, the lack of institutional continuity; a substantial number of the Marshal Office's ROP staff are newly recruited employees who need to repeat the learning process that took place in the 2004–2006 programming period. This led to delays in launching the ROPs across the country, which was undeniably reminiscent of the problems with IROP; by May 2009 the regions managed to spend only 6.0 per cent of the targeted amount of EU fund absorption by the 16 ROPs that year, which contrasted with the relatively faster absorption rate under centrally administered programmes (Niklewicz 2009).

Additionally, the lack of transparency conducive to irregularities and conflicts of interest also remains a major issue for the implementation of ROPs, especially regarding the process of project selection. In Lower Silesia, for instance, 13 out of 83 experts assessing submitted projects are linked with consultancies that prepare project documentation for beneficiaries (Kokot *et al.* 2009), which creates a situation particularly prone to corruption. Similar developments can be observed in the case of centrally managed operating programmes, such as in the 'Infrastructure and Environment' programme where roughly one third of experts assessing submitted project bids also offer consulting services to beneficiaries.

Finally, the Government's persistent determination to maintain control over regional authorities' actions suggests there is a continuing risk of perpetuating centralization tendencies, or the 'IROP syndrome'. In fact, the Government attempted to interfere in the drafting of procedures for ROP management, which caused frustration amongst regional authorities responsible for programme delivery. As one of the regional officials put it: 'The degree of control and interference of the central government in a region's action remains almost unchanged' (Wałbrzych Municipal Office 2007). This chimes with the doubts expressed by Bachtler and McMaster (2008) on the prospects for strengthening regions or regional authorities' position in the multi-level governance of SF implementation as a result of the regionalization of SF management. Indeed, the conservative-populist parliamentary coalition (formed in May 2006), which was hostile to regions' autonomy over SF management, introduced a right of veto for the Voivods into draft law for the 2007–2013 programming period; this 'veto', they argued, could be used in the case of disagreement with regional authorities' decisions regarding project selection. This decision has resulted in protests by regional officials, rightly considering the veto measure as an attempt to limit their active role SF implementation and a proof of government distrust. Finally, as a result of the European Commission's intervention, the right of veto along with other dispositions limiting regional autonomy, including the requirement of ministerial approval for actions submitted by regional authorities and the appointment of the Regional Monitoring Committee by the Voivod, were not included in the updated legislation (Law from 6/12/2006, *Dziennik Ustaw*, 227/1658). Thus, regardless of Government's commitment to retain trusteeship over the regions, these recent events suggest that whilst the regionalization of SF management could favour further decentralization it would be a long and painstaking process.

Civic involvement or emergence of technocratic networks?

The implementation of SFs has led to institutional adjustments, which could constitute a basis for the emergence of regions as the main architects of regional policy in Poland. Even so, one could doubt that the sole creation of regional authorities and the imposition of rules constraining these authorities' responsibilities in drafting multi-annual planning and involving various actors in decision-making automatically would lead to the adoption and internalization of rules of collaborative and inclusive regional governance.

Policy measures favouring inclusion and cooperation of various public and private regional actors are implemented across various countries, which reflects the popularity of 'new regionalist' concepts such as 'institutional thickness' (Amin and Thrift 1994), 'learning region' (Florida 1995) or 'associational economy' (Cooke and Morgan 1998) among Western policy-makers. The 'partnership principle' also echoes this 'new regionalist' thinking (Bachtler and McMaster 2008). Its imposition as part of the European SF framework is expected to trigger such developments. The realization of the 'partnership principle' among new Member States could, in fact, contribute to the strengthening of local democracy through stakeholder engagement of multi-level governance activities in the design and implementation of development policy, providing policy-makers with specific knowledge and information on diverse areas of policy concern as well as the developmental needs of concerned territories.

That said, one could express doubts concerning the transferability of partnership-based solutions across differentiated countries and regions. In fact, nothing guarantees that regions in which a similar policy is implemented will follow a similar path and respond in a similar way to policy guidelines imposed by central government or Brussels. Moreover those policy measures, which aim at strengthening regional networks, often draw on the experiences of leading Western regions (e.g. Silicon Valley, Third Italy or Baden-Württemberg) whose success is due to a set of region-specific relational assets (Lovering 1999). Again, this casts doubt over their transferability to different socio-cultural contexts, where such assets might not exist (cf. Stead and Nadin Chapter 7). Therefore one could question whether compliance with the 'partnership principle' actually favours participation of non-State actors in regional policy delivery in Poland; a country that has been characterized by low levels of 'social capital', and by politicized and clientelistic administrative procedures (cf., for example, Baldersheim and Swianiewicz 2003; Swianiewicz and Lackowska 2007).

A 'caricature' of partnership?

The partnership requirement is a major novelty in the Polish context, and in some respects it has appeared to work well and has been perceived by regional authorities as useful and beneficial to the SF programming stage, for example. The 'partnership principle' has made regional officials realize that consulting interested parties, such as business associations, local officials and NGOs, can be helpful particularly in gathering important information and expertise needed to design the ROP and, more generally, to deliver regional development policy. Some regional officials have been committed to consultations of the draft ROP for Lower Silesia, and have carried them out thoroughly and by various means, including conferences, online surveys or informal consultations with experts and stakeholders. In other respects, however, the compliance with the 'partnership principle' appears to be more ambiguous.

The difficulties in adopting partnership-based working at the implementation stage of SFs can be illustrated by the awkward functioning of the Regional Steering Committee (RSC) in Lower Silesia, an institution expected to fulfil EU requirements regarding inclusion of local authorities and social partners in the process of SF distribution during the 2004–2006 programming period. The RSC participated in project selection as part of IROP and was composed of representatives of Government, regional and local authorities, academia, social partners, businesses and NGOs. The participation of such a large variety of actors potentially could enhance the process of project selection as a result of the expert knowledge and/or 'hands-on experience' of members of the Committee. However, the author's findings, which echo official evaluation documents (Wolińska *et al.* 2005: 28–9), suggest that the RSC did not allow non-state actors to participate or to have any significant impact on the outcome of the debates and the choice of projects. Instead, the debates were dominated by local authorities' representatives who considered the RSC an arena for lobbying in favour of their own EU-funded projects or gaining information that could be useful in acquiring European grants. Also, the outcome of the debates was somewhat futile, considering that it was not binding for the final decision by the Board of Voivodship. Furthermore, there were no clear selection criteria for the members of the RSC, allowing the Marshal to side with criteria according to political allegiances and interests (Regional Steering Committee 2006).[5] Thus in theory the RSC complies with the 'partnership principle' as it enables participation of various regional actors in SF distribution, but in practice these actors have little influence on the process.

That said, the introduction of RSCs across Polish regions corresponded with a certain step forward in terms of promoting transparency and social control of administrative decision-making. NGO representatives, participating in RSCs, engaged in relations with regional and local officials, and attempted to circulate the information on the outcomes of debates among their peers. According to an NGO representative on the Lower Silesian RSC, their presence in the Committee involved obliging regional officials to refrain from overtly favouring certain projects (Regional Steering Committee 2006, 2007). In fact, NGOs have resorted to 'public blaming' in the local media, which apparently has prevented certain abusive practices in the distribution of EU grants. In November 2004, for example, when the Lower Silesian Board of Voivodship replaced eight out of 26 members of the RSC (including NGO representatives) with individuals closely connected to political parties forming the coalition in power in Lower Silesia, over 200 regional NGOs signed a protest letter published in press. As a consequence, the dismissed NGO representatives were reappointed (ibid.). The RSCs ultimately were short-lived. Instead of attempting to enhance the functioning of the RSCs, as was suggested in official (Wolińska *et al.* 2005) and independent expert reports (Dworakowska *et al.* 2006), the Government decided to suppress these bodies in order to simplify and speed-up the decision-making process in the 2007–2013 programming period. Such formalized partnership was in fact considered by Polish officials as an unwanted complication and a waste of time (Grosse 2006). Consequently, more pragmatic, yet also much less open and transparent approaches to SF distribution on the basis of ad hoc consultations of stakeholders and experts has been adopted for the implementation of ROPs.

These developments suggest that it might be relatively easy to establish new institutions, such as the RSCs, and thus produce higher levels of inter-institutional interaction between regional stakeholders. Nonetheless, it may turn out to be more difficult to make these newly created institutions work in a context characterized by centralism, clientelism and a traditional lack of cooperation between State and civil society. These findings also resonate with Bruszt's argument who suggested that one could observe 'layering' (or 'change in continuity') in the CEE Member States; that is 'emergence of change on the margins, implying local rule transformation within basically unchanged institution that does not challenge the dominant characteristics of the mode of governance' (2008: 620). This argument also appears to be confirmed in the way that SFs have impacted upon the interactions between various actors of regional governance.

Mobilization of actors around the SF: technocratic networks?

The implementation of SFs in Polish regions has undoubtedly triggered considerable mobilization of actors from both public and private sectors. Partnerships between SF beneficiaries, training for beneficiaries, sessions of partnership committees and public hearings concerning ROPs' priorities have provided unprecedented and numerous opportunities for different actors to interact, cooperate and foster contacts. Following observations and interviews conducted in Lower Silesia, informal SF-oriented networks of regional and local officials, business associations, NGOs, experts and consultants emerges. Actors across different regional institutions involved in SF distribution not only often know each other, but also have similar backgrounds and/or experiences (often due to participation in the implementation of pre-accession funds), and share a common enthusiasm, if not pride of being involved in SF distribution (Lower Silesia Voivod Office 2006; Wrocław Municipal Office 2006; Stowarzyszenie Inicjatywa dla Przedsiębiorczości 2006; Stowarzyszenie Sanatorów 2006). However, can one expect these networks to forge durable links between public actors, enterprises and NGOs, and thus to have positive externalities in terms of the emergence of a vibrant civil society participating in decision-making at a regional level? Can one consider these networks as a basis for future regional *élite* actively involved in policy-making or as nascent 'epistemic communities' disposing of knowledge and know-how that could be used in designing policy?

One should not overestimate the contribution of these networks to the strengthening of civil society in Polish regions, recognizing that relations between regional actors are far from being based on reciprocal trust. In the

Polish context 'as soon as money is at stake, problems with cooperation between partners begin' (Regionalne Centrum Wspierania Inicjatyw Pozarządowych 2006). Construction of such relations might be a matter of time; however, a stable institutional framework is required, which can regulate interactions between public and non-state actors (Wrocław Municipal Office 2006). Yet in the Polish context such a framework has been either missing or frequently changing.

Undoubtedly, a growing number of actors such as regional officials, various public or private beneficiaries of EU grants as well as consultants offering services to the latter or academics are increasingly involved in networks concerned with the administration and implementation of SFs. These networks are loose and informal, and their members are capable of putting forward their preferences or variably influencing regional authorities' decisions, depending on their 'knowledge resources' (cf. Adams *et al.* Chapter 2). However, these emerging networks are oriented towards technical questions related to the acquisition of EU grants. 'One should not confuse improvement and construction of technical know-how in fund-raising or management of the SF with building and improvement of skills in terms of making of regional policy' (Grosse 2006). Thus, the participation in networks is interest-driven, as it appears that most actors seek contact with other policy stakeholders in order to maximize their chances of benefiting from EU grants.

For instance, SFs offer a novel source of funding that attracted the attention of numerous NGOs. Thus they were encouraged to undergo organizational changes, to professionalize in order to be able to develop potentially eligible projects and also to communicate with their peers as well as officials distributing the grants to access information helpful in acquiring funding (Regionalne Centrum Wspierania Inicjatyw Pozarządowych 2006; Stowarzyszenie Sanatorów 2006; Stowarzyszenie Inicjatywa dla Przedsiębiorczości 2006). However, the potential drawback is that NGOs adapt their agendas in many cases to the priorities of SF programmes that can lead them to abandon their initial aims and/or fields of activity (Regionalne Centrum Wspierania Inicjatyw Pozarządowych 2006). Moreover, the actors that most actively participated in consultations of the Lower Silesian ROP were representatives of local communes, who had a successful record of EU-funded projects and were keen to influence or shape the regional funding programme according to their interests. Whilst other actors, such as poorer peripheral communes or weaker NGOs, who lack the capacities to prepare eligible projects, or who cannot afford to cover the match-funding and hence do not see opportunities from the SF, are often not at all interested in participating in these consultations. For the same reasons these actors also ignore other SF-oriented *fora* or 'knowledge arenas' (ibid.) that can enable access to information and participation in policy-making such as the partnership committees. These findings chime with Bruszt's argument (2008), which claims that stakeholder involvement in regional level policy-making in CEE countries can be difficult because of the poor organization and insufficient skills of peripheral communes and non-state actors.

Thus, SFs can stimulate multi-level and cross-scalar agent interactivity, which consequently can lead to the emergence of nascent regional governance structures. Yet the cooperation between the actors involved in SF-oriented networks is interest-driven and somewhat 'shallow'. Could these regional networks, though, be considered as emergent 'epistemic communities' (Haas 1992) or 'advocacy coalitions' (Sabatier 1998) exerting a significant influence on policy-makers' choices? The author's findings suggest that those actors involved in implementing EU funding programmes have built up an expertise in acquiring grants and carrying out projects funded by the distributors of SFs. Therefore these actors possess a practical know-how, which can be valuable for regional policy-makers. In other words, the European SF framework has prompted local and regional authorities administering these funds to carry out public consultations on programming documents or to enable participation of various actors in monitoring procedures that can create opportunities for access to policy-makers. In fact, the latter is one of the more effective means of influencing the policy process by 'epistemic communities of professionals with recognized expertise and competence in a particular domain and an authoritative claim to policy-relevant knowledge within that domain or issue-area' (Haas 1992: 3). What is more, Lower Silesian authorities perceive the EU-imposed consultations on ROPs as beneficial; that is, particularly useful for them as a means of gathering information and enhancing the fit between the regional needs and priorities outlined in the programme (Lower Silesia Marshal Office 2007). Altogether, this is a testament to the internalization or (re) institutionalization of SF-oriented norms and a shift towards 'evidence-based' policy-making by those actors who have built up an expertise in acquiring grants and carrying out projects funded by the distributors of SFs.

Zito (2001) additionally has argued that 'epistemic communities' also tend to be more successful in influencing decision-makers in the case of policy uncertainties or potentially controversial policy actions, which appears to be the case of SF distribution and implementation in Lower Silesia. In fact, regional policy is a relatively new domain for Polish policy-makers, and the design and implementation of ROPs are novel tasks for regional authorities keen to access expertise and competence in particular policy domains. Furthermore, as Hall suggests (1993: 280, paraphrased from Zito 2001: 590), policy-makers are more receptive to new ideas and external advice in a situation when there is dissatisfaction with previous policies or high media and political pressures. This also reflects the case in Polish regions where there was widespread frustration of regional officials with the centralized and rigid governance of IROP during the 2004–2006 programming period. In fact, the effective use of European funds became an object of strong media pressure as well as an important issue in local, regional and even national elections. Hence, the effective implementation of European funds became a criterion against which voters could judge the performance of Government and/or sub-national authorities.

Nonetheless, the interest-driven participation in the SF-oriented networks hardly involves any wider community representation. In other words, many actors are excluded in practice and those who participate in SF-oriented networks represent their often narrowly defined interests. For instance, communes' or non-State actors' contribution to the preparation of SF programmes is not based on any prior discussion or agreement on common views among interested parties. Rather, these communes or non-State actors are concerned mostly with obtaining the largest allocation of funding for their project interests. Additionally, despite a certain degree of SF-oriented mobilization within the third sector, the presence of NGOs in these networks remains relatively weak. Thus if one could qualify these emerging networks of technocrats, regional and local political actors, consultants and entrepreneurs as a nascent 'epistemic communities', their formation around the distribution and implementation of SFs might not be more profound than a concern for the absorption and acquisition of funds respectively.

Conclusions

The implementation of SFs in Poland has led to diverse and sometimes indefinite outcomes at distinct levels of territorial governance. At the national level, both the vagueness of the European Commission's recommendations concerning administrative reform and its reluctance to consign the task of formulating regional operational programmes to relatively young regional authorities offered the Government an opportunity to impose solutions suiting its best interests and consequently favouring the (re)centralization of power in line with its institutional legacies of Communist-era bureaucracy.

Regarding the regional level, the findings suggest that, despite a number of difficulties with the implementation of SFs, the imposition of the EU cohesion policy framework has forced regional authorities to learn and adjust their practices. This consequently led to the improvement of their organizational capacities in the management of regional development policy, and could lead to the strengthening of their position vis-à-vis Government control (see Bachtler and McMaster 2008). Therefore, the institutional changes associated with the arrival of SFs in Poland could contribute to a reassessment of the regions as major actors of regional policy and eventually, in the longer term, could favour emancipation from the state's trusteeship; further research into this reassessment (i.e. the regionalization of SF management) would need to be placed in a longer temporal perspective. These dynamics run contrary to observations at the national level. Yet additional research would be necessary in order to assess both outcomes in the context of ROP implementation during the current 2007–2013 programming period. It remains unclear, however, how regions will cope with the variety of challenges involved in the implementation of these programmes.

Finally, the apparent concerns over the impact of SFs on intra-regional governance and participation among various stakeholders in decision-making processes remain. On the one hand, the introduction of the 'partnership principle' involved the creation of novel *fora* or 'knowledge arenas' for the participation of stakeholders in the administration and implementation of SFs, and improvements to the transparency of administrative decision-making and the mobilization of regional actors. This has created conditions conducive to fostering new relationships between various regional actors and the emergence of informal SF-oriented networks that could be considered as nascent 'epistemic communities' in possession of useful practical knowledge of SF distribution and implementation. What is more, there appears to be a shift toward an 'evidence-based' form of planning whereby these informal networks have demonstrated their capacity to prepare ROPs whilst drawing on a range of stakeholder input. On the other hand, the partnership arrangements put in place in Polish regions have failed to ensure a genuine participation of non-State actors in the process of SF distribution and the aforementioned informal networks can hardly be considered as representing the 'public voice'. This casts doubt on the transferability of policy measures based on 'new regionalist' recipes and the usefulness of partnership as a tool for stimulating the participation of multiple non-state actors in the delivery of regional development policy in Poland.

Notes

1 For monthly reports on implementation of the SF see Ministry's of Regional Development website (accessed February 2007): www.mrr.gov.pl.
2 Quoted from MRD's website: www.mrr.gov.pl/english/Strony/default.aspx (accessed May 2009).
3 It should be stressed, however, that further investigation would be necessary to fully elucidate this issue.
4 For an outline of the system designed for SF implementation in the 2007–2013 period see the National Strategic Reference Framework 2007–2013 (Ministry of Regional Development 2007: 93–102).
5 See also Wolińska *et al.* 2005: 30–31.

References

Adams, N., Cotella, G. and Nunes, R. (2010) 'Territorial knowledge channels in a multi-jurisdictional policy environment: a theoretical framework', in N. Adams, G. Cotella and R. Nunes (eds) *Territorial Development, Cohesion and Spatial Planning: Knowledge and policy development in an enlarged EU*, London: Routledge.

Aïssaoui, H. (2005) 'L'élargissement européen au prisme des fonds structurels: vers une européanisation de la gestion publique du territoire de Pologne?', *Politique européenne*, 15: 61–84.

Amin, A. and Thrift, N. (1994) *Globalization, Institutions, and Regional Development in Europe*, Oxford: Oxford University Press.

Bachtler, J. and McMaster, I. (2008) 'The EU cohesion policy and the role of the regions: Investigating the influence of the Structural Funds in the new Member States', *Environment and Planning C: Government and Policy*, 26: 398–427.

Bafoil, F. and Hibou, B. (2003) 'Les administrations publiques et les modes de gouvernement à l'épreuve de l'européanization: une comparaison Europe du Sud, Europe de l'Est', *Les Etudes du CERI*, 102. Online. Available HTTP: www.ceri-sciencespo.com/cerifr/publica/etude/2003.htm (accessed February 2007).

Bafoil, F. and Lhomel, E. (2003) 'La préparation aux fonds structurels de l'UE, les exemples de la Pologne et de la Roumanie', *Le Courrier des Pays de l'Est*, 1033: 28–38.

Baldersheim, H. and Swianiewicz, P. (2003) 'The institutional performance of Polish regions in an enlarged EU', in M. Keating and J. Hughes (eds) *The Regional Challenge in Central and Eastern Europe*, Brussels: Peter Lang.

Beaumelou, F. (2004) 'Le Fonds social européen, un outil d'adaptation des compétences?', *Annales des Mines*, November: 68–71.

Börzel, T. (2006) 'Deep impact? Europeanization and Eastern Enlargement', in A. Kutter, and V. Trappmann (eds) *Das Erbe des Beitritts*, Baden-Baden: Nomos.

Brusis, M. (2002) 'Between EU requirements, competitive politics, and national traditions: Re-creating regions in the accession countries of Central and Eastern Europe', *Governance*, 15(4): 531–559.

Bruszt, L. (2008) 'Multi-level governance – the Eastern Versions: Emerging patterns of regional development governance in the new member States', *Regional and Federal Studies*, 18(5): 607–627.

Cooke, P. and Morgan, K. (1998) *The Associational Economy: Firms, regions and innovation*, Oxford: Oxford University Press.

CEC – Commission of the European Communities (2008) *European Union Public Finance*, 4th Edition, Luxembourg: Office for Official Publications of the European Communities.

Czernielewska, M., Paraskevopoulos, C. and Szlachta, J. (2004) 'The regionalization process in Poland: an example of Shallow Europeanization?', *Regional and Federal Studies,* 14(3): 461–495.

Dąbrowski, M. (2008) 'Structural funds as a driver for institutional change in Poland', *Europe-Asia Studies*, 60(2): 227–248.

Dworakowska, A., Bar, M., Cyglicki, R., Gula, A., Małochleb, M., and Smolnicki, K. (2006) *Przejrzyste fundusze strukturalne*, Kraków and Wrocław: Instytut Ekonomii Srodowiska, CEE Bankwatch Network, Dolnoslaska Fundacja Ekorozwoju.

EC – European Council (1988) *Framework Regulation – Council Regulation (EEC) No 2052 of 24 June 1988 on the tasks of the Structural Funds and their effectiveness and on coordination of their activities between themselves and with the preparations of the European Investment Bank and other existing financial instruments*, OJ L 185, 15 July 1988, Luxembourg: Office for Official Publications of the European Communities.

—— (1993) *New Coordination Regulation – Council Regulation (EEC) No 2082/93 of 20 July 1993 Amending Regulation (EEC) No 4253/88 laying down provisions for implementing Regulation (EEC) No 2052/88 as regards the coordination of the activities of the different Structural Funds between themselves and with the operations of the European Investment Bank and the other existing financial instruments*, OJ L 193, 31 July 1993, Luxembourg: Office for Official Publications of the European Communities.

Ferry, M. (2004) 'Regional Policy in Poland on the eve of EU membership: Regional empowerment or central control?', *European Policies Research Papers*, 53. Online. Available HTTP: www.eprc.strath.ac.uk/eprc/cv_mf.cfm (accessed February 2007).

Ferry, M. and McMaster, I. (2005) 'Implementing Structural Funds in Polish and Czech regions: Convergence, variation, empowerment?', *Regional and Federal Studies*, 15(1): 19–39.

Florida, R. (1995) 'Towards the learning region', *Futures*, 5: 527–536.

Goetz, K., (2005) 'The new Member States and the EU: Responding to Europe', in S. Bulmer and C. Lequesne (eds) *The Member States of the European Union*, Oxford: Oxford University Press.

Grabbe, H. (2001) 'How does Europeanization affect CEE governance? Conditionality, diffusion and diversity', *Journal of European Public Policy*, 8(6): 1013–1031.

—— (2003) 'Europeanization goes East: Power and uncertainty in the EU accession process', in K. Featherstone and C. Radaelli (eds) *The Politics of Europeanization*, Oxford: Oxford University Press: 303–327.

—— (2006) *The EU's Transformative Power: Europeanization through conditionality in Central and Eastern Europe*, Basingstoke: Palgrave Macmillan.

Grosse, T. G. (2004) *Polityka regionalna Unii Europejskiej. Przykład Grecji, Włoch, Irlandii i Polski*, Warsaw: Instytut Spraw Publicznych.

—— (2006) Interview with the author on 28 July 2006.Warsaw.

Haas, P. (1992) 'Introduction: Epistemic communities and international policy coordination', *International Organization*, 46: 1–35.

Hall, P. (1993) 'Policy paradigms, social learning, and the state: The case of economic policymaking in Britain', *Comparative Politics*, April: 275–96.

Harrison, J. (2006) 'Re-reading the New Regionalism: A sympathetic critique', *Space and Polity*, 10(1): 21–46.

Hughes, J., Sasse, G. and Gordon, C. (2004) 'Conditionality and compliance in the the EU's eastward enlargement: Regional policy and the reform of the sub-national government', *Journal of Common Market Studies*, 42(3): 523–551.

Illner, M. (1998) 'Territorial decentralisation: An obstacle to democratic reform in Central and Eastern Europe?', in J. D. Kimball (ed.) *The Transfer of Power: Decentralisation in Central and Eastern Europe*, Budapest: Local Government and Public Service Reform Initiative.

—— (2002) 'Multilevel government in three East Central European candidate countries and its reforms after 1989', EUI-RSCAS Working Papers, 7. Online. Available HTTP: www.iue.it/RSCAS/WP-Texts/02_07.pdf (accessed February 2007).

Keating, M. (2006) 'Territorial government in the new Member States', in W. Sadurski, J. Ziller and K. Zurek (eds) *Après Enlargement. Legal and political responses in Central and Eastern Europe*, Florence: European University Institute.

Kokot, M., Niklewicz, K. and Nowaczyk, M. (2009) 'Pomogą napisać wniosek i wygrać dotację', *Gazeta Wyborcza*, 70, 24 March 2009.

Lepesant, G. (2005) *La mise en oeuvre de la politique régionale en Pologne*, Paris: CERI. Online. Available HTTP: www.ceri-sciencespo.com/archive/jan05/artgl.pdf (accessed February 2007).

Lovering, J. (1999) 'Theory led by policy: the inadequacies of the "new regionalism" (illustrated from the case of Wales)', *International Journal of Urban and Regional Research*, 23: 379–95.

Lower Silesia Marshal Office (2006) Interview with the author on 20 April 2006. Wrocław.

—— (2007) Interview with the author on 7 November 2007. Wrocław.

Lower Silesia Voivod Office (2006) Interview with the author on 13 April 2006. Wrocław.

MacLeod, G. (2001) 'Beyond soft institutionalism: Accumulation, regulation and their geographical fixes', *Environment and Planning A*, 33: 1145–1167.

Ministry of Regional Development (2007) *National Strategic Reference Framework 2007–2013, in Support of Growth and Jobs (National Cohesion Strategy)*. Online. Available HTTP: www.funduszestrukturalne.gov.pl/NR/rdonlyres/2BD5B9B6-767E-473C-B198-496FDEC4DFED/42148/NSRO_an_20_07.pdf (accessed January 2009).

Niklewicz, K. (2009) 'Fundusze z UE. Nie jest dobrze', *Gazeta Wyborcza*, 149, 27 June 2009.

Pallagst, K. M. (2006) 'European spatial planning reloaded: Considering EU enlargement in theory and practice', *European Planning Studies*, 2/2006: 253–272.

Paraskevopoulos, C. and Leonardi, R. (2004) 'Introduction: Adaptational pressures and social learning in European regional policy-cohesion (Greece, Ireland and Portugal) vs. CEE (Hungary, Poland) countries', *Regional and Federal Studies*, 14(3): 315–354.

Putnam, R., Leonardi, D. and Nanetti, R. Y. (1993) *Making Democracy Work: Civic traditions in modern Italy*, Princeton: Princeton University Press.

Radaelli, C. (1999) *Technocracy in the European Union*, London and New York: Longman.

Regionalne Centrum Wspierania Inicjatyw Pozarządowych (2006) Interview with the author on 10 April 2006. Wrocław.

Regional Steering Committee (2006) Interview with the author on 19 April 2007. Wrocław.

—— (2007) Interview with the author on 6 July 2007. Wrocław.

Regulska, J. (1997) 'Decentralisation or (re)centralization: Struggle for political power in Poland', *Environment and Planning C: Government and Policy*, 15(2): 187–208.

Sabatier, P. (1998) 'The advocacy coalition framework: Revisions and relevance for Europe,' *Journal of European Public Policy*, 5: 98–130.

Schimmelfennig, F. And Sedelmeier, U. (eds) (2005) *The Europeanization of Central and Eastern Europe*, Ithaca, NY: Cornell University Press.

Sedelmeier, U. (2006) 'Pre-accession conditionality and post-accession compliance in the new Member States: A research note', in W. Sadurski, J. Ziller and K. Zurek (eds) *Après Enlargment. Legal and political responses in Central and Eastern Europe*, Florence: European University Institute.

Stead, D. and Nadin, V. (2010) 'Shifts in territorial governance and the Europeanization of Spatial Planning in Central and Eastern Europe', in N. Adams, G. Cotella and R. Nunes (eds) *Territorial Development, Cohesion and Spatial Planning: Knowledge and policy development in an enlarged EU*, London: Routledge.

Stowarzyszenie Inicjatywa dla Przedsiębiorczości (2006) Interview with the author on 24 April 2006. Wrocław.

Stowarzyszenie Sanatorów (2006) Interview with the author on 24 April 2006. Wrocław.

Swianiewicz, P. and Lackowska, M. (2007) *Cohesion Policy Making in Polish Regions: Creeping decentralisation*. Report prepared for the SOCCOH Project. Online. Available HTTP: http://wwww.lse.ac.uk/collections/ESOCLab/Documents/Past%20SOCCOH%20Presented%20Papers/lisbon%20paper%20POLAND.pdf (accessed December 2008).

Wałbrzych Municipal Office (2007) Interview with the author on 29 October 2007. Wałbrzych. Lower Silesia.

Wolińska, I., Klimczak, T., Niedoszewska, A., Lenkiewicz, E. and Czyż, P. (2005) *Analiza wybranych elementów systemu implementacji ZPORR pod kątem określenia potencjału regionów do wdrożenia zdecentralizowanego systemu zarządzania RPO*, Warsaw: Ministry of Regional Development.

Wrocław Municipal Office (2006) Interview with the author on 14 April 2006. Wrocław.

Zito, R. (2001) 'Epistemic communities, collective entrepreneurship and European integration', *Journal of European Public Policy*, 8(4): 585–603.

10 Cross-border communities or cross-border proximity?

Perspectives from the Austrian–Slovakian border region

Beatrix Haselsberger and Paul Benneworth

Introduction

In the last two decades, spatial planning in Europe has been wrestling with the implications of the Single European Project, recognized in the European Spatial Development Perspective (ESDP – CEC 1999) as well as in the spatial agenda for European territorial development, both documents envisaging a polycentric territorial structure with a multi-level urban hierarchy (DE Presidency 2007). Central to the 'polycentrism' concept is the fact that subordinate territories benefit from connections to node cities, even across borders reflecting a reality that many border areas are actual or potential urban hinterlands for foreign cities. Therefore, cross-border planning lies at the heart of a successful territorial agenda for European competitiveness and cohesion.

In the past (booming and stable) Europe, different actors across territorial borders, dependent on different systems sharing common problems and interests (cross-border pollution, land-use planning, security issues, border workers), tried to collaborate to find effective solutions. Any current decline in collaboration resulting from the recession counters the post-1957 trend of increasingly intense cross-border collaboration. Currently more than 70 cross-border regional organizations exist in Europe, and 32 per cent of EU citizens inhabit border areas comprising 40 per cent of EU landmass (Janssen 2006). Virtually all local authorities in these areas are involved in cross-border cooperation.

Yet the renown of cross-border regions, such as Öresund (Denmark–Sweden) – highlights the rarity of effective cross-border planning arrangements. First, early cross-border cooperation was based on largely informal ('gentleman's') agreements reliant on goodwill (Haselsberger 2007). Second, the later established legal frameworks enabling bi- and multi-national agreements based on public law, were constrained by cross-border regions' embedding within national planning spaces. Lacking capacities to influence and challenge their respective national planning conventions, the scope of cross-border arrangements to achieve effective territorial management is restricted by the coherence between national and local planning visions.

Frameworks like the Madrid Convention or INTERREG may enable institutional spaces to mediate between competing national interests thereby supporting cross-border planning. However, Jensen and Richardson (2004) argue that INTERREG's most influential element has been the creation of European macro-regions articulating (often highly influential) multi-national spatial visions. But this embodies a top-down notion of spatial planning, with limited space for distinctive cross-border arrangements emerging from the bottom-up (Faludi and Waterhout, 2002; Jensen and Richardson, 2004). Furthermore, this implication cuts across other great European planning trends already highlighted in Chapter 7 by Stead and Nadin and in Chapter 8 by Marot, namely 'subsidiarity', 'regionalization' and 'devolution'. This multi-level conundrum, with top-down elements dominating bottom-up, undermines development of grassroots institutional spaces for cross-border planning.

Our concern is to explore this bottom-up dimension and, in particular, the conundrum of relatively few promising cross-border 'epistemic communities' (Haas 1992) able to influence their respective national planning systems and cultures. We argue that, despite a recent softening tendency, most European borders are still highly rigid, hindering substantive interaction from whence an 'epistemic community' could emerge. Current policy instruments are modest, based upon one-off projects, and we therefore look beneath the meso-scale, the 'epistemic community', to its micro-scale analogue, the 'community of practice' (Wenger 1998) to understand progress in cross-border planning practices, and in particular whether current cross-border integration measures have encouraged the stabilization of cross-border networks exerting influence elsewhere within planning governance networks.

We explore this question as follows. First, we unpack the complex concept of 'border', distinguishing two kinds of effects, namely peripherality and division. We then consider how borders change in time, distinguishing geographical-cartographic shifts from changes to meanings imposed on borders' functions and roles. We contend that bottom-up cross-border planning structures have lagged behind transnational planning visions' evolution, and therefore have been unable to challenge border regions' fundamental problems (remoteness, peripherality, lack of 'critical mass'). We then question whether cross-border initiatives could stimulate an evolution in borders' form and meaning at the national scale, populating cross-border institutional spaces with actors and plans, which simultaneously become salient within national planning systems and cultures. The chapter closes with a discussion of different experiences from the Austrian–Slovakian border region.

Importance of borders in a European planning context

To understand the problematic of cross-border cooperation, it is first necessary to unpack the notion of border, defining more precisely what these lines demark and denote. Borders play a meaningful role in everyday life both consciously and subconsciously: the term 'border' is among the top 3,000 spoken and the

2,000 most written English words (Haselsberger 2008). Yet, users of the word 'border' do not always appreciate its multiple meanings or appropriate uses.

In the majority of cases, the notion 'border' expresses any kind of 'limit'. This is not necessarily wrong, but underplays the term's explanatory power. Sack (1986) argues that borders define, classify, communicate and control territories – assigning things to particular spaces, and regulating cross-border movements and access to specified areas. Territorial borders are – in their most general sense – a means of control, using bounded geographical spaces, private (the school playground, the workplace, the neighbourhood) or public (the nation-state territory, the electoral district, the administrative region). Moreover, borders assume different meanings and functions within territories and societies depending on internal and external changes and pressures.

The term 'border' often is used synonymously with 'boundary' and 'frontier', despite all three terms having their own particular meaning. Parker (2006) highlights the interrelation of the concepts of borders, boundaries and frontiers: borders and frontiers constitute 'boundary sets' of various boundary types (i.e. geographic, political, social, cultural or economic). At their most extreme, clear differences emerge: first as a hard, static and linear dividing element (e.g. nation-state border), and second as a soft, fluid and zonal element (e.g. a border area) (see Figure 10.1).

Two features characterize a border area; it is the end point for a nation-state's sovereignty, and it is removed from a nation's socio-economic core, producing two distinct territorial planning problems. A territory located at the physical edge of a nation-state may experience reduced interactions with its natural hinterlands over the border, reducing social and economic vitality. These border areas also suffer a remoteness from national policy-makers' pressing concerns, often manifested in lower levels of public investments.

The challenge for cross-border partnerships is to address both issues, working across an *edge line* peripheral to national policy-makers' imaginations. Yet borders are ambiguous, hiding a range of tensions and contradictions. National borders often seem 'fixed' and taken-for-granted as shaping everyday activities, identities and reference points. Irredentist movements manifest a reification of national cultures, justifying territorial border change as reflecting the popular will of the nation-state. This raises the question of the homogeneity of national culture and its agency.

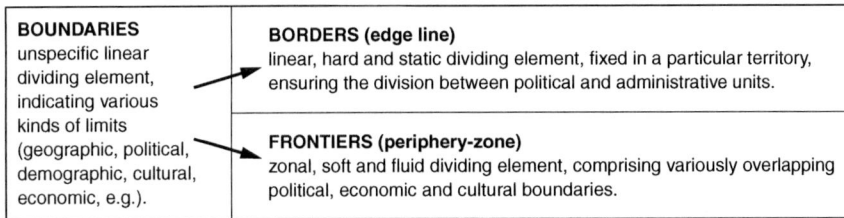

Figure 10.1 Borders – boundaries – frontiers (source: Haselsberger 2008).

Despite the reification of nation-state borders, Europe, has always been a continent of unsettled territorial (political) borders, experiencing pressures of fragmentation, whilst also being subject to grand unification projects. Both processes involved wars, violence or coercion, creating new (political) borders (Tilly 1990). It is here useful to further distinguish two types of territorial border-change (see Table 10.1), typically observed in the geographical-cartographic location of a border, and its functions (meanings and roles).

Although borders often simultaneously evolve along both dimensions, these two different types of changes are not *a priori* interrelated. Sometimes the functions and meanings imposed on borders change while the borders remain geographically fixed, such as during Slovakia's accession to the Schengen border area in December 2007. Conversely, the accession of three new Member States in the 1995 expansion of the EU shifted the EU's external cartographic border without altering its meaning as the edge line of a space allowing free movement of goods and people.

The first type of territorial border-change (geographical-cartographic location) is exceptional, requiring military conquest, post-war treaties or local plebiscites, yet are more common than frequently imagined. But at the same time, Europe bears the 'scars of history', with its physical and human geography continually reshaped by history, environment, politics, culture, economic interests, and national prestige and identities (Haselsberger 2008). Europe is home to a class of borders '*drawn for historical reasons which have [in many cases] ceased to be reasons*' (CoR 2007: 17, emphasis added). There are many physical borders in contemporary Europe which no longer correspond to the differences originally delineated. Consequently, their meanings evolve inconsistently, reflecting historic events rather than gradually transforming. Redrawing physical borders can be unleashed by political crises or tensions, and includes 'upgrading' formerly internal borders to nation-state borders as with the dissolution of Czechoslovakia. Creating, drawing or re-drawing of nation-state borders in geographical terms is typically a 'top-down' exercise by political and military elites.

The second type of territorial border-change, in terms of functions and meanings, is intangible albeit more continuous in evolutionary terms, with 'bottom-up' influences interacting with the 'top-down'. Borders' functions change over time, regulating the movement of people and commodities. These changes can be shaped by wider influences such as national policies, 'globalization' or emerging cross-national entities such as the European Union, along with greater local desire for cross-border interaction (a consideration of family ties, kinship, employment and culture). This is precisely the case with the border areas (hereafter border regions) of the Russian Kaliningrad enclave (cf. Fritsch Chapter 15), and the territorial border between Lithuania and Poland after 2004.

The dichotomy of these two types of border-change helps to focus the problematic of European cross-border planning. Indeed, cross-border cooperation emerged at a time of territorial border-change in both geographical-cartographic terms ('hard' edge line borders) as well as in function, meanings and roles ('soft' geographical borders). Whereas the former is evidence in the expanding 'Single

Table 10.1 Main categories of territorial border-changes

Subject of change	Degree of change	Emergence	Implementation	Recognition
geographical location	hard change (e.g. building up of new barriers in geographical terms)	wars; violence; coercion	top-down, through political and military elites	strong influence – visible in the territory (e.g. border controls)
function, meanings and roles of fixed geographical borders	soft change (e.g. regulating the permeability of existing borders)	regulations; agreements; negotiations	combination of top-down and bottom-up	intangible; (mostly) invisible

Source: Authors' elaboration.

Market', the previous internalized borders of the Single Market Project take on a softer and more fluid character in the latter. And yet, despite increasing emphasis placed on cross-border cooperation through INTERREG and associated programmes, the limits to cross-border cooperation are evident, symbolized by disappointments surrounding the transformative affect of the Öresund Bridge on the meaning of the Zealand-Scania border (Maskell and Törnquist 1999.).

Our central focus is how weak cross-border interaction and border change affects a wider European spatial agenda. This editors of this volume are concerned with the roles of 'epistemic communities' in transforming spatial planning practice in Europe, seeking to better understand the 'politics of expertise' driving the emergence of a (still-voluntary) evolving European territorial agenda. In this light we explore cross-border communities, arguing bottom-up cross-border planning structures have lagged behind the evolution of transnational planning visions, and therefore been unable to challenge border regions' fundamental problems. Our first contention, following Jensen and Richardson (2004), maintains that Europe's dominant cross-border 'epistemic communities' are cross-national rather than cross-regional (cf. Razumeyko Chapter 16). Despite the European Grouping of Territorial Cooperation (EGTC) instrument, there are no well known examples where bottom-up cross-border planning has become significant in higher-level planning arenas. We contend that this reflects the reality that whilst barriers across borders have softened, they constitute the kinds of multi-jurisdictional policy environments that nevertheless inhibit regional interactions. Multi-lateral institutions such as ESPON or the Council of Ministers have learned to avoid these problems through their long experiences in negotiating around cross-border issues that also impinge upon critical national interests, as evident in the case of the European Spatial Development Perspective.

Cross-border planning in a multi-jurisdictional policy environment

Unsurprisingly, modern European bottom-up cross-border cooperation dates to the Treaty of Rome (1957) establishing the European Economic Community. The first formal cross-border cooperation in this vein was the so-called 'Euregio', established in 1958 as a cooperative association between municipalities in North Rhine Westphalia (Germany), and Overijssel and Gelderland (The Netherlands) to address problems commonly experienced in their respective border regions. In 1980, the Council of Europe proposed what became the Madrid Convention – a treaty between a set of European countries as a first step toward cross-border cooperation structures in public law. The convention, signed by 20 countries and updated with two additional protocols, provides a legal framework for bilateral and multi-national cross-border cooperation agreements. The Madrid Convention allowed cross-border bodies to achieve legal personality; although decisions by these bodies are binding only on the public authorities within the cross-border area concerned.

The 1990s saw increasing *formal* cross-border cooperative institutions across Europe, partly credited to INTERREG Community Initiative, set up in 1990, and funding cross-border cooperation. EU enlargement to Austria, Sweden and Finland, and duty-free's abolition later this decade, brought significant new border regions as well as creating new economic problems for internal market border regions. Most recently, the creation of the EGTC allows cross-border arrangements to develop a distinct legal personality, allowing all cross-border regions to enjoy the benefits of legal personality previously reserved to those regions with a Madrid Convention arrangement.

Yet, the extent to which top-down transnational planning dominates European policy and research agendas is striking. One area of top-down cross-border planning introduced in the 1990s was the Trans-European Networks (TENs), where the Commission decided to promote a series of massive transnational infrastructure investments. National partners each had their own investment priorities for these projects, very closely matched to their respective national planning priorities and concerns. Later this TENs experience shaped the tactics adopted by DG XVI in developing a European spatial agenda.

Jensen and Richardson (2004) link the negotiations between national planning perspectives and subsequent attempts to articulate a European Spatial Development Perspective. They highlight two competing concepts emerging: the (long-standing) idea of the 'Blue Banana', proposed by the French (Brunet 1989), and the Germans' 'Bunch of Grapes' (Kunzmann and Wegener 1991). The TEN experience proved that southern European Member States would not countenance anything that implied their peripherality, fatally damaging the 'Blue Banana' model, with the 'Bunch of Grapes' emerging after the Potsdam conference (Faludi and Waterhout 2002). It is this version of cross-border working – the transnational/top-down – that dominates European thinking. Some instruments do permit bottom-up working, including INTERREG IIIa and IVa, and EGTC. However, we characterize these instruments as *additional* to national planning activities, whilst top-down transnational activities have *determined* national planning decisions.

Cross-border 'epistemic communities' – top-down or bottom-up?

Given that 'epistemic communities' are emergent communities, arising through purposive interaction, we first must consider what kind of purposive planning interactions may emerge where different systems with their own rationales and logics are juxtaposed. We contend that, given the enduring prevalence of national planning cultures and traditions, and despite a convergence of languages and processes of planning (Zonneveld 2005), purposive interactions are necessary in solving problems that cannot be (more) easily be addressed within the *national* governance scale.

Through this interaction toward together solving a complex problem, planning authorities build mutual understanding alongside shared routines and practices, which become foundations for further cooperation and interaction. The accumulation of these shared understandings, activities (routines and practices) and meanings also may influence external partners, particularly nationally. This may enable the exercise of influence reshaping national planning perspectives which frame border regions as peripheral. In short, cross-border cooperative arrangements may evolve into 'epistemic communities', using – as elsewhere in this volume – Haas's (1992: 2) criterion of helping 'to formulate policies through [the] framing of alternatives, [and the] implications of possible actions'. Building these 'epistemic communities' can be regarded as emergent from a series of negotiated outcomes addressing particular problems that might simultaneously encompass pragmatic, technical and idealistic dimensions.

'Epistemic communities' emergent nature provides a means to explore the emergence of a cross-border scale within contemporary European spatial planning practice. As previously noted, the European spatial scale emerged ignoring the complexities associated with borders, adopting a view of borders as either 'closed' (external) or 'open' (internal), a false duality rooted in a singular view of either a 'Europe of Places', or a 'Europe of Flows' (after Castells 1996). But this superficial understanding of borders denies their more complex and shaded realities: cross-border planning communities emerge from real interactions between partners who may occupy more or less coterminous juridical, organizational, cultural and cognitive planning spaces.

Of Europe's 70 cross-border institutional arrangements, relatively few have a direct competency for cross-border planning adding value to the respective national planning scales (Haselsberger 2008). In this context, three preceding points seem salient: first, the enduring hardness of borders, second, the disappointing progress to date with building up cross-border activities, and third, the relative absence of bottom-up cross-border 'epistemic communities'. We ask whether such communities – capable of influencing actors within their national planning systems – have been prevented from emerging. This fundamental question is addressed by asking two operational questions:

- Can cross-border arrangements, deriving from an 'epistemic community', interact with and rebalance national and European planning perspectives and agendas?
- Do cross-border learning communities for territorial development's knowledge practices provide a sufficiently robust basis for the functioning of policy networks?

We propose using a 'community of practice' theoretical framework to address these questions, enabling exploring the emergent characteristics of cross-border European planning arrangements, and whether they can be considered as 'epistemic communities'. First, this underlines that the success of cross-border cooperation is strongly dependent upon often underestimated bottom-up forces. Conversely, the 'community of practice' approach assists exploring the extent to which top-down interactions (e.g. those promoted by transnational INTERREG policies) represent a step in the process of the evolution of cross-border 'epistemic communities'.

'Community of practice' perspective on cross-border planning: building internal proximity as a pre-condition for effective external influence?

The idea of a 'community of practice' (Wenger 1998) is rooted in theories of experiential learning, in turn connected to a broader set of socio-economic shifts in the nature of contemporary knowledge production and social organization. Given knowledge's increasing importance to human society, organizational capacities to create knowledge are critical determinants of economic success and 'quality of life' (cf. Czapiewski and Janc Chapter 14). Unlike traditional forms of capital, land, labour and machinery, knowledge capital is embodied in people, and transmitted through personal relationships.

Nonaka and Takeuchi (1995) make a key distinction between 'codified' knowledge, easily written down and transmitted, and 'tacit' knowledge, best transmitted through face-to-face contact and interaction. 'Tacit' knowledge is required in finding solutions to complex problems and situations, drawing on teamwork, cooperation and networking. But there is an increasing appreciation that those communities who work together on shared challenges build up a 'tacit' knowledge base within the problem-solving community. The community and its knowledge can become an integral element of a solution (Wenger 1998).

Etienne Wenger popularized the phrase 'communities of practice' in his eponymous 1998 book, which described these resultant communities. His work studied a number of workplaces dealing with difficult and confusing situations, particularly how employees made sense of their work, of the world, and their shared solutions to problems. 'Communities of practice' manifested solutions in different ways, often embedding knowledge in the social rituals performed by employees in the course of their work. The stories that employees told, often about the first time a solution was used, helped transmit to newer employees the 'right' ways of solving problems, and were an important element of the 'communities of practice' collective solutions. These communities, according to Wenger, had a hierarchy of established core members and newer peripheral members or employees. Once initiated into the periphery of these communities, new employees could became more central to community life as they acquired the knowledge necessary for community participation. Once a core community member, they in turn became the ones 'telling the stories'.

Although Wenger's work was confined to single organizations, much work subsequently has looked at so-called 'networks of practice' or communities that build up across institutional boundaries (e.g. Benner 2003). Boschma (2005) highlights that the ease with which actors can transfer knowledge, develop relationships and network depends on their proximity – not only geographic/al/ cartographic, but also cognitive, organizational, social and institutional. In other words, 'networks of practice' must have sufficient 'proximity' to allow interaction, and develop a series of norms and routines to support that interaction.

The frontier effect of a border can be regarded as reducing proximity between geographically proximate agents, particularly along cognitive and social axes as well as institutionally. Repeated interaction may build familiarity that in turn creates cognitive and social proximity. Thus a cross-border 'community of practice' might build up various dimensions of 'proximity' through collective understanding and a shared knowledge base, creating the basis for collective problem definition, strategies, priorities, projects, and languages and effective cross-border planning. In such circumstances, the 'community of practice' development creates a foundation that allows other proximities – organizational and institutional – to emerge. Sufficient 'proximity', internal to the cross-border community, as well as good external connections with national planning agents, appears to be a necessary and essential foundation for an 'epistemic community'.

From our perspective, cross-border institutions to date have failed to exert external influence in their respective national planning systems and cultures. Our argument is that this results from a lack of cross-border cohesion or 'proximity' preventing the effective representation of cross-border interests in the complex multi-jurisdictional environments of national planning systems. We argue that the 'border' is itself instrumental in cross-border planning, as an agent potentially undermining cohesion. Boschma's framework provides a means to understand how negative border impacts are circumvented by local action which builds proximity, creating internally coherent cross-border communities with capacity to represent border region interests within wider planning 'epistemic communities'. This is based on a heuristic understanding of Euregios operations, building common experiences of working together, articulating shared visions, developing common plans, winning project funding, shaping mainstream funding, and ultimately building a cross-border governance space, albeit articulated within corresponding national and European planning spaces.

Thus a cross-border community involves building 'proximity' between regional partners, or an institutionalization process through which accumulated knowledge and learning provides capacities assisting shared material outcomes. We include juridical proximity in addition to the other classifications of 'proximity' (following Boschma 2005) because of the importance of legal systems and cultures in determining cross-border planning interaction.

We suggest that the emergence of cross-border 'epistemic communities' can be regarded as a journey in which relationships materialize, and are subsequently institutionalized and embedded within practice. The relationships between cross-border 'networks of practice' and 'epistemic communities' are akin to 'networks of practice' generating a stage on the journey towards 'epistemic communities'. We break this institutionalization down into four stages – progressing from no interaction to a superficial interaction, the emergence of a cross-border network of practice and the institutionalization of a cross-border 'epistemic community'.

In Table 10.2 we differentiate between different stages of community formation, using various dimensions of 'proximity' (i.e. juridical, social, institutional, organizational and cognitive) to understand the relationship of proximity to cross-border community formation. The table offers an 'ideal type' categorization of regional situations to illustrate the scope of this relationship. Thus an analysis on the basis of this categorization may be able to identify what has proven difficult to address in cross-border community formation alongside barriers remaining in completing a well functioning cross-border 'epistemic community' within the multi-jurisdictional policy environment of spatial planning in Europe (cf. Adams *et al.* Chapter 2).

We argue barriers to interaction have inhibited developing 'proximity' between regional partners, preventing the emergence of cross-border 'communities of practice' able to influence national planning systems. Considering proximity's relationship to cross-border community formation provides a means to explore the mechanisms that policy-makers use in attempting to stimulate cross-border communities. Are the tools encouraging cross-border planning practices in Europe also able to support varying dimensions of 'proximity'? What tools, instruments and regulations can foster interactive learning?

To explore these questions we present a highly stylized reading of one cross-border (INTERREG) project, to explore the particular relationship of 'proximity' to cross-border community formation. This allows an exploration of whether 'proximity' dynamics have enabled a functioning 'community of practice' to emerge as a precursor to an 'epistemic community', or whether it has restricted community formation to the level of superficial integration or lower.

Lessons of the Austrian–Slovakian KOBRA projects

This case study draws on three projects' results, undertaken under the KOBRA acronym between 2003 and 2006. We present them as a synthetic narrative with features asserted rather than demonstrated, as details of the KOBRA research have been published elsewhere (cf. Schaffer *et al.* 2008; Dillinger 2008; Haselsberger 2008). We use the synthesis to illustrate the difficulties and challenges of building up 'proximity' within cross-border regions. The KOBRA projects focused on a joint future perspective for Bratislava city-region and the Austrian rural hinterland along the Austria–Slovakian border, a border largely ignored historically (cf. Figure 10.2). In an enlarging European Union, however, this area's location at the heart of Europe offers great potential to become a dynamic and increasingly important border area. In this section we present a simple, static overview of KOBRA, exploring various dimensions of 'proximity' in the project planning process.

The two capitals of Bratislava (Slovakia) and Vienna (Austria), 'twin cities' 60 km apart, together with a number of other growing cities nearby (such as Brno – Czech Republic – and Györ – Hungary) comprise the CENTROPE Euroregion, assembling parts of the Czech Republic, Slovakia, Austria and Hungary, with a population of 7 million and a workforce of 2.7 million. The area covered by the KOBRA projects within this Euroregion consist of 14 Austrian municipalities immediately adjacent to the Slovakian border and the city of Bratislava (see Figure 10.2); whilst these 14 municipalities have a total population of 22,000, the total population of Bratislava is 430,000 across five administrative districts.

Table 10.2 Potential dimensions of cross-border community-building by sophistication level

	No integration (level 1)	Superficial integration (level 2)	Cross-border network of practice (level 3)	Cross-border 'epistemic community' (level 4)
Collective learning mechanisms (organizational)	Working on common projects and experiencing cultural gulfs	Learning-by-doing in delivering INTERREG and Euregio structures and activities	Shared languages understanding, problem definition, strategies, projects priorities	Active participation in multiple national planning systems
Legal framework (juridical)	The two legal systems operate independently with no recognition of the others	Attempts made to identify similar levels for cooperation, other partners recognised as stakeholders	There is some coordination of the two different planning systems at sub-national level	The two legal systems are completely coordinated and scheduled to run together
Political commitment and leadership (social)	Cross-border planning is largely ignored in political discourse	There are aspirations and interest towards cooperation	Regional leaders regularly sustain a momentum for the partnership with informal meetings and agreements	There is a cross-border planning organ with serious representation, responsibility and power
Shared problems and services (social)	Cross-border service delivery restricted to emergency and rare situations	Realism of current state of integration reflected in plans extrapolated to future	Cross-border intelligence used to allow services to be provided across region borders	Active cross-border planning of services and all infrastructure services

Planning outcomes (institutional)	The other nation omitted or ignored in spatial planning documents	Sub-national plans are made with consideration for neighbours but without negotiation	The sub-national plans each draw on a shared body of cross-border intelligence	There is an overarching cross-border plan that shapes/determines lower-tier plans
Availability of funding (institutional)	Opportunistic use of funding e.g. INTERREG to deliver 'pet' projects	Stream of sub-national project funding but dependent on external sources	Cross-border activities planned and budgeted out of own resources	Cross-border planning sustained through permanent regional budgets
Shared languages and understanding of planning cultures (cognitive)	No attempts to build up shared knowledge and connections between similar levels over border	A familiarity with language and structure of others' practices lacking cultural interpretation	Good knowledge of how the two systems and planning outcomes join up, 'who does what'	Diffusion of terminology from supra-plan into local activities. Shared knowledge and understanding, building up of reciprocal trust
Communities (associations) and cultures of planning (cognitive)	Special 'festival' (ribbon-cutting) meetings, exchange visits and seminars	Consultations between different groups as part of a wider stakeholder consultation irregularly, only if necessary	Regular informal meetings between officers and members to address shared problems and future visions	Range of formal forums/platforms where cross-border partners meet and do planning's 'serious business'
Infrastructure connections (geographic)	There is a hard, uncrossable border between the two regions	There are limited points of connection between transport infrastructures	There are well coordinated and extensive cross-border linkages	There is a single regional infrastructure maximising interaction

Source: Authors' elaboration (dimensions after Boschma 2005).

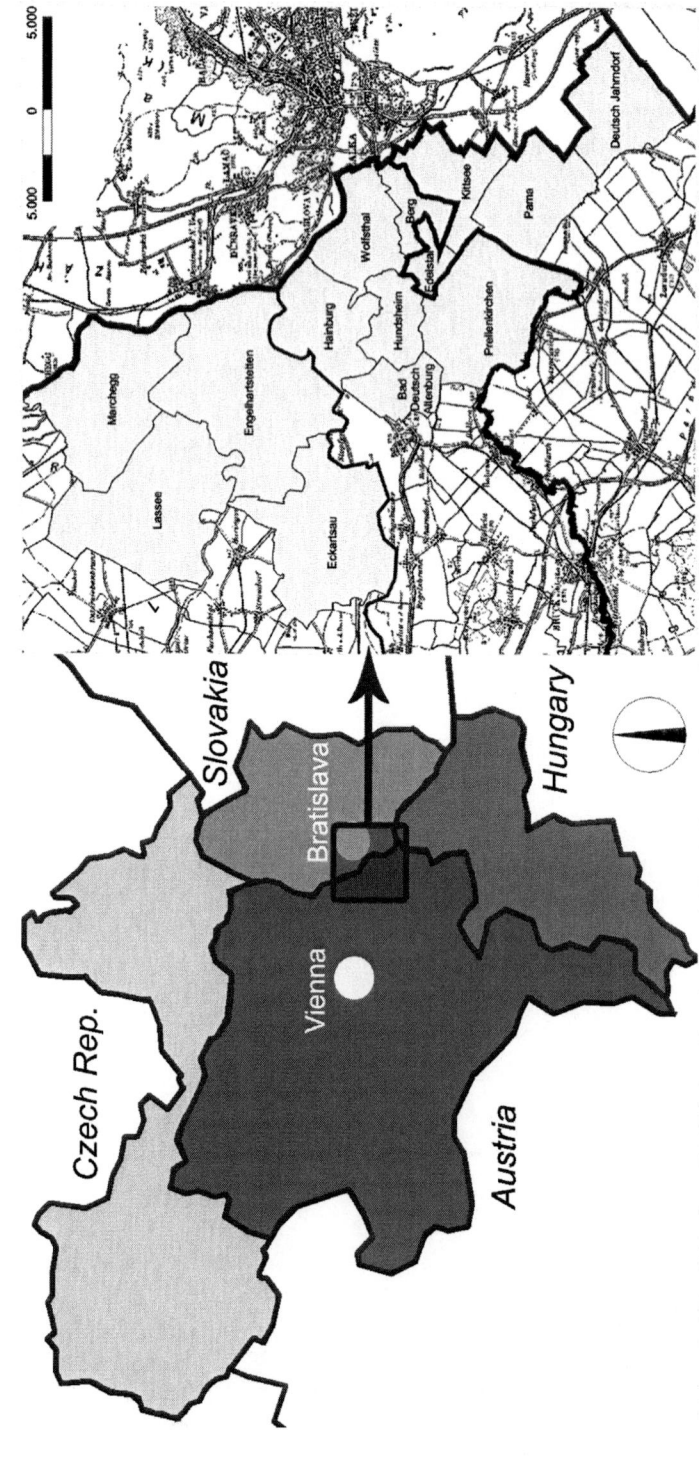

Figure 10.2 KOBRA project region (source: Authors' elaboration (after Vienna University of Technology – KOBRA project reports)).

The Austrian–Slovakian border has shifted throughout post-Westphalian history both in location terms as well as function and meaning. Austria and Slovakia were united from 1867 to 1918 in the Austria-Hungarian Empire. The Treaty of St. Germain divided this area, creating the newly independent country of Czechoslovakia. After the Second World War the 'Iron Curtain' structurally separated these two closely related regions until 1989. The enclosure of Austria's eastern border by the 'Iron Curtain' led this area to be regarded as the 'dead-end of the east', mirrored by the Czechoslovakian perspective of this border area as the 'dead-end of the west'.

The 1989 end of the Soviet Bloc and the Iron Curtain's disintegration facilitated new developments in this region, along with Austria and Slovakia's accession to the EU (1995 and 2004) and Schengen (1998 and 2007 respectively). However, this short history fails to capture the cognitive and emotional barriers that remain as a result of 60 years of separate territorial development dynamics, barriers manifested in mutual antipathy and distrust, which are hindering contemporary cooperation.

The KOBRA projects were initiated in 2003 (prior to Slovakia's EU accession) in three separate phases (the last phase concluding in December 2006). The first phase (2003–2004) was undertaken within the INTERREG project JORDES+ (Joint regional development strategy for the Vienna-Bratislava-Györ Region), focusing on creating a shared (cross-border) knowledge base by collecting and comparing country specific data as the basis for the development of a shared vision for this cross-border area.

The second phase (2004–2005) focused upon two interrelated objectives for the Austrian border area: first, identifying strategic regional development concepts to coordinate different land use demands and, second, forming a shared regional identity. In the course of this phase, the KOBRA strategic development concept emerged as one of the most important decision-making guidelines for planning processes and activities in this area. KOBRA's innovative planning approach, drawing a shared knowledge base, enabled the Austrian border area to develop a common set of strategic development criteria across its 14 municipalities – including more active cooperation with Bratislava.

The third phase (2005–2006) was an INTERREG IIIA (Austrian–Slovakian) initiative, drafting a cross-border master plan for the Austrian–Slovakian border area. This third phase was animated by local agents, who desired cross-border cooperation in this area to overcome remaining barriers. The main phase focus was dedicated to landscape, recreation and tourism, as well as delivering concrete cooperative cross-border projects. The broad knowledge base of previous KOBRA projects and consultations with local key players allowed involved actors to easily agree on what should happen 'over the border' for their own benefit. However, in the context of different planning traditions and cultures, only a few cross-national activity ideas were mobilized given agents' general fear of losing control over development in their respective territories. Therefore, the regional committee for phase was restricted to three 'small', politically palatable projects – a pedestrian and cyclist bridge, the (re)establishment of a historical route and a sculpture garden. In effect, both sides agreed to take a small step forward rather than do nothing, leaving the more pressing and politically sensitive planning concerns for subsequent project discussions. We now turn to explore the particular relationship of 'proximity' to cross-border formation throughout the KOBRA project phases.

Classifying experiential learning in KOBRA projects

KOBRA provided a basis for consolidating cross-border interaction and developing a 'network of practice'. However, the previous project outline hides much detail necessary to fully appreciate both progress and shortcomings concerning consolidation. Closely reading this simple overview highlights an immediate tension between 'big' cross-border cooperation and planning aspirations, and 'small' project outcomes – namely a bridge, a historical route and a cultural landmark. Nevertheless, these projects emerged out of discussions undertaken amongst regional partners over the impacts of untrammelled growth of Bratislava on the quality of living and accommodation, and on the environment and culture of the hinterland region. This discussion evolved and produced a set of technologies, maps, forums and projects – 'codified' knowledge about cross-border planning. But we argue that the more interesting story emerges in the 'tacit' knowledge between the partners involved in articulating solutions to their regional concerns (Wollansky 2008). In this section, we examine how particular dimensions of cross-border 'proximity' (following Boschma 2005) were manifested through KOBRA's phases in the context of its legal framework, political commitment and leadership, and planning outcomes.

Legal framework and juridical 'proximity'

KOBRA's legal framework stipulated that project development activity could begin as a relatively minor task within the INTERREG JORDES+ project (referred to as the first phase in this chapter) and subsequently evolve through a further INTERREG project (to which we refer as the third phase). The first phase was a technical data gathering exercise creating preconditions for a shared project vision. Legally speaking, this first phase was carried out under the auspices of the parent project (JORDES+) drawing on the prior JORDES legal agreements, which provided access to rather substantial sums for building transnational cooperation

The second phase was a purely Austrian affair, primarily financed by two Austrian Länder (states), Lower Austria and Burgenland through Planning Community East, which worried that these small municipalities lacked substantive planning capacity, and were overlooked by prior Austrian planning acts. Planning Community East is eastern Austria's regional planning committee, comprising the Länder Lower Austria, Burgenland and Vienna. This second phase was intended to create a shared inter-municipal Austrian vision (within 14 Austrian authorities).

The Planning Community East together with the State Governments of Burgenland and Lower Austria as well as partners in Vienna and Bratislava prepared the ground for an expert discussion of existing local and regional plans to define and map functional zones and regional focus measures. Especially the mission statement on the 'Biosphere region and green centre' was considered and advanced, by assessing areas and sites for their special relevance – with regards to ecology, settlement development, raw material extraction, agriculture, industry – from a national, regional and community perspective.

(Wollansky 2008:2)

These first two phases created a situation of a functioning inter-municipal organization on the Austrian side, when Bratislava was only interested in collaborating with Austrian authorities to address urban sprawl, congestion and flood-plain management. Nevertheless, this small, rural inter-municipal organization was able to coordinate with partners in the Slovakian capital city and city-region of Bratislava. This institutional progress between the two national partners consequently led to KOBRA's third phase – an INTERREG project involving Austria's newly formed inter-municipal organization.

More importantly, despite the cross-border dimension, progress was most marked in the second phase, when the project's operational sphere was a purely Austrian affair. One interpretation could suggest that Planning Community East acted to address a perceived lack of organizational capacity among the 14 municipalities participating in JORDES+. In other words, creating a new inter-municipal organization sought to overcome the potential for governance failure. We consider this concern in terms of creating the necessary organizational and juridical 'proximity' between national partners – creating two (more-or-less) equal bodies that could work together across the border to articulate a collective position.

Shared problems, and political commitment and leadership

The most comprehensive contribution by KOBRA was to effectively articulate the challenges facing the Austrian KOBRA municipalities trapped between two capital cities – adjacent to one (Bratislava) and beyond the attention of the other (Vienna). The KOBRA municipalities belong to the states of Lower Austria and Burgenland, with Vienna city uninterested in this eastern border region, its eastwards urban interest marked by the airport in Schwechat.

The Austrian municipalities' main concern was that Bratislava's urban sprawl would spread into rural Austrian border villages, leading to suburbanization, the rise of commuter settlements, and second-house occupation by Bratislava residents. In turn, urban sprawl could also drive the loss of rural land, countryside landscapes and the municipalities' and the region's distinctive appearance and identity. KOBRA helped these Austrian municipalities deal with this perceived threat and its implications in two principal ways. First, as a group of 14 very small municipalities, they identified they shared many of the same problems and challenges, recognizing that cooperation rather than competition made the most sense. Second, they realized the need to engage with Bratislava to resolve their concerns because urban sprawl's drivers lay over the border.

A further dimension came through the realization that ideal solutions were restricted partly by partners' negative perceptions. Bratislava regarded Austria as a pressure valve for congestion and development pressures undermining its competitiveness and attractiveness. Austria regarded Bratislava as a source of negative overspills, of new residents and tourists potentially destroying the area's environmental quality without due compensation. This situation highlights another important element of collective learning, namely the recognition that perceptions vary substantially across borders. This suggests that there was effective cognitive 'proximity' between national partners, whereby their mutual restrictions and limitations were identified.

The various phases encouraged the formation of a committed group of Austrian local leaders, keen to take advantage of their new central position in Europe and to position themselves appropriately in the Austrian–Slovakian dialogue. Initially, common Austrian leadership was challenging as the 14 municipalities were more accustomed to competing with one another, requiring the two Länder and Planning Committee East to initiate the process toward cooperation with Bratislava. Although the main focus of the first two phases was directed at stimulating interest in mutual cooperation among the 14 Austrian municipalities, it also involved sensitizing partners to the opportunities for collaboration with Slovakia, important given some Austrian partners had never visited Bratislava. These initial efforts included study tours of current development projects as well as presentations of land-use plans for Bratislava.

The second phase particularly helped to enthuse and energize the local Austrian leadership to undertake the third phase: there was a much broader and, for the first time, genuinely cross-border leadership that enabled the three above-mentioned projects to emerge. This third phase had to be led by Austrian partners because Bratislavan actors were focused principally on two development interests. First, Bratislava had developed a floodplain management plan in which the Austrian territory provided reserve floodplain land. Second, the city partners intended to profit financially by allowing high-value executive housing to be developed in the remaining green areas along the Austrian–Slovakian border. These projects had a profound impact on the Austrian municipalities, and Bratislava was unwilling to discuss them with its cross-border partners – a situation that created a sense of antipathy among the Austrian partners with respect to their Bratislavan counterparts.

This situation had immediate consequences for the degree of local autonomy that Austrian partners were willing to concede to Slovakian planners for a joint border regional planning structure. Bratislava's national-level aspirations and development interests created a boundary to further collaboration. When partners in cross-border partnerships are not working along an ideal set of relationships inevitably there will be tensions in cooperation, which may stem from external pressures such as national and European-level decisions.

Planning outcomes

The development of a shared vision for spatial development between national partners was the most significant cross-border planning outcome of the third KOBRA phase. However, the framework was developed around knowledge gathered at different project phases. Therefore its effectiveness is directly related to the activities undertaken throughout the project. As Wollanksy (2008) notes, there was a fundamental split in interests between the pro-development coalition in Bratislava – aiming to develop exclusive up-market real estate in an area of natural beauty, and an Austrian landscape-preservation coalition – keen on contributing to the ecological network initiative of the 'European Green Belt' that runs from the Barents to the Black Sea. In the end, the pro-development coalition abandoned its plans as some KOBRA areas were protected by European Union natural habitat conservation directives.

The shared vision demonstrated the need to reconcile interests in concentrated urban growth and targeted development within city-hinterland areas to prevent the loss of character associated with urban sprawl. The master plan developed for landscape, recreation and tourism reflects work undertaken to balance these competing interests. Together the strategic plan and the institutional arrangement between national partners encouraged investment in these activities through mutual benefit: a more competitive Bratislava generates higher residential tax revenues whilst increasing the demand for Austrian tourist activities.

Claims of shared vision, however, must not be exaggerated given the projects' extremely modest outcomes. Returning to the distinction made between 'tacit' and 'codified' knowledge, the 'codified' shared understanding (i.e. the master plan) has relatively limited value and demonstrates relatively little accrual of 'proximity' toward cross-border community formation. However, this 'codified' understanding would suggest 'proximity' had accrued were there to be strong evidence that this shared vision between national partners had successfully shaped funding streams. This reinforces the earlier point that success is critical to the development of 'proximity' – but that what can be achieved successfully depends on what has hitherto been delivered.

Cross-border planning communities and culture

The KOBRA case study highlights how different barriers can be nested within cross-border planning activities. After phase 2, the Austrian mayors – then highly enthusiastic and motivated – were keen to start cross-border cooperation with Bratislava. However, there was significant political resistance in Bratislava to this approach, making it extremely difficult for the Austrian partners to initiate a genuine cross-border community. In fact, when Bratislava could not get its desired solutions to its physical planning problems (flooding and housing), additional organizational platforms were developed to break the antipathy between the two partner groups. This illustrates the potential for the emergence of barriers challenging sustained success in cross-border collaboration and cross-border community formation.

KOBRA (which started in 2003) represents a notable attempt to exploit new cross-border opportunities particularly in light of the fact that Slovakia did not join the EU until 2004. It clearly demonstrates the indispensability of a shared knowledge-base for cross-border cooperation activities and organizational proximity. As we noted earlier, the lack of experience and competence in cross-border collaboration demanded the creation of an inter-municipal organization for developing a shared knowledge base. This emphasizes that it was not solely the Austria–Slovakia border (edge-line) which complicated the cooperation between national partners, but also the fact that the Austrian KOBRA region itself was characterized by administrative planning barriers between the two Austrian Länder.

A considerable effort by actors, who were not themselves the municipalities, was invested in the creation of a knowledge base for the Austrian KOBRA region. This 'codified' knowledge then had to be absorbed and owned by the KOBRA municipalities to integrate them effectively within an inter-municipal organization articulating a shared institutional vision into which other regional and national planning actors could be enrolled. This learning process not only involved the simple transmission of 'codified' knowledge, but it also required a learning process encouraging social 'proximity' between municipalities.

Both groups of partners regarded each other as the cause of their problems, which may partly explain the initial antipathy. It is important neither to underestimate the practical consequences of that antipathy, which greatly hindered the exchange of information across the border, nor to neglect resistance which arose because of national-level pressures from within their own national planning systems and cultures. This stresses the point that the deep-rooted cultural dimension of borders is neither flexible nor easily manipulable: there can be multiple overlapping barriers across various dimensions of 'proximity', which can present significant problems in developing effective collaboration despite the economic rationale and organizational pressure for cooperation.

Discussion

In this chapter on cross-border community formation we question why bottom-up cross-border 'epistemic communities' have failed to emerge, despite the apparent softening of European borders in the wake of the 'Single European Project'. By closely examining the KOBRA project, it becomes immediately clear that the formation of cross-border relationships is an extremely difficult and complex process. Despite geographic 'proximity', several barriers and organizational asymmetries prevented partners from easily working together. Arguably, the least of these barriers were the differences in the formal planning systems. The most significant barrier was national and regional planning authorities' persistent fear of losing control over 'their' territories under a cross-border institutional arrangement.

It was into this context of complex overlaying barriers and organizational asymmetries that a series of KOBRA INTERREG projects were introduced. The project assumed that if the right information could be assembled in front of the right partnership, then the right priorities and decisions for cross-border planning could be determined. There is also an implicit dimension to this assumption that expects an institutionalization of the cross-border 'epistemic community' dimension as a consequence. We argue that the failure of these communities to immediately emerge is a function of the opaque nature of these barriers and cultures, which worked against the introduction of effective cross-border planning.

There are three key points that come out of the preceding analysis, highlighting the more complex and embedded nature of cross-border learning processes. First, community formation is an uncertain process with actors requiring reasons to work together effectively. Second, multi-level governance of spatial planning is an increasingly crowded institutional space, and thus the weaknesses in developing strong cross-border relationships may reflect the fact that strong 'epistemic communities' already exist at a range of 'territorial governance' levels. Finally, 'proximity' is not a simple variable in a cross-border situation. Whilst some kinds of 'proximity' may build up in cross-border planning activities, this may in turn highlight the absence of other elements of 'proximity'.

Whilst having good reason to cooperate is a prerequisite for effective cross-border communities, this significantly simplifies a more complex reality. Funding was clearly a motivation for cross-border partnership, notably a desire or need to access INTERREG funding. However, the cross-border partnership was not initiated from within the Austrian KOBRA region. Rather it emerged from Austrian central planning authorities' pressure on local municipalities, whose organizational capacity grew over time to call upon the participation of municipal authorities in Bratislava. It reflected what these authorities felt was desirable and legitimate – the Austrian authorities expecting rural municipalities to behave less parochially, and Slovakian authorities strategically pursued interests in up-market real estate development. Support from these national-level organizations provided KOBRA partners with the necessary technological knowledge and support. This agent interactivity represented a new planning scale, as well as illustrating how existing actors at multiple scales helped to realize this new planning scale; it was not cross-border interactions that were most powerful in determining these relationships.

This raises the second point, which suggests that there could be a functional limit to the multiple scales of 'territorial governance' in a planning process. Multi-level spatial planning governance is increasingly crowded institutionally, and the reliance on existing actors in this crowded space appears to reduce 'proximity' between cross-border agents by flattening out the importance of cross-border relationships. This raises the question whether new cross-border planning spaces have failed to emerge as a consequence of a lack of demand for them or the limited capacity that they might bring to cross-border planning. In fact, there is a tendency within feature-driven planning (e.g. planning for river systems) where national systems remain important (Janssen 2009), raising the question about whether the future for cross-border regions remains contingent on the necessity of cross-border planning.

Lastly, the KOBRA case study highlights the multiple co-existing dimensions of 'proximity', which enable and constrain cross-border community formation. We began by indicating that softening of borders does not necessarily imply different actors are brought together more closely across borders. Clearly, better cross-border working is central to efforts to drive European competitiveness and solidarity, ensuring all regions benefit from Europe's economic success. But this raises the question of whether a new 'Single European Project' – and perhaps a new Lord Cockcroft – are necessary to ensure that it is not just borders that are softened but that Europe does deliver – in the romantic language of the Treaty of Rome – an ever closer Union between the peoples of Europe. A shift from thinking about border softness to 'proximity' could help reignite the popular dimension of the European project that has been all but lost in the Byzantine wrangling around the technocratic Constitutional Convention.

Confusing or constructive complexity?

The preceding discussion highlights the complexity of the many levels on which barriers and obstacles to cross-border working exist. In part, our framework in Table 10.2 is a useful way to 'peel back' the dimensions along which cross-border communities might progress in terms of their collective learning and organizational capacity to influence national planning cultures and systems. The framework also makes clear the relative poor progression toward genuine cross-border planning in a region that is seen as comparatively successful in terms of particular INTERREG projects. The framework also suggests that if effective cross-border activity is to take place, building real 'proximity' along a range of dimensions is necessary to encourage collective solutions to shared problems albeit perceived differently by different groups of partners. What we cannot answer in this analysis is whether higher levels of cross-border 'proximity' would result in a cross-border 'community of practice' evolving into an 'epistemic community' – placing cross-border issues more centrally within national planning debates and legislation.

To return to our main issue, the overall story is that a multi-level approach may be too 'flat' to properly perceive the real issues around the emergence of new (in this case cross-border) scales of 'territorial governance'. 'Proximity' is one of the determining variables of this nuanced exploration into new forms of 'territorial governance', but another is the asymmetry between partners *within* national planning systems. Even in the case of Bratislava, which as a capital city occupies a prime place in the national planning culture, its capacity to address cross-border issues were severely compromised by a need not to cross the red line of the inviolability of national planning sovereignty. Unless particular care is taken to emphasize these points, then an unduly optimistic message can emerge about the rate and substance of progress toward cross-border planning in Europe.

In this we are reminded of Lagendijk and Oïnas's (2005) admonition in telling 'happy family stories' about the emergence of new tiers of regional governance or regional development coalitions. By this they mean 'harmonious cooperation between a variety of firms, authorities and other organizations' widely critiqued for failing to adequately represent a more complex reality (Lagendijk and Oïnas, 2005: 12). The reality of cross-border arrangements is complex, progress has been slow, and thus it makes little sense to talk seriously of cross-border 'epistemic communities'. This is a key finding: positive stories of cross-border planning must be candid about their success or otherwise in shaping their wider regional and national systems, and ultimately their regions' place within them.

And yet there clearly has been a sense of progress – in ways that echo progress found in other similar cross-border regions. Our argument is that one problem for bottom-up cross-border arrangements has been that they are of a different scale to the top-down arrangements. INTERREG IVC – territorial cooperation – has high profile sponsors at the highest (national) levels with participants actively opting-in to arrangements. It is unsurprising that these arrangement are highly successful and influential – it is unsurprising that an 'epistemic community' can coalesce around a group of powerful actors. But for the 'ordinary' border regions, cross-border cooperation is framed by the fact that you cooperate with – for better or for worse – your adjacent regions. It therefore seems unreasonable to demand the same high standard of outcomes for such ordinary activities as those generated by leading powerful regions that already have the ear of their policy-makers.

And it is from this standpoint that we draw our main policy conclusion concerning European spatial policy, reiterating the tension that exists between a bottom-up and a top-down version of Europe as evident in policies such as INTERREG. If multi-level governance is to deliver on European integration and localization, then it must be a bottom-up version of multi-level governance – not only informed by the positions and interests of selected coalitions of the powerful, but also by the interests, networks, coalitions and opportunities that ordinary regions face. This is not purely a question of financial resources; bottom-up policy measures receive €5.6 billion (2007–2013) in European Structural Funds whilst top-down and horizontal measures between them receive €2.2 billion, and in previous rounds the balance has been similar. Other forces are here at work, and it is beyond the scope of our chapter to analyze why. However, clearly if bottom-up cross-border planning is to become an effective feature – and even a pillar – of the European planning landscape in the near future, then more thought must be given to developing the learning arenas of cross-border communities into 'epistemic communities' with the knowledge, legitimacy and salience to demand better consideration of their needs within Europe's emerging multi-level planning space.

References

Adams, N. (2008) 'Convergence and policy transfer: an examination of the extent to which approaches to spatial planning have converged within the context of an enlarged EU', *International Planning Studies*, 13(1): 31–49.

Adams, N., Cotella, G. and Nunes, R. (2010) 'Territorial knowledge channels in a multi-jurisdictional policy environment: a theoretical framework', in N. Adams, G. Cotella and R. Nunes (eds) *Territorial Development, Cohesion and Spatial Planning: Knowledge and policy development in an enlarged EU*, London: Routledge.

Anderson, A., O'Dowd, L. and Wilson, T. M. (2003) 'Culture, co-operation and borders', *European Studies*, 19: 13–29.

—— (eds) (2005) *New Borders for a Changing Europe. Cross-border Cooperation and Governance*, London: Routledge.

Benner, C. (2003) 'Learning communities in a learning region: the soft infrastructure of cross firm learning networks in Silicon Valley', *Environment & Planning A*, 35(10): 1809–1830.

Boschma, R. A. (2005) 'Proximity and innovation. A critical assessment', *Regional Studies*, 39(1): 61–74.

Brunet, R. (1989) *Les Villes "Européennes". Rapport pour la DATAR*. Paris: La Documentation Française (RECLUS/DATAR).

Castells, M. (1996) *The Rise of the Network Society, The Information Age: Economy, Society and Culture. Vol. I*, Oxford: Blackwell.

CEC – Commission of the European Communities (1997) *The EU compendium of spatial planning systems and policies*, Regional development studies 28, Luxembourg: Office for the Official Publications of the European Communities.

—— (1999) *European Spatial Development Perspective: Towards Balanced and Sustainable Development of the Territory of the EU*. Luxembourg: Office of the Official Publications of the European Communities.

CoR – Committee of Regions (2007) *The European Grouping of Territorial Co-operation – EGTC* (Study carried out by GEPE under the supervision of Professor Nicolas Levrat in the context of the CoR's research programme).

Czapiewski, K. and Janc, K. (2010) 'Accessibility to education and its impact on regional development in Poland', in N. Adams, G. Cotella and R. Nunes (eds) *Territorial Development, Cohesion and Spatial Planning: Knowledge and policy development in an enlarged EU*, London: Routledge.

Davoudi, S. (2006) 'Evidence-based planning: rhetoric and reality', *DisP*, 165: 14–24.

Dillinger, T. (2008) *KOBRA 2010*. Vienna: Vienna University of Technology.

Egeraat, C., van, McCafferty, D., Bartley, B. and Creamer, C. (2007) 'Towards the development of all-island spatial databases', *Regions*, 267: 23–25.

DE Presidency (2007) *Territorial agenda of the European Union: Towards a more competitive and sustainable Europe of diverse regions – Agreed at the occasion of the informal ministerial meeting on urban development and territorial cohesion on 24/25 May 2007*. Online. Available HTTP: www.bmvbs.de/Anlage/original_1005295/Territorial-Agenda-of-the-European-Union-Agreed-on-25-May-2007-accessible.pdf.

Fabbro, S. and Haselsberger, B. (2009) 'Spatial planning harmonisation as a condition for cross-national co-operation. The case of the Alpine-Adriatic area', *European Planning Studies*, 17(9).

Faludi, A. and Waterhout, B. (2002) *The Making of the European Spatial Development Perspective. No masterplan*, London: Routledge.

Fritsch, M. (2010) 'Interfaces of European Union internal and external territorial governance: the Baltic Sea Region', in N. Adams, G. Cotella and R. Nunes (eds) *Territorial Development, Cohesion and Spatial Planning: Knowledge and policy development in an enlarged EU*, London: Routledge.

Gabbe, J. (1999) 'Co-operation along Internal Borders of the European Union', *Lace Magazine*, 4: 5–6.

Haas, P. M. (1992) 'Epistemic communities and international policy coordination', *International Organization*. 46(1): 1–35.

Hart, A. and Wolff, D. (2006) 'Developing local "communities of practice" through local community-university partnerships', *Planning Practice & Research*, 21(1): 121–138.

Haselsberger, B. (2007) 'European territorial co-operation: regions of the future', *Regions*, 267: 6–8.

—— (2008) 'Co-operation beyond borders after the death of distance', *Regions*, 270: 10–12.

—— (2009) 'Back to the future: a new planning agenda?', *Town Planning Review*, 80.

Healey, P. (1997) *Collaborative Planning. Shaping places in fragmented societies*, London: Palgrave MacMillan.

Janssen, G. (2006) *Europäische Verbünde für territoriale Zusammenarbeit*, Berlin: LIT Verlag.

Janssen, J. (2009) *Modelling Qualitative Information for Strategic River Management: Necessity, feasibility and utility*, Enschede, NL: WEM.

Jensen, O. B. and Richardson, T. (2004) *Making European Space. Mobility, Power and Territorial Identity*, London: Routledge.

Keating, M. (2004) *Regions and Regionalism in Europe*, Cheltenham: Edward Elgar Publishing.

Kunzmann, K. and Wegener, M. (1991) *The Pattern of Urbanisation in Western Europe 1960–1990*. Report for the Directorate General XVI of the Commission of the European Communities as Part of the Study 'Urbanisation and the Function of Cities in the European Community'. Dortmund: IRPUD.

Lagendijk, A. and Oïnas, P. (2005) 'Proximity, external relationships and local economic development', in A. Lagendijk and P. Oïnas (eds) *Proximity, Distance and Diversity: Issues on economic interaction and local development*, London: Ashgate.

Marot, N. (2010) 'New planning jurisdictions, scant resources and local public responsibility: delivering spatial planning in Slovenia', in N. Adams, G. Cotella and R. Nunes (eds) *Territorial Development, Cohesion and Spatial Planning: Knowledge and policy development in an enlarged EU*, London: Routledge.

Maskell, P. and Törnqvist, G. (1999) *Building a Cross-Border Learning Region*, Copenhagen: Copenhagen Business School Press.

Müller, V. (2003) *25 years of the Euregio Council: Retrospective of a political organ in a small Europe*, Gronau: Euregio.

Nadin, V. and Stead, D. (2008) 'European spatial planning systems, social models and learning', *DisP*, 172: 35–47.

Nonaka, I. and Takeuchi, H. (1995) *The Knowledge-creating Company*, Oxford: Oxford University Press.

O'Dowd, L. (2001) 'Analysing Europe's borders', *IBRU Boundary and Security Bulletin*, 2: 67–79.

—— (2002) 'The changing significance of European borders', *Regional and Federal Studies*, 12(4): 13–36.

Oïnas, P. and Lagendijk, A. (2005) 'Towards understanding proximity, distance and diversity in economic interaction and local economic development', in A. Lagendijk and P. Oïnas (eds) *Proximity, Distance and Diversity: Issues on economic interaction and local development*, London: Ashgate.

Paasi, A. (1998) *Territories, Boundaries and Consciousness. The changing geographies of the Finnish-Russian border*, New York: John Wiley and Sons.

Parker, B. J. (2006) 'Toward an understanding of borderland processes', *American antiquity*, 71(1): 77–100.

Razumeyko, N. (2010) 'Strategic Planning Practices in North-West Russia: European Influences, Challenges and Future Perspectives', in N. Adams, G. Cotella and R. Nunes (eds) *Territorial Development, Cohesion and Spatial Planning: Knowledge and policy development in an enlarged EU*, London: Routledge.

Sack, R. (1986) *Human Territoriality, Its Theory and History*, Cambridge: Cambridge University Press.

Schaffer, H., Ringler, C. and Pürmayr, K. (2008) *KOBRA: Urban Regional Co-operation Vienna-Bratislava*, Vienna: Mecca Consulting.

Shaw, D. and Sykes, O. (2004) 'The concept of polycentricity in European spatial planning: reflections on its interpretation and application in the practice of spatial planning', *International Planning Studies*, 9(4): 283–306.

Stead, D. and Nadin, V. (2010) 'Shifts in territorial governance and the Europeanization of spatial planning in Central and Eastern Europe', in N. Adams, G. Cotella and R. Nunes (eds) *Territorial Development, Cohesion and Spatial Planning: Knowledge and policy development in an enlarged EU*, London: Routledge.

Temple, J. (1998) 'The new growth evidence', *Journal of Economic Literature*, 37(1): 112–156.

Tilly, C. (1990) *Coercion, Capital and European states AD 990–1990*, Oxford: Basil Blackwell.

Van Houtum, H. (2000) 'An overview of European geographical research on borders and border regions', *Journal of Borderland Studies*, 15(1): 57–83.

Wenger, E. (1998) *Communities of Practice*, Cambridge: Cambridge University Press.

Wollansky, I. (2008) 'KOBRA 2010 Urban-Rural-Cooperation Bratislava: Urban-rural linkages enhancing European territorial competitiveness', Brussels: DG REGIO.

Zonneveld, W. (2005) 'Expansive spatial planning: the new European crossnational spatial visions', *European Planning Studies*, 13(1): 137–155.

Part III

Addressing increasing disparities and inequalities in the new regions of Europe

Editors' introduction to Part III

Neil Adams, Giancarlo Cotella and Richard Nunes

One of the most significant challenges facing the EU today is how to address the apparently increasing disparities between regions within many Member States. It is likely that the pursuance of socio-economic and territorial cohesion across the EU territory will have serious implications at numerous territorial levels. In light of this, the European Commission and the Member States clearly anticipated the territorial impacts that accompanied the accession of significantly less prosperous regions to the EU in the successive enlargements in 2004 and 2007 (CEC 1996, 2004). However, it would appear that whilst such impacts at the EU level provide a difficult challenge for EU cohesion, the problems facing national and sub-national levels are going to be equally challenging, if not more so. The increased focus on the Lisbon Agenda promoting economic competitiveness appears to be driving centralization tendencies and an increased concentration of population, activities and resources within a limited number of larger urban areas in many Member States, and in particular in the CEE countries. These phenomena appear to be taking place at an ever increasing pace since the start of the transition process and this has significant implications for territorial development. There seems therefore to be a paradox whereby current policies, whilst reducing disparities at the EU level between Member States, are in many cases fuelling increasing disparities within them (Ezcurra *et al.* 2007).

The evolution of spatial policy in the EU since the publication of the European Spatial Development Perspective (CEC 1999) has seen a transition from concepts such as balanced and polycentric development to the more recent concepts of territorial cohesion and territorial capital. Though such concepts have been widely debated, particularly among the planning community in the 'old' Member States, the only real consensus amongst those engaged with spatial planning in Europe is that there is no precise definition of what these terms actually mean (Faludi 2006). The abstract nature and generative capacity of such concepts, whereby they mean different things to different people, will undoubtedly lead to multiple interpretations as stakeholders at different levels and within different contexts interpret them to suit their own ends (Adams 2008). Evers claims that this flexibility should be seen as an advantage and argues that if spatial planning is employed to support a substantively vague and piece-meal approach (e.g. enhancement of territorial capital, promotion of territorial cohesion etc.) in a manner that effectively skirts the issue of redistribution, it can maximise its political capacity and contribute to supporting the larger European project.

(Evers 2007: 313)

On the other hand, this ambiguity creates significant challenges to those seeking to apply such concepts and deal with the realities of their practical implications, as identified by Shaw and Sykes (2004) in relation to the concept of polycentricity.

The ambiguity of much of the terminology within the European regional policy and spatial planning discourse tends to reflect the apparently contradictory nature of simultaneously pursuing competitiveness and cohesion (cf. Tewdwr-Jones Chapter 3). Such contradictions appear to be encapsulated and reinforced by the increased emphasis on the competitiveness-based aims of the Lisbon Agenda over the equity and sustainability focus of the politically less influential Gothenburg Agenda. The forces of globalization and the increasingly neo-liberal agendas adopted by many EU Member States provide a context within which the increased emphasis on the competitiveness aspects of the Lisbon Agenda are likely to further exacerbate disparities between winning and losing regions within many countries and this appears to be particularly relevant to CEE. Current evidence suggests that the winning regions are likely to be the metropolitan regions that possess locational advantages and sufficient critical mass to drive regional development. The losing regions are generally likely to be those without large metropolitan cities and those in geographically peripheral locations. It is therefore important for these non-metropolitan regions to learn to identify and sustainably exploit the specific characteristics that make them unique and in order to do this they will need to be able to identify and harness their territorial potentials. The term 'territorial capital', whose roots may be traced back to the local development theories of the 1980s and 1990s, has re-emerged within the European spatial policy discourse to affirm the importance of European diversity and basically is to be understood as an umbrella term covering the unique characteristics of a specific territory. Waterhout (2008) relates territorial capital to both tangible and intangible factors, the latter being clearly difficult to quantify. This is reflected by the quantitative nature of much of the territorial knowledge or knowledge resources generated by the European planning community in recent years and particularly in the context of ESPON. Clearly one of the biggest current challenges for the European planning community generally in knowledge arenas such as ESPON is to generate more qualitative knowledge resources and in this context the concept of territorial capital could be useful. One of the most frequently used definitions of territorial capital is:

A region's territorial capital is distinct from other areas and is determined by many factors (which) ... may include ... geographical location, size, factor of production endowment, climate, traditions, natural resources, quality of life or the agglomeration economies provided by its cities. Other factors may be 'untraced interdependencies' such as understandings, customs and informal rules that enable economic actors to work together under conditions of uncertainty, or the solidarity, mutual assistance and co-opting of ideas that often develop in small and medium-size enterprises working in the same sector (social capital). Lastly there is an intangible factor, 'something in the air', called the environment and which is the outcome of a combination of institutions, rules, practices, producers, researchers and policy-makers, that make a certain creativity and innovation possible. This 'territorial capital' generates a higher return for certain kinds of investments than for others, since they are better suited to the area and use its assets and potential more effectively.

(OECD 2001)

The concept of territorial capital allows for opportunities to promote an indigenous approach to regional development as a means of strengthening regional competitiveness (Pike *et al.* 2006), and is therefore particularly attractive to those regions outside the major metropolitan areas as they often have more limited potential and face greater challenges in the pursuance of such goals. In this sense, the concept has some similarities with the concept of polycentric development that in the wake of the *ESDP* (CEC 1999) was the dominant storyline in European spatial planning. In common with many concepts associated with spatial planning over the years, the lack of a precise definition of the concept and the diversity of the tangible and less tangible elements, which could be considered to be part of an area's territorial capital, leads to flexibility but also to uncertainty for those trying to operationalize the concept in practice. However, what is clear is that identifying and harnessing territorial capital is a prerequisite for achieving the full potential of a region. As a result, the interpretation, evolution and practical application of the concept currently constitutes a significant challenge for those engaged in spatial planning in Europe. The process of enlargement has intensified this challenge and provides an opportunity to assess the potential of spatial policy to start to address the regional imbalances prevalent in many CEE countries. In this concern, the *Green Paper on Territorial Cohesion* (CEC 2008) represents the most recent attempt by the European Commission to generate debate about the meaning and interpretations of territorial cohesion and will potentially ultimately result in some flesh being put onto the currently rather ambiguous bones of the principle. The Green Paper is also significant in the sense that it would appear to be an attempt to engage a wider group of stakeholders in the territorial cohesion debate, broadening what Waterhout (Chapter 4) refers to as the 'territory matters coalition'.

Kunzmann (2008) claims that European territorial development currently appears to be characterized by three megatrends: metropolization, fragmentation and polarization. Given the socio-economic and spatial characteristics of many CEE countries, coupled with the ongoing transition process, the spatial development trends referred to by Kunzmann are particularly relevant in this part of Europe. Such processes are characterized by a high degree of complexity and imply the interaction of diverse perspectives. Having examined some of the relevant institutional and governance aspects of the multi-jurisdictional policy environment of the EU in Part II, this part aims to shed some light on a more contextual dimension, exploring some of the most significant spatial, economic and social challenges currently facing Europe. Increasing regional disparities within many Member States imply that current policy has until now been unable to reconcile the dual pursuance of competitiveness and cohesion at diverse spatial scales. Future policy responses are likely to be formulated by an ever increasing diversity of agents whose role and influence will be determined to a large degree by their effectiveness in utilizing new and emerging territorial knowledge channels. That is why the editors of this volume perceive the role of various types of expert communities and broader coalitions to be so important. As discussed in Chapters 1 and 2, the editors are seeking to provide a more robust framework than the notion of epistemic communities as put forward by Haas (1992) in order to try to explain how policy is currently framed. It is within this context that the contributions in this section should be read. Starting from a general discussion of some of the key concepts in the European spatial planning discourse, the authors discuss specific aspects of these and how the expert and professional communities have evolved and engaged in diverse transnational and national arenas in order to influence these processes.

The contribution by Karel Maier (Chapter 11) explores the interpretations, contradictions and practical implications of some of the key current concepts in European spatial planning from a CEE perspective. In addition the author seeks to assess the evolution and emergence of expert and professional networks and communities in CEE countries, their engagement with the wider European spatial planning discourse and the role they play in the relationship between knowledge and policy development. As mentioned in Chapter 1, EU enlargement has created numerous challenges and greatly increased the diversity of the EU and the heterogeneity of the landscape within which spatial planning is practiced. In response to these challenges the rhetoric of EU regional policy identifies territorial cohesion among its key policy aims and as an important means of promoting economic competitiveness. Nevertheless, the increased internal disparities within many Member States suggest that the simultaneous pursuance of balanced territorial development at different spatial scales has until now proved to be an elusive goal. The ongoing transition process in CEE countries combined with the influence of the Soviet/socialist legacy and the desire to reduce the prosperity gap with the West complicate the situation further. Concepts such as polycentric development, territorial cohesion and territorial capital have emerged at different times within the European spatial planning discourse as a potential means of addressing the growing disparities between and within less favoured European regions. Maier argues that this debate has been dominated by the planning community in the 'old' Member States and examines the reasons for this and for the limited debate of such issues in CEE countries. In light of this ambiguity, the application of such concepts is highly complex, partly due to ongoing debates about their actual meaning and practical implications which are continuously (re)shaped within the European planning community.

Within this context the author seeks to assess the meaning of such concepts from a CEE perspective and in so doing makes a valuable contribution to the current debate. The respective roles of policy-makers, practitioners and academics in CEE countries in the spatial planning and development discourse are discussed both at the EU level and at the level of individual Member States. The author examines the 'retention' and 'merger' scenarios put forward by Pallagst (2006 and Chapter 6) within this context, arguing that elements of both may be appropriate for different policy goals or in relation to different parts of the heterogeneous landscape of the enlarged EU. The chapter provides a CEE perspective on those concepts underpinning the European spatial planning discourse and explores the complexities of the cohesion agenda and its implications for the new Member States. In so doing, it discusses diverse ways in which the professional and expert communities in CEE could evolve and the potential implications these evolutions could have for future spatial policy development.

The contribution by Kule *et al.* (Chapter 12) examines the rhetoric and reality of spatial policy and territorial development in Latvia. As fully fledged Soviet Socialist Republics, the Baltic States of Estonia, Latvia and Lithuania were in many ways more fully integrated into the Soviet Union than other CEE countries. Despite similarities, not least in relation to collective recent memories, the three countries are different in many ways and this includes the way in which they approach spatial planning (Adams 2006). The specific characteristics of the country and the trends that have emerged during the transition and transformation process following Latvian independence and since the collapse of the Soviet Union, provide a highly relevant context within which to think about territorial cohesion and interregional disparities. The highly monocentric nature of the country (Meijers *et al.* 2007) means that Latvia represents an extreme example of what appears to be happening in many CEE countries. Latvia experienced consistently high levels of economic growth in recent years until the recent economic crisis saw it plummet into one of the worst recessions in Europe. Growth was driven predominantly by the Riga capital region, whilst the non-metropolitan regions (Kurzeme, Vidzeme, Zemgale and Latgale) continued to lose human resources and activities at an alarming rate with significant implications for territorial development. In many ways, therefore, Latvia experienced a reduction in social, economic and territorial cohesion and, in the case of its non-metropolitan regions, a reduction in competitiveness relative to the capital region. This imbalance and the strong monocentric character of the nation significantly reduce the potential of the non-metropolitan regions and put the apparent simultaneous pursuance of cohesion and competitiveness into perspective. Furthermore, the apparent embracement of the European planning discourse notwithstanding, the involvement of the Latvian spatial planning community within supranational knowledge arenas such as ESPON has until now been limited due to practicalities and financial realities. Nevertheless, an examination of recent regional and spatial policy in Latvia reveals many similarities to EU policy goals, evident in many national and regional planning documents that promote cohesion and more balanced patterns of development. However, despite these similarities, the reality reflects a host of cross-scalar tensions surrounding spatial concepts such as polycentricity, suggesting that the promotion of Riga as an international centre and driver of development with the intention of narrowing the prosperity gap between the national level and the EU average will continue to be prioritized.

As Latvia continues to experience the effects of the Soviet legacy (Paalzow 2006), the discussion commences with an examination of the complexities of the transition and transformation process, so as to provide the context within which some of the highly fluid socio-economic and institutional characteristics have emerged. In line with the rationale for this book, the authors explore the interplay between knowledge and spatial policy development in Latvia, analyzing the evolution of the professional and expert communities engaged in spatial planning arenas and the influence of processes of internationalization and Europeanization. These processes have provided opportunities for the Latvian planning community to engage with diverse knowledge arenas and a number of these are discussed. The main territorial guidance documents produced at the European level (such as the *ESDP*, the *Territorial Agenda* and the recently published *Green Paper on Territorial Cohesion*; CEC 1999, DE Presidency 2007 and CEC 2008 respectively) are explored in the light of their relevance for contextual territorial challenges. Partly in contrast to other contributions to this volume (cf. Chapter 5 by Finka and Chapter 11 by Maier), the authors argue that European spatial planning has had a significant impact and influence and that the European spatial planning discourse has been widely debated among the Latvian planning community. The discussion provides valuable insights into the cross-scalar and multi-jurisdictional tensions implicit in the simultaneous pursuance of national economic competitiveness and territorial cohesion and of the potential of these and other relevant concepts and policies at the national, regional and local levels to address the ever growing disparities between metropolitan regions and more geographically peripheral regions.

The final two contributions in this section, by Pawel Capik (Chapter 13) and by Konrad Czapiewski and Krzysztof Janc (Chapter 14), examine specific elements of territorial capital as potential drivers of regional development, respectively in relation to the attraction of foreign direct investment (FDI) and to the diffusion of education opportunities. As already emphasized by Tewdwr-Jones (Chapter 3), the attraction of FDI plays an important role in regional development, as FDI has traditionally been perceived as an important source of capital, technology and employment for regions undergoing structural change. This has inevitably led to increased competition between countries and also between different regions within countries. Numerous regional authorities have responded by actively promoting and marketing their regions in an attempt to beat the competition and attract higher levels of FDI. It can be argued that a determining factor in the success of any such promotional strategy is likely to depend on the extent to which it can be tailored to the specific territorial capital of a particular region. However, Capik argues that most regional authorities appear to make little effort to understand the endogenous potentials of their territories, often leading to a 'one-size fits all' approach in adopted strategies in an attempt to mirror successful Western experiences. Evidence suggests that regional promotion practices developed by those seeking to reinvent the post-industrial cities of the Western economies require adjustments to make them more appropriate to the CEE reality. However, the level of importance assigned by the regional authorities to this still somewhat new policy tool varies. As with all instruments with a competitive element, place promotion results in winning and losing regions in terms of FDI attraction, generally corresponding to metropolitan and non-metropolitan regions respectively.

The perception of FDI as some sort of panacea and as a means of driving economic growth and increasing economic competitiveness has led to most CEE countries actively pursuing this elusive mobile capital. Despite an extensive body of literature on themes such as marketing and promotion, as well as theories of exogenous and endogenous regional development, there appears to be a deficiency of knowledge resources based on systematic cross-national studies to assist policy development. This implies that policies and approaches are often insufficiently grounded in a robust knowledge base backed up by empirical evidence generated by professional or expert communities. The author of Chapter 13 examines the extent to which limited knowledge resources in relation to both endogenous potential and competitors underpins key decisions in relation to policy development with little attention given to tailoring solutions sensitively to specific local contexts. Capik explores these issues in the context of CEE competitiveness-based regional promotion and explores the determinants of approaches adopted by Czech, Polish and Slovak regional authorities to the FDI attraction process. He examines the extent to which effective promotion communities capable of promoting context-sensitive solutions are emerging and reflects on the importance of effective channels and networks between the increasingly diverse series of actors, arenas and institutions involved in these processes. In this concern, Tewdwr-Jones (Chapter 3) argues that one of the key challenges for the European planning community is to deliver approaches, strategies and policies that will enable mobile capital to become embedded within a specific regional context, in his words to promote 'a more embedded form of economically-aware spatial governance'.

The final chapter in this section (Chapter 14) examines the role of education as an element of territorial capital and as a potential driver of regional development, focusing on the Polish experience. The development of human resources potentially has a key role to play as a driver of regional development and constitutes a specific element of the territorial capital of a region. It can be argued that access to educational opportunities is an important determining factor in developing the potential of such human resources. Whereas the Lisbon strategy stresses the important role played by investments focusing on raising education levels in the overall framework of a competitive Europe, the strong focus on successful economic areas that characterizes the overall flavour of the document translates in many cases to a lack of emphasis on the improvement of education opportunities within less favoured regions. This differential access to educational opportunities implies that certain areas will be disadvantaged in terms of development potential and this in turn may contribute to further fuelling increasing regional disparities and a further exacerbation of the current mega-trends of metropolization, fragmentation and polarization being witnessed in the EU (Kunzmann 2008). The differential access to education in Poland is explored within the context of the spatial characteristics of the country and the potential implications are examined for the main development centres and the more geographically peripheral and rural areas. In contrast with other CEE countries such as Latvia, Poland is characterized by one of the most polycentric urban systems in the EU (ESPON 2005a, 2005b). However significant disparities are apparent in both the rates of development and the spatial distribution of and accessibility to higher education between the main urban centres and more geographically peripheral and rural regions. The authors explore the interdependencies and the relationship between these two factors and reflect on the approach adopted in Poland for embedding education policy within wider regional development policy. The authors argue that, if more balanced patterns of regional development are to be achieved in Poland, then it is essential that access to educational opportunities are improved significantly for the rural youth. They reflect on the potential implications of these findings for future territorial development and explore different options available in terms of policy development, funding and approach. An essential element of the spatial approach adopted by the *ESDP* (CEC 1999) was the promotion of 'joined-up' thinking and persuading sectoral actors to think about the spatial implications of their actions and spending programmes and this will resonate with actors in other parts of the EU in their pursuit of more joined-up forms of government (Alden 2006). The ongoing debates regarding equity and efficiency, competitiveness and cohesion, and the appropriate balance between investing in hard infrastructure and soft infrastructure to develop human resources, illustrate the enduring relevance of this discussion in the context of CEE.

References

Adams, N. (2006) 'National spatial strategies in the Baltic States', in N. Adams, J. Alden and N. Harris (eds), *Regional Development and Spatial Planning in an Enlarged EU*, Aldershot: Ashgate.

—— (2008) 'Convergence and policy transfer: an examination of the extent to which approaches to spatial planning have converged within the context of an enlarged EU', *International Planning Studies*, 13(1): 31–50.

Alden, J. (2006) 'Regional development and spatial planning', in N. Adams, J. Alden and N. Harris (eds), *Regional Development and Spatial Planning in an Enlarged EU*, Aldershot: Ashgate.

CEC – Commission of the European Communities (1996), *Scenarios of Spatial Development of Central and Eastern European Countries*, Luxembourg: DG-Regio.

—— (1999) *European Spatial Development Perspective: Towards balanced and sustainable development of the territory of the EU*. Luxembourg: Office of the Official Publications of the European Communities.

—— (2004) *Third Report on Economic and Social Cohesion: A new partnership for cohesion: convergence competitiveness cooperation*, Brussels: Commission of the European Communities.

—— (2008) *Green Paper on Territorial Cohesion – Turning territorial diversity into strength*, Brussels: Commission of the European Communities.

DE Presidency (2007) *Territorial Agenda of the European Union: Towards a more competitive and sustainable Europe of diverse regions – Agreed at the occasion of the informal ministerial meeting on urban development and territorial cohesion on 24/25 May* 2007. Available at HTTP: www.bmvbs.de/Anlage/original_1005295/Territorial-Agenda-of-the-European-Union-Agreed-on-25-May-2007-accessible.pdf (accessed March 2010).

ESPON (2005a) *ESPON 1.1.1 Potentials for Polycentric Development in Europe – Final report.* Luxembourg: ESPON.

—— (2005b) *ESPON 1.1.3 Enlargement of the European Union and the Wider European Perspective as regards its Polycentric Spatial Structure – Final report.* Luxembourg: ESPON.

Evers, D. (2007) 'Reflections on territorial cohesion and European spatial planning', *Tijdschrift voor Economische en Sociale Geografie*, 2008, 99(3): 303–315.

Ezcurra, R., Pascual, P. and Rapun, M. (2007) 'The dynamics of regional disparities in Central and Eastern Europe during transition', *European Planning Studies*, 15(10): 1397–1421.

Faludi, A. (2006) 'From European spatial development to territorial cohesion policy', *Regional Studies*, 40(6): 667–678.

Haas, P. M. (1992) 'Introduction: Epistemic communities and international policy co-ordination', *International Organization*, 46(1): 1–35.

Kunzmann, K. (2008) 'Futures for European Space 2020', *Journal of Nordregio*, 2(8).

Meijers, E. J., Waterhout, B. and Zonneveld, W. A. M. (2007) 'Closing the GAP: Territorial cohesion through polycentric development', Refereed Articles, Oct 2007, no 24, *European Journal of Spatial Development*. Online: available at www.nordregio.se/EJSD/refereed24.pdf (accessed March 2010).

OECD (2001) OECD Territorial Outlook, OECD Publishing.

Pallagst, K. (2006), 'European spatial planning reloaded: considering EU enlargement in theory and practice', *European Planning Studies*, 14(2): 253–272.

Paalzow, A. (2006) 'Barriers to regional development in the new Member States: the Latvian experience', in N. Adams, J. Alden and N. Harris (eds), *Regional Development and Spatial Planning in an Enlarged EU*, Aldershot: Ashgate.

Pike, A., Rodriguez-Pose, A. and Tomaney, J. (2006) *Local and Regional Development*, Abingdon: Routledge.

Shaw, D. and Sykes, O. (2004) 'The concept of polycentricity in European spatial planning: reflections on its interpretation and application in the practice of spatial planning', *International Planning Studies*, 9(4): 283–306.

Waterhout, B. (2008) *The Institutionalisation of European Spatial Planning*, Delft: IOS Press.

11 The pursuit of balanced territorial development

The realities and complexities of the cohesion agenda

Karel Maier

Introduction

This chapter focuses on the meaning of the spatial development concepts that are shared among the politicians and the planning community of the European Union (EU), as seen from the perspective of the East-Central European (ECE) countries, with occasional reference also to Eastern Europe. For the purposes of clarity, we include the Czech Republic, Hungary, Poland, Slovakia and Slovenia, and in many respects also Eastern Germany and non-EU Croatia in East-Central Europe. We make this distinction to distinguish ECE from Eastern Europe, which consists of the Baltic States, Bulgaria and Romania and the ex-Yugoslavia states that were not classified in the former category. These countries were not centrally involved in formulation of current EU spatial development concepts, but accepted the agendas that evolved around these concepts as part of their accession obligations. The discourse on European territorial cohesion and balanced development originated in the 'old' EU member states and retains a much higher profile amongst academics in these countries than amongst academics in the 'new' EU even now. The objective of this contribution is therefore rather to raise some issues that may not be clearly expressed due to the uneven level of their discussion in different parts of the EU-27. In the first section of the chapter the concepts under consideration are outlined. The following section explores the frameworks, complexities and realities of the territorial cohesion agenda for ECE before the application of these concepts in the context of ECE reality is considered in more detail.

Despite a shared recent history, ECE countries are more diverse than many outsiders may realize. The roles, priorities and viewpoints of their policy-makers, practitioners and academics may be different from what their partners from the 'old' EU expect. The discourse amongst the European planning community (Waterhout 2008) in relation to cohesion and spatial development policy has been ongoing in Western Europe for decades (Faludi 2007) allowing a degree of shared comprehension of the meaning of the concepts and the role of relevant policies. The planning community in ECE appears to be rather fragmented, consisting of evolving 'communities of practice' (Wenger 1998) rather than the 'epistemic communities' (Haas 1992) that have been discussed in the context of European spatial planning by Pallagst (2006) (cf. Pallagst Chapter 6 and Adams *et al.* Chapter 2). The extent and nature of the integration of the diverse planning communities in 'old' and 'new' Europe will be influential in terms of future EU spatial development policy and overall European integration as the 'new' EU seeks to catch the West economically and conceptually. The diversity of the EU increased significantly with the accession of the ECE countries. New patterns of territorial polarization and disparities have emerged along with revised spatial structures, new mobility patterns and coverage in terms of services and infrastructure. Enlargement has also affected the way issues such as cohesion and balanced, sustainable territorial development are perceived and dealt with. Within this context some of the relevant concepts will be examined in more detail in the next section.

Understanding the terminology of European spatial planning

A number of concepts and terms have taken a central place in the European spatial planning discourse, including cohesion, disparities, polycentrism and territorial capital. The original meaning of the word 'cohesion' is far removed from its current use in the EU documents. Webster's New World Dictionary (1999: 272) suggests that to cohere is to stick together as part of a mass, to be consistent, to become or stay united in action or to be in accord. Cohesion in an EU context clearly has a positive connotation as a desirable objective of EU policies. Several fundamental EU documents mention cohesion including the proposed Constitution and the so-called Lisbon Treaty (Treaty of Lisbon 2007: Article 2), within which economic, social and territorial cohesion is defined as a competence shared between the EU and the member states.

The consensual nature of these documents, however, means that although cohesion is frequently mentioned, it is never clearly defined. The European Spatial Development Perspective (ESDP: CEC 1999) dealt with cohesion in terms of equal access to public amenities and services as a right for all EU citizens. Polycentric development was presented as a means of achieving this right in physical space. However, as pointed out by Faludi (2000: 249) the ESDP policy process constituted an 'anarchic field', with 'uncertainty regarding content as well as on the positions of the various actors', leading to the emergence of 'an 'epistemic community', admittedly with its roots in Northwest Europe'. Evers also pointed out that

> despite the additional legal and political legitimacy, there is still no consensus about the actual meaning of the term. At present, there seem to be two major competing interpretations: one related to the cohesion-oriented goals of the EU's regional policy, and another stemming from ideas of efficiency.
>
> (Evers 2007: 304)

Even when a definition is agreed and accepted it is left to national governments to attribute their particular meaning to the concept in the practical implementation. Evers claimed that 'it may be wiser to applaud the fact that the meaning of "territorial cohesion" is still ambiguous, rather than rushing to give it a precise definition' Evers (ibid. 313). The recent Green Paper on Territorial Cohesion, however, implies a need to work towards a more widely recognised definition (CEC 2008: 11). In this chapter we use the term to describe a desirable state of the territory in which disparities do not exceed the scale and amount that would undermine the sustainable development of the community, the physical environment and the economy.

Unlike territorial cohesion, the issue of disparities has a more precise meaning in relation to inequality or difference in rank, amount or quality. When related to economics it refers to an 'inequality between internal and external purchasing power of currency' or an inequality in payment conditions or prices (Diderot 1999: 251). These definitions imply no immediate judgment on the desirability or threat connected to the concept. Disparities may originate in natural diversity or they may be created as a result of human activities, attitudes and values. In the modern world of networks, nature-based disparities still exist but the human-made disparities leading to polarization appear to be a more dynamic feature. Castells (1989) analyzed increasing polarization in cities, leading to disparities, and this can also be witnessed at higher territorial levels of regions, nation states and the European continent. The issue of disparities is discussed in the Territorial Agenda (DE Presidency 2007a) and in the Third and Fourth Reports on Social and Economic Cohesion (CEC 2004, 2007). In this context disparities is presented as a potential and a challenge, and a distinction is made between diversity, which can be a means to achieve improved competitiveness in Europe, and inequalities that may challenge European, national, regional and local cohesion at various spatial levels.

Polycentrism was introduced as a central concept in ESDP in 1999 (Meijers *et al.* 2007) as a means of promoting territorial cohesion and counterbalancing disparities and the existing concentration of economic and human capital in the European core of the Pentagon (the 'Pentagon' refers to the EU's economic core demarcated by the five cities of London, Paris, Milan, Munich and Hamburg, cf. Waterhout Chapter 4).

> Polycentric urban development at both the inter-regional and intra-metropolitan levels similar to that suggested by the European Spatial Development Perspective may be the appropriate way to construct a consistent spatial strategy at the same time sustainable in economic, social and environmental terms.
>
> (Camagni 2002, quoted in Camagni 2007)

However, some scholars question the weak theoretical underpinning of the polycentric concept. Davoudi pointed out that 'only some [...] polycentric metropolitan regions already started bottom-up cooperation and set up governance structures for collective decision making, while others still remain as a normative agenda' (Davoudi 2003: 982). Similarly, Copus (2001: 548) questions the benefit of the 'normative' polycentricity as a policy arguing that it 'might create an illusion of "balanced development" at a broad brush scale, whilst presiding over, or even exacerbating, polarization on a more localized scale'. Hall and Pain (2006: 208) distinguish morphological and functional polycentricity. Morphological polycentricity is defined as referring to the geographical distribution of towns and cities of different size. Morphological polycentricity however does not imply functional polycentricity, 'which refers to flows of information and organization of firms'. Building on this classification, the authors point out how morphologically polycentric regions are rather weak in terms of intra-regional functional linkages, arguing that balanced development can hardly be associated with polycentrism (Hall and Pain 2006: 209). The ESPON 1.1.1 and ESPON 1.1.3 projects also question a simplified association between polycentricity, cohesion and sustainability (ESPON 2005a, 2005b). The issue has become even more challenging in the context of the recent EU enlargements as the proportion of the population living in non-central EU regions has increased dramatically. When dealing with regions with different spatial and functional profiles, we can assume that the concept of functional polycentricity may have different references as well.

The concept of territorial capital has also emerged in the European spatial planning discourse and placed increased emphasis on the role of endogenous resources in regional development. According to the European Commission

> each region has a specific 'territorial capital' that is distinct from that of other areas and generates a higher return for specific kinds of investments than for others, since these are better suited to the area and use its assets and potential more effectively.
>
> (CEC 2005:1)

As a result 'Territorial development policies (policies with a territorial approach to development) should first and foremost help areas to develop their territorial capital' (ibid.).

Camagni deals with the concept from the point of view of its economic utility in Capello *et al.* (2008). Each region is expected to have something unique or, at least, specific to market and trade with. Effective regional development policies should therefore help to identify and develop these sometimes hidden endogenous resources and commercialize them for the benefit of the regional economy and community, instead of providing perpetual support to lagging regions. The concept assumes that there are endogenous, marketable and competitive resources in each region, that the number and character of the competitive resources can be adjusted to the effective demand and that the products can be delivered to the customers at competitive terms. There is no general consensus about the first assumption (cf. also Czapiewski and Janc Chapter 14) whilst the second and third may prove difficult to comply with where less developed markets coincide with less developed transportation infrastructures. In general, all the above-mentioned concepts share a certain vagueness when related to spatial development. The shared history of their use in the EU arenas makes them meaningful and comprehensible to experts operating within 'epistemic communities'. As this history started long before the accession of the new EU members, interpretation in the context of these new member states needs attention and this will be the focus of the following sections of the chapter.

Frameworks for the territorial cohesion agenda in East-Central Europe

In contrast to the highly fluid and rapidly changing economic and social environment, physical frameworks for societal and economic life, represented by settlement structure and infrastructures, are characterized by their inertia and anchorage. Some of the reasons for the current situation in ECE countries will be examined in this section as well as some of the resulting constraints for the future.

Regional policies and development under central planning

Centrally directed regional planning with a direct link to state investment policy was the major instrument for achieving the aims of economic and social homogeneity under the pre-1989 regimes. The state investment monopoly resulted in investments being directed towards less developed parts of the country, often in Eastern areas that were closer to the Soviet Union, which was the preferred supplier of raw materials and energy as well as the main customer for products. The emphasis on economic and social homogeneity led to the concept of balanced and homogeneous spatial pattern that would equalize access to jobs and services for all. Christaller's central place theory was often applied (Christaller 1966) in a simplified manner adapted to Fordist methods of control and management. National capitals were at the top of the multi-level urban hierarchy and the scale of regions and sub-regions, as well as the number of levels, reflected the size of a particular country. The deliberate effort to develop a spatially balanced hierarchical system of centres had to be fuelled by the continuous interregional redistribution of huge amounts of resources. In this way morphological polycentricity was successfully achieved at the basic level of small towns.

Extensive efforts were made to ensure a balance between the distribution of jobs and services and the distribution of the population so that they were equally accessible to all. The industrialization of rural areas was promoted to provide additional jobs and in order to stabilize local population levels (Matoušek 1986; Enyedy 1996). The planning system also involved the strict control of land-use, leading to compact cities and towns with high residential densities. A clear contrast between urban and rural areas was typical for urban fringes. Policies promoting 'concentrated de-concentration' in city regions, with industrial satellites of central cities, were introduced in the 1960s and 1970s. However, the policy leading to spatially balanced local centres and industrialization in rural regions proved to be economically counterproductive and the contradiction between egalitarian ideology and pragmatic needs of the economy was never entirely resolved. Personal linkages among people were not in the interest of the totalitarian regimes and time was not valued so highly in a non-market economy context. The development of infrastructure therefore focused on the transportation of bulk goods via rail and followed the main flows of raw materials and products nationally and within the Soviet domain.

Assets and challenges of the 1990s' transition

When the constraints of central control were released, ECE countries were immediately confronted with numerous challenges that the West had been confronted with over a number of years: the collapse of public finance of the 1970s, deregulation and privatization of the 1980s, shared governance responsibilities of the 1990s. The newly emerging democracies were expected to manage these challenges almost instantly with reforms guided from a single power centre in a weak, immature and often unfriendly institutional environment (Sýkora 1999). In some cases foreign direct investments (FDI) became the almost exclusive growth factor in some ECE countries during this economic transformation (cf. Tewdwr-Jones Chapter 3; Capik Chapter 13). The qualified local workforce, low wages and relaxed regulations attracted investors and led to re-industrialization in certain regions with specialization in some areas, predominantly in car production. The spill-over effect of large-scale FDI manufacturing investments also helped smaller local producers who succeeded in replacing the lost Soviet markets by supplying the new FDI-born producers with components for their production. While the service sector located predominantly in the national capital cities, new industrial plants often emerged outside metropolitan areas adjacent to transportation hubs. The location of FDIs contributed to increasing regional disparities within the countries except in rare cases where a more spatially aware policy of investment incentives directed the investments to problem regions, often as part of the EU pre-accession provisions. As a result polarization has been one of the most tangible effects of the transition process, increasing throughout the 1990s and becoming a permanent feature of the 2000s (Meijers *et al.* 2007).

The speed and extent of the change exceeded the limits of acceptance of many people, leading politicians to slow down, reduce or even abolish the earlier neoliberal reform attempts. Following the deep tradition of egalitarianism and state paternalism that extended beyond the period of communism, people expect state involvement in social disparities even taking into account the higher costs of solidarity. On the other hand, disparities tend to be more widely accepted among political élites than in the 'old' EU member states and policies aiming at their mitigation are strongly constrained by surviving ideological standpoints belonging to early-1990s laissez-faire rhetoric. As the credit of public institutions has remained low, values of own control, property and informal networks are highly appreciated. Families and local social relationships still retain their significance as mutually supporting networks especially in rural parts of the countries and among lower social layers of society. This results in low spatial mobility of people within the country, despite the disadvantages stemming from looming territorial disparities.

Spatial management and role of planners

Planning activities in most ECE countries were divided between physical land-use planning and regional planning under Communism. The former was related to the historical tradition of 'urbanism' (*Städtebau*) that had its roots in Central Europe and the latter dealt with social and economic aspects. The economic and social policy of ECE countries in the first half of the 1990s was driven by a desire for radical change, liberalization, privatization and the introduction of market forces, in other words it was spatially blind. The increase in spatial disparities and the influence of EU policies persuaded the national governments of ECE to introduce regional policies to tackle this problem (Maier 1999; Melecký 2008). Effective regional policies were repeatedly jeopardized by neo-liberal oriented politicians with claims that they constrained market forces.

The distinction between physical planning and regional management has generally survived in terms of planning practice. Urbanists usually have an architectural background and are responsible for making statutory (land-use) plans whereas regional planners are often economists or geographers and planning administrators come from a diversity of backgrounds. Consequently, the sense of belonging to a 'community of practice' (Wegner 1998) is weak. The transformation from central control towards a market-driven economy and democratic society necessarily affected the very concept of planning and, consequently, the planning profession. The mission of planning or the planning doctrine (Faludi 2009) became unclear when the totalitarian Fordism of scientific production of social welfare failed. As a result three different potential doctrines competed initially among Czech planners. First, environmental planning promoted by 'advocacy coalitions' (Sabatier 1998) close to ecological movements, second was the urbanist movement and, finally, those who saw planning as a means of promoting development (Maier 2001). Responsibility for planning also often shifted between ministries responsible for the economy, the environment or the interior and many land-use planning activities were outsourced to the private sector where planners served their clients rather than seeking sustainable solutions. Generally speaking only the statutory planning administration function remains in the domain of public service.

Private sector urbanists are usually required to be members of national associations of architects and/or planners in order to make statutory plans. The chambers have the legal right to set admission criteria and are responsible for guaranteeing the quality of the professional services offered by their members. There are also associations of urban and regional planners and some of these groups in ECE have recently become members of the European Council of Town/Spatial Planners (ECTP). Such professional associations may constitute an appropriate platform for debates on the issues of sustainable development, territorial cohesion and competitiveness. However, many planners in ECE share the general view that sustainable development is a target that can be aimed for only when economic parity with the West has been achieved.

Whilst the regulatory power of land-use planning remains quite strong, its strategic influence on spatial development remains weak and is dominated by the desire for economic growth. For many politicians economic growth appears to have become the exclusive criterion for success, with planning reduced to the provision of land and infrastructures for investment. Environmental and cultural issues are usually treated as external constraints, and social aspects are considered outside the development oriented planning agenda. As a result, numerous current agendas have not developed any spatial dimension (e.g. demographic change). Many decision-makers equate any planning initiatives, apart from making plans for infrastructure provision, with pre-1989 regional planning control. The marginal role of planners in the 'old' EU member states in the 1980s (Tewdwr-Jones and Phelps 2000) appears to be being repeated in a post-1989 ECE obsessed with deregulation and flexibility inspired by British Thatcherism.

Another key issue in the emergence of professional networks is the evolution of professional education. Dedicated planning courses are at different stages of development throughout ECE. The independent or semi-independent planning schools that have emerged in most ECE countries tend to be part of wider programmes and the architecture dominated professional associations tend to favour graduates from architecture schools. Regional planners are usually economics graduates with limited training in spatial and environmental aspects. The consolidation of a 'community of practice' under such conditions is extremely difficult and territorial cohesion remains marginal in public and political agendas. The general perception of planning as a bureaucratic nuisance means that planners have little influence in debates about spatial development and it is often left to environmental oriented 'advocacy coalitions' to oppose developments on a project by project basis. Paradoxically, spatial policy is now being confronted by problems, such as suburbanization, urban sprawl and the loss of distinction between urban and rural areas, which have only emerged since the end of the socialist era during which they were managed more effectively. Certain features of regional policy that were abolished in the early 1990s appear to be being reintroduced as part of the EU cohesion policies. In the next section the extent to which the current situation provides a basis for balanced territorial development within the enlarged EU will be discussed.

Potentials, constraints and current trends in East-Central Europe

Effective implementation of the cohesion agenda in the new EU member states will require a deeper understanding of the realities and local contexts in these countries. Some initiatives, including ESPON, have contributed towards the integration of ECE countries in this context. The aim of this section is to provide a useful, albeit not comprehensive, insider's view to supplement this knowledge. Debate amongst the planning community on spatial development issues remains limited in ECE countries and the discussion in this section of the chapter therefore represents personal experiences and debates, often unsupported by published material.

With the exception of Poland, countries in ECE are generally similar in size to relatively small countries such as Belgium, the Netherlands or Denmark but have a population density closer to more geographically peripheral countries like Spain, Portugal or Greece. The interactions between these factors have a significant impact on spatial structures and spatial development trends. Recent studies on ECE suggest that both morphological and functional polycentricity develops and acts in different ways at different spatial levels (REPUS 2007; Mulíček and Sýkora, 2008), as indicated in Table 11.1.

The pre-existing national urban hierarchies and networks offer significant potential upon which to build and the apparent monocentricity of these small countries on the macro-regional level is fully appropriate as long as it is complemented by a second tier of regional centres.

The size of functional regions is determined by the accessibility of their centres, which in turn depends on the capacity and quality of transport and communication networks. The weak penetration of high quality infrastructure in ECE is reflected in the much faster decline in economic prosperity between core and periphery in the 'new' compared to the 'old' EU when measured from the fringe of the European Pentagon (CEC 1999; ESPON 2006a, 2006b). Immense efforts have been made to overcome the remoteness of ECE countries and these efforts have been supported through EU co-financing from PHARE, ISPA (after 2000) and the Cohesion Fund (since 2004). As a result new motorways and airports have strengthened connectivity of national metropoles to the hubs of the West. However, the connectivity between centres within ECE has not experienced such a dramatic improvement, suggesting a reinforcement of monocentric tendencies focusing on the Pentagon rather than a transition to a more polycentric pattern. Investments in rail infrastructure have reduced travel times and increased the frequency of westbound trains from Prague but improvements have been much more limited for eastbound trains. It is apparent that the preferences of linkages to the West shared by the ECE countries coincided in this respect with the policies of the EU-15 in the pre-accession period before 2004.

The more peripheral non-metropolitan areas have not profited from the positive effects of new infrastructures at all. Accessibility of rural peripheries has not improved and in some cases it has declined, especially in relation to public transport. Many local railway lines have been abandoned and local bus services reduced in rural regions, thus excluding some people living in remote regions from the job market. Long distance commuting is either no longer possible or has become too time consuming and costly. A 'tunnel effect' has also emerged along many major transportation routes which also excludes places along the route from the benefits of improved services. The resulting multi-level pattern of accessibility exacerbates interregional and intra-regional disparities. Although the relevant national policies vary, there is a common trend in ECE countries for education and health services to be reduced in less populated rural areas. In combination with the reduction in transport services in the same regions this encourages a downward spiral of decline.

Table 11.1 Characteristics of polycentricity patterns in East-Central Europe

Spatial level	Morphological polycentricity characteristics	Functional polycentricity characteristics
Supra-national centres (national capitals and other major cities)	National capitals are evenly spread in ECE and in Poland the network is complemented by other major centres (Kraków, Wrocław, Gdańsk, Poznań). These are divided spatially, however, from Eastern and South-eastern European capitals which historically belonged to the Russian and Ottoman Empires	Functional linkages of ECE supra-national centres are directed towards the European Pentagon rather than to each other and therefore functional polycentricity of these centres remains a potential for the future
National/inter-regional	National networks of regional centres have been developed deliberately in the past, adjusted to the size of the individual countries. These networks have gaps in peripheral areas where the regional centres are small or missing	All ECE countries have a strong urban hierarchy with national capitals on top. The transition of the 1990s emphasized and reinforced the privileged position of the capitals and capital regions
Intra-regional	Developed sporadically and particularly in regional industrial agglomerations (Upper Silesia, North Bohemia, Saxony)	Emerges occasionally (following morphological polycentricity) to enhance the scope of regional services and specialized professional jobs. It can counterbalance (but not compete with) the scale and attractiveness of a capital city. Island-like polycentric systems exist outside the attraction zones of regional centres that compensate for the absence of a single strong centre
Local	Exists almost everywhere in rural areas of the countries; it is challenged by: (a) shrinkage and collapse of settlement system in declining, de-populated peripheries; (b) urban sprawl in hinterlands of metropoles.	Functional monocentricity is a prevailing pattern. Polycentricity only emerges where no strong regional centre is available *and* a dense network of local transportation routes is available

Source: Author's elaboration on REPUS 2007; POLYREG 2008.

Two main features appear to have emerged from the phenomena described above, which have exacerbated regional disparities within all ECE countries and look likely to persist for the foreseeable future. First, there is a remarkable gap between economic development and prosperity of metropolitan areas and the relative stagnation or even decline in all other parts of the countries. Second, it is clear that the relative prosperity of the non-metropolitan areas declines from west to east (REPUS 2007: 15). Old industrial regions with large brownfields are considered particularly weak, offering cheap and available housing but no jobs. The relatively low cost of living attracts socially deprived groups while young and well educated people leave, further exacerbating the gap in human resources potential between booming capital metropolitan regions and declining old industrial and peripheral rural regions. Such increased disparities can also be detected within urban areas and urban regions with a declining social mix in urban residential neighbourhoods and social exclusion in emerging urban and rural ghettoes. Recent retail trends illustrate these processes. Massive and rapid expansion in retail floorspace in urban areas has dramatically reduced demand for goods and services in small local shops, undermining employment and social structures in smaller centres and rural areas. Although this process is familiar in many EU countries, the sheer pace of this evolution in ECE countries has exacerbated the impacts.

Generally, accessibility to Western markets has been the precondition for prosperity since market liberalization. Growth rates have been higher in more open and accessible regions, but also in initially less developed countries (CEC 2007: 9).

The small size of the ECE countries and their previous separation from each other (not only along the former Iron Curtain but to lesser extent also within the former Soviet Bloc) created vast stretches of former borderlands that appeared to have significant potential after the formal barriers had been withdrawn. However, as the contribution by Haselsberger and Benneworth in this volume identifies, almost two decades later the expectations of cross-border integration have not been fulfilled or have been so only in a fragmented way. The borderlands are often structurally weak and share typical features of peripheries such as poor accessibility, low population density and low educational attainment. Despite the long-running subsidies for development in these areas many problems remain. This is the case not only in the former Eastern Bloc countries but also in the border areas of Germany (Bavaria) and Austria (Upper and Lower Austria, Burgenland), as a result of the former Iron Curtain effect. The potential impact of reducing this border effect should not be overestimated, especially where the national border coincides with a natural barrier or it divides ethnic groups without a history of mutual contacts (newly populated regions after the original population had been transferred as the consequence of World War II events).

The initial impetus of the crossing point economy in the 1990s was fuelled by price and prosperity differences between neighbours. Its actors were mostly from outside the region and their activities were often connected with the grey or black economy. However, the introduction of the Schengen Agreement and the strengthening of the economies in 'new' member states (until recently) means that borderland regions must find a more sustainable source of prosperity. Borderlands where historical regions with strong centres had been divided by the borders of nation states may have significant potential whereas the hopes for revitalization may not be fulfilled for a long time where cross-border urbanized areas are situated in old industrial regions that are now in decline. Reintroducing the functionality of all cross-border regions will be complex and will need to overcome institutional and language barriers and in many cases also old grievances. The possibility of cross-border integration leading to cohesion therefore depends not only on physical and economic potentials but also on the political setting, and here interests and objectives of national politicians and regional interests may prove significant. The complexity of understanding the EU spatial development concepts and notions developed within the EU-15 and applying them to an ECE context is now apparent and this will be explored in more detail below.

EU concepts and strategies and East-Central European reality

Building on the discussion about the reality in ECE countries, this section explores how these concepts and strategies may be 'read' by the 'new' EU member states. The relatively weak theoretical and research basis for planning in ECE countries is reflected by the fact that it is generally research from Western European scholars that deals with the spatial consequences of EU enlargement (integration?) and EU policies on the new EU members. It is hoped that this chapter and those by Finka and other CEE contributors in this volume may contribute to opening interesting alternative perspectives.

Conceptualization of and integration in European spatial system

There have been several attempts to conceptualize the spatial structure and development perspectives of the ECE region but they have generally generated little interest outside limited parts of the planning community. Most of these conceptualizations were based on a shared history and certain cultural similarities from the period before national states had been established. Generally they promoted a diverse region with the potential for polycentric development and offered visions of networks which could counterbalance and even compete with the European Pentagon in the future. Gorzelak (1996) tried to conceptualize a vision of the 'Boomerang' as an ECE counterpart to the 'Blue banana' predecessor of the European Pentagon (RECLUS 1989; cf. also Pallgast Chapter 6). The Boomerang consisted of a chain of centres between Gdańsk and Budapest. Optimal conditions to develop as major European centres were identified for Prague and the triangle Vienna/Bratislava/Budapest. The author also identified the regions around Łódź and Szczecin as the 'black holes' of socio-economic development as well as a general drift towards the West, especially in the Polish part that was oriented strongly towards Berlin. More recently, the INTERREG project REPUS (2007) concluded with a vision of a new development axis connecting Gdańsk, Warsaw,

Crakow/Katowice, Vienna, Ljubljana and Milan, as a complementary tangent to the development axes rayed from the European core. Regardless of such conceptualizations the reality is that the actual development of ECE space has not paralleled that of the EU core. This is clearly illustrated by the continued domination of flights from ECE countries towards the EU Pentagon. Studying data from airlines demonstrates that the share of the Pentagon-oriented flights from ECE capitals has been increasing in the last decade as a result of EU integration, from between 30 to 35 per cent in 2002 to an average of 49 per cent in 2009. This evidence suggests that EU enlargement has not changed the uni-polar functional pattern of Europe.

Translation of EU visions and concepts

Although the list of prospective new member states was almost complete in 1999 when the ESDP was adopted, the document is only fully relevant to the EU-15. This was due to the limited and incompatible nature of data on spatial development in the then candidate countries and the underdeveloped institutional and professional linkages to ECE spatial planning and policy networks. Pallagst nevertheless insisted that the

> central ESDP concept of polycentricity applies for all Europe, although the ESDP is an offspring from the western European discussion. [...] Polycentricity is rather inclusive, offering even peripheral areas the opportunity to be equally represented on the European map. Polycentricity might thus have the quality to be applied to central and eastern European countries in future.
>
> (Pallagst 2006: 253)

Camagni on the other hand expressed reservations about the apparent easiness of extending broad spatial principles to the new member states. He noticed the

> polarized and regionally concentrated character of the new industrialization and development phase triggered by the accession to the Union, [...] will probably continue in the next decade. [...] Political attention being directed to competitive cores as well as [...t]he excessive concentration of economic growth in a few areas is likely very rapidly to create tensions on the local labour markets and land markets [...].
>
> (Camagni 2007)

Significantly, the debate regarding the integration of ECE planners into the European planning community (cf. also Waterhout Chapter 4) has occurred predominantly amongst academics from the 'old' EU. The concepts of EU-wide spatial planning policies have not been much debated in national forums in ECE or in an (hypothetical) ECE regional platform. The debate inside the ECE countries has focused primarily on the utilization of EU funding.

Three scenarios for the future development of Europe were developed in the ESPON project 3.2. The scenarios were based on options between strengthening cohesion and strengthening competitiveness (ESPON 2007). The competitive scenario indicates less cohesion at the European and national scales with particularly negative consequences for the remote regions. It is likely that the Eastern periphery of the EU could more closely resemble their non-EU neighbours than the prosperous EU core in the competitiveness scenario. The cohesion scenario on the other hand indicates a more prosperous and more integrated Eastern part of the EU.

The mismatch between territorial levels of competitiveness and cohesion is reflected in politicians' standpoints. Politicians in the 'new' member states emphasize national competitiveness, i.e. EU-wide cohesion, as being more important than the internal cohesion within their countries. Politicians in the more affluent north-western part of the EU on the other hand are more concerned with the global competitiveness of the EU and the potential threat to stability if disparities within countries increase significantly. The issue of competitiveness versus cohesion is highly relevant in ECE and Eastern Europe. Policies promoting EU competitiveness may mean focusing only on the main metropolitan areas in these countries, as gateways to economies driven by technology, knowledge and information. In contrast other regions will be required to utilize their comparative advantages in terms of cheap labour costs and low land and rent prices. In this context the evolving spatial mega-trends of metropolitanization, fragmentation and polarization (Kunzmann 2008) will take on a new significance in ECE. Cohesion objectives would be seriously challenged in peripheral areas that are simultaneously challenged by poor accessibility, low population density and low prosperity. The anticipated increases in energy prices may even strengthen the vicious circle of high costs to access markets and thus question the reasons for investment, emphasize local incomes and, consequently, diminish local customer markets.

The ability of the concept of polycentric development as a means for territorial cohesion and social equity in Europe was promoted in the Second and Third Reports on Economic and Social Cohesion (CEC 2001, 2004). However, it would appear that there is little evidence to support this. Hall concluded that 'balanced spatial development does not necessarily result in social equity and quality of life' (Hall and Pain 2006: 209). The Fourth Report on Economic and Social Cohesion identified other factors as being more important in determining regional competitiveness including sound macro-economic and structural policies, the efficiency and effectiveness of public administration and the quality of infrastructure (CEC 2007: 86–7). The 'new' EU member states share a scarcity of energy resources with their 'old' EU partners and this makes them dependent on external supplies, mostly from countries of the former Soviet Union. The economies of the countries may soon be exposed to the new challenge of a new level of energy prices as well as other imported resources. While the service-based economies of metropolitan areas may be able to adapt to higher prices for energy and other imported resources, the energy-demanding manufacturing sector in non-metropolitan regions may be severely hit.

Another concept that has been mentioned increasingly in the EU discourse dealing with the cohesion/competitiveness agenda is the concept of territorial capital. At first sight this is a concept that appears to offer opportunities to ECE countries generally. The policy of local and regional branding may also prove difficult to implement in the peripheral regions of ECE and particularly Eastern Europe. Previously the branding of local or regional products, wherever it had existed in ECE and Eastern European countries, was restricted to national markets but conditions have changed as local enterprises have been overtaken by multinational companies and retail outlets have become dominated by international chains. Although the highly specialized 'daughter branches' of multinationals that emerged in ECE and Eastern European countries may remain competitive, they may also be vulnerable in times of economic recession and decline. In addition, such enterprises tend to be located in the more accessible parts of non-metropolitan regions rather than in the remote periphery.

The ability of tourism to act as an engine for the revitalization of the peripheral areas also needs closer consideration. Such an approach is likely to be highly selective geographically and benefit only selected locations with profits often being transferred out of the region. The quality of jobs generated by mass tourism is also usually limited, whilst significant pressure is applied to the natural and social environment. The smaller scale alternative 'soft' tourism model is more environmentally friendly and could complement other local activities; this would appear to be more appropriate for peripheral rural regions. However, even the 'soft' approach requires a variety of services and skills that are often lacking in such areas and the incomes generated are usually only sufficient if used to supplement income from other work. It is essential for these areas to build upon the relatively high quality of life in local and regional centres to retain young, educated and skilled people. Improved accessibility to national and regional centres needs to be counter-balanced by local access to high quality education, health and social services and jobs (cf. Czapiewski and Janc Chapter 14). A locally rooted, proud and educated population with a strong sense of identity will be the best territorial capital for non-central and rural regions of Europe. In the long run, agriculture and forestry, plus value-added activities connected to them may become an important component of a sustainable economy for the remote peripheries that is able to compete with imports from outside Europe. However, this is only likely to happen if transportation and labour costs increase for the non-European products.

EU strategies and implementation of EU policies

Pallagst (2006) identified two scenarios for the future development of spatial planning on the European level. The first scenario, 'retention', suggested that EU development perspectives will continue to be developed based on Western European experience. The Eastern part of the EU will be treated as one topic of its own, which has to be conceptualized in a separate way. This would assume that 'the EU funding is channelled to the eastern part of Europe in a different way from the western part [...] however, the gap between east and west is continuing [... and] a mental barrier between eastern and western European countries would remain' (Pallagst 2006: 268).

The second scenario, 'merger', would involve a closer integration between the planning communities in the 'old' and 'new' EU member states. The idea of a 'Europe of bits and pieces' as it was described for Western Europe (Curtin 1993) would be extended to the eastern part and a new 'epistemic community' of European spatial planning would emerge. The 'merger' scenario would appear to relate more closely to the cohesion scenario discussed earlier, whilst the 'retention' scenario appears to relate more closely to the competitive scenario. The 'merger' scenario sounded attractive in the pre-accession period especially for the accessing countries where the "Return to Europe" was one of the slogans of 1989. In reality the accession turned out to be a rather one-sided process in which the accessing countries had to adopt EU requirements and accession preparations resembled a race to fulfil these requirements, sometimes without in-depth internal discussion or full understanding of the consequences. This was fuelled by a hope that the acceptation of western standards would remove all restrictions, which later proved not to be fully the case. As a result EU policies and reforms have been implemented rather superficially in some cases. The central question remains whether an actual integration of new members will occur, and if so, which kind of integration this could be. The 'merger' scenario would appear to be a starting point for the further conceptualization of EU policies towards ECE in order to harness the diversity of the EU and promote European integration. Simultaneously, features of the 'retention' scenario may be more appropriate in respect to certain peripheral regions. A single-minded pursuit of the 'merger' scenario may have a negative impact on cohesion at the national level, whilst a single-minded pursuit of 'retention' may lead to a feeling of second-class membership amongst the 'new' member states and, in the long run, to a disintegration of the EU idea. It is important that the integration implied in the 'merger' scenario does not erase specific existing features where they reflect the above-mentioned national, regional or local circumstances and does not lead to the creation of large second-class areas where the 'retention' scenario remains dominant.

Experience from the pre-accession as well as the early post-accession period appears to have influenced the background paper for Territorial Agenda of EU, the Territorial State and Perspectives of the European Union (DE Presidency 2007b). This document recognized the increasing diversity of the EU territory and, consequently, it identified various themes for consideration. The differences in the territorial potential of Northern and Southern Europe were identified along with the implications for their future development and the approaches necessary to address the future challenges. The second relevant theme identified the need for special attention for Eastern Europe as it catches up to the West only in relative terms. Finally the continuing growth of the urban-rural dichotomy was identified, whereby many urban areas will be developing on the account of rural areas. The background paper also recognized the disparate territorial allocation of foreign direct investments leading to increased regional disparities and gaps in relation to large companies and weak local businesses. The diverse trends of 'top' and 'tail' regions and an emerging polarization within cities and city regions were mentioned as major issues relevant to the ECE member states.

The disparities mentioned above resulted from weak or even absent national spatial policies in countries that were unprepared for the pressures of market forces. EU pre-accession funding provided an incentive to adopt national regional policies prior to the commencement of funding for new hard infrastructure. It will be important to consider the long-term consequences of these infrastructure investments. Major infrastructure projects such as the Trans European Networks (TEN) will clearly help to integrate metropolitan regions in ECE into global and international networks although this is likely to exacerbate the relative disadvantage of the remote, peripheral regions still further. National and regional governments in ECE are unable to compensate peripheral regions for this exclusion as their resources are required to co-finance the EU programmes. Even in cases where the EU programmes leave sufficient flexibility to target financial assistance, local decision makers often prefer spectacular and highly visible projects rather than small tailor-made projects in remote areas with a small electorate. The 2007–2013 programming period provides a unique opportunity for the 'new' EU member states to improve infrastructure using EU funds. Unfortunately however, the necessity to absorb EU funding takes precedence over strategic thinking regarding their optimal use (cf. Dąbrowski Chapter 9 in relation to the use of the structural funds in Poland). In addition, the requirements to show tangible results may be leading to funds being spent on hard infrastructure rather than on soft infrastructure that could have a more beneficial long-term impact. It is easier to demonstrate the impact of a new road than it is to demonstrate the benefit of improved institutional capacity, governance structures or social capital, even if this in the long-term may be more beneficial due to the development of associated professional and social networks. In this context, the populism of national and regional politicians who enjoy opening new roads, the belief of planners in transport infrastructures as a panacea to remoteness and the pragmatism of EU administration may be mutually reinforcing.

Unlike the enlargement, European integration is not an act but a process and this process will extend far beyond 2013. Success will require substantial time, resources and good will amongst the various stakeholders and spatial development is just one component in this context. Some conclusions will be drawn on this discussion in the final section of the chapter where practical ways of reconciling EU aims with the ECE reality will be discussed.

Reconciling EU regional policy aims with East-Central European reality

Key issues for implementation of European strategic objectives

The importance of nation states in ECE and Eastern Europe should not be underestimated. Language and cultural barriers will remain important for large parts of the population even if all formal barriers disappear. It appears that European integration emphasizes the importance and leading role of the European core for the rest of Europe and we can assume that ECE and probably also Eastern Europe will become increasingly more integrated into the European spatial functional system. If we accept these assumptions, it is unlikely that a 'new Europe' with its own parallel spatial network will emerge in the East. It is more likely that ECE is and will remain on the fringe of the EU core (in the cohesion scenario) or outside the core (in the competitive scenario). It is important to understand that 'retention' is not a matter of spatial pattern but rather of political setting and epistemology.

Context sensitivity determines that it is not possible to develop a universally applicable policy to promote sustainable development and territorial cohesion in ECE and Eastern Europe. The vague definition of the key concepts of the EU spatial policy toolkit means that it is likely that the new EU member states will develop their own interpretations. Potentially therefore, they may pay lip service to the vaguely defined objectives of the EU and to debates about competitiveness and cohesion that have generally been conceptualized in the 'old' EU. They may prefer to pursue their specific national and local political interests, which may be influenced by large national or multinational companies. This situation cannot be dealt with effectively by any Brussels-made control system but will require the promotion of democratic control supported by local civic groups, 'advocacy coalitions' and 'communities of practice'. Effective strategies should lead to tailormade policies dealing simultaneously with spatial challenges at national, regional and local levels. The existing spatial structure of individual countries should be recognized and respected, requiring a more flexible approach to regional policy. The level to which EU funding is distributed does not always correspond to the actual level of regional governance that generally is in the best position to identify specific regional challenges and solutions. It could be argued that NUTS III regions are more appropriate than NUTS II as EU partners in certain countries of ECE. Working with regional development agencies at NUTS III level may enhance their institutional capacity in-situ allowing more tailored solutions to specific regional problems.

Equity versus efficiency and identification of priorities

The ongoing efficiency versus equity dilemma of regional policy is highly relevant in the ECE context, particularly in relation to their rural peripheries. The choice remains either to support weak regions on account of overall equity or to stimulate growth in selected, (relatively) prosperous centres/regions as engines of regional development. However, we need to understand what we mean by weak and prosperous centres/regions. If we apply Western criteria then the regions requiring assistance and the scale of the problems to be addressed will be immense and the cost therefore would be economically unsustainable. In addition, such an approach could be counterproductive and result in dependency syndrome. A focus on suitable regional and local centres may be more effective and allow small-grained and place-focused policies that will stimulate dynamics in keeping with the specific national hierarchies of centres. The regional centres of intermediate regions are particularly crucial for sound regional policies aimed at counterbalancing over-heating national capitals as the regional centres can serve as gateways to the rest of the country. However, such an approach would be inappropriate where accessibility and spatial distribution of suitable centres is poor. In such cases it may be more effective to support services in smaller local centres and to promote local spatial accessibility of public services to maintain competitive standards and quality of life for local people.

The initial volatility of the 1990s transformation required a form of crisis management as ECE countries continuously reacted to various emergencies such as the collapse of entire industrial branches. In principle ECE countries now have the opportunity to pursue more strategic policies for sustainable development. The previous desire to attract any kind of FDI to any location could be replaced by a more structured regional policy seeking to support investments that reflect specific regional potentials. Traditional infrastructure investments in improved railways, roads, airports and utilities remain the major priority for regional support in ECE, causing tension with more ecological and environmentally friendly modes of transport and technology. In addition to improving external accessibility and the accessibility of metropolitan centres, rural accessibility also requires attention. Generally this requires the improvement of existing infrastructure and services, sometimes even their reintroduction, rather than building new infrastructure. Investments to improve access to information and communication technologies (ICT) can compensate, at least partially, for geographical remoteness and peripherality. However, it is likely that improving the servicing of such regions will require ongoing assistance rather than one-off investments. The gradual improvement of physical infrastructures in the ECE and East European countries will allow regional policies to focus more on investments in 'soft' infrastructure supporting public services and human resources. Investments in educational, health and social infrastructure will improve the quality of life and create qualified employment opportunities in regional and local centres that could prevent further the marginalization of peripheral areas and help to retain young educated people. The outflow of such people is currently a major threat to the implementation of the Lisbon strategy in these regions. However, such investments require a long-term commitment and continuity in policies and instruments in order to be successful rather than the continuous changing of policy direction often sought by those in political power.

Power relations and participation of communities of practice in wider epistemic communities

The principle of subsidiarity should be applied in territorial governance according to the specific spatial and functional patterns of the countries and regions in ECE. Smaller functional regions also need to have a say, including smaller administrative units in remote peripheries. This is particularly important to balance the spending on large-scale prestigious infrastructure projects that are loved by national politicians in favour of less spectacular, small-scale improvements, or mere stabilization, in terms of quality of life. The power balance in economically and institutionally less powerful regions often favours less responsible investors promoting projects of questionable social, environmental and also economic benefit to the welfare of the region. EU policies should seek a balanced consideration of all projects by encouraging suitable arenas for debate for the various networks and communities active in this area. The weak and fragmented 'communities of practice' in many ECE countries often consist of small groups of academics and practitioners from a small number of planning consultancies that focus on research and national and EU-funded projects. It is possible that a community of Europe-oriented spatial planners will emerge from the nationally constrained agenda of planning practice, although such a community would not necessarily represent the views of the mainstream business-oriented planning practice who ultimately implement EU and national spatial development policies and strategies. Power relations are crucial in determining to what extent different groups set agendas and have real influence and decision-making power. The theoretical discourse in relation to concepts such as 'epistemic communities', 'communities of practice' and 'advocacy coalitions' is relevant here and it is important to remember that these groups are not necessarily mutually exclusive. It is possible for individual practitioners to be members of more than one 'community of practice', whilst at the same time a member of a given community can also be part of an 'advocacy coalition'. These coalitions are the entities at the periphery of or even within 'epistemic communities' that challenge or verify the knowledge claims of 'epistemic communities'. A purposeful and deliberate support will be necessary to develop a robust institutional network for EU-coherent spatial planning and territorial management, including higher education and life-long learning as a precondition for viable national components to the EU-wide 'epistemic community'.

Towards spatial development policies for a cohesive and competitive East Central Europe

Without compromising the central aim of EU-wide cohesion, EU spatial development policies require different priorities in different types of regions reflecting their historical evolution and current context. It is possible to differentiate between policies appropriate for metropolitan areas, centres of non-metropolitan regions, rural areas and peripheral remote regions in ECE.

Metropolitan centres should serve as national gateways and a link with the EU core. In order to achieve this they require the same quality of services and accessibility to the European core as that which the centres in the European core have with each other. In addition, the ECE metropolitan centres should be connected with each other to increase networking choice and opportunities without necessarily having aspirations to become an alternative or counterbalancing network to the European core. Successful metropolitan regions need coordinated management and infrastructure investment on the level of their functional regions in order to tackle the problems caused by recent haphazard development. The introduction of effective regional metropolitan management will require experience and knowledge from the EU core that is capable of uniting local interests. Currently existing institutional boundaries form a barrier in cities such as Prague, Budapest and Warsaw where the capital cities are separated from their functional regions and this needs to be addressed.

Centres of non-metropolitan regions can potentially provide a counter-balance to the metropolitan centres in terms of business and employment opportunities, services and other facilities related to quality of life. To achieve this they need good accessibility to the metropolitan centres and to each other. They need to be able to provide sufficient social infrastructure (education, culture, health) to serve their own region and, ideally, be able to offer certain high level services to the national and even international arena. The regions should seek their specific role in the global economy whilst simultaneously diversifying production and services in order to maintain not only their short-term competitiveness but also their economic robustness and sustainability.

Kunzmann (2007) distinguishes between different types of peripheries and different types of small and medium sized towns and it is essential that policies in rural regions are appropriate to the characteristics of specific areas. The decline of services in local centres in rural areas situated on major transportation corridors can be compensated by improved access to regional centres, on condition that the potential 'tunnel effect' of improved major transportation routes can be avoided. Remote peripheral regions that are lacking in strong centres require special attention. The size and occurrence of these regions increases with the distance from the European core, ultimately forming an almost continuous fringe belt on the Eastern EU border. A fundamental improvement of transportation links to more populated and more prosperous areas of the EU will not be feasible in foreseeable future and therefore a combination of specific measures are required. Local service centres need to serve as anchors for stabilizing population and to promote functional networking in order to multiply this capacity wherever possible. These local centres also need to be easily accessible to and from their hinterlands. The accessibility to ICT in peripheral regions, which reflects the poor accessibility to other types of infrastructure, needs to be addressed urgently and continuous support also needs to be offered for regeneration by local 'grass-roots' business initiatives as part of local civic society. Cross-border areas in remote regions constitute a specific case and their potential should be individually assessed. Generally such potential should not be overestimated in the case of similarly deprived neighbouring regions. The Nordic EU peripheries focus on access to services and amenities as a precondition for quality of life rather than a physical connection to distant centres and this can provide an inspiration to peripheries in Eastern Europe.

Individual regions must have the flexibility to apply a specific strategy and relevant measures as part of a tailor made policy. Any uniformity in proposed strategies and policies may ultimately prove counterproductive by increasing competition among the peripheral (sub)regions for scarce resources (e.g. tourist visitors, clients for the same agricultural products). Individualization of the economic profile of particular sub-regions combined with its diversification can contribute to the robustness of the regional economy. The development of appropriate tailor-made strategies will require effective regional and local governance involving the participation of educated and dedicated planners in cooperation with local communities, possibly in the form of 'advocacy coalitions'. Such coalitions may require assistance from 'communities of practice' to help them to interpret, verify or validate expert knowledge from wider 'epistemic communities' in order to be able to formulate effective and appropriate local strategies. Apart from perseverance, such an approach will require support and pressure in the form of carrots and sticks from the EU whilst the national or regional level will have an essential coordinating role. Assistance is required that will promote sustainable activities with long-term positive effects until the positive effects themselves are able to sustain the activity. It will be important to avoid forms of support that will lead to the emergence of dependency syndrome. The strengthening of local and regional platforms to discuss sustainable development in the local/regional context should be understood as an integral part of the EU-supported 'refurbishment process' of the new member states. The creation of suitable arenas should promote the evolution of 'epistemic communities' of spatial planning. In the meantime existing and emerging 'communities of practice' and 'advocacy coalitions' require long-term support to be able to participate in a learning process by building and implementing the policies that affect them.

References

Adams, N., Cotella, G. and Nunes, R. (2010) 'Territorial knowledge channels in a multi-jurisdictional policy environment. A theoretical framework', in N. Adams, G. Cotella and R. Nunes (eds) *Territorial Development, Cohesion and Spatial Planning: Knowledge and policy development in an enlarged EU*, London: Routledge.

Castells, M. (1989) *The Informational City*, Blackwell.

Camagni, R. (2002) 'On the concept of territorial competitiveness: sound or misleading?', *Urban Studies*, 13: 2395–2412.

—— (2007) 'Interregional disparities, territorial policies and city networks in New Member Countries of the EU', presented at Bled, 26–27 July 2007, unpublished.

Capello, R., Camagni, R., Chizzolini, B. and Fratesi, U. (2008) *Modelling Regional Scenarios for the Enlarged Europe*, Berlin: Springer.

Capik, P. (2010) 'Regional promotion and competition: an examination of approaches to FDI attraction in the Czech Republic, Poland and Slovakia', in N. Adams, G. Cotella and R. Nunes (eds) *Territorial Development, Cohesion and Spatial Planning: Knowledge and policy development in an enlarged EU*, London: Routledge.

CEC – Commission of the European Communities (1999) *European Spatial Development Perspective: Towards balanced and sustainable development of the territory of the EU*. Luxembourg: Office of the Official Publications of the European Communities.

—— (2001) *Unity, Solidarity, Diversity for Europe, its People and its Territory. Second report on economic and social cohesion*, Brussels: Commission of the European Communities.

—— (2004) *A New Partnership for Cohesion, Third Report on economic and social cohesion*, Brussels: Commission of the European Communities.

—— (2005) *Territorial State and Perspectives of the European Union*, Scoping document and summary of political messages.

—— (2007) *Growing Regions, Growing Europe: Fourth Report on economic and social cohesion.* Brussels: Commission of the European Communities.

—— (2008) *Green paper on Territorial Cohesion – Turning territorial diversity into strength,* Brussels: Commission of the European Communities.

Christaller, W. (1966) *Central Places in Southern Germany,* Englewood Cliffs: Prentice Hall.

Copus, A. K. (2001) 'From core-periphery to polycentric development: Concepts of spatial and aspatial peripherality', *European Planning Studies,* 9(4): 539–552.

Curtin, J. (1993) 'The constitutional structure of the EU: a Europe of bits and pieces', *Common market law review,* 30(1): 17–69.

Czapiewski, K. and Janc, K. (2010) 'Accessibility to education and its impact on regional development in Poland', in N. Adams, G. Cotella and R. Nunes (eds) *Territorial Development, Cohesion and Spatial Planning: Knowledge and policy development in an enlarged EU,* London: Routledge.

Dąbrowski, M. (2010) 'Institutional change, partnership and regional networks: Civic engagement and the implementation of the Structural Funds in Poland', in N. Adams, G. Cotella and R. Nunes (eds) *Territorial Development, Cohesion and Spatial Planning: Knowledge and policy development in an enlarged EU,* London: Routledge.

Davoudi, S. (2003) 'Polycentricity in European spatial planning: From an analytical tool to a normative agenda', *European Planning Studies,* 11(8): 979–999.

DE Presidency (2007a) *Territorial Agenda of the European Union: Towards a more competitive and sustainable Europe of diverse regions – Agreed at the occasion of the informal ministerial meeting on urban development and territorial cohesion on 24/25 May* 2007. Online. Available HTTP: www.bmvbs.de/Anlage/original_1005295/ Territorial-Agenda-of-the-European-Union-Agreed-on-25-May-2007-accessible.pdf.

—— (2007b) *The Territorial State and Perspectives of the European Union: Towards a stronger European territorial cohesion in the light of the Lisbon and Gothenburg ambitions – A background document to the territorial agenda of the European Union.* Online. Available HTTP: www.bmvbs.de/Anlage/original_1005296/The-Territorial-State-and-Perspectives-of-the-European-Union.pdf.

Diderot (1999) *Všeobecná encyklopedie* (Universal Encyclopaedia), Vol 2, Prague: Diderot.

Enyedy, G. (1996) 'Urbanisation under socialism', in G. Andrusz, M. Harloe and I. Szelenyi (eds) *Cities after Socialism,* Oxford: Blackwell: 100–118.

ESPON (2005a) *ESPON 1.1.1 Potentials for Polycentric Development in Europe – Final report.* Luxembourg: ESPON.

—— (2005b) *ESPON 1.1.3 Enlargement of the European Union and the Wider European Perspective as regards its Polycentric Spatial Structure – Final report.* Luxembourg: ESPON.

—— (2006a) *ESPON Synthesis Report III – Territory matters for competitiveness and cohesion,* Luxembourg: ESPON.

—— (2006b) *ESPON Atlas – Mapping the structure of the European territory.* Bonn: Federal Office for Building and Regional Planning, BBR.

—— (2007) *ESPON Project 3.2 – Scenarios on the territorial future of Europe.* Luxembourg: ESPON.

Evers, D. (2007) 'Reflections on territorial cohesion and European spatial planning', *Tijdschrift voor Economische en sociale geografie,* 99(3): 303–315.

Evers, D., Tennekes, J., Borsboom, J., van den Heiligenberg, H. and Thissen, M. (2009) *A Territorial Impact Assessment of Territorial Cohesion for the Netherlands,* The Hague/Bilthoven: Netherlands Environmental Assessment Agency (PBL).

Faludi, A. (2000) 'Strategic planning in Europe: Institutional aspects', in W. Salet and A. Faludi (eds) *The Revival of Strategic Spatial Planning*, Amsterdam: Royal Netherlands Academy of Arts and Sciences: 243–258.

—— (2007) 'Making sense of the territorial agenda of the European Union', *European Journal of Spatial Development*, 25. Online. Available HTTP: www.nordregio.se/ EJSD/refereed25.pdf.

—— (2009) 'A turning point in the development of European spatial planning: The territorial agenda of the European Union and the First Action Programme', *Progress in Planning*, 71(1): 1–42.

Finka, M., (2010) 'Evolving frameworks for regional development and spatial planning in the new regions of the EU', in N. Adams, G. Cotella and R. Nunes (eds) *Territorial Development, Cohesion and Spatial Planning: Knowledge and policy development in an enlarged EU*, London: Routledge.

Gorzelak, G. (1996) *The Regional Dimension of Transformation in Central Europe*, London and Bristol: Regional Studies Association.

Haas, P. M. (1992) 'Introduction: Epistemic communities and international policy co-ordination', *International Organization*, 46(1): 1–35.

Hall, P. and Pain, K. (eds) (2006) *Polycentric Metropolis: Learning from Mega-City Regions in Europe*, London: Earthscan.

Haselsberger, B. and Benneworth, P. (2010) 'Cross-border communities or cross-border proximity? Perspectives from the Austrian–Slovakian border region', in N. Adams, G. Cotella and R. Nunes (eds) *Territorial Development, Cohesion and Spatial Planning: Knowledge and policy development in an enlarged EU*, London: Routledge.

Kunzmann, K. (2007) *Medium-sized Towns, Strategic Planning and Creative Governance in the South Baltic Arc*. Online. Available HTTP: www.sebco.eu/wm_files/wm_ pdf/kunzmann_discussion_paper.pdf (accessed September 2009).

—— (2008) 'Futures for European space', *Journal of Nordregio: European Space 2020 Planning, Energy and Transport*, 2(8).

Maier, K. (1999) 'Wirksamkeit der bisheringen und zukunftingen Instrumente zum Abbau der regionalen Disparitäten in der Tschechischen Republik', in *Gleichwertige Lebensbedingungen in Mittelosteuropa – ein tragfahiges Konzept für die Raumordnung?*', Akademie für Raumforschung und Landesplannung Hannover, 253: 135–144.

—— (2001) 'Plánování v post-plánované společnosti: Kdo potřebuje urbanisty?' in *Urbanismus a územní rozvoj*, 1/2001. Brno: ÚÚR.

Matoušek, V. (1986) *Dosavadní vývoj a tendence rozvoje sídle v ČSSR*, Brno: VÚVA.

Meijers, E., Waterhout, B. and Zonneveld, W. (2007) 'Closing the gap: territorial cohesion through polycentric development', *European Journal of Spatial Development*, 24. Online. Available HTTP: www.nordregio.se/EJSD/refereed24.pdf.

Melecký, L. (2008) 'Regionální disparity a politika soudržnosti v Maďarsku', *Regionální disparity*, 3/2008, Ostrava: VŠB-TU.

Mulíček, O. and Sýkora, L. (2008) *POLYREG: Reciprocal Relations and Integrated Poly-centric Settlement Systems*. Research paper. Brno: Masaryk University.

Pallagst, K. (2006) 'European spatial planning reloaded: Considering EU enlargement in theory and practice', *European Planning Studies*, 14(2): 253–272.

—— (2010) 'The emergence of "Epistemic Communities" in the New European land-scape: Some theoretical implications for territorial development and the spatial agenda of the EU', in N. Adams, G. Cotella and R. Nunes (eds) *Territorial Development, Cohesion and Spatial Planning: Knowledge and policy development in an enlarged EU*, London: Routledge.

RECLUS (1989) *Les villes europeénnes: Rapport pour la DATAR*, Montpellier: RECLUS.

REPUS (2007) *Strategy for a Regional Polycentric Urban System in Central Eastern Europe Economic Integrating Zone. Final Report*, Budapest: VÁTI.

Sabatier, P. A. (1998) 'The advocacy coalition framework: revision and relevance for Europe', *Journal of European Public Policy*, 5(1): 98–130.

Sýkora, L. (1999) 'Local and regional planning and policy in East Central European transitional countries', in M. Hampl (ed.) *Geography of Societal Transformation in the Czech Republic*, Prague: Charles University.

Tewdwr-Jones, M. (2010) 'Cohesion and competitiveness: the evolving context for European territorial development', in N. Adams, G. Cotella and R. Nunes (eds) *Territorial Development, Cohesion and Spatial Planning: Knowledge and policy development in an enlarged EU*, London: Routledge.

Tewdwr-Jones, M. and Phelps, N. A. (2000) 'Levelling the uneven playing field: Inward investment, inter-regional rivalry and the planning system', *Regional Studies*, 34(5): 429–440.

Treaty of Lisbon (2007) *Treaty of Lisbon amending the Treaty on European Union and the Treaty establishing the European Community*, 3/12/2007.

Waterhout, B. (2008) *The Institutionalisation of European Spatial Planning*, Delft: IOS Press.

—— (2010) 'European spatial planning: current state and future challenges', in N. Adams, G. Cotella and R. Nunes (eds) *Territorial Development, Cohesion and Spatial Planning: Knowledge and policy development in an enlarged EU*, London: Routledge.

Webster's New World Dictionary (1999) Cleveland and New York: Simon & Schuster.

Wenger, E. (1998) *Communities of Practice: Learning, Meaning, and Identity*, Cambridge: Cambridge University Press.

12 The rhetoric and reality of pursuing territorial cohesion in Latvia

Laila Kule, Zaiga Krisjane and Maris Berzins

Introduction

Latvia provides an interesting case study in relation to any discussion about territorial cohesion and interregional disparities. As with all Member States, both those who joined the European Union prior to 2004 and those who have joined since, the concept of territorial cohesion is still relatively vague and remains open to interpretation. Until the recent economic downturn, the consistently high levels of economic growth experienced in Latvia over a number of years were driven by the Riga capital region. The non-metropolitan regions (Kurzeme, Vidzeme, Zemgale and Latgale) are unable to compete with the economic, social and cultural dominance of the capital and this clearly has significant implications for spatial development. As a result, Latvia is experiencing increasing internal regional disparities between Riga and the rest of the country and the relative competitiveness of the non-metropolitan regions is being reduced.

Furthermore, Latvia has undergone a dramatic transition during the turbulent times following independence and the collapse of the Soviet Union. Policy-makers and the planning community have had to readjust the planning system in a highly fluid context after the breakdown of the socialist system and the emergence of numerous spatial challenges during the transition period. The absorption of EU funding is a priority for the Government and, in order to meet this challenge, a number of national planning documents have been prepared, such as the National Development Plan (NDP) 2007–2013 (LCM 2006) and the draft Sustainable Development Strategy 2030 (MRDLG 2008). The latter document will include a National Spatial Development Perspective that will promote the simultaneous pursuance of cohesion and competitiveness. An analysis of spatial planning documents in Latvia reveals the considerable influence of European spatial planning, particularly the European Spatial Development Perspective (ESDP – CEC 1999) and, to a lesser degree, the Territorial Agenda (DE Presidency 2007a). Policy-makers in Latvia are simultaneously seeking to reduce regional disparities and promote more balanced and polycentric development, while at the same time relying on the international competitiveness of Riga to drive national growth. In this sense, Latvia encapsulates the paradoxes in terms of the dual pursuance of competitiveness and cohesion, which are apparent at both the EU level and within individual Member States (cf. Tewdwr-Jones Chapter 3 and Maier Chapter 11).

Exploring the elements introduced above, the first section of the chapter provides an overview of the transition and transformation process in Latvia from the end of the Soviet period, including the evolution of the institutional and socio-economic context. The origins of professional and expert communities and networks in the field of spatial planning and the extent to which they have become internationalized is then discussed in the following section, where the role and evolution of Latvian networks and communities in diverse learning contexts provided by the enlargement and the resultant processes of Europeanization are assessed. The penultimate section discusses the potential application and interpretation of the concept of territorial cohesion in the Latvian context. Finally some reflections are provided on the extent to which there are similarities or differences in the rhetoric and reality of Latvian spatial development policy.

Transition and transformation

Latvia is located in North-east Europe and shares its eastern external EU border with the Russian Federation and Belarus. Partly due to its location in what has long been something of a transitional zone between the East and West, the country has experienced a particularly turbulent history, most of which it has shared with its closest neighbours Estonia to the north and Lithuania to the south. It is not possible to understand the complexities of a country such as Latvia without first having some insight into the recent past that has been so influential in the country's development. After the collapse of the Russian Empire and as a result of the First World War and the fight for independence, modern Latvia was established in 1918. It remained independent until 1940 when, along with the other Baltic States, it was annexed by the Soviet Union. After 1945 all three formerly independent Baltic States were incorporated into the Soviet Union as Soviet Republics. The Soviet system evolved over the years, but its main characteristics did not change with most aspects of life dominated by the Communist Party ideology that promoted the centralized command economy, suppression and militarism. Throughout the Soviet Union, industrial and military priorities took precedence over human and environmental priorities. Accessibility and mobility were restricted as was access to maps and other geographical and territorial data. There were numerous restricted areas where access to the public was denied, including much of the Baltic coastline that formed an external border of the Soviet Union.

The economic performance of the Baltic States between the two World Wars was comparable to many advanced European countries and post-1945 they were among the most developed parts of the Soviet Union. Latvia has been faced with the legacy of Soviet regional policy since independence in 1991 and the policy system inherited from the Soviet Union was clearly not equipped to deal with the rigours of a market-based economy. Soviet socio-economic development and planning was dominated by a sectoral approach with organizations integrated into all-Soviet structures, which had significant implications for spatial development. The result was a highly centralized yet fragmented system of state planning, with the regional and local levels reduced to an administrative role that consequently had little regard for local context.

Soviet regional policy and its instruments were not clearly defined or transparent and, as a result, the public had little opportunity or reason to understand them. Soviet regional policy attempted in many ways to achieve territorial equity and balance between different parts of the country. A variety of instruments were used to try to achieve these aims, which included the industrialization of the periphery, limiting the growth of large cities, the coercive movement of labour, the subsidization of energy and transport costs as well as agricultural production, and the provision of basic services. However, the dominance of large urban centres and the discrepancies and disparities between rural and urban areas continued despite these measures. Fuchs and Demko claimed that industrially advanced socialist societies often exhibit marked spatial socio-economic inequalities, arguing "that these [inequalities] persist in large measure because socialist decision-makers have generally placed a higher value on growth, productivity, and efficiency than on equity" (Fuchs and Demko 1979: 317). They conclude that the persistence of such spatial inequalities, in both socialist and capitalist societies, suggests that these are long-term problems and that the processes which create these inequities may be cumulative and self-reinforcing.

In many ways Latvia is dominated by its capital city Riga. In 2007 Riga had approximately 722,500 inhabitants, i.e. 32 per cent of the total Latvian population, almost seven times larger than the second city Daugavpils (CSBL 2009). During the Soviet period, the intense growth of industry and the status of the area as one of the wealthiest and culturally most European in the country attracted much migrant labour to the Baltic States and to Riga in particular. The introduction of the policies of 'openness' (*glastnost'*) and 'reconstruction' (*perestroika*) throughout the Soviet Union after 1985 provided opportunities for transformation, and independence movements became more active in each of the Baltic States. What were initially relatively small and disorganized groups evolved into mass movements with widespread public support (Bleijere *et al.* 2006; Lieven 1993). The rapid pace of events left little time for extensive public discussions on future development as change came as 'a great surprise' (Agnew 2001), particularly to the outside world. As a result, early reform processes lacked coordination and organization, and discussions were often fragmented and delayed (King *et al.* 2004).

Institutional reform has been ongoing since independence. In 1995 there were 568 municipalities, seven republican cities and 26 administrative districts. This created a highly fragmented local governance context that persisted despite Government incentives for small municipalities to amalgamate. Melluma (1997) argued that the justifications used in the political debates were weak compared to the collective memories of the population who regarded the numerous changes of administrative borders between 1941 and 1967 as an instrument to diminish local identity. The discussions about reform of the district and regional levels were also highly contentious. The administrative districts (*Soviet rayon*) were initially imposed by Moscow and, as a result, they were perceived by many as an extension of Soviet power (King *et al.* 2004). In addition, the districts were also perceived to be too small to effectively deal with sub-national issues, which forced local municipalities to cooperate concerning regional infrastructure and services. The institutionalization of these regional arrangements occurred outside formal legislation, with executive bodies registered under the law of non-governmental organizations through the tacit support of the relevant Ministry. These voluntary arrangements were formalized and five distinct planning regions were formally established in 2003, although, in reality, this formalization of regional planning was retrospective and simply confirmed the existing situation at the time. Each of the planning regions established a regional development agency, overseen by a regional development council comprising representatives from the municipalities, socioeconomic stakeholders, academia and the NGO sector. The most recent reforms implemented in 2009 saw the abolition of the 26 administrative districts and the seven Republican cities, and a significant reduction in the number of local municipalities. These territorial jurisdictions were replaced by a two-tier system that consisted of five planning regions, and 109 local municipalities and 9 cities whereby the former district functions (civil defence, specialized social care and education) have been passed down to the local level. In addition to their regional spatial planning and regional development functions, it is possible that this newly established regional level will take over the regional transport function from the former districts as well as cultural and other functions from the national level. However, the authors were unable to confirm this potential development in regional responsibilities at the time of writing this chapter (MRDLG 2009b). Nevertheless, the responsibility for reviewing local plans has been delegated by the Ministry to the regional level (Pužulis 2008). A summary of the revisions of the institutional structure is provided in Table 12.1, while the planning regions and former administrative districts are displayed in Figure 12.1.

The demographic situation in Latvia is also complex, with population falling not only due to negative migration rates, but also due to a drastic decrease in birth rates. Eglīte (2007) claims that the decrease in birth rates is related to the specific ethnic and age structure of the population because of large-scale immigration from other parts of the former Soviet Union. As a result, the composition of the population has changed dramatically. Currently 60 per cent of the population are Latvian, compared to 77 per cent in 1935, and 28 per cent are Russian, compared to 9 per cent in 1935 (CSBL 2009). The Russian population is generally concentrated in larger cities and in rural areas of the Latgale region. The

Table 12.1 Institutional structure in Latvia pre- and post-reorganization in 2009

Territorial level	Pre-2009 legislation	Post-2009 legislation
Regional	5 planning regions	5 planning regions
Sub-regional	26 districts; 7 republican cities	–
Local	522 municipalities	118 municipalities, including 9 cities

Source: Authors' elaboration.

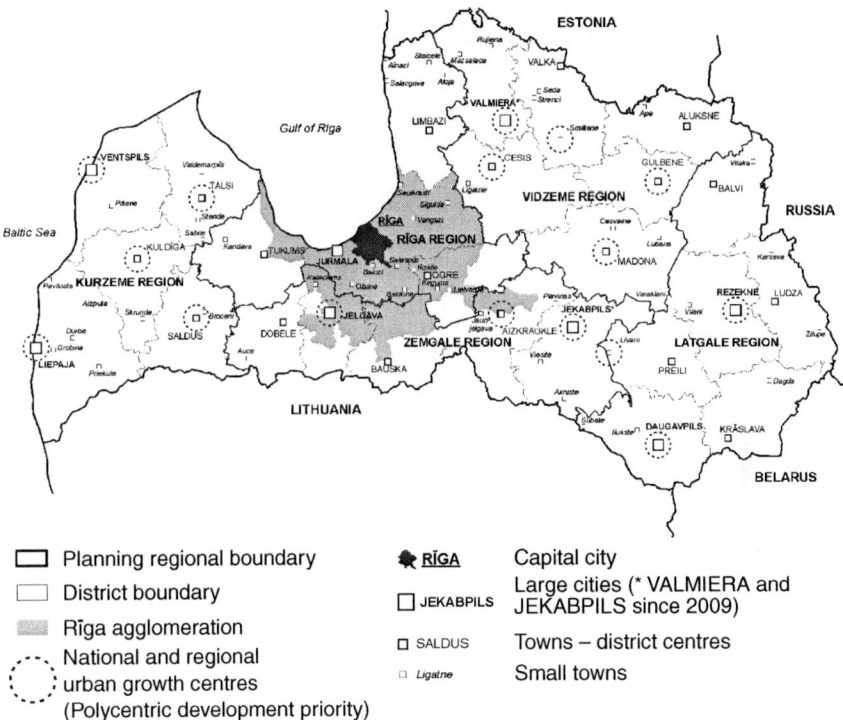

Planning regional boundary

District boundary

Rīga agglomeration

National and regional urban growth centres (Polycentric development priority)

★ RĪGA — Capital city

☐ JEKABPILS — Large cities (* VALMIERA and JEKABPILS since 2009)

☐ SALDUS — Towns – district centres

☐ Ligatne — Small towns

Figure 12.1 Latvian planning regions Riga, Kurzeme, Zemgale, Vidzeme and Latgale and former administrative districts (abolished in 2009) (source: University of Latvia on base map provided by GIS Latvia and Envirotech Ltd.).

higher proportions of Latvians in rural areas in the rest of the country is possibly one of the reasons why the Latvian national identity is predominantly based on rural and natural symbols, and the term *rural* in political discourse quite often has been used interchangeably with national ones (Bunkse 1992, 1999; Schwartz 2007; Borg 2006, Kūle 2008). The nature and extent of the population decline is clearly demonstrated in Tables 12.2 and 12.3.

Latvia has undergone deep structural reforms in order to catch up to developed countries and to satisfy the conditions for accession to the EU. The main goal of Latvia's economic development policy, before and after the EU accession, has been to achieve stable, balanced and sustainable economic growth measured in terms of GDP. The EU Pre-accession funds, Cohesion Fund and Structural Funds provided a unique opportunity to facilitate structural reforms, to stimulate growth and to provide the infrastructure required to support this growth. However, social and economic disparities appear to be deep rooted, and significant differences in rates of development persist. Paalzow (2006) has discussed the asymmetric patterns of development and the obvious core-periphery disparities in Latvia, whilst Krauklis (2000) has distinguished three typologies in

Table 12.2 Percentage population changes in Latvia 1959–2008

	Population changes in Latvia, %				
	1959–1970	1970–1979	1979–1989	1989–2000	2000–2008
Latvia	11.6	6.0	6.1	−12.2	−4.7
Riga	21.2	12.0	9.0	−19.1	−6.5
Pieriga	19.3	11.0	11.1	−5.4	6.0
Kurzeme	9.7	3.9	4.3	−13.7	−6.0
Zemgale	8.7	4.4	5.6	−9.0	−3.3
Vidzeme	3.2	−2.2	2.8	−6.4	−7.8
Latgale	−1.4	−1.5	−0.3	−9.6	−10.5

Source: Aut\hors' elaboration on CSBL 2009.

Table 12.3 Total population in Latvia 1990 and 2008

Area	Total population		
	1990	2008	% change
Latvia	2,668,140	2,270,894	−14.9
Riga City	909,135	717,371	−21.1
Pieriga	378,728	380,347	0.4
Kurzeme	365,733	303,618	−17.0
Vidzeme	272,289	237,803	−12.7
Zemgale	319,944	283,484	−11.4
Latgale	422,311	348,271	−17.5

Source: Authors' elaboration on CSBL 2009.

terms of diverse development trajectories in Latvia: (1) the differences between the capital Riga and the rest of Latvia, (2) the differences between the urban and the rural areas, and (3) the differences between Latgale and the other regions. The extent of these disparities and the concentration of human and economic capital in Riga city, and the surrounding Pieriga region is evident from the figures in Table 12.4. In the following section of this chapter, this brief sketch of transition and transformation in Latvia is further explored through the emergence of various networks in the field of spatial development and the internationalization of spatial planning.

Emerging networks, increased internationalization and access to learning contexts

Origins of Latvian planning community

The Latvian independence movement that ultimately contributed to the collapse of the Soviet Union had its roots in the environmental movement. Initially the movement started to gather momentum in response to the proposed construction

Table 12.4 Disparities between statistical regions in Latvia measured by share of population, GDP and long-term investment

Area	Share of population (%)		Share of GDP (LVL) (%)		Share of long-term investment (LVL)[a] (%)	
	1990	2008	1995	2006	1997	2007
Latvia	2.67 mln	2.279 mln	2,615 mln[b]	11,172 mln[b]	1,167 mln	4,404 mln
Riga City	34.1	31.6	46.5	55.3	51.7	47.4
Pieriga	14.2	16.7	12	13.1	11.9	21.2
Kurzeme	13.7	13.4	14.9	10.4	5.7	6.4
Vidzeme	10.2	10.5	6.9	6.6	17.1	10.4
Zemgale	12	12.5	8.8	7.2	7.4	8.3
Latgale	15.8	15.3	10.9	7.4	6.2	6.3

Source: CSBL 2009.

Notes
a Long-term investment in intangible assets, residential houses, other buildings and structures, cultivated assets, technological machinery and equipment, other fixed assets and inventory, as well as fixed asset formation and the costs of unfinished construction and capital repairs.
b At current prices.

of a hydroelectric power station on the Daugava River. Intense public scrutiny of the project was initiated by an article by Dainis Ivāns (Ivāns and Snips 1986, 1989) who later became elected chairperson of the Latvia Popular Front in 1988. The Popular Front was a civic movement that attracted widespread popular support and ultimately played the key role in the re-establishment of Latvian independence. There were numerous other examples in the period where the environmental movement was able to form an 'advocacy coalition' (Sabatier 1998) able to mobilize public support against industrial and municipal pollution of the Baltic Sea (Šulce 1988), the environmental and ecological problems caused by military training sites and against projects such as the Riga underground railway construction (Briedis and Strautiņš 1988). In some cases the networks and 'communities of practice' (Wenger 1998) in Latvia today can trace their roots back to the coalitions formed at this time.

Richardson (2001) has claimed that the role of experts in policy arenas is particularly relevant in situations with high levels of uncertainty. Albrechts (1999) and Gross (2000) have emphasized the important role that planners can have in times of turbulent social transformation because they can act as catalysts, initiators and facilitators of change. Kuus (2007) has claimed that the role of human agency is often underestimated in post-communist transformation because these types of transformations generally tend to be driven by agency power. According to Healey (2006a: 303), Gidden's structuration theory can be used for 'exploring territorially-focused governance transformation processes'. However, when this consideration of agency power is applied to a post-communist transformation period, the flow of ideas and frames of reference seem to contradict the flow of material resources and formal regulatory power, which are reduced dramatically or removed altogether. In other words, networking, based on professional or other interests, played an important role in the transition period when formal institutions and their linkages were contested and weak. In fact, intellectuals, with claims to certain types of knowledge, have been highly influential in forming and transmitting discourses in post-socialist Central and Eastern European (CEE) countries (Kuus 2007). Take the concept of 'epistemic communities' (Haas 1992), for example, which has been applied to European spatial planning by Pallagst (2006) and further elaborated and discussed in various contributions in this book. Haas emphasizes that

> recognizing that human agency lies at the interstices between systemic conditions, knowledge and national actions [...] an approach that examines the role of knowledge-based experts or 'epistemic communities' play in articulating the cause-and-effect relationships of complex problems, helping states identify their interests, framing the issues for collective debate, proposing specific policies, and identifying salient points for negotiation.
>
> (Haas 1992: 2)

Spatial planning was poorly codified as knowledge during the Soviet period. At the time, there was no specific spatial planning education programme at university level, only specialized courses aimed at architects, geographers and economists. Tacit knowledge often prevails over codified knowledge in spatial planning thus strengthening the role of experts (Håkanson 2005) in 'their expertise and competence on technical aspects of problems that are needed to make qualitative decisions' (Haas, 1992: 2–3). This shared tacit knowledge, values and normative principles, relating to spatial development problems and solutions, framed the planning 'epistemic community' in Latvia during the Soviet period. According to Haas (1992) and Adler and Haas (1992), 'epistemic communities' generally can be characterized by both mental inertia and the search for innovation. Such mental inertia can be identified in the context of the Latvian planning community in the immediate post-Soviet period by an obsession with pre-war planners despite the prevailing Soviet planning paradigms of high-rise large-scale housing estates. The ideas of Arnolds Lamze, the Chief Planner for Riga City in the inter-war period who was influenced by the English Garden City movement (Lamze 1926, 1932; Apsitis, 1989), were cited by Soviet planners and particularly by Gunars Melbergs who was the Chief Planner-Architect in the Riga City Master Plan Division between 1957–1999 (Melbergs 1969, 1979, 1995). Under his leadership at the end of the 1980s, when control from Moscow was starting to weaken, plans were prepared for suburban development in the open rural areas adjacent to Riga City. The planned development of single family homes in the suburbs was clearly not in accordance with Soviet ideology and planning doctrine and fostered much debate amongst the planning community (Krastiņš 1980, 1992; Lejnieks 1989a, 1989b).

The new and emerging institutions at the time relied on former Soviet experts. Chief architects of cities and districts, collective farms and large enterprises, chief economic planners of the Latvian State Planning Committee, land survey-ors and other specialists from research and design institutes were prominent in the field of spatial development. The diversity of experts involved was partly due to the lack of a postgraduate spatial planning education that has only recently been established in Latvia. Therefore spatial planning as a profession has strug-gled to establish an identity (cf. Maier contribution Chapter 11). The Latvian Spatial Planning Association, which currently has approximately 60 members, was established as a non-governmental organization in 1996. And the profile of spatial planning and regional development amongst professionals and policy-makers in the public and private sectors has risen more recently because of an increased awareness of the spatial challenges facing the country and also because of the accession to the EU.

Western planning ideas generally came to the Soviet realm through formal channels, such as the central research, planning and design institutes in Moscow or Leningrad (St Petersburg) or through review magazines. Latvia was a 'Soviet socialist republic' and therefore was integrated into the Soviet Union more than other socialist CEE countries that remained formally independent. Thus travel and contacts outside the Soviet Union were more difficult for Baltic citizens despite their proximity to neighbouring socialist countries (Peterlin and Kreit-mayer McKenzie 2007). Some informal contacts were established through foreign study trips that exposed the participants to ideas and approaches from outside the Soviet realm. Such contacts were highly valued mainly because they were so limited and provided a rare opportunity to share and discuss 'know-ledge' in informal seminars and discussion groups. The Latvian planning community also had informal contacts with the Latvian diaspora, including prac-ticing planners whose contacts were particularly extensive during the transition period. Bleijere *et al.* (2006: 392) estimated that approximately 130,000 Latvians were in exile in the West after World War II. However, the planning community, amongst these exiles, was not organized and consisted simply of a group of indi-viduals who occasionally exchanged professional literature or organized study tours and seminars; they were primarily based in Canada, USA, Australia, Germany and the Nordic countries (Bunkse 1979; Grava 1993; Roze 1991, 1995). Nevertheless, expatriates are often a useful knowledge transfer mechan-ism, particularly for transferring tacit knowledge (Bonache and Brewster 2001). A variety of projects were stimulated by the exile community including a study of metropolitan planning in capital cities of the Baltic States, financed by the Canadian Government and implemented by the Canadian Urban Institute. As time went on, however, there were numerous other opportunities for networking in the post-Soviet world and reliance on the exile community decreased. Some exiles moved back to Latvia and became active influential members of the Latvian planning community, while others remained in exile albeit continuously active in projects and research on the Baltic States (Bākule and Siksna, 2009).

Healey (2006) has noted that new concepts, approaches and ideas often have to overcome initial resistance before becoming accepted. And Jaakson (1996) has questioned the extent to which the skills of Soviet planners would be transferable to a market economy and the new political and economic reality. In light of these two perspectives, there is debate in the academic literature about the learning capacities of societies at different stages of development. On the one hand, Kuus (2004) argues that societies in transition have a greater propensity for learning due to deep structural changes and uncertainties, whilst Putnam (1993) and Healey (1999) have argued that actions of society are embedded in past experiences and are path-dependent. In the Latvian case, the interest of the planning community during the Soviet period on pre-war international experiences in urban and regional planning was broadened, after independence, with an interest in contemporary international good practice. This change was due to exposure to, and participation in numerous transnational planning initiatives. As mentioned previously, policy-makers may be more inclined to call on an 'epistemic community' during times of uncertainty. During such times the 'epistemic community' is not only a knowledge bearer and adviser to decision makers, but also can become directly involved in the institutionalization of specialized knowledge. This is supported by evidence from Latvia where a core of civil servants emerged from the Latvian planning community, some of whom became local and national politicians. These were largely younger members of the planning community, seen as trustworthy (also by the Latvian exile community and Western institutions) and open to new ideas due to their age and limited experience under the Soviet system (Manning and Poljeva 1999). The next section will focus on the internationalization and Europeanization of spatial planning in Latvia, exploring how this international community and the European integration processes have influenced spatial planning in practice.

Internationalization and Europeanization of spatial planning in Latvia

Adler (1992) has argued that transnational 'epistemic communities' are most likely to be involved in the transfer of knowledge and ideas from the international to domestic scenes in fields characterized by uncertainty and complexity. This seems to be the case of spatial planning in CEE countries, where debates on spatial development has played an important role in the post-Soviet period (Paalzow 2006; Petrakos 2001; Adams 2008). The collapse of the Soviet Union and the re-establishment of independence in Latvia opened the door to a multitude of initiatives involving the international community that offered opportunities for knowledge transfer and learning. In this section we will examine some of the key 'knowledge arenas' (cf. Adams *et al.* Chapter 2) in relation to spatial planning: the Vision and Strategies around the Baltic Sea (VASAB) initiative, various bi-lateral cooperation initiatives and the ESDP process.

As mentioned in the previous section, some of these international contacts were initiated toward the end of the Soviet period by the emerging environmental movement and also by the Latvian community in exile. In 1990 the Coalition for a Clean Baltic Sea was established to unite the environmental concerns of civil society in different countries around the Baltic Sea. NGOs and local, regional and national governments from the Nordic countries, Germany, the Netherlands, France and the Flemish Region of Belgium also became active from 1990 onward, funding capacity building initiatives and other forms of cooperation. The Nordic countries and particularly Germany were quick to recognize opportunities to use the change in regime to promote development and cooperation, and to implement extensive environmental clean-up on the eastern shore of the Baltic Sea. The enthusiasm of the international community was shared by many in Latvia, as Latvian organizations sought integration into different international networks, markets and institutions (Lauristin and Vihalemm 2009; Osis 2004). After much debate, a neo-liberal inspired shock therapy approach was adopted, the benefits and dis-benefits of which have been much debated in the academic literature (King 2003). However, the period of economic growth that followed also was characterized by fragmentation and a decrease in social cohesion, which left some academics to question why a more gradualist approach had not been adopted as had been the case in Western Europe in the post-War period (Ivanova 2007; Sommers 2009).

Yet the VASAB 2010 strategy, a Swedish initiative started in 1992, sought to promote a more comprehensive and integrated approach to activities relating to the Baltic Sea (cf. Fritsch Chapter 15). The aim of VASAB was to learn about the spaces, and development prospects and problems around the Baltic Sea through knowledge sharing and joint spatial planning activities. Latvia was active in VASAB from the beginning and thus Latvian planners became part of a transnational community that demonstrated some characteristics of an 'epistemic community'. Initially, planners in the eastern Baltic saw VASAB as a valuable channel and source of knowledge on planning in the West. VASAB provided many in the Latvian planning community with their first opportunity to learn first-hand about spatial planning systems and approaches in other countries. Seminars and consultations were organized in Latvia to discuss draft policy documents and prepare a coordinated Latvian response, which helped to raise awareness within the Latvian planning community, regional and local governments and sector ministries about the importance of spatial development issues at the level of the Baltic Sea Region (BSR). VASAB priorities were defined by the Spatial Development Committee of the BSR (ibid.) that was made up of representatives from the various national ministries responsible for spatial planning. VASAB members from the eastern coast of the Baltic Sea emphasized the importance of activities to promote knowledge and policy transfer, though these activities rarely corresponded with the priorities of the Western neighbours' who considered them to be national home-work. VASAB and the various pre-accession instruments became the main 'knowledge arenas', within which Latvia was able to learn in relation to integration into European structures. Recently, the political importance and influence of VASAB appears to be declining due to lower political commitment and lack of implementation instruments. The EU Strategy for the Baltic Sea Region (CEC 2009) is the first comprehensive strategy covering several Community policies, which is targeted on a 'macro-region' and where the European Commission has taken a leading role (cf. Fritsch

Chapter 15). The new Strategy is undoubtedly a competing political initiative for VASAB and currently appears to be the more favoured of the two strategic initiatives. However, a ministerial conference was held in October 2009 to discuss the latest VASAB draft policy document, the Long Term Perspective (VASAB 2009), which sketches a spatial perspective for the BSR until 2030. The continuation of the ministerial conferences and publication of policy documents demonstrates that despite a reduced political influence, VASAB currently remains an important forum. It provides spatial planners in the BSR an arena to exchange ideas, but perhaps more importantly it provides a context within which Eastern European members, such as Russia and Belarus, are able to participate on equal terms.

Foreign aid, in the form of bilateral agreements, also provided opportunities at this time for knowledge transfer and capacity building despite weak coordination and frequent delays in activities. These initiatives were donor initiated and the Latvian Government at the time had little influence over the priorities that the donors identified. Therefore, some of the projects had marginal value as donors had their own research, political or even personal agendas and priorities. A number of actions focused on environmental protection, improving the foreign investment environment and promoting democracy. The projects usually supported the local or regional level with little assistance from national level institutions. 'Experts' from Canada, Finland, Denmark, Sweden, Germany, the Netherlands and Flanders, were all active in spatial planning projects from the early 1990s onward in partnership with a wide variety of national, regional, district and local actors in Latvia. These activities and the interactions with the Latvian planning community were clearly influential in the design of early Latvian spatial policy and legislation, which bore a resemblance to the comprehensive integrated approach favoured in parts of Scandinavia, Germany, the Netherlands and Flanders (Adams 2008).

From the mid-1990s onward, European spatial planning had started to gain momentum and consequently Latvia became more involved in activities and debate about spatial planning at the EU level. Although European spatial planning emerged primarily from a (North) West European context (Pallagst 2006: 269), dissemination of information via seminars, working groups and publications also provided opportunities for learning in the transition countries (cf. Finka Chapter 5). Healey claims that this knowledge generation creates meanings around which attention may be mobilized as 'systems are not given, but are made, in complex interaction between the imaginary and the material world' (Healey 1999: 113). Latvia participated in the consultation process for the ESDP and this document significantly increased interest in spatial policy among Latvian politicians and planners at different levels. Both the Noordwijk draft document (CEC 1997) and the final version adopted in Potsdam (CEC 1999) were translated into Latvian and extensive discussions on the ESDP were organized between 1998 and 2000. The Latvian planning community was critical that the chapter focusing on enlargement seemed to disregard the needs of and opportunities offered by CEE countries. Furthermore many issues relevant to these countries, such as the role of natural and historical heritage, the potential of small and medium-sized towns and the specific challenges created by monocentric urban systems, were not covered sufficiently or at all. Dostal (2000) has noted that there was a degree of consensus between the then accession countries in relation to these deficiencies in the ESDP, and the same impression has been confirmed by a more recent ESPON research project on the application of the ESDP (ESPON 2006). However, the ESDP has been recognized by Latvia as a valuable learning resource in terms of both its adopted spatial approach as well as a reliable source of information for spatial policy options – with particular regard for the importance of reliability in the context of cross-border knowledge transfer (Evaristo 2007). In fact, the spatial principles promoted in the ESDP, such as polycentric development and urban-rural partnerships, became highly influential in Latvian policy documents, including the National Development Plan (NDP) 2007–2013, the Latvian Sustainable Development Strategy 'Latvia 2030' and the spatial plans of the five planning regions.

In addition, ESPON has provided another potential arena within which the Latvian planning community has had the opportunity to engage in European spatial planning discourse. However, the participation of Latvian organizations in both ESPON 2006 and so far in ESPON 2013 has been extremely limited. There has been some research done within Latvia to review the results of the ESPON 2006 Programme and the relevance to Latvia. Research also was undertaken to assess the potential of the 2013 Programme in relation to Latvia, and to identify Latvian spatial development priorities in terms of research. Though the extent of the dissemination of results is unclear as there is still no formal mechanism established to disseminate ESPON news and results. Therefore, participation in, and the impact of ESPON has been limited in Latvia. And a general lack of commitment from government, in terms of encouraging international research cooperation, not to mention the weak links between politicians and the research community, are significant barriers that still need to be overcome. The situation has been exacerbated by drastic cuts in research budgets in the context of the global financial crisis. The low priority for international research is also reflected by the fact that Latvia is currently the only EU country not to be a member of the European Science Foundation. However, there are plans to improve the dissemination of ESPON information to the Latvian planning community, which represents a potential opportunity for the future. Furthermore, until now the limited impact of ESPON in Latvia has been reflected in relation to the most recent EU reference documents for spatial development, i.e. the Territorial State and Perspectives of the European Union (DE Presidency 2007b) and the Territorial Agenda (DE Presidency 2007a). Although Latvia was involved in the process to prepare these documents, they were generally perceived to add little to the Latvian spatial planning discourse because concepts, such as the notion of polycentric development that is already embedded in spatial policy in Latvia (cf. Marot Chapter 8), remain implicit aims in the new documents. In the next section the debate around the concept of 'territorial cohesion' in Latvia will be discussed.

Relevance and application of territorial cohesion in Latvia

Green Paper on Territorial Cohesion

The Latvian Ministry of Finance (2009: 8) commented on the future of the EU Cohesion policy in response to the Fourth Report on Economic and Social Cohesion (CEC 2007), calling for a separation of the 'territorial cohesion' concept from the 'territorial development' concept. The Ministry expressed doubts about mixing Cohesion Policy and the Lisbon Strategy in the context of EU development, underlining that, despite the ongoing ambiguity over the concept of 'territorial cohesion', it is apparent that this notion requires both internal and external border regions to be given support to address low levels of development. Evers (2007) has claimed that the ambiguity in relation to the concept of 'territorial cohesion' should be perceived as an advantage rather than a problem. To support his thoughts, he claims the strength of the concept lies in its ability to simultaneously appeal to affluent and less affluent areas of the EU, depending on whether a competitiveness or a cohesion-based interpretation is used. Indeed, many members of the European spatial planning community, including the Latvian planning community, welcomed the opportunity to open a debate on the concept introduced by the Green Paper on Territorial Cohesion (CEC 2008). Almost 400 responses were received from national, regional and local governments, European institutions and programming bodies, social and economic partners, interest groups, academic institutions and individuals from throughout the EU and beyond. The Latvian national response was prepared by the Spatial Co-ordination Group that was established by the Ministry of Regional Development and Local Government (MRDLG) in March 2008, involving representatives responsible for structural funds and planning from the sector ministries, the five planning regions, Riga City Council, the Union of Local Governments and the Asociation of Latvian Large Cities. The Co-ordination Group undertook consulations and organised seminars for relevant stakeholders, including social and economic partners and local governments (MRDLG 2009a). As noted earlier, ESDP principles and terminology have strongly influenced Latvian policies, though generally the term 'territorial cohesion' is not widely used in Latvian policy documents. The influence of the ESDP is reflected in the Latvian response, which promotes an equity-based interpretation of 'territorial cohesion' and uses much of ESDP terminology. The Ministry defined 'territorial cohesion' as

> horizontal guidelines for sustainable and coordinated development of all EU regions oriented towards provision of equal standards of quality of life and access to the basic services for citizens by paying special attention to the less developed regions to enhance their competitiveness.
>
> (MRDLG 2009a: 1)

In other words if disparities between regions are to be reduced, subsidiarity and support to less developed regions are seen as crucial principles. Other important aspects mentioned in the response include the competitiveness of less developed regions, territorial cooperation, the promotion of polycentric development, urban networks and urban–rural partnerships, bottom-up planning and the implementation of region-specific strategies that capitalize on the unique territorial capital of each individual region. Moreover, the Latvian response emphasizes the importance of applying the concept and principles of 'territorial cohesion' to national development strategies and claims that this is the case in relation to the National Development Plan (NDP) 2007–2013 (LCM 2006), the National Strategic Reference Framework (NSRF) 2007–2013 and three operational programmes (LCM 2008, 2009a, 2009b), as well as the ongoing process to prepare the National Spatial Development Perspective (MRDLG 2008).

In addition to this coordinated national response, a number of transnational interest groups with Latvian partners also submitted responses to the consultation. The focus of the interest groups was diverse, covering issues such as innovation, metropolitan areas, social cohesion, rural development, environment and nature protection and local governance. Interestingly, despite the diversity of interests all of these groups welcomed the Green Paper and were generally positive about the concept of 'territorial cohesion'. Many of the submissions also demonstrated a number of recurring themes and focused strongly on aspects in relation to spatial equity, balanced development and horizontal policy coordination. The Council of European Regions and Municipalities, including the Latvian Association of Local and Regional Governments emphasized the importance of the horizontal, cross-sector and integrated nature of 'territorial cohesion' (MRDLG 2009c; LALRG 2009). Even groups more focused on innovation and competitiveness were extremely positive about the concept. The Lisbon Regions Network, for example, identified 'territorial cohesion' as the crucial link between the competitiveness focus of the Lisbon Agenda and EU cohesion policy (Lisbon Regions Network 2009). Two of the submissions by groups including Latvian partners were submitted by groups with a specific planning and urban development focus. One was submitted on behalf of VASAB and the other on behalf of the European Forum of Architectural Policies; the latter included three Latvian partners: the Ministry of Culture, the State Inspection of Heritage Protection and the Latvian Association of Architects. Interestingly the European Forum of Architectural Policies argued for an increased institutionalization of ESPON to strengthen the evidence base for spatial planning and also for an increased role for the expert community in the pursuit of 'territorial cohesion'. The organization of consultations by the MRDLG, involving the planning regions and local authorities, and the submissions by numerous interest groups, involving Latvian partners (especially those focusing on spatial planning and urban development as mentioned above), is a clear indication that the Latvian planning community is increasingly engaging in current European spatial planning discourse.

Which 'territorial cohesion' for Latvia?

Increasingly, the Latvian planning community and other communities in Europe are beginning to think about the interpretation of 'territorial cohesion' and its implications for their own national contexts. The Netherlands Environmental

Assessment Agency undertook a Territorial Impact Assessment (TIA) of territorial cohesion for the Netherlands (Evers *et al.* 2009), identifying various policy options for the possible implications of a variety of interpretations of 'territorial cohesion' in the Netherlands: as socio-economic convergence, as economic competitiveness, as rural potential, as spatial planning and as policy coordination. Evers *et al.* conclude that none of the interpretations examined would have a dramatic effect on territorial development in the short to medium term in the Netherlands. The application of a similar TIA methodology to Latvia may reveal dramatically different results due to the significantly different geographic, socio-economic and political context. In fact, the examination of the Latvian national response to the Green Paper on Territorial Cohesion discussed earlier in this section reveals that socio-economic convergence is the most dominant theme in the interpretation of 'territorial cohesion' put forward by the Latvian Government. The response states that:

> considering that social and economic disparities between Member States are still significant, we emphasize that also after complementing the contents of Cohesion Policy with a territorial dimension, it is important to maintain its original purpose – decreasing the differences in social and economic development levels, thus promoting the less developed regions.
>
> (MRDLG 2009a: 2)

Thus in the context of the economic situation in Latvia and in light of the importance given to closing the prosperity gap with Western Europe, this focus is perhaps not surprising. However, any interpretation of 'territorial cohesion' as a solution to socio-economic disparities in Europe raises the question as to which level this interpretation should be applied. Whilst between 1994 and 2007 the gap between Latvia and more wealthy European countries was decreasing and all regions experienced economic growth, the capital region was outperforming the other regions by a considerable margin, and increasing regional disparities within the country and potentially threatening territorial cohesion in the long term (Adams *et al.* 2006). Furthermore, there are numerous indications that EU-regional policy, aiming for economic convergence between Member States, promotes the concentration of economic development in a small number of larger centres and consequently increases internal disparities within many Member States (Ezcurra *et al.* 2007; Churski 2008; Brown *et al.* 2007; Heyns 2005), which is clearly relevant to Latvia.

These complexities and challenges are also highly relevant if the interpretations of 'territorial cohesion' as spatial planning or as rural potential (Evers *et al.* 2009) are applied to Latvia. Similarly, an interpretation of 'territorial cohesion' as a means of improving policy coherence will be equally challenging due to the dominance of deeply entrenched sectoral interests. On this particular point of 'territorial cohesion' as policy coherence, Evers *et al.* (2009) identified two policy options: the application of TIAs to new EU policies and the possibility of more flexibility for Member States in terms of the implementation of EU sector policies. Both of these could potentially be beneficial for Latvia, but the potential of the latter policy option is dubious in a context where sectoral interests remain dominant. Although there is no clear evidence that better governance and institutional change will ensure development (Goldsmith 2007), Latvia has undertaken considerable institutional reform in the hope that the increased scale of regional and local governments will be more efficient and improve policy coordination and coherence, both horizontally between different sectors and vertically between different levels of governance. However, despite the adoption of regional spatial plans, the planning regions still possess only limited institutional and financial capacity, which is likely to continue to hamper their effectiveness for the foreseeable future.

The dominance of Riga in the context of this part of the Baltic States has long been recognized (Sleinis and Sleinis 1938). The inherited spatial structure of Latvia means that any discussion regarding a balanced settlement structure must begin by acknowledging the disparities between the capital city and the rest of the country. With the exception of the six former republican cities that had populations between approximately 35,000 and 105,000 in 2009 (CSBL 2009), the sub-regional centres are represented by medium and small towns (usually with a population between 10,000 and 20,000) that are unable to compete at the international or even the national level. Coupled with the numerous (although decreasing) small farms and villages in rural areas, this provides a challenging context for any spatial development policy, particularity in terms of service and infrastructure provision. Rural development issues are traditionally high on the political agenda and rural service provision is highly contentious due to the importance of rural areas in the Latvian national identity. In this context, if a specific EU policy was introduced to address the multiple challenges facing rural areas that are geographically and economically peripheral, an interpretation of 'territorial cohesion' as rural potential could offer significant opportunities to Latvia.

Riga operates as the capital city of Latvia as well as the gateway to the Baltic States because of its scale and geographic position. As discussed earlier in this chapter, the increasing economic and demographic dominance of Riga is reflected in other areas such as education. During the Soviet period there were only two higher education establishments (Daugavpils and Liepaja) located outside the Riga-Jelgava cluster. However, the geographical distribution of higher education opportunities since 1991 has become more diverse with institutions in other regional cities – Valmiera, Rezekne and Ventspils. Despite this, 89 per cent of students and 87 per cent of academic staff remain concentrated in Riga and Jelgava (Ministry of Education and Science 2008). The complexity of demonstrating a direct causal link between level of education and rates of development has been identified as an area for concern in the National Strategic Reference Framework (NSRF 2007–2013) (cf. also Czapiewski and Janc Chapter 14). In addition, the capital region is characterized by intense migration and significant daily commuting patterns from areas within approximately 90 minutes drive of the capital, which includes almost the entire Riga Planning

Region and much of Zemgale Planning Region (Krisjane *et al.* 2004). Deficiencies in the quality and efficiency of the transport infrastructure prevent higher levels of labour mobility and 'therefore intra-regional differences can sometimes be more marked than interregional differences' (Vet *et al.* 2000: 66). Nevertheless labour mobility has contributed to the equalization of earnings and reducing unemployment in some parts of Europe, but Heyns (2005) claims that this is less so in CEE countries.

The presence of the Baltic Seaports of Ventspils and Liepaja in the Kurzeme Region usually promote Kurzeme to second place behind Riga in terms of economic development, but without the ports, economic performance in this region is similar to Zemgale and Vidzeme regions. The Latgale Region in the east of the country has traditionally lagged behind the other regions for a variety of reasons (Paalzow 2006; Adams *et al.* 2006; Krisjane 2005; Norkus, 2007). Petrakos (2001) claimed that adjustments in transition countries appear to be more rapid in metropolitan regions and also in western regions of CEE countries that are closer to the borders of Western European EU countries. The eastern location means that Latgale has an external EU border shared with Belarus and the Russian Federation and in distance it is also located furthest from the capital city and from the coast. A Territorial Development Index (TDI) is used in Latvia as an instrument to identify areas most in need of state support. The TDI ranks areas to determine eligibility for support from EU and national funding programmes (Vaidere *et al.* 2006). The TDI consistently identifies a high concentration of such areas in Latgale although the resulting state support has done little to reduce disparities.

Schön (2005) states that the influence of the ESDP is evident in many national policy documents. Research by Meijers *et al.* (2007) suggests that the reduction of disparities to enhance cohesion is central to territorial policy in 14 European countries including Latvia. They calculated the primacy rate for each country, which is the extent to which the capital region diverged from the average of the other so-called functional urban areas. Latvia was ranked first in terms of primacy rate for GDP and second in terms of population. This calculation suggests that Latvia, Portugal and Greece are the three most monocentric Member States in the EU. In their research Meijers *et al.* examined various national policy documents and concluded that Latvia was one of a number of countries where the main focus was on reducing disparities between the capital and the rest of the country – despite its high primacy rate and long-held consideration of polycentric development in spatial policy. According to Yamazaki-Honda (2005), priorities in many countries are shifting toward growth and competitiveness and away from redistribution type policies as already evident in Latvia. This may suggest a move toward an interpretation of 'territorial cohesion' as economic competitiveness (Evers *et al.* 2009), implying perhaps less emphasis on balanced development and more emphasis on harnessing territorial capital and targeting growth areas, or in other words Riga (cf. Finka Chapter 5 and Tewdwr-Jones Chapter 3). The focus on growth is also reflected in the long-term conceptual policy document *A Growth Model for Latvia: People First* (Latvian

Parliament 2005) that opts to pursue what it calls a 'people and knowledge-centred growth scenario' in a 'multidimensional and long-term approach'. Some consider this document to be a turning point for national development policy and a move away from the investor centred, short-term and sectoral policies of the past. However, the promotion of increased growth in Riga, in the anticipation that this is the most efficient means of raising national competitiveness and that the benefits will spill-over into the rest of the country, seems to remain the dominant paradigm. In fact, new development planning legislation identified this document as a framework for other planning documents in 2008. However, the recent economic downturn dramatically has altered the situation in the short-term and it is possible that the priorities of the Latvian NDP will have to be revised as a consequence of this recent turn of events.

Whilst it is far beyond the scope of this chapter to undertake a full TIA on the impact of 'territorial cohesion' in Latvia, this clearly would be a useful exercise. Though in light of the issues discussed in this section, it would appear that 'territorial cohesion', depending on how it is ultimately interpreted at different levels, could have a more significant impact in Latvia than it is likely to have in the Netherlands according to Evers *et al.* (2009).

Rhetoric or reality, some reflections

The discussion has demonstrated that an examination of the evolution of policies relevant to spatial development in Latvia is highly complex and requires not only inside knowledge about the country but also an ability to place this evolution within the contexts of both post-socialist transition and EU accession. The highly fluid political landscape, whereby fragile coalition governments have risen and fallen with alarming regularity, means that numerous national policy documents and priorities have been abandoned before they have been implemented. GDP in Latvia collapsed simultaneously with the collapse of the Soviet economy and in 1995 GDP was only 49 per cent of 1990 levels. A period of unprecedented growth followed between 1994 and 2007 stimulated by substantial levels of foreign capital and investor friendly neo-liberal policies. Between 2001 and 2006 GDP grew on average by over 8 per cent per year. Recently however, Latvia has plummeted into the worst recession in the EU with the global financial situation hitting Latvia harder than any other Member State. GDP decreased by 5 per cent in 2008 and was expected to decrease by 18 per cent in 2009 (all data from CSBL 2009). In fact, Sommers (2009) has claimed that the current crisis represents the weakening of society and the hyper-individualism of the past two decades – introduced by the Anglo-American led Washington Consensus; what some have referred to as the neo-liberal 'shock therapy' in Eastern Europe (Sokol 2001) has, in the case of Latvia, turned into truly shocking therapy.

After the long accession process during which Latvia strove to fulfil the requirements of the *acquis communautaire* in relation to institutional structure, regional policy and territorial organization (Brown *et al.* 2007; Bachtler and McMaster 2008), Latvia's experience raises as many questions as it provides answers. Questions remain in relation to the suitability of GDP growth as the main indicator for economic competitiveness, the sustainability of FDI driven growth and the potential for spill-over effects from dynamic to less dynamic regions. Economic competitiveness that will foster economic growth and increase employment and living standards has, since 1991, been a part of political declarations of various national governments. However, Latvian GDP per capita was still only 56 per cent of the EU-27 average in 2008, significantly less than the neighbouring Baltic States Lithuania (61 per cent) and Estonia (68 per cent). According to this indicator only Romania (46 per cent) and Bulgaria (40 per cent) are less prosperous (EUROSTAT 2009). Although economic restructuring has seen the emphasis move from industry and the primary sector to services, the economic context in Latvia remains complex. Ivanova (2007) and Pavlinek (2004) have both questioned the dominance of a transition paradigm whereby foreign capital is assigned the role of principal agent of economic restructuring. They also cast doubt on the anticipated spill-over effects, claiming that, whilst such an approach may have encouraged trade, it did not necessarily facilitate favourable economic and technological conditions. On the contrary, Ivanova (2007) claims that an overemphasis on foreign capital at the expense of endogenous potential may have limited development potential and lead to increased spatial disparities where metropolitan areas have taken advantage of their more accessible position at the expense of peripheral non-metropolitan areas (Pavlinek 2004; Hardy 1998). Brown *et al.* (2007) also claim that global investors will favour local economies that have similar supply structures to their home economies, which promise the maximum return on their investments (cf. also Capik Chapter 13). Therefore, in many cases, these investors will tend to avoid lagging regions regardless of the institutional modernization in, and state aid policies directed at them.

The NDP 2007–2013 (LCM 2006) and the Draft Latvia Sustainable Development Strategy (MRDLG 2008) are viewed by some as documents and processes that may be able to overcome traditional sectoral fragmentation, and facilitate more coordinated public investment and policy. However, others fear that the continuous changes in Government, limited institutional and financial capacity and limited human resources will continue to significantly hamper national, regional and local planning in Latvia (Vanags 2005). Adams has noted that Latvia was a fairly extreme example where 'the conflict between genuine integrated and long-term planning and sectorally structured governments working to election timetables has in reality proven impossible to reconcile' (Adams 2008: 43). The current financial crisis is forcing sectors to reduce public spending and to seek new partnerships and ways of working. The MRDLG is also searching for new instruments to foster territorial partnerships between sectors and municipalities in order to implement place-based and accessibility improving measures. Pužulis (2008) hopes that the condensed regional level will improve policy coordination and ensure that regional interests are taken into account at the national level. Regardless of which of the interpretations for 'territorial cohesion' put forward by Evers *et al.* (2009) is applied in Latvia, it would seem clear that more coherent and transparent decision-making processes, particularly in the field of public investments and service provision, would be a positive step in facilitating it. The Latvian planning community have an opportunity to continue the 'territorial cohesion' debate initiated by the Green Paper within the context of the country's ongoing National Spatial Development Perspective process. Debate about nationally important spatial development issues has been restricted in recent years because prevailing EU enlargement priorities and neo-liberal political ideals stopped the preparation of the National Spatial Plan several years ago. The process was stopped despite support from local and regional level actors and the planning community, and despite the preparation of a National Spatial Planning Concept (LCM 1998), sectoral studies and stakeholder seminars between 1997 and 2002. There was no political will to address issues such as suburbanization, land speculation and development of nationally important areas during the property boom. Though some of the studies, developed during the national planning exercise, were used to inform municipal, district and regional plans as well as various sectoral documents and legislation in relation to civil defence, forestry, agriculture and nature protection. Thus, ironically, despite the lack of a national plan, control of development in certain areas is relatively powerful, suggesting that the impact has been far more severe in relation to a lack of coordination of spatial policy between different levels and in relation to certain sectors such as transport. Nevertheless, it remains to be seen whether the current political commitment to producing a national spatial perspective will be successful.

The priorities in the NDP 2007–2013 (LCM 2006) were formulated taking account of regional disparities within the country, which have included horizontal cross-cutting priorities to try to address this issue. However, success will depend on the numerous actors involved in utilizing EU and national funds. The NDP allocated 8 per cent of the EU Structural Funds and Cohesion Fund for the 'Polycentric Development' priority that seeks to stimulate the competitiveness of both Riga and regional cities and towns. This in itself is an illustration of the influence of EU spatial policy. Furthermore, the regeneration of deprived areas as well as the promotion and stimulation of international competitiveness are key priorities in Riga. International competitiveness is now measured as a ratio of average GDP per capita of other capitals in the BSR – Copenhagen, Stockholm, Helsinki, Vilnius and Tallinn (baseline of 2004 was 29 per cent). And, apart from Riga, 17 other urban growth areas have been identified as centres of national or regional importance (see Figure 12.1). Although the selection of these growth areas was based on regional planning activities, the lack of supporting economic and territorial evidence and justification has led to scepticism in some quarters as to why these centres were chosen instead of others. In private, some officials admit that the selection was premature and unfair, and amendments are being considered.

As the discussion has illustrated, the activities and networks in relation to VASAB and the ESDP have significantly influenced spatial policy in Latvia both in terms of the content of the documents and also in terms of institution building at both national and regional scales. In this context both VASAB and the ESDP process have provided 'knowledge arenas' (cf. Adams *et al.* Chapters 1 and 2) and have also contributed significantly to the evolution of a 'community of practice' amongst Latvian planners. It is too early to judge the effectiveness of the institutional reform introduced in 2009 but future success may well depend on whether the Government have the commitment to strengthen the planning regions sufficiently to make them an effective tier of governance. An effective working relationship between Government and the research community requires a degree of political stability that has been absent in Latvia since independence. The 'community of practice' that has emerged is capable of debating national issues and operating in international networks, but a higher priority from the Government for international research will be required before Latvia can play a full and active role in initiatives such as ESPON and the European Science Foundation. The availability of planning courses at three Latvian universities will undoubtedly strengthen the skills pool and enrich the Latvian 'community of practice' in time. However, the limited institutional and financial capacities of research institutions remain a significant barrier to regular and effective participation in activities such as ESPON, which could hamper the evolution of the Latvian planning community in the international arena. Financial reality dictates that, while the Latvian Government is aware of the importance of participation in research activities, it is not currently a priority for the country. The Government is striving to strengthen policy coordination and coherence both vertically, between different levels, and horizontally, between different sectors, not to mention considering the introduction of territorial impact assessments as a means of promoting 'territorial cohesion'. Still, in terms of policy coordination, there is much work to be done. Progress is currently hampered as certain sectors use different territorial subdivisions compared to the planning regions and thus it is extremely difficult to coordinate activities or even to assess the levels and impacts of spending.

The current financial crisis is forcing the Government to reduce public spending, whereby improving multi-level governance and strengthening horizontal and vertical partnerships is one widely discussed option. Furthermore, the MRDLG, in its response to the Green Paper on Territorial Cohesion (MRDLG 2009a), emphasizes the importance of investing in infrastructure and communication, education and health services as means of promoting territorial cohesion in Latvia. They also call for the further institutionalization of relevant activities if territorial cohesion is to be pursued effectively. And the Ministry of Finance (2009) argue that key challenges in relation to sustainable development and global competitiveness cannot be addressed simply through the EU and other funding programmes; they call for a systematic revision in policy and legislation on the one hand, and in public administration and ways of thinking on the other. It remains to be seen what role the 'community of practice' in Latvian spatial planning will play in this process. Clearly a degree of commitment and stability at the level of Government will be required if this 'community of practice' is to operate effectively and become fully integrated into an international 'epistemic community'.

References

Adams, N. (2008) 'Convergence and policy transfer: An examination of the extent to which approaches to spatial planning have converged within the context of an enlarged EU', *International Planning Studies*, 13(1): 31–49.

Adams, N., Cotella, G. and Nunes, R. (2010) 'Spatial planning in Europe: the interplay between knowledge and policy in an enlarged EU', in N. Adams, G. Cotella and R. Nunes (eds) *Territorial Development, Cohesion and Spatial Planning: Knowledge and policy development in an enlarged EU*, London: Routledge.

Adams, N., Cotella, G. and Nunes, R. (2010) 'Territorial knowledge channels in a multi-jurisdictional policy environment. A theoretical framework', in N. Adams, G. Cotella and R. Nunes (eds) *Territorial Development, Cohesion and Spatial Planning: Knowledge and policy development in an enlarged EU*, London: Routledge.

Adams, N., Ezmale, S. and Paalzow, A. (2006) 'Towards balanced development in Latvia: The experience of the Latgale Region', in N. Adams, J. Alden and N. Harris (eds) *Regional Development and Spatial Planning in an Enlarged European Union*, Aldershot: Ashgate.

Adler, E. (1992) 'The emergence of cooperation: National epistemic communities and the international evolution of the idea of nuclear arms control', *International Organization*, 46 (1): 101–145.

Adler, E. and Haas, P. M. (1992) 'Conclusion: epistemic communities, world order, and the creation of a reflective research program', *International Organization*, 46(1): 367–390.

Agnew, J. (2001) 'How many Europes?: The European Union, eastward enlargement and uneven development', *European Urban and Regional Studies*, 8(1): 29–38.

Albrechts, L. (1999) 'Planners as catalysts and initiators of change: The new Structure Plan for Flanders', *European Planning Studies*, 7(5): 587–603.

Apsitis, V. (1989) 'Pie Lielrīgas šūpuļa', *Literatūra un Māksla* 11. 8 February.

Bachtler, J. and McMaster, I. (2008) 'EU cohesion policy and the role of the regions: Investigating the influence of Structural Funds in the New Member states', *Environment and Planning C: Government and Policy*, 26: 398–427.

Bākule, I. and Siksna, A. (2009) *Rīga ārpus Nocietinājumiem: Pilsētas plānotā izbūve un pārbūve/Riga beyond the walls: City planned growth and transformation from 17th century to the First World War*, Rīga: Neputns.

Bleijere, D., Butulis, I., Feldmanis, I., Stranga, A. and Zunda, A. (2006) *History of Latvia: The 20th century*. Riga: Jumava.

Bonache, J. and Brewster, C. (2001) 'Knowledge transfer and the management of expatriation', *Thunderbird International Business Review*, 43(1): 145–168.

Borg, E. A. (2006) 'The Latvian market constructed: Approaches towards independence, consumerism, symbolic leadership and market planning', *Baltic Journal of Management*, 1(1): 67–81.

Briedis, J. and Strautiņš, E. (1988) 'Rīgas metro svaru kauss', *Cīņa*, 7 February.

Brown, D. L., Greskovits, B. and Kulcsar, L. J. (2007) 'Leading sectors and leading regions: Economic restructuring and regional inequality in Hungary since 1990', *International Journal of Urban and Regional Research*, 31(3): 522–42.

Bunkse, E. V. (1979) 'The role of humane environment in Soviet urban planning', *Geographical Review*, 69 (4): 379–394.

—— (1992) 'God, Thine Earth is Burning: Nature attitudes and the Latvian drive for independence', *GeoJournal*, 26(2): 203–209.

—— (1999) 'Reality of rural landscape symbolism in the formation of a post-Soviet, postmodern Latvian identity', *Norsk Geografisk Tidsskrift*, 53: 121–138.

Capik, P. (2010) 'Regional promotion and competition: an examination of approaches to FDI attraction in the Czech Republic, Poland and Slovakia', in N. Adams, G. Cotella and R. Nunes (eds) *Territorial Development, Cohesion and Spatial Planning: Knowledge and policy development in an enlarged EU*, London: Routledge.

CEC – Commission of the European Communities (1997) *European Spatial Development Perspective*: First Official Draft. Presented at the informal meeting of Ministers responsible for spatial planning of the member states of the European Union. Nordwijk, 9 and 10 June 1997.

—— (1999) *European Spatial Development Perspective. Towards Balanced and Sustainable Development of the Territory of the EU*, Luxembourg: Office for Official Publications of the European Communities.

—— (2007) *Growing Regions, Growing Europe: Fourth Report on Economic and Social Cohesion*, Bruxelles: Commission of the European Communities. Online. Available HTTP   http://ec.europa.eu/regional_policy/sources/docoffic/official/reports/cohesion4/index_en.htm (accessed 9 September 2009).

—— (2008) *Green Paper on Territorial Cohesion – Turning Territorial Diversity into Strength*, Brussels: Commission of the European Communities. Online. Available HTTP: http://ec.europa.eu/Regional_policy/consultation/terco/index_en.htm (accessed 3 March 2009).

—— (2009) Communication from the Commission to the European Parliament, the Council, the European Economic and Social Committee and the Committee of the Regions concerning the European Union Strategy for the Baltic Sea Region. Online. Available HTTP: http://ec.europa.eu/regional_policy/sources/docoffic/official/communic/baltic/com_baltic_en.pdf (accessed 1 August 2009).

Churski, P. (2008) 'Structural Funds of the European Union in Poland – Experience of the first period of membership', *European Planning Studies*, 16(4): 579–607.

CSBL (2009) Central Statistical Bureau of Latvian Databases. Online. Available HTTP: http//www.csb.gov.lv (accessed 7 September 2009).

Czapiewski, K. and Janc, K. (2010) 'Accessibility to education and its impact on regional development in Poland', in N. Adams, G. Cotella and R. Nunes (eds) *Territorial Development, Cohesion and Spatial Planning: Knowledge and policy development in an enlarged EU*, London: Routledge.

DE Presidency (2007a) *Territorial Agenda of the European Union: Towards a More Competitive and Sustainable Europe of Diverse Regions*. Agreed on the occasion of the Informal Ministerial Meeting on Urban Development and Territorial Cohesion in Leipzig on 24 and 25 May 2007. Online. Available HTTP: www.eu-territorial-agenda.eu/Reference%20Documents/Territorial-Agenda-of-the-European-Union-Agreed-on-25-May-2007.pdf (accessed 9 September 2009).

—— (2007b) *Territorial State and Perspectives of the European Union: Towards Stronger European Territorial Cohesion in the light of the Lisbon and Gothenburg Ambitions*. Background Document for the Territorial Agenda of the European Union. Online. Available HTTP: www.eu-territorial-agenda.eu/Reference%20Documents/The-Territorial-State-and-Perspectives-of-the-European-Union.pdf (accessed 9 September 2009).

Dostal, P. (2000) 'The European spatial development perspective and the accession countries: Polycentric guidelines versus uneven spatial development', *Infromationen zur Raumentwicklung*, 3/4: 183–192.

Eglīte, P. (2007) 'Regional differences of depopulation in Latvia', *Geogrāfiski Raksti/ Folia Geographica.* 12: 169–174.

ESPON (2006) *Application and Effects of the ESDP in the Member States. Final Report,* Luxembourg: ESPON. Online. Available HTTP: www.espon.eu/mmp/online/website/content/projects/243/366/index_EN.html (accessed 1 August 2009).

Eurostat (2009) GDP per capita in PPS – GDP per capita in Purchasing Power Standards (PPS). Online. Available HTTP: http://epp.eurostat.ec.europa.eu/ (accessed 10 September 2009).

Evaristo, J. R. (2007) 'Knowledge transfer across borders: A process model', *Knowledge and Process Management,* 14(3): 203–210.

Evers, D. (2007) 'Reflections on territorial cohesion and European spatial planning', *Tijdschrift voor Economische en Sociale Geografie,* 99 (3): 303–315.

Evers, D., Tennekes, J., Borsboom, J., van den Heiligenberg, H. and Thissen, M. (2009) *A Territorial Impact Assessment of Territorial Cohesion for the Netherlands.* Netherlands Environmental Assessment Agency (PBL): The Hague/Bilthoven. Online. Available HTTP: www.pbl.nl/en/publications/2009/territorial-impact-assessment.html (accessed 1June 2009).

Ezcurra, R., Pascual, P. and Rapun, M. (2007) 'The dynamics of regional disparities in Central and Eastern Europe during transition', *European Planning Studies,* 15(10): 1397–1421.

Finka, M., (2010) 'Evolving frameworks for regional development and spatial planning in the new regions of the EU', in N. Adams, G. Cotella and R. Nunes (eds) *Territorial Development, Cohesion and Spatial Planning: Knowledge and policy development in an enlarged EU,* London: Routledge.

Fritsch, M. (2010) 'Interfaces of European Union internal and external territorial governance: The Baltic Sea Region', in N. Adams, G. Cotella and R. Nunes (eds) *Territorial Development, Cohesion and Spatial Planning: Knowledge and policy development in an enlarged EU,* London: Routledge.

Fuchs, R. J. and Demko, G. J. (1979) 'Geographical inequality under socialism', *Annals of the Association of American Geographers,* 69(2): 304–318.

Goldsmith, A. A. (2007) 'Is governance reform a catalyst for development?' *Governance: An International Journal of Policy, Administration, and Institutions,* 20(2): 165–186.

Grava, S. (1993) 'The urban heritage of the Soviet Regime: The case of Riga, Latvia', *Journal of the American Planning Association* 59(1): 9–30.

Gross, M. (2000) 'Adapting Western style regional planning to Russia: The University of Massachusetts–Pskov Region Partnership', *European Planning Studies,* 8(5): 619–630.

Haas, P. M. (1992) 'Introduction: Epistemic communities and international policy coordination', *International Organization,* 46 (1): 1–35.

Håkanson, L. (2005) 'Epistemic Communities and cluster dynamics: On the role of knowledge in industrial districts', *Industry and Innovation,* 12(4): 433–463.

Hardy, J. (1998) 'Cathedrals in the desert? Transnationals, corporate strategy and locality in Wroclaw', *Regional Studies,* 32(7): 639–652.

Healey, P. (1999) 'Institutionalist analysis, communicative planning, and shaping places', *Journal of Planning Education and Research,* 19: 111–121.

—— (2006) 'Transforming governance: Challenges of institutional adaptation and a new politics of space'. *European Planning Studies,* 14(3): 299–320.

Heyns, B. (2005) 'Emerging inequalities in Central and Eastern Europe', *Annual Review of Sociology,* 31: 163–97.

Ivanova, M. N. (2007) 'Why there was no 'Marshall Plan' for Eastern Europe and why this still matters', *Journal of Contemporary European Studies*, 15(3): 345–376.

Ivāns, D. and Snips, A. (1986) 'Par Daugavas likteni domājot', *Literatūra un Māksla*, 17, October: 10–12.

—— (eds) (1989) Domu Daugava. Sirdsdaugava, Rīga: Avots.

Jaakson, R. (1996) 'From Marx to market: Deciding the urban form of post-Soviet Tallinn, Estonia', *Journal of Urban Design*, 1(3): 329–355.

King, G. J., Vanags, E., Vilka, I., and McNabb, D. E. (2004) 'Local government reforms in Latvia, 1990–2003: Transition to a democratic society', *Public Administration*, 82(4): 931–950.

King, L. (2003) 'Shock privatization: The effects of rapid large-scale privatization on enterprise restructuring', *Politics and Society*, 31: 3–30.

Krastiņš, J. (1980) *Jūgendstils Rīgas arhitektūrā* [*Art Nouveau in Riga Architecture*], Latvijas Dabas un pieminekļu aizsardzības biedrība, Rīga: Zinātne.

—— (1992) Latvijas Republikas buvmaksla. Riga: Zinātne.

Krauklis, A. (2000) 'Living with diversity in Latvia: People, nature and cultural landscape', *Folia Geographica*, 8: 1–14.

Krisjane, Z. (2005) 'Latvia: a centre oriented country in transition', in Muller, B., Finka, M. and Lintz, G. (eds) *Rise and decline of industry in Central and Eastern Europe*, New York: Springer: 131–153.

—— (2007) *Darbaspēka ģeogrāfiskā mobilitāte*, Riga: Latvijas Universitate un Latvijas republikas Labklajibas ministrija. Online. Available HTTP: www.darbatirgus.gov. lv/?id=211&top=33&sa=89 (accessed 9 September 2009).

Krisjane, Z., Bauls, A. and Vilcins, A. (2004) 'Changing patterns of population mobility', *Folia Geographica*, 12: 66–73.

Kūle, L. (2008) 'Concepts of rurality and urbanity as analytical categories in multidimensional research', *Proceedings of the Latvian Academy of Sciences B*, 62(1/2): 9–17.

Kuus, M. (2004) 'Europe's Eastern expansion and the reinscription of otherness in East-Central Europe', *Progress in Human Geography*, 28 (4): 472–489.

—— (2007) 'Intellectuals and geopolitics: The "Cultural Politicians" of Central Europe', *Geoforum*, 38: 241–251.

LALRG – Latvian Association of Local and Regional Governements (2009) Latvijas Pašvaldību savienības Reģionālās attīstības un sadarbības komitejas 2009. gada 20. janvāra sēdes protokols Nr. 133. Online. Available HTTP: www.lps.lv/Komitejas/ Regionalas_attistibas_un_sadarbibas_komiteja/ (accessed 9 September 2009).

Lamze, A. (1926) 'Kāda izskatīsies Rīga pēc 50 gadiem', *Jaunakas Zinas*, 146.

—— (1932) 'Territorijas problema Lielrigas izbuve', in T. Liventals and V. Sadovsks (eds) *Riga ka Latvijas galvaspilseta*, Riga: Rigas pilsetas valdes izdevums: 769–805.

Latvian Parliament (2005) '*Latvijas izaugsmes modelis: Cilvēks pirmajā vietā*', Adopted by the Latvian Parliament on 20 October 2005. Online. Available HTTP: www.nap.lv/ eng/attistibas_planosana/latvijas_izaugsmes_modelis/ (accessed 9 September 2009).

—— (2008) *Latvian Development Planning Law*, adopted by the Latvian Parliament on 8 May 2008. Online. Available HTTP www.likumi.lv/doc.php?id=175748 (accessed 9 September 2009).

Lauristin, M. and Vihalemm, P. (2009) 'The political agenda during different periods of Estonian transformation: External and internal factors', *Journal of Baltic Studies*, 40 (1): 1–28.

LCM – Latvian Cabinet of Ministers (1998) Latvijas Nacionālā plānojuma koncepcija (prot. nr.4 36.§). akceptēta. Prepared by the Ministry of Environmental Protection and

Regional Development and accepted by the Cabinet of Ministers on 27 January 1998. Online. Available HTTP: www.vestnesis.lv/index.php?menu=doc&id=47431 (accessed 9 September 2009).

—— (2006) *National Development Plan 2007–2013*. Approved by the Latvian Cabinet of Ministers Regulations no. 564 on 4 July, 2006. Online. Available HTTP: www.nap. lv/eng/ (accessed 9 September 2009).

—— (2007) *Valsts stratēģiskais ietvardokuments 2007.-2013.gada periodam [National Strategic Reference Framework (NSRF) 2007–2013]*. Approved by the Cabinet of Ministers of the Republic of Latvia on 23 October, 2007. Online. Available HTTP: www.esfondi.lv (accessed 9 September 2009).

—— (2008) *1.darbības programma 'Cilvēkresursi un nodarbinātība' (ESF)*, Prepared by the Ministry of Finance in 2009 and approved by the Cabinet of Ministers on 20 February 2008. Available HTTP: www.esfondi.lv/page.php?id=492 (accessed 9 September 2009).

—— (2009a) *2.darbības programma "Uzņēmējdarbība un inovācijas" (ERAF)*, Prepared by the Ministry of Finance in 2007 and approved by the Cabinet of Ministers on 16 July 2009. Available HTTP: www.esfondi.lv/page.php?id=493 (accessed 9 September 2009).

—— (2009b) *3.darbības programma „Infrastruktūra un pakalpojumi"*, Prepared by the Ministry of Finance in 2007, modified by the Cabinet of Ministers on 17 June 2009. Available HTTP: www.esfondi.lv/page.php?id=494 (accessed 9 September 2009).

Lejnieks, J. (1989a) Rīgas arhitektūra/Riga's architecture, Rīga: Avots.

—— (1989b) 'Jūrmalas ģenerālais plāns 1989 [Jurmala Master plan]', *Latvijas Arhitektūra*, 96–97.

Lieven, A. (1993) *The Baltic Revolution*, New Haven: Yale University Press.

Lisbon Regions Network (2009) *Response to the Green Paper on Territorial Cohesion*, Online. Available HTTP: http://ec.europa.eu/regional_policy/consultation/terco/pdf/4_ organisation/69_lrn_en.pdf (accessed 1 August 2009).

Maier, K. (2010) 'The pursuit of balanced territorial development: The realities and complexities of the cohesion agenda', in N. Adams, G. Cotella and R. Nunes (eds) *Territorial Development, Cohesion and Spatial Planning: Knowledge and policy development in an enlarged EU*, London: Routledge.

Manning, P. A. and Poljeva, T. (1999) 'The challenge of management development in the Baltic States in the twenty-first century', *Journal of Management Development*, 18(1): 32–45.

Marot, N. (2010) 'New planning jurisdictions, scant resources and local public responsibility: Delivering spatial planning in Slovenia', in N. Adams, G. Cotella and R. Nunes (eds) Territorial *Development, Cohesion and Spatial Planning: Knowledge and policy development in an enlarged EU*, London: Routledge.

Meijers, E. J. Waterhout, B. and Zonneveld, W. (2007) 'Closing the GAP: Territorial cohesion through polycentric development', *European Journal of Spatial Development*, 24. Online. Available HTTP www.nordregio.se/EJSD/refereed24.pdf (accessed 3 March 2009).

Melbergs, G. (1969) 'Arhitekta A.Lamzes darbi Rigas plānošana un apbūve', in O. Tilmanis, O. Buka and J. Vasiljevs (eds) *Arhitektūra un pilsētbūvniecība Latvijas PSR: Rakstu krājums* I, Riga: Zinatne: 95–104.

—— (1979) 'Dažas mājoklu celtniecības problēmas pilsētekoloģijas skatījumā', in O. Buka *et al.* (eds) *Latvijas PSR Pilsētu arhitektūra*. Riga: Zinātne, 132–140.

—— (1995). 'Arnolds Lamze, 1889–1945', in O. Buka and J.Lejnieks (eds) *Latvijas arhitektūras meistari*, Riga: Zvaigzne, Rīgas Tehniskās Universitātes Arhitektūras fakultāte: 148–156.

Melluma (1997) 'Par Latvijas administratīvi teritoriālo reformu', *Latvijas Vēstnesis*, 66/67. Online. Available HTTP: www.vestnesis.lv/index.php?menu=doc&id=42512/ (accessed 9 September 2009).

Ministry of Education and Science (2008) Reģistri un statistika. Online. Available HTTP: http://izm.izm.gov.lv/registri-statistika.html (accessed 3 May 2008).

Ministry of Finance (2003) National Development Plan (Single Programming Document) Objective 1 Programme 2004–2006. Approved by the European Commission on 18 December 2003. Online. Available HTTP: www.esfondi.lv/upload/05-saistosie_dokumenti/spd_en_09112006.pdf (accessed 9 September 2009).

—— (2009) Informatīvais ziņojums par viedokļa sagatavošanu publicēšanai Eiropas Komisijas reģionālās politikas dienesta mājas lapā. Online. Available HTTP polsis.mk. gov.lv/LoadAtt/file37504.doc (accessed 9 September 2009).

MRDLG – Ministry of Regional Development and Local Governments (2008) Latvijas ilgtspējīgas attīstības stratēģija līdz 2030.gadam: Pilnveidotā 1. redakcija [Draft Latvia Sustainable Development Strategy 2030, Online. Available HTTP: www.latvija2030. lv/upload/lias_1redakcija_pilnv_final.pdf (accessed 9 September 2009).

—— (2009a) *Latvia's Position on the European Commission's Green Paper on Territorial Cohesion 'Turning Territorial Diversity into Strength'*. Approved by the Cabinet of Ministers of the Republic of Latvia on 17 February, 2009. Riga: Ministry of Regional Development and Local Governments. Online. Available HTTP: http://ec. europa.eu/regional_policy/consultation/terco/pdf/2_national/27_latvia_en.pdf(accessed 9 September 2009).

—— (2009b) *Rajonu pašvaldību reorganizācijas plāni*. Online. Available HTTP: www. raplm.gov.lv/pub/index.php?id=1729 (accessed 30 July 2009).

—— (2009c) Ikgadējās sarunas ar Latvijas Pašvaldību savienību. Online. Available HTTP: www.raplm.gov.lv/pub/index.php?id=1740 (accessed 30 July 2009).

Norkus, Z. (2007) 'Why did Estonia perform best? The North-South gap in the post-socialist economic transition of the Baltic States', *Journal of Baltic Studies*, 38 (1): 21–42.

Osis, U. (2004) Starp divām pasaulēm, Rīga: Jumava.

Paalzow, A. (2006) 'Barriers to regional development in the new Member States: The Latvian experience', in N. Adams, J. Alden and N. Harris (eds) *Regional Development and Spatial Planning in an Enlarged European Union*. Aldershot: Ashgate.

Pallagst, K. (2006) 'European spatial planning reloaded: Considering EU enlargement in theory and practice', *European Planning Studies*, 14(2): 253–270.

Pavlinek, P. (2004) 'Regional development implications of foreign direct investment in Central Europe', *European Urban and Regional Studies*, 11(1): 47–70.

Peterlin, M. and Kreitmayer McKenzie, J. (2007) 'The Europeanization of spatial planning in Slovenia', *Planning, Practice and Research*, 22(2): 455–461.

Petrakos, G. (2001) 'Patterns of regional inequality in transition economies', *European Planning Studies*, 9(3): 359–383.

Putnam, R. (1993) *Making Democracy Work, Civic Traditions in Modern Italy*, Princeton: Princeton University Press.

Pužulis, A. (2008) 'Reģiona attīstības uzraudzība. Iespējas un risinājumi', *Latvijas Architektūra*, 2: 142.-145.

Richardson, J. J. (2001) 'Policy-making in the European Union', in J. J. Richardson (ed.) *European Union. Power and Policy-Making*, London: Routledge.

Roze, A. (1991) 'Bez nopietnas pieejas visas ieceres nogrims ikdienas problēmās', pierakst. Ralfs Vīlands. *Jūrmala*, 1 August, 6.

—— (1995) 'Rīgas reģiona saskaņota plānošana' *Latvijas Vēstnesis*, 153.
Sabatier, P. A. (1998) 'The advocacy coalition framework: revision and relevance for Europe', *Journal of European Public Policy*, 5(1): 98–130.
Schön, P. (2005) 'Territorial cohesion in Europe?' *Planning Theory and Practice*, 6(3): 389–400.
Schwartz, K. Z. S. (2007) ' "The occupation of beauty': imagining nature and nation in Latvia', *East European Politics and Societies*, 21(2): 259–293.
Sleinis, I. and Sleinis, M. (1938). Dzintarzeme – dzimtene: Latvijas dabas un kultūras vērojumi. 2 iespiedums. Rīga: Valtera un Rapas akc.sab.apgāds.
Sokol, M. (2001) 'Central and Eastern Europe a decade after the fall of state-socialism: Regional dimensions of transition processes', *Regional Studies*, 35 (7): 645–655.
Sommers, J. (2009) 'Economic crisis and social turbulence in the Baltic States, the Baltic riots: "Existing Thatcherism" and the Washington Consensus', *Global Research*, January 19, 2009. Online. Available HTTP: www.globalresearch.ca/index. php?context=va&aid=11877 (accessed 1 August 2009).
Šulce, I. (1988) 'Cilvēki sadevās rokās', *Literatūra un Māksla*, 9 September: 3.
Tewdwr-Jones, M. (2010) 'Cohesion and competitiveness: the evolving context for European territorial development', in N. Adams, G. Cotella and R. Nunes (eds) *Territorial Development, Cohesion and Spatial Planning: Knowledge and policy development in an enlarged EU*, London: Routledge.
Vaidere, I., Vanags, E., Vanags, I. and Vilka, I. (2006) Reģionālā politika un pašvaldību attīstība Eiropas Savienībā un Latvijā. Rīga: Latvijas Universitātes Akadēmiskais apgāds, Latvijas Statistikas institūts.
Vanags, E. (2005) 'Development of local government reforms in Latvia', *Viesoji Politika ir Admininistravimas*, 13: 15–24. Online. Available HTTP http://internet.ktu.lt/lt/ mokslas/zurnalai/vpa/z13/1648–2603–2006-nr13–15.pdf (accessed 9 September 2009).
VASAB (2009) *VASAB Long-Term Perspective for the Territorial Development of the Baltic Sea Region*, Draft of 19 March 2009 for Public Consultation. Online. Available HTTP: www.vasab.org/documents.php?go=display&ID=63 (accessed 1 August 2009).
Vet, J., M. de, Boot, L. and Hollanders, M. (2000) *Regional Policy in Estonia, Latvia and Lithuania: Main Report*. On behalf of DG Regional Policy, European Commission. Rotterdam: NEI Regional and Urban Development in cooperation with Estonian Institute of Future studies, Latvian Academy of Science Institute of Economics, Lithuania Economic Research Centre.
Wenger, E. (1998) *Communities of Practice: Learning, Meaning, and Identity*, Cambridge: Cambridge University Press.
Yamazaki-Honda, R. (2005) 'Territorial Policy in OECD Countries', *Planning Theory and Practice*, 6(3): 406–409.

13 Regional promotion and competition

An examination of approaches to FDI attraction in the Czech Republic, Poland and Slovakia

Paweł Capik

Introduction

The past two decades have brought about profound changes to the range of spheres of socio-economic life in Central and Eastern European (CEE) countries. Transition to a market economy, integration with the global economy and accession to the European Union (EU) have all offered significant opportunities, but have equally been sources of multiple challenges for public administrations at all levels of the administrative hierarchy. After initial years of considerable hardship and declining output, gradually these countries started recording successes in restructuring their economies, legal environments and institutional frameworks (Ivanička and Ivanička 2007). The period of initial downturn has been succeeded by growth years (curbed only recently by the global financial crisis), decreasing inflation, increased political stability and concurrent efforts fostering integration with the world economy.

These changes have been taking place in the peculiar circumstances where globalization processes are reducing the significance of national boundaries and 'regions more so than nations, become major competitors on the global market place' (Stanilov 2007: 32). Recent EU enlargements have promoted such processes in two ways: (1) by increasingly empowering regions to shape their destiny in legal and administrative terms and partially in financial terms, and (2) facilitating the operations of international capital and consequently contributing to the creation of new cross-national regionalization patterns often with little regard for national borders. Both of these processes are aimed at encouraging the integration of new Member States with other areas of the EU, effectively contributing to an increased competitiveness of the Union, a daunting task considering the size of the areas and the scale and complexity of their problems (cf. Maier Chapter 11). The process of integration is obstructed by a number of difficulties, two of which provide part of the context for this chapter. First, the issue of socio-economic and territorial disparities discussed by Kule *et al.* in Chapter 12 and Maier in Chapter 11 characterize many of the most recent entrants. Second, the decentralization of administrative powers and responsibilities, particularly those closely associated with regional development, has a very short history (Pallagst and Mercier 2007) and arguably is still far from being concluded. However, this does not mean that regional and local municipalities are not actively involved in bringing their territories in line with the rest of their respective countries (and subsequently the other EU Member States) and securing prosperous futures for their territories. While the specific ways of doing this vary from country to country, as illustrated by discussions in many chapters in this volume, some general directions can be identified. One of them undoubtedly has been the general openness towards multinational enterprises (cf. Tewdwr-Jones Chapter 3).

In line with the wider principles established at the initial stages of transformation (e.g. the Washington Consensus) foreign multinationals were considered as one of the key means to achieve progress and lead to structural upgrade. Many countries, often with the support of EU funding, have established national investment promotion agencies initially as the main and the only agent in charge of attracting foreign direct investments (Young 2004). With the progressing decentralization (Gorzelak 2003), regional and local authorities have come to realize more recently the potential associated with the multinational enterprises (MNE). Many of them, either on their own initiative or with some external stimulus (e.g. creation of a special economic zone) have begun to actively promote their areas, with a view to attracting mobile companies (Florek 2004; Capik 2007). Simultaneously, MNEs started to recognize opportunities offered by CEE markets and become interested in efficiency gains opportunities (Artisen-Maksimenko 2000; Turnock 2005). Perceiving MNEs as a potential source of capital, employment and innovation, or in other words a quick solution to prolonged structural problems, regional authorities became increasingly interested in attracting mobile companies. Their attractiveness and growing popularity have inevitably led to increased competition between countries and between different regions within each of the countries. Numerous regional authorities have become increasingly active in promoting and marketing their regions in an attempt to beat the competition and attract higher levels of FDI. It can be argued that a determining factor in the success of any such promotional strategy is likely to depend on the extent to which it can be tailored to the specific territorial capital of a particular region. Yet most regional authorities appear to make little effort to understand the endogenous potentials of their territories, in most cases leading to a 'one-size-fits-all' approach in the strategies adopted, often in an attempt to mirror successful western experiences. However, emerging evidence suggests that regional promotion practices developed by those seeking to reinvent the post-industrial cities of the western economies require adjustments to make them more appropriate to the reality of places in CEE.

One such area where the modifications are necessary and recently became more evident is the administration of promotion, including the engagement of formal organizations and inclusion of informal institutions. Regional authorities do not operate in a vacuum, and indeed over the past decade a considerable number of other public and private organizations have become directly or indirectly involved with promotional activities. Whilst arguably the emergence of this wider promotion community can be seen as an initial stage in the creation of a competitive region, the evidence presented later in the chapter suggests that we should not hasten to draw this conclusion just yet. The set of institutions involved, as well as the extent of their involvement, varies from country to country. Nevertheless in general the group usually includes local municipalities, regional development agencies, associations of MNEs, and individual large multinationals interested in expanding their supplier and customer base (Capik 2007). The scale and impact of local municipalities' activities in this context have been elaborated elsewhere (cf. Florek 2004; Jarczewski 2007). However, despite the emergence of such a promotion community, it is the regional authorities responsible for territorial development who effectively remain at the centre of these complex policy networks. It can be argued that there are a number of practical and administrative reasons for this. Regional administrations link the tacit knowledge and 'territorial capital' of the different locales with the possibility to tap into the networks of national organizations and influence them. Furthermore, despite often considerable financial constraints and limited fiscal powers, regional levels of administration to a large extent design and implement development strategies, which more and more often include an explicit promotional element.

It is therefore the promotional activities performed by the regional authorities that are the primary focus of this chapter. In general this contribution aims to advance the debate on FDI promotion and its selected procedures and mechanisms within the 'place marketing' framework in the context of emerging 'epistemic communities' of agents for FDI promotion. By doing so the chapter focuses on horizontal and vertical dimensions of the organization of promotional activities and selected strategic aspects of FDI attraction schemes, including but not limited to the identification and knowledge of national and international competition in regions of the Czech Republic, Poland and Slovakia. The initial part of the chapter discusses the conceptual issues of place promotion, highlighting inconsistencies and deficiencies in the current literature. Next the specific context of CEE place promotion is explored. The findings of the empirical research are presented in the latter part of the chapter which draws attention to the emergence of 'promotion communities', followed by conclusions and recommendations for further study. The presented discussion is a result of initial desk-based research complemented with study of the FDI promotional activities of regional authorities in the Czech Republic, Poland and Slovakia. Secondary data has been sourced from national statistical offices, national banks and national investment promotion agencies. Primary data was obtained in the form of a postal survey to all 38 CEE regional authorities (14 regional authorities in Czech Republic, 16 in Poland and 8 in Slovakia), all of whom responded. The chapter focuses on arguably the cornerstone of regional promotion, namely the strategic issues of organization and competition identification, in an attempt to shed some light on the emerging promotion community and to enhance the knowledge base for future policy decisions.

The case for FDI promotion in the regional development context

In corporate environments, promotion is a direct way in which an organization tries to communicate with its various audiences with the aim of moving forward a product, service or an idea in a distribution channel. It attempts to influence the knowledge, attitudes and behaviour of its recipients (Stanley 1977; Brassington and Pettitt 2003). Promotion mix comprises the following five elements: (1) advertising, which can be defined as any paid form of non-personal, mass communication. Personal selling (2) on the other hand, involves interpersonal communication in the form of field, retail or door-to-door selling. Sales promotion (3) engages short-term schemes stimulating the purchase of the promoted object, while publicity and public relations (4) involve coordinated activities building good relations with many interest groups, not just the customers (Burnett 1993; Kotler and Armstrong 2001). Direct marketing (5) borrows from the elements discussed and involves creating one-to-one relationships with individual customers in the mass markets. Additionally Belch and Belch (2004) distinguish a sixth element of promotion – internet marketing, which relies on the interactive media and allows 'back-and-forth flow of information whereby users can participate and modify the form and content of the information they receive in real time' (Belch and Belch 2004: 20). Essentially then, promotion aims to communicate the qualities of a given product or service and persuade the target customer to purchase it (Kotler and Armstrong 2001). The question arises of how it could be understood within a regional policy context when the 'product' is a socially and economically diversified multidimensional space, i.e. a region?

Place promotion has a long and eventful history dating back to the ancient pilgrimages (Beinart 2001), through the settlement encouragements during Viking times (Ashworth and Voogd 1990) and increasingly systematic practices that have evolved over the last one and a half centuries (Ward 1998), to gradually more specialized activities aimed at attracting specific target groups. Ashworth and Voogd (1994) recognized that in more recent times, and within the context of various conceptual developments including the competitive cities, competitive regions and civic boosterism agendas, those involved with and responsible for urban and regional development have increasingly engaged with marketing techniques generally and with promotion in particular. Such activities play an increasing role in the attempts of a particular locality to manage the impacts of globalization, epitomized by mobile industries and political change (Young and Kaczmarek 1999). If place marketing is understood as customer-oriented regional policy, it can be concluded that promotion is a vital instrument of such a policy. Invariably it is informed by and benefits from other aspects within the marketing approach which offers place promoters practical expertise and techniques to distinguish their areas from the competitors. In order to achieve this a range of activities are necessary including unique and targeted advertising, successful public relations activities, negotiations with investors and an attractive and coherent set of investment incentives and post-investment services (Gold and Ward 1994; Fitzsimons 1995; Wells and Wint 2000; Zanatta *et al.* 2006).

There is a higher degree of consensus about the role and suitability of the application of regional promotion than on its actual impact on regional development. As Bradley *et al.* (2002: 62) identify: 'We know little of the actual importance of place promotion to the actual decision making process of its intended audiences.' For various reasons there is little consensus on the effectiveness of any of the regional promotion tools. Importantly there appears to be an absence of credible and systematic research into the evaluation of the effectiveness of promotional practices. Underlying it, however, there is lack of clear, accepted methods for such evaluation (especially in case of image campaigns), which at least in part is caused by the relatively limited critical interest of academics (and practitioners) in this long performed, yet still little understood practice. Also the debate on the effectiveness of various incentives schemes is ongoing. Specialized literature on FDI promotion suggests that public incentives are not the most important factor in determining a country's attractiveness for investors (Zanatta *et al.* 2006), however, as Navaretti and Venables (2004) stress, they can influence the MNEs final decision when all other factors are comparable for competing locations. Other studies also provide enough evidence to suggest that place promotion can have an impact on location decision making. Burgess and Wood's (1988) study of the promotional effort in relation to London Docklands concluded that the majority of small and medium sized companies that relocated into the area were in some way influenced by the promotion campaign by the London Docklands Development Corporation. It was clear, the authors argue, 'that advertising had played a significant role in attracting small companies to the Enterprise Zone [...], and the rate relief offered in the Enterprise Zone was a significant factor' (Burgess and Wood 1988: 101).

Place promotion is clearly a highly complex activity and the process encounters multiple obstacles. The costs in terms of financial and other resources of promotional activities, as well as their questionable effectiveness, are amongst the main problems that those involved in promotion need to tackle (Young and Kaczmarek 1999). Indeed the continuous budget constraints have often constituted the key problem for regions and localities in CEE. More recently resources from the structural funds have provided welcome support for some, bringing other issues, many of which have been experienced by other places around the world, to the fore. Burgess (1982) and Burgess and Wood (1988) claim that the major operational difficulty that many places are facing is the lack of coherence of their promotional actions resulting in production of a fragmented image and an unstable (and therefore unreliable) investment climate. As will be discussed in the latter parts of the chapter, this issue is highly relevant to the CEE regions.

A well designed regional promotion campaign should meet numerous conditions (Lodge 2002; Rainisto 2003; Quelch and Jocz 2005; MIGA 2006) and the internal coherence of promotional efforts and the adequate targeting and recognition of competitors are critical in this respect (Kotler *et al.* 1999). Promoters require a substantial amount of knowledge in order to be able to promote a place successfully and this requires means of generating knowledge and also the effective application of this knowledge in practice. For instance, in order to persuade the potential investors about the advantages of locating their business in a particular region, the authorities (and other promoters) first need to develop a profound understanding of the specific territorial capital of the region (cf. Maier Chapter 11) and clearly define unique selling points of their place product(s). Additionally efforts to attract FDI need to be a part of a wider development strategy seeking to achieve particular development goals of the different stakeholders within the regional community. For example some places while granting investment incentives require investors to recruit highly skilled workers locally and to cooperate with local research institutes and universities (Zanatta *et al.* 2006). Furthermore targeting a region's actions increases the chances of internal coherence of the promotional activity, increases the efficiency of often limited disposable funds by directing investment flows into priority sectors (Wells and Wint 2000) and avoids situations when everything is promoted to everybody (Kotler *et al.* 1999). Recognizing competitors and their activities allows the regional authorities to prepare distinctive and unique packages for targeted investors. It also helps to position and distinguish the region's offer and to appraise the reasons behind the popularity of a region with investors in relation to its competitors.

Different places – same promotional aims

Young and Lever (1997) considering promotion as an 'an important element of entrepreneurialism of the city', assert that promotion campaigns are designed to increase the knowledge and understanding of a place. Based on the points presented earlier and evidence shown in the latter part of the chapter, the aspect of 'knowledge and understanding' in the first instance refers to the organizations involved with the promotion of the area, who need to develop it in order to be able to convincingly pass it on to the targeted audiences. Paddison (1993: 340) gives promotion a broader role 'rather than advertising per se', and argues that promotion seeks to rebuild and reconstruct the image of the place, i.e. influence and shape a particular kind of knowledge of the place in the eyes of external audiences. Supporting this argument Wu (2000) indicates that in the case of places, promotion presents and represents a new image to raise the competitiveness of the area. Such images tend to be selective, generalized and reaching into the future rather than reflecting the 'here and now' of the region. Invariably image campaigns are constructed on a preselected core idea using a set of characteristics (image staples) supported by a variety of promotional tools and channels, including imagery and slogans. Hence we hear communicated histories about 'innovative region', 'region of the future' or 'green region' and so on. The aim of image recreation is to eliminate the adverse knowledge and negative images held by external audiences, i.e. overcome the negative perceptions of the industrial past, backward economic structure, lack of growth potential, and only subsequently and indirectly to attract investment. This interpretation, however, is unnecessarily limited to just one type of place, namely the post-industrial, which largely implies the city scale, or city-region at most. Despite many examples in the academic literature supporting this argument (e.g. Madsen 1992; Goodwin 1993; Holcomb 1993; Young and Kaczmarek 1999; Wu 2000), some promotional activities have been undertaken with various degrees of success in other types and scales of places – as documented by Ward's (1998) historical analysis of promotional materials of states (e.g. Georgia, Michigan), metropolitan areas (e.g. Atlanta, Baltimore) and towns (Blackpool, Spa) in the United States, the UK and selected countries of continental Europe. Also Florek (2003) offers substantial evidence of the involvement of local communities in Poland in generic place promotion and Jarczewski (2007) explains local promotion efforts aimed at investment attraction. Furthermore Endzina and Luneva (2004) explore the issues around the recent branding strategy of Latvian government agencies.

Van den Berg *et al.* (2002: 107) argue that 'image and identity are important promotion factors, but cannot by themselves change the general perception of a city or a region'. Therefore place promotion cannot stand on its own and should be considered as an addition, albeit vital, to a broader development strategy and everyday life of a region (Borchert 1994). 'Every aspect of public policy from street cleaning to the provision of housing, from equal opportunities to public transport, from the award of public contracts to sewage outfalls can be made to bear the imprint of place selling ethos' (Ward 1998: 3). Indeed, the publicizing of the features and advantages of places acts alongside other elements such as financial packages, infrastructure improvements and land and facility provisions in an attempt to influence economic decision makers (Young and Lever 1997; Kotler *et al.* 1999; Lever 2001). Place promotion therefore includes all or a purpose-defined selection of the presented promotion mix tools used in conjunction with place development policies fostering (i.e. promoting) the activities of selected target groups – be it tourists, settlers or investors.

Place promotion and FDI attraction

Loewendahl (2001) distinguishes four consecutive stages of investment promotion, all requiring the promotional agents to construct new, purpose-oriented knowledge or the application of knowledge created in one of the preceding stages: (1) strategy and organization (development policy context, structure of investment promotion, competitive positioning, sector targeting strategy), (2) lead generation (targeted promotion), (3) facilitation (project handling) and (4) investment services (after-care, product improvement, monitoring, evaluation). While the initial stage is concerned with planning and strategy setting, the remaining three involve concrete actions and activities and could thus be called promotion per se. Consequently regional promotion is aimed at investment attraction and aims to achieve three interrelated objectives – the improvement of the image of a place in the eyes of the investment community (image-building activities aimed at potential investors, investment consulting firms and banks, amongst others), the direct generation of investment and the provision of investment and post-investment services. In their study Wells and Wint (2000) identify the different phases of FDI promotion. Initially the relevant authorities are more concerned with image-building activities and gradually move towards investment generation and service provision. However, such a gradual approach unnecessarily extends the time-span of investment promotion attempts, increasing the risk of losing out on some of the projects captured 'in the mean time' by competing areas. All three objectives are interlinked and should not be considered as substitutes but rather as complementary. Image building is a very complex and time-consuming process. Some of the necessary techniques and tools are also used in achieving the other two remaining objectives. Investment generating activities (e.g. investment missions, road-shows, seminars, 'sales' presentation; Wells and Wint 2000) can and should be used to create an image of a region as a place welcoming for the investors. This picture can be further strengthened by the swift provision of adequate services for both potential and current investors.

From a regional development perspective, apart from image improvement (or indeed creation) activities, a set of investment incentives needs to be included in effective FDI attraction schemes. For over three decades now, national governments have increasingly adopted measures to facilitate the entry of foreign companies. Next to the liberalized legal frameworks for foreign entities and guarantees for repatriation of investment and profits (regulatory incentives), tax (fiscal) incentives and investment subsidies (financial incentives) are amongst the most common measures (UNCTAD 2000, OECD 2003). Already in the mid 1990s over 100 countries were providing various FDI incentives and many more have introduced such incentives since then (Blomström and Kokko 2003). To foster regional development, national governments delegate some of the incentive granting powers to regional jurisdictions. The main benefit of giving the lower administrative level a freer hand lies in the more intimate knowledge of the socio-economic situation (industries and individual investment projects) that is available locally (OECD 2003). This necessities the involvement of various local and regional participants (formal organizations and often informal institutions) creating an environment and an opportunity for the emergence of a regional promotional community, whose task is to articulate and communicate the potential of the region in the most effective way.

Deficiencies in the current debate

The growing literature on place promotion, marketing and, more recently, branding, remain insufficient to create a sound foundation for academic discussion and practical applicability (Anholt 2002). In fact, what is particularly relevant in the context of the debate presented in this book, there seems to be a lack of a systematic approach and empirical evidence supporting the theoretical base with real-life arguments, making the whole concept appear to be an unreliable and still little-understood panacea (Papadopoulos and Heslop 2002). Despite evolving over a number of years, FDI promotion remains a largely under-explored subject since the majority of studies commonly focus on general image campaigns and more recently place branding efforts. There is also a limited diversity in existing research considering the spatial coverage of such activity. Existing works are mainly concerned with the post-industrial cities in developed economies, with the majority of examples coming from Western Europe (e.g. Sjøholt 1994; van den Berg *et al.* 2002), particularly the UK (e.g. Madsen 1992; Young and Lever 1997; Daskou *et al.* 2005) and the United States (e.g. Holcomb 1993; Kotler *et al.* 1993; Rainisto 2003). CEE examples are only recently starting to emerge in the current place marketing, promotion and branding discourse. This is caused by two inter-linked factors. First, it is the effect of short history or indeed lack of such prac-tices and, second, the embryonic academic interest in this subject. Young and Kaczmarek's (1999) evaluation of promotion activities in Łódź (yet another post-industrial city) is one of the very few examples of more comprehensive research in CEE countries. Studies concerned with FDI promotion are comparatively scarce although Young (2004) offers an insight into the FDI attraction activities of CzechInvest, the Czech national investment promotion agency. In his later work the author scrutinizes the different general practices of place marketing at a range of administrative levels in selected CEE countries (Young 2005).

In these circumstances, this chapter aims to further the current academic debate by offering analysis of empirical findings concerned with FDI promotional activ-ities performed by the regional authorities in the context of the emerging promo-tion communities in the Czech Republic, Poland and Slovakia. As evidenced by many recent examples (including Hyundai-Kia and Hankook's locations and fre-quent law amendments aimed at increasing attractiveness of the national business environment), the three countries find themselves competing for FDI projects.

Regional promotion and FDI attraction in the Central Eastern European context

Throughout the 1990s CEE countries became a popular FDI destination. A few years of slowdown after the turn of the century were followed by considerable growth of investment flows to the region following EU enlargement (see Table 13.1). When deciding where to establish their activities MNEs often consider locations in one of the three countries: Czech Republic, Poland and Slovakia (Helinska-Hughes and Hughes 2003). Once the country has been selected, trends up to now indicate that the capital city and its immediate surroundings are the favoured location (Domański 2001; Young 2004). This contributes to increasing national disparities, i.e. the further growth of the core areas at the cost of already disadvantaged and more geographically peripheral regions (cf. Tewdwr-Jones Chapter 3, Kule *et al.* Chapter 12 and Maier Chapter 11) and this has important implications for other regions within the country. Competition for FDI takes place not only on an international level but also intra-nationally. This requires actions from those responsible for FDI attraction at both national and regional level in order to avoid the situation where some localities are 'regular losers' in development terms (Young 2005).

Table 13.1 FDI flows and percentage of stock in Central-Eastern European capital-city regions

	FDI flows ($ million)				*% of FDI stock in capital city region[a]*		
	2000	*2003*	*2005*	*2007*	*2000*	*2003*	*2005*
Czech Republic	4.9	2.1	11.6	9.1	47.6[b]	46.2	46.7[c]
Poland	9.3	4.1	10.4	17.6	n.d.	30.0	n.d.
Slovakia	2.0	0.7	2.1	3.3	60.4	69.2	67.1

Sources: www.czechinvest.org, www.sario.sk, www.paiz.gov.pl, UNCTAD 2002, UNCTAD 2005, UNCTAD 2008.

Notes
a No data for years after 2005.
b Flows.
c 2004 data.
n.d. – no data available.

When preparing and performing their FDI promotional activities CEE countries face numerous specific challenges, which are further reinforced once the promotional activities are performed by the regional authorities.

Every place has an image, however its impact and range are geographically uneven. While some places boast worldwide recognition, others are known locally or nationally at best (Anholt 2006). Some of the major cities in CEE countries, such as Prague or Cracow, are increasingly recognized globally as popular tourist destinations. Growing business traffic and FDI inflows offer opportunities to build a positive image of the country in the minds of potential investors. All too often however, such an image is constructed based on the experience of the capital city and possibly its immediate vicinity. This is likely to be an obstruction for the provincial regions aiming to raise awareness and create their image amongst global investors. The majority of the regions in the Czech Republic, Poland and Slovakia therefore face a difficult task of overcoming the country and/or its capital city image. This often involves refuting national stereotypes and prejudices dominated and conditioned by the post-war history of the area.

The economic dominance of the capital city regions is another obstacle in promoting non metropolitan CEE regions as highly rewarding FDI destinations. Furthermore there is competition from other regions within, but also outside the country. The level of precision in defining the actual target group(s) poses another difficulty. Additional barriers relate to the administrative division of powers and responsibilities vested with regional and local authorities, their limited experience and competence in promotional activities and only limited cooperation between promotional agencies (Capik 2006). In the next section, selected FDI promotion issues and activities performed by the Czech, Polish and Slovak regions in these peculiar circumstances will be examined.

Multiple dimensions of promotion organization

Regional promotion, predominantly managerial, is also a political process (Paddison 1993) involving a range of actors and agencies, all characterized by different tacit knowledge and posing questions about their responsibilities, interdependence and the coordination of actions. It is a multi-scalar procedure and, as evidence to date suggests, its vertical and horizontal organization differs greatly (e.g. Burgess and Wood 1988; Young and Kaczmarek 1999; Lever 2001; Florek 2004; Young 2005). In an ideal scenario the principle of subsidiarity dictates that in a bottom-up approach to regional development, it would be imperative for the regional authorities to have a leading role in initiating and coordinating FDI promotional activities. They should link national and local FDI promotion efforts, which requires budget and staff commitment and also a vision and integration of the promotional activities with wider development goals. As will be demonstrated below, such (ideal) circumstances are rarely observed in CEE reality.

The results of the research indicate that the majority (60 per cent) of the CEE regions investigated have a designated office within regional authorities responsible solely for regional promotion. However, there are considerable differences between the countries. Only three out of eight Slovakian and seven out of fourteen Czech regions claim to have promotional offices, while in Poland only three out of sixteen regions do not have one. The quality of those offices is considered to be average, indicating the regional authorities' awareness of scope for improvement.

Half of the offices are inadequately staffed and staff qualifications vary across the three countries. The majority of the staff have good regional economic development university education in comparison to training in marketing and promotion (see Table 13.2). Practical experience in both areas is assessed less favourably. This could reflect the fact that the majority of the employees in the promotional offices are fairly young and inexperienced and come from an economic rather than marketing background. Polish promotional offices scored highest in terms of quality while Slovakian ones achieved lowest marks. The generally medium and low scores may be a reason why the majority of regional authorities (85 per cent) use external consultants in order to inform both policy and practical approaches. In the Czech Republic regional administrations tend to commission private consultancy firms, whereas Polish and Slovakian regions tend to rely on academics, regional companies and local municipalities. This creates the potential for the further evolution of a 'community of practice' (Wenger 1998) that ultimately may have the potential to evolve into an 'epistemic community' (Haas 1992), although the current ad hoc and purpose-driven nature of the contacts make it impossible to classify them as such at this time. The findings presented above, especially the number of regions actually having promotional offices within their administrative structures, emphasize the relative novelty of regional promotion in CEE. The fact is additionally highlighted by the fact that only half of regional administrations evaluate their promotion activities internally and none are subject to appraisal by any external organization.

Table 13.2 Evaluation of staff training and experience

	Marketing and promotion				Regional and economic development			
	Czech Republic	Poland	Slovakia	Average	Czech Republic	Poland	Slovakia	Average
Training	3.16	4.33	3.5	3.66	3.66	4.83	3.5	3.99
Experience	3.66	4.09	3.0	3.58	3.66	4.08	3.0	3.58

Sources: Author's research.

Notes
1 Scale 1 (low) – 5 (high), only full marks were allowed. Table provides average marks.

Contrary to the impression one may get studying 'place marketing' and investment promotion literature, FDI attraction is a multi-agent process requiring regional authorities to develop relationships with a variety of partners in the region and beyond. Evidence suggests that the nature of such relations is often purpose-driven or related to a particular task environment. Whereas relationships with organizations that influence the business climate tend to be collaborative, the nature of the relationship with local municipalities or business services organizations tend to be more top-down or consultative at best. Alternatively the relationship may be more competitive in nature or may be limited to a simple exchange of experiences. The main driver behind the development of such relationships is a desire of the regional authorities to control and consult those 'beneath' the regional administrative level and to influence those 'above' and parallel. Invariably, some of these relationships and mechanisms have been developed in knowledge arenas related to other task environments such as planning and strategy development, while others emerge as new and are explicitly promotion focused. Whatever the current nature of relations, the ability to generate spontaneous associations and/or participate in more permanent networks oriented towards achieving strategic objectives, arguably remains the key to successful promotion (Domański 1997).

Apart from regional authorities, a number of other public and private agencies often exist who are involved either directly or indirectly in regional promotion aimed at FDI attraction. For example in Britain local councils remain the main organizations, formerly often supported by the Urban Development Corporations in some areas. Other public or semi-public agents (e.g. airports, trade fairs, conventions centres), private organizations such as Chambers of Commerce and other ad hoc organizations then gather round them (Ward 1998). Although the regional authorities are not necessarily cooperating closely with all such institutions they should ideally be aware of their existence and operations to try to effectively manage the promotional activities (Bickl 2004; Young 2005). Again, the reality often diverges from the ideal scenario.

In CEE countries the number of organizations involved varies as does the nature and extent of their relations with the regional authorities. The evidence suggests that Polish regions operate within wider networks than their Czech and Slovak counterparts. Contrary to Loewendahl's (2001) argument, the wider networks (up to four organizations in the Czech Republic, six in Poland and five in Slovakia) are not conditioned by factors directly linked with perceived investors' preferences. There also appears to be no detectable correlation between the size of the region, the levels of prosperity and unemployment or the proportion of national FDI and the size of the networks within which they operate. Instead the participation in wider networks would appear to be influenced rather by less tangible cultural factors and reflects regional political arrangements.

Apart from regional authorities the promotion community commonly includes other public organizations, notably regional development agencies (RDAs). However, Polish regional authorities also differ from their Czech and Slovakian counterparts, in that none of them consider the national investment promotion agency as part of their networks. In all but two of the 16 Polish regions the RDAs are involved with FDI attraction whereas only half of the Czech and Slovakian RDAs participate in such activities. The dissimilarity of Polish practice and its more clear regional and purpose-oriented focus is further emphasized by the fact that one in two regional authorities mention regional tourist boards as their partners compared to one in three of the Czech and one in four of Slovakian authorities. Additionally special economic zones and technology parks are more common promotion partners of the authorities in Poland compared to the other two countries.

The representation of private capital within the promotion communities, although fairly widespread, is somewhat sporadic. The inclusion of Chambers of Commerce by four regions and fairs and exhibitions companies by another two regions serve as rare exceptions. Equally civil society also forms an under-represented group. Only two of the surveyed regions (Dolnoslaśkie in Poland and Karlovovarský kraj in the Czech Republic) identify civic organizations involved with promotion. This situation is clearly distant from the highly idealistic circumstances presented by Kotler *et al.* (1999) that stress the importance of very broad participation in promotion ranging from taxi drivers, individual tourist agents and industrial associations, to societal groups and investment promotion agencies. Equally it is contrary to the theoretical propositions underpinning the notion of 'epistemic communities' promoted by the editors of this book, which seeks to extend the concept beyond the restricted group of experts to engage a wider representation of diverse stakeholders.

Notably not all the organizations indicated by the authorities are directly involved with FDI promotion. Nonetheless the fact that regional authorities recognize their activities suggests a degree of coordination in terms of promotion between the different target groups, which can only strengthen the message for potential investors. However, the coherence between the actions and messages transmitted by different agencies is often only superficial (Capik 2007). Moreover, even in the view of the regional authorities the level of coordination of promotional efforts between themselves and the various organizations is satisfactory (43 per cent) rather than very good (26 per cent). Typically, Polish and Czech regions differ also in this respect. While 54 per cent of Czech regions assess the coordination as satisfactory, 64 per cent of the Polish ones judge it to be good or very good, a view shared by a comparable percentage of Slovakian regional authorities. The evidence suggests that neither the size of the networks or their qualitative composition impact the level of coordination between its members. Furthermore the assessment of the regional authorities is not related to regional share of country's FDI stock or to economic performance of the region. The reasons for an overall more synchronized approach must therefore lay elsewhere, possibly in the nature of individual relationships or political arrangements. However, when requested to indicate the best and worst partner institutions, the CEE regional authorities mainly refrained from providing information. Over 80 per cent of them did not indicate the organization with which the cooperation is worst, and 60 per cent failed to name the most effective partner. Those which provided the information in the Czech Republic and Poland most commonly praised the regional development agencies and in Slovakia the national tourism board. There is also no individual type of organization that the Czech and Polish authorities complain about, while universally for the Slovakian regions the national investment promotion agency remains the most troublesome partner.

The promotion networks discussed above have a rather horizontal structure, in other words they involve agencies operating on a regional level, with the vertical dimension extending only upwards to include the national investment promotion agencies and the national tourist boards. This needs to be complemented by the 'downward' extension of the FDI promotion networks to include the key organizations on a sub-regional level, namely the numerous local urban and rural communities. It can be argued that local municipalities, perhaps more than other sub-regional organizations, need to be incorporated into the networks of regional authorities due to their powers and direct interest in FDI attraction (Jarczewski 2007; Drahokoupil 2007). Research by Young and Kaczmarek (2000) demonstrated that 63 per cent of Polish municipalities undertake some form of promotional activity and over 80 per cent of them see attracting FDI as their main function. Although research by Florek (2003) clearly indicated that over 70 per cent of local municipalities consider investors to be their most important target group, not all municipalities are equally active in FDI promotion, with the larger urban ones tending to be more dynamic than the rural ones.

CEE regional authorities seem to be aware of the importance of local municipalities and 30 per cent of them claim to consult regularly with all urban and rural localities in relation to promotional activities. Furthermore, 47 per cent consult some local municipalities (up to half of them), while a quarter of regional authorities do not involve local administrations in their promotional activities. Interestingly, the existence of consultations (or lack thereof) is not related to the size of the region or the number of municipalities within the region, i.e. regions comprised of a smaller number of municipalities are no more likely to consult some or all of them than the areas consisting of a higher numbers of municipalities. Once again this practice differs between the three countries. The involvement of all local municipalities is most common in Poland (44 per cent). In contrast Czech regions tend to be much more selective in their choice of local partners and on average consult just over 10 per cent of local municipalities. In Slovakia both approaches are equally popular, but the more selective regions on average consult 30 per cent of localities. There appears to be no correlation between the number of localities which the regions involve in their FDI promotion and the number of partner institutions on the regional level, i.e. the regional authorities are equally likely to develop their promotional networks horizontally and vertically.

These results should however be treated with caution. Considering the vast numbers of local municipalities (2,478 in total in all 38 regions, on average more than 150 in each of the regions in Poland) it is difficult to assume real and equal participation of all local communities in the promotional actions of their region.

Nevertheless the Polish regions seem to be more outward-oriented and are more likely to cooperate with others than their Czech and Slovak counterparts and this is consistent with earlier findings and other research into other aspects of regional policy formulation and governance (e.g. Myant and Smith 2006). More dynamic localities may have a significant impact not only on the promotional strategy of a particular region but can overshadow images of others and the whole the region (Madsen 1993). Therefore the objective of involving localities in the regional authorities FDI promotion is twofold. First, it should guarantee that local needs are fairly represented and, second, their participation helps to ensure the coherence of the promotional efforts, which is arguably one of the main success factors (Loewendahl 2001; Kotler and Gertner 2002).

Just over 50 per cent of the regions believe that no single locality dominates its promotional activities. However, a comparable amount claim that some local areas either dominate or significantly impact their promotion. Most often it is the regional capitals or other large cities that dominate, while rural areas rarely have major influence on the activities of the regional authorities. The importance of regional capitals is further emphasized in the context of image and promotional spending. For example some of the Polish regional capitals and other big cities often spend more on promotion (generally) than do the regional authorities. For example promotional spending in Szczecin and Warsaw in 2007 reached $7.3 million, while Poznań expenditure totalled $992,000 (Rzeczpospolita 2007). In contrast the FDI promotion budgets of the corresponding regional authorities in 2004 totalled $54,000, $292,000 and $81,000 respectively. Consequently it gives some grounds for the conviction expressed by over 45 per cent of CEE regional authorities that the perceptions of the region are dominated by those of their capitals. In addition a further 11 per cent claim that the image of the capital city significantly overshadows the regional image. Only 14 per cent of regions also point to other main cities and none mentions any rural locality.

The local municipalities which have a major impact on the image of a region are typically consulted by the regional authorities (80 per cent of cases). However, despite significantly influencing the perceptions of the region, they do not automatically dominate their promotion. There were only six cases where regional authorities admit that their promotion is subjugated to the capital city which also overshadows the image of the region.

Generally then, the two objectives identified earlier are met, albeit at different levels. The involvement of localities in the regional promotion is biased towards the bigger urban communities. Usually, however, no individual community, including the regional capitals, is overrepresented in the promotion of the region.

Utilising international networks for FDI promotion

The collaboration networks of regions frequently extend beyond national borders. While such cooperation has traditionally often been dominated by the educational and cultural agenda (especially within the EU), subsequently other issues have come to the fore (e.g. environmental protection). More recently the

CEE regions are increasingly involved in networks and partnerships fostering economic development, be it by the means of export promotion or twinning for public policy design. Such cooperation can either be institutionalized and legally sanctioned (e.g. Euroregions, Association of European Regions) or come in form of less structured associations and initiatives (e.g. partner regions, Innovating Regions in Europe). Invariably however, despite other primary objectives, such groups offer potential for the promotion and FDI attraction (Young 2005). Therefore it is important for CEE regions to participate in these groupings and from the FDI perspective specifically the ones oriented towards economic issues. This would increase the international visibility of the region and extend the networks of potential partners and would also provide a platform for exchanging experiences and expertise. CEE regions are involved in bilateral partnerships, but also in multilateral associations. In fact all regions report having mutual partnership arrangements and four in five participate in alliances of usually pan-European scale. The most common amongst the latter type are the Assembly of European Regions and Committee of Regions. Both of these are characterized by intense political involvement in the European process. Another popular grouping indicated by the regional authorities is the Euroregions. With the exception of individual interior areas in the Czech Republic and Poland, all of the CEE regions constitute a part of at least one Euroregion, fostering transnational cooperation in environmental protection, cultural exchange and economic cooperation. In addition every Czech, Polish and Slovakian region reports its involvement in economic cooperation with other areas. Some of those partnerships are utilized to foster trade or exchange promotional experience, as discussed earlier, while others serve as a promotion tool itself. From the perspective of target markets and competition discussed in the subsequent part of the chapter, it is interesting to examine the geographical scope of such relations.

CEE regions cooperate on economic issues with regions in a wide variety of different EU and non-EU countries. The most popular of these types of relationships are with regions in large and strong European economies such as France, Germany and Italy. Areas in neighbouring countries were the second most common, albeit with significantly less regions indicating this type of cooperation. The geographical coverage of economic partnerships varies between the three countries. While Polish regions operate within more diverse networks, on average each Polish region has partnership arrangements with areas in six different countries, cooperation of Slovakian and Czech regions are usually limited to four and three countries respectively. The evidence also suggests that Polish regions cooperate more actively with areas in countries further afield (including China, India and South Korea) and in Eastern Europe, notably Ukraine, but also the Russian Federation.

Recognizing competition

Achieving a competitive edge over others remains one of the main factors determining the extent of involvement in promotion activities (Ward 1998). It is surprising therefore that the regional authorities tend to have only limited knowledge in relation to their competitors and to their own potential competitive edge. The place authorities are aware of certain qualities desired by the investors, but they show limited familiarity with the characteristics of their national and international competitors (Burgess 1982; Young and Lever 1997). Fretter (1993) notes that authorities make little effort to understand their competitors and as a result use similar if not identical approaches to promote divergent types of regions with different endowments and potential advantages. The current findings seem to question earlier research results, at least on the surface. The regional authorities in CEE claim to have a high awareness of national competition and are often capable of identifying the reasons behind it. Only 13 per cent of regions have difficulty with naming their rivals (see Figure 13.1), while over a third recognize neighbouring regions as their main competitor for FDI projects. Just a few percentage points less perceive the capital city region as their main competitor within respective nations. Again however, the results differ between the three countries. Half of the Polish regions point to their neighbours as their main rivals, while in the Czech Republic this is the case with only two out of 14 regions. Prague (region) is identified as the main competitor in FDI attraction by 36 per cent of Czech regions. Despite the highest concentration of FDI stock in Bratislava (see Table 13.1) only a quarter of Slovakian regions have identified the capital as their main competitor. In comparison 25 per cent of Polish regions see themselves in competition for mobile companies mainly with Warsaw. The reasons for this situation are likely to be diverse. Slovakian regional authorities understand that Bratislava is beyond their reach and constitutes what Kotler *et al.* (1999) call a superior competitor. This view is strengthened by the capital itself, which (like Prague and the surrounding region) believes that it has no serious competitors for FDI projects in the country. Warsaw's position on the other hand is contrary to the situation of the other two national capitals, reflecting the city's less dominant position in the national context. The regional authorities acknowledge the existence of the competition in Poland but Warsaw's

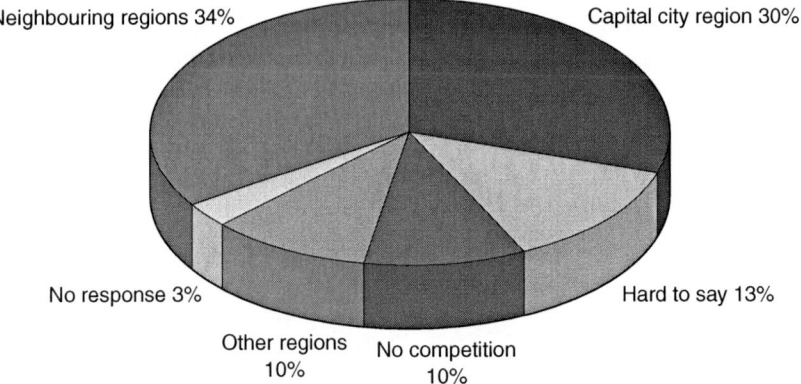

Figure 13.1 Main national competitors for regions (source: Author's elaboration).

dominance in levels of FDI stock is less evident and means that the regions often see their immediate neighbours as the main source of competition. This also reflects the somewhat incorrect conviction about the relative homogeneity of the country.

The main reason for the Czech, Polish and Slovakian regional authorities to feel competition from other regions in their respective countries relates to infrastructure deficiencies. In addition, 60 per cent of Polish and 40 per cent of Slovakian regions feel that they suffer from an inferior image in comparison to their competition, an opinion shared by only 20 per cent of their Czech counterparts. Almost half of the Polish regions and a quarter of Slovakian regions admit that their competitors are promoted better than themselves. Such views were expressed by just one regional authority in the Czech Republic.

International competition

The level of international competition awareness varies across the CEE regional authorities and between other organizations involved with FDI promotion. Perhaps the only common view is that the regions and localities of all three countries compete with other nations in CEE (Capik 2006). Over a half of the CEE regional authorities surveyed, mainly the Slovakian (76 per cent) and Polish (56 per cent) authorities, see themselves competing with neighbouring nations, while a third of them (mainly Czech) point to the remaining countries in more broadly defined CEE, including Bulgaria, Ukraine and Romania. The regions investigated felt that they are less competitive than their CEE counterparts but for different reasons than was the case in relation to national competitors. The regions stress the competition results primarily from labour market disadvantages such as inflexibility and cost inefficiency. Almost a third of the regions (mainly Polish and Slovakian) also point out to infrastructure deficits and the better connectivity and accessibility of their rivals. Czech regions additionally feel that unstable reforms and inadequate FDI incentives put them in a disadvantaged position. This again indicates how much Czech regional authorities rely on and are dominated by CzechInvest (Young 2004, 2005; Capik 2007).

The empirical evidence suggests that promotion activities performed by international competitors and their images are less important for CEE regions. This additionally highlights the need for regional authorities to perform effective promotion activities to out-compete national rivals and influence the flows of international capital in order to correct the uneven FDI stock distribution often fostered by the national investment promotion agencies. The evidence suggests that actors are aware of their competitors and, to a degree, this questions the findings of earlier studies. Regional authorities are often very aware of the existing competition and can identify competitors' features which put them in a disadvantaged position. However, the closer the competitors are located the better knowledge of their advantageous characteristics, which suggests that regions tend to rely on general, common knowledge rather than any systematic research.

Conclusions

Regional promotion aimed at FDI attraction is by no means a straightforward process of integrating marketing tools and principles into regional development policies. Promotion serves rather as a link between the two. Using selected marketing-based practices it can improve the efficiency of FDI attraction policies by strengthening the integrity of undertaken activities and implemented policies. However the level of importance assigned by the regional authorities to this still somewhat new policy tool varies. As with all instruments with a competitive element, this consequently results in winning and losing regions in terms of FDI attraction. As a consequence, the subsequent development of the losing regions can be compromised, contributing to further increase of interregional disparities which have become very apparent particularly after the recent enlargements of the EU.

Increasing FDI flows to CEE countries remain concentrated in and around capital cities and national investment promotion agencies persistently fail to address this situation. Progressing decentralization in a regional policy setting, albeit characterized by different pace and scope in the Czech Republic, Poland and Slovakia, has presented regional authorities with new opportunities also in the area of FDI attraction. Across the three countries these opportunities are capitalized upon at varying levels, but never fully. Two interlinked issues are closely associated with this situation. First, while the number of agencies and organizations involved in promotion increases, this is not accompanied by a satisfactory development of links, relationships and networking activities among them, therefore seriously hampering the consolidation of efficient promotion communities. In some instances the regional authorities take on the leading role, particularly in Poland, yet a dominant position of the national investment promotion agencies (especially in the Czech Republic and to a lesser degree in Slovakia) remain the key obstacle in fostering the development of a comprehensive bottom-up approach. While in theory national investment promotion agencies could act as a facilitator of the regional promotional effort, and a nucleus of the promotion community, all too often, guided by ignorance, they chose to act on their own, which at best does not help the consolidation of the promotion community but sustains its fragmentation.

Following the perspective adopted by the authors of the present volume, it is interesting to underline how the analyzed phenomena revealed a twofold dimension of the aspects of knowledge in regional promotion activities. Promoters' knowledge of their territorial capital and ways to effectively emphasize it remains limited. Despite their stated self-confidence and some encouraging evidence in the form of increasing recognition of competitors and their advantages, the same is usually true for regional administrations familiarity with various strategic and operational aspects of FDI promotion practice. Arguably a number of reasons contribute to this situation, most important amongst which seems to be only evolving expertise-driven, apolitical culture of decision making, inadequacy of financial resources as compared to the range of responsibilities and inefficient or non-existent inter-institutional links. Although the levels of existing knowledge and new knowledge creation are relatively limited, knowledge exchange occurs only sporadically due to the poor inter-agency links. The increasing number of place promoters within a region therefore does not constitute the appearance of a fully operational promotion community, as the links and networks between the agents are rarely in place.

The extent of the situation identified above varies between the three countries. In the Polish case regional authorities and other organizations seem to be working more closely and more coherently, while the national investment promotion agencies tends to dominate FDI attraction activities in the Czech Republic and Slovakia. At the national scale, the current level of development and wealth of a region seem to have little influence on the scope and coherence of its promotional effort, suggesting that the regional authorities are aware of the advantages of promotion and its potential to enhance the development of their areas and to bridge the disparity gap. Conversely it reflects the hubris of the more prosperous regions that seem to be convinced that even without engaging in promotion the investments will keep flowing their way. CEE regions are new players in the game of place selling and as such offer immense research opportunities. Further research is required to investigate the longitudinal development of regional FDI promotion communities and the effectiveness of their strategies. Such studies would provide the long awaited empirical evidence to demonstrate the vital role of different actors in promotion and ultimately wider regional development, as until now such actions remain based on assumptions.

Acknowledgements

I would like to express my thanks to the AESOP-YA Bratislava Conference participants for their feedback on the preliminary version of the chapter during and outside the conference sessions. Further I owe a debt of gratitude to the book editors, whose comments were critical in drafting of this chapter. My thanks also go to my PhD supervisors at the University of the West of Scotland for their valuable comments on the early version of the chapter.

References

Anholt, S. (2002) 'Forward', *Brand Management*, 9(4–5): 229–239.
—— (2006) 'Is place branding a capitalist tool?', *Place Branding*, 2(1): 1–4.
Artisen-Maksimenko, P. (ed.) (2000) *Multinationals in Eastern Europe*, Houndmills: Macmillan Press.
Ashworth, G. J. and Voogd, H. (1990) *Selling the city: marketing approaches in public sector urban planning*, London: Belheven Press.
—— (1994) 'Marketing and place promotion', in J. R. Gold and S. V. Ward (eds) *Place Promotion: the use of publicity and marketing to sell towns and regions*, Chichester: John Wiley & Sons.
Beinart, J. (2001) 'Image construction in premodern cities', in L. J. Vale and S. B. Warner Jr (eds) *Imagining the City – continuing struggles and new directions*, New Brunswick, NJ: CUPR.

Belch, G. E. and Belch, M. A. (2004) *Advertising and Promotion: an integrated marketing communications perspective*, Boston: McGrawHill.

Bickl, M. (2004) *Image Management in Old-Industrial Regions: policy learning, governance and leadership in North East England and the Ruhr*, PhD Thesis, Durham: University of Durham.

Blomström, M. and Kokko, A. (2003) *The Economics of Foreign Direct Investment Incentives*, Working Chapter 168, Stockholm: Stockholm School of Economics.

Borchert, J. G. (1994) 'Urban marketing: a review', in *Abhandlungen – Antropogeographie Insitut für Geographische Wissenschaften*, Band 52, Berlin: FU Berlin.

Bradley, A., Hall, T. and Harrison, M. (2002) 'Selling cities: promoting new images for meeting tourism', *Cities*, 19(1): 61–70.

Brassington, F. and Pettitt, S. (2003) *Principles of Marketing*, Harlow: Prentice Hall.

Burgess, J. (1982) 'Selling places: environmental images for the executive', *Regional Studies*, 16(1): 1–17.

Burgess, J. and Wood, P. (1988) 'Decoding Docklands: place advertising and decision-making strategies of the small firm', in J. Eyles and D. M Smith (eds) *Qualitative Methods in Human Geography*, Cambridge: Polity.

Burnett, J. J. (1993) *Promotion Management*, Boston: Houghton Mifflin.

Capik, P. (2006) 'Regional promotion strategies and network models in competing regions – FDI attraction mechanisms in Central Eastern Europe', *CIRM 2006 Proceedings*, Manchester: Manchester Metropolitan University.

—— (2007) 'Organising FDI promotion in Central-Eastern European regions', *Place Branding*, 3(2): 152–163.

CzechInvest: www.czechinvest.org.

Daskou, S., Thom, C. and Boojihawon, D. (2005) 'Marketing a city: Glasgow, city of architecture and design', *Global Business and Economics Review*, 6(1): 22–37.

Domański, T. (ed.) (1997) *Marketing terytorialny; Strategiczne wyzwanie dla miast i regionów*, Łódź: Uniwersytet Łódzki.

Domański, B. (2001) *Kapitał zagraniczny w przemyśle Polski*, Kraków: IGiGP Uniwersytetu Jagiellonskiego.

Drahokoupil, J. (2007) *The Rise of the Competition State in Central and Eastern Europe: The politics of foreign direct investment*, PhD Thesis, Budapest: Central European University.

Endzina, I. and Luneva, L. (2004) 'Development of a national branding strategy: the case of Latvia', *Place Branding*, 1(1): 94–105.

Fitzsimons, D. S. (1995) 'Planning and promotion: city reimaging in the 1980s and 1990s', in W. J. V. Neill, D. S. Fitzsimons and B. Murtagh (eds) *Reimaging the Pariah City: Urban development in Belfast and Detroit*, Aldershot: Avebury.

Florek, M. (2003) 'Territorial marketing: theoretical issues and empirical survey in wielkopolska communes', *Quaderno di ricerca*, 2: 1–28.

—— (2004) 'Możliwości zastosowania narzędzi marketingu w gminie (w kontekście wyników badań w gminach regionu wielkopolskiego)', in H. Szulce (ed.) *Obszary i możliwości wykorzystania marketingu*, Poznań: Zeszyty Naukowe AE.

Fretter, A. D. (1993) 'Place marketing: a local authority perspective', in G. Kearns and C. Philo (eds) *Selling Places; the city as cultural capital, past and present*, Oxford: Pergamon Press.

Gold, J. R. and Ward, S. V. (eds) (1994) *Forward, in Place Promotion; the use of publicity and marketing to sell towns and regions*, Chichester: John Wiley & Sons.

Goodwin, M. (1993) 'The city as commodity: the contested spaces of urban development', in G. Kearns and C. Philo (eds) *Selling places; the city as cultural capital, past and present*, Oxford: Pergamon Press.

Gorzelak, G. (2003) 'Economic and social cohesion in an enlarged EU: Comments on the post-socialist transformation', *EPRC Symposium materials*, Glasgow.

Haas, P. M. (1992), 'Introduction: Epistemic communities and international policy coordination', *International Organisation*, 46(1): 1–35.

Helinska-Hughes, E. and Hughes, M. (2003) 'Joining the competition: Central and Eastern European challenge to established FDI destinations?', in N. Phelps and P. Raines (eds) *The New Competition for Inward Investment*, Cheltenham: Edward Elgar.

Holcomb, B. (1993) 'Revisioning place: de- and re-constructing the image of the industrial city', in G. Kearns and C. Philo (eds) *Selling Places; the city as cultural capital, past and present*, Oxford: Pergamon Press.

Ivanička, K. Sr and Ivanička, K. Jr (2007) 'Regional growth dynamics in Central and Eastern Europe in the socio-economic and geographic context of a post-socialist reality', in K. Stanilov (ed.) *The Post-Socialist City: urban form and space transformations in Central and Eastern Europe after socialism*, Dodrecht: Springer.

Jarczewski, W. (2007) *Pozyskiwanie inwestorów do gmin*, Warsaw: Wolters Kluwer.

Kotler, P., Apslund, C., Rein, I. and Haider, D. H. (1999) *Marketing Places – Europe: how to attract investments, industries, residents and visitors to cities, communities, regions and nations in Europe*, London: Pearson Education.

Kotler, P. and Armstrong, G. (2001) *Principles of Marketing*, Upper Saddle River NJ: Prentice Hall.

Kotler, P. and Gertner, D. (2002) 'Country as brand, product and beyond: a place marketing and brand management perspective', *Brand Management*, 9(4–5): 249–261.

Kule, L., Krisjane, Z. and Berzins, M. (2010) 'The rhetoric and reality of pursuing territorial cohesion in Latvia', in N. Adams, G. Cotella and R. Nunes (eds) *Territorial Development, Cohesion and Spatial Planning: knowledge and policy development in an enlarged EU*, London: Routledge.

Lever, J. (2001) *The Effectiveness of Place Imagery in English Local Authority Inward Investment Promotion – an evaluation*, MPhil Thesis, Manchester: Manchester Metropolitan University.

Loewendahl, H. (2001) 'A framework for FDI promotion', *Transnational Corporations*, 10(1): 1–42.

Lodge, C. (2002) 'Success and failure: the brand stories of two countries', *Brand Management*, 9(4–5): 372–384.

Madsen, H. (1992) 'Place marketing in Liverpool: a review', *International Journal of Urban and Regional Research*, 16: 633–640.

Multilateral Investment Guarantee Agency (MIGA) www.fdipromotion.com/toolkit/user/content_page.cfm.

Maier, K. (2010) 'The pursuit of balanced territorial development: the realities and complexities of the cohesion agenda', in N. Adams, G. Cotella and R. Nunes (eds) *Territorial Development, Cohesion and Spatial Planning: Knowledge and policy development in an enlarged EU*, London: Routledge.

Myant, M. and Smith, S. (2006) 'Regional development and post-communist politics in a Czech region', *Europe-Asia Studies*, 58(2): 147–168.

Navaretti, G. B. and Venables, A. J. (2004) *Multinational Firms in the World Economy*, Princeton: Princeton University Press.

OECD (2003) *Checklist for Foreign Direct Investment Incentives Policies*, Paris: OECD Publications.

Paddison, R. (1993) 'City marketing, image reconstruction and urban regeneration', *Urban Studies*, 30(2): 339–350.

Pallagst, K. and Mercier, G. (2007) 'Urban and regional planning in Central and Eastern European countries – from EU requirements to innovative practices', in K. Stanilov (ed.) *The Post-Socialist City: urban form and space transformations in Central and Eastern Europe after Socialism*, Dordrecht: Springer.

Państwowa Agencja Informacji i Inwestycji Zagranicznych: www.paiz.pl.

Papadopoulos, N. and Heslop, L. (2002) 'Country equity and country branding: problems and prospects', *Brand Management*, 9(4–5): 294–314.

Quelch, J. and Jocz, K. (2005) 'Positioning the nation-state', *Place Branding*, 1(3): 229–237.

Rainisto, S. K. (2003) *Success Factors of Place Marketing: a study of place marketing practices in northern Europe and The United States*, Espoo, Helsinki.

Rzeczpospolita (2007) Więcej na reklamę miast, 20.11.2007.

Sario: www.sario.sk.

Sjøholt, P. (1994) 'The city of Bergen: image and marketing', in G. O. Braun (ed.) *Managing and Marketing of Urban Development and Urban Life*, Berlin: Dietrich Reimer Verlag.

Stanilov, K. (2007) 'Political reform, economic development, and regional growth in post-socialist Europe', in K. Stanilov (ed.) *The Post-Socialist City: urban form and space transformations in Central and Eastern Europe after Socialism*, Dordrecht: Springer.

Stanley, R. E. (1977) *Promotion Advertising, Publicity, Personal Selling, Sales Promotion*, Prentice-Hall Englewood Cliffs, N.J.

Tewdwr-Jones, M. (2010) 'Cohesion and Competitiveness: the evolving context for European territorial development', in N. Adams, G. Cotella and R. Nunes (eds) *Territorial Development, Cohesion and Spatial Planning: Knowledge and policy development in an enlarged EU*, London: Routledge.

Turnock, D. (ed.) (2005) *Foreign Direct Investment and Regional Development in East Central Europe and the Former Soviet Union*, Aldershot: Ashgate.

UNCTAD (2000) *Tax Incentives and Foreign Direct Investment – a global survey*, ASIT Advisory Studies No. 16, Geneva: United Nations.

—— (2002) *World Investment Report 2002: Transnational Corporations and Export Competitiveness*, New York: United Nations.

—— (2005) *World Investment Report 2005: Transnational Corporations and Internationalisation of R&D*, New York: United Nations.

—— (2008) *World Investment Report 2008: Transnational Corporations and the Infrastructure Challenge*, Geneva: United Nations.

Van Den Berg, L., Braun, E. and Otgaar, A. H. J. (2002) *Sports and City Marketing in European Cities*, Rotterdam: Euricur.

Ward, S. V. (1998), *Selling Places: the marketing and promotion of towns and cities 1850–2000*, London: E&FN Spon.

Wells, T. L. Jr and Wint, A. G. (2000) *Marketing a Country – promotion as a tool for attracting foreign direct investment*, FIAS Occasional Chapter 13, Washington: IFC-MIGA.

Wenger, E. (1998) *Communities of Practice: learning, meaning, and identity*. Cambridge: Cambridge University Press.

Wu, F. (2000) 'The global and local dimensions of place-making: remaking Shanghai as a world city', *Urban Studies*, 37(8): 1359–1377.

Young, C. (2004) 'From place promotion to sophisticated place marketing under post-socialism: the case of CzechInvest', *European Spatial Research and Policy*, 11(2): 71–84.

—— (2005) 'Place marketing for foreign direct investment in Central and Eastern Europe', in D. Turnock (ed.) *Foreign Direct Investment and Regional Development in East Central Europe and the Former Soviet Union*, Aldershot: Ashgate.

Young, C. and Kaczmarek, S. (1999) 'Changing the perception of the post-socialistic city: place promotion and imagery in Łódź, Poland', *The Geographical Journal*, 165(2): 183–189.

Young, C. and Lever, J. (1997) 'Place promotion, economic location and the consumption of city image', *Tijdshrift voor Economische en Sociale Geografie*, 88(4): 332–341.

Zanatta, M., Costa, I. and Filippov, S. (2006) *Foreign Direct Investment: key issues for promotion agencies*, UNU Policy Brief, 10, Maastricht: UNU-MERIT.

14 Accessibility to education and its impact on regional development in Poland

Konrad Ł. Czapiewski and Krzysztof Janc

Introduction

The development of human resources potentially has a key role to play as a driver of regional development and constitutes a specific element of the territorial capital of a region. Following on from this, it can be argued that accessibility to educational opportunities is an important determining factor in developing the potential of such human resources. Whereas the Lisbon Strategy (CEC 2005) stresses the important role played by R&D (research and development) investments in the overall framework of a competitive Europe, especially those focusing on raising education levels, the strong focus on successful economic areas translates in many cases to a lack of emphasis on the improvement of education opportunities within less favoured regions. Uneven accessibility to education implies that certain areas will be disadvantaged in terms of development potential and this in turn may contribute to further fuelling regional disparities and exacerbating the current mega-trends currently being experienced in the EU (cf. Finka, Stead and Nadin, Maier in this book). Poland provides an interesting context within which to analyze these issues because, like many EU Member States, Poland is experiencing significant disparities between the biggest urban centres and their immediate vicinities, and the peripheral areas. There is also a distinct difference between the western and the eastern parts of the country, the former being characterized by a greater number of urban centres (notably Wrocław, Poznań, Szczecin), whilst the latter contains significant internal differentiation, with no urban area of national importance except for the capital. Notwithstanding the disparities mentioned above, Poland possesses one of the most balanced and polycentric settlement systems in the EU (ESPON 2005a, 2005b) (see Figure 14.1). ESPON studies have also demonstrated how the 'university system in Poland is the most polycentric in Europe' (ESPON 2005b: 100) due to the strong association with the national settlement structure and having benefited from a highly dynamic development through last decades. Nevertheless, despite the exponential increase in the number of academic centres and enrolled students, the Polish tertiary education system[1] is still affected by several factors limiting its spatial accessibility and the consolidation of qualified human capital in specific areas. The scarce development and quality of transport and ICT infrastructure networks, insufficient aids to support the access of disadvantaged social groups and the lack of jobs for highly educated people in peripheral areas all provide specific challenges in this context.

Building on the above considerations, the present chapter develops two main themes. First, the authors introduce the role of human capital in promoting regional development and explore the different dimensions of accessibility to tertiary education in relation to the development of human capital in a specific area. This involves analysis of the evolution of the spatial distribution of tertiary education institutions in Poland and the degree to which the educational level of the population is correlated with the level of regional development.[2] On the basis of this investigation, the chapter examines policy responses in the field of education and their potential impact on future regional development. These issues are examined over a period of four recent decades with special attention to the processes of systemic transformation, that is 'transition from the centrally planned economy to the market economy and formation of the market-based conditions for the

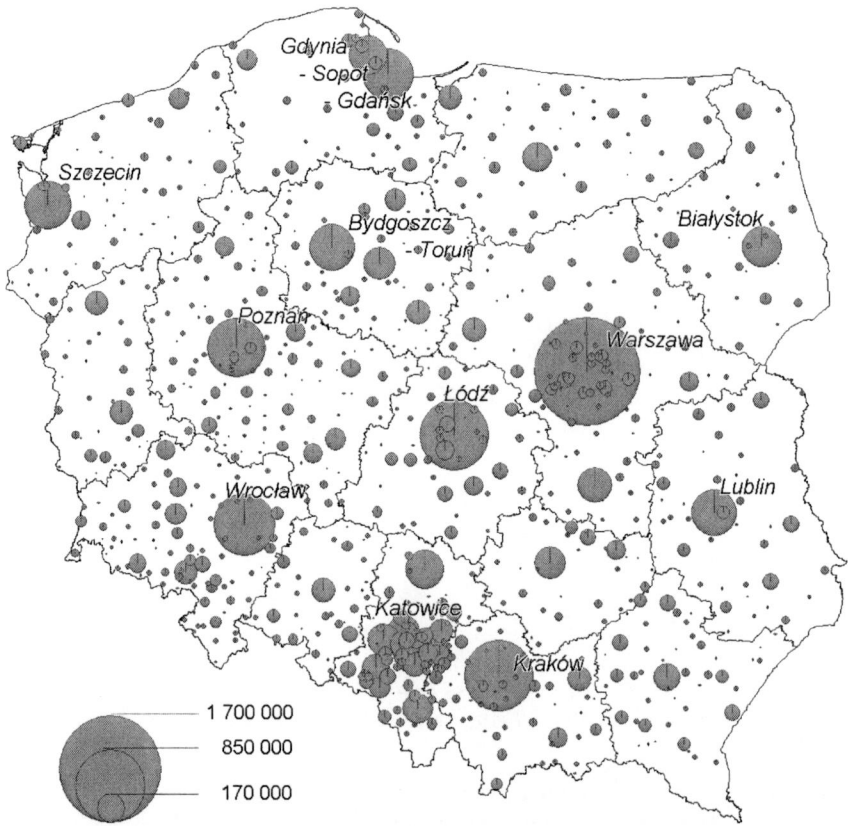

Figure 14.1 Towns and numbers of their inhabitants in Poland (source: Authors' elaboration on basis of data from Central Statistical Office (GUS)).

functioning of all the economic entities' (Nasiłowski 1995: 17, translation). Detailed analysis is carried out of the spatial accessibility to education and its potential implications for the development capacities of individual areas of Poland, treating it as one of the essential elements influencing the development of qualitative properties of human resources. The authors then reflect on the potential implications of these findings for future territorial development in Poland and explore different options available in terms of policy, funding and approach. In conclusion the authors argue that if more balanced patterns of regional development are to be achieved in Poland, then it is essential that access to educational opportunities are improved significantly in rural and peripheral areas.

Accessibility to education and its implications for regional development

A crucial aspect of contemporary socio-economic processes is constituted by their close association with location and the features related to it, i.e. the unique local resources that constitute the so-called territorial capital of a specific area (cf. Maier Chapter 11). These are the features of places, which are the expression of appearance of specific, often deeply rooted resources, distinguishing one area from another (see Bathelt *et al.* 2004; Storper and Venables 2004). Various authors have demonstrated how social systems that are strictly localized in space and partly immobile can play a pivotal role in influencing the development capacities of an area. In other words, as argued by Gössling and Rutten (2007), '*milieu* matters'!

Human resources are one of numerous variables that play a key role in regional development. They can constitute either a barrier to or a stimulation to the development of a specific region, depending on their quantity and quality (for example, see de la Fuente and Ciccone 2003; Lee *et al.* 2004; Tondl and Vuksic 2003). In order to foster development effectively, it is important to pay attention to the factors that influence the concentration of those people whose role is crucial in promoting economic development. From the point of view of contemporary development processes, one of the key indicators of human capital is the educational level of the population. An adequate proportion of educated people (Horváth 2005) is thought to be key in terms of achieving economic success. It is also argued that spatial proximity may enhance collective learning processes, due to the short distance between actors facilitating knowledge and information sharing (cf. Boschma and Lambooy 1999; Törnqvist 2004). As noted by von Hayek (1945) economic success takes place largely with the application of knowledge, which facilitates rational assessment of the situation and a realistic formulation of own goals. Similarly, according to Romer (1990) for economic growth it is not an area with a large number of people that is of significance but an area with a high proportion of well educated residents.

Whereas some authors argue that research organizations like universities seem to have a less dominant position in the diffusion of information and knowledge than is commonly thought, their important function as suppliers of 'knowledge workers' cannot be denied (Lambooy 2004). Furthermore, Drucker and Goldstein (2007) identify a variety of other important functions of universities such as promoting regional leadership, positively influencing the regional *milieu* and facilitating knowledge transfer. It is therefore important from a socio-economic development perspective, that institutions providing knowledge and competence such as schools, universities and research institutes are developed and enhanced (Hilpert 2006). Earlier studies by the current authors suggested that an area featuring a high proportion of persons with higher education usually shows higher economic potential, displaying higher numbers of businesses, lower joblessness rates as well as higher revenues and the local budgets (Janc and Czapiewski 2005). At the same time, the limited development opportunities of some regions may be determined by their lack of qualified human resources. The importance of the spatial differentiation of accessibility to tertiary education therefore becomes important in this context. Identification of the spatial patterns essential for this question makes it possible to effectively translate scientific knowledge on socio-economic processes in planning and the monitoring of regional development.

In contemporary, well developed democratic societies, education is by definition a public and thus generally accessible good. However, as a result of economic pressures, education at tertiary level is also a scarce good and is not evenly accessible to all potential students. The question of equity of access may relate to several aspects, namely to the issue of differences in participation rates to higher education among groups of students according to gender, socio-economic background, region of residence or disability. In order to explore the issue of accessibility to tertiary education in relation to the development of the human capital of a specific area, it is essential to 'unpack' the notion of accessibility. The different dimensions of accessibility can be divided into socio-economic factors and spatial factors. Socio-economic factors relate to the economic conditions of specific groups of people and to their relation to the possibility to access tertiary education. Particular elements affecting access to tertiary education in this respect are the level of the tuition fees and the existence of economic aid programmes. Numerous sociological surveys on the tertiary student population suggest that a key factor determining access to tertiary education is the educational attainment of parents. It is argued that families with low levels of attainment in education face not only economic barriers but also psychological barriers connected with negative self-evaluation and a lack of confidence. Spatial factors include barriers that inhibit access to tertiary education in relation to the place of residence of potential students. This category includes the possibility for residents of a specific area to access tertiary education and this is influenced by the quality of the transportation network, the travel and accommodation costs and by the possibility to benefit from e-education services at home. Furthermore, in relation to the consolidation of qualified human capital in a specific area, a crucial role is played by the existence of job opportunities that will prevent highly educated people emigrating once they have graduated.

The remainder of the chapter is dedicated to exploring the relationship of accessibility to higher education with the level of socio-economic development in Poland. The following section presents the characteristics of the transformation of the tertiary education system in Poland since the 1970s, highlighting the main barriers in terms of accessibility. Next there is an analysis of the interdependencies between the differentiation in the level of education and the spatial patterns of development. Building on this investigation, the authors then discusses the potential impact of policy responses in the field of education on future regional development.

Development and accessibility of tertiary education in Poland

In this section there is an analysis of the transformation of tertiary education institutions in Poland and the evolution of their spatial distribution. As the formation of knowledge resources in society is a long process, it was decided to explore the evolution of the Polish tertiary education system over a number of years. Three essential time points were considered, in which different economic, political and social circumstances existed. In 1970 the socialist regime was in power in Poland and this had significant consequences in the education domain and resulted in high demand for a specific kind of manpower – mainly low-skilled people employed in heavy industry. The second year selected for the analysis is 1993 during the initial phase of the socio-economic transformation. Significant changes in virtually all the spheres of social and economic life started to make a visible impact on the attitudes towards the level of education and the meaning of knowledge in business processes, as well as in society in general. The final year selected for analysis was 2002, by which time the Polish economy could be referred to as a market economy, this meaning the presence of private ownership protected by a commercial law, a corporate structure of industry, an independent financial system and the active participation of foreign firms in the domestic economy (cf. Lipton and Sachs 1990).

The university network of Poland is strongly associated with the highly polycentric settlement structure that derives from a long-standing tradition of polycentric development strategies (Korcelli 2005; Meijers *et al.* 2007). For the same reasons, the spatial distribution of academic centres has benefited from a highly dynamic development. There were already 23 towns in which tertiary education institutions were located by 1970, while 13 other towns hosted branches and local departments. This situation persisted until the breakdown of the socialist block and at the beginning of the 1990s 33 towns hosted tertiary education institutions and 21 towns had branches and local departments. The systemic transformation resulted in changes leading to a dynamic increase in the number of schools and their branches so that in 2002 as many as 133 localities could be considered academic centres (i.e. hosting at least one tertiary education institution in the form of either a school or its branch). The exponential increase in the number of university and college level schools at the beginning of the 1990s is primarily related to changes in the legislation, which for the first time permitted the establishment of private education institutions. The first private universities started to appear as early as 1991 following the approval of the new legislation and these mainly flourished in middle-sized towns (Nowosielska 2002). Many of the public universities as well as some of the private ones started to open an increasingly larger number of branches and departments. This phenomena is associated both with the necessity of satisfying the demand for higher education in smaller towns as well as with the limited capacity of lecture halls in the main university centres. It is worth emphasizing that the process of increasing of the number of tertiary education facilities could be regarded as spontaneous as there has been no national policy concerning the spatial aspects of the development of university education. This dynamic growth was linked more with the drive to satisfy the increasing demand for university education, as in the period analyzed half of the young people in the age of 19–24 years took up tertiary studies.

The increase in the number of tertiary education institutions, which is ongoing, also resulted in an increase in the number of students. The biggest increase of the respective numbers took place in large academic centres due to the presence of the required infrastructure, staff and local demand (Figure 14.2).

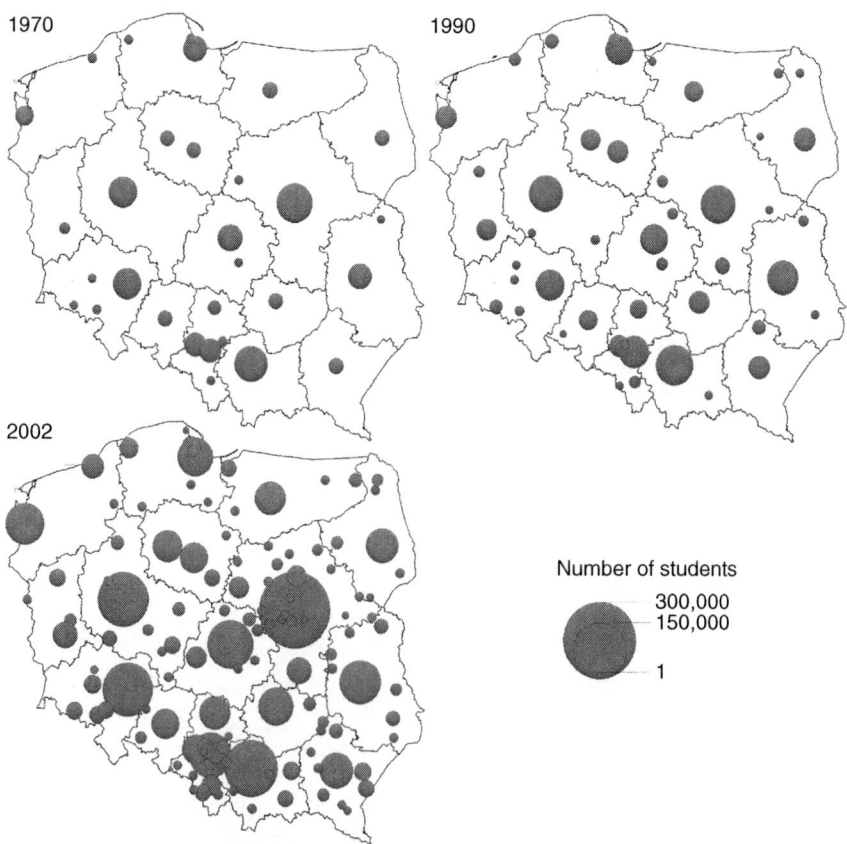

Figure 14.2 Number of students in Poland in the years 1970, 1993, 2002 (source: Authors' elaboration on basis of data from Central Statistical Office (GUS)).

In 2002 the greatest number of students concentrated in Warsaw (300,000), with three other centres (Cracow, Poznań, Wrocław) also attracting high numbers of students (130,000–150,000). Alongside a couple of other towns, these centres host the highest numbers of university-level schools and offer the best choice in terms of directions of study. In addition they are attractive to students due to their prestigious 'study climate', access to culture and leisure opportunities, scientific resources (libraries, archives, bookshops) and to entertainment.

Uneven accessibility to tertiary education opportunities

The transformation of Polish tertiary education in the last decades is very significant. Between the years 1970 and 2002 the share of persons with higher education increased from less than 3 per cent to roughly 10 per cent (Figure 14.3). Distinct relations may be observed between the process analyzed and the settlement network. Tertiary education institutions started to gradually emerge in smaller towns with the highest increase being visible in the surroundings of the largest traditional academic centres. This is due on the one hand to the limited mobility of the teaching staff who are concentrated in the largest centres and on the other hand to the establishment of new schools in locations of highest demand. However, several university institutions appeared also in peripheral centres and despite many of them belonging to the private sector and thus requiring tuition fees they became more accessible for the inhabitants of the peripheral areas.

Although there has been considerable progress broadening and expanding participation in higher education, serious concerns persist as regards equity of access. Enrolment levels in tertiary education grew by 161 per cent between

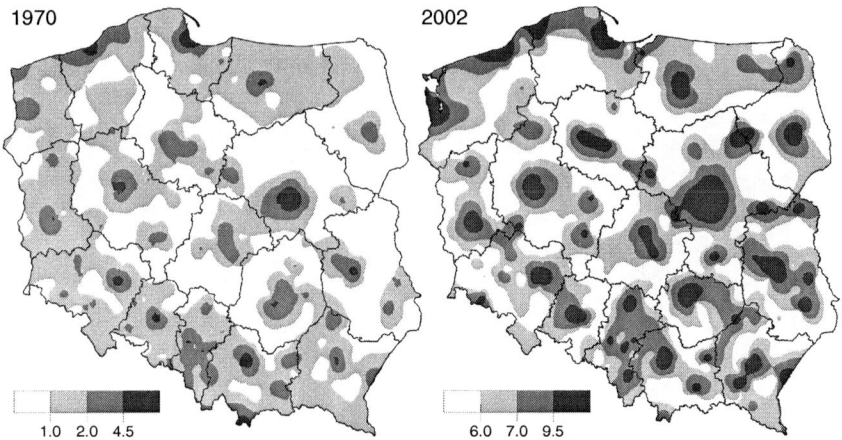

Figure 14.3 Shares of population with higher education in Poland in the years 1970 and 2002 (source: Authors' elaboration on basis of data from Central Statistical Office (GUS)).

1995 and 2003, the highest growth rate among OECD countries (Fulton *et al.* 2005). Such rapid expansion could potentially lead to a range of equity outcomes as the newly opened-up places in tertiary education should in principle increase opportunities for disadvantaged students to attend. However, the strategy was driven by deregulation and de-concentration with little or no space for measures to promote equal accessibility. The situation has been exacerbated by limited investments in transport infrastructure and reductions in the frequency of public transport in rural areas.

The historical context is also important as a determining factor in the density of the network of academic centres. In 1970 one can distinctly identify areas of the country where there was no easy access to academic centres. These areas where academic centres are lacking coincide with the border areas of the former partitions of Poland from the nineteenth century when lands were taken in by Russia, Prussia and Austria and with the then peripheries of the country (Werwicki 1994). Despite the constantly increasing density of the network of academic centres in recent times, the areas with poor accessibility to these centres were still visible in 2002 and this had an obvious impact on the proportion of the young people from certain areas in the population of students. It is also apparent that the increase in the level of higher education was very different for the urban and rural populations. Jakubowicz (2004) noted that every fifth inhabitant of the town had higher education while in the countryside only every twentieth. The urban young account for 78 per cent of the students on full-time courses who started studying in 2003 while students of rural origin account for 22 per cent of the total. Hence, the population structure in terms of the levels of education depends strongly upon the share of the urban population and upon the structure of the population according to the occupational activity. The changes in the pattern of spatial differentiation of the proportion of population with tertiary education are not significant. In 1970 this share did not exceed 1 per cent in the majority of the territory of Poland. One can clearly see the locations of towns and their immediate vicinities in contrast with the remaining areas. In 2002 the concentration of the best educated population in urban centres is still visible although there is also a distinct territorial growth of the areas around towns, featuring higher proportions of people with higher education than in the remaining areas. This process ought to be attributed to the increased accessibility to higher and secondary schools, to suburbanization processes and to the development of activities requiring educated labour in the peripheries of large towns.

While the highest education levels are observed within the areas situated in the vicinity of large urban centres and in particular in regional capitals, the least advantageous situation exists in the areas between such zones that can be labelled 'intra-regional peripheries of economic development' (cf. Rosner 2007; Czapiewski and Janc 2009). These areas experience various disadvantages including limited accessibility to the tertiary education institutions and limited job opportunities for highly-educated people, which in turn stimulates outmigration of the most highly educated people. Positive balances of the migration of persons with higher education are recorded for all the biggest towns and their surroundings. On the contrary, almost the whole territory of eastern Poland including the areas located between large towns, are in danger of progressive peripheralization due to the brain drain phenomena. In the case of migration of persons with higher education there is a higher than average tendency towards the concentration in places offering the opportunity of achieving success in life, i.e. in large towns (cf. Bański 2004). In addition, this process is suggested not only by strong data about migration (Janc 2009) but also by 'softer' data about the willingness of people to migrate from places offering fewer opportunities (Table 14.1). It is worth emphasizing that inhabitants of rural areas are more willing to change the place of residence than inhabitants of towns and that younger persons are more willing to move than older people. The most striking aspect, however, is the willingness of jobless inhabitants of rural areas with university education (68 per cent of the respective population studied) to move.

Having explored the evolution of Polish tertiary education institutions during the last decades and the impact of accessibility barriers on the spatial distribution of qualified human resources, in the next section the interdependencies between the level of education and the spatial patterns of territorial development of the Polish territory will be explored.

Interdependencies between level of development and level of education

In the early parts of the chapter, the spatial differentiation of educational levels was illustrated and the necessity of overcoming this current spatial dichotomy was emphasized, which would require improving the accessibility of tertiary

Table 14.1 Jobless persons willing to change place of residence in rural and urban areas according to age and education, 2000

Category	Total number of jobless in given category willing to change place of residence (%)	
	Town	*Countryside*
Total	**25.4**	**34.4**
According to age, years		
18–24	39.5	49.5
25–34	26.2	32.0
35–44	19.2	24.0
45–64	17.5	17.3
According to education		
Tertiary	32.5	68.4
Secondary	23.7	30.0
Basic professional training	24.7	34.4
Primary and incomplete primary	28.3	34.8

Source: *Badanie Aktywności Ekonomicznej Ludności*, Central Statistical Office.

education services. The aim of this section is to investigate the extent to which an improvement in the education level of inhabitants and the socio-economic development performance of peripheral regions is realistic. This does not necessarily imply any cause-effect relationship between the level of education and the economic performance of a specific area. Rather, it explores the positive coexistence of the two factors and suggests that a look at spatial patterns of the level of tertiary education within the overall spatial policy and planning for territorial cohesion remains a highly relevant issue.

When trying to determine the level of regional development, it is important not only to compare individual regions (*vide* important studies of ESPON, widely analyzed in Waterhout's Chapter 4) but also to get insight into their internal differentiation. This is clear if one considers how spatial polarization processes may be observed at different levels – between centre and periphery, between different regions, within urban areas and so on. In this respect, one of the contemporary processes observed is an increasing polarization between metropolitan and non-metropolitan regions. As Jałowiecki puts it

> metropolises functioning in network settings are mutually connected more strongly than with their own surrounding hinterland. Their surroundings undergo fast peripherization, preserving only a definite significance as the reserve of poorly skilled manpower and, in contrast, as place of residence and recreation for wealthy inhabitants. Consequently, one can observe polarization between the centre – the metropolis, and its surroundings – the closer and farther periphery.
>
> (Jałowiecki 2007: 146, translation)

Studies conducted by Wojnicka *et al.* (2005) show that regions with higher internal differentiation are the areas with above average GDP per capita, with higher number of growth centres, higher growth rates and higher levels of prosperity. These observations can be generalized by stating that the higher the level of economic development of a region, the higher the probability of distinct differences between the 'core' and the 'periphery'. Considering the possibility for planning to stimulate development, cognition of the intra-regional differentiation is therefore constitutive for the capacity of understanding the conditioning of differentiation at a broader scale. Knowledge, acquired through these analyses is most often applied in regional development of provinces (identification of problem areas, areas of outmigration and commuting areas) because national documents do not tend to cover such regional or local issues. It is for this reason that the reference units for this research are the 380 counties of Poland (*powiaty*, NUTS 4 level).

Socio-economic development patterns of the Polish space

A set of indicators was selected allowing for a comprehensive description of the essential features of the spatial structure of the country in order to determine the level of socio-economic development. The indicators related to aspects such as entrepreneurship, demographic structure, wealth, the labour market and absorption of European Union funds. The following indicators were applied:

Entrepreneurship of the population:

- number of registered businesses per 1,000 persons in productive age 2005–2006;
- number of registered businesses from sections J, K, L, M of the Statistical Classification of Economic Activities in the European Community[3] per 1,000 persons in productive age 2005–2006;

Prosperity of the local communities:

- revenues of the state budget from personal income tax (PIT) per capita 2005–2006;
- effectiveness of businesses: revenues of the state budget from the corporate income tax (CIT) per person in productive age 2005–2006;
- unemployment rate 2006;
- the number of long-term unemployed (over two years) as a proportion of the total number of unemployed 2005–2006;

Absorption of EU funds:

- EU funds per capita 2006;

Demographic factors:

- age dependency ratio: number of persons in pre-productive and post-productive age per person in productive age, for 2006;
- migration balance: average for the years 2005–2006.

The method of Principal Component Analysis (PCA) was applied in order to reduce the number of variables, i.e. a data reduction method allowing for the reduction of a dataset containing a large number of possibly correlated original variables down to a small number of uncorrelated underlying factors (for interpretation and details of the method cf. Rogerson, 2006). Use of PCA made it possible to determine three synthetic components (after Varimax rotation), describing the level of socio-economic development of Poland (Table 14.2).

The first component identified, explaining 42 per cent of variance present in the features considered, can be interpreted as an indicator of social and economic success. It is most closely associated with the features related to entrepreneurship and wealth. Negative correlation is displayed by the features, whose high values signify negative phenomena (dependency ratio, proportion of long-term unemployed). The second component (explaining close to 14 per cent of the

Table 14.2 Results of application of principal component analysis to variables describing
level of socio-economic development of Poland

Feature/variable	Component 1	Component 2	Component 3
Entrepreneurship – business services	0.88		
Entrepreneurship	0.85		
Dependency ratio	−0.82		
Wealth of local communities	0.74	0.42	
Unemployed for more than two years	−0.59		
Joblessness		−0.82	
Migration balance		0.70	
EU funds acquired			0.71
Business efficiency	0.42		0.53
% of explained variance	**41.6**	**13.6**	**12.3**

Source: Authors' elaboration.

Note
Only values of loads exceeding 0.4 are shown in the table.

joint variance) is most strongly linked with joblessness and migration balance. Here a causal connection takes place, as a rate of lower joblessness is connected with higher positive migration balance. The third component, which explains 12 per cent of the joint variance, is most closely associated with business efficiency and EU funds and this provides some indications of the effectiveness of the institutions active in a given area. Interestingly, as far as the absorption of EU funds is concerned, no relevant correlations have been shown in relation to the first two components. This is potentially attributable to the limited time-span of the available data and this is discussed further in the following paragraphs.

The spatial differentiation of the first component, describing success in socio-economic development, allows for the confirmation of the image of differentiation of Polish space in two essential dimensions (Figure 14.4). First the situation is better in the urban units and in the case of large towns and their immediate vicinities. As mentioned earlier in the chapter there is also a clear dominance of western regions over those located in the eastern part of the country. The evidence suggests that only regional capitals are well developed in eastern Poland resulting in significant internal disparities. These disparities have their roots in centuries-long differentiation of the levels of socio-economic development, stemming mainly from the historical divisions of the present-day territory of Poland and the differentiation of the economic structures across Poland. The area stretching along the Baltic Sea coast is particularly interesting due to the intensive development of tourism in this area.

Location with respect to the boundaries of the country appears to be another important factor. The areas situated along the German border feature higher levels of entrepreneurship and business-related service. It would appear therefore that this border does not constitute a barrier but rather stimulates development and facilitates economic success. This is despite the fact that institutionalized cross-border Polish-German cooperation has been limited, as indicated by Ciok *et al.* (2008) in relation to the limited activities in the relevant INTERREG IIIA programme. Nevertheless, although the development of the border areas is often associated with informal activities and location advantages, more specific non-economic outcomes of territorial cooperation programmes, such as the trigger of innovation diffusion processes, have also contributed to the success mentioned above (cf. also Haselsberger and Benneworth Chapter 10). Importantly, the western areas of Poland are inhabited by an altogether younger population with the opposite being the case in the east (Gawryszewski 2006). The majority of the eastern border separates Poland from Belarus and Ukraine that are non-EU countries outside the Schengen area and with lower levels of development and prosperity. In this case the border does form a barrier to development, hindering the free flow of people, goods and ideas.

The spatial distribution of the values of the second component partly follows the first one. This may be explained if one considers that the variables associated with it, namely unemployment and migration balance may be considered to a high extent spatial complements of socio-economic success.

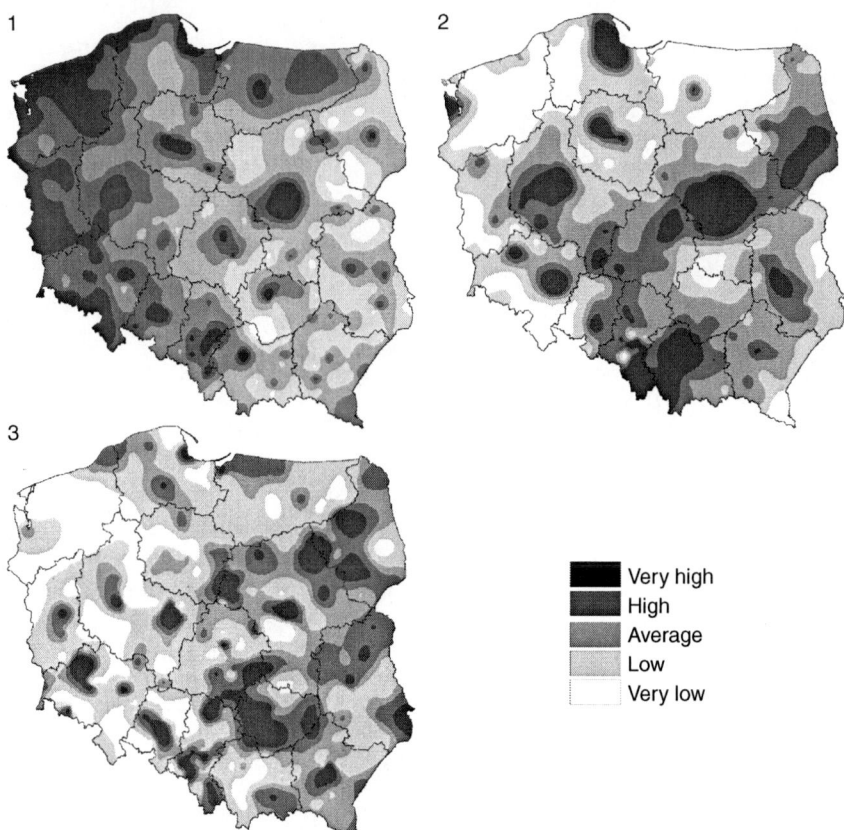

Figure 14.4 Spatial differentiation of values of the three components (source: Authors' elaboration on basis of data from Central Statistical Office (GUS)).

The third component relating to business efficiency and EU funds features less distinct spatial dispersion. This is associated with the fact that the features, composing this component have a less explicit spatial character and do not reveal coherent spatial patterns. First, as we consider the performance of businesses, it is important to emphasize that the values observed are influenced by the presence of larger companies. The location of a large company bringing high revenues (very often associated in Poland with the extraction of natural resources) results in an increase in the value of the respective indicator. The presence of such enterprises is of course very often desirable, since they bring an increase to the wealth of the inhabitants and stimulate the development of entrepreneurship. As far as the EU funds are concerned, it should be highlighted that the available data relates only to the year 2006. This makes comparison with other years impossible, while it must be kept in mind that this particular variable is subject to high temporal variability. A significant proportion of these funds have been spent in the initial phase on investments in infrastructure in Poland. As a result it is important to bear in mind the fact that in the less urbanized areas (eastern part of Poland) the value of means per capita can be higher for the same value of investment projects. There appears to be a strong positive correlation between the level of education of self-government authorities and the level of absorption of EU funds. Previous work by the authors examining data for the years 1990–2003 demonstrated that a higher educational level of the councillors is reflected in a higher volume of acquired EU funds (Czapiewski and Janc 2007). Similarly, studies by Dołzbłasz and Raczyk (2007), concentrating on absorption of INTERREG IIIA means in Poland (along the Polish-German and Polish-Czech borders), also identified this correlation.

Exploring the correlation between education and development

In this section evidence collected in search of a spatial correlation with the level of education will be explored. Several potential correlations can be found by comparing the spatial pattern of socio-economic development with that concerning the domain of tertiary education. As mentioned earlier in this chapter, the distribution of tertiary education institutions corresponds distinctly to the distribution of the main cities as a consequence of the highest demand for educational service and highly educated manpower in large towns. Table 14.3 provides the

Table 14.3 Interrelations between components describing level of socio-economic development and educational level in Poland (values of Pearson correlation coefficient)

	Tertiary	Secondary	Basic professional training	Other
Component 1	0.70	0.70	−0.20	−0.79
Component 2	0.28	0.16	−0.01	−0.28
Component 3	0.37	0.31	−0.34	−0.22

Source: Authors' elaboration.

values of the Pearson linear correlation coefficient[4] for the four possible levels of education and the three principal components identified in relation to the 380 counties in order to show these relations with a greater precision. It is particularly significant that the highest levels of education (tertiary and secondary) are positively correlated with all the components describing the individual dimensions of the socio-economic success. The two lowest levels of education display a negative association with the components obtained. The respective values indicate the direction of relation taking place between the level of education of the population and the socio-economic situation of an area. It is interesting to note that there is practically no distinction as to the strength of the association between the tertiary and secondary education. This is a consequence of the ongoing shortage of highly skilled specialists that is primarily attributable to the very low starting point at the beginning of socio-economic transformation in 1989 and as a result persons with only secondary education are still over-represented at high levels in economic life. We should also emphasize the strong negative interdependence between the first component and the lowest educational level (−0.79), implying that areas with the highest proportion of people with the lowest level of education are characterized by the poorest economic situation. The majority of these areas are rural and particularly the mono-functional strictly agricultural areas.

Relatively homogeneous groups were obtained by dividing the set of units into five groups according to the proportion of urban population with each of them containing 75–76 units.[5] By analyzing the values of the Pearson linear correlation coefficient between the level of socio-economic success (first principal component) and the level of education for the particular groups of urbanization levels we can identify the following relations (as shown in Table 14.4):

- the correlation between socio-economic success and the level of education strongly depends on the share of urban population;
- the highest value of correlation is observed between the share of the population with higher education and the group of units with the highest degree of urbanization, which implies the significance of an appropriate environment (here: the strongly urbanized areas) for the creation and attraction of human capital;

Table 14.4 Interrelations between first component, describing level of socio-economic development and education level in Poland, depending upon share of urban population (values of Pearson correlation coefficient)

Urbanisation degree (%)	Tertiary	Secondary	Basic professional	Other
1 (below 27.5)	0.33	0.14	0.63	−0.63
2 (27.5–39.0)	0.26	0.11	0.53	−0.61
3 (39.0–52.5)	0.25	0.23	0.20	−0.44
4 (52.5–70.0)	0.25	0.34	−0.15	−0.23
5 (exceeding 70.0)	0.64	0.43	−0.47	−0.59

Source: Authors' elaboration.

- for the remaining four classes of urbanization (1–4) the interrelation with the share of population having tertiary education is decidedly lower and does not change significantly, so that one can speak of an important gap between the areas having truly urban character and the remaining areas.

The relations observed indicate the areas characterized by disadvantageous conditions in terms of development. Primarily these consist of those featuring low levels of educational attainment of the population. The observed correlation between the level of the socio-economic development and the educational level brings about quite an important problem, the possibility of the accumulation of the negative characteristics. At the other extreme there are areas displaying high potential of producing, attracting and retaining the most valuable human resources. The discussion in the remainder of the chapter will focus on the implications of these issues for policy-making and the Polish approach to regional development policy will be discussed with particular reference to its educational dimension.

Discussing Polish approach to education within wider regional development policy

The correlation described above between the education level of inhabitants and socio-economic development may be attributed to a spatial coexistence of the different factors. On the one hand the specific conditions of some regions contribute to attracting more enterprising people and on the other hand such people, mostly young and well educated, play a crucial role in the consolidation of those successful conditions in the regions. This spatial diversification has clear implications for territorial development and cohesion as it naturally implies the existence of 'growth poles' and 'less favoured areas' with different development potentials.

The national Concept for the Spatial Development of the Country (CSDC – Koncepcja polityki przestrzennego zagospodarovania kraju. GCSS 2001), pre- pared by the Government Centre for Strategic Studies on the basis of a set of analyses developed during the second half of the 1990s (cf. Korcelli 2005), identi- fies territorial cohesion as the main aim of Polish regional policy. Several other national guidance documents for regional policy reinforce the importance of the role of territorial cohesion including the National Development Plan (NDP) 2007–2013 that forms the main guidance document for EU and national expendi- tures for the period 2007–2013 (IGPNDP 2005) and the forthcoming National Spatial Management Concept (NSMC) for the years 2008–2033 (NSMC 2008)[6] that is currently being prepared. These latter two documents in particular were pre- pared by teams that display characteristics of an 'epistemic community' focused on regional development and spatial planning (cf. Haas 1992, quoted in Pallagst 2006, and also Pallagst Chapter 6). This team is composed of experts originating from numerous circles (societal, academic, ministerial, self-governmental) and dis- ciplines (geographers, planners, economists). The NSMC in particular will be the result of a discourse developed within this expert group and once approved it is expected to constitute the fundamental premise for the Polish Government in the domain of spatial policy.

The documents seem to consider territorial cohesion as an important instrument to support economic competitiveness (cf. also Evers *et al.* 2009: 29–36). The CSDC focuses on two apparently conflicting objectives, on the one hand a more liberal efficiency goal aimed at rapid national economic development and on the other hand a more regulative equity aim, focusing on the limitation of growing regional disparities. This situation reflects existing tensions between the objectives of economic growth and territorial cohesion discussed by Tewdwr-Jones and others in this book. This is also partly due to the numerous channels opened between the redaction of the background document of the study and the ESDP process (ESPON, 2006) leading to the adoption of the two concepts with an equivalent weight although this appears to have been at the expense of the clarity of the document itself (Korcelli 2005). The mission of the NDP, in the wake of the renewed Lisbon Strategy (CEC 2005) is to promote rapid economic growth as a result of a reinforced corporate and regional ability to compete, increased employment and a higher level of economic, social and territorial cohesion (IGPNDP 2005: 39). The document affirms how a steady economic growth is indispensable to improve competitiveness and to reduce the development gap with the other Member States. At the same time it identifies regional and spatial policies as important instruments to achieve domestic economic objectives and balancing out territorial and social development opportunities. Some doubts on the future effectiveness of the NDP 2007–2013 still persist, however, as objectives and priorities do not seem to be translated into an adequate action plan for implementation (Grosse 2005) and the three dimensions of cohesion are respectively reduced to a measure of GDP, employment and transfer time thus reducing the operative dimension of the concept itself (IGPNDP 2005).

The primary guidance document for the development of the Polish territory, the NSMC 2008–2033 (NSMC 2008) adopts the competitive turn of the contemporary EU spatial discourse (further details can be found in Waterhout Chapter 4 and Tewdwr-Jones Chapter 3). The document promotes strengthening the competitive position of the main urban centres and regions of Poland in the European space whilst preserving the polycentric structure of the settlement system and development of a knowledge-based economy. The NSMC, similar to other national documents, also interprets the objective of territorial cohesion as functional to economic growth. The implementation of this vision is to be based on the network of the largest Polish cities: Warsaw, Cracow, the Upper Silesian conurbation, Wrocław, Poznań, Łodz and the Tri-City (Gdańsk/Sopot/Gdynia). The vision also promotes the role of other important centres including Bydgoszcz and Toruń, connected by multi-modal infrastructure systems to form an interrelated open system, the so-called Central Hexagon (Figure 14.5). The mutual linkage of the main cities in Poland is to be conducive to the appearance of the effects of synergy and development of high value added activities. In this way it is hoped to achieve a more competitive position among the regional networks of metropolitan centres in Europe in terms of functions fulfilled and the quality (standard) of spatial development (NSMC 2008).

During the social debate generated by the document a number of controversies emerged, primarily generated by regions outside of the Hexagon, underlining the importance of what Dühr (2007) referred to as 'the power of being on the map'. However, it is important to stress that the Hexagon does not aim to represent a region but rather refers to the aim of improving connections between the largest cities. The NSMC strives for a consolidation of the existing polycentric network and to improve the accessibility of the main cities of the Hexagon from the peripheral regions. This idea constitutes an alternative to the scenarios of development of urban settlement systems in Europe produced by the ESPON 3.2

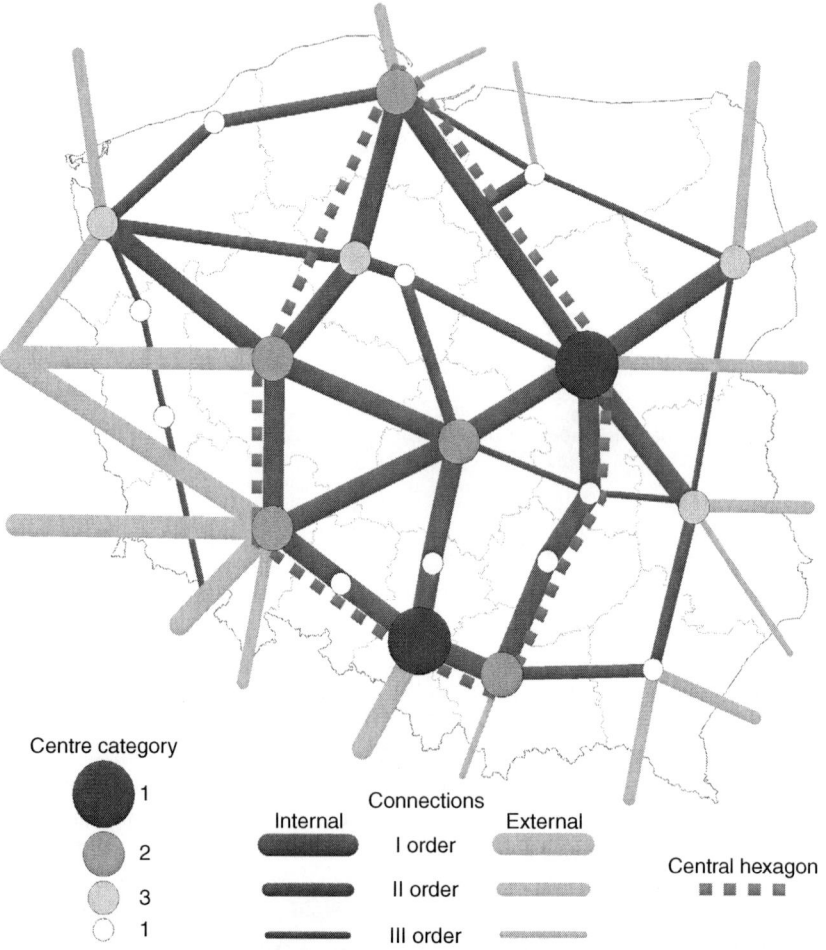

Figure 14.5 Model of central hexagon and functional connections between cities (source: NSMC – National Spatial Management Concept 2008).

project, indicating a highly probable extension of the concentration of the advanced knowledge-based economy over directions that bypass the territory of Poland to the North and South (ESPON 2007). It is possible to detect the will of Polish scientists and policy-makers to debate existing development visions produced within the European planning community (cf. Waterhout Chapter 4) and this may imply a potential merger of the community itself and the contamination of its work.

Whereas the elements above illustrates a reflection of the EU discourse on national policy-making, the influence of EU spatial concepts on sectoral policies is less apparent and the spatial dimension is discussed only to a limited extent in many sectoral documents. Despite the increase in education centres and the number of students being consistent with EU goals the process has primarily been spontaneous and due to the reforms during the transformation rather than being guided by regional and spatial policy.

The Strategy for the Development of Education (Strategia rozwoju edukacji na lata 2007–2013), prepared by the Ministry of Education and approved by the Polish Government as a part of the National Development Plan 2007–2013, explicitly mentions the large number of tertiary education institutions and the highly differentiated supply as one of the strong assets of Polish education (SDE 2005). Nevertheless, the document does not include any 'spatial' measure focused on increasing accessibility of tertiary education. The only exception is represented by the so-called 'special educational zones', which are to be established by 2013 in areas where specific educational problems exist: areas of low population density and with a high proportion of pupils with educational start-up hardships due to poor social and living conditions (SDE 2005). Such areas are supposed to receive special financial aids to allow for a partial reduction of the differences in the opportunities for learning that exist between rural and urban youth. The Ministry of Education have also tried to stimulate discussion between the universities on future development potentials for Polish tertiary education in the Strategy of development of university education in Poland until 2010 (Strategia rozwoju szkolnictwa wyższego w Polsce do roku 2010. SDUEP 2002). Although the document appears to be viewed favourably by the academic community, it exists only in the form of a concept and does not foresee any direct implementation measures. This lack of concrete financial measures, the limited consideration of demographic prognoses and the way it conforms to the Bologna Declaration have all provided ammunition for critics.

As mentioned previously, there has been no attempt to elaborate a spatial strategy for the development of tertiary education. Domestic and EU resources devoted to this field are mainly focused on the improvement of quality and adaptation of the curricula to the requirements of the changing economy, and towards the modernization of educational infrastructure (cf. the Strategy for Socio-Economic Development of Eastern Poland until 2020 – Strategia rozwoju społeczno-gospodarczego Polski Wschodniej do roku 2020. SSEDEP, 2008). The approach of the Government appears primarily to focus on the improvement of standards and quality of education and research and does not produce relevant efforts in the direction of the improvement of accessibility to tertiary education. This is also highlighted by the World Bank Report on Tertiary Education in Poland (World Bank, 2004) where, although accessibility is mentioned amongst the major issues, the enhancement of quality and innovation are listed as the most promising policy approaches. On the other hand awareness of the differences between the levels of socio-economic development and the role played in this context by tertiary education is constantly present in national spatial documents and guidance (cf. the CSDC, GCSS 2001; the NDP 2007–2013; IGPNDP 2005; and the NSMC, NSMC 2008) and this demonstrates that accessibility to education remains a highly relevant issue.

Overcoming existing disparities can be seen in the equalization of the educational opportunities of persons inhabiting both the development centres and the peripheral areas and this would eliminate existing barriers. Given that these barriers are not only physical but also social, financial, mental and connected with the digital divide, comprehensive solutions to this problem must be developed and pursued through different complementary actions: (1) an improvement of transport infrastructure connecting peripheral areas to academic centres, (2) an increase in investments in ICT infrastructure, (3) the provision of financial support for students coming from disadvantaged areas and (4) the enhancement of the multi-functionality of peripheral areas in order to stimulate the creation of jobs for highly educated people. The Concept for the Spatial Development of the Country recognizes the insufficient internal spatial accessibility of the regional centres due to the poor state of infrastructure and lack of the necessary investments. The document states that spatial policy ought to be implemented in particular through stimulation of increased mobility of students and the young. Similarly, the NDP 2007–2013 explicitly aims at the improvement of the accessibility of higher education for the youngsters from the rural areas and the poorest communities in towns and cities and from deprived post-industrial and post-military areas (IGPNDP 2005: 51).

The approach of the government is evolving from subsidies to investments and towards rural rather than agricultural policy and these are priorities in the Programme of Development of Rural Areas 2007–2013 (Plan Rozwoju Obszarów Wiejskich 2007), that build upon The New Rural Paradigm: Policies and Governance (2006) of the OECD as a new tool for strengthening the endogenous potential of rural areas. As far as the financial support for tertiary students is concerned, state support is provided in repayable and non-repayable form according to the prescription of the Law on Higher Education of July 2005. Funds for non-repayable types of student support have expanded, and the proportion of the student population receiving some form of publicly subsidized grant reached 25 per cent in 2005 compared with 14 per cent just three years before. Furthermore, all students in the tertiary system are now eligible for public student support (Fulton *et al.* 2007). Nevertheless, the measures undertaken do not show an explicit spatial dimension and target the entire country. In this context, the 'special educational zones' mentioned in the SDE 2007–2013 constitute an interesting step forward. In addition various programmes are being introduced aiming to develop new ways of studying primarily based on distance learning. If this is to be successful then it will clearly be necessary to reduce the digital divide and the diffusion of ICT (Piwowarski 2008). Recent years have seen a highly dynamic development of the European programme of e-Twinning (linkage and cooperation of schools in Europe with the help of the ICT). At the beginning of 2009 there were close to 7,000 Polish schools in the programme out of a total of 52,000 European schools participating (see www.etwinning.net). E-learning is also present in the university sector: in 2002 the Polish Virtual University was established and numerous universities also conduct part of their activities via the internet. Initiatives are being implemented to address the 'digital divide' between the core and peripheral areas (especially the remote peripheries). Examples of such initiatives include the *ikonk@* programme (establishment of the local so-called web-reading-rooms in rural areas) and the e-VITA and e-VITA II programmes (establishment of the local web access points in rural areas and training of the inhabitants in the use of the internet). The Operational Programme 'Human Capital' 2007–2013 (Program Operacyjny 2007) emphasizes the importance of distance learning, especially in the context of training for companies and accessibility of tertiary education. Polish national expenditure in R&D still only accounts for the 0.7 per cent of GDP, which is significantly below the European average and the 3 per cent threshold mentioned in the Lisbon Strategy (CEC 2005) and this is another issue that the Government need to address.

The range of initiatives discussed in this section illustrates how specific actions have been introduced in recent times to reduce the disparities in terms of accessibility to tertiary education in Poland. Nevertheless, as argued by Grosse (2005: 7–8), sectoral thinking still dominates policy-making activity. 'Polish administration is naturally inclined to operate in a departmental manner. This gets in the way of proper coordination and synergy of Government endeavours. At times it creates competition for power and money between the various branches of the administration' and thus inhibits a true spatial coordination of the different sectoral interventions.

Concluding remarks

The discussion in the previous sections allows us to draw some tentative conclusions on the approach pursued by the Polish Government to the transformations of Polish education and to assess it vis-à-vis the current regional development situation and trends. First, it is important to stress how Polish tertiary education has changed dramatically since the fall of communism and how it has adapted rapidly to the requirements of the market economy. In a short time, Poland has managed to join the ranks of countries with a modern, responsive and creative system of tertiary education (Fulton *et al.* 2005). Serious concerns still persist however, in relation to equity of access although this has yet to emerge among the priorities of policies that relied considerably more on the expansion of overall enrolment. Clearly the exceptional growth of enrolment levels could potentially lead to increasing opportunities for students coming from disadvantaged areas. However, the question remains as to whether regional structures actually undergo transformation due to the development of the higher-education sector or the latter has been to a greater degree dependent upon the existing structures. The authors would argue that this is actually a bilateral relationship. On the one hand, specific conditions have to be in place in order to allow for a successful strengthening of the tertiary education level. On the other hand, the increase in the number of highly educated persons contributes to the consolidation of the territorial capital of a specific area. As argued by Maier in Chapter 11 a 'locally rooted, proud and educated population with a strong sense of identity will be the best territorial capital for non-central and rural regions of Europe'. This offers considerable potential to develop both the tangible and intangible resources attached to a specific territory as well as stimulating entrepreneurship and business activity.

The cumulative nature of the development factors causes a barrier to growth that appears hard to overcome. The territorially rooted and specific characteristics of some locations predestine them to play the role of engines of regional development and it is to be expected that the gap will continue to increase between the winning and losing regions. In this context, the growing dichotomy of the Polish space constitutes a serious challenge in regard to the process of strengthening the territorial capital of areas with a weak socio-economic structure (see Faludi 2006; Kunzmann 2006). Any discussion of regional development priorities begs the rhetorical question of to what extent it is possible to overcome the deeply embedded disparities between the core and peripheral areas. Poland, along with many other CEE countries, has now passed through the transition shock. Whereas economic policy of the 1990s focused on macroeconomic issues, structural reform has recently become increasingly important in order to correct those regional disparities that have grown considerably during the transformation period and to promote enhanced development in lagging regions. The policy approach to the education sector certainly has a role to play in this framework through the improvement of individual learning and the development of human capital (Dubarle 2002). The OECD review on the role of higher education in regional development highlighted the fact that in times of increasing globalization, growth and development continue to cluster around specific regions that have a high concentration of skilled and creative workforce and the infrastructure for innovation. In this context tertiary education institutions can help their cities and regions become more innovative and globally competitive.

It would seem appropriate for the Polish Government to develop a comprehensive and coherent vision to guide future policy development. The years since 1990 have been occupied with responding to the exceptionally rapid growth in demand and trying to introduce a comprehensive framework of governance and quality assurance culminating in the new Law on Higher Education in 2005. Now that the speed of growth has slowed and the groundwork for the system has been tested and revised, this would be an excellent time to set out a clear statement of the strategic aims which should underpin future policy in the medium to long term. In this context issues of equitable accessibility need to become more prominent in national debates and policy-making. Although enhancing quality remains important, it should be remembered that in every education system the opportunity to acquire the highest grades is not equally distributed. A society seeking to optimize its talents needs to balance the demand for merit with the imperative of equity (Fulton *et al.* 2005). The extent to which the Government can simultaneously promote quality, equity and responsiveness while pursuing creativity and enterprise in the tertiary education system provides a significant challenge for the Polish Government. Unfortunately, the Education Development Strategy linked to the National Development Plan for 2007–2013 appears neither comprehensive nor widely debated. In addition its non-binding status has severely hampered its impact. It will be essential that the development of any vision involves the full range of internal and external stakeholders and potential beneficiaries and not only those who make use of tertiary education as it now exists.

Public and private enterprises need the opportunity to reflect on and articulate their needs, not only for newly qualified graduates but for continuing education and training, lifelong learning in the broadest sense and the full range of other services which tertiary education can be expected to provide. Furthermore, it will be particularly important to ensure that the emerging vision is discussed and shared by the full range of national and regional/local government ministries and agencies with an interest in any aspects of tertiary education. It will be necessary to improve coordination between the Ministry of Science and Higher Education and other relevant ministries and agencies. In the context of evidence-based policy it can also be argued that any more coherent and systematic approach to accessibility should be evidence-based using both targeted research and routine data gathering. Such evidence can be used to assess where equity problems arise and to explore the extent to which these are related to income constraints, insufficient student support or constraints related to transport or ICT. Such an assessment would require the systematic collection and spatialization of data in order to identify both territories and social groups in need of support and the knowledge gained would allow the development of appropriate mechanisms to reduce inequalities in access to tertiary education. In order to reduce inequities in the access to tertiary education the policy response should include initiatives in four areas. First, the spatial accessibility of the academic centres should be improved through improvement of the transportation network. Reducing journey times from rural areas to towns by car or public transport would result in increasing use of the services available in towns. Although over €20 billion is being devoted to Polish transport-related policies within the framework of the Operational Programme 'Infrastructure and Environment' these investments give priority to transport infrastructure of European significance aiming to strengthen the embeddedness of the main urban centres within the EU urban system rather than at the improvement of national and regional transport infrastructures.

The second issue relates to the decentralization of the educational services by capitalizing on the opportunities offered by modern ICT. The Polish Government already promote a number of initiatives aimed at addressing the 'digital divide' between towns and rural areas but more could be done in relation to strengthening the R&D base, which is currently well below the EU average. The third point is to improve financial assistance provided to needy students and although several incentives are already in place, the student support system should be expanded and diversified in order to further target people coming from disadvantaged areas. The final recommendation relates to strengthening existing relations between universities, government and business. This is a fundamental element of the process creating a territorial knowledge pool even in less successful regions (cf. Benneworth and Charles 2005; Arbo and Benneworth 2007). The enhancement of the multi-functionality of peripheral areas through the creation of high quality jobs to retain and attract people with tertiary education would also strengthen the human capital in peripheral areas.

In summary, policy-makers appear increasingly to recognize the importance of knowledge and education as crucial inputs to achieving economic growth. Tertiary education institutions are considered as externalities or critical factors of structural competitiveness that regions can tap into in order to enhance their development opportunities and increase their comparative advantages in the global market. However, doubts remain as to the sustainability of promoting financial flows toward infrastructure or subsidizing non-economically oriented activity as an effective instrument of regional development policy. Experience from elsewhere (cf. Gundlach 2003 in relation to Eastern Germany) suggests that it is more important to invest in people, not only in terms of enhancing knowledge with direct economic benefits but also in terms of enhancing skills and capacity that will enable more effective conversion of the existing territorial capital into positive effects for the social and economic sphere. The future development potential of peripheral areas will be determined to a large degree by the quality of their human capital and this would be enhanced by more spatially balanced education opportunities. Structural change is ongoing in Poland, as in other CEE countries and the EU funding that is currently available offers a unique opportunity that needs to be transformed into visible effects. If the Polish Government are to achieve cohesive regional development then more appropriate allocation and coordination of institutional actions and financial means, especially in the domain of the qualitative development of human resources, will be required.

Notes

1 The paper is focused on tertiary education institutions. Terms such as 'universities' and 'higher education institutions' are used throughout the paper, all of them meaning tertiary education institutions. For further details on the categories of tertiary education institutions, see Fulton *et al.* 2007.
2 That aim has to be understood as a geographical investigation in regional disparities (diversification) of level of socio-economic development of subregions and educational

level of inhabitants, and as well searching for an answer about spatial correlation (coexistence) of both features.

3 The Statistical Classification of Economic Activities in the European Community is a European industry standard classification system. Section J (Information and Communication), K (Financial and Insurance Activities), L (Real Estate Activities), M (Professional, scientific and technical activities) (NACE Rev. 2).

4 The Pearson linear correlation dictates the strength and direction of a linear relationship between two random variables. Coefficient is always between −1 and 1 inclusive. −1 means perfect negative linear correlation, 0 means no correlation and +1 means perfect positive linear correlation.

5 It is worth emphasizing that in group 5 (share of urban population in excess of 70 per cent) only 11 units do not display full urbanization (100 per cent).

6 At the time of preparing this chapter, the *National Spatial Development Concept* is undergoing social debate and has not yet been accepted by the government.

References

Arbo, P. and Benneworth, P. (2007) *Understanding the Regional Contribution of Higher Education Institutions: A Literature Review*, OECD Education Working Papers, no. 9, OECD Publishing.

Bański, J. (2004) 'Contemporary Transformations of the Rural Space in Poland: Selected Problems', in A. D. Kovacs (ed.) *New Aspects of Regional Transformation and the Urban-Rural Relationship*, Pecs: Centre for Regional Studies of Hungarian Academy of Sciences: 20–35.

Bathelt, H., Malmberg, A. and Maskell, P. (2004) 'Clusters and Knowledge: Local Buzz, Global Pipelines and the Process of Knowledge Creation', *Progress in Human Geography*, 28: 31–56.

Benneworth, P. and Charles, D. (2005) 'University Spin-off Policies and Economic Development in Less Successful Regions: Learning from Two Decades of Policy Practice', *European Planning Studies*, 13(4): 537–557.

Boschma, R. (2005) 'Proximity and Innovation: A Critical Assessment', *Regional Studies*, 39: 61–74.

Boschma, R. and Lambooy, J. G. (1999) 'Evolutionary Economics and Economic Geography', *Journal of Evolutionary Economics*, 9: 411–429.

CEC (2005) *Working Together for Growth and Jobs: A New Start for the Lisbon Strategy.* COM 24 (05), Luxembourg: Office for Official Publications of the European Commission.

Ciok, S., Dołzbłasz, S., Leśniak, M. and Raczyk, A. (2008) *Polska – Niemcy. Współpraca i konkurencja na pograniczu* (*Poland – Germany. Co-operation and Competition in the Border Region*), Studia Geograficzne, no. 81, Wrocław: Uniwersytet Wrocławski.

Czapiewski, K. Ł. and Janc, K. (2007) 'Education as a Factor that Diversifies the Possibilities of Economic Development in Poland', *Central European Journal of Architecture and Planning, Alfa Spectra STU*, 11(2): 29–35.

—— (2009) 'Internal Peripheries of Socio-Economic Development in Poland', in A. D. Kovacs (ed.) *Old and New Borderlines/Frontiers/Margins*, Discussion Paper, Pecs: Hungarian Academy of Sciences.

de la Fuente, A. and Ciccone, A. (2003) *Human Capital in a Global and Knowledge–based Economy*, Paris: European Commission.

Dołzbłasz, S. and Raczyk, A. (2007) 'New versus Old Cross-Border Cooperations Programmes in the Example of Polish-Czech and Polish-German border areas', *EUROPA XXI*, 16: 153–165.

Drucker, J. and Goldstein, H. (2007) 'Assessing the Regional Economic Development Impacts of Universities: A Review of Current Approaches', *International Regional Science Review*, 30(1): 20–46.

Dubarle, P. (2002) 'Learning as a Tool for Regional Development. The Case of Central and Eastern European Countries', Paper presented at the International Seminar *Education and the Future. Knowledge, Education and Territorial Development in Central and Eastern European Countries*, Trieste, 8–9 November.

Dühr, S. (2007) *The Visual Language of Spatial Planning: Exploring Cartographic Representations for Spatial Planning in Europe*, London: Routledge.

ESPON (2005a) *ESPON 1.1.1 Potentials for Polycentric Development in Europe – Final report*. Luxembourg: ESPON.

—— (2005b) *ESPON 1.1.3 Enlargement of the European Union and the Wider European Perspective as regards its Polycentric Spatial Structure – Final report*. Luxembourg: ESPON.

—— (2006) *ESPON Project 2.3.1 – Application and Effects of the ESDP in the Member States – Final Report*. Luxembourg: ESPON.

—— (2007) *ESPON Project 3.2 – Scenarios on the Territorial Future of Europe – Final Report*, Luxembourg: ESPON.

Evers, D., Tennekes, J., Borsboom, J., van den Heiligenberg, H. and Thissen, M. (2009) *A Territorial Impact Assessment of Territorial Cohesion for the Netherlands*, The Hague/Bilthoven: Netherlands Environmental Assessment Agency (PBL).

Faludi, A. (2006) 'From European Spatial Development to Territorial Cohesion Policy', *Regional Studies*, 40(6): 667–678.

Finka, M. (2010) 'Evolving Frameworks for Regional Development and Spatial Planning in the New Regions of the EU', in N. Adams, G. Cotella and R. Nunes (eds) *Territorial Development, Cohesion and Spatial Planning: Knowledge and policy development in an enlarged EU*, London: Routledge.

Fulton, O., Santiago, P., Edquist, Ch., El-Khawas, E. and Hackl, E. (2007) *OECD Reviews of Tertiary Education. Poland*, OECD, Paris.

Gawryszewski, A. (2006) 'Demographic Development', in M. Degorsky (ed.) *Natural and Human Environment of Poland, A Geographical Overview*, Warsaw: IGiZP PAN: 125–142.

GCSS – Government Center for Strategic Studies (2001) 'Koncepcja polityki przestrzennego zagospodarovania kraju', *Monitor Polski*, 26, 503–595.

Gössling, T. and Rutten, R. (2007) 'Innovation in Regions', *European Planning Studies*, 15(2): 253–270.

Grosse, T. G. (2005) 'Assessment of the National Development Plan 2007–2013', *Analysis and Opinions*, (30).

Gundlach, E. (2003) 'Growth Effects of EU Membership: The Case of East Germany', *Empirica*, 30: 237–270.

Haas, P. M. (1992) 'Epistemic Communities and International Policy Coordination', *International Organization*. 46(1): 1–35.

Haselsberger, B. and Benneworth, P. (2010) 'Cross-border Communities or Cross-border Proximity? Perspectives from the Austrian–Slovakian Border Region', in N. Adams, G. Cotella and R. Nunes (eds) *Territorial Development, Cohesion and Spatial Planning: Knowledge and policy development in an enlarged EU*, London: Routledge.

Hayek, F. von (1945) 'The Use of Knowledge in Society', *American Economic Review*, 35: 519–530.

Hilpert, U. (2006) 'Knowledge in the Region: Development Based on Tradition, Culture and Change', *European Planning Studies*, 14(5): 581–599.

Horváth, G. (2005) 'Regional Disparities and Competitiveness in Central and Eastern Europe', *EUROPA XXI*, 13: 9–25.

IGPNDP – Interministerial Group for the Preparation of the National Development Plan (2005) *National Developmen Plan 2007–2013*, Varsavia.

Jakubowicz, E. (2004) 'Edukacja a kapitał ludzki', in S. Ciok and D. Ilnicki (eds) *Regionalny wymiar integracji europejskiej*, Przekształcenia regionalnych struktur funkcjonalno-przestrzennych, vol. VIII/1, Wrocław: IGiRR UWr: 359–366.

Jałowiecki, B. (2007) 'Metropolie jako bieguny rozwoju', in G. Gorzelak (ed.) *Polska regionalna i lokalna w świetle badań EUROREG-u*, Warszawa: Wyd. Naukowe Scholar: 143–162.

Janc, K. (2009) *Zróżnicowanie przestrzenne kapitału ludzkiego i społecznego w Polsce*, Rozprawy Naukowe Instytutu Geografii i Rozwoju Regionalnego Uniwersytetu Wrocławskiego, no. 8, Wrocław: IGiRR UWr.

Janc, K. and Czapiewski, K. (2005) 'Wykształcenie czynnikiem wspierającym rozwój gospodarczy obszarów wiejskich', *Studia Obszarów Wiejskich*, 8, Warszawa: IGiPZ PAN: 69–84.

Kaufmann, V. (2005) *Re-Thinking Mobility: Contemporary Sociology*, Hampshire: Ashgate.

Korcelli, P. (2005) 'The Urban System of Poland', *Built Environment*, 31(2): 133–142.

Kunzamann, K. (2006) 'Spatial Development and Territorial Cohesion in Europe', in U. Altrock, S. Guntner, S. Huning and D. Peters (eds) *Spatial Planning and Urban Development in the New EU Member States: From Adjustment to Reinvention*, Aldershot: Ashgate: 19–30.

Lagendijk, A. and Lorentzen, A. (2007) 'Proximity, Knowledge and Innovation in Peripheral Regions. On the Intersection between Geographical and Organizational Proximity', *European Planning Studies*, 15(4): 457–466.

Lambooy, J. G. (2004) 'The Transmission of Knowledge, Emerging Networks, and the Role of Universities: An Evolutionary Approach', *European Planning Studies*, 12(5): 643–657.

Lee, S. Y., Florida, R. and Acs, Z. (2004) *Creativity and Entrepreneurship: A Regional Analysis of New Form Formation*, Discussion Papers on Entrepreneurship, Growth and Public Policy, Jena: Max Planck Institute.

Lipton, D. and Sachs, J. (1990) 'Creating a Market Economy in Eastern Europe: The Case of Poland', *Brookings Papers on Economic Activity*, 1: 75–133.

Maier, K. (2010) 'The Pursuit of Balanced Territorial Development: The Realities and Complexities of the Cohesion Agenda', in N. Adams, G. Cotella and R. Nunes (eds) *Territorial Development, Cohesion and Spatial Planning: Knowledge and Policy Development in an Enlarged EU*, London: Routledge.

Meijers, E. J., Waterhout, B. and Zonneveld, W. (2007) 'Closing the Gap: Territorial Cohesion through Polycentric Development', *European Journal of Spatial Development*, no 24. Online. Available HTTP: www.nordregio.se/EJSD/refereed24.pdf.

Nasiłowski, M. (1995) *Transformacja systemowa w Polsce*, Warszawa: Wydawnictwo Key Text.

Nowosielska, E. (2002) 'Higher Education and the Urban System. The Case of Poland in 1990s', *Geographia Polonica*, 75: 85–110.

NSMC – National Spatial Management Concept (2008) *Koncepcja przestrzennego zagospodarowania kraju do roku 2033 – projekt ekspercki*, Non-Governmental document, Warszawa: Ministerstwo Rozwoju Regionalnego.

Pallagst, K. M. (2006) 'European Spatial Planning Reloaded: Considering EU Enlargement in Theory and Practice', *European Planning Studies*, 14: 253–272.

—— (2010) 'The Emergence of Epistemic Communities in the New European Landcape: Some Theoretical Implications for the Spatial Agenda of the EU' in N. Adams, G. Cotella and R. Nunes (eds) *Territorial Development, Cohesion and Spatial Planning: Knowledge and Policy Development in an Enlarged EU*, London: Routledge.

Piwowarski, R. (2008) 'Modele edukacji dla potrzeb Koncepcji Przestrzennego Zagospodarowania Kraju', *Ekspertyzy na potrzeby KPZK*, 4: 396–415.

Plan Rozwoju Obszarów Wiejskich na lata 2007–2013 (2007) Warszawa: Ministerstwo Rolnictwa i Rozwoju Wsi.

Program Operacyjny Kapitał Ludzki (2007) Warszawa: Ministerstwo Rozwoju Regionalnego.

Radaelli, C. M. (1995) 'The Role of Knowledge in the Policy Process', *Journal of European Public Policy*, 2(2): 159–183.

Rogerson, P. A. (2006) *Statistical Methods for Geography*, London: Sage.

Romer, P. M. (1990) 'Endogenous Technological Change', *Quarterly Journal of Economics*, 98: 71–102.

Rosner, A. (ed.) (2007) *Zróżnicowanie poziomu rozwoju społeczno-gospodarczego obszarów wiejskich a zróżnicowanie dynamiki przemian*, Problemy Rozwoju Wsi i Rolnictwa, Warszawa: IRWiR PAN.

Stead, D. and Nadin, V. (2010) 'Shifts in Territorial Governance and the Europeanization of Spatial Planning in Central and Eastern Europe', in N. Adams, G. Cotella and R. Nunes (eds) *Territorial Development, Cohesion and Spatial Planning: Knowledge and Policy Development in an Enlarged EU*, London: Routledge.

Storper, M. and Venables, A. J. (2004) 'Buzz: Face-To-Face Contact and the Urban Economy', *Journal of Economic Geography*, 4: 351–370.

SDE (2005) *Strategia rozwoju Edukacji na lata 2007–2013*, Warszawa: Ministerstwo Edukacji Narodowej i Sportu.

SDUEP (2002) *Strategia rozwoju szkolnictwa wyższego w Polsce do roku 2010*, Warszawa: Ministerstwo Edukacji Narodowej i Sportu.

SSEDEP (2008) *Strategia rozwoju społeczno-gospodarczego Polski Wschodniej do roku 2020*, Warszawa: Ministerstwo Rozwoju Regionalnego.

Tewdwr-Jones, M. (2010) 'Cohesion and Competitiveness: The Evolving Context for European Territorial Development', in N. Adams, G. Cotella and R. Nunes (eds) *Territorial Development, Cohesion and Spatial Planning: Knowledge and Policy Development in an Enlarged EU*, London: Routledge.

Tondl, G. and Vuksic, G. (2003) 'What Makes Regions in Eastern Europe Catching Up? The Role of Foreign Investment, Human Resources and Geography', *ZEI Working Paper*, B12, Bonn.

Törnqvist, G. (2004) 'Creativity in Time and Space', *Geografiska Annaler, Series B: Human Geography*, 86: 227–244.

Waterhout, B. (2010) 'European Spatial Planning: Current State and Future Challenges', in N. Adams, G. Cotella and R. Nunes (eds) *Territorial Development, Cohesion and Spatial Planning: Knowledge and Policy Development in an Enlarged EU*, London: Routledge.

Werwicki, A. (1994) 'Potencjały naukowe w Polsce w 1990 roku i ich rozmieszczenie', *Zeszyty IGiPZ PAN Warszawa*, 21: 37–76.

Wojnicka, E., Tarkowski, M. and Klimczak, P. (2005) *Przestrzenne i regionalne zróżnicowania ośrodków wzrostu. Polaryzacja a wyrównywanie szans rozwojowych. Przesłanki dla kształtowania polityki regionalnej państwa*, Gdynia-Rzeszów: Ministerstwo Rozwoju Regionalnego.

World Bank (2004) *Tertiary Education in Poland*, Raport No 29718, Warsaw: World Bank.

Part IV

Learning from experiences beyond the border

Editors' introduction to Part IV

Neil Adams, Giancarlo Cotella and Richard Nunes

There has been an increasing awareness of the importance of the external dimension of EU policy generally and, more importantly considering the context for this book, in relation to territorial governance in particular. The changing nature of borders in times of globalization, an issue already put forward by Haselsberger and Benneworth in this volume (Chapter 10), suggests how it has become crucial to look at the wider European and global context and try to learn from experiences beyond the external EU border. Similarly, while discussing different types of peripheries, Kunzmann (2008) emphasizes the importance of the EU understanding its external dimensions. This external dimension of EU territorial governance provides the focus for this final part of the book which examines one of these external dimensions, namely the eastern external border of the EU and, more specifically, the border with the Russian Federation. The inclusion of this part of the book is premised on the editors' belief that any discussion of the complex cross-scalar and multi-jurisdictional policy environment of planning in the EU-27 would be incomplete without a consideration of the new border with the Russian Federation and former Soviet republics. Part 4 therefore seeks to provide some initial insights into the complexities of the Russian dimension in relation to cooperation on spatial development issues and the production and sharing of knowledge that can influence policy development and practice on both sides of this external border.

Major international and national processes in the last 20 years, such as the collapse of the Soviet Union, the eastwards enlargement of the EU and the re-emergence of the Russian Federation as a global power, have changed the geo-political map of Europe beyond recognition. There is little doubt that the relationship between the EU and the Russian Federation is becoming increasingly important at many levels and in many ways due to the geographic position and size of the latter and the extent of its influence and natural resources. However, a complex set of historical, political and cultural differences and tensions make this relationship far from straightforward. The contributions presented here, far from pretending to constitute any comprehensive examination of these complexities, aim to provide a 'first glimpse' at a little known transnational space of socio-cultural and economic relations that pose significant territorial implications for the EU as well as for the wider European continent.

The contributions provide an insight into some of the socio-political and cultural realities and complexities of the post-Soviet world and indicate the potential opportunity for mutual learning and increased understanding. In this context, it is important to underline how the history of Russia in the last 70 years has been closely entwined with that of other CEE countries within the context of the socialist block and, after 1989, of its enduring Soviet legacy. As a result, many of the challenges being faced in the Russian Federation are reminiscent of realities that remain strongly connected culturally with the post-socialist countries that have since joined the EU, as well as with new EU neighbours such as Belarus and Ukraine. The process of transition since the collapse of the Soviet Union has been rapid and dramatic. Whilst a healthy body of literature has emerged in planning-related academic publications in Western Europe focusing on the transition process in CEE (cf. Thomas 1998; Ovin 2001; Gorzelak *et al.* 2001; Petrakos 2001; Krakte 2002; Paalzow 2006), relatively little of this material has related specifically to post-Soviet Russia. The complexities of planning in post-Soviet Russia are immense. Planning is situated between competing tensions of an expert-centred Soviet style approach and an incremental development driven market-based approach and includes a complex mixture of eastern and western planning ideals (Tynkkynen 2009). Tynkkynen argues that power is central in Russian planning and that knowledge and expertise has a clear role in serving the needs of certain elite groups. Here the challenges and responses to the transition process merit discussion, both because of the number of similarities as well as of the significant differences, and for this reason the inclusion of this section of the book appears to be particularly relevant also in relation to CEE countries.

However, in an age when it could be argued that borders are in many ways becoming an increasingly abstract concept (Williams 2003; Blatter 2004), the engagement of Russia into emergent expert and professional communities presents both challenges and great potential. The characteristics of the Soviet regime where planning was highly centralized meant that the Soviet planning system was in many ways incompatible with the demands of a post-Soviet market-based society (Iyer 2003). In addition market-based systems require a mature and coherent institutional infrastructure that was lacking initially in the Russian Federation and in the other former soviet and socialist countries, therefore leading to a wide diversity of approaches being adopted (Golubchikov 2004). In this context Adams (2008) argued that it may be somewhat naive to expect complex concepts and practices such as strategic planning, transparency, inclusion and stakeholder engagement to be embraced in post-Soviet states when they are problematic enough in mature democracies. In addition it is far from certain the extent to which such practices are appropriate in such dramatically different contexts. Whilst the relationship between the EU and Russia is highly complex, a variety of formal and informal networks and arenas have emerged that offer opportunities for cooperation and mutual learning. The degree to which policy is evidence-based or indeed evidence is policy-based is debatable, especially within the contentious context of world politics. Nevertheless, on the basis of the contributions in this book, the editors would argue that the further evolution of the expert and professional communities and arenas throughout the European continent is an ongoing and worthwhile process that can foster mutual learning and potentially be highly beneficial in many fields including spatial planning and territorial governance.

As mentioned in Chapter 1, it is possible to detect an increasing awareness at the European Commission of the importance of clarifying the place of the EU in the global environment and this clearly requires an exploration of the realities beyond its external borders. This increasing awareness is illustrated by the two recent calls for proposals for ESPON projects and the anticipated projects under the 7th Framework Programme focusing on the external and global dimension of the EU. This section seeks to offer some preliminary insights into the complex relationship between the EU and the Russian Federation from both perspectives and to elaborate on some of the main themes analyzed during the first three parts of this book in this context. The difficulties and complexities of establishing effective epistemic communities and communities of practice and the enduring effects of borders within the EU have been discussed at length and in varying contexts in the different contributions to this book. A number of authors have also explored and discussed the retention and merger scenarios in the context of enlargement and their relevance to those communities in the new Member States (cf. the contributions of Pallagst, Finka and Maier in this volume). The exploration in this final section takes this discussion to a new level, as in principle it may still be possible to adopt the two scenarios to conceptualize the potential interaction of expert and professional communities in an EU–Russian context. Although the authors in this section do not focus on this aspect specifically, it would be reasonable to assume that the merger scenario would be undermined by the existing physical and political borders but also due to significant psychological, institutional and cultural borders that exist between the EU and the Russian Federation. The divisions between actors and the limited permeability of the Austrian–Slovakian border discussed by Haselsberger and Benneworth in Chapter 10 would seem to suggest that effective integration and cooperation between Russian and EU expert communities and networks would be more difficult to achieve. Nevertheless, as evidence presented in the chapters of the present section shows, a set of established cooperation initiatives, mainly promoted under the flag of the EU and of the Council of Europe, seems to provide some room for a lukewarm optimism in relation to mutual learning and the generation of mutually beneficial knowledge arenas and resources in the future.

Offering themselves an opportunity for mutual learning, the discussions in these chapters suggest a degree of permeability of the new EU Eastern border, building on the diffusion and reciprocation of formal and informal policies and practices as well as on the global character of many territorial trends affecting European regions. Together the contributions shed some light on the complex cross-scalar and multi-jurisdictional tensions and difficulties that characterize the relationship between the EU and the Russian Federation. An understanding of some of these issues may be beneficial and indeed necessary if effective cooperation at lower spatial scales is to be immune from sporadic high-level geopolitical tensions. Relations between the EU and the Russian Federation are all too often characterized by such geopolitical tensions in relation to issues such as foreign policy and energy, as well as a mutual misunderstanding and mistrust. The complexity of the relationship has been increased with the re-emergence of Russia as a major power on the global stage and the subsequent re-centralization of power in the Russian Federation discussed by Fritsch (2009). Regular fluctuations in relations between the EU and the Russian Federation provide a challenging context for ongoing cooperation at lower institutional levels and in diverse arenas and jurisdictions. Numerous and diverse knowledge arenas have emerged within which the various multiple bodies and organizations engaged with aspects relevant to spatial development cooperate. The influence of these diverse knowledge arenas depends to a degree on the status, influence and power of the various actors within their own institutional structure. In this context, the influence and role of CEMAT, where the Federal Ministry of Regional Development is active, appears to have more status in Russia than the VASAB initiative where Russia is represented by regional and local actors rather than actors from the Federal level. The complexities and fluctuations in these high-level relationships can be interpreted as a threat but also as an opportunity for the evolution of networks and communities operating in knowledge arenas dealing with issues more relevant to lower territorial scales.

It is within this complex cross-scalar and multi-jurisdictional environment that the contributions in this section of the book are set. The contribution by Matti Fritsch focuses on the Baltic Sea Region (BSR) and the role that the Russian Federation has played within this well established arena of cooperation. The geographical proximity of Finland to the Russian Federation and the well established bilateral links and cooperation between the countries means that the Finnish experience can provide valuable insights into the potentials and complexities of relations with the Russian Federation. In many ways Finland has a different relationship with the Russian Federation than other Member States, even those who, like Finland share a land border with their large eastern neighbour. The transition from a status as Soviet Socialist Republics to members of the EU and NATO, coupled with tensions in relation to significant Russian minorities and transit issues, mean that relations between the Baltic States and Russia are complex and often tense. Although historical relations between Russia and Finland have also seen conflicts, in more recent times a more pragmatic and cooperative relationship has emerged. This special relationship between the two countries means that Fritsch is well placed to provide valuable insights into the potentials, opportunities and complexities of cooperation with Russian actors. The author emphasizes the usefulness of the BSR as a lens through which these issues can be explored due to the fact that both the internal and external dimensions of EU territorial governance are present. In addition, the BSR also illustrates the complexity and cross-scalar nature of the interactions between actors trying to operate within the all too rigid confines of cross-border institutional realities.

Fritsch examines two initiatives to explore these issues. First, he examines the long standing VASAB initiative that has operated as a knowledge arena within which regional actors from the Russian Federation have played an active role since the early 1990s. VASAB is characterized by the formulation of long-term vision and strategies for 11 countries around the Baltic Sea, including the non-EU Member States of Russia, Norway and Belarus (VASAB 2009). The approach adopted to spatial planning in VASAB is highly strategic and, in this sense, is similar to approaches familiar to the north-west European planning community in relation to the ESDP and transnational spatial visions prepared under the INTERREG programme. More recently the European Commission has shown an increasing interest in macro-regions and the BSR has been seen as a pilot region in the context of the EU Strategy for the Baltic Sea Region in which the Commission has played an active leading role (CEC 2009). This focus on macro-regions illustrates the current emphasis on 'soft spaces' referred to in Chapters 1 and 2. The recently published Strategy forms the second initiative considered by Fritsch. The Strategy provides an interesting comparison to VASAB due to the countries and actors involved and the approach adopted and reveals much about the complexities of the relationship between the EU and Russia, as well as the evolution of territorial governance in an EU and a wider European context. The more pragmatic and action-oriented approach adopted in the EU strategy for the BSR compared to the aspirational style of VASAB documents supports the view of the more general shift in planning style discussed in Chapter 1.

The complexities of cooperation and achieving joint actions between the EU and the Russian Federation are explained and the implications of this for the future of territorial governance in the EU are assessed. Fritsch's contribution also sets the context for a more detailed examination of the evolution of strategic planning within the Russian Federation in the second chapter in this part of the book. The contribution by Natalia Razumeyko examines the emergence and evolution of the practice of strategic planning within the Russian Northwest Federal District and, more specifically, in the city of St Petersburg. The chapter provides a further brief insight into an aspect of the planning realities in the part of Russia that shares a common land border with the EU. This part of the country has been referred to as the most European part of Russia, due to its geographical proximity and interactions dating back to Tsarist times, but also partly due to the history of cooperation and initiatives with regional and local actors in EU Member States. As editors we feel that no discussion of spatial development in Europe would be complete without considering the Russian dimension and this is even more so in the context of the BSR, within which St Petersburg is by far the largest city, as mentioned in the chapter by Fritsch. St Petersburg is the second largest city in the Russian Federation and is a highly significant centre for economic activities, culture, education, and most importantly in the context of this book, knowledge. It is therefore not surprising that there is a significant concentration of actors and expert and professional networks and communities in the city that are active in international, national and regionally relevant knowledge arenas and are responsible for generating considerable knowledge resources in the Russian context. This chapter therefore provides valuable insights into the permeability of this part of the EU external border in terms of knowledge transfer as the author examines the evolution of strategic planning and the challenges and obstacles of applying strategic planning by public bodies in practice. Tynkkynen (2009) argues that the emergence and popularity of strategic planning in St Petersburg is in itself evidence of this permeability and western influence. The author applies a framework to conceptualize the diversity of approaches adopted in the application of strategic planning in Russia and assesses some of the implications of this as well as exploring the role of expert and professional networks and communities within this context.

In many ways this book is itself evidence of the existence of an expert community that crosses this eastern external EU border and actors from St Petersburg have been active in this process. Like a number of contributors to the volume, the author of the final chapter in this section participated in a meeting organized in 2007 in Bratislava by the Young Academics Network of the Association of European Schools of Planning (AESOP), that focused on the engagement with and between CEE countries and at which the idea for this book was born. The following year the network was strengthened and extended when a second meeting was organized in St. Petersburg and involved the participation of a number of Russian actors. It is difficult to assess how many similarly informal networks are active although in the field of spatial planning the number is likely to be small. Such networks are characterized by frequent fluctuations in the intensity of interaction, and in both the levels and composition of the membership. On the other hand, they are also likely to be able to be flexible and adaptable and have the potential to become more formalized from time to time in the context of specific arenas. Such informal networks do not possess the influence or indeed the desire to directly influence spatial policy development but nevertheless they form an important component of the wider European planning community and can potentially make valuable contributions to the wider spatial planning discourse by generating and debating knowledge resources. These rather low key interactions also generally have the ability to operate in spite of any high-level geopolitical tensions that may arise at the level of the EU and the Russian Federation. In the longer term this may have a beneficial impact on the integration of professional and expert communities and on knowledge transfer although the scale of the barriers suggests that the merger scenario outlined elsewhere in this book would be an unrealistic goal. The cross-border nature of spatial development trends and challenges however, implies that both informal and more formalized arenas, networks and coalitions have significant potential to promote mutual learning. There is little doubt that the spatial planning and spatial development discourse on both sides of the eastern external border would be enriched as a result and that actors from North-west Russia generally, and St Petersburg in particular, will have a significant role to play in this process.

References

Adams, N. (2008) 'Convergence and Policy Transfer: an examination of the extent to which approaches to spatial planning have converged within the context of an enlarged EU', *International Planning Studies*, 13(1): 31–50.

Blatter, J. (2004) 'From Spaces of Place to Spaces of Flows? Territorial and functional governance in cross-border regions in Europe and North America', *International Journal of Urban and Regional Research*, 28 (3): 530–548.

CEC – Commission of the European Communities (2009) *Communication from the Commission to the European Parliament, the Council, the European Economic and Social Committee and the Committee of the Regions concerning the European Union Strategy for the Baltic Sea Region.* Available at HTTP: http://ec.europa.eu/regional_policy/sources/docoffic/official/communic/baltic/com_baltic_en.pdf accessed March 2010.

Fritsch, M. (2009) 'European Territorialization and the Eastern Neighbourhood: Spatial development co-operation between the EU and Russia', *European Journal of Spatial Development*, 35. Available at HTTP: www.nordregio.se/EJSD/refereed35.pdf accessed March 2010.

Golubchikov, O. (2004) Urban Planning in Russia: Towards the market, *European Planning Studies*, 12(2).

Gorzelak, G., Ehrlich, E., Faltan, L. and Illner, M. (eds) (2001) *Central Europe in Transition. Towards EU membership.* Warsaw: Regional Studies Association – Polish section.

Iyer, S. D. (2003) 'The Urban Context for Adjustments to the Planning Process in Post-Soviet Russia: Responses from local planners in Siberia', *International Planning Studies*, 8(3): 201–223.

Krakte, S. (2002) 'The Regional Impact of EU Eastern Enlargement: A view from Germany', *European Planning Studies*, 10(5): 651–64.

Kunzmann, K. (2008) 'Futures for European Space 2020', *Journal of Nordregio*, 2(8).

Ovin, R. (2001) 'The Nature of Institutional Change in Transition', *Post Communist Economies*, 13(2): 133–146.

Paalzow, A. (2006) 'Barriers to Regional Development in the New Member States: the Latvian experience', in N. Adams, J. Alden and N. Harris (eds) *Regional Development and Spatial Planning in an Enlarged European Union*, Aldershot: Ashgate.

Petrakos, G. (2001) 'Patterns of Regional Inequality in Transition Economies', *European Planning Studies*, 9(3): 359–383.

Thomas, M. J. (1998) 'Thinking about Planning in the Transitional Countries of Central and Eastern Europe', *International Planning Studies*, 3(3): 321–333.

Tynkkynen, V. P. (2009) 'Planning Realities among Practitioners in St Petersburg, Russia – Soviet traditions and Western influences', in J. Knieling and F. Othengrafen (eds) *Planning Cultures in Europe: Decoding cultural phenomena in urban and regional planning*, Farnham, Surrey: Ashgate.

VASAB (2009) *VASAB Long-Term Perspective for the Territorial Development of the Baltic Sea Region*, Draft of 19 March 2009 For Public Consultation. Available at HTTP: www.vasab.org/documents.php?go=display&ID=63 accessed March 2010.

Williams, J. (2003) 'Territorial Borders, International Ethics and Geography: do good fences still make good neighbours?', *Geopolitics*, 8 (2): 25–46.

15 Interfaces of European Union internal and external territorial governance

The Baltic Sea Region

Matti Fritsch

Introduction

As several authors already argued in earlier chapters of this book, the recent eastern enlargement of the European Union (EU) is reshaping the European spatial planning agenda to a significant extent. North-eastern Europe in general and the Baltic Sea Region (BSR) in particular have become items of specific interest in this respect, as the region includes 'old' and 'new' as well as non-Member States. Within this context, the analysis in this chapter focuses on collective action and processes of learning and knowledge transfer in territorial governance in the BSR. Various forms of territorial development policy carried out at multiple levels of governance and an increasing awareness of, and an interest in territorial issues at the EU level constitute important elements of the territorialization of the European space (Fritsch 2009). This process of territorialization entails a politically laden visioning process of how the European space should develop both internally (into a more integrated space) as well as vis-à-vis its external neighbourhood (relations with neighbouring states and regions) (ibid.). In this respect, the BSR can be seen as a particularly interesting and challenging arena where these processes of internal and external territorialization are played out at a macro-regional level. Internally, the macro-region's unprecedented integration as a result of the EU membership of the majority of its littoral states, the existence of numerous forms of collaborative organizations and networks, the apparent dissolving of the barrier effects of borders (cf. Haselsberger and Benneworth Chapter 10) and the subsequent reconnection of links that have been cut off during the Cold War provide a fertile ground for spatial integration in the BSR. However, the process of territorialization of the EU in general and in the BSR in particular also includes an intricate external dimension. This mainly refers to Russia's geographic location as a non-EU littoral state (and major regional power) and its involvement and obvious interest in the development of, and cooperation within the BSR.

Acknowledging the BSR's special status as an arena where the internal and external dimensions of EU territorial governance come together, the focus of attention in this chapter rests on territorial governance initiatives, which mainly emanate from within the EU territory, and their interrelationship with other large regional power and territorial entities in the region (i.e. the Russian Federation). Although it is clear that many other initiatives and actions exist in relation to territorial governance in the BSR, the long-running *Vision and Strategies Around the Baltic Sea 2010* (VASAB) and the more recent and, at least on paper, novel *EU Strategy for the Baltic Sea Region*, which, if successful, may serve as a model for other macro-regions in Europe, are used as case studies.

The wider aim of this chapter is therefore to examine how initiatives of mutual learning and knowledge exchange as well as policy-making in territorial governance have been deployed and carried out between a variety of actors in the BSR and to examine the extent to which the Russian dimension has been either excluded or included in these activities. The chapter is structured as follows. First, the internal and external dimensions of EU territorial governance will be explored in a wider context. Second, the territorial features and specificities of the BSR will be highlighted. Third, spatial planning cooperation and territorial governance in the BSR will be analyzed with regard to its external and internal dimensions by focusing on two territorial governance initiatives (VASAB and the EU Strategy for the Baltic Sea Region) that deal with knowledge production and exchange as well as policy transfer in multi-level networks. Finally, conclusions will be drawn on the presented discussion.

Internal and external dimensions of European Union territorial governance

The territoriality of the EU political project and the territorial shape of the BSR have undergone significant change during the last two decades. The 1995 and 2004 accession rounds included the accession of Finland, Estonia, Latvia, Lithuania and Poland, countries that are both littoral states of the Baltic Sea as well as sharing common borders with the Russian Federation. As noted by the editors in the introduction to section 4 of this volume, this has presented the EU with new social, economic and environmental challenges as well as a new territorial context. Having extended into North-Eastern Europe, the EU has been presented with a new, and explicitly territorial, 'Russian dimension'. This new and direct territorial interrelationship between the two territorial entities is today signified by a land border approximately 2,400 km long, including, with the Kaliningrad oblast, a Russian exclave completely surrounded by EU territory. As a result of this territorial proximity and the relative vibrancy in multilateral as well as bilateral cooperation between the EU Baltic Sea states and Russia since the early 1990s, the centre of gravity of EU-Russian territorial relations today can be deemed to be located in the BSR.

This new territorial context has also been accompanied by an increasing interest at regional, national and the EU level in the development of European macro-regions, arguably as a consequence of the accession-induced vastly enlarged EU territory and the resultant increasing territorial diversity, but also by an increasing interregional competition due to processes of globalization. This also relates to the wider-ranging question of the future development of the European political space or, in other words, its territoriality. In this context, the increasing interest in European macro-regions can be taken as an indication of an increasing politico-territorial practice towards what Sami Moisio (2003) calls *power fragmentation*. According to Moisio (2003, drawing on Joenniemi 2000), the territorial result of this development trajectory would resemble the spatial model of a 'Europe of Olympic Circles', consisting of different but interdependent European regions that also integrate external territorial dimensions by blurring existing East-West divisions and treating Russia in a non-discriminating manner. Antola (2009), for example, argues that through processes of regionalization there are currently five mega-regions emerging in the EU. In addition to the BSR, the regions identified by Antola are the Mediterranean Olympic Circle, Visegrad cooperation, Danube Region and the circle of Western Europe. Moisio pitches this regionalist conceptualization of the European space against another possible model of a 'Europe of Concentric Circles', which would be the result of centralized powers that would emanate from the core towards the peripheries and exclude Russia from the European project. The question of how either the model of a 'Europe of Olympic Circles' or the model of a 'Europe of Concentric Circles' is visible in territorial governance initiatives in the BSR is at the heart of the investigation in this chapter.

European macro-regions have found their procedural and institutional expression in recent initiatives such as the *EU Strategy for the Baltic Sea Region* – the first EU-led macro-regional strategy launched by the EU, and the European Strategy for the Danube – a more recent macro-regional strategy built around the territorial assets of one of the most important inland waterways in the EU. In the above initiatives, the European Commission has played a key role. In the context of the BSR, this signifies a clear departure from the earlier apprehensiveness on part of the EU to develop distinct approaches and sets of policies for this macro-region (Joenniemi 2008). It also clearly represents manifestations of the EU's growing interest in territorial frameworks and strategies for specific parts of its territory. This is related to the operationalization of territorial cohesion through the encouragement of strategic territorial cooperation and coordination at a variety of territorial levels (cf. also Haselsberger and Benneworth Chapter 10).

However, European macro-regions are not closed territorial entities as generally they extend into non-EU territory and, thereby, exhibit important spatial interdependencies also with adjacent non-EU regions such as trade, transport infrastructure and, particularly in the case of Russia, energy relations. Not surprisingly then, the EU has long shown an interest in the development of its neighbouring areas and has facilitated policy transfer and provided funding opportunities in order to support and stabilize transition and transformation processes to democracy and a market economy in both pre-accession states as well as in countries that are not foreseen to become EU members in the near future (Williams 1996). EU instruments used for this purpose include TACIS, PHARE, the INTERREG Community Initiative and, more recently, the Instrument for

Pre-Accession Assistance (IPA) and European Neighbourhood and Partnership Instrument (ENPI). However, despite an increasing understanding at the EU level that EU policies have certain territorial impacts – which, in turn, results in a need for these policies to be spatialized or territorialized (Evers *et al.* 2009) – these instruments, with the exception of the INTERREG IIC and INTERREG IIIB programmes, did not have particularly strong territorial focus, especially in their external dimensions.

However, there exists a variety of channels for cooperation at multiple levels of governance between the EU and Russia in territorial governance issues. This, for example, includes the European Conference of Ministers responsible for Regional Planning (CEMAT) in which Russia recently held the Presidency and enjoys a high status. CEMAT is perceived as an important arena for pan-European exchange on spatial development issues. There are a variety of other important and long-lasting as well as ad-hoc arenas of cooperation. VASAB, which will be the focus of attention in a later part of this chapter, has provided North-West Russia with a lasting voice in spatial development in the BSR since the mid-1990s. At even lower echelons of governance, the 'Baltic Euroregional Network' (BEN), which was financed by the BSR INTERREG III B Neighbourhood Programme and aimed at the promotion of spatial development and territorial integration in the BSR by strengthening Euroregions through continuous capacity-building and sharing of experience, can be mentioned as an example of sub-national and multilateral cooperation. As a direct result of this cooperation the Russian/Belarusian dimension of the project was further strengthened by the launching of the 'Baltic Euroregional Network – East' project in 2007. Also on a bilateral level between Finland and North-West Russia there have been both nationally and regionally driven initiatives on spatial development cooperation, which, however, have remained at a rather rudimentary and exploratory level (cf. Fritsch 2011).

Recently, interest in the external dimension of territorial development at the EU-level is also visible through the ESPON research programme, where several projects deal with the EU's position in wider territorial settings. With regard to the importance of 'evidence' to inform this debate, ESPON is, for example, launching projects on *Territorial cooperation in transnational areas and across internal/external borders* and *Continental territorial structures and flows (globalization)* as part of its ESPON 2013 programme (ESPON 2009a, 2009b). With regard to the 'Visions of Europe in the World' (ESPON 2007: 57–83), part of a report produced as part of the ESPON 2006 Project 3.4.1 that aimed to trace the role and place of Europe in the world, has attracted considerable interest, distilling four different visions from the current debate on spatial planning in the EU. These visions range from the conceptualization of the European territory as a protected and closed territory ('continent' vision) with an emphasis on internal territorial cohesion and securitization against external threats, to an 'archipelago' vision that is based on networked non-territorial relations rather than geographical proximity. As such, these visions are both the result of and, more importantly, influence and inform the debate among the 'epistemic community' concerned with EU territorial development – both in its external and internal dimensions. It must be borne in mind that the 'visions' set out for Europe in the world was not part of the official assignment from the ESPON Monitoring Committee – which consists of representatives of the Member States as well as the European Commission – but was based on the initiative and work of individual ESPON partners, particularly Beckouche and Grasland from the University of Paris (cf. Beckouche and Grasland 2008). However, hoping that the visions 'would raise the awareness of the territorial dimension of the global context of Europe' (ESPON 2007: 59), the Monitoring Committee decided to grant exceptional permission to include the visions in the ESPON report. Here we can witness firsthand how evidence produced in a specific knowledge arena – the ESPON research network – has turned into a knowledge resource for policymakers at the EU level – via the ESPON Monitoring Committee – that supports the opening up of new areas of investigation and the formulation of ideas, i.e. the EU's territorial relations with its wider neighbourhood.

The European Commission's interest in the external dimension of territorial governance and regional policy is also illustrated by the fact that the Commission signed a Memorandum of Understanding with the Ministry of Regional Development of the Russian Federation in May 2007, aiming to establish a 'Dialogue on Regional Policy'. The Memorandum stresses that 'questions regarding regional and territorial become ever more important, not only because the EU and the Russian Federation share common borders but also because both cover territories of continental scale which leads to similar large scale problems' (CEC 2007). Among the objectives set out in the Memorandum are cooperation and exchange on regional policies, multi-level governance and specifically collaboration within the ESPON and CEMAT frameworks. However, to what extent these objectives have been put into practice is uncertain, although it is, at this point in time, too early to cast judgement over these aspects.

A complexity in analyzing spatial planning and territorial governance in Europe and its macro-regions also concerns the ambiguity and vagueness of the policy field of European spatial planning itself, which has been referred to as a 'strange animal' (Rusca 1998: 37. For detailed analysis of spatial planning as a concept see Böhme 2002; Giannakourou 1996; Faludi 2002). In relation to the governing of territorial development at supranational scales, it also should be mentioned that the EU has no statutory rights in this policy field and as such is only one among many actors (cf. Waterhout Chapter 4). Consequently, the EU is, to a significant extent, dependent on Member States, regional governments and local authorities; that is, those actors/organizations where actual competencies in spatial policy and planning actually lie. This renders European spatial planning a policy field that incorporates a peculiar mix of regional, national/ bilateral, and pan European/supranational cooperation initiatives, which, in turn, emphasizes the *multi-level* nature of (territorial) *governance* in the EU (Hooghe and Marks 2001). Thus, a variety of actors and organizations located at different territorial levels are involved in the shaping of ideas and discourses on the territorial development of the EU. Waterhout (2008: 204) put forward the idea of territorial governance as a more appropriate term for current spatial planning activities at the EU level and this can be understood as a process of collective action with a territorial focus, as also promoted by Healey (2006) in the context of urban regions. Undoubtedly, this conceptualization is also appropriate in the macro-regional territorial context in which the BSR is located. 'Collective action' emphasizes the concern of, initiative by, and cooperation within a set of actors for the good of a given territory; that is, to search for solutions to commonly and collectively perceived territorial problems and challenges (Bagnasco and Le Galès 2000).

Also, against this background, the BSR represents a particularly interesting region as a highly collaborative environment with a plethora of organizations at transnational, sub/regional and city levels, which has already been active since the early 1990s and has provided a fertile ground for activities and initiatives in the field of territorial governance.

Territorial features of and cooperation in the Baltic Sea macro-region

The BSR is an increasingly visible macro-region in the territorial structure of the EU. The region is generally perceived by regional and national stakeholders, as well as the European Commission, as a dynamic, collaborative, but also diverse region that grapples with its past as a divided macro-region. According to EU figures, the BSR contains 23 per cent of the EU population (106 million inhabitants), but only an aggregated GDP of 16 per cent (EU-27) (CEC 2008a). This can be compared to the 'Pentagon', which has been identified by the ESDP (CEC 1999) as the 'core area of the EU' shaped by London, Paris, Munich, Milan and Hamburg – and thus also includes parts of the BSR, which, according to ESPON figures, contained 32 per cent of the population and produced 46 per cent of GDP in 2002 (ESPON 2006).

Political, social, economic and, ultimately, territorial development in the BSR have been turbulent in the recent past. The disappearance of the 'Iron Curtain' and the accession of the majority of Baltic Sea states to the EU, made it possible for the BSR to emerge as a macro-region on the map of Europe and to develop into an increasingly integrated space. This was facilitated by an increasing permeability and openness of borders, the harmonization of economic practices and the removal of unnecessary obstacles between Member States brought about by European integration and this has led to the opening up and creation of new or formerly existing markets (Nijkamp 1995). The removal of obstacles between traditional trading routes between regions and cities and the subsequent socioeconomic integration in the BSR reflects the area's tradition of close economic and political cooperation since medieval times, represented by historical trading blocs such as the Hanseatic League. Indeed, as Scott (2002: 142) argues, much of the emergence of the BSR as a macro-region, particularly during the 1990s, had 'as much to do with historical relationships as with an acute sense of mutual interdependence'.

Despite strong economic development since the early 1990s, the BSR remains a region that suffers from socio-economic disparities, as still today an East-West divide is clearly discernible (see Hanell and Neubauer 2005; Schmitt and Dubois 2008). As such, the BSR can be seen as regional, *en miniature* variant of the East-West disparities that are part of the rationale for the investigation in this book (cf. Adams *et al.* Chapter 1 and Maier Chapter 11, both in this book). The BSR indeed includes some of the most economically successful, innovative and prosperous regions in Europe, such as the capital regions of Helsinki and Stockholm as well as Denmark and northern Germany, but also some of the economically most lagging regions of the EU in the Baltic States and Poland. Thus, despite the progress made in the former Eastern bloc countries, a significant gap between the western and eastern shores of the Baltic Sea still exists. A North-South divide can also be identified in the form of significant differences in population densities as well as infrastructure provision and accessibility. Particularly, the northern sparsely populated areas have long been seen as an area of specific problems that relate to the existing settlement pattern and economic structures, and thus have been spatially and psychologically somewhat removed from the more southern areas.

Numerous single and multi-issue networks of cooperation and learning, supported by joint research into spatial integration in the BSR,[1] have sprung up in the macro-region during the last 20 years. These networks have been fuelled by the development prospects provided by potential integration of traditional economic regions, again forming new markets and re-establishing traditional lines of communication that were cut off during the Cold War. The sheer volume of sometimes overlapping collaborative action at a variety of territorial scales and in any conceivable sector has prompted many observers to speak of an emerging Baltic Sea regionalism and regionalization (cf. Scott 2002; Joenniemi 2000). This also relates to the fact that the formation of the BSR was not a State-based project and thus was part and parcel of regionalist agendas within the EU (Wæver 1992, cited in Moisio 2003), which included a general re-scaling of competencies, responsibilities and initiatives from national to sub-national and supranational levels, and the subsequent formation of multi-scalar environments (Brenner 1999). The majority of the voluntary platforms for cooperation, learning and knowledge exchange, which have been set up in the BSR, contain an explicit East-West dimension and seek to overcome the divisions and disparities brought on by the 'Iron Curtain' between the Eastern and Western blocs and national borders in the region. As such, these platforms represent 'knowledge arenas' and channels of knowledge exchange between the heterogeneous set of BSR countries and actors in a variety of sectoral fields. However, the focus of these platform initiatives has changed significantly over time. The initial emphasis on 'development aid' for the countries on the eastern shore has shifted towards a more functional cooperation between equal partners. Particularly, the accession of most BSR countries to the EU has significantly re-formulated collaboration and provided new outlooks and perspectives but also a renewed search for the actual purpose of Baltic Sea cooperation (Schymik and Krumrey

2009). In fact, this has been put forth as one reason for the need of an EU-led BSR Strategy. Given the continuing divisions in the BSR, it is no surprise that many collaboration initiatives specifically focus on what is generally termed 'spatial integration'. The focus on territorial or spatial integration or 'territorial cohesion', to use the EU vocabulary, raises the importance of joint, cross-border and transnational territorial governance in this macro-region. In this context, the EU apparently aims to provide an overarching framework for territorial development in the region with the Baltic Sea Strategy, which brings together sectoral policies (horizontal integration) and actors from different territorial levels (vertical integration) into a coherent whole.

Rhetoric concerning the external dimension of spatial integration and territorial development in the BSR has for quite some time already emphasized the Baltic Sea as an 'inland sea' of the EU. This has to be seen against the general background that, despite the increasing amount of cooperation and spatial integration in this region, a politically heterogeneous and geopolitically complex picture remains. The EU, especially with the 2004 accession round, has enlarged its territory to the doorstep of the Russian Federation and has gradually extended both its soft and hard power into northern Europe. In addition, the Kaliningrad Region – a subject of the Russian Federation, which is completely surrounded by the territories of EU member states, is located in the BSR, forming a Russian exclave in the EU territory. The Baltic countries, formerly part of the Soviet Union, have recently joined both the EU and NATO. As such, the development of the Kaliningrad region is high on the agenda of both the Russian Federation and the EU. Indeed, in its Country Strategy Paper 2007–2013 on the Russian Federation, the European Commission expresses its concern that '[Kaliningrad] skew[s] the development of the Baltic region' (CEC no date: 8). In addition, although Russia is one of the few non-EU members of the BSR, the Russian city of St. Petersburg is the largest metropolitan conurbation in the macro-region and surpasses many BSR states in terms of population potential. Finally the Federal District of Northwest Russia is one of the economically most advanced regions within the Russian Federation (cf. Razumeyko Chapter 16) from which a significant amount of its imports and exports are currently channelled through the Baltic Sea. Within this context, and from a Russian point of view, the conceptualization of the Baltic Sea, as an intra-EU macro-region and, as such, a realm of EU policy-hegemony, may neglect the strategic importance that the Sea has for Russia in terms of being a 'window' to the West as well as a transport and energy corridor to Europe and the rest of the world.

Territorial governance in the Baltic Sea Region

Having outlined the general framework for territorial governance in the BSR, it is now possible to analyze how cooperation in spatial planning, or more appropriately in the context of this paper 'territorial governance', has been and is being deployed and carried out between a variety of actors in the BSR in concrete terms and to examine the extent to which the Russian dimension is included or excluded in arenas of knowledge exchange (learning) and policy implementation and evaluation (practice). Despite this chapter's focus on two distinct major initiatives, it should be borne in mind that there are a number of other territorially focused collaborations at work in the BSR. A number of INTERREG-funded projects dealing with territorial governance issues, such as the Baltic Euroregional Network mentioned earlier in this chapter as well as the 'COMMIN – The Baltic Spatial Conceptshare' project, which aims to provide knowledge and the interchange of experiences within the field of spatial development with a particular focus on the comparison of planning systems in the BSR, can be mentioned as examples. The focus in this section however is specifically on VASAB and on the EU Strategy for the Baltic Sea Region.

Visions and strategies around the Baltic Sea

Visions and Strategies around the Baltic Sea 2010 (VASAB) was launched in 1992 shortly after the collapse of the Soviet Union and during a phase of enthusiasm brought about by the geopolitical changes in the BSR and it has been the most important spatial planning initiative in the BSR for almost two decades. The duration of the initiative illustrates how transnational networks of cooperation and learning have been set up in the BSR long before EU enlargement incorporated much of this macro-region. VASAB adheres to the 'traditional' delineation of the BSR including eight EU Member States (only the Northeast of Germany is represented), Norway, Belarus and Northwest Russia. Since its inception, the key aim of this intergovernmental network of eleven countries has been the promotion of cooperation on spatial planning and development in the BSR. The organizational structure of VASAB is strongly based on the national level of governance, which is structured on meetings of the Conferences of Ministers responsible for spatial planning as well as the groundwork carried out by the Committee on Spatial Development of the BSR (CSD/BSR). Stemming from its organizational disposition, VASAB is based on a principle of aligning national systems of spatial planning, and as such constitutes transnational rather than supranational cooperation in planning issues (Groth 2000). Despite its emphasis on national levels of decision-making, work carried out within the VASAB framework has frequently extended its network of cooperation to actors at other levels and positions of vertical (as well as horizontal) scales of governance in the BSR, such as sub-national actors, research institutions as well as private actors. Consequently, VASAB has contributed to the formation of a wide platform for knowledge exchange and interplay between research and policy-making. This extension of the network towards non-ministerial stakeholders was particularly important for the production of the 'evidence' – for which the ministerial levels did not have a sufficient knowledge and resource base – needed for the drawing up of the four key strategic planning documents that have emerged from the VASAB process. These documents include the original VASAB 2010 report, adopted in 1994, the VASAB 2010+ report, adopted in 2001 and more analytical than the original report, and the Gdansk declaration in 2005, which emphasized the cross-border dimension of spatial planning in the BSR (Schmitt and Dubois 2008). Currently, VASAB is in the process of drawing up a new visionary document – the VASAB Long Term Perspective (LTP) – which is planned for adoption in autumn 2009.

VASAB's approach to spatial planning cooperation in the BSR is an example of what often has been called symbolic or visionary planning (Scott 2002; Groth 2000; cf. also Nadin 2002). According to Scott (2002: 145), symbolism plays a key role in policy decisions, agenda setting and collective action, which, in the context of policy fields as complex as spatial planning or territorial governance, will have to be based on interregional interaction, open collaboration and consensus-building. Thus, in its approach, VASAB is quite close to the ESDP. Both the ESDP process and VASAB produced strategic planning documents that set out grand lines and strategic frameworks for the spatial development of their respective regions (EU-15, BSR). VASAB in particular provided what Nadin (2002, based on Shipley and Newkirk 1999) calls a *mission statement* for future spatial integration between Western and Eastern Baltic Sea countries. However, implementation of the, often rather modest, goals set out in these frameworks was generally hampered by their relatively weak institutional setting (Groth 2000) and the abstract and visionary nature of the documents. Although VASAB is based on traditional national-level governance that has been extended to include a variety of other actors, it has provided a concerted view on spatial planning measures, and served as an important forum for debates on the future of spatial development for the BSR.

Despite the fact that VASAB was the brainchild of Sweden and, at least in early days, had an overwhelmingly 'Western' bias (Jaakson 2000), both eastern and external dimensions of territorial governance have been continuously prominent in the initiative and Northwest Russia has been an active member in VASAB since its inception. The Leontief Centre in St. Petersburg has been the key link in cooperation with Russia because it provides Russia's representative to the VASAB Committee on Spatial Development of the BSR (for information on the Leontief Centre and the administrative structure of North-West Russia, see Razumeyko Chapter 16). Indeed, the various activities of the Centres have been instrumental in integrating a (North-Western) Russian dimension into the spatial planning community in the BSR and, in turn, has introduced Russian practitioners, researchers and policy-makers to Western practices. However, despite the active involvement of Northwest Russia in the VASAB activities, Russia's regional representation, as opposed to the national/ministerial representation provided by most other members – illustrates a somewhat asymmetric setting. Indeed, VASAB representatives are struggling to raise awareness of VASAB at the Federal level and to gain the invaluable support of the Ministry for Regional Development in the current Russian political climate of re-centralization (Fritsch 2009).

Recently, the East-West window project, which has been brought to a conclusion in late 2008 and has been embedded within VASAB and funded by INTER-REG IIIB BSR, has been an important element in the integration of the Russian dimension into territorial governance of the Baltic Sea whilst serving as an evidence base for the VASAB Long Term Perspective currently under preparation. The project's main aim was to promote territorial integration of the North-West Russia and Kaliningrad into the Baltic Sea Region through joint spatial planning and development actions in priority fields such as business development, transport and ICT development, as well as in sea-use planning and Integrated Coastal Zone Management (VASAB 2009).

The fact that several ministries, research institutes and universities as well as private agencies from both the EU and non-member states have been involved in the project demonstrates how multiple levels of governance have been integrated into this platform for the exchange of evidence, ideas and practices in territorial governance. In turn this facilitates further integration within the spatial planning 'epistemic communities' both across institutional borders as well as the external border of the EU.

EU strategy for the Baltic Sea Region

It has been argued earlier in this chapter that the EU (particularly the European Commission) has shown an increasing interest in the territorial governance of its macro-regions. The recent EU Strategy for the BSR is a strong manifestation of this trend. Based on an earlier report published by the European Parliament, the Council of the EU, i.e. the heads of State or Government of the Union's Member States and the President of the European Commission, on 14 December 2007, invited the European Commission to

> present an EU strategy for the Baltic Sea region at the latest by June 2009. This strategy should inter alia help to address the urgent environmental challenges related to the Baltic Sea. The Northern Dimension framework provides the basis for the external aspects of cooperation in the Baltic Sea region.
>
> (EC 2008: 17)

At this point in time, the Strategy consists of a Communication on the Baltic Sea Strategy, which is accompanied by a detailed Action Plan that guides the implementation of the Strategy and sets out around 80 actions and flagship projects grouped around 15 priority areas. The Strategy rests on four key pillars for subsequent action, which aim to make the BSR (1) an environmentally sustainable place; (2) a prosperous place; (3) an accessible and attractive place, and (4) a safe and secure place. The Strategy does not open up significantly new areas for cooperation with these thematic foci because they do not differ much from the priority areas set out in other national and supranational cooperation initiatives. For example, the Council of the Baltic Sea States sets out the (1) environment, (2) economic development, (3) energy and (4) education and culture, and civil security and the human dimension, as its long-term priorities for BSR cooperation.

Significant emphasis in the EU Strategy for the BSR is placed on the environmental dimension, which is already illustrated by the fact that this theme has been placed first in the list of the priority areas and specifically mentioned in the assignment by the Council of Europe. Nevertheless, the BSR Strategy also focuses on economic and trade issues, accessibility, transport and communication as well as environmental and social safety. These areas have been identified by the European Commission as the most relevant fields of action for tackling the prevalent problems and finding 'concrete solutions to these challenges'. Nevertheless, despite the four thematic areas, the Strategy has a distinctly intersectoral spirit to it by stressing that all pillars are interlinked and interdependent and relate to a wide range of policies.

Turning from this brief introduction to the Strategy's content to the rationales behind it, an obvious question is why the EU (the European Council in conjunction with the European Commission) chose to make the BSR the locus of its first macro-regional strategy, potentially serving as a model for future strategies. It should be remembered, however, that the European Commission showed an interest in the BSR by drawing up the much more modest BSR Initiative as early as 1996 (CEC 1996). The rationales for action were obviously based on the common territorial challenges related to environmental degradation and socio-economic disparities and the existing vibrant, but recently stalling (cf. Schymik and Krumrey 2009) cooperation and the EU membership of the majority of the littoral states. In addition, the Baltic Sea itself was certainly perceived as a functionally integrating factor. The extent to which the BSR is in fact a functionally integrated region, particularly in comparison to other European macro-regions, is of course a matter of debate. Nevertheless, the same approach (i.e. the promotion of integration in European macro-regions that are grouped around certain territorial resources), appears to be taken in relation to the Danubian Strategy, which has been conceived around an important inland waterway. Indeed, the BSR Strategy stresses that it '[follows] the territorial cohesion proposals of the Commission in the Green Paper of October 2008, whereby interventions are built around the needs of *functional* regions rather than according to predetermined financial and administrative criteria' (CEC 2009a: 6, emphasis added).

In contrast to VASAB, the link between the EU Strategy for the BSR and what generally is referred to as European spatial planning is less clear, and it may be useful to understand the Strategy as a tool for EU territorial governance rather than spatial planning. This is, first, due to the fact that the European Commission (i.e. a key driving force behind the Strategy) has no formal competencies in the policy field of spatial planning. In addition, the spatial planning 'community of practice' was not directly involved in the drafting of the Strategy, which took place in-house at the European Commission and was supported by an extensive consultation process. Second, the BSR Strategy has little resemblance to symbolic and visionary spatial planning as exercised by the ESDP or VASAB. Instead of grand visions, the Strategy is an action-oriented framework (it could also be referred to as a 'rolling action plan') that aims to provide coherence and reduce overlap for project implementation in the BSR. Nevertheless, the Strategy certainly relates to a spatial planning agenda as it actively aims to encourage horizontal (between sectors) and vertical (between different levels of government) integration, and to combine environmental, social and economic objectives – all integral elements of a spatial planning agenda. In addition, the BSR Strategy is linked to the policy objective of territorial cohesion, which generally is seen as a new inroad strategy for the European Commission into the spatial planning policy field, for which it has repeatedly failed to obtain competencies from the national governments. Indeed, as pointed out by Faludi (2008), the inclusion of the policy objective of territorial cohesion into the (Lisbon) Reform Treaty, when adopted, will give the EU the right of initiative under the Community method in territorial cohesion matters. This right of initiative ultimately could serve as a vehicle for achieving a stronger role in European territorial governance in the future.

Currently, however, conclusions with regard to the direct interrelationship between the BSR Strategy and the policy objective of territorial cohesion are difficult to draw. First, the BSR Strategy is still at a very early phase because it officially has yet to be adopted. Second, the concept of territorial cohesion itself is still in its formative phase and there is no established understanding of what territorial cohesion actually means and entails (Waterhout 2008; Evers *et al.* 2009). Nevertheless, in its Action Plan, the European Commission indentifies the EU Strategy for the BSR as 'a key instrument in promoting territorial cohesion with both land and maritime dimensions' (CEC 2009b). To further the concept, the European Commission recently launched a consultation round by publishing a Green Paper on Territorial Cohesion (CEC 2008b), to which the Baltic Sea Strategy also directly refers. A significant number of northern European research institutes/think tanks (Damsgaard *et al.* 2008), national governments and regional councils from the BSR have taken up the challenge and expressed their views on an understanding of the concept. Despite the ambiguities around the policy objective of territorial cohesion, the BSR Strategy, as the first EU strategy for a specific macro-region, potentially provides the EU with a new tool to shape spatial policy-making in a significant manner. In turn this may help to flesh out the policy objective of territorial cohesion to a significant extent. Indeed, the Communication explicitly states that the BSR Strategy represents an 'innovative policy instrument, which could serve as a good example of efforts to achieve common EU objectives and a more effective coordination of territorial and sectoral policies based on shared territorial challenges' (CEC 2009a: 6).

The BSR Strategy is politically strong and important from an institutional viewpoint, due to the fact that it has been instigated and prepared within the highest formal structures of the EU. It may thus be argued that, at least on paper, the BSR Strategy benefits from a strong institutional setting within which it has been prepared. However, despite the strong involvement of the European Commission, the Member States and regional governments also have an important role in this initiative by lending political support and acting as implementers of the Strategy's goals. Germany and, particularly, Sweden, but also Denmark and

Finland, were major driving forces behind the development of the BSR Strategy. The locations of the two stakeholder conferences in Sweden (Stockholm, September 2008) and Germany (Rostock, February 2009), reflect this division of labour. Both Sweden (Prime Minister Frederik Reinfeldt) and Germany (Chancellor Angela Merkel) have also promoted and endorsed the Baltic Sea Strategy at the highest political level; the Strategy is scheduled for adoption during the Swedish EU presidency in the second half of 2009.

Despite the above-mentioned political strength of the BSR Strategy, its accompanying Action Plan is not equipped with dedicated financial resources nor does it create new institutions. This acknowledges or echoes those arguments put forth by stakeholders during the consultation process on the BSR Strategy, which was carried out by the European Commission. Here, it had been found that the 'general view is that no new institution should be created at the level of the BSR, but that the existing ones should be somehow involved in the decision-making process as well as in the implementation process' (DG Regio no date: 1). As a consequence, the implementation of the Strategy's objectives hinges on already existing organizations and authorities – of which plenty exist in the BSR – and funding instruments such as the European Territorial Co-operation instrument, the Structural Funds and national/regional sources of funding. Not surprisingly, the lack of additional funding from the EU in the form of a dedicated funding instrument was regarded as a weakness by several consulted stakeholders (DG Regio no date). Interestingly, these occurrences could be regarded as a direct consequence of the difficult process of institutionalization of European spatial planning or, in other words, of what is commonly referred at as 'the competence issue' (cf. Waterhout 2008 and Chapter 4).

Although at this point in time it is still relatively uncertain how the implementation of the Strategy will be governed, it is interesting to note that the European Commission, merely by leading the effort to develop such a strategy, appears to be taking territorial development matters more firmly into their own hands. According to the results of the European Commission's consultation process (DG Regio no date), this generally was seen as a strength, rather than a weakness or even a threat, because the Commission is regarded as a sufficiently strong actor for real change in the BSR – transcending national interest for the benefit of the wider territorial context of the BSR. It is indeed appropriate to speak of 'implementation' of the Strategy rather than 'application', which has been used more widely in the context of the ESDP and VASAB, as the Strategy represents an action and project-oriented initiative rather than a symbolic and abstract 'mission statement'. Undoubtedly, this element represents a novelty in the European spatial planning field, which may eventually lead to higher effectiveness of EU-led strategies in terms of their ability to produce concrete impacts.

If the Baltic Sea Strategy represents a novel and potentially important new instrument in territorial governance for the BSR, it is important to ask in which way the Strategy conceptualizes its interrelationship with non-EU members in general and the Russian dimension in particular, and how it relates to other channels of EU-Russia cooperation at supranational, national and sub-national levels. This question of how the Russian dimension is included in, or excluded from communities of research, policy and practice in territorial governance firmly relates to discussions on the future of European political space (i.e. territorial development as introduced at the beginning of this chapter). As mentioned earlier, the Baltic Sea often is seen nowadays as an inland sea of the EU. The Communication on the Baltic Sea Strategy avoids this choice of words, though it is clearly stressed that the vast majority of the countries surrounding the Baltic Sea are members of the EU. Nevertheless, the Communication on the Baltic Sea Strategy reinterprets the 'traditional' geographical delineation of the BSR, as applied in the VASAB and the Council of the Baltic Sea States contexts, for example, where the BSR consists of 11 EU members and non-member countries – in important ways. In the Strategy, the targeted region is defined as only including the actual littoral countries (i.e. excluding the countries of Norway and Belarus). The Communication on the BSR Strategy states that 'overall, it concerns the eight Member States bordering the Baltic Sea' (CEC 2009a: 5). As such, the Strategy has a relatively unambiguous internal spirit. Nevertheless, it should be borne in mind that the Communication also stresses that the cooperative extent of a region depends on, and can be extended to the topic at hand. The inward-looking character of the Strategy is understandable given that the comprehensive and binding nature of the EU framework for the Baltic Sea must be built on common structures of governance and available funding, which, despite streamlined procedures as part of the ENPI programme, still poses challenges to its external dimension. It could also be argued that the Baltic Sea Strategy is, at least on paper, a politically strong document prepared at the highest levels of EU decision-making, obviously making it difficult to extend its reach into the external neighbourhood. In this respect, the Baltic Sea Strategy Action Plan indeed stresses that 'the strategy cannot dictate action to third parties: rather it indicates issues on which cooperation is desirable and proposes fora where this discussion and cooperation would take place' (CEC 2009b: 3). It can be assumed that the Commission is referring to existing collaborative initiatives with Russian representation, which is indeed compelling with regard to the pre-existing, numerous and well-functioning channels of cooperation, such as VASAB, HELCOM and the Council of the Baltic Sea States.

However, on a higher EU-Russia level, the Baltic Sea Strategy does not appear to open up new avenues of cooperation. Instead the Northern Dimension, which was launched as official EU policy in 1998, is a common framework for the promotion of dialogue and concrete cooperation in Northern Europe between the EU, Iceland, Norway and Russia as the 'external arm' of the BSR Strategy. However, at this point in time, it remains unclear how the Northern Dimension and the BSR Strategy will be integrated and how they will serve each other in practice, especially as the Northern Dimension is narrower in focus by comparison. This raises the issue of national interests in relation to territorial development in the BSR and the wider European North. Indeed, despite subsequently having been mainstreamed into EU policy, it is interesting to note that the

Northern Dimension initially was a Finnish initiative in the service of Finnish national interests (cf. Moisio 2003). In other words, whereas Finland has kept a low profile in the initiative, Sweden was the key driver behind the EU Strategy for the BSR. This may be understood as Finland's keen interest in developing external relations with its large neighbour Russia, whereas Sweden has opted for a more internal and inward-looking territorial conceptualization of the European North in general and the BSR in particular. Thus both initiatives together could be interpreted as a compromise between internal and external interests that exist amongst EU Member States. In fact, it could also be argued that utilizing the Northern Dimension as the external arm of the BSR Strategy reinforces the internal spirit of the Strategy; this would be due to the fact that the Northern Dimension generally has been regarded as a vehicle of foreign policy between the EU and Russia rather than a regional, integrative initiative (cf. Moisio 2003). Seen from this angle, it might be questioned whether the EU is truly interested in integrating Russia and the Russian dimension into its territorial governance initiatives, policy networks and extended 'epistemic communities'. If indeed the EU (Commission) assumes a stronger role in territorial development policy and governance in the future, this particularly becomes an important issue to consider.

Conclusions

Currently, at the EU level, macro-regional territorial development and governance in the BSR is the centre of attention. However, the territorial setting of the BSR is intricate because it includes the geopolitically and territorially sensitive Russian dimension – including the Kaliningrad enclave issue – which works against a conceptualization of the Baltic Sea as the inland sea of the EU. As a consequence, the territorial setting in the BSR in general and the EU's Strategy for it in particular serve as a test-bed for the EU's willingness to integrate this Russian dimension into its territorial governance. As it stands now, it can be argued that through the Strategy's unambiguously internal spirit, despite (unclear) reference to the Northern Dimension as its external arm, the EU is unwilling or, more likely, unable to encourage the integration of the Russian dimension into BSR territorial governance. This is a pragmatic approach and explicable in respect of the wider complexities of general EU-Russian relations and matters of statutory competence. This, however, does not mean that Russia is entirely excluded from territorial governance in the BSR, since a large number of national as well as sub-national cooperation initiatives that involve Russian partners are at work in this macro-region and are also ultimately involved in the implementation of the EU Strategy for the BSR. As has been shown, there exists a long tradition of collaborative and collective action in the form of transnational cooperation and networking with strong horizontal integration between research, policy and practice in the BSR. Initiatives such as VASAB have been eager, as typical for collaborative networks set up during the integrative spirit of the early/mid-1990s, to include Russia and its epistemic and policy communities into their work.

The wider dilemma of EU-Russia cooperation – signified by the reliance on existing national and sub-national channels of cooperation – may become problematic if the EU indeed assumes a stronger role in territorial governance in the future, which would require an opening up of new and direct arenas of cooperation between the EU and Russia in macro-regional territorial contexts. As such, it appears that the inclusion of Russian dimension in the territorial governance of the BSR, and the epistemic communities active therein, is the most challenging at the top-end (EU-Russia level) of this multi-level policy field. The described challenge notwithstanding, its effective engagement represents a unique opportunity in terms of promoting further integration within the European continent.

Note

1 Work carried out as part of NEBI Yearbook series that deals with a variety of topics related to integration in the North European and Baltic Sea areas represent a key example in this respect.

References

Adams, N., Cotella, G. and Nunes, R. (2010) 'Spatial Planning in Europe: The Interplay between Knowledge and Policy in an Enlarged EU', in N. Adams, G. Cotella and R. Nunes (eds) *Territorial Development, Cohesion and Spatial Planning: Knowledge and Policy Development in an Enlarged EU*, London: Routledge.

Antola, E. (2009) *EU Baltic Sea Strategy – Report for the Konrad-Adenauer-Stiftung London Office*, London: Konrad-Adenauer-Stiftung. Online. Available HTTP: www.kas.de/wf/doc/kas_16867–544–2–30.pdf.

Bagnasco, A. and Le Galès, P. (2000) 'European Cities: Local Societies and Collective Actors?', in A. Bagnasco and P. Le Galès (eds) *Cities in Contemporary Europe*, Cambridge: Cambridge University Press: 48–73.

Beckouche, P. and Grasland, C. (2008) 'North-South Regionalism: A Challenge for Europe in a Changing World', in A. Faludi (ed.) *European Spatial Research and Planning*, Cambridge: Lincoln Institute of Land Policy: 195–223.

Brenner, N. (1999) 'Globalization as Re-territorialization: The Re-scaling of Urban Governance in the European Union', *Urban Studies*, 36(3): 431–451.

Böhme, K. (2002) *Nordic Echoes of European Spatial Planning*, Stockholm: Nordregio.

CEC (1996) Baltic Sea Region Initiative: Communication from the Commission, SEC/96/0608, Brussels: Commission of the European Communities. Online. Available HTTP: www.ena.lu/communication-commission-baltic-sea-region-initiative-10-april-1996–020005738.html.

—— (1999) *European Spatial Development Perspective: Towards Balanced and Sustainable Development of the Territory of the EU*. Luxembourg: Office of the Official Publications of the European Communities.

—— (2007) Memorandum of Understanding for Establishing a Dialogue on Regional Policy between the Ministry of Regional Development of the Russian Federation and the European Commission. Online. Available HTTP: http://ec.europa.eu/regional_policy/international/pdf/mou_russia_en.pdf.

—— (2008a) Commissioner Danuta Hübner and Swedish Prime Minister Fredrik Rein-feldt launch debate on EU strategy for Baltic Sea Region, Press Release. Online. Available HTTP: http://europa.eu/rapid/pressReleasesAction.do?reference=IP/08/1430.

—— (2008) Green Paper on Territorial Cohesion – Turning Territorial Diversity into Strength, Brussels: Commission of the European Communities. Online. Available HTTP: http://ec.europa.eu/regional_policy/consultation/terco/paper_terco_en.pdf.

—— (2009a) Communication from the Commission to the European Parliament, the Council, the European Economic and Social Committee and the Committee of the Regions concerning the European Union Strategy for the Baltic Sea Region. Online. Available HTTP: http://ec.europa.eu/regional_policy/sources/docoffic/official/commu-nic/baltic/com_baltic_en.pdf.

—— (2009b) Commission Staff Working Document – Action Plan, SEC(2009) 712, Brus-sels: Commission of the European Communities. Online. Available HTTP: http://ec.europa.eu/regional_policy/sources/docoffic/official/communic/baltic/action2009.pdf.

—— (no date) Country Strategy Paper 2007–2013 – Russian Federation, Online. Availa-ble HTTP: http://ec.europa.eu/external_relations/russia/docs/2007–2013_en.pdf.

EC – European Council (2008) European Council Presidency Conclusions, 16616/1/07 REV 1, Online. Available HTTP: www.consilium.europa.eu/ueDocs/cms_Data/docs/pressData/en/ec/97669.pdf.

Damsgaard, O., Dubois, A., Gløersen, E., Hedin, S., Rauht, D., Roto, J., Schmitt, P. and Steineke, J. M. (2008) *Nordic Inputs to the EU Green Paper on Territorial Cohesion*, WP 2008:4, Stockholm: Nordregio.

DG Regio (no date) *EU Strategy for the Baltic Sea Region – Report on the Public Con-sultation*. Online. Available HTTP: http://ec.europa.eu/regional_policy/consultation/baltic/doc/summary_baltic_consultation.pdf.

ESPON (2006) *Territory Matters for Competitiveness and Cohesion Facets of Regional Diversity and Potentials in Europe ESPON Synthesis Report III*, results by autumn 2006, Luxemburg: ESPON. Online. Available HTTP: www.espon.eu/mmp/online/website/content/publications/98/1229/file_2471/final-synthesis-reportiii_web.pdf.

—— (2007) *Europe in the World – Territorial Evidence and Visions*, ESPON Project 3.4.1, Luxemburg: ESPON. Online: Available HTTP: www.espon.eu/mmp/online/website/content/publications/98/1681/file_4002/EIW_light_25–3–25008.pdf.

—— (2009a) Call for Proposals 'Territorial cooperation in transnational areas and across internal/external borders'. Online. Available HTTP: www.espon.eu/mmp/online/website/content/programme/1455/1496/2621/2628/index_EN.html (accessed Septem-ber 2009).

—— (2009b) Call for Proposals 'Continental territorial structures and flows (globaliza-tion)'. Online. Available HTTP: www.espon.eu/mmp/online/website/content/pro-gramme/1455/1496/2621/2628/index_EN.html (accessed September 2009).

Evers, D., Tennekes, J., Borsboom, J., van den Heiligenberg, H. and Thissen, M. (2009) *A Territorial Impact Assessment of Territorial Cohesion for the Netherlands*, The Hague/Bilthoven: Netherlands Environmental Assessment Agency (PBL).

Faludi, A. (2002) 'Positioning European Spatial Planning', *European Planning Studies*, 10(7): 897–909.

—— (2008) 'European Territorial Cooperation and Learning/Reflections by the Guest Editor on the Wider Implications', *DISP*, 172, 44(44): 3–10.

Fritsch, M. (2009) 'European Territorialization and the Eastern Neighbourhood: Spatial Development Co-operation between the EU and Russia', *European Journal of Spatial Development*, 35. Online. Available HTTP: www.nordregio.se/EJSD/refereed35.pdf.

—— (2011) 'Re-connecting Territorialities? Spatial Planning Co-operation between Eastern Finnish and North-West Russian Sub-national Governments', in H. Eskelinen, I. Liikanen and J. W. Scott (eds) *The EU-Russia Borderland*, London: Routledge.

Giannakourou, G. (1996) 'Towards a European Spatial Planning Policy: Theoretical Dilemmas and Institutional Implications', *European Planning Studies*, 4(5): 595–614.

Groth, N. B. (2000) 'Urban Systems between Policy and Geography', *Regional Studies*, 34(6): 571–580.

Hanell, T. and Neubauer, J. (2005) *Cities of the Baltic Sea Region – Development Trends at the Turn of the Millenium*, Stockholm: Nordregio.

Haselsberger, B. and Benneworth, P. (2010) 'Cross-border Communities or Cross-Border Proximity? Perspectives from the Austrian–Slovakian Border Region', in N. Adams, G. Cotella and R. Nunes (eds) *Territorial Development, Cohesion and Spatial Planning: Knowledge and Policy Development in an Enlarged EU*, London: Routledge.

Healey, P. (2006) 'Transforming Governance: Challenges of Institutional Adaptation and a New Politics of Space', *European Planning Studies*, 14(3): 299–320.

Hooghe, L. and Marks, G. (2001) *Multi-level Governance and European Integration*, Lanham: Rowman & Littlefield.

Jaakson, R. (2000) 'Supra-national Spatial Planning of the Baltic Sea Region and Competing Narratives for Tourism', *European Planning Studies*, 8(5): 565–579.

Joenniemi, P. (2000) 'Bridging the Iron Curtain. Cooperation around the Baltic Rim', *Journal of Borderland Studies*, 15(1): 168–186.

—— (2001) 'Changing Politics along Finland's Borders: From Norden to Northern Dimension', in P.-L. Ahponen and P. Jukarainen (eds) *Tearing Down the Curtain, Opening the Gates: Northern Boundaries in Change*, Jyväskylä: SoPhi.

—— (2008) 'Border Issues in Europe's North', in T. Diez, M. Albert and S. Stetter (eds) *The European Union and Border Conflicts – The Power of Integration and Association*, Cambridge: Cambridge University Press.

Maier, K. (2010) 'The Pursuit of Balanced Territorial Development: The Realities and Complexities of the Cohesion Agenda', in N. Adams, G. Cotella and R. Nunes (eds) *Territorial Development, Cohesion and Spatial Planning: Knowledge and Policy Development in an Enlarged EU*, London: Routledge.

Moisio, S. (2003) 'Back to Baltoscandia? European Union and Geo-Conceptual Remaking of the European North', *Geopolitics*, 8(1): 72–100.

Nadin, V. (2002) 'Visions and Visioning in European Spatial Planning', in A. Faludi (ed.) *European Spatial Planning*, Cambridge MA: Lincoln Institute of Land Policy.

Nijkamp, P. (1995) 'Borders and Barriers in the New Europe: Impediments and Potentials of New Network Configurations', in H. Coccossis and P. Nijkamp (eds) *Overcoming Isolation: Information and Transportation Networks in Development Strategies for Peripheral Areas*, Berlin: Springer Verlag.

Razumeyko, N. (2010) 'Strategic Planning Practices in North-West Russia: European Influences, Challenges and Future Perspectives', in N. Adams, G. Cotella and R. Nunes (eds) *Territorial Development, Cohesion and Spatial Planning: Knowledge and Policy Development in an Enlarged EU*, London: Routledge.

Rusca, R. (1998) 'The Development of a European Spatial Planning Policy – A Learning-by-doing Experience in the Framework of Intergovernmental Co-operation', in C. Bengs, and K. Böhme (eds) *The Progress of European Spatial Planning*, Stockholm: Nordregio: 35–47.

Schmitt, P. and Dubois, A. (2008) *Exploring the Baltic Sea Region – On Territorial Capital and Spatial Integration*, Stockholm: Nordregio.

Schymik, C. and Krumrey, P. (2009) 'EU Strategy for the Baltic Sea Region – Core Europe in the Northern Periphery?', Working Paper FP 1, Stiftung Wissenschaft und Politik, Berlin: German Institute for International and Security Affairs.

Scott, J. W. (2002) 'Baltic Sea Regionalism, EU Geopolitics and Symbolic Geographies of Co-operation', *Journal of Baltic Studies*, 33(2): 137–155.

Shipley, R. and Newkirk, R. (1999) 'Vision and Visioning in Planning: What do these Terms Really Mean?', *Environment & Planning B*, 26(4), 225–236.

VASAB (2009) *VASAB Long-Term Perspective for the Territorial Development of the Baltic Sea Region*, Draft of 19 March 2009 For Public Consultation. Online. Available HTTP: www.vasab.org/documents.php?go=display&ID=63.

Wæver, O. (1992) 'Nordic Nostalgia: Northern Europe after the Cold War', *International Affairs*, 68(1), 77–102.

Waterhout, B. (2008) *The Institutionalisation of European Spatial Planning*, Amsterdam: Delft University Press/IOS Press.

—— (2010) 'European Spatial Planning: Current State and Future Challenges', in N. Adams, G. Cotella and R. Nunes (eds) *Territorial Development, Cohesion and Spatial Planning: Knowledge and Policy Development in an Enlarged EU*, London: Routledge.

Williams, R. H. (1996) *European Union Spatial Policy and Planning*, London: Chapman.

16 Strategic planning practices in North-West Russia

European influences, challenges and future perspectives

Natalia Razumeyko

Introduction

Over the last 15 years a significant number of Russian regions and municipalities have started to introduce strategic planning as an important tool for managing territorial development. However, despite there being a variety of definitions of the term discussed in academic literature in Russia, there is as yet no real consensus on the meaning of 'strategic planning'. For instance, Zhikharevich (2006), the Director of Resource Centre for Strategic Planning at the Leontief Centre identifies the following characteristics of strategic planning: an independent development led by the local community where the aims, objectives and strategic priorities seek sustainable development in a competitive environment. For the purposes of this chapter this definition needs further elaboration to fully capture the characteristics of strategic planning. In order to do this, a review of relevant planning literature from Western Europe is useful. Dimitriou and Thompson (2007) point out that one of the aims of strategic planning is to provide a framework based on goals and objectives that allows a systematic approach to planning and resource allocation. In addition they identify both stability and flexibility as important characteristics of the planning process if strategic planning is to be effective. Given the growing relevance of strategic planning in the Russian context, the present chapter aims to examine the emergence of this practice, focusing on North-West Russia where certain actors have been particularly active in this field. In doing so, the chapter will identify the main challenges facing local authorities in the application of strategic planning in practice, as well as explore the emergence of knowledge networks and communities related to strategic planning. In the context of the interplay between knowledge and policy, as outlined in the editors' introduction to this book, the analysis will reflect on the different organizational approaches to the application of strategic planning and on the potential and implications for emerging 'epistemic communities'.

Strategic planning has become a new practice for both local authorities and for civil society in the Russian Federation, as previously they have had neither the experience and skills nor a tradition in participatory planning and independent policy-making. Before the political and economic transition, in the former

Soviet command and control system, strategic planning was not practiced at the city level, as independent local planning and financing was not permitted. Responsibility for urban development was granted to the state authority, which had competence to implement and coordinate national urban development policies. Urban development was managed exclusively from the outside. General settlement schemes and general plans, which determined the spatial allocation of settlements, enterprises, services and recreation zones, were designed and approved by central government before being passed down for territorial implementation. Cities and municipalities were not considered economically independent administrative units and therefore public consent for implementation of externally drafted strategies was not required.

As mentioned by Stead and Nadin in Chapter 7, St Petersburg has been something of a pioneer in the field of strategic planning in Russia, working with international partners to develop its first Strategic plan in 1997. The St. Petersburg experience later inspired a significant number of other regions and municipalities of the Russian North-West to proceed with similar initiatives. The term North-West in this context refers to the North-Western Federal District (NWFD) of the Russian Federation. It is one of the seven federal districts of Russia, which consists of the northern part of European Russia and contains nearly 10 per cent of the national population at approximately 13.5 million (North-West Federal District 2009). The NWFD consists of 11 political subdivisions (regions): Arkhangelsk Oblast, Nenets Autonomous Okrug, Kaliningrad Oblast (with no land connection to the rest of Russia), Republic of Karelia, Komi Republic, Leningrad Oblast, Murmansk Oblast, Novgorod Oblast, Pskov Oblast, Federal City of Saint Petersburg, Vologda Oblast. The federal districts are an administrative level made up of different regions, operating for the convenience of the Federal Government. The NWFD is fifth out of seven federal districts in terms of GDP, producing 10 per cent of national GDP, although it is third out of seven in terms of GDP per capita. The NWFD also has the highest degree of urbanization in Russia with 82 per cent of the population classed as urban across the 1836 municipalities of the District. The City of Saint Petersburg historically has been the main centre in Russian North-West, making it the recognized centre of the Federal District.

In the next section the current situation with regards to strategic planning in North-West Russia will be discussed. This will be followed by an outline of some of the challenges, and the roots of these challenges, to the effective application of strategic planning. The chapter will then consider the extent to which new planning communities and networks are emerging in decision-making arenas with particular reference to the concepts of 'epistemic communities' (Haas 1992) and 'communities of practice' (Wenger 1998). On the basis of this discussion, four organizational approaches to strategy and policy-making will be identified within the Russian context, as well as an assessment of the implications of these approaches for these communities and networks before some final conclusions are drawn on the future of strategic planning in Russia.

Evolution of strategic planning in Russia

The application of strategic planning mechanisms by local governments in Russia generally pursues a typical set of objectives, including development of a new positive vision of the city's future, identification of long-term strategic development goals, objectives and priorities, and consolidation and integration of local stakeholders and civil society for further social and economic growth of the city based upon jointly developed strategic priorities. It is important to emphasize that while at the end of 1990s strategic planning was often considered to be a 'new fashion' in local government, today the awareness of both the necessity and the advantages of strategic planning principles, practice and process is increasing amongst regional and local officials. In this context it is interesting to underline how this understanding came earlier to those municipalities that were in close cooperation with EU networks (i.e. Leningrad region, Pskov region, city of Kaliningrad) and had the opportunity to participate in a number of planning projects such as the local development strategy within TACIS programme in 2001. This implies a degree of porosity of EU borders when it comes to the exchange of knowledge and good practices. At the same time it should be clearly understood that while European cities used strategic planning for the purpose of strengthening competitiveness, the social and economic context within which Russian municipalities apply this technique is totally different due to the period of rapid transition. The difficulties of transferring so called 'good practice' have been widely discussed in the academic literature, especially where there is a significantly different context between the donor and recipient countries. From an EU perspective some of these forms of cooperation constituted an external Europeanization of EU governance approaches beyond its borders. In recent years, however, as the Russian Federation has grown in status and confidence on the world stage, the desire within Russia to accept such practices has been reduced (Fritsch 2009).

The evolution of the role and perception of strategic planning as an important management instrument over the last 15 years has increased demand for the creation of regional and local development strategies. As Waterhout has identified in Chapter 4, diverse types of communities and networks have emerged in the EU in recent years and despite the different context a similar process can be identified in North-West Russia where two main types of knowledge community can be distinguished. On the one hand, diverse types of professional networks have emerged with similar characteristics to the 'communities of practice' discussed by Haselsberger and Benneworth in Chapter 10. These networks tend to focus on the accumulation and exploitation of knowledge in a given field in Russia. On the other hand, expert or 'epistemic communities' have also started to emerge focusing on the exploration of a new field of knowledge, in this case strategic planning. Currently, however, there does not appear to be any linguistic equivalent for the term 'epistemic community' in the Russian language. It is therefore perhaps not surprising that a review of relevant academic literature in Russia also failed to discover discussions of the 'epistemic community' concept in a Russian context. Hence, this part of the following investigation can be considered as an attempt to fit internationally recognized terminology with the Russian context.

According to the definition by Haas (1992) it can be argued that the community active in the field of strategic planning in North-West Russia is part of a wider 'epistemic community', with a specific knowledge-based expertise within the strategic planning domain. This statement arises from the definition of an 'epistemic community' according to which its members share knowledge about social phenomena in the area for which they have a reputation for competence (Haas 1992), even though they might come from a number of different disciplines associated with economics, political science or public administration. At the same time we need to make a distinction between members of professional planning networks, which could potentially evolve into an 'epistemic community' in the field of strategic planning, and members of bureaucratic bodies inside the local administrations that are also involved in the planning process. As has been identified by Waterhout and others in this volume, different types of communities and networks are difficult to define precisely and, whilst these members of the bureaucratic bodies are members of professional networks, they are not normally planning policy entrepreneurs. In other words, though they may be part of a wider network, they would not necessarily be considered as part of an expert community in the field. An 'epistemic community' can be interpreted as an umbrella term under which transnational networks of experts with common values and principled beliefs, interact to generate and circulate new ideas in respective areas of application. In the absence of informal professional networks, planning decision making and strategy development and implementation tends to be ad hoc and subject to the compulsion of regional and local politicians. At this point in time there are no widely accepted standards for local strategic planning decision making in Russia. In some municipalities, strategy development is subject to debate and discussion exclusively between local administration and selected stakeholders. In neighbouring municipalities this discussion may be more open and transparent, involving both experts and a broader group of stakeholders. Therefore the preparation of a local development strategy and the increasing complexity of strategy design, require significant discussion and support and this could be stimulated and facilitated by increased engagement with the planning community nationally and internationally. Zito (2001) identifies specific circumstances under which 'epistemic communities' occur. In the Russian context local planning policy-makers tend to seek advice from recognized experts either in situations of great uncertainty or in the case of the absence of any competent planning staff with relevant skills inside the local administration. In cases where this knowledge is controversial or where it does not fit with the dominant political strategy, this expert community and the role of knowledge tends to be marginalized. Where this happens, it is more appropriate to talk about an underpinning of an already taken decision followed by the search for evidence to support the course of action identified by politicians. In the next section some of the challenges hampering the effective application of strategic planning in Russia are explored.

Challenges and their roots

An analysis of the experiences of local governments in the NWFD demonstrates that Russian municipalities traditionally face a common set of obstacles in relation to the implementation of strategic planning. These include (1) a shortage of reference material and lack of a standardized approach, (2) a legal vacuum, (3) a lack of reliable data, (4) the conservatism of local administrations, and (5) a lack of financial resources. The shortage of specialist reference materials available in municipalities distant from the large cities and a considerable diversity in technical approaches to strategic planning have resulted in a lack of consensus and clarity in terms of what is commonly perceived as the characteristics of strategic planning and strategy development and implementation. Cities and municipalities of the NWFD are relatively well off in terms of access to information compared to other more remote territories of the Federation. This is attributed to the leading role of St Petersburg in terms of access to information, the availability of educational workshops, conferences, qualified experts and, moreover, the opportunities for raising new sources of project funding. However, the lack of consensus over what constitutes strategic planning remains an issue. An analysis of local planning documents from administrations in the NWFD reveals that many of these works lack the characteristics that would distinguish them as strategic documents. For example, many of these 'strategies' are more of an action plan than a strategy and are often developed in a vacuum with little or no public discussion and/or consideration for sources of finance.

The presence of a legal vacuum, whereby none of the levels of authority (Federal, regional or local) have created a sufficient legal basis for strategic planning procedures or a framework of necessary complementary documents and requirements is the second common problem. As a result, the documents have no clear legal status, which in the Russian context is usually necessary if there is any hope that implementation is to be achieved. A strategic document is protected (to a degree) from the direct influence of election cycles only if it has sufficient legal status to secure its place in the local government system. Thus, in terms of the legal status of strategic documents, it is important that a regional/ local development strategy is adopted by a representative power and obtains the status of regional/local law. In fact, Russian experience shows that in situations where a legislative body has not adopted a strategy it is either never fully implemented or simply ignored. The status of a strategy becomes even more important if local authorities seek to link the implementation of strategic priorities to the local budget. These strategic documents simply do not work in the absence of legal adoption by a representative body; this is particularly relevant for municipalities with budget deficits and weak political leadership. We also should bear in mind the fact that in the current Russian reality, regardless of whether the rule of law obliges public officials to undertake a particular action, there is no guarantee that legal requirements will be carried out as intended, if at all. If a requirement is not legally binding, then the chances that it will be carried out are virtually non-existent. Then again, mandatory status does not necessarily depreciate the flexibility of territorial strategies given that they can be regularly adapted and reviewed as necessary at various stages in an implementation process (Dimitriou and Thompson 2007).

There is another side to this challenge. Current Federal legislation has not provided a clear definition of what constitutes 'territorial strategic planning'. On the face of it this gives a lot of freedom to municipalities in designing and elaborating of their own unique planning systems and approaches. However, Russian practice demonstrates that the exclusion of the municipal level of planning from the Federal legislative process leads to municipalities' reluctance to take the initiative, which has a consequential negative effect on the promotion of strategic planning. To an extent all sides of this challenge are relevant for the overwhelming majority of Russian cities and municipalities, particularly considering the significant improvements required of the legislation in these jurisdictions. It is also worth mentioning that some of the other challenges discussed here are a consequence of this legal vacuum at both local and regional levels.

The third key problem refers to the lack of reliable data, which constitutes a serious obstacle for any planning initiatives – not just for strategy drafting. The development of a new system of municipal statistics is currently underway in the Russian Federation. Until now the lack of effective and reliable statistics has meant that there have been few resources available to inform local decision making. There are a number of reasons for this lack of reliable statistics, including under-financing of municipal data collection (funded from local budgets), limited quality of technical assistance and a limited system of social and economic development indicators for municipalities. Statistics in the Russian Federation are a State competence whereby statistical departments in municipal administrations are responsible for data-collection and regional committees are responsible for its analysis and dissemination. Therefore, they are usually based on Federal State Statistics Service requirements and not on local demands when regional committees supply data to municipalities. The municipality is required to purchase statistics from national statistics agencies if they need large amounts of data. The lack of reliable and comparable statistical data therefore remains a significant problem for communities and networks trying to influence policy.

The conservatism of local administrations is the fourth challenge to the implementation of strategic planning, but for obvious reasons was not mentioned by politicians. In some territories local officials still have preconceived negative views about strategic planning as a management tool, maintaining the view that drafting a local development strategy is the prerogative of prosperous local communities. This is the mindset of administrators who feel that strategic planning is not their concern and that it distracts them from the essentials of local governance. In turn this can lead to situations where local bureaucracy is not interested in the application of strategic planning principles and procedures, especially if the latter is not required and controlled by higher levels of government. Official apathy also generates little demand for new academic research in the fields of strategic planning, and local social and economic development. An underestimation of the potential need for strategic planning, and the insufficient activity of regional and municipal authorities in the sphere of strategic planning may be due, at least in part, to the recently adopted legal provisions that limit their power. The Federal Law 'On general principles of municipal self-government organization in the Russian Federation' does not refer to strategic planning at this level. In this respect many municipalities of the NWFD are advanced in terms of strategic planning initiatives compared to those in more remote parts of the country. The proximity of *big neighbour* St Petersburg not only enhances development opportunities but has also provided opportunities for them to learn about strategic planning and to integrate strategic planning processes into their local governance system.

The fifth and last problem, possibly the most significant, is the permanent under-financing of strategy design and implementation processes. Strategic planning is an expensive initiative. And the larger the scope of local community involvement the higher is the cost: the Moscow city strategy cost an estimated 3 million dollars (BN.RU Gazeta 2007). Grant funding provides the primary source of raising funds for strategy design in small cities and municipalities and a variety of national and international organizations have provided grants on a competitive basis. The TACIS Programme, Eurasia Foundation, Open Society Institute, EUROGRAD Institute, the World Bank, USAID, EBRD, Ford Foundation, Moscow Public Science Foundation, Leontief Centre and UN-HABITAT are among the most active donor organizations in Russia. There is a significant shortage of funding for planning purposes at the local level, which can be explained by the continuous deficit of local budgets, though the larger city administrations and regional authorities often have considerably more funds for such activities, largely resulting in publicly funded initiatives. Other factors and problems that hamper the evolution of effective strategic planning in the Russian Federation include a lack of professionalism between municipal managers, a lack of project development and strategic management skills, and an excessive reliance on budgetary support. However, a detailed consideration of these factors is beyond the scope and word count of this chapter.

An 'epistemic community' as a new actor in the planning decision-making arena

Haas (1992) emphasized that 'epistemic communities' are more likely to emerge in countries with well established institutional capacities for public administration, science and technology, and are also more ikely to be present in economically advanced democracies with a significant number of scientists in the country (Haas 1992). The experience of Russia as a transition country and a young democracy would appear to support this view and such 'epistemic communities' have had only limited influence on the evolution of strategic planning practice in comparison to their influence in established EU countries. Nevertheless, in a situation similar to that discussed by Maier in Chapter 11 in the context of CEE countries and by Haselsberger and Benneworth in Chapter 10 in the context of cross-border networks in Austria and Slovakia, initial signs indicate that networks of planning experts and professionals are beginning to emerge and these potentially could evolve into 'epistemic communities'.

One of the primary driving forces in the establishment of such expert networks in the field of territorial and strategic planning in the NWFD has been the Leontief Centre, the International Centre for Social and Economic Research in St Petersburg established in 1991. It is a non-profit, self-financing independent research and consulting organization that operates as a think tank on market reforms in St Petersburg and the rest of Russia through its active involvement in numerous international (EU funded and non-EU funded) initiatives. Besides its research and coordinating activities, the Centre provides consulting and methodological support to the government of the Russian Federation and to the administrations of Russian regions and municipalities in the development of scientifically well grounded socio-economic programmes, draft laws and effective mechanisms of strategic management. Currently the partnership network of the Centre encompasses 34 countries, 150 Russian cities, 80 international and more than 300 Russian organizations. The Centre employs 70 staff, including recognized academics and practitioners as well as support staff. The core principles of the Centre philosophy, which in many ways are similar to various communities and networks discussed here, embrace an openness to cooperation, a willingness to share research findings, and an emphasis on partnership and networking (Leontief Centre 2009).

Since 2004, the Centre has also been organizing annual distance learning programmes on administrative capacity building. The programme, entitled 'Municipal Government', is aimed at civil servants of Federal, regional and municipal levels, specialists of consulting organizations and members of NGOs, both in the Russian Federation and in the countries of the Commonwealth of Independent States (CIS). The programme aims to familiarize participants with new approaches, techniques and instruments of city management, including a specifically tailored strategic planning module. One of the main areas of specialization is territorial planning undertaken by the Resource Centre for Strategic Planning. The Resource Centre is one of the key non-governmental organizations that maintains methodological support for strategic planning as well as advice to local and regional authorities on the development of strategic plans for municipalities and regions. It was established in 2000 as a cooperation initiative between the Leontief Centre and the Eurasia Foundation. The Centre was established within the organizational structure of the Leontief Centre, bringing together highly qualified experts alongside 'knowledge resources' in relation to methodological and practical information on territorial strategic planning, and promoting consultations, informational support and training for regional and local officials. An informal virtual network of experts on strategic planning is among the Centre's initiatives, which provides advisory support, research and methodological services in the field of territorial strategic planning. The Centre also maintains a website on strategic planning in the cities and regions of Russia (www.citystrategy.leontief.ru/), which has become a platform for information exchange and access to a wide variety of academic and practical material on strategic planning.

The 'Annual All-Russia Forum of Strategic Planning Leaders', held in St Petersburg, is one of the most powerful instruments employed by the Centre to help strengthen cooperation networks and share experience between cities and regions. It has been recognized as one of the most effective forms of cooperation and communication of regional and municipal authorities on the support and promotion of territorial strategic planning. In 2008 the Forum was organized jointly by the State Duma of the Russian Federation, the Federal Ministry for Regional Development and the Federal Ministry for Economic Development, the St Petersburg City Administration, the Centre of Strategic Research and the ICSER Leontief Centre. On the one hand the participation of the Duma and the Federal ministries reflects the widespread support for the Forum at the state level, indicating the importance of communication and knowledge sharing in the political agenda. But while their involvement encourages a more official atmosphere and indicates high level Government support, it also potentially discourages some groups from either discussing their full range of problems or from participating altogether. Fritsch (2009, cf. also Fritsch Chapter 15) identifies the importance of the capacity and level of the participants in determining the potential influence of such activities in these cooperation arrangements. Normally members of these networks are representatives of cities, municipalities and regions, and heads or deputy heads of economic divisions within these administrations. The international community is also often represented by the EU, the Assembly of European Regions, South-Eastern Finland, the Union of Baltic Cities, and the Eurasia Foundation. Forum organizers claim that the Forum aims to enhance balanced and sustainable development of the regions and cities of Russia by improving the system of strategic planning for territorial development, supporting coordination and public dialogue on long-term development priorities and creating and promoting up-to-date standards of planning. The vision of the Forum as a networking and learning platform provides wider opportunities for discussions of new instruments for strategic planning and socio-economic development, and for dialogue and information exchange between leading actors in strategic planning processes. The Forum provides an arena for debate, bringing the positions of government ministries and State agencies on priorities for long-term development into the public realm and stimulating discussion of State regional policies. It also provides round-tables and workshops for all participants, even those from the most remote regions, who want to share experiences and to become acquainted with international good practice and instruments.

The Centre for Strategic Research (CSR) North-West is another foundation that plays an important role in the network of planning experts and other professionals. The Centre was established in 2000 as an independent public organization by the Centre for Strategic Research (Moscow) with Government ministries and departments, regional and local administrations, public and research organizations, and business structures among its partners. The consultation activities of the Foundation extend far beyond the boundaries of the NWFD to more than 20 regions throughout Russia.

The examples of the Resource Centre Forum and the CSR North-West in the evolution of territorial strategic planning practice throughout Russia suggests that involving professionals from diverse planning networks or 'communities of practice' has helped some municipalities to achieve a common approach to the practice of strategic planning. The evidence suggests that those local administrations that choose to avoid engaging with these professional communities and networks often fail to achieve their strategic aims because of a lack of expertise and an inability to operationalize effective instruments in relation to public participation. The 'communities of practice' among these administrations, who fail to engage with other professional communities and international networks are relatively nascent to the evolving context of strategic planning practice in Russia. However, they do have the potential to evolve and to integrate with international 'epistemic communities' in the future in the same way as the 'communities of practice' referred to by Maier in Chapter 11 and the cross-border networks referred to by Haselsberger and Benneworth in Chapter 10.

Despite the long history of planning in Russia, strategic planning organizations still tend to draw on EU experiences for strategic planning approaches and public participation instruments. At the same time it is important to note that the 'second wave' of strategic documents in Russia (post 2002) have mostly been developed on the basis of Russian experience and international knowledge adapted to local specific contexts with the direct engagement of Russian planning staff. Also, as a transition country in the CIS, Russia has been responsible for transferring cumulative planning knowledge to cities and regions of other transition states. This has been achieved mostly through Russian international networks and initiatives, including the above-mentioned institutional arrangements of the Leontief Centre and Eurasia Foundation. In fact, this could be taken to imply potential for future international Russian-speaking 'epistemic communities' to emerge with the aim of informing policy in the Russian Federation and CIS countries.

Moreover, geopolitical events in the last 20 years have dramatically altered power relations in Europe. In the field of spatial planning, the European Conference of Ministers Responsible for Regional Planning (CEMAT) involves 47 European countries and provides an established arena within which spatial development matters on a pan-European scale are discussed. From an EU perspective, Fritsch (2009) refers to CEMAT as the bridgehead to non-EU Europe and participation on the Russian side is high-level, with the Federal Ministry of Regional Development the main actor. CEMAT has also produced principles that provide a basis for sustainable spatial development, which in turn guide regional and local strategies. By contrast, most EU initiatives with the Russian Federation tend not to have direct high-level State participation in Moscow. These initiatives are nevertheless important, however, and it is worth considering some of the key ones here. There appears to have been a change in attitudes to pursuing cooperation initiatives with EU partners over the years. In the middle of the 1990s, Russian regions started to become actively involved in a number of initiatives in cooperation with EU institutions and individual EU Member States or regions in the field of spatial planning. This represented a clear shift from a passive to a more active approach to cooperation. Regions and municipalities of the North-West (Leningrad, Kaliningrad and Pskov Oblasts) were targeted territories that became "pilot regions" for numerous projects under VASAB, TACIS and INTERREG. Though with the exception of TACIS, these initiatives have contributed more to territorial development and strategic planning concerns in neighbour regions than to the field of local strategy-making. Nevertheless, they have helped to foster and stimulate the evolution of international professional planning networks and cooperation. The key impact of active participation in joint EU-Russian initiatives is likely to be the development of new patterns of social partnership and interaction between local administrations, stakeholders, local citizens and the wider expert communities and networks on both sides of the border. Therefore there appears to be a basis for the existing diversity of professional communities or 'communities of practice' and international networks, involved in the practice of strategic planning, to evolve into an 'epistemic community'. There are clear indications that this evolution may be underway although, due to specific socio-political conditions in the Russian Federation, the possibility of an 'epistemic community' remains uncertain as disparate groups seek to clearly identify their role and scope in the evolving context of strategic planning in the country.

Having examined the evolving role of 'epistemic communities' within the Russian context, especially in relation to the NWFD, the following section will begin with a discussion of a typology of strategy-making processes applied in Russian municipalities and the potential impact of these approaches on the involvement of professional or expert communities in the planning process. This discussion will also explore the extent to which the planning process is open to multilateral dialogue between various interest groups within local communities, and the impact different forms of communication on the process may have in terms of obtaining (financial) support from key stakeholders. This discussion of the typology of strategy-making processes is then followed by a closing look at the influence of these approaches on funding opportunities.

Organizational approaches to strategy-development

On the basis of research undertaken by the author, it is possible to identify four distinct approaches to strategy-making amongst the authorities of the NWFD. This section will briefly examine these approaches in light of their implications for policy-making and the potential emergence of 'epistemic communities' as well as for the likely funding arrangements for development strategies. The following discussion will argue that the type of approach adopted in a particular case will determine, to a degree, which actors and stakeholders are permitted to participate in a particular arena. Also, this view maintains that what is permitted or classed as 'evidence' will determine the degree of legitimacy of particular knowledge claims. The following approaches to strategy-making will be discussed: administrative, elitist, populist and democratic.

Administrative approach

The first organizational approach to strategy-making can be defined as an *administrative approach*, which has been used widely in small towns with around 20–40,000 inhabitants. This approach implies that the strategy development process is carried out in exceptional isolation, by a very narrow body inside the local administration. In fact, many Russian local officials adhere to the opinion that 'nobody among the citizens knows the current local situation better then we' and that the 'community's concern is a qualitative implementation of taken decisions' (Vinogradov and Erlikh 2001). The population, stakeholders and various representative groups are neither informed about the progress nor even partially involved in the strategy adoption. That is, no sitting at the bargaining table, and no public advertisement or public hearings. At best, some of the most influential local economic agents are informed afterwards. This approach is common in conditions characterized by a lack of public participation traditions among a disorganized, demotivated and weak civic society, a lack of legally binding provisions on the processes of strategy-making and implementation, and a lack of strong local political leadership. Generally, the only source of funding for such a closed municipal strategy drafting and implementation process is a local budget. From a financial point of view, this approach appears to be the least expensive as it does not require fees to be paid to urban and strategic planning experts and consultants. As a rule, funds come from a subsidized budget with restricted sources of income for the advertising and promotion of a new strategic document in the mass media. The evidence suggests that the outcome of the planning process (i.e. development strategy or strategic plan, vision and priorities) under an administrative approach tends to be unbalanced and lacking focus and quality, therefore providing a rather ambiguous framework for future development. At the stage of strategy implementation there will be little opportunity to identify problems, or to evaluate and review them. The administrative approach leaves little or no room for reciprocal learning, or for the improvement of participatory planning skills among local officials and citizens. In the long term this can result in mistakes that easily could have been avoided or rectified. In most cases a change of political leadership will lead to the abandonment of strategy implementation as management succession is not provided. The question of whether such a planning mechanism should be termed as 'strategic planning' at all remains open. The role of planning networks within this type of planning organization is minimal as knowledge and experts' expertise remains unclaimed.

Elitist approach

The second of the four types can be defined as an *elitist approach*. This approach is characterized by a participatory planning process that is restricted to the local administration and local business elite. Employment of this technique of planning decision-making implies that the city administration tries to mobilize local resources on the one hand and to fulfil statutory provisions for community involvement on the other. Such cases usually involve the invitation of a narrow circle of local stakeholders in the development of a strategic initiative. The selection of potential stakeholders for establishing an alliance with local authorities generally occurs according to the preferences of the highest standing local officials – as opposed to the principles of representative democracy. Pallai considers this cooperation as a 'government capture' (Pallai 2006), whereby officials and local economic agents enter into collusion for future mutual benefits (cf. Dąbrowski Chapter 9). The planning process lacks transparency, leaving unselected interest groups and the local community excluded and unrepresented in the process. This process is conducted exclusively with a provisional project group that forms a self-selecting and self-serving 'knowledge arena' (cf. Adams *et al.* Chapter 2). As long as planning decision-making occurs within the scope of an elitist approach in the interests of a small group of involved actors, its strategic development outcome(s) lacks the community ownership of a 'community based strategy'. As a result, this type of strategy-making approach generates unnecessary tensions between local administrations and the communities they serve, and questions the credibility of the development strategy.

In relation to community involvement in the planning process, we have to bear in mind that the direction of local development in the Soviet system was determined and managed solely by the state, and that the establishment of public participation mechanisms, methods and procedures was not necessary or required. In the context of urban planning Golubchikov (2004) refers to a crisis and stagnation in the early 1990s as it became clear that new approaches to planning would be required to deal with the transition to a market-based economy. The development of more participatory forms of strategic planning only commenced in the 1990s, recognizing that a new culture of democracy in planning practice needed to be locally developed and incorporated. However, numerous planning initiatives continue to take place within an amorphous de-motivated social environment whereby local residents do not strongly identify themselves with their hometowns as a result of Soviet resettlement policies and the state's unwillingness to take responsibility for participatory forms of local strategic planning and development. Thus the consequential amorphous mentality of local civil societies continues to be characterized by a lack of organizational capacity, and by the reluctance or a weak self-determination to engage in consensus building for the protection of common interests.

The elitist approach to strategic planning is highly relevant for mono-economic small and medium-size cities, or for those municipalities with a small number of large-scale enterprises that contribute the lion's share of revenue to the local budget. In these conditions, on the one hand, local administrations cannot ignore the interests of main economic agents and a priori must take them into consideration. On the other hand, smaller stakeholders tend to be more reluctant to participate, believing that the new strategy will have little beneficial impact for small businesses and other small-scale interests. Typically, there are two types of funding relevant for this model. Either the process is joint-financed through a combination of local budget resources and participating stakeholders, or it is funded entirely by the stakeholders. The potential risks of such an approach to strategic planning are evident. Under such conditions there is little adherence to the principle of balanced public participation in the planning process. The strategy tends to lack any element of an integrated approach, is unlikely seek an equitable treatment of diverse community interests and is likely to neglect social and environmental issues in favour of economic concerns. This distorted form of strategic planning, which excludes a large part of a local community, results either in a failure to properly implement the developed strategy or to have any significant impact on local community development in the long term. As with the administrative approach, it is difficult to recognize many of the principles of strategic planning in the elitist approach because the strategy-making process is manipulated in the interests of a minority group of stakeholders on the one hand and a local administration on the other. Furthermore, the potential for the participation of professional networks is limited and restricted to those organizations that are in partnership with local decision-makers as well as those responsible for the implementation of strategic documents.

Populist approach

The next approach to the development of a local strategy can be defined as a *populist approach*. This type of strategic planning is characterized by strong publicity and advertising campaigns in the mass media as well as public forums, focusing on strategic planning generally and a specific strategic initiative or document in particular. Often the development strategy is associated with a new local political leader or leadership, and is highly promoted during the election campaign, albeit a public relations exercise in many cases. The drivers of the process do not strictly adhere to strategic planning methodology or principles within the scope of a populist approach, but they tend to use the label of strategic planning for individual political benefits. With particular regard for this approach, both unilateral and multilateral ways of financing are applicable. Sometimes the process can be partially or fully assisted by funds from an election budget, or it can be financed by election campaign donors or similar outside funding sources. The disadvantages of donors driving planning initiatives are well known. The context of the drafted strategy is often deliberately simplified and often constitutes a wish list of good intentions or a political declaration whereby the identified perspectives are not integrated with, or adapted to specific local conditions. Moreover, strategic development priorities tend merely to reflect the interests of privileged local stakeholders despite provisions for 'public participation' in some cases. Again, the application of a populist approach is unlikely to lead to the full implementation of an inclusive and integrated strategy.

Democratic approach

The final type of strategic planning can be referred to as the *democratic approach*. Unlike the types discussed above, this approach is characterized by comprehensive citizens' involvement in the strategic planning process. Large numbers of communities all over the country have endeavoured to incorporate this type of approach into their local governance system. As discussed by Stead and Nadin in this volume, St Petersburg, as something of a pioneering Russian city, applied a democratic model of strategic planning in 1996. This particular model drew upon planning mechanisms from successful experiences in Barcelona and Munich. The knowledge transfer involved the use of international consultants and the sharing of good practice experiences between experts and officials of the participating cities. However, the significantly different institutional and cultural contexts of these successful experiences challenged agents' ability to implement these democratic forms of strategic planning in St Petersburg. Nevertheless, grant funding has been one of the most important resources in the successful incorporation of a democratic approach to strategy-design processes. A variety of national and international organizations have provided grants on a competitive basis for this purpose, although the substantial part of financial support has been obtained from foreign governments, local administration budgets and research institutions in the case of larger cities (with one million or more inhabitants) and regions. Research by the author, based on the analysis of 19 municipalities, suggests that approximately 58 per cent have chosen this latter form of financial assistance.

Normally, the application of the democratic approach implies that at least a local network of planning professionals will participate in the development process on a regular basis. Where there is a lack of local experts, it may be necessary for temporary external consultants to participate in the strategy-making process. Due to the popularity and increased use of external consultation, specific attention to both Russian and foreign supporting organizations and experts is required. In cases where funding is provided by foreign sponsorship, it is often a condition of the grant approval that international experts participate (possibly jointly with local consultants) at some stages in the process. However, despite the undoubted value of such participation, Russian experience demonstrates some key disadvantages of cooperation with overseas planners and consultants. Paradoxically the previous professional experience of these experts, which is the reason they have been asked to participate, can also be a disadvantage from a Russian perspective. In other words, foreign experts naturally tend to present knowledge and experiences that have been obtained in a social, institutional, political and cultural context that differs greatly from Russian realities and experiences. Little or no attention is given to differences in the treatment of strategic planning or the specific local context because these international experts have a highly superficial knowledge of both Russian Federal and local legislation at best. All of these factors substantially reduce the effectiveness of international consulting and emphasize the complexities of policy transfer discussed widely in the academic literature (Adams 2008). However, there are two key disadvantages that need to be underlined with regard to the use of Russian consultants. The first fault of local administrations occurs when obtaining financial support for the purpose of a new local planning initiative; local administrations commission external planning organizations to prepare their strategies without fully or actively participating in the process themselves, consigning them to the role of outside observers. Consequently the quality of the product is often limited because important local socio-economic development considerations have not been taken into account and important local knowledge remains un- and/or under-utilized. The second disadvantage relates both to Russian and overseas consultants whereby these temporarily employed 'parachuted' consultants (Pallai 2006) are not involved in strategy implementation. Often the question of whether the strategy is realistic or achievable in the local context is given little attention in such cases because there is little incentive for consultants to ask such questions; once the strategic document has been approved, the same approach and the same methodology will be applied as they move to the next city or district.

Thus the extent to which expert community and planning professionals are involved in the strategy design process is likely to be different in each of the approaches discussed. The extent of this involvement is predetermined by the scope of centralized local power and control on the one hand, and social and economic conditions of territorial development on the other. Clearly there is limited scope for the involvement of expert communities in the case of an administrative approach. The *knowledge and evidence* required to support strategic initiatives are produced by local administrations with little or no opportunity for public debate because they are rooted typically in the interests of particular politicians. Also, the contribution of expert communities is limited in the application of elitist or populist approaches. Again the knowledge and evidence necessary to support strategic initiatives is created and debated by a limited group of stakeholders in relation to their own needs. The elitist approach often implies outside consultancy at the stage of strategy development where planning knowledge is required to serve the needs of an established political and/or business order. The final strategic document is assembled by participating professionals within a pre-determined framework. In other words, the strategy becomes an instrument for achieving political goals, leaving planning knowledge and experiences to be politicized and modified at will. The involvement of planning experts does not guarantee the adequate use or legitimization of knowledge and evidence. Subject to the need for context sensitivity, strategy-making within the scope of a democratic approach offers the most significant opportunities for meaningful debate, and for knowledge creation and transfer. The strengthening of democratic traditions in decision-making processes will facilitate the widening of professional networks, whilst moving beyond knowledge in the interests of limited stakeholder groups to a broader application of community interests on the whole.

Conclusion

This chapter has explored some of the complexities of the evolution of strategic planning in the Russian Federation. It is important to remember that a vast centralized system of territorial planning with an extensive network of planning professionals was in place before the collapse of the Soviet Union, although all planners were state-employed. In the post-Soviet period between 1990 and 1995, during which all planning initiatives were perceived with suspicion, the professional planning community lost a significant number of highly qualified specialists because their services were no longer in demand. However, the re-application of professional knowledge and skills to new social and economic realities, and to an extent the restructuring of the planning profession has accompanied the revival of strategic planning and other forms of planning practice in post-Soviet Russia.

The main discussion of this chapter began by examining the emergence of strategic planning in Russia with a specific focus on the NWFD. On the basis of this examination, some of the main challenges facing local authorities in the practice of strategic planning were identified. There appears to be a number of critical barriers that currently prevent strategic planning from becoming fully integrated into the local governance system. These barriers consist of the existence of a legal vacuum, the diverse interpretations and applications of strategic planning, the under-funding of new planning initiatives and the negative perceptions of the need and potential for strategic planning. Also the recently adopted Federal Law on general principles of the organization of municipal self-government, which limits municipal power in the sphere of strategic planning, has discouraged the full engagement of some administrations in the long-term planning of territorial development. Nevertheless, despite the relatively long tradition in planning during Soviet Russia, some of these challenges were pre-determined by the absence of successful experience and the lack of a long-standing tradition in strategic planning. In this sense the Russian Federation has much in common with other former Soviet and socialist countries in CEE as can be seen elsewhere in this book.

A discussion of the emergence of different types of professional and expert networks and communities related to strategic planning follows the above exploration of strategic planning in Russia. The emergence of strategic planning in Russia and particularly in the NWFD has been driven, to a degree, by the City of St Petersburg, which was the first to adapt EU and American strategic planning methods and techniques to the Russian context. This has produced a unique planning model from which other Russian regions and municipalities as well as other countries of the former Soviet Union can learn. However, any 'territorial governance' model adaptation will have to reflect the local context in each case. The importance of St Petersburg is also evident in the emergence of professional and expert networks and communities in the field of strategic planning. Many of these are concentrated in St Petersburg but supply their services far beyond the border of the NWFD. This immediately brings to light the different organizational approaches to the practice of strategic planning and the potential for, and implications of emerging 'epistemic communities', which has been discussed in the final part of this chapter. The diversity of organizational approaches in relation to strategic planning reflects the conditions in contemporary Russia whereby each administration perceives the issues of local government and self-government in a different way. In order to apply strategic planning practice more effectively, a change in institutional and administrative culture will be required to overcome the barriers that have been identified, including the amorphous and demotivated social environment, corruption, legal shortcomings, credibility gaps in government – community relations, permanent budget deficits and a lack of local administrative accountability.

Thus it has been argued in this chapter that professional planning networks, which have emerged from the ruins of the Soviet planning system, have gained a solid experience in the application of new methods and techniques in strategic and other forms of planning. If new networks and communities are to be given the opportunity to emerge, then existing networks need to be given the opportunity to evolve within different contexts from the local to the transnational. In some ways, Russia may be in a strong position to develop such networks with other Russian speaking CEE countries such as Belarus and Ukraine. Also the evolution of international networks inside and outside the EU will be important at all levels of governance. Sub-national cooperation between lower levels of government and experts that can avoid the potential geopolitical tensions and conflicts of higher level relations are extremely important in fostering such networks. In the long-term there is evident potential for Russian planning 'communities of practice' to become fully integrated into these wider international networks of professionals and experts or 'epistemic communities'. In turn these networks can act as mediators and transfer knowledge and experience from the transnational community to local power institutions in the forms of effective policy advice. Enlarging networks and the further evolution of an 'epistemic community' will result in a broader application of their research and the integration of this knowledge into local planning decision-making on a regular basis. However, if the evolution identified here is to become a reality, much remains to be done.

References

Adams, N. (2008) 'Convergence and Policy Transfer: An Examination of the Extent to which Approaches to Spatial Planning Have Converged within the Context of an Enlarged EU', *International Planning Studies*, 13(1): 31–49.

Adams, N., Cotella, G. and Nunes, R. (2010) 'Territorial Knowledge Channels in a Multi-jurisdictional Policy Environment. A Theoretical Framework', in N. Adams, G. Cotella and R. Nunes (eds) *Territorial Development, Cohesion and Spatial Planning: Knowledge and Policy Development in an Enlarged EU*, London: Routledge.

Bauzer, V. and Hidebach, H. P. (2002) 'Uchastie grazhdan v upravlenii i planirovalii gorodskogo razvitia', in *Ekonomicheskie strategii aktivnich gorodov*, St. Petersburg: 137–148.

BN.RU Gazeta (2007) *Razrabotka strategii razvitija Moskvi do 2025 goda oboidetsa v \$3 milliona*, in BN.RU Gazeta 13.07.2007. Online. Available HTTP: www.bn.ru/news/2007/07/13/15677.html (accessed June 2009).

Dąbrowski, M. (2010) 'Institutional Change, Partnership and Regional Networks: Civic Engagement and the Implementation of the Structural Funds in Poland', in N. Adams, G. Cotella and R. Nunes (eds) *Territorial Development, Cohesion and Spatial Planning: Knowledge and Policy Development in an Enlarged EU*, London: Routledge.

Dimitriou, H. and Thompson, R. (2007) *Strategic Planning for Regional Development in the UK*, London: Routledge.

Fritsch, M. (2009) 'European Territorialization and the Eastern Neighbourhood: Spatial Development Co-operation between the EU and Russia', *European Journal of Spatial Development*, Mai 2009, 35. Online. Available HTTP: www.nordregio.se/EJSD/refereed35.pdf (accessed July 2009).

—— (2010) 'Interfaces of European Union Internal and External Territorial Governance: the Baltic Sea Region', in N. Adams, G. Cotella and R. Nunes (eds) *Territorial Development, Cohesion and Spatial Planning: Knowledge and Policy Development in an Enlarged EU*, London: Routledge.

Golubchikov (2004) 'Urban Planning in Russia: Towards the Market', *European Planning Studies*, 12(2): 229–247.

Grinchel, B. M. and Kostileva, N. E. (2002) *Aktualnie problemi strategicheskogo planirovaniya v rossiyskikh gorodakh*, St. Petersburg.

Haas, P. (ed.) (1992) *Knowledge, Power and International Policy Coordination*, Columbia SC: University of South Carolina Press.

Haselsberger, B. and Benneworth, P. (2010) 'Cross-border Communities or Cross-border Proximity? Perspectives from the Austrian–Slovakian Border Region', in N. Adams, G. Cotella and R. Nunes (eds) *Territorial Development, Cohesion and Spatial Planning: Knowledge and Policy Development in an Enlarged EU*, London: Routledge.

Ianovskii, A. E. (ed.) (2000) *Uchastie grazhdan v formirovanii strategii ekonomicheskogo razvitia goroda. Opit proekta*, Obninsk.

Innes, J. E. and Booher, D. (2000) *Public Participation in Planning: New Strategies for the 21st Century*, Berkeley CA: University of California at Berkeley.

Jounda, N. (2004) *Evolution of Local Development Policymaking in Russia: From Administrative Planning to Public Policy?*, Budapest.

—— (2004) *Local Development in Russia: From Administrative Planning to Participatory Policymaking*, Budapest.

Jounda, N. and Zhikharevich, B. (2003) *How to Develop a Strategic Plan? A Practical Guide*, St. Petersburg.

Kemp, R. L. (ed.) (2008) *Strategic Planning for Local Government: A Handbook for Officials and Citizens*, Jefferson NC: McFarland.

Leontief Centre (2008) *Annual report 2008*. Online. Available HTTP: www.leontief.ru/news/?n_id=710 (accessed May 2009).

—— (2009), www.leontief.ru/about_eng (accessed June 2009).

Linkolla, T. (2000) 'Strategicheskoe planirovanie i rossiyskie municipaliteti' in *Strategicheskoe planirovanie v rossiyskikh municipalitetakh* (Strategic planning in Russian municipalities), Moscow.

Maier, K. (2010) 'The Pursuit of Balanced Territorial Development: The Realities and Complexities of the Cohesion Agenda', in N. Adams, G. Cotella and R. Nunes (eds) *Territorial Development, Cohesion and Spatial Planning: Knowledge and Policy Development in an Enlarged EU*, London: Routledge.

Mani, S. (2006) 'Epistemic Communities and Informed Policy Making for Promoting Innovations: The Case of Singapore', in L. Box and R. Engelhard (eds) *Science and Technology Policy for Development, Dialogues at the Interface*, London: Anthem Press.

North-West Federal District (2009) Official Webpage. Online. Available HTTP: www.szfo.ru/section/30/federalynyy_okrug.html (accessed June 2009).

Pallai, K. (2006) 'How can Strategies Become Destructive?', in M. Schrenk (ed.) *International Conference on Urban Planning and Regional Development*, Conference proceedings, Vienna.

Razrabotka strategii razvitiya Moskvi do 2025 goda (Development of the Moscow city strategy till 2025). Online. Available HTTP: www.bn.ru/news/2007/07/13/15677.html (accessed June 2009).

Resource Centre of Strategic Planning at Leontief Centre. Online. Available HTTP: www.citystrategy.leontief.ru (accessed May 2009).

Rohchin, V. E. and Chekalin, V. S. (1995) *Regionalnoe i municipalnoe planirovanie. Chast I. Regionalnoe planirovanie*, St. Petersburg.

Stead, D. and Nadin, V. (2010) 'Shifts in Territorial Governance and the Europeanization of Spatial Planning in Central and Eastern Europe', in N. Adams, G. Cotella and R. Nunes (eds) *Territorial Development, Cohesion and Spatial Planning: Knowledge and Policy Development in an Enlarged EU*, London: Routledge.

Tosics, I. (2003) *Strategic Planning in European cities*. Online. Available HTTP: www.urbaneconomics.ru/events.php?folder_id=87&mat_id=61&page_id=1382 (accessed may 2009).

Vinogradov, V. N. and Erlich, O. V. (2001) *Vovlechenie obschestvennosti goroda v razrabotky i realizatsiu strategicheskogo plana: teoria, praktika, technologii*, St. Petersburg.

Waterhout, B. (2010) 'European Spatial Planning: Current State and Future Challenges', in N. Adams, G. Cotella and R. Nunes (eds) *Territorial Development, Cohesion and Spatial Planning: Knowledge and Policy Development in an Enlarged EU*, London: Routledge.

Wenger, E. (1998) *Communities of Practice: Learning, Meaning, and Identity*, Cambridge: Cambridge University Press.

Zhikharevich, B. S. (2006) 'Desiat let gorodskim strategiam v Rossii', *Russian Expert Review*, 2(16). Online. Available HTTP: www.rusrev.org/content/review/default.asp?shmode=8&ida=1198&ids=125 (accessed June 2009).

Zhikharevich, B. S. and Limonov, L. E. (2003) *Territorialnoe strategicheskoye planirovanie pri perekhode k rinochnoy ekonomike: opit gorodov Rossii*, St. Petersburg.

Zito, A. (2001) 'Epistemic communities, European Union governance and the public voice', *Science and Public Policy*, 28(6): 465–476.

17 Territorial knowledge channels

Contexts for 'situated learning'

Neil Adams, Giancarlo Cotella and Richard Nunes

Introduction

This book has opened a knowledge perspective on the exploration of stability and change of policy development in the enlarged European Union (EU) through the presentation of a set of both theoretical and empirical contributions, with particular regard for Central and Eastern Europe (CEE) in the run up to, and aftermath of the 2004 and 2007 enlargement rounds. This exploration into 'the role of knowledge in the policy process' (Radaelli 1995) is a consideration of the interplay of knowledge and policy development within the polyarchic, multi-level and cross-scalar policy landscape of spatial planning in Europe, examining how data, ideas and argument translate into the powers that shape or 'frame' (Schön and Rein 1994) the course of spatial policy development through organizational structures or 'arenas of action' (Steinmo *et al.* 1992; Hall and Taylor 1996; Lowndes 1996).

We have suggested a framework for conceptualizing this interplay of knowledge and policy development in Chapter 2, and have maintained that formal and informal multi-level institutional arrangements can influence policy development as a result of having acquired the power to shape or frame new policy considerations or safeguard existing policy approaches. Alternatively this policy development process can be influenced through persuasive expert opinion (epistemic communities) or external political pressures from advocacy groups and professional communities of practice.

The analysis of the evidence and the considerations presented in the different chapters suggests that the evolution of spatial planning in Europe constitutes a highly complex process that is influenced by an extremely diverse set of variables, the challenges of which extend beyond the 'hard' formal boundaries of Member States and of the EU. The attention of both the editors and the contributors has been directed toward the crucial role played by European spatial planning in this process, as both a set of tools and practices put in place at the EU level to achieve specific territorial goals and as a complex process of development and consolidation of discursive elements that 'trickle down' to influence spatial planning activities in the various domestic contexts. The various contributions clearly illustrate the extent to which different elements of European spatial planning have influenced the evolution of territorial governance arrangements and operations in the different domestic contexts and even beyond EU borders. For instance, European territorial cooperation (together with previous INTERREG initiatives) has offered an experimental platform to explore the creation and transformation of partnerships or informal (soft, ad hoc) and formal (hard, regulatory) spatial governance arrangements (cf. Waterhout Chapter 4; Stead and Nadin Chapter 7; Haselsberger and Benneworth Chapter 10; Fritsch Chapter 15). European Territorial Cooperation is one of a set of evolving knowledge arenas of European spatial planning as well as a driver of action-oriented projects. And therefore it is a mainstream tool in spatial development on a European scale of metagovernance (Faludi 2006). A similar discourse is valid for the ESPON programme, which plays a role as both a knowledge arena in its own right whilst at the same time generating numerous other project related knowledge arenas that focus on specific issues (Adams *et al.* Chapter 1; Waterhout Chapter 4). The debate on the operational complexities of the territorial dimension of the cohesion objective provides another knowledge arena that performs a similar role (cf. Adams *et al.* Chapter 1; Tewdwr-Jones Chapter 3; Waterhout Chapter 4; Maier Chapter 11; Kule *et al.* Chapter 12; Czapiewki and Janc Chapter 14).

From these observations an appreciation of planning as 'both a form of governance and metagovernance' (Haughton *et al.* 2010) calls for an understanding of the links between metagovernance systems, and the 'soft' and 'hard' spaces discussed in Chapter 1. These links relate to the co-evolution of knowledge and policy development, to contested knowledge, and to the overlapping and conflicting communities of actors and arenas which interact with planning systems in a multi-jurisdictional policy environment. These issues are contextualized within the contemporary academic debates in relation to Europeanization (cf. Conzelman 1998; Olsen 2002; Radaelli 2004; Radaelli and Saurugger 2008) – more specifically in relation to the Europeanization of spatial planning (cf. Böhme and Waterhout 2008) – and questions over the extent of convergence of policy approaches or the institutionalization of policy transfer (Adams 2008; Stead 2008; Stead and Nadin Chapter 7). In the context of this discussion, the emphasis of this book has been placed on knowledge, or more specifically on the 'territorial knowledge communities' responsible for the production of 'knowledge resources' (data, ideas, persuasion and argument), and their interface with new and existing 'knowledge arenas' via 'territorial knowledge channels' (Nunes *et al.* 2009; Adams *et al.* Chapter 2).

Building on the theoretical framework extensively discussed in Chapter 2, this concluding chapter provides some reflections on the individual contributions when viewed through the interpretive lens of the knowledge perspective of this book. First, a brief summary of the main elements of the adopted framework is presented. Then, the evidence and considerations proposed by the different authors are examined in the light of three complementary strands that constitute entry points to the adopted knowledge perspective, namely the interplay and co-evolution of knowledge and policy development, the role of data, ideas and argument (knowledge resources) in policy development and the uncertainty, interpretation and path-dependency of evolving institutional arrangements (knowledge arenas). Finally a conclusive section reflects on the added value of the adopted approach, revisiting the presented elements in the light of the future for spatial planning in and beyond the enlarged EU.

A knowledge perspective in the development of spatial policies in Europe

The evidence presented in the different contributions illustrates how the interface of knowledge and policy development constitutes an issue of pivotal importance. The diverse mechanisms for the transmission of knowledge into the policy process are situated at this interface and depend on the interaction of a complex set of knowledge and power logics. The conceptualization of this interplay (cf. Adams *et al.* Chapter 2) has stressed the need for a broader exploration of the extent of engagement or of the nature and character of the links within and between diverse communities of actors with particular emphasis on the close relationship between knowledge and interests. Incidentally, this book has taken a path emerging within planning and, more broadly, in public policy research circles, which focuses on knowledge (inclusive of research) as data, ideas, argument and persuasion (Weiss 1986, Majone 1989). Departing from Haas' (1992) definition and usage of the concept of 'epistemic communities', with its particular emphasis on the 'usable knowledge' (Haas 2004) made possible through internal 'validity checks' of the shared knowledge base among expert professionals, we have emphasized the need to broaden the spectrum of participating stakeholders through the additional consideration of extra-community links (cf. Haas 1990; Radaelli 1999; Zito 2001a, 2001b; Waterhout Chapter 4). This immediately raises the complex issue of the competing institutional and discursive logics of 'reality tests' (Haas 1990) or 'knowledge claims' (Rydin 2007), which has led to the adoption of a knowledge perspective in consideration of other communities of actors such as 'advocacy coalitions' and 'communities of practice' under the concept of territorial knowledge communities.

This preliminary consideration has taken the agent interactivity implicit in these different communities to be the products of coordinated activity in the form of networks, seminars, conferences and meetings, which can help to institutionalize activities through the establishment of new routines. At the same time, these processes may lay new foundations for questioning established beliefs or values, or policy stability as precursors of policy change, exploring what this represents in terms of the confluence of, and tensions between evidence-based causal beliefs and value judgments in policy context-sensitive settings. More importantly, it is also the agent interactivity across these territorial knowledge communities whereby a member of a community of practice can simultaneously have a role in advocacy or the validation of knowledge within other networks or communities in a multi-jurisdictional policy environment (cf. Figure 2.2, Table 2.1). This is particularly relevant to the spatio-temporal context of this book; that is, the turning points created by EU enlargement for both the contexts of diverse spatial planning approaches in Europe and the evolving context of European spatial planning, which have generated new 'policy windows' (Kingdon 1995) in the European territorial governance arena (cf. Adams *et al.* Chapter 2; Waterhout Chapter 4; Pallagst 2006 and Chapter 6).

Both the described knowledge perspective and this consideration of agent interactivity provide impetus to the suggested notion of knowledge resources and its generation and mobilization through arenas whereby knowledge is validated and verified, or debated. As outlined in Chapter 2, the intersection of these two entities is a consideration therefore of both 'knowledge and information' and 'power and preferences' as key variables of the understanding of policy change, and/or investigations into the extent to which institutional and organizational forces take on the powers to shape or frame policy (cf. Adams *et al.* Chapter 2 and Conzelman 1998 on 'knowledge' and 'conflict' models). In other words, how, when and to what extent territorial knowledge communities engage with different knowledge arenas to advance, inform or legitimize policy agendas or approaches ('policy images', cf. Chapter 2) through the strategic use of knowledge resources.

The knowledge conduits or 'transmission belts' (Haas 2004) through which knowledge is generated and mobilized can be found at the intersection of knowledge resources and knowledge arenas, or territorial knowledge channels in our terminology (cf. Adams *et al.* Chapter 2). These territorial knowledge channels manifest themselves as either formal or informal multi-scalar institutional arrangements of European territorial governance and take the form of advisory boards, committees, working groups and coalitions. They constitute the confluence of diverse territorial knowledge communities with varying degrees of influence, which press for stability and change in policy development with evidence-based causal beliefs, and/or value-based and 'evidence-informed' argument (Davoudi 2006) (cf. Figure 2.1). This consideration of the potential links within and between territorial knowledge communities, of consensual/disputed or absent knowledge bases and shared/unshared interests, has clear implications for how different knowledge arenas link with the 'hard' regulatory spaces of planning systems, and the 'soft spaces' of territorial governance beyond the geographical and professional boundaries of these systems.

This implies that territorial knowledge channels can take on sub-national, national or supranational characteristics as well as more complex multi-level or cross-scalar forms, which are subject to both formal and informal institutional influences that may both enable and constrain the creation, transformation and destruction of these channels.

It is important to stress that the proposed knowledge perspective is also sensitive to temporal and socio-cultural elements. On the one hand, the influence of these territorial knowledge channels is likely to be highest when new policy windows emerge, evoking responses from a diverse range of actors on particular policy areas or issues. On the other hand, the attitude and capacity of domestic actors to consolidate particular policy areas or issues may foster or hamper their ability to identify or create the appropriate knowledge arenas through which they can access or convey knowledge resources as well as take part in testing and validating knowledge and scrutinizing the rules of policy evaluation. Several contributors have suggested that the policy windows opened as a result of the latest EU enlargements have significantly influenced the evolution of spatial planning in the former candidate countries (cf. Finka Chapter 5; Pallagst Chapter 6; Maier Chapter 11), through the introduction of EU-inspired elements within domestic legislative frameworks (cf. Finka Chapter 5; Marot Chapter 8; Dąbrowski Chapter 9) and contextual discourses (cf. Kule *et al.* Chapter 12; Capik Chapter 13; Czapiewski and Janc Chapter 14), and through the adoption of ideas and approaches transferred from old Member States (cf. Capik Chapter 13; Stead and Nadin Chapter 7). At the same time, the 'weak and fragmented character' of territorial knowledge communities in CEE countries (Maier Chapter 11) appears to have hampered the emergence of an 'Eastern European perspective' within the European spatial planning discourse (cf. Janin Rivolin and Faludi 2005; Cotella 2007a, 2009a). A more ambiguous but less pronounced interaction also can be detected between the EU and the Russian Federation (cf. Fritsch Chapter 15 and Razumeyko Chapter 16); although its link to EU enlargement is perhaps more tenuous.

Territorial knowledge channels therefore are the products of agent interactivity, spatio-temporal context and socio-cultural influences, and all of these factors potentially have implications for their effectiveness as generators and drivers of knowledge, and as contexts for 'situated learning' (Lave and Wenger 1991). In the multi-jurisdictional policy environment of the EU, the resultant learning within internal territorial governance spaces is a function of a large number of dynamic territorial knowledge channels that can stimulate or condition the 'vertical', 'horizontal' and 'circular' processes of Europeanization (cf. Adams *et al.* Chapter 2; Stead and Nadin Chapter 7); that is, the learning and conflict outcomes influenced by ongoing debates in relation to the simultaneous embrace of, and apprehension and confusion over different rhetoric as well as other institutional constraints. The complexity of this situation is exacerbated when applied to the numerous 'soft spaces' of EU territorial governance (cf. Haughton *et al.* 2010; Haselsberger and Benneworth Chapter 10) and particularly when applied to the external dimension of EU territorial governance (cf. Fritsch Chapter 15). In the next section the evidence presented by the different contributors in relation to the above discussion will be contextualized.

Exploring territorial knowledge channels in an enlarged EU

The dynamic context introduced earlier requires a consideration of the manner in which knowledge resources are tested within knowledge arenas and channeled into the complex forces shaping spatial development policies. This consideration includes, but is not limited to the discursive formation of adopted spatial planning practices (cf. Majone 1989; Dabinett and Richardson 2005; see also Fischer and Forester 1993; Hajer and Wagenaar 2003 on 'discursive analysis'), and the turning points or newly framed policy issues and opportunities made possible through the forces acting upon the course of policy development on the back of

EU enlargement. These forces are born out of debates about knowledge resources, the dynamics of uncertainty, and the interpretation of problems and path-dependency (knowledge arenas). Thus their interplay with policy development is crucial to an understanding of existing and evolving policy contexts of incremental change (path-dependency) as well as the more radical path-shaping policy change that periodically punctuates or breaks with a state of policy stability or 'institutionalized policy monopoly' (Meijerink 2005).

Following on from the exploration and discussion of relevant academic literature necessary for the development of the theoretical framework for this book, it is possible to identify three complementary strands among the contributions to this volume: (i) the interplay and co-evolution of knowledge and policy development, (ii) the data, ideas, argument and persuasion in policy development, and (iii) the uncertainty, interpretation and path-dependency of existing, evolving and new institutional arrangements. Each of these different strands, which link implicitly to the adopted knowledge perspective of the theoretical framework, and have informed the individual contributions, is now explored more in detail.

Epistemic communities and the interplay and co-evolution of knowledge and policy development

The first strand examines the complex interplay between knowledge and policy development and the implications that this has had for the evolution and role of the territorial knowledge communities engaged in spatial planning in Europe. First, there is a discussion of the extent to which any component of these diverse communities (Table 2.1) can be identified as an epistemic community. Second, the need to broaden engagement and the importance of addressing the East-West dimension is explored before finally turning the focus to the extent of CEE engagement in spatial planning in Europe.

The European planning community: an epistemic community?

The European planning community is a broad, difficult to define and heterogeneous group (Waterhout 2008). Several thousand partners have participated in INTERREG projects under the umbrella of territorial cooperation and the same is true, though in lower numbers, for projects undertaken as part of the ESPON programme. Their involvement has been structured on numerous networks and communities of actors that have an undeniable impact particularly on the internal, but also on the external dimensions of European territorial governance albeit difficult to measure. The communities of actors behind European territorial cooperation and ESPON are set within a European spatial planning organizational framework, which consists of different, and to some degree, interacting circles. Waterhout identifies an 'inner circle' of ESDP planners, new territorial cohesion policy-makers, new Member States, INTERREG and ESPON programme monitoring officials, and local and regional policy-makers on transnational projects. Waterhout also identifies a second or 'outer circle' of stakeholders such as the EU Parliament, Committee of the Regions, interest and lobby groups or advocacy coalitions, researchers and commentators (2008 and Chapter 4). In the context of these two circles, the heterogeneous and political character of committees, organizations and working groups suggests that an EU level epistemic community of like-minded academics, practitioners and policy-makers with recognized expertise or policy-relevant knowledge in the domain of European spatial planning is difficult to identify. However, if a European spatial planning epistemic community does exist, Waterhout suggests it should be conceived as a group of consultants, researchers and officials who are well acquainted and occupy key positions in Member States or organizations such as ESPON, INTERREG or DG Regio. They are likely to be, as stressed elsewhere in this book, acquainted through social interaction within select 'venues' (Sabatier 1988) or knowledge arenas, and consequently able to use their politically or academically influential positions to shape or frame policy development or invoke new policy images through the generation and mobilization of knowledge resources. Furthermore, as these individuals may have several concurrent roles and responsibilities (e.g. contact point/national representative for arenas such as ESPON, European Territorial Cooperation initiatives, CEMAT etc.), they also have the opportunity to facilitate the channeling of knowledge resources developed within a particular knowledge arena into other arenas. As discussed in the previous sections, the scale and heterogeneity of contemporary networks require a combination of complementary theoretical explanations that can begin to address the 'relational complexity' (Healey 2006) of policy development and its interface with knowledge, expanding the intra-community knowledge focus of epistemic communities in an effort to provide a broader base of intersecting knowledge resources and arenas that are not limited to expert knowledge.

Broadening engagement and addressing the East-West dimension

The need to broaden the base of knowledge resources and their generation and co-evolution with policy development within and across diverse arenas parallels the need to broaden engagement with European spatial planning (cf. Stead and Nadin Chapter 7; Finka Chapter 5). Spatial planning is constantly confronted by new challenges (such as climate change, demographic decline etc.) in addition to the introduction of new terminology as illustrated in the transition from 'polycentric development' to 'territorial cohesion'. This has important implications for the need to engage a wider group of stakeholders and non-experts, despite the apprehension and confusion these new challenges and terminology can cause among planners and non-planners alike. In light of recent developments in the maturing and increasingly institutionalized environment of European spatial planning (Waterhout 2008, Chapter 4), this need to broaden engagement to a wider group of stakeholders is concomitant with an increasingly heterogeneous and ever evolving landscape of spatial planning in Europe at all territorial scales from the supranational to the local (Adams *et al.* Chapter 2 and Introduction to Part II). In other words, European spatial planning and the landscape of spatial planning in Europe have taken on uniquely distinct turning points concomitantly with the latest rounds of EU enlargement, respectively shifting from the 'spatial' focus of the legacy of the ESDP to a 'territorial cohesion' emphasis, and adding an indisputable East-West dimension to the already heterogeneous landscape (Pallagst 2006 and Chapter 6). This has significant implications for the territorial cohesion policy window or future windows of opportunity for the 'territory matters coalition' discussed by Waterhout (Chapter 4) as well as for the overhaul of regional policy post 2013, which was invoked by the Constitutional Treaty, the Sapir and Barca reports, and the Financial Perspectives 2007–2013 (respectively Sapir *et al.* 2004; Barca 2009, EC 2005) and currently sustained by the recent ratification of the Lisbon Treaty.

With particular regard for the new East-West dimension within the already heterogeneous landscape of spatial planning in the EU, the opening of the Iron Curtain and subsequent reform processes in CEE countries in the run up to accession in 2004 and 2007 – in addition to post-enlargement structural funding reform – has resulted in a major development impulse for European spatial planning. Namely, it has invoked a significant impulse for territorial development and in turn for spatial planning, which the EU has encouraged further through linkages to prioritized funding regimes. On the other hand, the mainstreaming of former INTERREG priorities notwithstanding, the focus on spatial planning of the new European territorial cooperation initiatives seems to be reduced (cf. Pallagst 2006). Be that as it may, the factors contributing to this development impulse are characterized by a neo-liberal agenda that has ensured a strong focus on FDI in the initial transition periods for CEE countries (cf. Tewdwr-Jones Chapter 3). It is therefore interesting to note how CEE regions have been increasingly involved in international economic development networks within and outside the EU, demonstrating the high priority being given to economic development in these countries (Capik Chapter 13). Potentially EU-oriented spatial planning communities may emerge from this development impulse and whereas these communities may or may not necessarily represent the views of mainstream business, the evidence presented in the contributions to this volume implies that existing communities of practice in many CEE countries remain 'weak and fragmented' (Maier Chapter 11; cf. Tewdwr-Jones Chapter 3 on the bypassing or potential marginalization of planning). Tynkkynen (2009) identifies an even closer alignment between business, development and planning in the context of the Russian Federation and the discussions presented by Fritsch (Chapter 15) and Razumeyko (Chapter 16) also suggest that existing communities of practice are characterized by similar weaknesses and fragmentation.

This is a matter of some concern in a context already marked by the contradictions and tensions between the dual aims of cohesion and competitiveness (Tewdwr-Jones Chapter 3), tensions that are encapsulated in various Member States including Latvia (cf. Kule *et al.* Chapter 12 and Paalzow 2006). The recent response to the *Green Paper on Territorial Cohesion* by the Latvian Ministry of Regional Development and Local Government (CEC 2009a) revealed a strong focus on addressing regional disparities within the country. At the same time, however, policy and funding continues to promote Riga as the principle international driver of national development, a choice that leads to further growth in internal disparities (Kule *et al.* Chapter 12; see also Capik Chapter 13 on the concentration of FDI). The same is true for the Polish context, where recent national spatial policy documents promote the simultaneous pursuance of cohesion and competitiveness whilst prioritizing the latter when it comes to operational decisions (Cotella 2009b; Czapiewski and Janc Chapter 14). The lacuna between rhetoric and reality (Adams 2008) appears to characterize components of both the internal and external dimensions of EU territorial governance. The extent to which territorial knowledge communities in CEE have engaged with spatial planning in Europe generally and European spatial planning in particular will now be examined.

Spatial planning in Europe: CEE engagement and influences

In light of the need for broader engagement in European spatial planning, this interplay and co-evolution of knowledge and policy development can be further likened to CEE 'new' Member States seeking to catch-up to the EU-15 both economically and conceptually (cf. Waterhout Chapter 4; Maier Chapter 11). This would imply CEE actively seeking to close the gap between the east and west (Pallagst 2006). Despite claims that suggest the integration between eastern and western epistemic communities seems to be solely a western academic concern (as highlighted by both Finka in Chapter 5 and Maier in Chapter 11), Pallagst (Chapter 6) explores the potential emergence of epistemic communities post-EU enlargement in two EU-level scenarios ('retention' and 'merger'). Whereas expert knowledge of CEE would be high in addition to the strong advocacy of policy issues in the former, networking and transnational cooperation would be a principle driver of the latter, thus reducing opportunities for the emergence of epistemic communities around CEE. Pallagst implies that the EU and the contemporary knowledge arenas of European spatial planning – ESPON, INTER-REG, the Territorial Agenda and the debate on territorial cohesion, promote 'merger' (cf. Maier Chapter 11 for opposing view). However, it is unclear how or indeed the extent to which these knowledge arenas may potentially fulfill this role both conceptually and in reality. In other words, it is hard to identify the forces contributing to the 'retention' and 'merger' scenarios in the different contexts as well as to identify the specific policy areas and issues where one of these scenarios – or of a third differentiated scenario somewhere between the two – may manifest as opposed to a collective regional response among CEE countries.

Building on the legacy of the ESDP, the contemporary knowledge arenas or 'pillars' of European spatial planning (Waterhout Chapter 4) have a unique role to play as institutional platforms for the generation and mobilization of knowledge, which in turn has prompted the evolution of existing arenas and/or the emergence of new ones. However, the policy impact of these arenas will vary from context to context, due to the highly heterogeneous reality of CEE. Kule *et al.* (Chapter 12) argue that the ESDP process stimulated debate in the Latvian context, which has subsequently influenced policy development and this implies significant levels of engagement with European spatial planning discourse as the recent responses to the *Green Paper on Territorial Cohesion* by Latvian organizations and networks demonstrate. There are also similarities with the Polish context whereby the influence of EU concepts and ideas on domestic spatial policy documents is evident (Czapiewski and Janc Chapter 14). Finka (Chapter 5) and Maier (Chapter 11) on the other hand argue that the reciprocal influence of European spatial planning on domestic policy development (the circular interactions referred to by Stead and Nadin in Chapter 7) has been limited, primarily due to the lack of effort by the EU level to effectively integrate a CEE dimension. In light of these opposing observations, it is unclear whether the evolving knowledge arenas of European spatial planning will encourage the consolidation of professional networks over matters of much needed policy change or the promotion of new policy images. Kule *et al.* (cf. also Tewdwr-Jones Chapter 3) suggest that planners can have an important role to play in times of turbulent social transformation such as those often offered by policy windows. However, the inability of CEE communities of practice to take on the powers to shape or frame spatial policy development or invoke new policy images due to their weak and fragmented nature appear to contradict this view. Finka (Chapter 5) and Pallagst (Chapter 6) also state that CEE experts are not yet as engaged in the ESPON arena as their Western European counterparts, despite the potential of ESPON as a platform for the generation and mobilization of epistemic communities for European spatial planning. One of the reasons for this limited engagement may be related to the lack of a professional 'sense of belonging' among 'communities of [planning] practice' (Maier Chapter 11; see also Handley *et al.* 2006 and Wenger 2000 on 'identity'). A lack of political will, commitment and/or financial resources by national governments also may be relevant here, particularly in the current economic climate where considerable pressure exists on scarce public finances (cf. Kule *et al.* Chapter 12 on the case of Latvia). The lack of experience and/or confidence for reasons that may be attributed to the poor integration of CEE with long existing, and evolving or new arenas for action may also be exacerbating the situation (Finka Chapter 5). The intricacies and complexities of EU territorial governance are exacerbated considerably when the external dimension is taken into account. This is illustrated by the differential levels of engagement and commitment of the Russian Federation to arenas such as CEMAT and VASAB and by the inability of the EU to engage the Russian Federation into its territorial governance arrangements in the context of the Baltic Sea Strategy (cf. Fritsch Chapter 15). The 'hard' nature of this physical, cultural and psychological external EU border suggests that the 'merger' scenario is even more unlikely in relation to this external dimension of EU territorial governance.

While many questions remain in relation to the extent of CEE engagement in European spatial planning and the evolution of territorial knowledge communities, there is a view that arenas such as INTERREG and ESPON have supported the creation and consolidation of epistemic communities in the field of planning. However, as identified by Stead and Nadin (Chapter 7), epistemic communities do not always possess the power to trigger Europeanization processes or to stimulate policy convergence or policy innovation. Once more this seems to echo the need for considering the wider group of stakeholders engaged in the process of policy development, as well as the intertwining of knowledge and power dynamics. Nevertheless epistemic communities can reinforce (e.g. through the bureaucratic power of an advisory committee) or constrain (e.g. through the framing of evidence-based policy options) perceived causal knowledge among stakeholder groups or influence the evolution and transformation of policy, notwithstanding the disputed nature of these expert knowledge claims. The unique contribution of this approach recognizes that these communities can formulate policy options/choices from an array of interests. Therefore, as discussed elsewhere in this book, a combination of complementary theoretical explanations that can begin to address the relational complexity of policy development and its interface with knowledge is necessary – expanding the intra-community knowledge focus of epistemic communities in an effort to provide a broader base of knowledge resources that are not limited to expert knowledge. In this light, the following section tries to unpack the suggested notion of knowledge resources through a detailed exploration of the role played by data, ideas, argument and persuasion in policy development.

Knowledge resources: data, ideas, argument and persuasion in policy development

The second strand of the knowledge perspective put forward by the book relates to the role of knowledge resources in policy development. First the influence and role of knowledge resources are examined before the focus turns to the types of knowledge resources that have to a greater or lesser extent become influential in the form of spatial visions, spatial metaphors and conceptualisations. Finally the discussion turns to the interaction of the knowledge and power dynamics that ultimately determine the influence and impact of these knowledge resources.

The influence and role of knowledge resources

Knowledge capital is embodied in people and transmitted through relationships with others; this is a key aspect of the interrelationship of both the 'tacit' and 'codified' qualities of knowledge (cf. Hasselsberger and Benneworth Chapter 10). However, if it is not 'usable' (Haas 2004) and accessible, knowledge is of no use on its own. The post-EU enlargement regional policy windows have witnessed a rise in the emphasis on territorial cohesion and on what Waterhout (Chapter 4) labels the territory matters coalition. The anticipated overhaul of regional policy will require that transformative capacity continues to be determined by social recognition, trust and legitimacy, and that spatial planning displays a capacity to learn and act upon this learning as part and parcel of a broader public engagement of spatial planning in Europe (Chapter 4). Pallagst

(Chapter 6) highlights that this engagement with a wider spectrum of stakeholders will be relatively new to the post-EU enlargement context for CEE as, until now, expert groups have dominated the European spatial planning arena (see also Finka Chapter 5). The extent to which this broader group will become engaged with territorial development issues remains to be seen especially where spatial ideas, concepts, metaphors and planning approaches can be seen as abstract and potentially working against sectoral interests.

This may begin to explain the reason why there appears to be a tendency to move away from abstract forms of strategic spatial planning toward more evidence-based and pragmatic forms of planning, i.e. getting things done. Such a move can be detected in the style of the recent EU Strategy for the Baltic Sea Region (Fritsch Chapter 15) that potentially offers a way forward for a 'soft' form of European spatial planning (Faludi 2010; cf. Haughton *et al.* 2010).[1] But the more gradual shift to evidence-based or even 'evidence-informed' (Davoudi 2006) policy development remains highly context sensitive (cf. Maier Chapter 11) by way of politically motivated deliberation (argument) and teleological (persuasion) tactics that generate and mobilize knowledge resources (see for example 'epistemic persuasion' in Haas 2004: 586). The ESDP (CEC 1999) and the Guiding Principles for Sustainable Spatial Development of the European Continent (CEMAT 2000), are two useful examples of knowledge resources that can begin to illustrate this fragmented and highly context sensitive setting in Europe. Whilst the knowledge resources embodied in the CEMAT document have been less influential than the strategic aspirational resource of the ESDP, CEMAT is seen by some countries as a more influential and important reference document (Fritsch Chapter 15, cf. also Stead and Waterhout 2008). This is certainly the case in relation to the external dimension of EU territorial governance and it can be argued that the document more truly reflects the realities of spatial challenges in the European continent. Paradoxically, despite the marginal role of CEE experts in the ESDP process (cf. Finka Chapter 5 and Pallagst Chapter 6), it has had a pivotal influence in some knowledge arenas in CEE. Kule *et al.* (Chapter 12) discuss the extent to which the ESDP has helped to persuasively advance arguments for new policy images, and to redirect approaches to territorial development and the addition of new dimensions to spatial policy in Latvia. This also seems to suggest, the importance of power dynamics notwithstanding, how knowledge resources, such as the ESDP, the EU Strategy for the Baltic Sea Region (CEC 2009b) and the Vision and Strategies Around the Baltic Sea 2010 (VASAB), have all had varied impacts as a result of the extent to which these strategic visions have been successfully argued, or the extent to which their interpretations have been persuasive. Maier (Chapter 11) likens this 'context sensitivity' to 'political setting' as well as 'epistemology', suggesting that there is a politicized setting for the knowledge base of causal beliefs (epistemic communities) as well as the value base of political choices (advocacy coalitions) bearing down on communities of practice in the form of policy images that constitute varied and sometimes contradictory spatial policy ideas and planning approaches, or the transfer of 'best and good practices' (Stead and Nadin Chapter 7).

As already stressed elsewhere in this book (Chapters 1 and 2), this context sensitivity merits an attention to the dynamic links between metagovenance systems, and 'soft' (informal) and 'hard regulatory' (formal) spaces; that is, the complex interplay of the knowledge resources embodied in 'social learning treaties' (Haas 2004) such as the ESDP, the European Territorial Agenda, the VASAB and the EU Strategy for the Baltic Sea Region, and their interpretation and subsequent application to and influence on policy. Additionally, the consideration of 'multiple streams', as an underpinning notion of the knowledge perspective adopted in this book (cf. Chapter 2), can offer useful insights into this interplay by singling out the value base of forces that can influence how problems are recognized and framed (politics stream), the causal beliefs underpinning varied and contradicting ideas and planning approaches with regard to those problems (policy stream), and the pragmatic albeit contested application of this knowledge and its inherent value judgments and causal beliefs (problems stream) (Kingdon 1995; Zahariadis 1999). Thus there is a need to recognize the cognitive boundaries and political parameters of policy learning (Dąbrowski Chapter 9), re-learning (Razumeyko Chapter 16), transfer (Stead and Nadin Chapter 7) and cooperation (Haselsberger and Benneworth Chapter 10) through the generation and mobilization of knowledge resources. So, for example, while the VASAB community has evolved over time and possesses some characteristics of an epistemic community, the extent to which this expert group will be able to continue to influence future policy in light of the recent and currently much more 'powerful' EU strategy for the BSR remains to be seen. Another area of ambiguity relates to the impact that the prominence of the new Strategy has on relations and interactions between territorial knowledge communities on either side of the EU external border with the Russian Federation (cf. Fritsch Chapter 15).

A storyline for CEE?

An understanding of knowledge as solely data (evidence or 'usable knowledge') and ideas therefore, does not begin to address some of the complexity implicit in the adopted understanding of knowledge resources particularly due to the above-mentioned context sensitivity of the dynamic, complex and politicized interplay of knowledge and policy development. Nevertheless, the influential role of storylines promoted by spatial concepts and metaphors in the policy development process is indisputable (see for example Dühr 2007). The CEE spatial metaphor of the 'Boomerang' (Gorzelak 1996, Pallagst 2006) is an example offering a unique conceptualization of CEE space, although it never achieved significant influence by being incorporated into important spatial visions such as the ESDP. The question of why other spatial metaphors such as the 'Blue Banana' (Brunet 1989), the 'Bunch of Grapes' (Kunzman and Wegener 1991) and the 'Pentagon' (Schon 2000) all had more of an impact on the European spatial planning discourse could be answered by the fact that, at the time of its publication, the 'Boomerang' space was not part of the EU. Although its underlying considerations were potentially relevant for the EU space, the fact that it was produced 'outside Europe' did not situate it within relevant knowledge arenas where similar metaphors and conceptualizations were discussed. Currently, both the 'New Banana' (SIC! 2006), which lies parallel to the 'Blue Banana', and the 'Europe of Olympic Circles' (Moisio 2003) offer new metaphorical spatial insights and conceptualizations of European space with special regard for the economic and conceptual catch up of CEE. Though in the absence of the relatively less influential 'Boomerang', the influence of ideas or storylines related to current 'generative metaphors' (Schön 1978) such as the 'New Banana' or the suggested scenarios of 'retention' and 'merger' (Pallagst 2006, Chapter 6) remain uncertain (see Finka Chapter 5; Maier Chapter 11 for sympathetic critiques).

So why has an influential storyline for CEE not emerged? As mentioned above, Pallagst (2006, Chapter 6) and more recently Tunka (2009) begin to address this question. The ESPON programme certainly has a role to play in this process and new representations of the enlarged EU space not only in terms of representation of current trends but also in relation to future development scenarios have already been produced (cf. the ESPON project 3.2, ESPON 2007). Still, as suggested elsewhere in this book, future research on the suggested scenarios of 'retention' and 'merger' – or alternatively a mixed scenario – will have to embrace what seemingly constitutes *many* storylines (cf. Sandercock 1998, 2003). In addition, these scenarios could potentially manifest differently and simultaneously across diverse policy areas and issues or policy development processes in CEE as a result of its context sensitive interface with knowledge resources and arenas. This re-emphasizes the need for European spatial planning to engage a wider group of stakeholders and non-experts despite the apprehension and confusion that precepts such as territorial cohesion can evoke. ESPON, as well as other knowledge arenas, will potentially play a crucial role in this process, which will be necessary if spatial conceptualizations and 'images' are to become more influential as a rationale for policy development and funding.

The contributions to this book illustrate how the generation of knowledge resources and spatial metaphors and conceptualizations, and their subsequent mobilization into influential visions on a European level can be traced to an entirely different context. On a regional level, Capik (Chapter 13) points to the focus on 'promotion campaigns' for the creation of images and the use of narratives and metaphors, which have been purposely generated by 'promotion communities' to overcome negative images of the past. Capik notes that there are few innovative context sensitive approaches to the attraction of FDI in CEE; that is, according to the author, regional authorities take limited consideration of their own 'territorial capital' or the 'endogenous potential of their territories' when mirroring successful western practices. The result is often a 'one-size fits all' approach, which is not consistent with a move toward evidence-based planning or 'evidence-informed' (Davoudi 2006) spatial policy development. Rather the knowledge resources component is found among the transfer of 'best and good practices' (Stead and Nadin Chapter 7), and the 'wooing process' of economic agents. As highlighted by Tewdwr-Jones, 'wooing major multinational companies, identifying land, the availability of cheap labour, the offer of incentives, and the hard sell between particular companies and individual city-regions are the factors that carve out customized spaces for businesses' (Chapter 3). In this concern, it appears that the use of mega projects or flagship projects in CEE countries are much more popular with politicians compared to small-scale tailor made projects for specific regions, mirroring a trend that has been affecting western Europe in recent decades (cf. Maier Chapter 11; Capik Chapter 13) and, as Tewdwr-Jones points out, planning systems are often by-passed by this process. Tewdwr-Jones argues therefore, that if spatial planning is to provide 'spatial certainty' and cohesion across and between territories, then spatial planning policy and financial incentives must be aligned more effectively in the future. Reforms and initiatives presented by Marot (Chapter 8) and Dąbrowski (Chapter 9) are good examples in this context, pointing out how much still remains to be done in CEE countries.

Knowledge resources and the power to shape spatial policy development

The potential range of multi-level institutional arrangements of territorial governance discussed above can present a planning system as a knowledge arena in addition to the many overlapping and conflicting arenas within a multi-jurisdictional policy environment. That is, the dynamic links between the metagovenance systems of EU funding and inward investment, and the 'soft' (informal) and 'hard regulatory' (formal) spaces of 'spatial governance arrangements' of planning systems and the overlapping/conflicting arenas with which they interact (cf. Haughton *et al.* 2010). Thus, the above-mentioned considerations of context sensitivity at EU, national and sub-national level suggest a complex, dynamic and politicized interplay of knowledge and policy development at the intersection of knowledge resources and knowledge arenas. On an EU level, the forces potentially pushing towards 'retention' and 'merger' – or a third differentiated scenario – remain unclear, not to mention the implications of one of these scenarios becoming dominant for different arenas of multi-scalar institutional arrangements of spatial governance in Europe (e.g. ESPON, planning systems and policy monitoring research or advisory organizations, cross-border institutions). Several issues emerge in relation to the transition of knowledge resources into the powers that shape or frame the course of spatial policy development, including the 'scant resources' found in professional skills and more broadly in organizational capacity as a consequence of the redesign and introduction of new planning jurisdictions (Marot Chapter 8), a poor or unestablished professional identity that lends itself to 'weak and fragmented communities of practice' (Maier Chapter 11), and a lack of cross-border cohesion or 'proximity' that prevents effective cross-border representation of issues (Hasselsberger and Benneworth Chapter 10). Moreover, these issues serve to re-emphasize the context sensitivity of a knowledge resources interface with policy development in light of the turning points of EU enlargement for both the contexts of diverse spatial planning approaches in Europe and the evolving context of European spatial planning. Finally they further contribute to the mounting academic research debate on the Europeanization of spatial planning approaches (cf. Stead and Nadin Chapter 7; Kule *et al.* Chapter 12) and convergence in the EU (cf. Stead and Nadin Chapter 7; Adams 2008; Healey and Williams 1993). The question therefore arises as to how territorial knowledge communities contribute to the transformation of institutional geographies of agent interaction as both institutionally enabling and constraining factors on policy development (cf. Dąbrowski Chapter 9, Marot Chapter 8 on state centralization in the face of regional decentralization). Bearing this question in mind, it is the symbiotic relationship between knowledge and interests evident in the complex set of power relations and struggles, and the uncertainty that dominates knowledge arenas within the cross-scalar multi-jurisdictional policy environment of the EU, which the next section will reflect upon.

Knowledge arenas: institutionalization, path-dependency and uncertainty

The final strand of the knowledge perspective proposed in this book relates to knowledge arenas. As identified earlier in the book, knowledge arenas are the environments where knowledge is contested, verified, validated or marginalized and where the rules for policy evaluation are established. First in relation to this strand the relationship between Europeanization, institutionalization and knowledge arenas will be explored before the challenges of engaging territorial knowledge communities are examined. Finally the extent to which territorial knowledge communities and some of the knowledge arenas relevant for spatial planning in Europe are becoming consolidated will be discussed.

Europeanization and institutionalization

Knowledge arenas operate at a variety of levels and in a variety of forms, and are the products of agent interactivity. In other words, they are the products of coordinated interaction in the form of networks, conferences and meetings, which can help to institutionalize activities through the establishment of new routines as well laying new foundations for questioning established beliefs or values. The extent to which such knowledge arenas are influential depends on a variety of factors including the ability 'to gain societal recognition, trust and legitimacy' (Buitelaar *et al.* 2007: 895) among a broad and often skeptical group of actors, and the ability to take advantage of the opportunities presented by relevant policy windows.

There are clear parallels between a conceptualization of knowledge arenas and the 'pillars' of European spatial planning discussed by Waterhout (Chapter 4). These pillars (the ESPON programme, the European Territorial Cooperation objective, the Territorial Agenda and the virtual arena manifest in the online consultation on the *Green Paper on Territorial Cohesion*), representing the programmes and initiatives around which European spatial planning is currently organized, all provide contexts within which knowledge relating to both European spatial planning and spatial planning in Europe is generated, contested, verified, validated or marginalized. In addition, all of these contexts generate the complex social structures (Lopez and Scott, 2000) – 'institutional' (rules, norms and routines), 'relational' (networks, conferences, meetings) and 'embodied' (value/belief systems) – through which interaction and negotiation takes place. The relevant interactions are characterized by the vertical, horizontal and circular reciprocation already introduced in relation to Europeanization processes (Adams *et al.* Chapter 2; Stead and Nadin Chapter 7).

These vertical, horizontal and circular interactions imply that there are a considerable number of other knowledge arenas at both the transnational level and within domestic contexts that are relevant to the field of spatial planning in Europe and that these arenas display a considerable degree of diversity in terms of characteristics, influence and degree of institutionalization. Those already mentioned in this section, relating to ESPON, European territorial cooperation, the Territorial Agenda and the on-going debate on territorial cohesion also display diverse degrees of institutionalization. INTERREG and ESPON are clearly institutionalized in the sense that they have formal organizational structures with norms, routines and values, promoting conditionality through the setting of rules and regulations that determine funding eligibility. It can be argued that the European Commission have used these initiatives creatively to gain influence over the policy field of spatial planning where they have no direct competence by linking them to its regulatory frameworks and funding streams. Despite having become part of an established policy landscape, however, these arenas are continually evolving and therefore characterized by degrees of dynamism rather than states of static equilibrium (cf. Baumgartner and Jones 1993, 2002 on 'punctuated equilibrium'; Adams *et al.* Chapter 2). The dynamics of such knowledge arenas can be illustrated by the evolution and change in emphasis in terms of priorities that both INTERREG and ESPON have displayed over time. In this context, these EU level arenas react, albeit often slowly, to the emergence of new debates and ideas. Other less institutionalized knowledge arenas, however, can display a higher degree of dynamism and can emerge, evolve and disappear in response to the emergence of these new debates and ideas. These types of arenas most frequently emerge in the more 'ad hoc' and 'soft' spaces of territorial governance or in response to the funding possibilities presented by more formal institutional arenas.

The degree of institutionalization does not necessarily determine the extent of the influence or the success of a particular knowledge arena in generating and mobilizing the knowledge resources discussed in the previous section. For instance INTERREG secretariats, despite displaying the characteristics of a high degree of institutionalization, do not have the capacity or indeed the remit to necessarily mobilize the vast expanse of diverse knowledge resources they posses and therefore to stimulate their operationalization. The more institution-alized knowledge arenas however, do have an important role in establishing common ground, guiding principles and a common terminology, which Pallagst (Chapter 6) refers to as a 'joint spatial planning language'. The inherent stability of much public policy and many policy images results in the above-mentioned policy equilibrium that will only be 'punctuated' under certain con-ditions. The extent of the influence of a particular arena depends on a variety of factors including the level and type of actors involved, institutional arrange-ments and their proximity to influential agents as well as the attractiveness of the knowledge resources that are generated under particular political agendas. The nature or quality of the knowledge resources that have been generated are, somewhat worryingly, not necessarily a key factor in determining this degree of influence. The widespread adoption of place promotion and flagship projects despite the lack of a robust empirical or knowledge base illustrates this concern (cf. Capik Chapter 13; Maier Chapter 11). In the context of the external dimen-sion of EU territorial governance the situation once again is even more complex. The participation of actors from the Federal level of the Russian Fed-eration in CEMAT compared to the participation of local and regional actors in the VASAB initiative implies differing levels of commitment to, and influence of these initiatives in the Russian context. The contribution by Fritsch (Chapter 15) also raises questions relating to the varying degrees of influence enjoyed by VASAB and the EU Strategy for the Baltic Sea Region, whereby VASAB cur-rently appears to be 'out of fashion' and taking a secondary role compared to the politically popular and more action-oriented EU strategy. The robustness and quality of the knowledge resources generated is often highly contested in a cross-scalar and multi-jurisdictional policy environment where actors, including central Government actors, often search for knowledge resources and influential contacts among different arenas, which can be used to support, advance or promote new policy aims or policy images. As Dühr *et al.* (2010) point out in relation to the various conceptualizations of European space, the generation of such knowledge resources is ultimately political in the sense that they will favour certain interests and be promoted by them. The new Polish National Spatial Management Concept (NSMC 2008) and the criticism matured among peripheral Voivodships around its vision are a clear example of such concerns (Czapiewski and Janc Chapter 14). The internal coherence between the context, goals and priorities of various actors and territorial knowledge communities can determine the nature of the interactions and to a large degree the usability (Haas 2004) and accessibility of the knowledge resources generated. The lack of robust cross-border institutions and networks highlighted by Haselsberger and Benneworth (Chapter 10) illustrates this as the actors within the Slovakian-Austrian border region pursued their own locally determined aims and priorities and this has significant implications and presents significant challenges for the future of 'soft' planning generally and particularly in the context of interactions between the EU and the Russian Federation and by definition also for other external EU borders.

Engaging territorial knowledge communities

An additional element of the diversity of knowledge arenas relates to the hetero-geneity in the type of actors and networks that operate within them and this has been taken to a new level with the emergence of the East-West dimension since enlargement. The theoretical basis of the conceptual framework presented in Chapter 2 draws on a number of relevant and complementary concepts, includ-ing epistemic communities, advocacy coalitions and communities of practice. Several contributions to this book have explored the extent to which different types of territorial knowledge communities have emerged within various domestic and cross-border contexts. The evidence that has been presented in the various contributions is inconclusive in relation to the emergence of epistemic communities despite the prevailing conditions in the EU generally and CEE countries in particular, appearing to favour the emergence of such groups. Zito (2001a) has claimed that epistemic communities tend to be more successful in influencing decision-makers in the case of policy uncertainties or potentially controversial policy actions. However, despite the prevailing uncertainty that has characterized the EU and particularly CEE in the post-enlargement period, there is little evidence in the case studies from the various contributors of epistemic communities emerging or having an influential effect on policy environments and processes. Many of the contributions in this volume discuss the uncertainties emerging in light of new post enlargement realities for 'environmental uncer-tainty' or 'process uncertainty' (Abbot 2005). With particular regard to the dis-cussion of the interplay of knowledge and policy development, both categories of uncertainty are closely linked. However, process uncertainty is the more closely associated with the role of knowledge in spatial policy development. This consists of uncertainties in knowledge of the external environment with demands for more research (e.g. epistemic argument/persuasion and evidence-based policy; Clarence 2002), uncertainties about appropriate value judgments with calls for more policy guidance from politicians, and uncertainties about future intentions of people and organizations in related fields of choice with requirements for more coordination with a broader spectrum of policy fields.

Tewdwr-Jones (Chapter 3) implicitly offers a complex politically sensitive setting for the link between these two categories of uncertainty in planning when he suggests the need to link the 'wooing process' of FDI to spatial policy and plan-ning. Waterhout (Chapter 4) offers a similarly relevant setting at the EU level in his assertion that the increased heterogeneity and the dramatic increase in the size of the 'European planning community' as a consequence of enlargement make it more difficult to identify epistemic communities in the sense that the Committee for Spatial Development constituted one in the context of the ESDP. This argument implies that, if an epistemic community in relation to European spatial planning does exist, then it is not contained within a specific knowledge arena. Rather the actors are active in various arenas, making them difficult to identify as an epistemic community. The contributions by Maier, Haslesberger and Benneworth, Dąbrowski and Capik all imply a degree of skepticism about the existence of identifiable epistemic communities in the contexts they explored. This unlikely existence can be attributed to different reasons, ranging from scarce cohesiveness and fragmentation among communities of practice (Maier Chapter 11), to differences in aims and goals (Haselsberger and Benneworth Chapter 10), to excessive economic sub-ordination of FDI or EU funding programmes (respectively Dąbrowski Chapter 9; Capik Chapter 13) to the realities of 'hard' external EU borders (Fritsch Chapter 15) and to uncertainty about organizational realities (Razumeyko Chapter 16). Nevertheless, many of the contributions argue that communities of practice are present and that members of these communities may have the potential to evolve into epistemic communities on condition that suitable arenas exist and that these community members can consolidate and access these arenas to support this process. Moreover, in addition to the issues raised above, it is important to highlight how the promoters of policy change must be able to seek out the most appropriate arenas in order to achieve their aims. Both Fritsch (Chapter 15) and Kule *et al.* (Chapter 12), for example, argue that a network with many of the characteristics of an epistemic community has evolved within the context of VASAB, but the emergence of the EU Strategy for the Baltic Sea Region provides a clear challenge to the influence of VASAB in the policy development arenas of the participating counties.

The 'merger' and 'retention' scenarios identified by Pallagst (Chapter 6) conceptualize the evolution of epistemic communities of 'old' and 'new' Member States. However, Finka (Chapter 5) questions the value of this approach, acknowledging that CEE networks and communities do not appear to be engaging fully with knowledge arenas that focus on European spatial planning (cf. Maier Chapter 11; Marot Chapter 8; Dąbrowski Chapter 9 for similar viewpoints). There is seemingly no real consensus about the reasons for this lack of engagement as a variety of possibilities are put forward. Maier (Chapter 10) argues that one of these possibilities can be linked to the 'weak and fragmented' nature of the planning community in many CEE countries, claiming that academics in the 'new' Member States have more pressing priorities than engagement within European spatial planning, preferring to focus on goals identified by policy-makers relating to economic development and convergence with average EU prosperity levels (cf. Davoudi 2006 on the extent to which policy drives research or vice versa). Kule *et al.* (Chapter 12) argue that the lack of formal engagement in Latvia is primarily due to a lack of central government commitment and financial constraints and this argument seems to be supported by the recent dramatic cuts in research and higher education budgets in Latvia and the fact that Latvia is the only EU Member State that is not a member of the European Science Foundation. There is evidence to suggest, however, that whereas it is currently more difficult for Latvian actors to become involved in the more formal knowledge arenas such as ESPON, they appear to be engaging more fully in the informal arenas as demonstrated by the number of Latvian respondents to the *Green Paper on Territorial Cohesion*. Furthermore, the 'weak and fragmented' nature of the planning communities of many CEE countries identified by Maier (Chapter 11) potentially limits the extent to which they are able to engage and/or influence the knowledge arenas of European spatial planning.

Consolidation or uncertainty?

The observations in this section suggest a challenging context for the future evo-lution of effective domestic arenas, which in turn makes it more difficult for these territorial knowledge communities to acquire the knowledge resource powers to shape or 'frame' policy development. Without these arenas it is diffi-cult for these communities to emerge and evolve, notwithstanding the co-presence of different communities in any given arena vying for political influence and in turn mutually reinforcing joint or opposing agendas (cf. Conzel-mann 1998 on knowledge and conflict models; Dabinett and Richardson 2005 on knowledge/ideas – power/legitimacy). As a result, there is a danger that the debate regarding European spatial planning will remain limited and marginal and that the associated communities will not evolve beyond project and issue related communities of practice and advocacy coalitions, which has clear consequences for the 'retention' an 'merger' scenarios proposed by Pallagst.

The consolidation of territorial knowledge communities in CEE would increase debate in relation to the 'pillars' of European spatial planning as a result of the engagement of a wider body of stakeholders. This could lead to the gener-ation and rethinking of knowledge resources, which would enrich the European spatial planning discourse and could potentially result in 'merger' scenarios over particular policy areas or issues. On the other hand, such attempts at the consoli-dation of territorial knowledge communities in CEE may result in 'retention' becoming the dominant scenario. The 'merger' scenario may have been attrac-tive to CEE countries during the pre-accession phase, as identified by Finka (Chapter 5), but the fragmented nature of the European planning community and the lack of suitable arenas may imply that 'retention' is the more likely scenario within specific policy areas, or over particular policy issues although 'retention', 'merger' and a combination of the two scenarios could emerge simultaneously. Clearly, diverse territorial knowledge communities and knowledge arenas are emerging, but their scope and effectiveness is often limited and uncertain. One of the key challenges for these communities will be to identify, create or become engaged with appropriate arenas within which they can have a more enduring influence on policy development.

Conclusions: territorial knowledge channels as contexts for situated learning

The knowledge perspective on stability and change in spatial planning policy development in Europe presented above has provided an interesting entry point to explore the nature and extent to which members of territorial knowledge com-munities engage and influence knowledge arenas. In turn, this consideration may be used to shed some light on the future of spatial planning in an enlarged EU. Faludi (2010) claims that European spatial planning has reached a turning point. On the one hand, the ratification of the Lisbon Treaty, and the consequent confir-mation of territorial cohesion as a shared competence between the EU and the

Member States has provided the European Commission with the possibility to make legislative proposals on territorial matters. Waterhout (2008 and Chapter 4) also points out that the territorial cohesion discourse offers new opportunities for spatial planning to engage with what he refers to as the 'territory matters coalition'. At the same time however, and the positive reactions to the consultation on the *Green Paper on Territorial Cohesion* notwithstanding, the debate about the future of cohesion policy is ongoing with many net contributors favouring the redirection of these funds from the Commission to national administrations. To all intents and purposes this would involve a renationalization of regional policy and by implication therefore, the removal of the need for European spatial planning as a means of programming in the pursuit of Community goals. Nevertheless, other indications suggest that the future of European spatial planning may be somewhat brighter. Net recipients of cohesion policy, including numerous CEE countries, seem unlikely to withdraw their support for its continuation and there appears to be a general consensus in favour of the European Territorial Cooperation objective which potentially suggests an increased budget in the future.

Although European spatial planning will continue to evolve, the shape and direction of this evolution is far from clear and the same can be said for the implications of this for the wider context of spatial planning in Europe. The difference between 'hard' and 'soft' spaces and 'hard' (regulatory) and 'soft' (strategic, informal and ad hoc) planning has been already discussed extensively in Chapter 1 and 2. Faludi (2010) argues that a shift towards 'soft' spatial planning is required in Europe and, in turn, a shift in the perceptions and understandings of planners towards a 'softer' understanding of space and planning. This could involve a proliferation of strategic and 'visioning' activities or of more pragmatic and action oriented initiatives; either would involve variable dynamic spaces not delimited by rigid administrative borders and may imply the need for a number of 'spatial plannings' (Haughton *et al.* 2010). Within this scenario, planners will need to learn how 'to package funds, spatial concepts and images, trusts and so forth' (Faludi 2010).

In this context, the process of production, consolidation and validation of knowledge resources and their interface with the process of policy development within relevant knowledge arenas has remained at the heart of the rationale for this book. Knowledge resources have to make their way through a sea of power logics in order to influence policy-making. This requires more than the production and analysis of evidence and, in the absence of a 'champion' with sufficient power and influence, needs to be supported by the creation of storylines or policy images and by their promotion within different knowledge arenas. Here a crucial role is played by territorial knowledge communities, supporting different and often conflicting spatial storylines underpinned by different evidence and logics. It is the interactions between such storylines and visions with these communities that eventually create revised knowledge resources that have the potential to influence policy development.

These considerations help us to further interpret the diverse evidence in relation to the spatio-temporal focus of this book, that is the impact of the eastwards enlargement of the EU on the complex environment of spatial planning in Europe. The presented scenario suggests that the influence of actors on spatial policy development seems to be connected with their participation in territorial knowledge communities and the territorial knowledge channels that are located at the interface of knowledge resources and arenas. The role that CEE experts will play in the process is uncertain. In the future, CEE planning agendas at the different domestic levels are likely to continue to be influenced by elements matured within the different knowledge arenas that constitute European spatial planning. At the same time networks of CEE experts do not currently appear to be consolidated enough to influence the validation of knowledge resources produced at the supranational level, due to their 'weak and fragmented' nature (Maier Chapter 11). Their fragmented nature in many CEE countries can potentially pose limits on the extent to which community members are able to engage and influence knowledge arenas. However, the increasing integration of CEE actors within ESPON and European Territorial Cooperation initiatives, as well as their contribution to the further definition of the operational detail of post 2013 cohesion policy may lead to a growing influence of CEE experts on policy development and the enrichment of the European spatial planning discourse more generally.

In this concern, territorial knowledge channels may be understood as 'contexts for situated learning', or in other words places where learning occurs due to the social interaction that takes place among the members of the context itself. In their role as relative newcomers and in view of their overriding focus on other priorities such as economic development, until now CEE actors have tended to operate at the margins of territorial knowledge communities. According to the rationale of Lave and Wenger (1991), this situation is likely to change and they are likely to exert an increasing influence within such communities as they move from the periphery to the centre over time. This overall understanding builds on the methodological insights into 'analyzing the governance of European space' (Böhme *et al.* 2004), which follows Majone (1989), who claimed that policy alternatives are based on value judgments that are argued in the course of public debate. The indeterminate variability of the situated learning dynamics through territorial knowledge channels within and between metagovernance systems, and the 'soft' (informal) and 'hard regulatory' (formal) spaces of the institutional arrangements of territorial governance can reflect power struggles, conflict and fragmentation inherent to territorial development and spatial planning as well as 'episodes' of integration, consolidation and convergence in Europe.

More generally, the theoretical framework for this book emphasizes the complexity of the policy development process within European territorial governance. We have, with the help of contributors, brought the subject matter closer to the spatial planning research arena as well as situating the subject in a particular spatial-temporal context. It remains to be seen whether the existing tensions between the pursuit of competitiveness and the desire for integration and cohesion will ever be reconciled in the increasingly challenging economic scenario for the EU. With the negotiations on the future of regional policy post 2013, the future of European integration seems to have reached another turning point that potentially endangers the future of any territorial dimension of community policy. Planners, as Faludi puts it (2010) 'can do little' about it, as the future of cohesion policy seems less subject to their will and more dependent on political judgment and the power dynamics in place among the Member States. The same can be said for both the internal and the external dimensions of EU territorial governance and the communities that operate within these dimensions. The valorization of the diversity of the EU is identified as a key aim in the most recent EU territorial reference documents where territorial diversity is referred to as a strength and a potential (DE Presidency 2007a, 2007b; CEC 2008). We would echo the views of Finka that a similar challenge exists for the territorial knowledge communities in Europe. The optimization of the respective strengths and potentials of these diverse communities and knowledge arenas throughout the EU will enable spatial planning in Europe to promote creative and innovative approaches to the challenges of territorial development and cohesion in an enlarged EU. The challenge will be for the territorial knowledge communities to generate relevant knowledge resources and to effectively bring about the appropriate territorial knowledge channels or governance arrangements as a means of adding value to wider discourses, influencing policy development and ultimately achieving more sustainable patterns of territorial development and cohesion. Nevertheless, it is our firm belief that the further exploration of the interactions between the different actors and communities involved in both the internal and external dimensions of EU territorial governance would appear to offer a way forward if the further consolidation of the European project is to be achieved.

Note

1 Cf. Hillier (2008) and Nilsson (2007) for retaining strategic visioning alongside evidence-based monitoring of planned futures and managing complex spatial planning processes respectively.

References

Abbott, J. (2005) 'Understanding and managing the unknown. The nature of uncertainty in planning', *Journal of Planning Education and Research*, 24: 237–251.

Adams, N. (2008) 'Convergence and policy transfer: an examination of the extent to which approaches to spatial planning have converged within the context of an enlarged EU', *International Planning Studies* 13(1): 31–50.

Barca, F. (2009) *An Agenda for a Reformed Cohesion Policy. A place-based approach to meeting European Union challenges and expectations*. Independent Report prepared at the request of Danuta Hübner, Commissioner for Regional Policy.

Baumgartner, F. R. and Jones, B. D. (1993) *Agendas and Instability in American Politics*, Chicago: University of Chicago Press.

—— (eds) (2002) *Policy Dynamics*, Chicago: University of Chicago Press.

Böhme, K. and Waterhout, B. (2008) 'The Europeanization of spatial planning', in A. Faludi (ed.) *European Spatial Research and Planning*, Cambridge (MA): Lincoln Institute of Land Policy: 225–248.

Böhme, K. Richardson, Dabinett, G. and Jensen, O. B. (2004) 'Values in vacuum? Towards an integrated multi-level analysis of the governance of European space', *European Planning Studies* 12(8): 1175–1188.

Brunet, R. (1989) *Les Villes 'Européennes'. Rapport pour la DATAR*, Paris: La Documentation Française (RECLUS/DATAR).

Buitelaar, E. A., Lagendijk, A. and Jacobs, W. (2007) 'A theory of institutional change: illustrated by Dutch city – provinces and Dutch land policy', *Environment and Planning A*, 39: 891–908.

CEC – Commission of the European Communities (1999) *European Spatial Development Perspective: Towards balanced and sustainable development of the territory of the EU*, Luxembourg: Office of the Official Publications of the European Communities.

—— (2008) *Green Paper on Territorial Cohesion – Turning territorial diversity into strength*, Luxembourg: Office for Official Publications of the European Communities.

—— (2009a) *Green Paper on Territorial Cohesion – Turning territorial diversity into strength*. Contributions to the Consultation. Online. Available HTTP: http://ec.europa.eu/regional_policy/consultation/terco/contrib_en.htm (accessed March 2010).

—— (2009b) Communication from the Commission to the European Parliament, the Council, the European Economic and Social Committee and the Committee of the Regions concerning the European Union Strategy for the Baltic Sea Region. Online. Available HTTP: http://ec.europa.eu/regional_policy/sources/docoffic/official/communic/baltic/com_baltic_en.pdf (accessed March 2010).

CEMAT – European Conference of Ministers Responsible for Regional Planning (2000) *Guiding Principles for Sustainable Spatial Development of the European Continent*. Online. Available HTTP: www.coe.int/t/dg4/cultureheritage/heritage/cemat/Version-Principes/rec-2002–1_en.pdf (accessed March 2010).

Clarence, E. (2002) 'Technocracy reinvented: the new evidence based policy movement', *Public Policy and Administration*, 17(1): 1–11.

Conzelmann, T. (1998) 'Europeanization of regional development policies? Linking multi-level governance approach with theories of policy learning and policy change', *European Integration Online Papers* (EIoP), 2(4), http://eiop.or.at/eiop/texte/1998–004a.htm.

Cotella, G. (2007) '(R)Evolution of Central and Eastern European spatial planning systems: trends towards divergence or uniformity?', in R. Nunes, E. Cidre and G. Cotella (eds) *Central and Eastern European Engagement: planning, development and sustainability. ALFA SPECTRA, Central European Journal of Architecture and Planning*, special issue, 11(2): 11–19.

—— (2009a) *Governance territoriale comunitaria e sistemi di pianificazione: Riflessioni sull'allargamento ad est dell'Unione europea*, Ph.D. tesi in Spatial Planning and Local Development, Discussed in May 2009 at Politecnico di Torino.

—— (2009b) 'Exploring the territorial cohesion/economic growth multidimensional field: evidences from Poland', in T. Markowsi, M. Kozak and M. Turala (eds) *Innovations and Space – an European and national approach*, Warsaw: Polish Academy of Science: 71–95.

Dabinett, G. and Richardson, T. (2005) 'The Europeanization of spatial strategy: Shaping regions and spatial justice through governmental ideas', *International Planning Studies*, 10(3): 201–218.

Davoudi, S. (2006) 'Evidence-based planning: rhetoric and reality', *disP*, 165(2): 14–24.

DE Presidency (2007a) *The Territorial State and Perspectives of the European Union: Towards a stronger European territorial cohesion in the light of the Lisbon and*

Gothenburg ambitions – A background document to the territorial agenda of the European Union. Online. Available online HTTP: www.bmvbs.de/Anlage/original_1005296/The-Territorial-State-and-Perspectives-of-the-European-Union.pdf (accessed March 2010).

——— (2007b) *Territorial Agenda of the European Union: Towards a more competitive and sustainable Europe of diverse regions – Agreed at the occasion of the informal ministerial meeting on urban development and territorial cohesion on 24/25 May* 2007. Online. Available HTTP: www.bmvbs.de/Anlage/original_1005295/Territorial-Agenda-of-the-European-Union-Agreed-on-25-May-2007-accessible.pdf (accessed March 2010).

Dühr, S. (2007) *The Visual Language of Spatial Planning: exploring cartographic representations for spatial planning in Europe*, London: Routledge.

Dühr, S., Colomb, C. and Nadin, V. (2010) *European Spatial Planning and Territorial Co-operation*, London: Routledge.

EC – European Council (2005) *Financial Perspectives 2007–2013*.

ESPON (2007) ESPON project 3.2 *Spatial Scenarios in Relation to the ESDP and EU Cohesion Policy* – Final Report, Luxembourg: ESPON.

Evers, D., Tennekes, J., Borsboom, J., Heiligenberg, H. van den and Thissen, M. (2009) *A Territorial Impact Assessment of Territorial Cohesion for the Netherlands*, Netherlands Environmental Assessment Agency (PBL). Online. Available HTTP: www.eukn. org/binaries/eukn/netherlands/research/2009/07/tia_tc_webversie.pdf (accessed March 2010).

Faludi, A. (2006) 'From European spatial development to territorial cohesion policy', *Regional Studies*, 40(6): 667–678, August 2006.

——— (2010 forthcoming) *Cohesion, Coherence, Cooperation: European spatial planning coming of age?*, London: Routledge.

Fischer, E. and Forester, J. (eds) (1993) *The Argumentative Turn in Policy Analysis and Planning*, Durham, NC: Duke University Press.

Gorzelak, G. (1996) *The Regional Dimension of Transformation in Central Europe*, London: Jessica Kingsley.

Haas, E. B. (1990) *When Knowledge is Power*, Berkley: University of California Press.

Haas, P. (1992) 'Introduction: Epistemic Communities and International Policy Coordination', *International Organization*, 46(1): 1–35.

——— (2004) 'When does power listen to truth? A constructivist approach to the policy process', *Journal of European Public Policy*, 11(4), August 2004: 569–592.

Hajer, M. and Wagenaar, H. (eds) (2003) *Deliberative Policy Analysis*, Cambridge: Cambridge University Press.

Hall, P. and Taylor, R. (1996) 'Political science and the three new institutionalisms', *Political Studies*, 44: 936–957.

Handley, K., Sturdy, A., Fincham, R. and Clark, T. (2006) 'Within and beyond communities of practice: making sense of learning through participation, identity and practice', *Journal of Management Studies*, 43(3): 641–653.

Haughton, G., Allmendinger, P., Counsell, D. and Vigar, G. (2010) *The New Spatial Planning: territorial management with soft spaces and fuzzy boundaries*, London: Routledge.

Healey, P. (2006) 'Relational complexity and the imaginative power of strategic spatial planning', *European Planning Studies*, 14(4): 525–546, May.

Healey, P. and Williams, R. (1993) 'European urban planning systems: diversity and convergence', *Urban Studies*, 30: 701–720.

Hillier, J. (2008) 'Plan(e) Speaking: a multiplanar theory of spatial planning', *Planning Theory*, 7(1): 24–50.

Janin Rivolin, U. and Faludi, A. (2005) 'The Hidden Face of European Spatial Planning: innovations in governance', *European Planning Studies*, 13(2).

Kingdon, J. W. (1995) *Agendas, Alternatives and Public Policies*, 2nd edition, New York: Harper Collins.

Kunzmann, K. and Wegener, M. (1991) *The Pattern of Urbanisation in Western Europe 1960–1990*. Report for the Directorate General XVI of the Commission of the European Communities as Part of the Study 'Urbanisation and the Function of Cities in the European Community'. Dortmund: IRPUD.

Lave, J. and Wenger, E. (1991) *Situated Learning: legitimate peripheral participation*, Cambridge: Cambridge University Press.

Lopez, J. and Scott, J. (2000) *Social Structure*, Buckingham: Open University Press.

Lowndes, V. (1996) 'Varieties of new institutionalism: a critical appraisal' *Public Administration*, 74(2): 181–197.

Majone, G. (1989) *Evidence, Argument, and Persuasion in the Policy Process*, Yale University Press.

Meijerink, S. (2005) 'Understanding policy stability and change. The interplay of advocacy coalitions and epistemic communities, windows of opportunity, and Dutch coastal flooding policy 1945–2003', *Journal of European Public Policy* 12(6) December 2005: 1060–1077.

Moisio, S. (2003) 'Back to Baltoscandia? European Union and geo-conceptual remaking of the European North', *Geopolitics*, 8(1): 72–100.

Nilsson, K. L. (2007) 'Managing complex spatial planning processes', *Planning Theory and Practice*, 8(4): 431–447.

NSMC – National Spatial Management Concept (2008) *Koncepcja przestrzennego zagospodarowania kraju do roku 2033 – projekt ekspercki*, non-governmental document, Warszawa: Ministerstwo Rozwoju Regionalnego.

Nunes, R., Adams, N. and Cotella, G. (2009) 'Policy framing and evidence-based planning: epistemic communities in the multi-jurisdictional environment of an enlarged Europe', RSA Annual International Conference, Leuven, Belgium, April 6–8.

Olsen, J. P. (2002) 'The many faces of Europeanization', *Journal of Common Market Studies*, 40(5): 921–952.

Paalzow, A. (2006) 'Barriers to Regional Development in the New Member States: the Latvian experience', in N. Adams, J. Alden and N. Harris (eds) *Regional Development and Spatial Planning in an Enlarged European Union*, Aldershot: Ashgate.

Pallagst, K. (2006) 'European Spatial Planning Reloaded: considering EU enlargement in theory and practice', *European Planning Studies*, 14(2): 253–272.

Radaelli, C. M. (1995) 'The role of knowledge in the policy process', *Journal of European Public Policy*, 2(2): 159–183.

—— (1999) 'The public policy of the European Union: whither politics of expertise?', *Journal of European Public Policy*, 6(5): 757–774.

—— (2004) 'Europeanization: solution or problem?', *European integration online papers* (EIoP), 8(16), Online. Available http://eiop.or.at/eiop/texte/2004-016a.htm (accessed February 2010).

Radaelli, C. M. and Saurugger, S. (eds) (2008) 'The Europeanization of public policies: new research directions', *Journal of Comparative Policy Analysis: Research and Practice*, 10(3).

Rydin, Y. (2007) 'Re-examining the role of knowledge within planning theory', *Planning Theory*, 6(1): 52–68.

Sandercock, L. (1998) *Towards Cosmopolis*, Chichester: Wiley.

—— (2003) *Cosmopolis II: mongrel cities in the 21st century*, London: Continuum.

Sabatier, P. (1988) 'An advocacy coalition framework of policy change and the role of policy-oriented learning therein', *Policy Sciences*, 21: 129–168.

Sapir, A., Aghion, P., Bertola, G., Hellwig, M., Pisani-Ferry, G., Rosati, D., Vinal, J., Wallace, H., with Butti, M., Nava, M., Smith, P. M. (2004) *An Agenda for a Growing Europe, the Sapir report*, Oxford: Oxford University Press.

Schön, D. (1978) 'Generative metaphor: a perspective in policy setting in social policy', in A. Ortony (ed.) *Metaphor and Thought*, Cambridge: Cambridge University Press.

Schon, P. (2000) 'Einfuhrung – Des Europaische Raumentwickslungkonzept und die Raumordnung in Deutschland', *Informationen zur raumentwicklung*, 3/4, I–VII.

Schön, D. and Rein, M. (1994) *Frame Reflection: toward the resolution of intractable controversies*, New York: Basic Books.

SIC (2006) Sustrain Implement Corridor, Interreg IIIB CADSES, Online. Available www.cadses.net/projects/apprpro.html?projectId=1475&topic=projects/apprpro (accessed March 2010).

SIC! Sustrain Implement Corridor (2006) 'Facts on the high-speed train for Saxony and Europe growing together', Online. Available www.landesentwicklung.sachsen.de/download/Landesentwicklung/Endbericht_SIC-Modul_Kurzfassung_en.pdf (accessed March 2010).

Stead, D. (2008) 'Assessing the convergence of National spatial planning systems in Europe', paper presented at the 4th joint conference ACSP-AESOP 'Bridging the divide: Celebrating the city', Chicago IL, 6–11 July.

Stead, D. and Waterhout, B. (2008) 'Learning from the Application of the ESDP: influences on European territorial governance', *disP*, 172(1): 21–34.

Steinmo, S., Thelen, K. and Longstreth, F. (1992) *Structuring Politics: historical institutionalism in comparative analysis*, Cambridge, New York: Cambridge University Press.

Tynkkynen, V. P. (2009) 'Planning realities among practitioners in St Petersburg, Russia – Soviet traditions and Western influences', in J. Knieling and F. Othengrafen (eds) *Planning Cultures in Europe: decoding cultural phenomena in urban and regional planning*, Farnham, Surrey: Ashgate.

Waterhout, B. (2008) *The Institutionalisation of European Spatial Planning*, Amsterdam: IOS Press.

Wenger, E. (2000) 'Communities of practice and social learning systems', *Organization*, 7(2): 225–246.

Weiss, C. H. (1986) 'Research and policy-making: a limited partnership', in F. Heller (ed.) *The Use and Abuse of Social Science*, Beverly Hills and London: Sage: 214–235.

Zahariadis, M. (1999) 'Ambiguity, time and multiple streams', in P. A. Sabatier (ed.) *Theories of the Policy Process*, Davis: University of California Press & Westview: 73–93.

Zito, A. R (2001a) 'Epistemic communities, collective entrepreneurship and European integration', *Journal of European Public Policy*, 8(4): 585–560.

—— (2001b) 'Epistemic communities, European Union governance and the public voice', *Science and Public Policy*, 28(6), December 2001: 465–476.

Index

Tables are indicated by *italic* type, figures and maps by **bold**.

eBooks – at www.eBookstore.tandf.co.uk

A library at your fingertips!

eBooks are electronic versions of printed books. You can store them on your PC/laptop or browse them online.

They have advantages for anyone needing rapid access to a wide variety of published, copyright information.

eBooks can help your research by enabling you to bookmark chapters, annotate text and use instant searches to find specific words or phrases. Several eBook files would fit on even a small laptop or PDA.

NEW: Save money by eSubscribing: cheap, online access to any eBook for as long as you need it.

Annual subscription packages

We now offer special low-cost bulk subscriptions to packages of eBooks in certain subject areas. These are available to libraries or to individuals.

For more information please contact webmaster.ebooks@tandf.co.uk

We're continually developing the eBook concept, so keep up to date by visiting the website.

www.eBookstore.tandf.co.uk